The
L/L Research
Channeling Archives

Transcripts of
the Meditation Sessions

Volume 13
May 30, 1993 to July 6, 1995

Don
Elkins

Jim
McCarty

Carla L.
Rueckert

Copyright © 2009 L/L Research

All rights reserved. No part of this book may be reproduced or used in any form or by any means—graphic, electronic or mechanical, including photocopying or information storage and retrieval systems—without written permission from the copyright holder.

ISBN: 978-0-945007-87-6

Published by L/L Research
Box 5195
Louisville, Kentucky 40255-0195

E-mail: contact@llresearch.org
www.llresearch.org

About the cover photo: *This photograph of Jim McCarty and Carla L. Rueckert was taken during an L/L Research channeling session on August 4, 2009, in the living room of their Louisville, Kentucky home. Jim always holds hands with Carla when she channels, following the Ra group's advice on how she can avoid any possibility of astral travel.*

Dedication

These archive volumes are dedicated to Hal and Jo Price, who faithfully and lovingly hosted this group's weekly meditation meetings from 1962 to 1975,

to Walt Rogers, whose work with the research group Man, Consciousness and Understanding of Detroit offered the information needed to begin this ongoing channeling experiment,

and to the Confederation of Angels and Planets in the Service of the Infinite Creator, for sharing their love and wisdom with us so generously through the years.

Table of Contents

Introduction 7
Year 1993 9
    May 30, 1993 10
    June 6, 1993 15
    June 13, 1993 19
    June 20, 1993 22
    June 21, 1993 26
    June 27, 1993 31
    July 10, 1993 35
    July 11, 1993 38
    July 18, 1993 42
    August 22, 1993 46
    August 29, 1993 52
    September 4, 1993 56
    September 5, 1993 61
    September 6, 1993 66
    September 12, 1993 70
    September 19, 1993 74
    September 24, 1993 79
    September 25, 1993 84
    September 25, 1993 93
    September 26, 1993 107
    September 26, 1993 117
    October 17, 1993 119
    October 31, 1993 123
    November 14, 1993 128
    November 21, 1993 133
    November 28, 1993 136
    December 12, 1993 140
    December 19, 1993 144
Year 1994 149
    January 2, 1994 150
    January 16, 1994 153
    January 23, 1994 158
    January 30, 1994 162
    February 6, 1994 170
    February 13, 1994 175
    March 13, 1994 178
    March 27, 1994 183

April 3, 1994	187
April 10, 1994	190
May 1, 1994	194
May 22, 1994	198
May 29, 1994	201
June 12, 1994	207
June 19, 1994	212
June 26, 1994	215
July 14, 1994	219
September 11, 1994	222
September 18, 1994	226
September 23, 1994	232
September 24, 1994	238
September 24, 1994	244
September 25, 1994	257
September 25, 1994	265
October 2, 1994	270
October 16, 1994	274
October 23, 1994	277
October 30, 1994	282
November 6, 1994	286
November 13, 1994	290
November 20, 1994	294
November 27, 1994	297
December 11, 1994	301
December 25, 1994	304
Year 1995	**308**
January 15, 1995	309
January 22, 1995	311
January 29, 1995	317
February 5, 1995	320
February 12, 1995	325
February 19, 1995	330
February 26, 1995	336
March 12, 1995	341
March 19, 1995	346
March 26, 1995	352
April 2, 1995	356
April 9, 1995	362
April 16, 1995	369
April 21, 1995	374
May 14, 1995	379

May 21, 1995	386
May 28, 1995	390
July 6, 1995	394

Introduction

Welcome to this volume of the *L/L Research Channeling Archives*. This series of publications represents the collection of channeling sessions recorded by L/L Research during the period from the early seventies to the present day. The sessions are also available on the L/L Research website, www.llresearch.org.

Starting in the mid-1950s, Don Elkins, a professor of physics and engineering at Speed Scientific School, had begun researching the paranormal in general and UFOs in particular. Elkins was a pilot as well as a professor and he flew his small plane to meet with many of the UFO contactees of the period.

Hal Price had been a part of a UFO-contactee channeling circle in Detroit called "The Detroit Group." When Price was transferred from Detroit's Ford plant to its Louisville truck plant, mutual friends discovered that Price also was a UFO researcher and put the two men together. Hal introduced Elkins to material called *The Brown Notebook* which contained instructions on how to create a group and receive UFO contactee information. In January of 1962 they decided to put the instructions to use and began holding silent meditation meetings on Sunday nights just across the Ohio River in the southern Indiana home of Hal and his wife, Jo. This was the beginning of what was called the "Louisville Group."

I was an original member of that group, along with a dozen of Elkins' physics students. However, I did not learn to channel until 1974. Before that date, almost none of our weekly channeling sessions were recorded or transcribed. After I began improving as a channel, Elkins decided for the first time to record all the sessions and transcribe them.

During the first eighteen months or so of my studying channeling and producing material, we tended to reuse the tapes as soon as the transcriptions were finished. Since those were typewriter days, we had no record of the work that could be reopened and used again, as we do now with computers. And I used up the original and the carbon copy of my transcriptions putting together a manuscript, *Voices of the Gods*, which has not yet been published. It remains as almost the only record of Don Elkins' and my channeling of that period.

We learned from this experience to retain the original tapes of all of our sessions, and during the remainder of the seventies and through the eighties, our "Louisville Group" was prolific. The "Louisville Group" became "L/L Research" after Elkins and I published a book in 1976, *Secrets of the UFO*, using that publishing name. At first we met almost every night. In later years, we met gradually less often, and the number of sessions recorded by our group in a year accordingly went down. Eventually, the group began taking three months off from channeling during the summer. And after 2000, we began having channeling meditations only twice a month. The volume of sessions dropped to its present output of eighteen or so each year.

These sessions feature channeling from sources which call themselves members of the Confederation of Planets in the Service of the Infinite Creator. At first we enjoyed hearing from many different voices: Hatonn, Laitos, Oxal, L/Leema and Yadda being just a few of them. As I improved my tuning techniques, and became the sole senior channel in L/L Research, the number of contacts dwindled. When I began asking for "the highest and best contact which I can receive of Jesus the Christ's vibration of unconditional love in a conscious and stable manner," the entity offering its thoughts through our group was almost always Q'uo. This remains true as our group continues to channel on an ongoing basis.

The channelings are always about love and unity, enunciating "The Law of One" in one aspect or another. Seekers who are working with spiritual principles often find the material a good resource. We hope that you will as well. As time has gone on the questions have shifted somewhat, but in general the content of the channeling is metaphysical and focused on helping seekers find the love in the moment and the Creator in the love.

At first, I transcribed our channeling sessions. I got busier, as our little group became more widely known, and got hopelessly behind on transcribing. Two early transcribers who took that job off my hands were Kim

Howard and Judy Dunn, both of whom masterfully transcribed literally hundreds of sessions through the eighties and early nineties.

Then Ian Jaffray volunteered to create a web site for these transcriptions, and single-handedly unified the many different formats that the transcripts were in at that time and made them available online. This additional exposure prompted more volunteers to join the ranks of our transcribers, and now there are a dozen or so who help with this. Our thanks go out to all of these kind volunteers, early and late, who have made it possible for our webguy to make these archives available.

Around the turn of the millennium, I decided to commit to editing each session after it had been transcribed. So the later transcripts have fewer errata than the earlier ones, which are quite imperfect in places. One day, perhaps, those earlier sessions will be revisited and corrections will be made to the transcripts. It would be a large task, since there are well over 1500 channeling sessions as of this date, and counting. We apologize for the imperfections in those transcripts, and trust that you can ascertain the sense of them regardless of a mistake here and there.

Blessings, dear reader! Enjoy these "humble thoughts" from the Confederation of Planets. May they prove good companions to your spiritual seeking. ☘

For all of us at L/L Research,

Carla L. Rueckert

Louisville, Kentucky

July 16, 2009

Year 1993

May 30, 1993 to December 19, 1993

Sunday Meditation
May 30, 1993

Group question: This afternoon we would like to know how we can balance our concerns for worldly survival and spiritual perception of the real nature of things; how we can discern what of our concerns deserve our attention and those which are perhaps a waste of time and cause a lot of excess worry. When we have concerns, what kind of a yardstick can we access to determine where we need to place our attention?

(Carla channeling)

I am Hatonn. Greetings, my friends, in the love and in the light of the infinite Creator. It is a great blessing to come into your circle of seeking, to enter into your vibratory harmonies, and to rest with you in seeking and faith. As always, we ask that each of you choose those thoughts which aid and discard the rest.

Your question about how to judge your own concerns about provisions for the physical well being and continuation is one which is important simply because in the pursuit of third-density lessons, all of which have to do with learning how to love, the issue of providing a supply of those things needed can be a key one. Your density has the strong tincture of yellow-ray concerns; that is, of concerns which involve the seeker in his participation in groups or institutional relationships. The going out to find work is a going out into the society, moving into and out of groups, other families, institutions who employ, and in each of these forays the mind is guided by that attitude which points like the arrow at the prevailing wind of attitude and internal bias.

The prayer which you repeated says, among other things, "give us this day our daily bread." Focus upon this request and see how simple and limited this request is. See, too, where the weight of attitude is shifted. The prayer is a reaching to the Creator, not to the institutions of your society and culture.

We would at this time transfer to the one known as Jim. In this particular channeling working we shall omit our signature at the end of each portion and simply begin with our identity. We ask each instrument to continue to be sensitive to the tuning and we ask each in the circle to aid in the clockwise energy flow of light, the light of desire, so that each entity's desire to seek further may blend into a constantly energized stream which feeds the contact and aids in the channeling process. We would now transfer to the one known as Jim. I am Hatonn.

(Jim channeling)

I am Hatonn. The attitude which prays that the daily bread be given as it is needed is an attitude which is not available to those of your peoples who feel that the world in which they live is one with which they must contend and wrest the …

(The second page of the original transcript is missing.)

(Carla channeling)

… become ladders and thoughts become structures, structures of logic upon which the entities which dwell in the darkness of flesh attempt to use those imprecise items you call words to express the relationship between the self and the Creator.

All of those within the Confederation of Planets in the Service of the Infinite Creator are those who are people of this mythology and people of this history. Yet time and space are not as they are in space/time when one attempts to delve beneath the surface of the story of the race of humanity upon Earth. Thusly, while we are real, we are also metaphysical as opposed to physical, just as your thoughts have no flesh but are as they are. So are we within your space/time continuum.

That which the entity Jehovah or Yahweh did among your peoples was within history and yet also of the quality of the thought that has no place within history. We say this in order to deflect the intellectual desire of the seeker of truth from aiming directly into this matter as though it were logical or linear. That which has to do with the relationship of consciousness in the personal sense with consciousness in the creative sense or the sense of being the Creator will always fly before any gust of wind that attempts to chase it and the more words that are thrown at it, the faster it will flee.

So, at the very beginning of anything that we say at this time, we ask that you understand that we are using analogy, and we are mixing mythology and historicity because that is the way the creation is melded within your illusion.

The entity, Yahweh—as the one known as Jim surmised within his question—was indeed one who had the plan of enabling those who wished to transfer to your planet with that move. The concept seemed to them fairly direct; that is, to improve the intelligence and the curiosity and the physical and emotional strength of the type of physical vehicle which had been the native physical vehicle for those within the Martian sphere. And, as was surmised, this entity discovered, to its discomfiture, that it had caused great distortion—worse distortion, shall we say—than the distortions would have been without the aid.

This kind of situation occurs at all levels of consciousness. The mistake is made. There it is. One cannot go back. One simply learns and moves forward. However, this people indeed did crave and wish for a continuing source of, shall we say, God-given help. Its expectations were very high because there had been interaction betwixt a god-like being and humans. The remarkable nature of this history speaks for itself.

The entity which succeeded the first Yahweh, calling itself by the same name and using the same frequency of light to express, simply continued to offer aid and comfort when it wished but with the ever increasing distortions towards belligerency and aggressiveness that is the hallmark of a negatively oriented being or culture. The echoes of this action which was transmitted long ago redounds even now and shall continue to echo and re-echo as long as there are those within third density within this sphere who wish to claim power and who seek a god of power.

Now, let us look at the promise first made and the promise that took its place. The hunger which many among your peoples have had revolves around knowing what is right. It is instinctive within your physical vehicle to watch out for the safety and the comfort of the body, the mind and the spirit. The continual proclamations and greatly detailed taboos, prohibitions, and schedules of sacrifice that characterized the relationship of your so-called Old Testament God constituted an order, a structure, a logic within which entities felt comfortable living. Through this structure they knew what was right. The tendency was to enunciate finer and finer point of law until all possible actions with ethical consequences or consequences of safety and health were covered and the entities within this system were safe.

We ask you to look about you within your present world scene and see the entities about you looking for a way to be safe. Look upon your leaders who wish to prohibit freedom in order to guarantee safety. The spirit of Yahweh is strong and it survives. It is part of that mixture of light and dark which makes up all that is. In other words, we are saying that entities continue to have a choice between the many laws of moral rectitude in such a logic as

Yahweh's. They can also choose a logic and a path which is not rational or linear, which does not hold, which does not insist, and which is not aggressive. This spirit was before the one known as Jesus the Christ. It exists, as does Yahweh, within each entity, for each of you is the universe. You are looking out at a world that is actually interior. Such is the illusion created by flesh.

In the testament of the one known as Jesus the place of the law is simply turned upon its head as the one known as Jesus is quoted as saying, "Man was not made for the Sabbath, but the Sabbath for man." The direction to love the one infinite Creator and to love each other self as the self is not a detailed, closed or encapsulated direction. It is specifically open-ended, and the one known as Jesus goes to some pains in the body of teaching that survives to impress upon those whom he taught that there is never an end to love. There is never the need to return to the old prescriptions and old taboos. These are not either/or situations but rather either/or processes, and as each student works upon its personal polarity perhaps it will aid the student to ponder and remember these two kinds of promises, these two kinds of ways of thinking. And perhaps this can be instructive in showing the way, the balance, when that way seems unclear.

We wish to tell you that your model of the universe is very, very limited. The attempt to nail down a history which is replete with metaphysical subject matter shall always be unending and full of lacunae, holes, gaps and spaces where there is no logic, there are no words, there is no road, there is no structure. Not that there is no structure, just that there is beyond all structure, love. The illusion is so very, very deep, for you are a dream, yet when you leave the flesh and enter a larger life you will still be a dream, for we also are but illusions, and ahead we see illusion. Yet always that siren call which beckons you and beckons us calls us all forward. And yet are we forward-going? We do not think so. We feel at this point the comfortable awareness that we do not know what is occurring. We only know how to be faithful to love. When it is accepted within the heart that nothing can be known and that a sea of confusion will always surround love, then the mind and the heart are better armed to take up the walk of the pilgrim who seeks truth, peace and love.

That call has come to many who wander within this world of yours at this time, listening for a sound, a tone, a letter from home, waiting, hardly hoping at some times, yet holding onto the faith that that which is within, that which is so hungrily sought, does exist. And we say to you, "Yes, love exists. Love is before, after, and around all that is." You do not seek an ephemeras. You seek that which is and that which exists perfectly. We encourage all lines of thinking which fascinate your minds, and we hope that we can, within your meditative periods, be with you as strengtheners of your own vibration. But we do continue to remark that the ways of seeking which are scholarly and of the mind yield a limited harvest. This is acceptable to us. We can look at what is possible within your world and see that it will be helpful and useful. And we encourage those who are drawn to this material, to this subject, to continue that process of thinking, meditating and reflecting, for these are helpful things not simply to the self, but in terms of service to others as well.

Let those truths that you seek remain small enough for you to remember that beyond all that can be understood or discussed is the truth, and that is a vibration which has created all that is and into which we hunger and yearn to move again. That should keep your intelligence and your heart on a sturdy road that has good perspective.

We would at this time transfer this contact to the one known as Jim. We do thank this instrument and leave it in love and in light. We are those known to you as Q'uo.

(Jim channeling)

I am Q'uo, and we greet each again in love and in light through this instrument. It is our privilege at this time to offer ourselves in the attempt to speak to any further queries. Is there another query at this time?

K: I understand you to say that there were two Yahwehs? The original who brought the entities from Mars to Earth and then a second entity using his vibration?

I am Q'uo, and am aware of your query, my brother. This is correct, with the second entity being of a negative orientation and utilizing the name of the first as a means of gaining control of the entities to whom the first Yahweh had spoken. Is there a further query, my brother?

K: The second Yahweh, then, gave the Laws of Moses to the people as well as the curses that attended them?

I am Q'uo, and this is correct, my brother. Is there a further query?

K: Ra said that the first Yahweh gave the Law of One in a very simple form to Moses. Is this the saying, "I am that I am," or was this the Ten Commandments, or something else? What was this exactly that he was talking about?

I am Q'uo, and am aware of your query, my brother. The entity, Yahweh, from the Confederation of Planets in Service to the Infinite Creator, was one who spoke with those entities from the Mars influence in a manner that reflected the unity of all creation and the attempt to be of service to others through this speaking, and intermingling, shall we say, the attempt was formed or fashioned in a way or in a philosophy that attempted to weave all experience, desires and expenditures of energy as portions of one great tapestry of energy, love and unity. All communications were based upon this simple recognition of the unified nature of all creation. It was the foundation upon which the interrelationship was built. Is there a further query?

K: The Ten Commandments were given by the second, negative Yahweh? Is that correct?

I am Q'uo, and am aware of your query, my brother. This is basically correct, for these commandments were seen as the pillars upon which would rest the many laws that would protect and guide the chosen people in a manner that was in accordance with the desires of the Orion-based Yahweh. These commandments included previous concepts given by the first Yahweh contact and then there was added unto those concepts a turning or twisting toward the negative orientation so that the commandments were, shall we say, then restrictions upon entities more than inspiration to affirmative or positive action and imaging of concepts. Is there a further query, my brother?

K: In the Old Testament we have this record of Yahweh speaking. It is a strong personality. Can we take this strong personality to be the creation of later editors or writers, or is this a faithful reproduction of the negative Yahweh?

I am Q'uo, and am aware of your query, my brother. We find in most instances there is, as you have surmised, the faithful reproduction of words spoken and recorded carefully. However, as in all recording by human hand there is the possibility of coloration or distortion which has occurred in some instances. Is there a further query?

K: Was the negative Yahweh responsible for the miracles on the journey out of Egypt such as the parting of the Red Sea, the manna from heaven, or the water from the rock? Or did these not happen at all?

I am Q'uo, and am aware of your query, my brother. We find here that there is some mixture of influence and there is some difficulty in interpretation, although much is carefully recorded and in a reasonably accurate manner. We would take this opportunity to remind each entity present that though the details of such an interaction are quite interesting upon many levels, that it is well to remember that the process of the evolution of the entities involved is one which is at its heart in accordance with the free will choices of the peoples of this time who, though laboring under dual influences, did have enough previous understanding of the heart of the evolutionary process being love and compassion that this positively oriented source of information was for the most part ignored by the majority of these entities who were evolving according to the energies set in motion …

(Side one of tape ends.)

(Jim channeling)

I am Q'uo, and am again with this instrument. As we mentioned previously, these entities had access to information of a positive nature but chose through their own free will to move with those energies which had originated with their experience on the red planet known to you as Mars, and there was, indeed, much interaction and influence offered to these entities by both positively and negatively oriented entities who were interested in the evolution of these Mars entities. Is there a final query at this time?

K: I would ask about what Ra said about giving some visionary information to some philosophers of ancient Greece about six hundred B.C. Can you tell me what this information pertained to and how it showed up in Greek philosophy?

I am Q'uo, and am aware of your query, my brother. And we would answer by suggesting that the Law of

One was the primary information given in the distortion of the ways of love and understanding, so that there were those philosophers within the Greek culture and experience which made this assumption the foundation of their philosophy and their view of the nature of creation, its purpose, direction and ultimate conclusion. Is there any further query?

K: Do we have time for some more?

I am Q'uo, and we would entertain one final query, my brother.

K: I am interested in Jesus of Nazareth. He often had the term, "Son of God" attributed to him. Is this to be taken literally or was this a reference to the Logos of Philo Judaeus of Alexandria, who often used that term for his Logos?

I am Q'uo, and am aware of your query, my brother. The phrase, "Son of God," or the phrase, "The Christed One," are means of expressing the kind of consciousness available to those who have been able to open the green-ray energy center in sufficient degree to feel and experience this creative force of love that has made all that there is. This quality of consciousness or attitude of beingness is the goal or opportunity which is offered each third-density entity as a means of passing from this illusion to the fourth density, where the study of this creative power of love is that which is the focus of all energy expenditure. Thus, the one known as Jesus was able to offer itself as a model or pattern by which entities could move their own consciousness to a larger view in which the acceptance of self and others as one being was far more easily facilitated.

We are those of Q'uo, and we would take this opportunity to thank again those who have gathered in this circle of seeking this day and who have graciously offered us the opportunity to speak our words and to share our thoughts in those areas that are of interest to you. We are always most grateful for this opportunity to walk with you upon this journey which all make together. At this time we shall take our leave of this instrument and this group, leaving each as always in the love and in the light of the infinite Creator. Adonai. Adonai.

Sunday Meditation
June 6, 1993

Group question: The question this afternoon has to do with the process of worry and prayer. It seems that when one worries overmuch about a situation, one is really sowing seeds for allowing that situation to take root and to sprout, to grow, to become more likely to be a reality. And the suggestion was made that a form of prayer might be the more helpful of the paths to choose in dealing with a situation that you are quite worried about; that talking out your worry to the Creator, to an angel, to a saint, to your higher self, to whomever, is much more helpful in creating the internal environment that not only gives you a peace of mind and a feeling of perspective, but sows the seeds of greater possibilities, so that that which you are concerned about has more chance of turning out in a favorable fashion rather than in the way which you fear that it might turn out, and the way which you tend to worry about. And we would like Q'uo's comments on the concepts of worry and its effect upon a situation, and the concept of prayer and its effect upon a situation.

(Carla channeling)

I am Q'uo. Greetings in the love and the light of the one infinite Creator. We are gratified to be with you this afternoon and to be that source called to your circle to comment upon your query concerning worry and prayer. As always, we request that personal discrimination be used as you listen to these thoughts, for we speak not as authorities, but as your brothers and sisters.

In responding to your query, we begin by observing the estate of your species and your density. It has been written that man is a little lower than the angels. What separates the estate of third density from that angelic host is an illusion in which the truth is hidden, so that the generator of either positivity or negativity is chosen—we correct this instrument—is chosen in faith alone, not because the circumstances of any situation are or become clear.

The essence of third density is the striving for clarity in the midst of unremitting confusion and darkness. In this situation it would be miraculous for any not to worry. There seems to be a continual stream of circumstance which cannot be controlled; efforts to control are often useless. In the absence of action that is effective the concern and returning to the concern is natural. Yet, as your question posited, it is true that over-concern and worry cooperate with what may be called desire-driven destiny in such a way as to more nearly solidify the matter about which the worry and concern is expressed.

We ask you to sit for a moment with the sheer inevitability of worrying circumstance. You have come into this density and into this incarnational experience fully aware of and willing to undergo the dropping of the veil of forgetting. Before your present physical vehicle was created, you chose this circumstance and this continuing line of circumstance. What about this was so valuable? The gem which you chose was this very veil of forgetting and the blindness of the choices you would be making within this density and this incarnation. It is to this present worrying moment that you have come, not by mistake or error and not by chance, but step by step you have moved hither in chosen blindness and each issue before you now is faced in this blindness.

What is the supreme value of this blind choice, but that it is blind. We emphasize this repeatedly because, although it feels as though those of spiritual discretion and learning will have a greater and greater ease and pleasantness of incarnational experience, yet, in terms of the matter which acts as catalyst, the reverse is true: the greater the activity of the seeker within incarnation, the more frequent the choices and the more heartily each choice is tested.

So, this situation which precipitates worry is the common coin of third-density incarnation, and as such, we recommend a quiet and contemplative consideration on each occasion in which worry arises of this fact. You did not come here to dispel worry and to be comforted; rather, you came into the arena of third density to strive in darkness. Your greatest sight is the blind but loving heart, for one sees with the heart the light which is not visible to the mind; for within the heart rests the spirit of love.

This spirit is a side of wisdom which has no words in your density, and it expresses its wisdom in the more and more purified emotions. When the seeker comes first to the conscious study of the processes of spiritual choice-making, at first the heart is less than optimally pure in its expression. The seeker begins, day-by-day and meditation-by-meditation, to empty out of the heart the less pure of that heart's contents, as though the heart were a pocket in which many things had been placed, some of which were not desirable. After a time meditating and seeking, the heart begins to be released from having to hold so much of that which is less than pure; and then the heart may begin to shed its wisdom upon the conscious mind. This purifying process is not short, and we do not wish to suggest that you must become consciously pure in heart. We simply encourage each to do the work of opening in meditation regularly and allowing the heart to empty itself of the petty trivia so that its strain may be deeper and ever more pure.

The path to the deep mind goes through what we call the heart. This is why we focus upon this word, "heart." We wish, centrally, to disengage the mind from the intellectualizing capacity of your brain, for although one may speak intellectually of spiritual truths, the truths are only true in and as a whole when they are felt rather than intellectually understood.

Now, we have placed you in the situation and legalized worrying to an extent. Yes, you shall worry; you shall not break this habit entirely. Yet, we have suggested that the truth of the situation is not best served by worrying.

What, then, is the manner of moving in harmony with desire-driven destiny in such a way as to make the most effective and positive choices? We ask that you recall from one of your holy works that the one known as Peter saw the one known as Jesus walking upon the water. Peter, it is written, was excited to see this miracle and leapt out of the boat to walk to his teacher. But then Peter realized that he was doing the impossible, and immediately he stopped walking upon the waves and began to sink; however, the one known as Jesus reached his hand to Peter, and Peter was again able to walk upon the water with his teacher.

This reaching of the hand to the infinite intelligence that is source and ending, is an image showing the essence of prayer. It is a direct communication with that which surrounds and makes possible the illusion now experienced. To pray is to organize the energies within the self and point them directly at communication with, and ultimate congruency with, the great Original Thought of Love.

Thusly, prayer needs not to be answered to be effective. It is not given that a seeker see clear answers to each and every prayer; rather, it is given that communication and interaction with the infinite and the divine is not only possible, but inevitable. Prayer organizes this direct communication and identification in a polarized way; worry makes the connection with the divine in an unorganized way. The very process of communicating with infinite intelligence causes the seeker to refine, reconsider, restate and begin to see the truer dimensions of that situation about which he has been concerned.

We do encourage more than prayer, however. The praying to be led is most helpful and efficacious; yet, there is also the great energy which dwells in this connection with infinity, which may then be released from intended communication as a reflex of this communication, as, if you will, an answer to prayer. To the open-hearted there comes that spirit which enlivens hope and faith; and in its turn, this faith organizes the intellectual mind so that it is more worry-resistant when next the situation causing worry arises.

The answer to prayer is not only the response of infinite intelligence to the matter for which intercession has been offered, but also a feedback which more and more informs the intelligence of that seeker who has prayed. Indeed, we would substitute for "prayer" the term "conversation," for prayer is a word which in your culture has many negative connotations concerning the feelings of lack of faith, lack of confidence, lack of worth, and similar shadows. It also is connoted with the concept of the elite, as though some were more able to pray or had more right to pray than others. We would instead call prayer a conversation with infinite intelligence. In this conversation, the seeker speaks his mind as it is given him to do. Infinite intelligence responds in silence and in power; and free will being observed, destiny moves on, affected to some degree by this interaction. More than this, he who converses with infinity grows more and more full of this energy which is the reflex of this conversation—the silent encouragement of the infinite for the seeker within illusion.

We would suggest that as the seeker moves through the illusion day-by-day, and repeatedly goes through the practice of worry, of noting the worry, and of turning to communicate this concern in an organized way to infinite intelligence, there is the self-contradictory need both to release the free will to circumstance and to enter into that worrisome situation in imagination, to turn and face that about which the seeker is worried. Again, this turning and facing of catalyst does not bring about simply an answer to prayer, but rather, it acts as a teaching aid, if you will, opening more and more the seeker's heart, enlarging the scope of the seeker's identity to itself, and bringing about more and more in the thinking patterns of the seeker an awareness of the self as a universal Self.

Much of what prayer and worry do is offer a definition or qualification of selfhood. Much of what seekers do in blind faith is seek and seek outwardly, reaching and reaching, yet learning more and more about the heart of the self, for the creation reflects that self, and those circumstances which are so obviously happening outside the self within the illusion are, in fact, reflecting part of the nature of the inner self.

Behold your own visions and all sense impressions not only as outer events, but also as a grand system of mirrors reflecting your own inner nature, for all that seems outer, all that seems divergent, all that seems to have this and that quality in and of itself, is that within the illusion which is positioned in a way that shall teach the seeker of his inner nature.

We join you in moving along this bewildering path. We encourage each in that cosmic conversation which shall reveal the seeker to itself, and the self to the infinite One.

We would close this sitting through the one known as Jim. We are those of Q'uo, and leave this instrument in love and light.

(Jim channeling)

I am Q'uo, and greet each again in love and in light. At this time it is our privilege to offer ourselves for the further query if those present have additional queries. Is there a query at this time?

Carla: I have a question. Let me see. I don't exactly know how to frame it. First of all, I would very much like to know—did I get any part of what you were trying to give me? It was very difficult to go through some of those concepts; and if I didn't, could you re-say them—whatever I didn't get— another way through Jim?

I am Q'uo, and we are quite pleased that you were able to move through what was indeed difficult conceptual framework, shall we say. This is not material that is easily apprehended, and we are happy that you have applied yourself with such determination and …

(Side one of tape ends.)

(Jim channeling)

I am Q'uo, and am again with this instrument. Is there a further query, my sister?

Carla: Yes. I think I grasp what you're saying about how worry is good to the extent that we need it to alert ourselves to the fact that we need to pray; and that prayer is good, or communication with the divine is good. But there is a trigger in there where you're worrying about something and you hope that you somehow could get a trigger in there, so that you move right on from worry to dealing with it in a prayerful and communicative way. And I think the original impetus for this question was, "What trigger can I use to point out to myself the fact that I'm worrying, and get me into a frame of mind in which I can do something about it?" What keeps us from just worrying and worrying and worrying? What kind of trigger can we put in our consciousnesses that alerts us to this in ourselves?

I am Q'uo, and am aware of your query, my sister. The threshold of worry, shall we say, varies from entity to entity. There are entities who feel comfortable only as they are able to worry about a situation. There are others who feel little distortion towards worry and allow whatever situation is occurring to continue with little concern for their part in the situation.

Each entity must determine when worry has begun to wear out one's ability to find peace and equanimity concerning a given situation. There is the necessity, as we have previously mentioned, of giving enough concern and worry to a situation to alert the deeper self that there is the need for creative problem-solving, shall we say. When an entity has thusly alerted not only the deeper levels of its own mind—reaching into that which is below conscious awareness—but has through this same process alerted those presences which serve as guides and teachers, then it is that these presences along with the more whole self must be allowed to present their comments, shall we say.

When these resources have been heard and whatever action that is possible has been taken—even if only to prepare for action—then it is that the entity must trust and have faith that all it can do and all that is appropriate to be done, it has done. By having this faith, the entity is affirming that all is, indeed, well, and has added that ingredient of faith into the mix of catalyst to serve as what you may call a kind of yeast that will affect the outcome, shall we say, in a manner which is most appropriate, considering the various qualities, energies and entities involved.

Is there a further query, my sister?

Carla: Just one. I sense that we could study this topic further to good advantage. Would you confirm that, if it's true?

I am Q'uo, and we agree that this is fertile ground for further consideration, for there is much of foundation attitude formation and its effect upon the external environment that reflects the nature of your illusion and the general field of that which you may call magic.

Is there a further query, my sister?

Carla: No, thank you, Q'uo. This has been an interesting session.

I am Q'uo, and again we thank you, my sister.

Is there another query at this time?

Questioner: No, not from me, Q'uo. It's been good to continue *(inaudible)*.

I am Q'uo, and we have also enjoyed this session. We feel that the queries which come from your mutual concern are those which are rich in possibility for study, and we study with you that which you seek, for are we not all One? We thank you, each of you, for your dedication, your courage, and your sense of proportion which you call humor. We are most grateful to be able to join you in your meditation and in your seeking of truth.

At this time we shall take our leave of this group and this instrument, leaving each, as always, in the love and in the light of the one infinite Creator. We are known to you as those of Q'uo. Adonai, my friends. Adonai. ☙

Sunday Meditation
June 13, 1993

Group question: The question this afternoon has to do with solitude. We would like to know what the value of solitude is to the seeker of truth and why it is that some people seem to need more solitude or others less, and are there any problems or pitfalls with too much or too little solitude? Is it sort of like dreaming in the sleep stage? Do you need so much of it?

(Carla channeling)

I am Q'uo. I greet you in the love and in the light of the one infinite Creator. Thank you for calling us to your circle of seeking that we may offer our thoughts to you on the subject of solitude.

(Pause)

We are those of Q'uo and apologize for refraining from speaking. This instrument is experiencing flares of pain which temporarily removed the instrument from tuning. We shall proceed but we'll attempt to be shorter than our usual lengthy discussion. This instrument feels that *(inaudible)* remains unlikely.

The uses of solitude are various. Thusly, there is not one clear answer to a question attempting to evaluate this condition. If the goal of the seeker is to assimilate truth, then certainly it may be seen that solitude has a part to play to some extent in this search. Perhaps looking at the question from the standpoint of what a seeker is working toward is helpful. If a seeker seeks to move its vibration more and more nearly into attunement with the one great original Thought whose vibration is called love, if the seeker already is feeling that it needs to seek more this growing attempt at a congruency between the vibration of the self and the greater Self, then the entity will look more favorably upon solitude and its right uses spiritually. If a seeker is considering itself as moving well in attunement, but needing the work of service for others, then the seeker will find solitude less spiritually appropriate. This is one clear and simple way of evaluating the spiritual uses of solitude in that, to be of manifested service to others, the servant usually must spend time with those others whom he serves.

However, within the cultural attitude—we correct this instrument—attitudinal ambiance which you enjoy at this space and time, it is very nearly guaranteed that those seeking solitude will not already be in a vibratory state congruent with the one great original Thought. It is probably that the entity may not even be seeking solitude for a spiritual reason, but rather seeking solitude as a surcease from suffering and pain of some kind. So let us look at the right use of this gift.

Perhaps the solitude which is often spoken of in your literature as the "desert experience," or "forty days and forty nights in the wilderness," in this situation, the seeker is in crisis. The seeker has been stimulated and its sensory systems overtaxed by wisdom, by sense perceptions, by the opinions of others. In this crisis, the seeker often typically must needs walk by itself in terms of sharing with another third-destiny entity the verdance and thirst of this journey.

As the old folk song says, "You've got to walk that lonesome valley. You've got to walk it by yourself. Ain't nobody else gonna walk it for you." This, my friends, is true to the best of our knowledge. You walk though the valley of the shadow of death as your holy work is quoted. And although you have your higher self and the inner planes, [entities] who come to your request, although in fact you are not alone ever nor cut off from the love of the infinite One, yet in terms of someone to help with the burden of the learning, each seeker perforce must do this work for and by itself.

The next great category of reasons people yearn for solitude is the category which is a dynamic of sensitivity. There are many to whom relating to the self has been in some way blocked. This usually occurs in the younger years of incarnation. Part of the young experience has caused the entity to seek solitude in order to be comfortable, for there is perceived the discomfort in company, and this discomfort builds up within such an entity. When such a one reaches a solitary place, there is the feeling of safety and of relaxation. It is almost as though the mind and emotions constituted another organ such as the lungs, and as the lungs need to breathe for the organism to live, so the entity must be solitary in order for the emotional and mental faculties to remain acute, for if this need is ignored, there is the equivalent lack of oxygen to the brain—that is, oxygen to the emotions and mind.

Such an entity is correct in assessing the need for solitude. However, it is well for a seeker of this character type to look well to the right use of solitude, for the potential is there for distraction and the lessening of the impact of this gift to the self by a lack of considered thought as to how to create within solitude.

"Create what?" this instrument asks us irritably. However we leave this a blank on purpose, for those who seek solitude are often given within that solitude, when it is used well, creations and fantasies of the heart, the mind, the emotions, and of the spirit.

Thusly, we say to those seekers whose way is solitary, be aware of the joy of this gift and if riches pour into you, pour them through yourself and into manifestation, so that that which has been given you and you alone in the darkness of the sanctum sanctorum within you may open-handedly allow such creation to occur through yourself and bless all who may hear or see.

There is that to be considered which is inclined towards the negative path of service to self in most desires for solitude, and the threads or the strain of this can be picked out and discovered by the seeker, that the times of solitude may become more productive. And we use the term "productive" to include, first of all, the lightening of the planetary consciousness. These service-to-self portions or threads or melodies, entwined within the tapestry of incarnational experience in solitude, occur naturally. This tendency to desire to be distracted is an artifact of the blockage of energy which is almost inevitable within the dense chemical distillery of the human frame.

The exhaustion of living occurs frequently, and certainly more frequently as the physical vehicle becomes more aged and less able. This is not to say that it is always service to self to allow the self to be distracted. Occasionally, and more for some than others, such distraction within solitude is salutary and salubrious, for this method enables one who is uncomfortable to achieve a more pleasant state of mind. However, the seeker may look carefully at the service-to-self entity's habit and custom of considering the self separate from all else. Solitude, you see, is among many other things, an illusion. There is no solitude in a full, teeming, living creation. The force of life about all is unbelievable, literally. You cannot even imagine how crowded the universe is. It bursts with life.

You dwell within a deep, deep illusion. Out of the unknown, yet felt, glory of the great Self within, you come to a realization that you wish to walk what this instrument would call the "King's Highway." You put your pack on your back, your walking stick in your hand, and you set out with one tunic and one pair of sandals. Your situation grants to you one opportunity after another to so choose your environment and your actions that you may be the most aware of the love of the infinite One, and may be most able to be a channel for that infinite vibration to others. It is completely dependent upon each situation, each entity, as to the appropriate amount of solitude. There is no one best way, just as there is no one best path.

However, there is one form of solitary practice [which] deserves notice above all else, and that is the solitude within in which one turns to the holy of holies within the self. In meditation, a link is sought in spiritual solitude. Through that solitude the seeking soul stretches out its purified desire, and the silence answers in thought too poignant, too profound, too deep for words. Treasure those moments with the infinite One, and know that each moment wherein the Creator has been sought is lightening the consciousness of your people and doing needed work in establishing the generation of an ever fuller light upon your sphere.

We would at this time transfer to the one known as Jim. We are those of Q'uo and we leave this instrument with thanks in love and light.

(Jim channeling)

I am Q'uo, and greet each again in love and in light through this instrument. May we say that it is a privilege to be able to utilize each instrument present in the dissemination of our thoughts and opinions in response to your queries. At this time we would ask if there may be any further queries to which we may respond.

Carla: You didn't say anything about when people are depressed and like to be off by themselves. I was wondering about that.

I am Q'uo, and am aware of your query, my sister. The second designation of the conditions that one may experience that would cause the seeking of solitude is that in which the entity is greatly sensitive to the movement of the world about it and feels, in a sense, easily jostled by the disharmonious vibrations, and which seeks the condition of solitude as a means whereby a refuge can be taken and the life pattern explored in a less threatening environment. The condition of depression, as you have called it, is a special example of this sensitivity that has been distorted by an imbalance of personal experience and the difficulty in processing a catalyst to clear the, shall we say, line to the inner self. When an entity experience—we correct this instrument—

experiences the condition of depression, there is [at] the one time over-sensitivity and yet there is the distancing or numbness, shall we say, to hope and to faith which causes the entity to feel the despair that will, at some point, cause the entity to retreat into a smaller, safer and solitary environment, much as the turtle retreats into the shell when danger is perceived. An entity with the feeling of despair in the mental and emotional energy systems oftentimes attempts to lick its wounds, shall we say, by seeking solitude.

Is there a further query, my sister?

Carla: No. Thank you very much, Q'uo.

I am Q'uo, and we thank you, my sister. Is there a further query?

(Pause)

I am Q'uo, and we thank each for offering the support for this circle of seeking and for searching the heart for the part each has to offer in bringing this query to us. We are full of gratitude at the opportunity to be with you in your seeking and to share with you that which we have found helpful in our own journey. At this time it is our great and joyous privilege to please the instrument known as Carla with a shorter than usual session. We realize that we speak at great lengths more frequently than not and we are happy that we are able to, at this time, offer a more succinct answer to your query.

We shall take our leave of this group at this time, leaving each, as always, in the love and in the light of the one infinite Creator. We are those known as Q'uo. Adonai, my friends. Adonai. ☙

L/L Research

L/L Research is a subsidiary of Rock Creek Research & Development Laboratories, Inc.

P.O. Box 5195
Louisville, KY 40255-0195

www.llresearch.org

Rock Creek is a non-profit corporation dedicated to discovering and sharing information which may aid in the spiritual evolution of humankind.

ABOUT THE CONTENTS OF THIS TRANSCRIPT: This telepathic channeling has been taken from transcriptions of the weekly study and meditation meetings of the Rock Creek Research & Development Laboratories and L/L Research. It is offered in the hope that it may be useful to you. As the Confederation entities always make a point of saying, please use your discrimination and judgment in assessing this material. If something rings true to you, fine. If something does not resonate, please leave it behind, for neither we nor those of the Confederation would wish to be a stumbling block for any.

CAVEAT: This transcript is being published by L/L Research in a not yet final form. It has, however, been edited and any obvious errors have been corrected. When it is in a final form, this caveat will be removed.

© 2009 L/L Research

Sunday Meditation
June 20, 1993

Group question: The question this afternoon has to do with the metaphysical appropriateness, or value, in consciously choosing the more difficult path when we are aware of more than one path facing us in a particular direction. Is there a value, metaphysically, to consciously choosing more difficult paths or more difficult catalyst and being able to find joy anyway?

(Carla channeling)

I am Q'uo. Greetings in the love and in the light of the one infinite Creator. We greet you with undiluted pleasure and thank you for calling us to your circle of seeking. It is our pleasure to share our thoughts on the subject of difficulty and would—we correct this instrument—we would ask of you only that you hear our thoughts with the awareness that they are our opinions and have no authority over you except that authority you give them because you recognize them as your personal truth.

Move with us in your mind to the gardens outside this dwelling place and gaze about you at the various flowers, bushes, shrubbery, grasses and trees. Walk along the brick pathways looking at the perfection in each leaf, each blossom, be it clover or rose, green thing or colorful. Turn towards the light and visualize the beauty of this tranquil environment. Listen to the songs of the small birds twittering in the trees. The Creator moves through each fiber of each thing whatsoever that your eye can fall upon. Shall the lilies find some labor to justify their existence? Indeed, in your holy works the teacher known as Jesus asks to behold the lilies for they are so lovely not even a great king could be dressed in such splendid apparel yet they had done no work, put out no special effort to gain this glorious beauty. It was simply the Creator's gift.

Turn within now to look at the self. How, within, is your self arrayed? What clothing do you use to dress your thoughts, your personality, your character? Is the character that is your inner self that which has come to you by taking thought or is this self of yours that which you have by some effort chosen? We ask you to see yourselves as natural creatures like the lilies and the roses. There is a beauty and a virtue in the self that is natural. There is a truth within which is given and by no thought can this truth be duplicated. Indeed, all who seek truth seek out in the world only as a reflection of the seeking within to strip away the illusions of shadow which cover from one's own inner eyes the truth that lies at the heart of self.

The spiritual journey is a journey of taking away those things which are not natural until the natural beauty, the natural truth of the self is at last uncovered and is able to stand free of the fetters of darkness and radiate as the light bulb. Let us then move to another image. The self is now the light bulb. It is in itself simply a clear, empty channel. When that which is exterior to the bulb places it in a position in which it can receive energy and then this pathway is opened the bulb becomes radiant. As the lily radiates in its fragrant color the love of the infinite One so does the creature of spirit, the natural man stand in its empty openness of heart and radiate the love and light of the infinite One.

You ask if one should choose difficulty in order to express love under more difficult circumstances. We say to you, rather, the circumstances are before each. There is a period where no choices seem to need to be made and the seeker expresses its nature in peace and harmony. Inevitably, however, the seeker comes to some choice. Say it is the choice of one activity over another. The activity, say, of riding the bicycle or the activity of listening to the concert of music. Shall the entity choose the physical effort of riding the bicycle or shall the seeker choose to sit quietly and listen to beautiful music? One is physically difficult, another is physically easy.

Do you then choose to ride the bicycle so that you may choose the difficult path? We suggest, rather, that the seeker consult its desire. Which activity is the more natural to it? Some would find the bicycling, though physically more difficult, yet still preferable because the nature of that particular seeker is to find joy in activity, in feeling the muscles working, the body moving and the harmonies and beauties of the natural second density creation of the infinite One delightful. Another seeker might well choose to listen to music and feel its inner nature expand in feelings of positive joy and praise at the beauty of the creation of the race of humankind in all of its harmony and its joyous expression.

This seeking for some way to intensify the offering of love to the infinite One has a long history among your peoples. There are those in every generation who seek to wear the hair shirt next to the skin, to make this creation uncomfortable in as many ways as possible so that joy will be found not in this world but in the Creator only and the world of the Creator which is not here. There are many seekers who instinctively attempt to find the hardest jobs, the most difficult and intractable people to befriend, all for the sake of the infinite One. To those who find this an expression of their true nature we say go and do that which is natural to you for the path to the infinite Love and infinite Light in its purest manifestation within your illusion is that path which is—we correct this instrument—which has attained most purely a realization of the natural self within.

There is no intrinsic value either in ease or in discomfort. There is no special learning in arbitrarily choosing the more difficult or the more easy paths. What the seeker is attempting to do is to attain the inner vibration which is most natural and true, which most expresses the core of the self, the heart of that which is infinite and everlasting.

Thusly, to one seeker one way is the most straight path to that original Thought. Each entity will have its own way of moving towards that vibration of love and light. Perhaps we would say that as each seeker attempts to vibrate in the vibration which is most close to the original Thought which is the Logos or the Love of the infinite One the attempt is aided not by questions concerning difficulty or ease but rather the seeking to express and echo the original Vibration is aided by those who are willing to become transparent to that original Vibration.

When one is transparent then all things whatsoever color one, touch one, affect one. When one opens in transparent trust and love allowing the radiance of the original Thought to pour through one then that which is natural to that entity simply is in front of that entity. The choice has been to bear witness to the infinite Creator. Thus, if this purely vibrating entity is offered either the bicycle or the concert the transparent entity simply gazes upon each activity with the question, "How may I serve in this environment?" If the entity vibrates more in love and praise while physically active then this is the greater path. If the transparent entity vibrates more radiantly as a passive listener then the entity joyously sits and serves in praise and thanksgiving for this beauty all about.

Now, when there are choices which are partaking of the incarnational level, such as the choice of life mate and the choice of worldly vocation, it may seem more difficult to determine which of two choices is the more natural choice, yet in this too we suggest the process of becoming transparent to the original Thought, becoming able to be a channel for that great original Thought, so that there is allowed the self the process of choosing that life mate or that vocation in which the entity might most deeply bear witness to the love and light of the infinite One. This takes more and more awareness of the true nature of the self. The Creator does not ask of its children that it choose those things which are unnatural. It rather allows complete freedom. However, it is our observation that the more a choice conforms individual nature with the more representative way of relating or way of working the more profound will be the expressions of praise and thanksgiving that become possible as this relationship or this vocational activity is pursued.

To all who may listen to the voice of spirit comes suffering, limitation, difficulty, loss and the experience of death. To any activity that the sons and daughters of the infinite One may move there comes the difficulty, the pain, the time in which stamina, nerve and determination are called upon. It is not necessary to choose a more difficult path for all paths will contain the difficulties which you have prepared for yourself. Each of you has great trials in the past and in the future. That is the nature of the illusion in which you have chosen to pursue the learning of the lessons of love. If you attempt to choose an easy path, difficulties shall come to you. If you attempt to choose the difficult path, difficulties will come to you. It is impossible to avoid them.

So the virtue lies not in choosing difficulty, for difficulty is inevitable. The choice well made is that choice which seeks the most opportunity for service to others. We do not find it necessary to encourage any to wear hair shirts and make themselves uncomfortable thereby, for each will be very uncomfortable and feel as though he were indeed wearing the hair shirt again and again throughout the incarnational experience. It is just as futile to attempt to avoid difficulty. Those who attempt to make their lives easier and choose the easier path will still find the same lessons learned and every single iota of difficulty experienced whether the attempt to avoid the experience is made or not. You cannot move from your own nature and your nature as you experience yourself will be that which recedes before your understanding's grasp.

We began this talk thinking of the flowers in the garden who turn towards the sun. Just so, we encourage each to consider itself as that which by its very nature turns towards the sun which is the one great original Thought. Unlike the lilies in the garden you in third density have legs, you are mobile, you can move and express with mind and heart by using your voice and in all of your communication ways, writing, singing, drawing and expressing again and again. In your expression seek to allow to drop away those things which you do not find to be congruent with the attempt to express that great original Thought. Sometimes this will occasion the choice of the more difficult way. Sometimes it will prompt the choice which seems the easier way. The choice, however, we encourage you to make on the basis of its rightness for you as you attempt to praise and serve the infinite One. Follow your nature and know that your nature is joy, light, peace and love. Yes, you shall strive, you shall find difficulty, you shall perform feats of overcoming difficulty and still bearing witness to the light, but in any choice between two paths follow your light, follow your joy, follow your nature so that you may be your own unique self, most wholly and most entirely.

As you give up yourself to service you simply seek to maximize that service by choosing those …

(Side one of tape ends.)

(Carla channeling)

We see that we have overspent our allotted time once again and apologize for this length. We sense a low energy within this group, however, we do thank each for opening this channel this day. Perhaps you may see in this activity the example you seek. There were two ways to work with that with which you came to this circle today. You came to this circle without a clear and intense desire to seek the truth. You could have chosen not to sit in this working yet you chose to be faithful to a practice which you consider a portion of your spiritual seeking, and you turned toward the light and sat in faith, hoping in faith that light would be given. In that energy you created that vehicle through which we were able to contact this instrument. Was it the more difficult of the two choices? We believe so, yet this is not why this choice was your proper choice but rather it is because the choice was made to be of service and to open the self to the seeking of truth. In this you fulfilled your nature as you understand it at this point in your development. We thank you for this attempt to seek to grow closer to the one original Thought. We thank you for allowing us to be of service by your seeking and allowing us to speak.

And as you leave this circle we ask you to look not for difficulty but for opportunity to bear witness to the light by your very nature. Thusly, may your beauty shine and the Creator manifest Itself in the outworking of your life. We leave each in the resting and abiding of that selfhood which is the true nature of all. We leave you in love and in light, holograms of the one infinite Creator. We are those of Q'uo. Adonai. Adonai. ✛

L/L Research

L/L Research is a subsidiary of Rock Creek Research & Development Laboratories, Inc.

P.O. Box 5195
Louisville, KY 40255-0195

www.llresearch.org

Rock Creek is a non-profit corporation dedicated to discovering and sharing information which may aid in the spiritual evolution of humankind.

ABOUT THE CONTENTS OF THIS TRANSCRIPT: This telepathic channeling has been taken from transcriptions of the weekly study and meditation meetings of the Rock Creek Research & Development Laboratories and L/L Research. It is offered in the hope that it may be useful to you. As the Confederation entities always make a point of saying, please use your discrimination and judgment in assessing this material. If something rings true to you, fine. If something does not resonate, please leave it behind, for neither we nor those of the Confederation would wish to be a stumbling block for any.

CAVEAT: This transcript is being published by L/L Research in a not yet final form. It has, however, been edited and any obvious errors have been corrected. When it is in a final form, this caveat will be removed.

© 2009 L/L Research

Special Meditation
June 21, 1993

Question for S: The question this afternoon has to do with walking through the valley of the shadow of death in our daily lives, and in our metaphysical apprehension of our lives. Can you talk to us about what it is like, metaphysically, to feel the feelings of hypocrisy, of being worn out, burned out, angry, resentful, feeling that the Creator and the creation have, more or less, let you down? That things aren't the way they should be?

(Carla channeling)

I am Q'uo. Greetings in the love and in the light of the one infinite Creator. What a privilege and a blessing it is to be with this group. To blend our vibrations with yours, and to welcome the one known as S. We are most blessed by this opportunity to share our humble service with you and thank you for calling us to this session of working. How radiant is this circle. How deeply does each wish to know the truth and to bear witness to it. The courage of those who choose to live a life governed by blind faith astounds us afresh each time we are able to blend with this dedication of self in a circle such as this one. We ask as you listen to our thoughts that you use discrimination and accept as truth only those things which seem to you to be your own personal truths.

We use this instrument's knowledge of the context of the phrase, "The valley of the shadow of death," to quote that part of one of your holy works, "Yea, though I walk through the valley of the shadow of death, I shall fear no evil for thou art with me. Thy rod, thy staff, comfort me."

This psalmist whose works have praised the infinite Creator and given voice to many a desperate prayer, spoke most truly of third-density incarnational experience. Third density is the first self-conscious density; therefore, it is the density in which consciousness deals with the paradox of life and death.

To the flower, there is only the experience of the moment. The flower is whole and entire. Each moment of its life, its nature is fixed. It responds to love and to light; it is moved by these things and flourishes and thrives, or wilts and dies in utter contentment with its lot for it knows only the seeking towards the light. Though these second-density creatures have no wit and no voice, yet they manifest wisdom, which is lost in the migration into third density.

The tasks of humankind, then, are marked by the first consciousness aware of its own surcease. This life and death is the first of many self-contradictory and paradoxical opposites or pairs of opposites that are met in this density of the valley of the shadow of death. The magnitude of this shadow and its complexity and reach is hidden from those of third density not yet ready to awaken to the call of the inner self, to make the choice of light or darkness. When a seeker first becomes aware of the hunger to know of the mystery it has apprehended then comes the time of the taking up of the journey of pilgrimage, which [is] the life lived in faith.

At each juncture, each pivotal choice, the entity who seeks first becomes aware of a new level of unknowing and then finds itself in the position of dealing responsibly with this new level of awareness. One word for this quantum move from level of awareness to a fuller level of awareness is called initiation. It may be called that or any other term as long as the seeker grasps that at this level there is the full flowering of previous work and study. The onset of a new awareness of the depth of the shadows of death is in this way a compliment which destiny pays to the seeker. For as the new level of unknowing strikes one, as one begins working with the raw materials of the universal self thrown up by this new awareness, all that has been learned before is now integrated into the wider and deeper awareness of that universal self. In this way, when a time of testing comes, this time, in addition to being a beginning, is also the servant well done, which resounds within the heart of self.

A seeker who has a keen awareness of suffering is also a seeker who has reaped the bloom and blossom of much effort before.

Do we then suggest you rejoice at the new awareness that bites like a sword at the consciousness? Yes, my friends, indeed, we ask you to turn to the one infinite Creator and offer thanks and praise. Then we ask further, that the seeker be aware that in addition to thanks and to praise there are those communications which the one infinite Creator delights in hearing. These are those confessions of anger, of disappointment, of sorrow, and of suffering. To share these gifts with infinite One, it is to give to this mystery the most precious of gifts, for as each emotion whatsoever goes through the continuing process of refining and purification, so does the infinite One become infinitely more than It was. This is the greatest gift, to share all things, seemingly positive and seemingly negative, in a continuing and honest, heartfelt dialogue with the infinite One.

This is a dialogue whose part is silence. This is the inner working of consciousness and it is a great gift that each offers, as each continues to seek steadily, doggedly, persistently, unwaveringly for the truth, the light, the fuller awareness of life moves to the heart.

We wish each of you to do this now. Focus the attention upon this energy center. Touch, if you will, into that pool of sorrow. You are a stranger in a strange land. You seek amidst the deepest illusion. You are lost in solitude of spirit, feeling abandoned, stranded upon an alien shore. Allow this sorrow to become intense and then give it to the infinite One.

We pause briefly …

(Pause)

We are again with this instrument.

As you allow these feelings their silent expression, there was the answering expression … silent and unmanifest. Truly, each sorrow is a treasure and the thankfulness and love of the infinite Creator speaks directly to that deep heart within, wherein lies a true intelligence and true knowledge.

This walk through the valley may be seen with the eyes of faith as other than it seems. It may, if the seeker chooses, gradually begin to seem not only the valley, but also the high place. Not only the dark path but also that path which streams, full of light, *(inaudible)*. Both perceptions are equally true and to refrain from seeing things both ways is to refrain from wholeness.

This instrument spoke earlier of a phrase we have used, "The healing of the incarnation." We feel that as a third-density incarnational experience begins to mature and to be shaped by the growing consciousness within one distortion is added to another. Until, bias upon bias, the life has attained its characteristic shape. Within this shape, in virtually every instance, there is a fairly regular system of distortions which need a certain kind of healing which is unique to each biased yet balanced entity.

As the self does enough work in consciousness to have the capacity of looking upon the life experience as a whole, then the opportunity comes to offer a new level of commitment to the spiritual path, or what this instrument would call "The King's Highway."

We do not urge any to make commitments that do not feel right to the seeker, but we suggest when that time of testing comes and the new lesson of love begins, there is the opportunity to turn deliberately and with greatest desire to the mystery of all that there is and say, "Yes, I accept this lesson and through harsh experience, rediscovering the joy at the heart of my self." Do not do this quickly or before there is the inspiration to make this commitment to the forces of life, evolution and destiny, but when there is that moment when the grand Quixotic quest is clearly seen and there is that foolish, heartfelt impulse to accept, again, the process of healing and self-forgiveness, then we encourage each to leap in joy and faith with that affirmation that through long experience can be carved out of what would otherwise be a wilderness of sorrow.

You cannot, of yourself, create order out of the chaos of suffering. Any manmade order imposed upon such, in order to avoid pain, also avoids further knowledge of the self and diminishes the self's capacity to know and heal the self's balance within.

The road recedes before each. It shall continue, as far as we are aware, to do so infinitely.

Turn in mind and heart so in strength then to that companion that is never absent, the higher self or spirit within. Welcome all those, such as we, who move in thought to love, support and undergird the seeking strength of those who call upon our names and turn ever and again to those precious ones whom you serve and who are for you companions upon the way. To love one another. To share one another's sorrows and to walk hand in hand, rejoicing and singing upon that precious, dim, shadowy walk through the valley of the shadow of death.

Life and death are but shadows. The Creator is all that there is. Rest then in shadow and in sunlight, and feel compassion flood you in your innermost being for your own courage, as you struggle with light and darkness and choose again and again, in blind faith, the manifested light.

We would at this time transfer this contact to the one known as Jim. We thank this instrument. We are those of Q'uo, and leave this instrument in love and light.

(Jim channeling)

I am Q'uo, and greet each again in love and in light through this instrument. It is a privilege at this time to ask if there might be any further queries to which we may speak. Is there another query at this time?

Questioner: I have a comment and see what you can say about it. A feeling this whole year has been that it has not been my third density personality, fourth density, whatever density personality that is going through the difficulties that I, in the past, have always gladly with light heart and, as Carla would say, as "keeper of the watchtower" offer back to the Creator gladly the hardships that I would travel and meet. But something has happened this year that has, I feel very firmly about, has affected my magical self, a part of me that I never really thought would ever be attacked, because of my utmost naiveté and faith and automatic turning to the light.

The valley and the shadows that I have been walking through have shaken the very foundation of my magical place, something that I find frightening. It's only been because of the habit of turning to the light that I have held on. Because I have heard self say, "No." And that in itself … something has happened, and it's only been in the reservoir of having led the life on the magical path that has kept a darkness at bay, but I am concerned because I am finding myself, my magical self, growing less purposeful in experiencing and giving back to the Creator the experiences of my magical identity, the purpose for my being here. I need to know more than just giving back to the Creator the experience that seems very arrogant, the purpose of my magical identity, because the price this year has been incredibly high and the pain, incredibly deep.

I am Q'uo, and we listened with great sympathy to the pain and anguish which you describe and we feel a great kinship with you, for each of you who walk through the valley of the shadow of death that is the third-density illusion walks with great courage and as you have said this day, a kind of naiveté, that is at once a shining light and a protection to those who walk in the valley of illusion.

We would hasten to suggest that it is not your magical personality that has suffered the blows that you have felt, for each entity such as yourself that has come to this illusion to serve in the light has a magical personality which is unblemished, as is yours. That which you have experienced as your magical personality is, in relation to your true magical personality, but the barest beginnings of a description of its fullness.

For as you work in magical sense in this illusion, you establish a contact with this personality that is truly magical in its essence. This contact is made of but the finest fibers of light and love, constructed with the greatest of efforts by you in your work that is metaphysical in nature. As you continue to travel this pathway, this light and love woven thread leading to the magical personality, you strengthen this pathway, Even the strongest of magicians, shall we say, in your third density illusion, touch only a portion of that personality which resides, safely and securely, within the six-density level of experience.

What you have felt in this past year, as you have described it, is more the pathway becoming less and less accessible, or so it would seem to you in your experience. Yet, may we also suggest that this pathway is accessible though it may seem to be not so accessible as previously. This is as because as you go through those experiences of difficulty which we have described as initiation, there is the changing perception of your third-density personality as it seeks for that which it once knew as a pathway, and finds brambles and stones and dryness of experience.

This is a part of this transformative experience which, when completed, will have served to temper even more precisely and finely that pathway which you travel to the magical personality, but there will be a new you, for the third-density entity which you have been, and are now, is that entity which is being transformed by the difficulties of the experience. Thus, the tempering is by fire and seems to destroy that which once was.

As the …

(Side on of tape ends.)

(Carla channeling)

I am Q'uo. We shall continue. Those of your friends and your guides and teachers are with you always and are aware of your difficulty and give aid where they can and guidance where it is possible. However, this particular kind of transformation is that which requires the one undergoing the transformation to seek with one's own efforts, as fully as possible. Thus, the darkness seems far more black and full of difficulty than has any previous experience.

However, we assure you, my sister, that there is aid at hand, and even though you feel there is no response to your call for assistance, there is the love and the light sent by all those whose honor it *(inaudible)* is to walk with you upon this journey.

We counsel you to have faith and take heart that in these times of trials and testings that you will survive. You will make the feeling of unity that once was yours become again as the steady state of your experience. This testing is a great gift that is given, both to you, as you experience it, and given by you to the Creator, as you are victorious in your testing.

We can say to you that you are doing well, though it may seem such is not the case. Be of good spirits, my sister, for we walk with you, always.

Is there a further query?

Questioner: No, thank you.

I am Q'uo, and we thank you, my sister. Is there another query, at this time?

Carla: I have one. You said, "Don't be afraid." You said it somewhere. "Take courage," I think you said and the verse says, "I will fear no evil." But it is scary. It is terribly frightening. It's terrifying, especially when you feel like the negativity's right within yourself and it's you and you're sort of attacking yourself, in the end.

I had that after Don died. I really just felt very suicidal and hopeless and the only thing that kept me going was, like S said, the habit of turning to the light. I just was determined to keep my faith, but it didn't make it the less hurtful or terrifying and I had lots of nightmares.

Is there some way that you can reduce the terror factor while you're having to go through it? I mean, I realize what you're doing is building a whole new personality that takes in the fruits of everything that was learned before and I know that means pain, because change always mean pain. But how can you get comfort when you're so wretched?

I am Q'uo, and am aware of your query, my sister. We must suggest that there is but little comfort in this transformation experience. There is the strength that comes from faith, continually exercised. Faith that there is an end to this experience. Faith that there is strength within to overcome that which seems to be overwhelming, and we can assure each of you that as you move from this illusion and look back upon your experiences here, you shall rejoice at those areas of darkness, that you have been blessed with light, with love, and with the faith in your journey and in your efforts and in the unity of all things.

Is there a further query?

Carla: No. Thank you very much for that.

I am Q'uo, and we thank you, once again, my sister. Is there another query, at this time?

(No further queries.)

I am Q'uo, and as it appears that we have exhausted the queries for the nonce, we shall once again express our great gratitude at being invited to join you in this circle of seeking. It is not often that we are able to bathe in these vibrations of harmonious interaction that are born at the meeting of these entities present. We especially are grateful for being able to speak with, and walk with, the one known as S.

At this time, we shall take our leave of this group and this instrument, leaving each, as always, in the love and in the light of the one infinite Creator. Adonai, my friends. Adonai. ✣

L/L Research is a subsidiary of Rock Creek Research & Development Laboratories, Inc.

P.O. Box 5195
Louisville, KY 40255-0195

www.llresearch.org

Rock Creek is a non-profit corporation dedicated to discovering and sharing information which may aid in the spiritual evolution of humankind.

ABOUT THE CONTENTS OF THIS TRANSCRIPT: This telepathic channeling has been taken from transcriptions of the weekly study and meditation meetings of the Rock Creek Research & Development Laboratories and L/L Research. It is offered in the hope that it may be useful to you. As the Confederation entities always make a point of saying, please use your discrimination and judgment in assessing this material. If something rings true to you, fine. If something does not resonate, please leave it behind, for neither we nor those of the Confederation would wish to be a stumbling block for any.

CAVEAT: This transcript is being published by L/L Research in a not yet final form. It has, however, been edited and any obvious errors have been corrected. When it is in a final form, this caveat will be removed.

© 2009 L/L Research

Sunday Meditation
June 27, 1993

Group question: We Earth-dwellers are exhorted to praise and worship our Creator by both our earthbound religions and extraterrestrial sources alike. It is inconceivable that the Creator would perform the stupendous feat of the creation simply in order to provide an adulating audience. Can you please explain this seeming enigma?

(Carla channeling)

Greetings in the love and in the light of the one infinite Creator. We are known to you as those of Q'uo. It is a privilege to be with you and to be called to respond to your queries. We thank you for this beneficial request. That is, we express that it is beneficial for us to be able to attempt to serve you in this way. We ask that if we do say that which you feel is beneficial to you, that you may consider this thought, but not the thought which you do not find helpful. Those thoughts which are not recognized by you, by your inner guidance, are thoughts to be left behind. With this understanding we may begin.

When in the primeval unity of the creation the Creator chose through free will to express Itself the creation was articulated. The proper response to this Being has in your culture formed around itself a large number of ways and means which are deemed to be appropriate so that one gives one's rightful response to a Creator which has chosen to manifest that which is the seeker. Each of these instructions seems wise and proper to some and inappropriate to others. Therefore it would seem that there is no consensus as to what the Creator Itself might want from Its creation.

This seems to be the situation; however, the Creator, as we feel this mystery, is unworldly and incompletely grasped by us, [and] seems to us not to desire any response over other responses, but rather, the Creator acts and continues in action rather than reaction. The seeker wishing to address the infinite One in most cases is addressing a logos or sub-logos, the love manifest, or some expression of love manifest, such as the higher self. To this higher self, still, no one mode of address is preferred precisely, rather the praise and thanksgiving are accepted without emotion.

Questioner: Then why do so many sources state that it is good and just to offer praise and thanksgiving to the infinite Creator?

I am Q'uo. The Creator created a great original Expression or Thought. This we have called the logos or love. This principle, this love, created all that there is by the quantizing articulation of light. Yet all that is created is of the nature of its parent source, which is love. The reason for offering love, appreciation, a blessing and thanksgiving to the infinite One is that the entity within incarnation is attempting to form its vibratory frequency more and more like that of the vibrational frequency of the one great original Thought, which is love. The closer the seeker comes to matching that vibratory frequency, the more that entity will be perceived as offering praise and thanksgiving. This is true far beneath any articulation of words or even what you consider thoughts. Rather, it is in the nature of the way creation is built. That is, original Thought expresses in love, thanks, blessing, praise and rejoicing. Thusly, it is not a Creator hungry for praise and thanks that requires homage of its worshippers, but rather it is love, it is reflected in love, and in that infinite reflection lies truth.

Questioner: We are also encouraged to fill ourselves with inner joy. To maintain a state of inner joy whilst entombed in the physical body and being constantly inundated with horrific scenes of worldwide death and destruction is far from easy. Would it be correct to say that we must endeavor to convert our feelings of anger and despair to those of compassion, for we do not experience these dreadful acts directly and we upset our equilibrium by becoming emotionally involved?

I am Q'uo. As the seeker moves into the world scene, it moves from that inner pathway which at times seems shadowed and at times seems a wonderful King's Highway into a theater, if you will, wherein there is all sorts of entertainment. Reliably, some of this entertainment will be terrible, horrific and pitiable. Provision is made within each of your cultures for sheltered places wherein the gentle entities, there protected, may not have to deal with the seeming ugliness of the world. Good and loving persons move into these cloistered environments and the purity of love generated by these protected ones is beautiful. However, some hardy souls there are, who though not personally starving, or hunted, or otherwise in terror and desperation, still allow these experiences occurring with others to have a substantial place in the waking consciousness.

Many of those who are riveted by the grisly side of the world scene are those which are attracted to the negative clustering emotions surrounding these events. This in turn makes more metaphysical darkness to appear around these happenings, which makes it seem even more appealing to protect the self, or those which are deemed most delicate, from having to experience, even in thought, these horrors.

However, it is our opinion that when the seeker feels called upon in its rhythms of being guided to bear witness to the universal nature of the self, the addressing of the self to the universal nature of the world which it inhabits is a very good entrance point into the challenging business of seeking to address the universal self, which must be done by those who wish to graduate into the density of compassion.

It seems foolish and inappropriate even to consider gazing with thanks or rejoicing upon such suffering, yet this too is a portion of the one infinite Creator. This too is perfect.

We would suggest that when the seeker is struck by this situation, it may be productive to enter into the life experience of an entity within that war or that starving population which has drawn the attention. In thought, the seeker may become one of those suffering. We suggest that it is helpful then to move deeply into that persona, to experience as intensely as imagination allows the suffering and horror of this situation. Not simply touching into the thought and then leaving, but staying with this suffering, keeping company with this suffering, embracing this suffering, exploring and affirming this suffering, until the whole vibration re-echoes with this suffering in its fullness.

When this is done to the extent possible by the seeker, then allow this frame of mind to be offered as the offering of money to the one infinite Creator, for this suffering has been suffering in love of the fellow self. This is a goodly presentation to the infinite Creator. Each time the seeker re-experiences this horror, the feelings of helplessness and powerlessness, being unable to aid the situation, then we suggest repeating this, embracing the full extent of this suffering.

It is well also to send light to these situations. This is work well done and we do not wish to discourage this practice in order to encourage the embracing of the unrelieved and unchanged and unhealed situation, rather we wish to enable a seeker to use the resource of its own structure, that is, there lies within each the deep mind structure as part of the archetypical mind, wherein each may suffer as each, each may experience anything whatever as each. There is that deep within the mind in which all entities within one influence are together, and the change from individual-to-universal-to-individual is but a blink or thought away. To move in sympathy into another's illusion fully is to take this black and bitter harvest, and in the way possible only to one which does this consciously and deliberately, to embrace the full travel and extent of suffering and so relieve by that imagining the bite of pain for all.

Questioner: In an earlier session, Yom commented on the fact that humankind finds the need to adopt a choiceless, compassionate position as deeply threatening. Is this sensed threat, that of loss of identity, brought about by the need to do the will of the Creator, or as Jesus said, "not as I will, but as Thou wilt"?

I am Q'uo. To those who do find the attitudes of non-judgment a threat, we would say that it is so, that these so threatened fail to perceive that the attitude of choiceless compassion can possibly express the truth, for within the incarnational experience it would seem that all things have some positive or negative aspect, that is, seldom do entities experience people and situations without some bias governing the way the situation or entity is perceived. To let go of this judgment and embrace non-judgment seems if not actually threatening, at least poor judgment. The entire world of observed data is based upon choices and judgment. This, not that, is the way to proceed. That, and not this, is the way to react skillfully. Indeed, an entity which embraces non-judgment may certainly be seen to lack the appropriate cultural responses.

Within the processes of creating and transforming one's consciousness there are paradoxical requirements for the seeker who is asked both to choose the manner of its seeking in polarizing and to attempt to apprehend all incoming data with no bias. Entities within incarnation will almost surely fail to express a complete lack of bias, but the paradox we wish to point out is that the seeker needs both to choose decisively the system of biases it wishes to encourage within the self and is at the same time attempting to see its catalyst more and more clearly, which involves removing both attraction and repulsion from the processes of perception.

To choose to be choiceless seems ultimately nonsensical, yet in the process of perception this is precisely what is required, and then, when perceptions have been formed, the seeker is required to move in a positive, purposeful way, either towards the light, metaphysically speaking, or towards the darkness.

The mind and metaphysical vehicle which is your second-density self does not involve itself with these niceties. Its instinct is to sort and catalogue all incoming catalysts and to give it importance in accordance with its agenda. That is, said impressions having to do with the survival of the physical vehicle are given priority over all other stimuli, and so forth, until the instinctual needs of body and brain are satisfied. To this entity it seems excessively poor judgment to withhold bias to maintain choiceless awareness. It makes no sense, and more than that does seem to represent a way of perception which could result in the cessation of life for the physical vehicle. If something is obstructing the air passages in a physical vehicle, it does not make sense to the physical vehicle to note this fact choicelessly. Action definitely seems necessary.

The threat of which the ones known as Yom spoke stems from this portion of the seeking entity. It is when work is beginning to be done in consciousness, when the second-density creature begins to work in harmony with the third-density consciousness which is your infinite selves, that the requirements of spiritual seeking begin to apply. Many there are among your peoples which at the present moment have no clear perceptions of their own infinite nature, or their eternal span of being. And to communicate from the spiritual being aware of non-sensation with that entity which is completely aware of its probable dissolution and ending of self seems impossible. Many entities attempting to walk the spiritual path are still deeply involved in that second-density consciousness which knows of its own dissolution, and the third-density consciousness then is much taken up with material having to do with catastrophes and difficulties, those things which we see in this instrument's mind labeled as "conspiracy theories" and the "last days syndrome." This is the effect of third-density consciousness, whose natural rhythms are based upon a choiceless awareness, interacting with, and acting as, second-density consciousness which has become aware of its forthcoming end.

The two consciousnesses, each of its kind, are excellent and express divinity. The mixture is confusing and creates confusion within the seeker. As the seeker becomes more and more familiar with how third-density consciousness actually feels, it may become more and more skillful at timely notings or notation of those thoughts which seem to be less than the desired third-density level. The seeker then can turn and gaze upon that which has been created in fear, that by which the consciousness without choice seems threatening, and can move to embrace that fear.

It is not skillful to drag one's consciousness into a fuller expression of compassion or understanding. It is far more skillful to stop when the threat is perceived, when the feelings are engaged that are called fear and other negative emotions, to turn and go to meet that fearful or threatened entity, to metaphysically put the arms around that entity and to witness with that entity each iota of pain, to accept this limited entity and to be one with it.

When this has been done the seeker may then move forward in praise and thanksgiving until it next finds its processes of perception in a snag or snare, feeling threatened and fearful. Then the same process may be begun, completed without hurry and the journey continued.

This constant turning back to keep the straggling portions of the self-awareness at one with those which would march ahead, is most diligently encouraged by us, for we are of the opinion that when the laggardly portions of the recording self are offered the same compassion offered to others in pain, the actual rate of spiritual learning is greater than the rate of true spiritual learning which is achieved by those entities which leap forward from good thought to good thought and ignore if possible any portions of the self which will not come along for the ride. This is living in a judgment of the self, and in the long run does hinder and seriously slow the seeker's steps.

We encourage each, therefore, to turn back again and again, always attempting to practice toward the self's fears, be they light or very deep in nature, with that love which is felt from the infinite Creator. Ministering to the self in this way, the universal nature of the self may in a graceful way, which is full of rhythms of compassion, be put forward and practiced more and more.

Is there one more query before we leave this instrument?

Questioner: No.

We are those whom you call Q'uo. It has been our pleasure and our privilege to work with this instrument and this group. We thank the one known as K, who has made it part of his practice to be a witness with this group. We thank this entity and are thankful for these queries which allow us to be of some humble service. At this time we would leave this instrument and this group, wishing all the utmost awareness of the love and the light of the one infinite Creator. Adonai. Adonai. ❧

Intensive Meditation
July 10, 1993

Second Session

(Carla channeling)

I am Hatonn. Greetings in the love and in the light of the one infinite Creator. We are privileged to be called to your group this afternoon and we thank you very much. For it is greatly enabling us to perform our service that you call upon us to share our thoughts.

We are especially glad to be working with the one known as M, for as our brothers and sisters of Laitos have noted, each voice which collaborates with our Source adds one more universe of potential ways to state the simple truth we come to bring to your peoples.

We would say a few words concerning the conditioning, so-called. The stronger conditioning can occur, spontaneously, however, we have used it in order to satisfy a channel who wished to have some indication that there was a contact.

One may request the conditioning and we attempt then to intensify its effect. It is, however, a byproduct, rather than something to which one can attach true importance. Its simply the effect of one life stream being overshadowed, or undershadowed, or combined with another energy nexus, such as ourselves.

In the case of a new channel, it can serve as a focal point when the conditioning is felt that can become to the instrument who chooses to use it that which is focused upon and deepened by attention. This adds to the self-confidence of the channel and it is our intention that its use might relax the channel which may be somewhat concerned about whether it is indeed receiving a contact.

You will notice that this instrument does not request conditioning, although it occasionally will receive a mouth movement or something of that kind. However, this instrument has much experience in learning to trust in the contact once the work of tuning and challenging has been done and perhaps we would encourage the new instrument to think of conditioning and indeed the concern about whether there is a contact, as part of a process whereby the instrument simply gains experience so that the process becomes known and the rhythm can be felt as the channeling continues from the first phrase.

However, for now, we are most happy simply to work on the basic fundamentals. The instrument needs to be very conscious of the tuning process and very interested in learning enough about the self to begin to find those techniques of tuning and becoming more purely desirous of service. The more carefully the instrument amasses knowledge of the self and the mental, emotional energies are exalted and raised, the better able that instrument shall be to hold a stable contact at the higher reaches of the range at which the instrument can relax as a steady state of consciousness within.

We ask about this circle to continually envision the light energy moving clockwise about the circle. For this functioning like a battery, if you will, does aid the new instrument and indeed any which are instruments in maintaining that steady contact which is so much at the heart of good channeling.

We ask the one known as M to relax and insofar as it is possible do as has been said this day several times, "go with the flow." This instrument would say, "Rome was not built in a day," and neither, my friends, are channels. So we, at this time, ask the one known as M to open to our presence and we would, at this time, like to transfer this contact to the one known as M. We are those of Hatonn.

(Inaudible)

(Pause)

(Carla channeling)

I am Hatonn, and am again with this instrument. This instrument was impatient to begin again, but we wished to work with the one known as M at some depth and we thank this instrument for allowing us to continue for a while.

We find that although we have a seemingly stable connection within the one known as M there is the desire to be sure that the contact is accurate and actual, and the desire not to guess. This is a praiseworthy attitude, which, in the case of one which is too closely attached to the desire to be sure, becomes that rigidity within which [one] can never be sure.

We would suggest that the first several times the contact is exercised, that the new channel begin with the greeting, "I am Hatonn." As the one known as S has said, although much can be greatly doubted about the experiences it is certain that we shall begin with our humble identification and the careful greeting in the name of the infinite One in love and light, in joy and in power beyond.

This certainly, the feeling of security slips away quickly, however, this beginning can be taken in—we correct this instrument—on faith and perhaps as has happened often before, something about the experience of venturing forth with these opening greetings may break that dam of concern which has hardened into too much strength for the needs of this circumstance. The group is a good protection against any real error and working with more experienced channels there is the certainty that a wrong step shall be quickly pointed out and repaired.

This instrument indeed is willing at any and all times to stop the session completely if that seems to be desirable and indeed this instrument has done so occasionally in the past.

So there is much support within this environment. This being said, we would again like to transfer this contact to the one known as M and say only a couple of sentences through this instrument.

We would now transfer this contact. I am Hatonn.

(M channeling)

I am Hatonn, and I greet you in the love and the light of the one infinite Creator. I have some difficulties … *(inaudible)*, but the connection is a stable *(inaudible)*. There are some principal difficulties that need to be addressed.

I leave this instrument, now. I am Hatonn.

(Carla channeling)

I am Hatonn, and am with this instrument, once again. We are most pleased and gladdened that the one known as M has indeed taken that leap from the cliff. We thank this instrument for its courage and feel very positive that although the contact is always a subtle thing, the one known as M begins now to be truly aware that thoughts do come into the mind of one who is willing to say one thing quickly and then hear another, say another, and so forth.

We would appreciate the circle's patience, because we would like to spend a bit more time working with our connection with this instrument to alleviate any discomfort …

We shall pause at this time. I am Hatonn.

(Pause)

I am Hatonn, and am again with this instrument. We have adjusted the connection and would ask the one known as M if the change was helpful

M: *(Inaudible).*

We shall continue to work with this tuning as we speak briefly through each instrument. Now we would enjoy the opportunity to speak further, though the one known as S. We leave this instrument and transfer at this time. I am Hatonn.

(S channeling)

I am Hatonn. We greet you again in the love and in the light of the infinite One through this instrument. It was with some amusement that this instrument greeted us. For it felt that had been thrown the "curve ball," so to speak, the normal pattern being that this instrument receives the contact from the one known as Jim. This instrument is accustomed to ready itself for this contact by focusing particularly upon the effort to control the material at hand.

To some extent, this is a crutch this instrument has requested and which we are most happy to cooperate with. However, it is the mark of a maturing instrument to be willing to take up the task of speaking with less and less expectation concerning what precisely it is that lies ahead, what precisely it is that will be said. There is always some degree of anticipation involved in the process of being an instrument as a certain horizon unfolds within the process of supplying words for the concept which blossom in the deeper or less conscious part of the mind.

This instrument is currently in the process of developing that greater faith and confidence that the concepts shall indeed continue to blossom even when a clear structure of thought has not been delineated or laid out beforehand.

This blooming of concepts within the deep mind is the manner in which our thoughts came to you, in the blended energies of our two selves. Thus, if one reaches down to the source it is not wholly possible any longer to distinguish self from self, as indeed within the process of this greeting we do not distinguish ourselves from those embracing energies of All That Is, the infinite and creative love which is source to us and to you all alike.

The fear which separates self from self shall gradually, my brothers and sisters in the light, fall away as do the petals of a spent blossom, even as the blossom closer to its heart continues to unfurl.

We encourage each in the process of tuning and of allowing this deeper self greater and greater access and greater and greater voice within the life experience, which is your gift to be able to enjoy at this time.

We now would transfer this control to the one known as Jim.

(Jim channeling)

I am Hatonn, and greet each of you in love and in light through this instrument. It has been a great privilege to be able to utilize each instrument this afternoon. We are especially gratified to have been able to initiate contact through the new instrument known as M. It is a great honor for us to be asked to provide our services in this regard and we wish to thank the one known as M with all our hearts.

At this time, we would ask the new instrument or any other entity who may have queries for us.

M: At the present time, I'm experiencing moods … *(inaudible)*.

I am Hatonn. We shall look at our vibrational harmonics and readjust, momentarily.

(Pause)

I am Hatonn. We would ask the one known as M if there has been any relief?

M: *(Inaudible)*.

I am Hatonn. We see that there is some discomfort from the position of the head and neck area that has resulted from the initial experience of voicing the thoughts transmitted. This is not unusual for a new instrument to find that the position of its body has, due to unfamiliarity, became a stress point. We shall work with your instrument and our contact with you in future work to attempt to alleviate this side effect of the newly experienced contact.

Is there another query?

Questioner: No. Not at this time. Thank you Hatonn.

I am Hatonn, and again we wish to thank each in this group for inviting our presence into this circle of seeking. We are overjoyed at this opportunity and thank each of you. We would take this opportunity to greet each again with our conditioning vibration and would at this time leave this instrument and this group in the love and in the light of the one infinite Creator. We are known to you as those of Hatonn. Adonai, my friends. ✾

L/L Research

L/L Research is a subsidiary of Rock Creek Research & Development Laboratories, Inc.

P.O. Box 5195
Louisville, KY 40255-0195

www.llresearch.org

Rock Creek is a non-profit corporation dedicated to discovering and sharing information which may aid in the spiritual evolution of humankind.

ABOUT THE CONTENTS OF THIS TRANSCRIPT: This telepathic channeling has been taken from transcriptions of the weekly study and meditation meetings of the Rock Creek Research & Development Laboratories and L/L Research. It is offered in the hope that it may be useful to you. As the Confederation entities always make a point of saying, please use your discrimination and judgment in assessing this material. If something rings true to you, fine. If something does not resonate, please leave it behind, for neither we nor those of the Confederation would wish to be a stumbling block for any.

CAVEAT: This transcript is being published by L/L Research in a not yet final form. It has, however, been edited and any obvious errors have been corrected. When it is in a final form, this caveat will be removed.

© 2009 L/L Research

Sunday Meditation
July 11, 1993

Group question: The question this afternoon has to deal with the fact that life seems to be composed of gains and losses, and we're wondering about how we can use the losses that we feel in our life as means by which to increase our spiritual seeking or our service or our knowledge of ourselves. In a world of dualities, how is this duality of gain and loss, especially the loss, of help and of a tempering quality, shall we say. How does it aid our spiritual evolution, or how can we use it to aid our spiritual evolution?

(Carla channeling)

I am Hatonn. Greetings to all in the love and in the light of the infinite Creator. It is our privilege and blessing to be with you this day. We are most grateful to be allowed to share our thoughts with you and to enjoy not only the blending of our vibrations, but also the beauty of your surroundings as we see them through your consciousnesses. You ask us to speak about a certain kind of harvest this day, that plenty which is reaped, and garnered, and treasured when the seeking conscious self is faced with loss.

We would at this time transfer to the one known as S. I am Hatonn.

(S channeling)

I am Hatonn. We give to this instrument the concept of passion, and we would note that passion has its sorrowful side as well as its joyful side. We find that a life lived with an eye only to joy is a life which is bereft of half of life's full passion. The task, not just for the conscious spiritual seeker, but for any who walk upon the highways and byways of this existence you now share, is to fully immerse oneself in the process of living, to accept life in all of its many colors and all of its many hues, to feel the full brunt and carry the full weight in all earnestness. To live a life of passion means to love living, and this includes even one's sorrow.

At this time we would transfer the contact to the one known as M, expecting that M shall give our greeting and then pass the contact to the one known as Jim. In the love and light of the one Creator, we are those of Hatonn.

(M channeling)

I am Hatonn, and greet you again in the love and the light of the one infinite Creator. Transfer now to the one known as Jim. I am Hatonn.

(Jim channeling)

I am Hatonn. The passion with which one lives the incarnation is that energy which assures one that there shall be the joy and the pain combined in full so that one may experience the total vibrational frequency of this illusion and have at one's disposal the full range of responses that one makes and which one may utilize in the formation of the character of the conscious spiritual seeker. Were there less range and choices, the seeker would have less to utilize in this construction. It is for advanced work, shall we say, that the seeker remembers that all is one, and that there is no true loss or gain, but a realization of unity that becomes more finely tuned as one feels the joy and the pain.

We shall now transfer to the one known as Carla. I am Hatonn.

(Carla channeling)

When the seeker beholds the harvest of joy, it seems natural and right to give praise and to offer thanks for the bounteous harvest which one may embrace with all of one's passion. However, this passion seems to grow weak and ineffectual when presented with the bounteous ingathering of deep and deeply felt loss. The passionate heart cannot reason how to embrace, to praise, and to give thanks for this plenty, although that same entity may easily observe how much this harvest is an aid to the seeker of truth and love as it looks back in memory to reconfigure for the mind's own understanding of self how the path to a new level of awareness was first graded and made passable by that very difficult harvest of loss.

We now transfer to the one known as S.

(S channeling)

I am Hatonn. The sense of loss bespeaks a separation. It is a separation, in the case of one who has died, that is easily understood, for one is no longer able to communicate in those old familiar ways with the beloved one. At a deeper level, however, the sense of separation registers as a kind of disharmony with all that is. One perhaps feels torn out of the sense that one may have had of being rooted in, or belonging to, an environment that is nurturing and welcoming, staring now at a hostile and unforgiving land. The separation then cuts quite deep.

We would at this time again transfer the contact to the one known as M, expecting once more that this instrument shall give our greeting, express whatever thought may come to mind, and then again pass the contact to the one known as Jim. We are those of Hatonn.

(M channeling)

I am Hatonn. I greet you in the love and light of the Creator. I would again transfer this contact to the one known as Jim. I am Hatonn.

(Jim channeling)

I am Hatonn. To feel the pain of loss is to feel, firstly, to awaken those inner sensing qualities that are also the same qualities that may experience joy. Loss is a way of sensitizing one's fine perceptions, shall we say. This, of course, also includes the necessity for healing the self that feels torn and overly sensitized to pain. The healing that works upon the pain comes when the feeling of loss is placed within a larger framework for the mind, the emotions, and the spirit to feel as whole, thus placing the entity within a harmonized universe, yet retaining the increased sensitivity to all stimuli. With this increased sensitivity, the seeker then goes forth to renew its gathering of the harvest of catalyst.

We shall now transfer to the one known as Carla.

(Carla channeling)

I am Hatonn. How hard it is for those in your illusion to become able clearly to perceive any sense of comfort or nearness of truth or spirit when this cutting edge has cleft the world that was in twain. It is as though the seeker were suddenly stranded upon a hostile beach, from which stretched forward mile upon mile, mile upon mile, nothing but heat, dust, dryness and the thirst and starvation that comes to one far too long unwatered and unfed. How to grasp that larger picture which sees the true value of this dark bounty? How to stay within that desert in authentic mindfulness, and from that desolation bring forth that thanks and praise that is, seen in retrospect, the faith at this point [that] is truly, utterly and completely blind.

We now transfer to the one known as S.

(S channeling)

I am Hatonn. Though the vocation of the wayfarer involves an inveterate blindness, yet still the seeker yearns to see; and through the tears of anguish and the groans of pain may make out a sense of a greater meaning lurking and looming behind the events, the very events, which seem otherwise so dark. The seeker, bereft of all comfort and alone, finds yet there is some prospect of help, some prospect of solace in knowing that there is a meaning and a value to the experience which is currently endured, though the precise nature of this meaning lies just beyond the outstretched fingertips.

While it would often seem, oh, so easy to have resort to the wisdom that this experience after all is but an illusion, the sense of loss but a temporary blip on an ephemeral radar screen, yet to resort to this feeling overmuch is simply to anesthetize the self and to rob it of the very experience which it seeks.

There is a universal passion that one may aspire to. Did the teacher known to you as Jesus the Christ not have a passion which reached out to the very sorrow of humanity itself? In order to appreciate the enormity of the task of this teacher, however, one must realize that the passion of the Christ was not a comfortable experience. It was not a wise experience, but it rather was an experience in which a humble seeker reached as deeply as it could reach into a compassion which opened as on to a floodgate of pain. The pain, my brothers and my sisters, was there to be felt. It is not to be circumvented.

At this time we would transfer the contact to the one known as M. We are those of Hatonn.

(Pause)

(Carla channeling)

I am Hatonn. We thank the one known as M and assure this instrument that the amount of seating or grounding that has been accomplished during this time of working is quite excellent. The new channel being opened is still delicate and the energy of the beginning of the message is much like your starting load upon your electrical appliances wherein a great deal of energy, more than is needed for running, is needed for starting to run. This opening intensity which is required at the beginning of a contact has fairly thoroughly numbed the channel, and this is quite normal. We therefore encourage the new instrument and suggest that each attempt at bearing this starting load, as it were, refines and deepens the channel which has been opened in a tuned and focused manner so that there comes the time when that starting load is easily borne and is not that which takes the full focus and energy of the instrument.

We would at this time transfer to the one known as Jim.

(Jim channeling)

I am Hatonn. The loss of any portion of that which is perceived as important within the life experience makes one equal, shall we say, to all those who have suffered such loss. It is hoped that by working with loss the seeker will develop compassion, first for the self and the healing of the self for the loss, then in compassion for others who feel the same kind of loss. Eventually, this will hopefully develop compassion for all entities who suffer any loss. And as the seeker looks deeper within its own being at the many experiences gathered during the incarnation, it begins to see that all entities share the same in this illusion: the joy and exhilaration of being alive and of gaining those things which have value in this illusion, and the use of such for the growing and serving of others then balanced with the pain of loss, the removal of that which one thought was irreplaceable and of inestimable value. To realize that all is but temporary and illusory causes the seeker to find a means to understand, to use a poor term, the meaning of the life as it is lived. This impetus to search is yet another great fruit of loss.

We shall now transfer to the one known as Carla.

Carla: Could we please sing "Row, Row, Row Your Boat"? Chocolate Bar *(a cat)* has just caught my attention and I'd like to retune.

(Song)

(Carla channeling)

I am Hatonn. We thank each for aiding this instrument in reestablishing the depth of contact that this instrument prefers. The purring of the kitten that shall mystify the scribe which places this message upon paper is that joy which rejoices in the …

(Side one of the tape ends).

(Carla channeling)

There is beyond this joy a passion and joy which contains a fullness which is the eventual realization of the great blessing of those desert times, those seemingly insufferable limitations, losses and agonies which take that which was the awareness of the self by the self and remove, while still living, that tissue of personal structure that seemed quite necessary.

The hollowing out of the rock by those forces of nature which cause the caves to be made, the hollowing out of clay which makes of the lump upon the potter's wheel the empty and waiting chalice … this hollowing, this refining, this harvest of that which shall be transformed—how painful, yet how full of the terrible beauty that is that which we greet you in—the one great original Thought which is love, love that is seen in creation, love that is seen in destruction, love that speaks with thunderclap, as well as flower and tree and bird. How blessed are those who suffer. With what riches are they furnished. Only the one who has found the strength to offer praise and thanksgiving, not in spite of but because of suffering, may speak the greater and transforming passion and joy that endures throughout experience.

We would, if we could, spend your time in whatever amount you allowed us. However this instrument requests that we move onward. May we say how exhilarating it is for us to be able to work in this way, to be able to use the mind's experience of each channel as we express our thoughts. We do thank each, and especially the one known as M, for the acceptance of our contact, and also for the desire each has to become ever more carefully and aimlessly aware of our contact, allowing our thoughts to flow throughout the group. This is indeed an advanced lesson, but we do feel that the results of such work are those which have the strong tendency to more and more balance those who function as channels in their willingness to be without need for knowledge of the portion of the information which is yet to come.

We would at this time open the meeting, therefore, for queries. If there is a query, please ask it at this juncture. I am Hatonn.

(Pause)

I am Hatonn. Again we thank each, and would at this time close through the one known as S. We leave this instrument in love and in light and transfer now. I am Hatonn.

(S channeling)

I am Hatonn. It is a source of tremendous joy for us to be able to participate in an offering which is like that of a table spread before a robust company of hungry guests. There are many servers at this table, and it is somewhat tempting for each who would serve to offer all that bounty the table has to supply. Yet it takes a certain faith in the greater process of serving and being served that one serves only that portion which is most readily available to one and leaves for others that service which is theirs to give in the conviction that all that shall be served shall in this manner find its home. We are most pleased.

We are most especially pleased to be able to greet the one called M into this robust company of guests and servers, for all serve. Those who remain silent serve just as surely as those whose tongues wag the most eloquently, vibrating with the joy of overt service. We, too, serve as we may, and we feel that it is most propitious now for us to serve again in silence. We are with any who request our presence in silent meditation. You need only ask. We are those joyful servants of the one infinite Creator, Hatonn. Adonai, my friends. Adonai. ❧

Sunday Meditation
July 18, 1993

Group question: The question this afternoon has to do with relationships and how we choose relationships. We think we know things about emotions, and intellect, and perhaps family before we get into relationship with people, but, in general, is there another level to the reason why we might choose to be in relationship with those people around us, something that would have to do with other parts of our being, our learning, our growth?

(Carla channeling)

I am Hatonn. Greetings to each of you in the love and in the light of the infinite Creator. We are most grateful to have been called to your group this afternoon and to be asked to share our opinions with you. This is of great service to us, for sharing our thoughts is the nature of our path of service at this time in our development and this opportunity is one for which we are grateful. We do request that each discriminate in listening to our thoughts and choose to consider only those thoughts which seem to the seeker to be of truth. We ask that other thoughts which do not find so happy a home be dropped and left behind, for each entity is his own best judge of what is true.

In speaking with you about relationships, we would begin with the concept of the vine with many branches. The branch that may represent one entity seems to have little to do with a far flung branch of that same rambling vine. And only as the path of growth is traced backwards to these two branches' common root can the branches begin to grasp the nature of the union which is the true nature of each entity's relationship to each. For there is truly one being and one great self, one great Thought which is love, (and in that creative love are all, and all of that love.)[1]

Yet, within that illusion which you now enjoy as your incarnative experience this union seems of the veriest folly and to be palpably untrue: how could two entities' deepest reality be union? None of this is at all apparent. And this is the very purpose of the illusion you now enjoy. It is important to you in your evolutionary path that you grasp no deep commitment to union, for it is in the illusion of differences and the working with situations in which the spiritual principles are tested that the lessons of love which you have incarnated to learn are brought forward and laid before each in patterns which engage the mind and heart and launch one, as it were, upon that road which you may call the spiritual path.

---

[1] The brackets enclosing this sentence and several others are in the original transcript.

(The seeker, having once begun this walk, attemp[s] to grasp what is true, attempt[s] to learn consciously to help the self along in this spiritual quest, and in this walk each spirit has its own solitude, its own pace, its own unique lessons to learn.) Each choice which comes before the seeking self is a new crux, a juncture, and from this juncture there are at least two and perhaps more paths which can be chosen. In making these choices the relationships which the seeker has shape and focus the seeker in the most efficient way in order to enable the most lucid choices to be available.

Each has expressed thoughts this day concerning the mystery of the call to relationship: why this branch of the vine? Why not another? Yet the path of each is a long one, and in its time—if we may use that term—the entities with whom each has relationships have been in relationship perhaps many times. Each time, each incarnational opportunity, the two, the seeker and its relation, have worked in the tips of the vine, as it were. And as each lifetime's choices deepen each entity, the two entities in relationship move about, being in different relation to each other, yet still working upon the harmonic, the euphonious, which more and more might be found to exist between the two seemingly separate entities. And each time the relationship deepens, each time the two selves involved are able to move farther down the vine whose identity is the common root, [both self and other-self come] a little bit closer to that unity which exists in the very heart of the root of this vine of being or consciousness.

Thusly can one entity so move one that the seeker finds itself in the deepest and most wrenching of emotions. "How could this depth be?" the seeker asks. "Why am I so vulnerable, so easy to wound, so easily happy, so desperately sad because of this one being?" Yet that one being and you may have worked many, many incarnational times in order that this depth of pain, of joy, this level of choosing love may be reached.

Each entity, in its relationship to others, has some degree of ability, depending upon previous history to some extent, to encourage, aid, exhort and support each in that entity's attempts to seek the truth. (And each entity which you, the seeker, faces may find in you that power to aid and change.) This is in the ideal sense love reflected in love, which is then reflected in love, and in each variation love speaks the same truth of unity.

I am Hatonn. We must pause as this entity is most dry in the mouth.

(Pause)

We may continue, and we thank you for your patience. One may look to the heavens, to the universal and seemingly far away level at which all is ideal, all is clear and there is no illusion, and think that there is no way to proceed to that level where all things are clear. How could each step, one foot after another on a slow and often uncomfortable path, lead to perfect light, perfect realization and unity? What does this cosmic grandeur have to do with the plodding human self?

Yet we feel that each of you is in truth a universe, a creation within, as infinite as can be imagined. That which you see outwardly, that which seems clearly to be real, is in the metaphysical sense far less real than the universe within. And it is in that inner universe that each may best position the self to attempt to maximize the opportunities to grow and to share the journey towards greater realization.

If you as a seeker can be aware of the goal of relationships, that is, to aid each other in learning the lessons of love, then each as seeker may have the beginnings of an idea as to how to proceed. For if each is seeking the truth of relationship, the truth lies in commonality. If a branch speaks to another branch of the same vine and says "You have poor leaves; your fruit is unacceptable; that twig is out of the question," you speak not only to that other twig but to your very own twig self.

Grasp, if you will, the thought that relationship is basically with the self. Each entity with which you are in relationship is basically a mirror reflecting to you your face, your nature, your, as this instrument would say, issues, your lessons. That which you admire and encourage you are encouraging in yourself. That which you judge and question in another you are questioning in yourself.

It takes much pain out of dealing with another if you can take responsible realization in the knowledge that that which you say to another is also true of the self. The more you are able to see and hold this dear the more clearly and purely may your service flow from you, for then if you are angry or upset, that issue lies within yourself, and you have removed from your speaking and actions to the other self the bitterness and the judgment. And that which flows from you then, even if it is a (home) truth, flows shiningly and clearly without the taint of anger or disappointment.

The lessons of love are infinitely many, yet, in each lesson the love is the same: one Principle, one Thought, one Logos. We call it love to you, yet that word is pallid. For the love that created all that there is is a thought infinite in intelligence and expressing itself in one creative nature, bound into manifestation by free will, and then seemingly many, infinitely many.

Yet each of you is as the hologram of this one original Thought. And as each seeker attempts to learn the lessons of love that previous biases have brought that seeker to, the goal is one. All entities seek from each unique viewpoint to grasp the same basic thought. And each is attempting more and more to express as consciousness in the vibratory rate of unity, unity in one thought, one love, which has birthed all that there is.

Each relationship consists of two entities who have so plaited their consciousness together time and time again that each is more able with the other's help to come a little closer to an approximation of some awareness of love. As you attempt to be of service in relationship allow that seemingly far away perfection that ideal love seems to be to color your thinking so that regardless of what you choose to do or say you have the sense of proportion which allows you to form, as well as possible, responses to each other that contain the openness to love that enables each to be a channel through which infinite love may flow.

The human heart, to use the instrument's language, has a very limited amount of love. The energy which created each and which is each entity's true being has infinite love, for love is the nature of consciousness at that level. More and more may you feel transparent to that infinite love and may each so open the heart that each may serve shiningly.

We thank this instrument for its service and would now transfer to the one known as Jim. We are those of Hatonn.

(Jim channeling)

I am Hatonn, and greet each again in love and in light through this instrument. At this time it is our privilege to offer ourselves in the capacity of attempting to answer any further queries which those present may have for us. Are there any queries at this time?

Carla: I have one. In choosing whether to speak or whether to be silent, there are things to be said for both avenues. Is there one way to look at choices like that where you could either speak a good word and maybe spark some thinking, or you could just be silent and pray about it, say, worry about it, whatever. Is there one way of doing that's better than the other?

I am Hatonn, and am aware of your query, my sister. In this regard we can only recommend that the path be taken which one feels is drawn by love. Whatever action or inaction is possible, imagine love being that which is most helpful to include. If you can move in love, then so move. If love would keep your silence, then remain silent.

Is there a further query, my sister?

Carla: No, Hatonn, that was a very succinct answer. Thank you very much.

I am Hatonn, and we thank you once again. Is there another query?

Carla: Well, I have—I have one more. We were talking earlier about how fragile relationships are, and I was especially thinking of a friend of mine that I've had since high school. In one letter that I sent her, I seemingly offended this person, and the relationship that had lasted for twenty-five years was suddenly no more. What's the purpose of that kind of heartache, spending so much time on a relationship and then having it break?

I am Hatonn, and am aware of your query, my sister. All experience has the purpose of extending those limits to love which you have within your being. Each of you feel pain, and each of you question the self as to whether there is love enough to heal. Thus, as you explore those reasons for pain, you will hopefully find reasons to heal. And this healing energy will have love as its primary force. Thus, each experience offers some opportunity for testing the limits of love, until the seeker at some point discovers that there are no true limits. However, this journey is long and offers much variety, shall we say.

Is there a further query, my sister?

Carla: Not for me, Hatonn. Thank you.

I am Hatonn, and we thank you, my sister. Is there another query?

R: I would just say to the brothers and sisters of Hatonn it's wonderful that we walk on the path together.

I am Hatonn, and we return the gratitude for joining on this path with you to the one known as R. And as it appears that we have exhausted the queries and perhaps those present as well, we shall take our leave of this instrument and this group, leaving each, as always, in the love and in the light of the one infinite Creator. We are known to you as those of Hatonn. Adonai, my friends. Adonai. ❧

L/L Research

L/L Research is a subsidiary of Rock Creek Research & Development Laboratories, Inc.

P.O. Box 5195
Louisville, KY 40255-0195

www.llresearch.org

Rock Creek is a non-profit corporation dedicated to discovering and sharing information which may aid in the spiritual evolution of humankind.

ABOUT THE CONTENTS OF THIS TRANSCRIPT: This telepathic channeling has been taken from transcriptions of the weekly study and meditation meetings of the Rock Creek Research & Development Laboratories and L/L Research. It is offered in the hope that it may be useful to you. As the Confederation entities always make a point of saying, please use your discrimination and judgment in assessing this material. If something rings true to you, fine. If something does not resonate, please leave it behind, for neither we nor those of the Confederation would wish to be a stumbling block for any.

CAVEAT: This transcript is being published by L/L Research in a not yet final form. It has, however, been edited and any obvious errors have been corrected. When it is in a final form, this caveat will be removed.

© 2009 L/L Research

Sunday Meditation
August 22, 1993

Group question: The question this afternoon has to do with our spiritual focus, or our spiritual attention span. R was concerned that he was going through his days only occasionally remembering that he was in an illusion and most of the time getting so caught up in work that he was thinking about nothing but the work. When he would get home he would be more able to remember that it was an illusion but wanted to know more how focus could help in his life. Carla was concerned that she was focused on too many projects and energy expenditures and by focusing on too many projects might not be able to do what she wanted to with any one of them, and I was concerned about the focus that a creative person or a skilled artisan of any kind uses in order to bring forth the creativity that is their expression, and also the practical focus of hanging your little toes on the side of the roof so you don't fall off. So we would like to know something about the spiritual attention span and the focus of our consciousness as we go through our daily round of activities.

(Carla channeling)

I am Q'uo. Greetings to each, and in the love and in the light of the one infinite Creator it is our blessing to be with you at this meeting, and we gratefully thank you for calling for this information. It is a blessing to us, for we are by this means able to offer our service, that of sharing our thoughts and opinions with those of your density who wish to work consciously upon the study of spiritual principles which animates and enlivens the incarnation, and creates a far more intensified and accelerated rate of potential spiritual evolution and transformation.

You wish to know more about lengthening the spiritual attention span. You wish that the weaknesses in your natures, the places where you perceive yourself less skillful, can be made stronger and more crystallized, and these are the wishes of one who seeks to do the work of consciousness in a conscious manner.

Each entity in your density works upon these spiritual principles in an unconscious manner and if you were to bury the self and the consciousness in all manner of distraction and labor, yet still would you move forward along the path of evolution. There is no ultimate resistance possible to the truth, no matter how greatly the truth has been deleted and biased as it has traveled through the increasing distortions away from the infinite oneness of unpotentiated Love. However, there is substantial percentage of this journey which can be walked at a quicker pace, shall we say, and we do encourage each to continue to work consciously.

This conscious working may seem to be repetitive, your questions may be perceived by you to be less than inspired. However, we ask each to continue asking, for it is to the persistent questioner that the universe reveals itself. Yet at the same time it is equally true that when the revelation occurs it shall occur not as you expected it. The transformations of the third density almost always come from an oblique angle and are not possessed of those obvious hints that this instrument would call "telegraphing the punch."

So, the situation as regards the basic seeking is that it is excellent to seek intensely and to practice a regularity of meditation, contemplation and prayer. But it is well to widen the inner definition of environment to include that spiritual environment into which each is permanently imbedded, in and out of incarnation. It is from this bedrock of spiritual selfhood that the moments of transformation shall rise and the angle of perceptions of these transformations shall almost always be confusing at first but not necessarily obvious. The state of mind, then, that we can recommend is that of the utmost intensity, and at the same time, that of one who is dancing in and out of the steps of living, feeling the rhythms that murmur through the endless hallways of self.

Firstly, there is that energy to recommend which does indeed take one out of the world while one is yet quite active within this same world. Indeed, it is a useful practice to find the triggers in the daily routine which fire almost automatically and act as reminders of who the true self is which is perceiving the experiences which you perceive and experience. What sort of triggers which each can think of within the daily round? Perhaps there is the bell that strikes, or the clock which strikes the hour. Perhaps there is one symbol which can be invested—we correct this instrument—by the seeking self with a mnemonic meaning, for instance, perhaps there is a doorway through which the seeker goes quite often. This seeker can then create a secondary illusion for this door, and in the mind it becomes a magical doorway. Each time the doorway is passed the reminder becomes visible and tangible. Each time there is that momentary opportunity which reminders offer to center the self and to orient the self with regard to that overarching principle of truth which is love and service.

The second principle requires that each who listens turn the self around mentally so that the self is seated in the portion which does work in consciousness. From this point of view you are gazing at the incarnation strictly with regard to the primary environment which is a spiritual environment. This environment is within each but it must be named, expected and sought before it can be perceived. Yet, once it is perceived, this environment recreates the day-to-day environment so that whatever the environment within the illusion yet the consciousness is to some degree stayed, settled and rooted in spiritual truth so that the self continues to vibrate in harmony with the one great original Thought while it is in the midst of the busy, humming day.

You may practice for these attitudes in various ways. We shall discuss a very few. In meditation, you may with the out breath visualize the bringing in of the truth, the light, the love, bringing in the truth of love in every circumstance. With the out breath, you may visualize the releasing of all spent energies, including those judgments and self-judgments, those businesses and distracted thoughts, so that with each outbreath there is the emptying of darkness and fatigue and the inbreathing of truth, love, light. Each—we correct this instrument—we would request each to, at this time, take a few deep breaths and practice this technique. We are those of Q'uo.

(Pause)

We are again with this instrument. We are Q'uo, and greet each in love and light once more. Perhaps you shall have felt the health being breathed in as the out breath cleansed the self of that which was used up. This cleansing of the energies does indeed strengthen the stability and the spiritualized awareness of the seeker. Each is familiar already with the basic principles of working with the day's experiences in such a way as to balance these experiences, but we would mention at this time that this a technique which is very useful for consistent and constant realignment of the self in the direction which the seeker perceives to hold more and more of truth. That technique is to, within meditation, allow the mind to ripple through the day's experiences, searching for those things which have distracted or attracted, repelled or drawn the self during that diurnal period. Those things which were perceived as negatively oriented, then, would be brought to the conscious mind and the memory replayed.

When the self feels that emotional distortion which was the initial reaction during the day's busy rush, this feeling or ideation shall be allowed to express and intensify within the emotional self, or more precisely, within that portion of complex of energies which is the self which deals with the emotional and mental perception, allow these feelings and ideations to become ever stronger until you feel they are well intensified. Then mentally lay down that emotion and sit with that emotion without any attempt being made to change it. Allow the complementary emotions and/or ideations to arise, allow the other side of the coin to become slowly visible. When the opposite of the first emotion is felt and has been respected and honored allow the thesis and antithesis, the original feeling and its complimentary one, to exist side by side within the mind's eye. Both of these things is you, for each self is universal and contains all that there is. If you see that you are both things then you may also see that you are neither. These events are then transitory, as is the entire incarnation which you now enjoy. Then all may be dropped aside, for by this route you have arrived at the position in mind and heart where you recognize that fundamental environment which is spiritual and which lies around, beneath, above and beyond any of your illusion characteristics, features or realities, so-called.

A third technique for increasing the focus is to choose to undertake a short visualization on a regular basis. Some entities prefer visualizations which are static, others those which flow. Whichever the seeker chooses, we recommend the object be simple. That is, if a specific object is chosen let it be a colored object, for instance a blue circle, or a red square, or a rose. One object. Demand of the self that it continually visualize this for, say, one of your minutes to begin with. At two week intervals, if the visualization is going well, begin to lengthen that time of gazing within at that visualized object. If the preference is for a flowing visualization let it be that of watching the waves upon the shore, or the clouds rolling past, or the gazing out at the passing countryside as though one were on a train, or in a small airplane within which one may look out and see the countryside. The time constraints are the same. This is difficult work, however, it has often had good results for those who are persistent.

A fourth technique is the technique of reduction. This is especially helpful when the seeker is facing more than it can do. The principle here is to reduce the point of view, the focus, shall we say, of attention until only the part which is in front of one is receiving notice. This often might be a matter of physical rearrangement of workplace, for instance, if the desk is full of several projects, allow the time to remove all but one project from the desk. This affects the point of view and makes it materially easier to do the mental work of reduction.

This should, for best results, be integrated with the meditative work on a daily basis for without this silent listening time the energy necessary to focus down upon that one thing which one wishes to do well now will often sorely flag. It is difficult to convince seekers how much work is done within those flawed meditations which to the seeker's own perception are not done very well. But we do assure each that it does not matter how one perceives the experience of meditation as being. What is perceived spiritually is the intensity of commitment of the continued attempt. Fidelity to the truth within one is won day-by-day, meditation by meditation, and distraction upon distraction.

The fifth and final of the techniques we would describe best as holy silliness or silly sanctity. Many are the third-density luminaries which have offered redemption to many souls by helping each entity spill forth the unhealthful tensions of perceptions, those perceptions which carry pain in their arms, burden and trouble each soul, and blessed is the entity which can learn to laugh. We recommend in the spirit of silly sanctity seeing any situation—we correct this instrument—of gazing at a situation which for some reason has involved you to the extent that you are exercising the emotions within you, and see this "gestalt" as a cartoon. Consider then what caption you would write under the picture of this moment. Allow the self to make a little fun of all of the emotions, all of the perceptions, all of the energies. It often will generate at first the kind of humorous caption which contains sarcasm, irony and bitterness. But as the work continues the seeker may well find itself generating gentler and more sweetly humorous captions as the lighting up of the whole environment begins to come more and more into [alignment] as the one great original Thought.

If you have difficulty feeling that laughter is holy, think back to the last time in which you laughed and laughed. Was there not a full feeling of receiving the expression of love, forgiveness and healing within the heart of that laughter? Laughter is the fire's communication with the Earth as mercy is the rain's communication with the Earth. Laughter first burns away pain, then it builds golden castles and offers to the joyous recipient the universe.

All of these techniques have in common the perception on our part, fundamentally, that there is a country within that is native. You are at home in this spiritual country which is reached only when one is willing to go deeper than the surface of things. With the will to recognize this comes the opportunity. We hope these techniques enable each to make use of the opportunity. Once this country within is truly sensed it can be re-entered in the split second that the thought …

(Side one of tape ends.)

(Carla channeling)

Work in consciousness tends to deepen feelings of isolation until it is seen that work in consciousness simply creates channels whereby memories and knowledge of that native land may be routed through the higher subconscious levels of mind to cross the threshold of consciousness and be perceived consciously as characteristics of whatever environment the seeker is inhabiting at any moment. There is nothing that is not full of glory and beauty and truth in the fundamental sense that higher truth, deeper truth, interpenetrates and shows the truth of all other environments of conscious living. By consciously becoming aware that as a seeker you are always in the native land of spirit and only visiting in the foreign land of incarnation, that incarnational web of perceptions shall be transformed. Where can the spirit not travel? It is said within your holy works "If I take the wings of the morning, yet you are there. If I go even to the depths of hell, yet you are with me." There is no unspiritual environment. It is only that instance of intent that lies closed between the seeker and the living of every moment in the presence of the infinite One.

We encourage each to seek the peace of moment by moment living. This shall serve you well as you seek your focus, and, indeed, this is the key to focus—to look not back nor forward except insofar as it is necessary to inform this present perfect moment. If the attention strays, then bring it back, and if you do this a million times in a day and still forget, then when you remember, bring it back. No judgment, no expression to the self of disapproval, just realign.

The habit is hard to make but once made it is even harder to break. May the joy of this journey enliven and transform your daily experience.

At this time we would transfer to the one known as Jim, and would continue with this instrument. We leave this instrument with thanks and transfer now. We are those of Q'uo.

(Jim channeling)

I am Q'uo, and greet each again in the love and in light through this instrument. At this time it is our privilege to offer ourselves in the answering of any further queries. Are there any further queries at this time?

Carla: I have a question, Q'uo. When I was on vacation, immediately that I started the journey, I began … the first time that I got involved in thinking about a spiritual question, I began getting a very strong signal. It seemed to be giving me very good information, but I had not tuned, I had not challenged, I had not asked for any channeling to be done. There were only two of us in the car and I did not want to channel without three. It was very persistent and that made me question its polarity. However, once I had explained this carefully within my mind the contact did stop as I requested, and has not resumed except on the way back. Again, I was relaxing in the car and I began thinking about some spiritual question and again this occurred. The strong contact, the very strong and clear flow of information, almost like I could read it, hear it. Very specific. Again I asked it to stop and it did, this time much less reluctantly.

I want to investigate what that was. Would it be in my best interest to work with it, using my own channel; would it be in my best interest to work with it using Aaron, Barbara's inner guide? Would it be in my best interest to let it go, as being most probably negative? And finally, the other option I guess is this … the way personal guidance is received, and should I now be looking at trying to more fully develop that inner guidance that I call the Holy Spirit?

I am Q'uo, and we are aware of your query, my sister. The response to this query is somewhat complex. We shall begin. Firstly, the inner guidance of which you have spoken is available to all entities through the serious and heart-felt seeking of information leading one along the path of spiritual evolution. The means by which any seeker is able to perceive the response of such guidance depends upon each seeker's avenues of opportunity, shall we say. The avenues of opportunity are those means by which any seeker has attempted to receive information or inspiration from those angelic presences which you may for convenience call guides.

Your particular means of perception moves along the line of your channeling ability, that is, your ability to clear a pathway through the conscious and subconscious mind, through which sources of information may move, be they the contact of Confederation entities such as we are or the movement of energies of those guides which look over your incarnational experience, or any other entity for that matter which may wish to communicate with you through this channeling ability.

The desire to know certain spiritual principles which you exhibited upon this recent journey, combined with your developing channeling ability, further combined with the substance which enhances your receptivity, allowed you to be aware of the response to your query in a much more immediate fashion than is normal, shall we say, for your experience. It is our opinion that it is indeed possible to work with these guides in furthering your own understanding, if we can use this misnomer, of your spiritual journey. However, it is our recommendation that the pursuing of this source of information and inspiration be accomplished under more normal, shall we say, conditions, such as those now utilized, that is, without the use of the enhancing substance that was a portion of your recent experience. The holding forth with the challenge is, of course, also necessary at each working, and it would be well that the group be numbered at least three. There is the possibility of receiving concept information using only your own tuning and energies, however, this information would remain in the form of concept rather than words being utilized to convey information. Thus, you would need to be able to remember the concepts for later elucidation and refinement in your conscious expression of them—words or images set to paper.

Is there a further query, my sister?

Carla: There is a query but I don't know if there is an answer right now, and that just has to do with why I would want to do this. I feel that I have in the Confederation entities an excellent source of information and I fail to really see why I would need a personal guidance, other than the Holy Spirit that I always trusted and that I probably felt was moving me around by hunch and by guess rather than by anything, kind of A, B, C … you know, out there where you can write it down and prove it. I always was satisfied to live my life that way and it's always worked so far. So for myself I never have desired to seek any further about guidance than just knowing that the Holy Spirit will guide me.

The reason that I thought to pursue this was monetary. I thought if I could in all conscience develop a good personal guide, as Barbara has Aaron, I could charge money for readings which I feel I cannot do with the Confederation's universal messages. So I kind of question whether I should move forward with this at all. I can ask your opinion, that is about as far as I can question on that. Do you have an opinion as to the excellence of offering people personal readings in general, and of my doing it specifically?

I am Q'uo, and I am aware of your query, my sister. We must withhold any opinion about this portion of your query, for it is a portion of your experience which must be left to your own discretion. We feel that you have already answered your query, and refer you to your own feelings.

May we respond to any other query, my sister?

Carla: No, I would just repeat the part in general. Is there in your opinion useful information, helpful information to be gained through personal guides that is unavailable to the universal guides? Concerning spiritual principles.

I am Q'uo, and again we move most carefully, wishing not to step over the boundary of infringement. For those who feel there is such value, indeed there is such value.

Is there any further query, my sister?

Carla: Are inner guides and universal guides one and the same?

I am Q'uo, and am aware of your query, my sister. In truth, are we not all one? We do not mean to be facetious, but refer you again to that which is the nature of your service and your journey.

Is there a further query, my sister?

Carla: No, thank you. Thank you very much.

I am Q'uo, and we thank you, my sister. Is there another query at this time?

(No further queries.)

I am Q'uo, and we thank each for the inspiration of your experience. We are gratefully blessed to have been able to join in this circle of seeking. We walk with you at all times and enjoy the diligence, the humor, and the patience with which you grapple in this illusion. It is an inspiring sight and we cannot express enough our admiration for your efforts. At this time we shall take our leave of this instrument and this group, leaving each, as always, in the love and in the light of the one infinite Creator. We are known to you as those of Q'uo. Adonai, my friends. Adonai.

L/L Research

L/L Research is a subsidiary of Rock Creek Research & Development Laboratories, Inc.

P.O. Box 5195
Louisville, KY 40255-0195

www.llresearch.org

Rock Creek is a non-profit corporation dedicated to discovering and sharing information which may aid in the spiritual evolution of humankind.

ABOUT THE CONTENTS OF THIS TRANSCRIPT: This telepathic channeling has been taken from transcriptions of the weekly study and meditation meetings of the Rock Creek Research & Development Laboratories and L/L Research. It is offered in the hope that it may be useful to you. As the Confederation entities always make a point of saying, please use your discrimination and judgment in assessing this material. If something rings true to you, fine. If something does not resonate, please leave it behind, for neither we nor those of the Confederation would wish to be a stumbling block for any.

CAVEAT: This transcript is being published by L/L Research in a not yet final form. It has, however, been edited and any obvious errors have been corrected. When it is in a final form, this caveat will be removed.

© 2009 L/L RESEARCH

SUNDAY MEDITATION
AUGUST 29, 1993

Group question: The question this afternoon has to with destiny. We are wondering if our destinies are fixed, more or less, or if we can affect our destiny. And we would like to know just a little bit about how destiny works and how it manifests in our lives.

(Carla channeling)

I am Q'uo. Greetings in the love and in the light of the one infinite Creator. We are most pleased to be called to this group to discuss destiny with you and we humbly thank each for allowing us to share our opinions through this instrument.

Our personal destiny, in the short term, is to await the call of spiritual seekers such as you, and to respond either through channels such as this one or in the dreamings of those who are seeking. Through this instrument's senses we feel the sun as its rays warm her and each of you through the window of your dwelling place. The light is golden and clear, the temperature balmy and warm. And it is easy to find—we correct this instrument—to feel that golden hours such as this shall never end. Yet each knows that the seasons will cycle around to the winter and where there is now golden warmth, there will one day, not too far away, be chill and cold where now the skies brim with light. This is the destiny of the home upon whose surface you live—to turn ceaselessly, moving through days and seasons and cycles.

So, too, it is with the beings which we could call heavenly bodies which are your true selves. Each, before the beginning of incarnation, has either of his own volition or with the aid of guidance chosen the lessons to be learned within the incarnation. This sets up one axis of event stream.

Agreements also have been made, before the beginning of incarnation, with each entity which shall be in key relationship to you—the mother and father, the brothers or sisters, the mate, the children. These relationships, be they informal—called friends—or formal—such as marriage and family—represent the perpendicular axis of what you could loosely call personal destiny.

Freedom of will is retained throughout the outworking of the long trail of a personal history. There is almost always far more than one option from which to chose at any juncture in which the seeker attempts to mold his destiny. One might, as this instrument has in the past, use the concept of a trip to Chicago. If three seekers go from Louisville to Chicago, they may well go three different ways. What is destined is the eventual arrival in Chicago. Within the bounds of this destination, free will may be used to choose the manner of conveyance and the rate of speed with which this destination is approached.

To move into a somewhat deeper consideration, we would suggest that the destiny may be thought of as that which comes into and captures the heart and the spirit within a seeker so that, even though many other options may be available, there is a sense of gazing into a lane or avenue which is simply more appealing than other options. Although a seeker has his destiny, that—we correct this instrument—it does not follow that the seeker knows or can fully know his destiny.

Consequently, when attempting to cooperate with destiny, as you discussed earlier, it is well to attempt to become ever more sensitive to that feeling of rightness, of clarity, and the feeling of fitting well into one particular option. When once this feeling is followed, then for those willing to live by faith and the feeling of rightness, the life may feel that it is being lived more and more without effort, more and more like the well-oiled rifle which accepts the bullet and powers it most swiftly and straightly to the target through all the air in between.

The spirit within has the capacity to live as the bullet does: swiftly, straightly, accurately and with substantial force. Even those who are without any sense of personal destiny may well find events quickening and becoming more simple, simply because there has been, for whatever reason, a willingness to move forward without resistance when change of some kind is seemingly necessary.

So, we would say to you that the greatest skill which the spirit may offer, when working with one's destiny, is that skill which surrenders the intellectual and logical modes of thought, and instead adopts a willing and flowing attitude which allows the seeker to feel its way until that which feels right within has been discovered.

The permeability of destiny to accident is variable, depending upon how far from the target or hub of destiny a seeker may be. When a lesson has just been begun, that is the equivalent of being in Louisville and having enough supply of money to afford a variety of ways to Chicago. As choices are made and the lessons go forward, that is, analogously, as Chicago is neared, there are fewer uncertainties about how the next few occurrences will unfold, for there is less room in which to work, less latitude concerning the approach to the, shall we say, punch line of the lesson.

And in terms of living and cycling into the end of your particular incarnation, this holds true, so that at the beginning of the incarnation, there is at least one locus or point at which the opportunity to end the incarnational lesson shall be great. This opportunity may come, however, more than once, and this is due to there being not one lesson upon most entities' agendas for an incarnation, but more than one. And after a certain minimum number of lessons, which varies, has been reached, there is the choice to allow this lesson to be the last or to work through another lesson. So we cannot say that the time of an entity's death is fixed. However, in the sense that there is perhaps one extra choice or perhaps two extra choices to be made and know, more than certainly the destiny awaiting each may be seen to be inevitable.

We are having some difficulty using this instrument at this time and would appreciate the retuning of the group. We shall pause for this to occur. We are those of Q'uo.

(Singing)

(Carla channeling)

I am again with this instrument. I am Q'uo. We thank this group for retuning, as this instrument had begun to slip in its focus, and we wish to revivify the strength and depth of the relaxation into which this instrument is best suited to maintain during a channeling working.

So you may see each entity's destiny as moving as does the bullet, straight and cleanly. However, although this makes no sense in terms of your physics, at the same time that destiny is bullet-like, it also varies in its travel depending upon the strength of the relations—we correct this instrument—relationships which intersect and interweave other entities with their destinies with one's own. If a true loner chooses continually throughout the incarnation not to seek company, that entity's destiny is completely undisturbed except by those changes which learned lessons might make to him.

However, most entities are much involved with the family and the mate and the family made with that mate. The dance of two whose destinies are intertwined is also straight and clean, yet somehow the tracks of two become one to the extent to which the other has become important to the self. As the choice of mate especially is made, the two tracks become fused, as the two enter into the relationship fully. Much confusion among your peoples has been, and continues to be generated because the mutually planned learnings of lessons for two entities within a relationship are ignored and the relationship splits before the lesson has been completed. Thusly, it is in our trip to Chicago scenario, as though the two arrived at Indianapolis and began to back up, to turn around, and to attempt to retrace the steps. However, destiny is such that Louisville, once having been left, no longer exists and cannot be returned to. No, those who avoid the work of a cooperation with destiny find not the exact same cycle repeated as the lesson is posed again. Rather, they will find the lesson to have been made more pointed, the difficulties more pronounced, and the options fewer.

You may see the effect of this walking away from the hard work of learning the lessons reflected in so many of your people who find themselves within what they feel to be an empty existence without rhyme or reason. Once a sufficient number of lessons have been avoided, it is very difficult to get into the rhythm of the dance which destiny, in its outwork, truly is.

This is an interesting subject and there is much to say concerning it. However, we feel this is as far as we wish to go this day. We encourage queries, and would transfer from this instrument to the one known as Jim for the remainder of this working. We are those of Q'uo, and leave this instrument in love and in light.

(Jim channeling)

I am Q'uo, and greet each again in love and in light through this instrument. At this time we would ask if there may be any further queries to which we may speak?

M: I have a question for Q'uo which concerns *(inaudible)* channel or getting *(inaudible)* seeker getting more *(inaudible)* to feeling *(inaudible)* in which case the factor I suspect that mediation would be used for *(inaudible)*. Are there some other ways or methods to encourage to make this feeling more obvious?

I am Q'uo, and am aware of your query, my brother. We can always be assured that to recommend meditation is to recommend a path that will eventually succeed, for in mediation all experience is available to the seeker for its examination and more full understanding. However, we may also turn the attention to utilizing the catalyst of one's daily round of activities. As one moves within the illusion and partakes in the destiny of the day, one may observe many opportunities to exercise the feelings in any fashion, whether it be to accentuate a certain aspect of feeling, or simply to open the heart to a greater sense of feeling in general. There is much that comes before the attention of every entity within your illusion upon a daily basis which can be utilized to expand the ability to feel and to sympathize and even to empathize with others and the plight that might befall them.

If you will look at the variety of catalysts that presents itself to you in any of your days, and concentrate upon any portion of the catalyst which calls from you the feeling of one emotion or another, it is as though the microscope has been applied to experience and all that is available in each experience is enhanced by your focused perception. This, done on a regular basis and aided by the further use of meditation, can allow the seeker to increase its appreciation of feeling in general and to refine its feelings of any particular nature.

Is there a further query, my brother?

Questioner: Yes. I have, like, this burr sticking out of my life. I have this thing about something that relates to what you talked about back there when there are two in a relationship and how their tracks, reaching Indianapolis, and then they try to backtrack. I don't get a clear question out of it. I'll just ask you if you can comment as much as you feel comfortable on that destiny as it relates to two entities who agree to work together in an incarnation. If it is too vague, just pass it up.

I am Q'uo, and we feel that we may speak briefly here. As two entities join their destinies in relationship there is the merging of two distinct paths. And as the work of relationship is accomplished by both entities when it is necessary, then the halves begin to merge so that eventually there is one path being traveled by two entities. Eventually, there is one path being traveled by one entity as the process is perfected.

Is there a further query, my brother?

M: No, I thank you for the comment, Q'uo. I don't come up with any good queries at this time.

I am Q'uo, and we thank you, my brother. Is there another query at this time?

Carla: Let me take a stab at restating the question that I think M had in mind. think he was wondering about what happens to a couple that splits. They can't go back and they can't go forward together. Either he was wondering how to avoid that or how to deal with it after it's happened.

I am Q'uo, and am aware of your query, my sister. When two entities find it impossible to continue in a relationship that has attempted to join each entity's path, there is the continuation of the journey for each entity upon separate tracks, shall we say. These entities then are as any other entities—that is, they have the choice of continuing as individual entities or of joining …

(Side one of tape ends.)

(Jim channeling)

I am Q'uo, and I greet each again in love and in light. We shall continue.

Thus, each entity would have the ability to create a path that would reflect its own individuality. This would include the possibility of again joining the path with the entity from whom the spilt was made if there has been sufficient repairing of the perception of the journey that would again allow this joining. Each seeker has complete free will at all times to continue its journey as it is, or to alter that journey to include any other entity's situations or opportunities.

May we speak further, my sister?

Carla: Yes. It is implied, I believe, by you and certainly it's stated by channels from Ra, that there is an advantage to joining forces with a mate in order to better pursue one's destiny. Is that so? And I wondered how does it strengthen one's abilities or improve one's ability to perceive the right, the path of the right, the simplest, the clearest, the straightest destiny?

I am Q'uo, and am aware of your query, my sister. As that portion of our principle which is made up of those of Ra has stated previously, those who of like mind together seek shall far more surely find. As that portion of our principle that is made up of Q'uo—but we would paraphrase: two heads are better than one. Thus, what one misses the other may find.

Is there a further query, my sister?

Questioner: No, it was very clear. Thank you.

I am Q'uo. Again we thank you, my sister. Is there another query?

Questioner: *(Inaudible).*

I am Q'uo, and we also appreciate the good humor with which this group accepts our contact, for we are often perceived as somewhat tedious and speak overlong as we have been reminded. But we can assure each that we take great pleasure in joining your group and we thank you with our whole heart for inviting our presence this day.

At this time we will take our leave of this group, leaving each in joy, in peace and in wonderment at the perfection of all creation. We are those of Q'uo, and we leave each in this great love and light at this time. Adonai, my friends. Adonai. ♣

L/L Research

L/L Research is a subsidiary of Rock Creek Research & Development Laboratories, Inc.

P.O. Box 5195
Louisville, KY 40255-0195

www.llresearch.org

Rock Creek is a non-profit corporation dedicated to discovering and sharing information which may aid in the spiritual evolution of humankind.

ABOUT THE CONTENTS OF THIS TRANSCRIPT: This telepathic channeling has been taken from transcriptions of the weekly study and meditation meetings of the Rock Creek Research & Development Laboratories and L/L Research. It is offered in the hope that it may be useful to you. As the Confederation entities always make a point of saying, please use your discrimination and judgment in assessing this material. If something rings true to you, fine. If something does not resonate, please leave it behind, for neither we nor those of the Confederation would wish to be a stumbling block for any.

CAVEAT: This transcript is being published by L/L Research in a not yet final form. It has, however, been edited and any obvious errors have been corrected. When it is in a final form, this caveat will be removed.

© 2009 L/L Research

Intensive Meditation
September 4, 1993

Group question: The question this session deals with the doubt that all the instruments feel as to whether or not the contact is actually themselves making up the information, or are they receiving information from an external source and simply relaying it. What is the best procedure for a new instrument to use to deal with this doubt?

(Carla channeling)

I am Oxal. Greetings in the love and in the light of the infinite Creator. We are privileged to come to join in your session of working and to share with you thoughts concerning doubt and its place in the channeling process.

We ask each to take the step backwards and gaze at the self as it is seated within your domicile. Note that within the entire life of experience of this small, fragile being that walks upon the surface of your planet, note the vulnerability and the lack of knowing.

Each entity chooses to live with free will made manifest strictly because no moral course of action can be proven to be correct. Each individual seeker walks his own path, balancing between doubt and the rational mind, and overzealous faith and an irrational mind. On the one hand, [there] looms a petty system of small correctnesses; on the other, the chaos of feelings allowed to have full sway without discipline. However, although both the intellectual and the zealot believe and feel that they have the truth and know it, neither knows the truth, nor does any other entity know the truth.

Within your vibrational system your environment is such that each entity may hope to become a witness to the truth, that is, as close to knowledge of truth as there is within your density, and indeed, those of higher densities may have far more well developed systems, however, if the gaze is just, the eyes shall see not provable truth.

Each life is lived either without faith, or with faith. The choice of those who choose to have faith is the nature and character of that faith. Being true to the self is important and this importance is far more easily seen when one realizes that, in any event, there is no knowing. There are no shortcuts to truth. Truth shall bloom within each seeker as does the desert flower and we encourage each to treasure and cherish this inner self planted in the desert soil of deep mystification. Praise it and the Creator, when a glimpse of that precious bloom is seen.

To be more specific and to aid in the channel's development of its instrument, we ask the instrument to consider that there must be the start somewhere. The way which is far mellower and seemingly easier is that way which simply requires that the new instrument sit in meditation each day and invite contact. However, we have developed opinions, as has this instrument, upon the subject through practice, and our current opinion at this point is that the one known as Carla is doing well to, shall we say, "Toss the new swimmer into the water." For no matter how long the interval is between deciding to take that first long step into the chasm of not knowing, nevertheless, when the first attempt is actually made, there will be that strong and substantial feeling of not knowing, feeling of alarm, even at the possibly or the possibly not glimpsed contact.

As this instrument has said, the experience of processing the words of a channeling message is quite like the process of ideation within an instrument's conscious mind. The concept of—we correct this instrument—the concept arises from the subconscious and passing through the threshold into consciousness is quickly or laboriously cloaked with logic and actual words, becoming a thought and then a spoken assertion or question. Consequently, there is no clear and provable way to know that a contact is positive and is the highest and best contact.

Also, this instrument has said a great deal of the total effort of an instrument is made prior to opening to channel as that instrument tunes itself more and more skillfully. Thus, in answer to the query concerning opening to channel, without sure knowledge, we may summarize by saying that there is no provable way to be sure one has made contact.

However, the most aid one can give oneself towards assuring itself that it will receive the appropriate contact is to focus and observe closely the results of tuning sessions. As the experience mounts, some particular ways or elements of a way of preparing shall show themselves to you as being the most efficient and efficacious means for you, personally. Note these and repeat the use of them until there has been developed within you a kind of awareness which is ritualistic. As you then go through the process over and over again, its ritualistic nature will reward you a familiarity of the deep mind. When the deep mind becomes aware that you are going through this ritual that deep mind will perforce open with much more balance and correctness of opening so that the way for the channeling is made well. Each entity, being on an unique path, will and must develop his system of or process of opening the channel in a protected way for himself.

We are glad to answer queries, before we move on, if there are any with regard to this basic point. May we develop this material further, my brother?

Questioner: No. I think that gave me enough to work with. Thank you.

We thank you, brother. Very well then. We would like then to move on to the portion of the session with the new instrument.

Very briefly, we remind the instrument that the way of moving forward in learning this skill lies in a balance between disciplined care at opening the channel and being able to take the process lightly enough that there is a relaxing and loosening of concern and worry, so that when contact is perceived, or hunched, the instrument feels free to make an error if it is wrong, and then simply begin.

We would also note that those of Latwii request that the new instrument be aware that there is no simple way for a discarnate entity to refrain from speaking if a contact is left open, consequently it is encouraged that when practicing the processes of tuning and challenging, that there be a polite request made, if necessary, after the greeting to move immediately to the closing, so that the channel is neatly and carefully guarding the conscious mind of the instrument.

The few sentences, perhaps, of other thoughts are not anything to concern the instrument about. However, it is more appropriate when practicing with three entities together that any message be politely, but firmly rejected.

This is, as we said, simply for the most respect to be expressed for the process of receiving a full message, that is, respect for the process of channeling and for the message itself.

We would like to speak at this time concerning love. The desire to speak of love to each present is always there, for that is at the heart of our message. We bring a simple message to your peoples, that love is. That "is" expresses its nature in all that there is and that each may accelerate the rate of its development and evolution by seeking more and more closely to match that original Vibration, which is love. However, this message is too simple to seize the minds and hearts of most of your peoples and so we speak in many ways concerning love. Therefore, we find this a good topic when the channel is exercised.

What we would enjoy doing, if it meet with each entity's approval, is simply to pass the channeling around, while each entity each entity receives a relatively short portion of the continuing message. We feel it shall give each the best opportunity to exercise its channel and also will give the somewhat more advanced channels the opportunity to work on their skills in harmonizing a message, which moves through several different sensibilities and frames of reference. This is a delicate and subtle skill once the initial practice opens this kind of channeling up within the mind of the more experienced channel.

"Love"—such a word in your language is almost guaranteed to become weak, for so many things are called "love" among your peoples. The word, therefore, loses more and more power as time goes on. However, the creative and sometimes terrible love of the infinite One is that strong and powerful love which we speak at love's bidding. All that you see was brought into manifestation and each when seeing the beauty of the natural world is gazing at a primary manifestation of love itself. For all beauty is wrought with that light which love created.

Many among your peoples walk down the lovely summer lane of trees, looking up at the sun which warms all, seeing no leaf, or small animal, or warmth of sun that might suggest that there is in the deity a most loving nature.

We would at this time transfer this contact to the one known as M. I am Oxal.

(M channeling)

I am Oxal. The beauty of nature has inspired many men and women throughout time. The love that flows through the trees and streams is the love of the Creator.

At this time, we will transfer to the one known as Jim. I am Oxal.

(Jim channeling)

I am Oxal. We shall continue. The love of the Creator enlivens all creation for there is no other thing than this love, formed in an infinite array of images, each exercising free will and moving in harmony with some with that same love. Thus, the dance of creation is the dance of remembering and experiencing this love.

We shall transfer now to the one known as Carla. I am Oxal.

(Carla channeling)

One way of looking at the process of learning to be of service is indeed the realization that the original gift, which any may give to another, is that gift of uncompromising and unstinted love. How difficult it is to move in one's mind from the many judgments and cautions of a people bound in fear, to relating to others as one who loves unconditionally, yet what a great gift this sheer love is. Somehow those who receive this gift recognize it, no matter how stumbling or seemingly imperfect the attempt may be.

We would now transfer to the one known as M. We are those of Oxal.

(M channeling)

I am Oxal. The love that is of the utmost importance is the love of self and to be free of self-judgment.

We will transfer at this point to the one known as Jim.

(Jim channeling)

I am Oxal. To judge the self is to place a bar against the love of self, and if one is unable to love the self, that one is, then, it is difficult to love any other self, for the connection with each other self is unity. Thus, it is important that each seeker discover that it contains not only what you may call the full array of human characteristics, both those thought of as acceptable and unacceptable, but the seeker must also discover that those portions of the self felt to be unacceptable are as acceptable as any other, for all are distortions of the one Creator set in motion that the one should know itself more fully with greater intensity and variety than would be possible should these distortions not exist. Therefore, it is to the seeker's benefit to begin the process of self-knowledge that will eventually lead to self-acceptance.

When the small self is accepted then this acceptance may move outwards, as the ripples in a pond from a thrown stone move outward, and begin to include entities within the circle of friends, entities beyond the circle of friends, until all is accepted as the Self, the one great Self.

We shall transfer now to the one known as Carla. I am Oxal.

(Carla channeling)

I am with this instrument. I am Oxal. Although seekers may wish they were not such universal entities, yet still each is. The concern of the spirit within, filtered through biases of moral good and evil, express themselves as concern that the self is far too unworthy of love to be loved. As a seeker becomes more clear and honest concerning the true nature of the perceived self within, there are always those times when the seeker must wrestle with the feelings of unworthiness. May we suggest to each that the one who feels unworthy is heavily judging.

The judgment, then, bars that door to love of which we spoke and the clinging to this self-opinion of apparent unworthiness can then stop an entity still in its tracks and gradually, even cause the entity to begin to back up and lose some awareness …

(Side one of tape ends)

(Carla channeling)

… and allow that loving nature to forgive the errors that are inevitable and to heal that sense of frailty that might make the seeker stumble against its own perceived misdoings.

Beyond all action and reaction lies love. We would transfer to the one known as M. We are Oxal.

(M channeling)

(Inaudible)

(Carla channeling)

We are again with this instrument. We are those of Oxal. We thank the one known as M for availing himself of our contact and wish at this time to work to adjust for any discomfort. We ask the one known as M to mentally express any discomfort and we shall attempt at this time to begin to make the small corrections in what this instrument would call "the hookup." We shall pause at this time for a brief time and then would transfer to one known as Jim, in order that any queries which have come up during this session might be addressed. We now pause. We are those of Oxal.

(Pause)

(Jim channeling)

I am Oxal, and am again with this instrument. At this time, we would ask if we may respond to any further queries?

Carla: If no one has a question, I have a small one and that is, would you speak anymore at all on the subtleties of working as an ensemble in harmony with other channels as opposed to working to offer one message with one contact?

I am Oxal, and am aware of your query, my sister. We find that the, as you call it, ensemble method of offering information is one which benefits both the new instrument and the more experienced instrument for the new instrument is offered both the support of the other instruments and the multiple opportunities to perceive the contact and then speak the words that are given.

This, then, is a more intensive means of learning this part and because of this intensity, the new instrument is developing the skill necessary to be an instrument on a dependable basis. The more experienced instrument also are exercised in their abilities to allow their contact to move freely between them and to speak without reservation.

Thus, both new and old instruments can benefit from this method and thus we offer it for the exercising of any instrument.

Is there a further query, my sister?

Carla: Another small one. I can always encourage people who want some kind of proof, subjective proof of contact, to ask for conditioning. I wonder if you of the Confederation have any problems whatsoever with this. Is there any reason why I should not suggest this?

I am Oxal, and we cannot think of any reason why this should not aid the new instrument who would wish a physiological signal that would indicate our presence and our desire to exercise the instrument. Such training ids are valuable, especially in the initial stages of learning the channeling process.

Is there any further query, my sister?

Carla: No thank you, Oxal. That's just all there is today.

I am Oxal, and we thank each for the great opportunity to work with the new and the more experienced instruments. We are not often able to join your group for our vibration is somewhat more obscure and less requested and we are full of joy at this opportunity. We shall be available for any future calling and we at this time shall take our leave of this group leaving each in that great ineffable light of the one infinite Creator. We are known to you as those of Oxal. Adonai, my friends. Adonai. ✺

L/L Research

L/L Research is a subsidiary of Rock Creek Research & Development Laboratories, Inc.

P.O. Box 5195
Louisville, KY 40255-0195

www.llresearch.org

Rock Creek is a non-profit corporation dedicated to discovering and sharing information which may aid in the spiritual evolution of humankind.

ABOUT THE CONTENTS OF THIS TRANSCRIPT: This telepathic channeling has been taken from transcriptions of the weekly study and meditation meetings of the Rock Creek Research & Development Laboratories and L/L Research. It is offered in the hope that it may be useful to you. As the Confederation entities always make a point of saying, please use your discrimination and judgment in assessing this material. If something rings true to you, fine. If something does not resonate, please leave it behind, for neither we nor those of the Confederation would wish to be a stumbling block for any.

CAVEAT: This transcript is being published by L/L Research in a not yet final form. It has, however, been edited and any obvious errors have been corrected. When it is in a final form, this caveat will be removed.

© 2009 L/L Research

Sunday Meditation
September 5, 1993

Group question: The question today has to do with how we open ourselves to the awareness of non-dedication to an outcome. When we do anything during a day, whether it's attempt to apply a spiritual principle to a situation, or earn money, or reflect upon ourselves—anything that we do—we tend to have a yardstick by which we measure the outcome, so that we set ourselves up with expectations for how the things shall be done and the final product that we produce. So, we're aware that if we can achieve the non-dedication to the outcome—open ourselves to whatever comes through our experience—that things tend to turn out a whole lot better than we could ever imagine. And when we put expectations on outcomes, then we tend to find that our experience isn't so harmonious, and we tend to judge ourselves. So we would like to know something about how to open ourselves to the awareness of acceptance of any situation and any process that we find ourselves in.

(Carla channeling)

We are those of Q'uo. Greetings in the love and the light of the one infinite Creator. It is a privilege and a blessing to be called to this session of working to share our service with you. We are humbly thankful and are happy, indeed, to share our opinions and experiences. We do, however, request that as we are not those with perfect authority, but rather seekers of truth such as you are, that each here present use his own discrimination in listening and taking to heart that which each hears. We would not be a stumbling block before any. With this understood, may we say that this particular session of working is a real treat for us, as each present brings something new to the vibratory patterns which we have become more and more familiar with through what you would call the passage of time. We thank each. And so, to our subject.

Picture, if you will, the tree in the early spring. It has been bare of all foliage except a few dead leaves for the long sleep of winter. As the air and earth gradually thaw, there is created within the living tree that life-giving food which pours upward and outward from the tree's roots, systematically feeding and encouraging growth in the whole tree with all of its members. As each bud begins to be distinct and to show its tiny head on each limb of each part of the great trunk of the tree, does each leaf consider what it shall do? Each small creation, each bud, being of second density, has full unconsciousness awareness of the perfection of the enormously complex process of developing the leaflet to the leaf, and the process occurs perfectly.

When third density begins, those entities which have been individuated from second density and are harvested to third density receive great gifts, whereas before, all awareness and knowledge was unconscious but full. So now, third density offers the gift of self-consciousness, of self-awareness, but there is a balancing gift as well, and that is that a veil is dropped between the conscious and the unconscious minds or levels of mind, so that there is no longer that perfect unconscious awareness of the perfection of processes which is occurring. The third density, then, is one which begins with the unconscious mind completely opaque.

Among your peoples, those entities which have by choice or by geographical design been left to form societies which are simple have been more successful in reaching a recommitted relationship with what we could call destiny, so that the attitude toward good and seemingly bad things remains one of cooperation and acceptance. However, a great majority of people within your culture do not lead and do not have the obvious opportunity to lead, simple lives—the life small enough to be lived in one place with the small tasks not associated with the earning of your money. These tasks become luxuries, and entities choose under great pressures to do so, to have ambitions and to pursue these ambitions, whether they be within the world of material supply or intellectual advancement or spiritual seeking.

The basic attitude is often that which seems obviously to be at work in the processes of the educating of the self throughout the school years—to read, to do, to learn, to gather, to amass, to become more aware. These ambitions create tremendous complexity. To relocate so that the living of the complex lifestyle is possible while retaining the attitude of one who lives a simple life is a seeking which is, we would say, close to universal among those entities who have consciously chosen to pursue the living of a life by faith rather than by words.

The one known as Jesus was a teacher whose words often addressed the process of choosing to be a pilgrim, seeker or disciple of truth during a busy incarnation. This entity often suggested the very difficult possibility—to look at, to choose—of actually becoming the whole and complete pilgrim, giving away all things of the world except one outfit of clothing, not worrying about money, taking to the road … And this is one good way to begin to simplify one's worldly, shall we say, concerns. However, the effects of an ethos or "cultural type" are subtle, and into any chosen lifestyle, no matter what its seeming simplicity, the cultural pressures to think along certain paradigms almost inevitably create as much complexity revolving around what this entity would call "chopping wood and carrying water" as they would create for a professional person with extended responsibilities. In other words, although choosing a simpler lifestyle may seem to aid in the development of a more harmonious attitude, any outer, physically described circumstance offers only the potential for such results. In each case, it is the mind of the seeker which creates that which it desires by desiring it.

What is the process of desiring? One, perhaps, could describe desire as "a falling in love with." Certainly, the desires of the heart are deeply felt and etched with the pen of love. The yearning for that centered, flowing, effortless living which each seeker has experienced at certain times is constant, and sometimes nearly overwhelming. How the seeker yearns to feel wholly connected with the wellsprings of life, light, love and truth! It is within each seeker's ability to so discipline the thoughts and the attitudes that, more and more, there is an increased potential for returning to a centered position of heart and mind, within which a true simplification of the improving of the centered stance is achieved.

Let us ask another question: What is each seeker's process of perception, for this question is the beginning of a more interesting way of approaching becoming that centered entity which each wishes to become. The processes of perception are enormously many. In order to perceive anything, the five physical senses are, at all times when an entity is awake, sending millions, literally millions, of bits of information all the time to that bio-computer which you call the brain. Your brain uses programming which it began receiving before coming out of the womb. In order to prioritize the incoming data, perhaps one or two percent of the combined total of all sense information is actually chosen for use in any moment, and the rest is stored in that very, very spacious storage which you may call the brain. Therefore, if an entity wishes to alter the attitude, it is a good idea, we feel, to address the question of what sense data achieves the priority to be considered by the conscious mind as the moments fly by.

How can a seeker communicate with that unconscious portion of the mind which filters sense perceptions? The entity simply communicates with that portion of the self. The beginning of this communication is silent meditation. This is different for each entity. Some are refreshed by one method of silent listening, another by a second, and so forth. Each path is good for that one entity; each is unique. To improve that communication, then, the beginning is to meditate in your own unique way, to be faithful to the remembering each in your own way. For you see, it is remembering who you are to sit in meditation for a few moments, and within that silence, however imperfectly you may feel you are keeping that silence, you are doing the equivalent of knocking at that door to the subconscious or deeper mind and saying, "Yes, I am ready for material from you, I hope, in this way, in this set of emotions and attitudes with which I come questing to this silence." And the deep mind hears and understands, and one more small step has been taken to move the seat of living from the brain and its intellectual circumstances to the heart, with its lack of justification and its purity of feeling, for the true wisdom lies within the emotions which are progressively purified by focus.

Once the habits have been set and experiences have been had of that feeling of life flowing freely, the feeling then can be, not created, but accessed by the seeker with more and more grace and ease, with simple repetitive—we correct this instrument—repetitive practice, for what you seek to be whole is already there, as each is truly aware. It is an allowing of that feeling to be there that is needed, an allowing that calls to your processes of perception and says, "I want information about love in this moment. Where is it? I want to be there working cooperatively with these energies."

We know that each will be self-disappointed many times. We encourage each to consider that this, too, is a lovely portion of a process by which change within is achieved for each grain of transformation, each new ability to choose spiritually based information rather than other priorities. Some that were priorities will be lost, and as the heart and mind change their habits, that which is old and stale must fall away. This is perceived as painful.

Consequently, what we are saying is that along with the flow of living life cooperatively with destiny, there is a continuing discomfort which comes from changing faster than other entities because that is what you wish to do. However, it is a simple choice to make for most who prefer being awake and in the conscious presence of the Infinite to being those who are asleep in a dream within the dream of incarnation itself, and do not ask themselves to do aught except flow along the lines of the society.

We do encourage each not only to partake in this speeding up process of conscious living, but we encourage and exhort each to find within the attitude a growing awareness of how love felt within is a channel through which the infinite love of the Creator may flow to others. Let that light within be. Let the self open and flow consciously, so that you may be part of the good in the lives of those whom you touch. Sometimes it is nothing more than a supportive smile to a stranger that makes the difference for that stranger that particular moment. As you are given grace to lift away from the stains of sorrow and toil into the ethereal beauty of that ever flowing love which is the Creator, remember to be generous, and know that that which comes through you is in utter abundance—completely unlimited in supply.

How, then, does this translate to not worrying about lacks of perfection? My friends, when one does remember that one is a portion of love, much begins to fall away. Work with these thoughts and be patient with the self. We believe you may one day look back and say, " Why yes, I believe I can feel the difference and see the progress." However, do not look for your getting better, but simply turn the heart and mind towards the infinite Creator, Whose creation expresses Its loving nature.

The trees now are in full leaf offering oxygen to each of you as you pass them offering to them, as you breathe, the carbon dioxide which the leaves need to grow. How loving and complete are the interrelationships of life to life! It is love reflected in love, over and over and over. The teacher known as Jesus said, "Let your light so shine before men that the Creator is seen, not you." We paraphrase, this instrument is reminding us. Let your light—let that light which flows through you—shine before all, and remember to enjoy that light as it pours through you.

We thank you for allowing us to speak, and we thank this instrument. We would at this time, transfer to the one known as *(name)* that we may offer questions an opportunity to be asked before we leave this group. Thusly, we do leave this instrument in love and light. We are those of Q'uo.

(Jim channeling)

I am Q'uo, and greet each again in love and in light through this instrument. At this time, it is our privilege to offer ourselves for any further query which those present may have for us. Is there a query at this time?

Questioner: I have a question. How does grace come into our lives and into our experience?

I am Q'uo, and am aware of your query, my sister. The quality of consciousness which you would call "grace" is that quality that is nurtured in each seeker, as the seeker is able to open itself to the awareness of the perfection of all creation. Thus, it is also a process of realization. You may, in a moment of great desire, fling all predetermined expectations to the wind and become as hollow as the pipe through which the water moves, and this water for you is grace. The movement of the Spirit aligning with your open heart causes the feeling of perfection, purpose, place and identity with all to occur, so that your experience is the perfect reflection of the one Creator smiling through your face.

Is there another query, my sister?

Questioner: Thank you very much, but no. I'll think about that. Thank you.

I am Q'uo, and we thank you, my sister. Is there another query?

Carla: I'm having trouble moving from … I understand what you're saying about, "re-think what your priorities are," but moving from just a commitment to doing that and a commitment to regular meditation, to a place in life where you really are OK with letting things be … I'm not real clear on how you put that into effect—how you actually, positively do that. Could you give me some light here?

I am Q'uo, and am aware of your query, my sister. Again, the persistent practice of remembering is that means whereby you begin to uncover your relationship to all things, discovering that that relationship is balance, is unity, is harmony. The seeker looks and seeks and asks and knocks many times at the door of understanding, and receives many times a glimpse to remind the seeker that there is a relationship of unity. This seeking is like unto moving from the conscious mind through that veil of forgetting, blazing a trail that can be traveled backward and forward into the subconscious mind which is full of the feeling of wholeness and unity. Thus, as you knock and seek, and repeat in heartfelt persistence this desire to remember, so do you remember that reality of unity. The process in your terms seems slow and …

(Side one of tape ends.)

(Jim channeling)

I am Q'uo, and am again with this instrument. We shall continue. As you continue to seek and to ask, so do you remember and receive the inspiration of that wholeness that is the true reality of your being. The process is filled, it would seem to you, with the pain of missing the mark, the slowness of repetition. Yet, in truth, this process is seen by us to be one of great vividness, great intensity, and great persistence, occurring in but the blink of an eye when seen from the eye of infinity.

Thus, the seeker is well counseled to depend upon the faith and the will—the rod and the staff—as it moves through that valley of darkness that is your incarnation, seeking the light upon the way.

Is there a further query, my sister?

Carla: Just one small one. Perhaps that's why I really love to sing so much. I do find sometimes when I'm singing, especially sacred music, that—I don't know, things sort of feel better, as if I am accessing that place where everything is whole.

I am Q'uo, and we shall comment briefly upon your comment. It is so that each seeker shall find an unique pathway through the veil of forgetting, and perhaps shall discover a number of avenues or entrances to the feeling of wholeness and one's complete and absolute connection to that unity. Thus does each entity channel a life experience distorted in more or less degree, and fashioned by the uniqueness of its own personality. Thus, each journey proceeds apace from every direction homeward to the center of unity.

Is there a further query?

Carla: No, Q'uo, thank you very much.

I am Q'uo, and again we thank you, my sister. Is there another query at this time?

(Pause)

I am Q'uo, and it appears that we have exhausted the queries for the nonce. Before we take our leave of this instrument and this group, we would wish to offer our conditioning vibration to the one known as *(name)*, and if this entity is willing we would speak our identification through its instrument and speak a few sentences following. We would at this time, then, transfer this contact to the one known as *(name)*. We are those of Q'uo.

(Pause)

I am Q'uo, and am again with this instrument. We feel that there is the work for us to do in adjusting our vibrations to those of the new instrument, and at this time we would leave this group and allow the complex known as Oxal to close this session of working, for this entity has already achieved some adjustment which allows more comfort to the new instrument. Consequently, we would bid this group hail and farewell, in the love and light of the One which is All. That All is Love, and all that comes from It is etched by light. Adonai. We are those of Q'uo.

I am Oxal. Greetings in the love and in the light of the infinite Creator. This instrument, you may note, has some difficulty with the strength of our signal; however, the one known as *(name)* finds it very comfortable, and this is why we are here. We wish to close this session encouraging each to put value in the self without reservation, for the love that is infinite can only shine through an entity which is comfortable enough to open a channel to that love. The heart engaged in clinging to concern has more difficulty opening to the love which is always present. If each could picture the inner self as a child which needs a hug, it would aid each in becoming able to love all that is. Those who attempt to do service work before they have successfully fallen in love with the self find themselves unable to access that flow which is infinite, and instead find themselves burning out and becoming exhausted spiritually. You are loved, each of you, and it is in that love that you truly reside. Finding that center is truly a matter of asking, and the asking is well to do each day if possible. We would now transfer to the one known as *(name)*. We are those of Oxal.

(? channeling)

I am Oxal. The love that we spoke of—the love of the inner child—is one which is close to the heart of the Creator. Have compassion for this inner child as you would any other. We leave this instrument now, and would transfer back to the one known as *(name)*. I am Oxal.

(Jim channeling)

I am again with this instrument. I am Oxal. As you begin to become used to ministering to your self, to that inner child, may each become aware, as if for the first time, of the universal inner child that is your common truth, for that which carries you about, thinks the thoughts of the world, and functions within the illusion is not the end of the self. Indeed, you may think of yourself as having two life forms: the second-density animal which faithfully serves and carries consciousness, thinks and makes decisions for the self is joined by the unlimited and infinite Self, which is the consciousness which is you and is also all others.

There is one consciousness. Yet, due to free will, that consciousness expresses within you in an unique way. As the little child is cared for, so is that awareness of what consciousness truly is. It is born within each. That spiritual self must be nurtured and cared for, for it is young. Each of you is, in one sense, an old soul. In another, in the sense that each is facing the lessons of third density, each is a new and untried spirit, newly conscious of self, newly conscious of the true nature of existence, and very hungry for more. Yet, this is a fragile child, and it exists in sometimes inhospitable climes. Therefore, love that inner identity and know those things that faith alone can give knowledge of. All is well. All will be well, and destiny will bring every harsh and sweet lesson which you need in order to grow. Turn to the sun which is love, and bloom gloriously.

Blessings to each as we, too, leave through this instrument. We leave you in love and in light, and in the care of each other and consciousness itself. My friends, you are not alone. Adonai. Adonai. We are those of Oxal. ✤

Intensive Meditation
September 6, 1993

(Carla channeling)

I am Oxal. We greet you in the love and in the light of the infinite Creator. It is a privilege to share this morning offering with you and we thank you for requesting our service at this time. The bright new energies of the day are most to enjoyable to us as we sense the many small sounds of your creatures, the birds as they sing at your windows. To hear with physical senses such as yours is a keen pleasure.

Before we would exercise the new instrument, we would say a few words concerning the so-called "armor of light." Were we to suggest that you protect yourselves in the spirit of fear, we would be treating you to poor advice. For truthfully, there is not anything or essence to fear in terms of negativity. However, the energies which each instrument seeks to employ are those which are those which have been potentiated greatly more and more intensely towards the polarity of service to others. It is in this mode of intention that the work of channeling is undertaken.

This desire places the instrument close to the source of light, and when one stands in very bright light, one casts a very visible shadow, sharp and black. In metaphysical terms, this shadow is to be respected. This instrument calls it the loyal opposition. The energies of service to self which offer their service to this planetary influence are most delighted when they can sway a channeled messages content to the point that the original intention to serve others is vitiated due to the mixed and increasingly service-to-self content of the messages received. This is done simply by the negative entity aping, or imitating the way the positive source was channeling in terms of both the way the channeling felt and the way the message was worded.

When a positive channel has been compromised in this way, and has become avid for more and more specific answers, the negative entity or energy offering this service simply continues to give more and more specific information, which, however, becomes less and less accurate. Eventually, due to the inaccuracy of the channelings, that particular attempt to be a servant of the light has been foiled.

There are simple things which one may do. In addition to inner cleansing and purification or what this instrument calls the tuning process and we would suggest some form of this protecting effort be used.

We have found it easiest to work with the seven energy centers by color in suggesting a visualization technique which is fairly clear and simple to generate. Picture the spine, mentally, and see the chakra points: red, then orange, yellow, green, blue, indigo and violet as those centers are located upon the spine.

Ask to see these energies and you shall see some representation of what your energies are like at that moment. If the energy is sluggish, ask it to spin, to rotate, and to brighten to clarify or in every way to suggest that is become clear and bright. And even insofar as that is possible with other energies, do this for each ascending energy center, until you see the chakras spinning like, shall we say, a beautiful, large roll of your Lifesavers.

After this has been visualized and you feel that your chakras are open and productive together, visualize the swirling together of the violet, swirled to the clockwise way to the red color and back to violet, so that you have a red-violet color, then visualize yourself being drenched in this red-violet ray, inside and outside every cell. This is representative of the body's protection of itself. Then move on to a visualization of the limitless light, or the white light that is pure and again drench yourself in this light, inside and outside in every cell. Breathe this white light in. Feel it move into every sense. Can you, as we describe this, sense even by one telling the clarifying energy of this procedure? If you do not feel brightened and strengthened by this visualization, we urge each to discover another representation which has this effect.

The use of the mind is poorly grasped among your peoples, yet we assure each that as entities work with visualizations such as these, these entities are using that skill which your minds, that is your consciousnesses, have in great abundance.

The benefit of such cleansing processes is perhaps best felt when one looks back upon an experience and is able to see that there was a positive addition of poise and peaceful feelings, which in turn aided the clarity of the contact.

We of Oxal have worked with few among your peoples for we are fifth density and are not often contacted, however, due to circumstances of, shall we say, kinship between the new instrument, the one known as M, and our particular vibration. We move into what, for us is a new area seldom visited, that being the opening of a channel.

We feel privileged to be offered this opportunity for service and express to the one known as M our affection and our enjoyment of this honor.

We also express that we feel our way here for we have not, as we said, become experienced at this most pleasant task, consequently, we do ask the one known as M to express mentally to us any discomfort or any other concern, which would be aided by the sharing … we must pause for this instrument to clear her throat.

(Pause)

This instrument just said to herself, "You talk too much." May we say to this instrument, that in terms of this contact, you talk just enough. We look for a way to more accurately aid in the new instruments perceptions of when to begin with a contact.

As we search this instrument's experience, we find that this instrument simply has a feeling, a sense of rightness. The equivalent in each instrument's way in sensing is what a new instrument needs to be looking for. Each time that the tuning and challenging procedures have been followed and a contact is initiated, allow some portion of the sensibilities to record, consciously, the way that induction of shared energy has felt and store this memory as high priority so that when that sensation is again experienced, it may be sensed in a quicker and heightened fashion.

Some who channel find it helpful to request some signal which this instrument would call conditioning, such as the involuntary opening of the mouth, or the movement of the tongue.

We feel this answers one persistent query in one way and we shall entertain further questions at the end of this session. As to what we hope to accomplish through channels such as this one and the one known as M, we hope to accomplish a witnessing of a very simple concept which we feel to contain all the truth we know. That concept is that there is one great original Thought, or vibration. That vibration is love. It created all that is, beginning with the first creation, the photon or what you call light. Graduated rotations of this light have articulated all physical phenomena whatsoever. Your world, your illusion, and all that you can imagine is made of light that is the manifestation of love.

When we greet you and leave you in love and in light, we carry with those words our feeling that this is all that there is. Now this is a very simple truth, but when we say you are love [and] that which you seek is love, become more and more conscious of that love and vibrate as that love vibrates, more and more closely resembling the vibration of the one original Thought, and all the paths to union with the infinite Creator shall be light and love. Entities say, "Yes, but how can I apply this in daily life?" and so we find our treasure in the storehouses of opinion and personal thinking, reading and evaluation which is in each instrument's mind. Using conscious channels such as this one, and the one known as M, we hope to tell our simple story in an infinitely various number of ways, knowing your that people are greatly individualistic in their needs and there cannot be too many ways to share this truth.

We pause to feel the energy dancing around the circle of seeking. The light which you gather is beautiful. We honor it as we transfer this contact to the one known as M. We are those of Oxal.

(M channeling)

I am Oxal. We again greet each in the Creator's eternal love and light. The love which is continually expressed from that which you call your sun in the form of light penetrates all that you see.

This light as it moves through the nature of creation can inform those entities who pay close attention to the seemingly mundane of life. The flight of a bird or the splash of a fish, when looked at closely, are expressions of that love.

(Pause)

(Carla channeling)

I am Oxal, and am again with this instrument. It is a helpful thing to remember that all form whatsoever, is love. If all is beautiful this is love, yet too, if there are things that seem unpleasant or harsh or difficult, this too is love. There is no escaping the unified nature of all that there is.

We would again transfer to the one known as M. We are those of Oxal.

(Pause)

(Carla channeling)

I am Oxal. We are again with this instrument and we say to the one known as M that this instrument has done well in sustaining the contact, in expressing our intended thoughts with style and accuracy. There is still the natural limit of ability to sustain the focus, however, we stress that this is peculiarly difficult work as is all work of this kind for the work of receiving spiritual information is abstract and metaphysical and takes place in utmost darkness. The light of what one may archetypically call the moon is the only light and this light is difficult that is it is difficult to see clearly in moonlight yet such is the way of spiritual teaching.

Therefore, be merciful to the self and realize that this work is careful and slow and in some ways never becoming easy. However, we believe that there is a call. We sense this call coming forth from your peoples for messages of light and love, words of truth and love, and therefore we welcome and hope only to assist such channels and we thank each who serves in this way.

We do not say that this service is greater than other services. We by no means suggest this yet this is one more way of sharing in the heritage of love with those about you and we thank each channel for without such, we could only speak in dreams and visions.

We would at this time transfer to the one known as Jim for the close of this session of working. We are those of Oxal.

(Jim channeling)

I am Oxal, and greet each again in love and in light through this instrument. At this time may we ask if there might be a query upon any mind to which we may respond?

M: I have one. As you were talking about protecting ourselves and the challenging process, I remembered reading in a newsletter about a challenging process, or even the voices that we hear and was wondering if I could get a little clarification on that because I spend a great deal of time speaking with my inner guidance and ever since reading that was a little confused as to how to approach that.

I am Oxal, and am aware of your query, my brother. When one hears voices or guidance from within it is well that you offer to these voices the challenge that asks if they come in the name of that quality for which you live most passionately and would die most willingly. This can be a simple process and need not take a great deal of your effort or your time, yet it is well that it be accomplished with a purity and intention at each communication. For as each seeker grows more fully open to the service-to-others polarity and gains in the power of this polarity, there will be attracted to the seeker those entities of a negative nature whose wish it is to control the power of this light now developing. The means by which such control is gained is that means by which we described at the beginning of this session, thus it is well to ask if whatever voice you hear comes in the name of [that] which you hold most dear.

Is there a further query, my brother?

M: Just a short one. Should this be done each time the voice is heard, or just the beginning of the conversation? And then assume that the person you are holding the conversation with stays the same?

I am Oxal. This is correct, my brother. At the beginning of each contact is the time for the challenge and the challenge then may respond as it will and be relied upon to be as it says it is for the remainder of that contact.

Is there a further query, my brother?

M: No, thank you.

I am Oxal, and we thank you, my brother. Is there another query?

(No further queries.)

I am Oxal. We give you our blessing and prosperity in your seeking, and we thank you again for asking us to join your morning offering and for allowing us to utilize the instruments here. It is a great honor to walk with you in this fashion. Know always that you are not alone for each has those guides and angels …

(Tape ends.)

L/L Research

L/L Research is a subsidiary of Rock Creek Research & Development Laboratories, Inc.

P.O. Box 5195
Louisville, KY 40255-0195

www.llresearch.org

Rock Creek is a non-profit corporation dedicated to discovering and sharing information which may aid in the spiritual evolution of humankind.

ABOUT THE CONTENTS OF THIS TRANSCRIPT: This telepathic channeling has been taken from transcriptions of the weekly study and meditation meetings of the Rock Creek Research & Development Laboratories and L/L Research. It is offered in the hope that it may be useful to you. As the Confederation entities always make a point of saying, please use your discrimination and judgment in assessing this material. If something rings true to you, fine. If something does not resonate, please leave it behind, for neither we nor those of the Confederation would wish to be a stumbling block for any.

CAVEAT: This transcript is being published by L/L Research in a not yet final form. It has, however, been edited and any obvious errors have been corrected. When it is in a final form, this caveat will be removed.

© 2009 L/L Research

Sunday Meditation
September 12, 1993

Group question: The question this afternoon has to do with the effect our constant pursuit of having enough money to survive and pay our bills causes in our spiritual seeking. We were wondering if that basic attitude of our working from 9 to 5 for most of the days of the week has an effect on our spiritual seeking, and we were wondering if there was another attitude that would have a more beneficial effect, keeping in mind that, well, I'll suggest that the Egyptians began some of their difficulties with disease and famine when they changed from the barter system and the common ownership of all things to private property and the institution of a monetary system. So we would like to know what the effect of our monetary pursuits have on our spiritual seeking and if there is an alternative attitude that may be more beneficial.

(Carla channeling)

I am Q'uo. Greetings in the love and in the light of the one infinite Creator. We are blessed to be called to your group this day. The sun streams into the domicile in which you sit, touching this channel's body with warmth, and we feel the metaphysical warmth of your welcoming to us. Thank you for this privilege. As always, we request that each entity use his personal discrimination in choosing those of our thoughts which may seem interesting to you. Leave others behind, please.

You ask if your monetary system has an effect on the life of the spirit. We may start by saying that it is clear that your sphere has great feelings concerning this system whereby a symbol of wealth is used in order to purchase goods or services. The globe upon which you dwell has in some form a monetary system regardless of where, in which culture, or at what level you may look.

Earlier, the one known as R was wondering if the brain was capable of giving good information considering that its makeup is a portion of the delusion. The brain is quite effective at dealing with problems within the illusions. One of the problems it perceives is the need for a supply of your money which not only shall cover the daily need, but shall also extend beyond that need to some possible future need for which there must be a supply which is more than enough for today.

As your peoples' cultures become more sophisticated, the perception of your bio-computer brain grows continually so that in the technically sophisticated culture which you now experience there is the universal perception that whatever is being received is probably not enough, for there is not enough extra.

We could encourage each to take the mind and lead it into a more wise configuration. However, the spiritual uses—we correct this instrument—the spiritual nature is not greatly linked with the bio-computer brain. The key, then, to a more elevated view of the relationship of money to the self is gained through the use of consciousness rather than the brain. To better gain access to a right relationship with money it is well to place concerns about finances within that holy of holies which lies within your deep mind. The consciousness of One is a consciousness of infinite plenty. The creation is full of all that there is. Every need has that which can meet the need. This consciousness of infinite supply sheds a welcome light upon the soul besieged by financial worries.

To backtrack, please move in mind to that prayer which began this session. You asked for daily bread. The teacher known as Jesus recommended that prayer include the concern over money. That is, that there be enough for today. If entities worried only when there was not enough for this day, a great deal of worry would cease and hearts would calm and feel soothed. However, though this is true, it is not definitively helpful because there is so much of world opinion which screams that enough for today is not at all a satisfactory end to concern.

But what if you were to alter the term "money" and subsume it in the term "energy"? When the term "energy" is used this may aid somewhat, for that which is energy does not need to be hoarded, but rather expresses its nature in its potentiation. Thusly, the general rule of thumb is that entities may do that which they must to gain enough energy to survive and be comfortable. This energy may be transmuted by those who see the spectrum of energies so that many things become money. And we feel sure that each can think of many instances where seemingly impossible things have occurred because of the trading of goods and services rather than the insistence upon some single form of energy.

Why, then, do entities feel that they must be concerned beyond today with money? For this is the place where concern over money does have a deep metaphysical result, [that is, thinking and worrying about the future.] Each is familiar with this habit of thinking, "Is there enough to pay this and this and this?" As each touches into this feeling, we suggest that each is gazing at a temporal being in fear that it may cease to exist, or that it may exist less comfortably.

Even with those who amass great quantities of money, the motivation continues to be at heart based upon fear. Indeed, money is but one example of the way persons within your culture perceive energy. We said earlier that the word "energy" would help those who hoard money, for they see that the use of energy is in being used, consumed or spent. But upon another level, those who have ambitions to gain power, for whatever reason, will amass as much extra power or energy as they can, there being no ceiling on the need for more.

In your culture, there has been more and more an unspoken assumption that there can never be too much energy, money, power, call it what you will, that there is literally no end to ambition or greed—all in the name of being more secure. Yet where is your security? In the bank which may fall? In the job which may cease? In the legal agreements which may be broken? Seek for that security, seek to amass energy saved against possible need, and feel the footsteps wander off the path.

The solution each day is to reorient the way of perceiving on a conscious level when you see yourself turning to that grasping concern for more than enough. Say to the self, "Let go of fear." We realize we speak to those who must work long hours in order to pay for food and lodging and all necessities and desired objects. Yet we suggest that those who do not need to spend long hours working are still just as capable of loosing sight completely of their true nature and of their true orientation with regard to plenty, if you must go to the place you would not wish, to do a job you would not choose. Yet, still, those who have no need but to please themselves spend at least as much of their time in fear.

The question of supply is perhaps the deepest chasm of irrational concern which seduces your peoples. In the face of this, we simply suggest that as the healthy regard for money is in being sure of the daily bread and then allowing concerns to fall away as appropriate, each simply move each day or each time he feels this concern into a conscious reorientation.

Step back now and gaze at the illusion. Money is a perfect symbol for this entire illusion. It is a polarized concept. Not only is it "more" and "less," but "all" and "nothing." To the prudent, there is more money and less money. To the large majority, there is the state called, "I have money," and the state called, "I don't have enough." It is all or nothing. Such is the radicalizing effect of fear.

Your situation surrounds you and seemingly would be obvious to you. Yet it is carefully structured, that is, the illusion is carefully structured so that you do not catch on to the depth of illusion. We praise this illusion in which you struggle, even though the struggle is not necessary in terms of sheer metaphysics. Within third density, each of you came to struggle, came to be confused and befuddled, came to develop fears, to do all the wrong things, to clutch and grasp at everything from money to ideas, feeling needy. And why? Because it is in working with these honest feelings that the entity within you, the spirit, the consciousness, may float about the being with all these concerns and may interact with it in such a way that consciousness is transferred into the working brain, the working mind.

Basically, your job here is to, within incarnation, begin to allow the programming of consciousness to replace the programming of your mind which deals with the illusion in a polarized manner. See the concern for money as the challenge it is. What consciousness does to this concern is to lend it the awareness that there is enough, for consciousness is infinite.

Celebrate your problems. They bring you to the point of desiring and seeking a higher truth. We encourage every discomfort of mind that leads you to seek and seek and seek again.

This entity just thought to itself that it tends to seek and seek and seek again to have enough money to spend. Very well, that seeking, too, may provide material for an entire lifetime. However, there is an alternative to seeking within the illusion. That is simply seeking the consciousness and its infinite plenty-essness.

We would at this time transfer this contact to the one known as Jim. We are those of Q'uo.

(Jim channeling)

I am Q'uo, and greet each again in love and in light. We would ask at this time if there might be any further queries to which we may speak?

Carla: I guess the only thing that I would say—it's not a question—is that in my mind, anyway, the situation where you've got somebody who is spending most of his day at work and he gets really tired and he says, "Well, how can I have time to seek spiritually when I'm just wearying myself at work?" I just don't feel that's been addressed entirely, and I was wondering if you could go into that. Because I see where it's consciousness, if we had a consciousness of plenty we'd be a lot better off, and, still, how do you find the time?

I am Q'uo. And am aware of your query, my sister. The time, as you experience it within your illusion, is oftentimes lacking for the pursuit of the metaphysical foundation for that which occurs in your physical illusion. And too often, for those who labor from sunrise to sunset, there is no time to consider the meaning of the life that seems so hard and unyielding. It is for these entities that there is a primary purpose for the life that includes nothing other than dedication to a goal and honing the desire to survive, not so much because this is of importance, but because the entity needs to focus its spiritual awareness upon a single concept. And, perhaps, at some point in this persistent practice, it will feel the need to move its awareness to a higher goal.

But for those who have the ability to survive without expending all of one's energies to do so, there is the luxury, shall we say, of being able to pursue the finer ramifications of the focus of spiritual awareness upon goals that are more intricately delineated. Each entity has this life agenda that provides for it the opportunity of that which is most important in its overall soul pattern. Thus, [for] those who are able to find their purpose within the illusion of supply and survival, there is the constant repetition of this opportunity.

Is there a further query, my sister?

Carla: No. Thank you, Q'uo.

I am Q'uo, and we thank you, my sister. Is there any other query at this time?

(Pause)

I am Q'uo, and we are most grateful to each present for inviting us to join your meditation this day. We are grateful to be able to offer that which is ours in metaphysical understanding in response to your heartfelt queries. We appreciate the difficulty of your illusion and the confusion that is, of necessity, experienced. We wish each well as each attempts to untangle the confusions that are the threads of your life pattern, and we assure each that your work is being accomplished with steady and sure hands whose Source moves beyond this illusion, and the work that is done stretches far beyond this illusion.

At this time we shall take our leave of this instrument and this group, leaving each, as always, in the love and in the light of the one infinite Creator. We are known to you as those of Q'uo. ✻

Sunday Meditation
September 19, 1993

Group question: The question this afternoon has to deal with what is sometimes called the spiritual desert-like experience, in which one feels that one is in a wasteland and that the sustenance or the spirit in whatever way it was perceived is no longer present, that one is not connected to, or really partaking in that same experience; a feeling of being isolated and alone, abandoned even. We've noticed also that in the rushing through our daily round of activities we can also create something like the desert experience, in which we're not connected to what we're doing and we're passing by so quickly that things and people just seems to be barely marking our days, and we're wondering if the desert experience has a purpose, if it's part of a spiritual cycle, and how we can be in that cycle and not be overly concerned about it, and just wondering in general what you might have to say about the spiritual desert experience.

(Carla channeling)

I am Q'uo. Greetings to each of you in the name of the One Who Is All. In love and in light we and you exist, and in that one creative love we greet you. In that pure and limitless light we salute you. We are asked to speak about the spiritual desert experience and are most happy to share our thoughts. However, we ask that each listen to these thoughts with the ear that is tuned by personal discrimination, for each person has his own truth, and to each person who hears that truth it seems as though it were being remembered rather than learned. If our thoughts do not evoke this feeling then we encourage each to lay them gently aside.

As you rest in this domicile upon this sun drenched day, listening to the small sounds of silence, there is the sensation of, shall we say, deceleration, as though the mind and its thoughts, which had been racing, were now slowed by the inactivity. We recommend meditation often, and our reason for doing so is precisely its effect upon the spiritual seeker, for the incarnational experience is one of action, and yet, if there is constant action, how can the fundamental nature of the pure self be felt or perceived? And without that self-knowledge, how then can the seeker move skillfully back into action in ways which address the deep concerns of seeking? How can one become more aware of one's true nature unless one is willing to sit with the self, listening to that inner silence through which spirit and guidance speak to the conscious mind?

The feeling of being not present is a deadening and disturbing sensation, for the essence of your human experience is intense and continuing experience of action taken and choices presented and made to involve yourself in this process of perceiving choices and then making them is to be involved in the most nearly central work of your density of conscious seeking. It fulfills a deep portion of your nature, both to focus upon these perceived choices and to find one's creative strength in applying choices already made. We say creative because this process of defining the self by its choices is peculiarly open to creative inspiration and insight.

When entities begin to feel hurried in the everyday life, there is the tendency to encourage within the self activities that numb the creative powers of perception. This is in order to avoid pain, for it is painful to spend the waking hours ceaselessly performing actions which the self feels are unimportant. Thusly, even when a meditation period is perceived by the self as being a failure because of an unremitting flow of inner noise, yet still the attempt to sit with the self and listen resensitizes the perceptions of self so that the self within feels stronger and more real. This in turn opens the inner door to the effect of that creative love which is the one great original Thought.

Thusly, one important way to approach the feeling of the spiritual desert experience is to place within the routines of each day those moments when the only goal is to sit with that inner reality and offer the self to the experience of being present with all that there is, for as you meditate you touch within that gate to eternal things, and the meditation becomes larger and larger until all the starry heavens dwell within the tiniest point of that meditative silence, and literally, the universe, the creation in totality, is tucked into the perception of self, and you are all that there is, and all that there is is part and parcel of your self.

For each of you perceives that he works upon the small self in the context of the day, the season, the moment, and these moments in the conscious mind seem to add up to a life too quickly experienced and are too soon over. When the self is feeling this disconnection, and the self feels less and less a portion of a beautiful creation, yet how to address the longing felt by one who does feel disconnected?

This instrument was speaking earlier of the feeling which her faith had given her within this spiritual desert experience, and we feel this is a good example of the ways seekers can use those choices already made. If one has the faith in one's previous perceptions and respects one's previous conclusions, this certainly aids materially in keeping an entity in balance. However, it is often that part of the desert experience is that one doubts and even rejects one's previous perceptions and feels to be—we correct this instrument—and feels itself to be stranded, having no continuing beliefs. It is not that the pilgrim soul wishes to turn upon its past and rend it, but rather that the experience of the spiritual desert seems to openly and lucidly delineate a self which has been taken out of all previous patterns which comforted, so that there is in the truth seeking heart of the pilgrim the solemn and sure belief that all previous states were now left behind. When one's context is not respected and a new one must be built, then there is a true desert experience.

Let us address this state of perception in which previous truths, previous patterns and previous emotions concerning spirit have been left behind, and the seeking self must be invented entirely. What would you do if suddenly you were not the sex you are, or the nationality that you are, the intelligence that you perceive in yourself, or the kind of entity you perceive yourself to be? Would these definitions of self, shall we say, then become irrelevant, or would the seeker need to reinvent each of these ways of thinking about the self? We suggest that the reason qualities such as nationality, sexuality and type of character are valued and are a part of each person's web of perception is that they are fundamental building blocks of that milieu in which you have come to learn the lessons of love. These are not things you outgrow in third density. These are tools you use often in attempting to better perceive the day-to-day nature of your world.

Thusly, the first thing to avoid when feeling annihilated and full of desert times is the casual flinging away of identity. The small changes of everyday identifications of self are not unspiritual. These homely truths of self are portions of the self which has come to learn those things which are greater than any description of that which goes into them can possibly encompass. You use these building blocks, and many, many other, not simply to distinguish the self from others or each entity from another, but to do work in consciousness in which words are given burdens greater than words can bear. This is the reason poetry and music are so compelling to those sensitive to the freight that they do carry, for the common places within the life do not remain common when one is sitting with them in faith that there is that nature of self which is more than its circumstances or its expression.

In music, the tones create words which carry more feeling, more deep emotion than could be explained. In poetry, the words themselves are twisted together until they make a rope stronger in evocative truth than the words used to make the rope. And when two hearts touch, whether silently or with words, a commerce is achieved from self to self that far outstrips the power of expression, for you are within an illusion in which every possible means of distraction is purposefully placed to allow the full travel of free will to give the self who seeks the largest stage upon which to improvise.

We do not encourage walking away from the world of too much to do. Not for long, my friends, for this is the world into which you came to learn the lessons of love, and this is the incarnation which is your present opportunity to, shall we say, achieve a state of realization which transforms the everyday into that which rings true.

The key here is to respect this incarnation, to respect the times of celebration and the times of suffering, however they may be perceived. You came into this illusion because you wished for these complications and distractions, not to look at them and then turn aside and move out of the world necessarily, but rather to so orient the self that the limitless and unbounded truth that overflows each moment may in the present incarnation be encouraged to express the deeper and deeper nature of the self which transforms all the everyday experiences into those freighted with that precious burden of the immanence of love.

When you feel most trivial, most dry and most disconnected, there is the natural tendency to turn away, to fill the time or the mind with something which may distract and release one from the uncomfort, the discomfort. Yet, we do suggest that these feelings be respected, that the time may be well spent, when the self simply sits with these feelings and honors the self as it expresses itself in these sometimes hard or uncomfortable feelings and thoughts. For you are here not to feel good all the time, but to attempt more and more to know the truth of each thing which is perceived, and to honor that truth. The sitting, the meditating, the high and holy words and work, yes, these are truth, but true too is the poorly done, the mishandled, the tumbled, the messed up, as this instrument would say. In the dirt and grime and struggling of day-to-day living lies the most transcendent beauty, the deepest passion, the most intense of perceptions of overarching infinity.

We therefore encourage each to continue in the desert times to hold in respect those positive frames of perception which temporarily seem to have been invalidated; but more than that holding of the past, to continue in a state of mind that does not contain the fear that this dry desert period will continue. If one may become fearless concerning one's state of mind so that discomfort is seen without fear, then the groundwork has been done for the present moment to touch the heart anew, so that that deep wisdom of the heart may transfigure the perceptive web and suddenly the self feels itself in green pastures, strengthened, straightened and strong once again.

We hope each may cultivate, not an indifference to the state of mind, but rather a willingness to appreciate the difficult times without asking that they be soon over …

(Side one of tape ends.)

(Carla channeling)

… *(inaudible)* is most fundamentally about respect. This incarnation is but a moment. You have treasure in your moments within this illusion. The unknowing of an incarnational experience is its most potent characteristic. Open your hearts without fear to these times and find yourself striding among the stars, yet still very much focused upon the daily life. You cannot do this by turning from the demands of the illusion, but in turning to them with love and without fear, for each perceives the nature as one who does work, and we say to you your first vocation is the creation and maintenance of your web of that which is true and that which is love.

We would at this time conclude through the instrument known as Jim. We thank this instrument and would leave it in love and light. We are those known to you as Q'uo.

(Jim channeling)

I am Q'uo, and greet each again in love and in light through this instrument. At this time it is our privilege to offer ourselves in the attempt to speak to any further queries which those present have for us. Is there a query with which we may begin?

Carla: I guess what I didn't hear in the previous part was if you have—if you have any suggestions that you can use to refocus quickly if your mind is really bugged and really bothered.

I am Q'uo, and am aware of your query, my sister. Each seeker will have had experience with a variety of inspirational material, be it that of the written word, the spoken word, the words of music, or of the appreciation of paintings and the appreciation of the natural surroundings themselves which will have been helpful in focusing the essential quality of the spiritual journey for this seeker. Thus, any of these previous experiences, having been crystallized in a word, a picture, or any passage whatsoever may be recalled at those moments when it is felt that there is no center to the life, no fabric that holds all together. We would recommend that those most favored and inspirational passages be recalled at this time and utilized for the refocusing of the attention and the sharpening of that which has become diffused and depleted.

Is there a further query, my sister?

Carla: Yeah, on a completely different level. I had no awareness of time going past this time and I hear that click on the tape recorder and I just couldn't believe it. What was different about how you—was there anything different about the way you were working with me that I should ponder? Because I—it was a little bit different as to how I experienced the contact.

I am Q'uo, and am aware of your query, my sister. We would refer you to that cycle of experience that you know as the cycle of the adept and remind you that there are portions of that cycle during which you are more able to practice your art, and it is during these favorable periods that you will find such practice less of an effort and more harmonious, shall we say. You will discover that the passage of time seems to be that which is rapid during such cyclical and enhanced periods.

Is there another query, my sister?

Questioner: One last one. I have heard from other channels, I've read in the spiritual literature of the New Age here and there that time is speeding up, that there's a difference in time. Do you think that there is a difference in time now, or do you think that there's a difference in people? Or is there a difference at all? Is it just what people always say?

I am Q'uo, and am aware of your query, my sister. We find that the measurement of your time periods is as it has always been. However, it is a phenomenon of your aging process that, as you continue to gain experience and years, that the passage of time seems to accelerate, for you have recorded in your memory much experience and are able to process that experience far more efficiently than when you were in the younger of your years and experience was more, it would seem, drawn out and the learning time progressed more slowly. Thus, we find the aging of your physical vehicles and the mental notation of that aging and gathering of experience to be the responsible factors in this perception.

Is there a further query, my sister?

Carla: No, Q'uo, and rub it in, why don't you? That's okay, that's okay. Thank you, Q'uo.

I am Q'uo, and we thank you, my sister, once again. Is there a further query at this time?

Questioner: I have a question, Q'uo, [on some feeling] that I remember. It seems that when I watch weather patterns—a storm, or when I feel wind blowing my hair around—it resonates with something in me, and I seem to be fascinated or riveted by it … very powerful. Are there some suggestions you can offer that I can ponder about this experience [so vividly observed]?

I am Q'uo, and am aware of your query, my brother. We again refer you to those younger years within this incarnation, during which there was a fascination with the patterns of weather as they move through your natural environment. There was an affinity for the natural elements and the activity that they brought as you were able to appreciate the effect that the patterns of weather brought to the environment about you. This effect was internalized in the changing of your own mental and emotional attitudes as the patterns of weather moved hither and yon. Thus, we would suggest that the continued fascination of these patterns in your experience harkens back to those earlier and more expansive years, that is, expansive in the growing sense of appreciation that was developing in your life pattern.

Is there a further query, my brother?

Questioner: No, not for now, Q'uo. I'd just like to thank you *(inaudible)*.

I am Q'uo, and we thank you, my brother. Is there another query?

Questioner: This isn't exactly a question, it's an observation. As I was listening to the words today I felt that my chest was vibrating—around the center of my chest or my esophagus was vibrating with each word. This is a very unusual and strange experience for me, and one that I haven't experienced before. I just wondered what was going on?

I am Q'uo, and am aware of your query, my sister. The phenomenon of which you speak was one in which you felt that there was some resonance of truth, shall we say, or application to your own experience by the words which were being spoken, thus this was your means by which the feeling of harmony was expressed, since you have developed in your own life experience the ability to utilize that portion of your physical vehicle to speak and sing those words of praise that have been written and recorded by various authors throughout the history of your peoples. Thus, this was simply your unique means of feeling a harmony with the basic message that was being given.

Is there a further query, my sister?

Questioner: No, thank you.

I am Q'uo, and we thank you, my sister. Is there a final query at this time?

Carla: I'd like to follow up on hers and ask, I've heard of the rising of the kundalini and all that, and I've also heard a lot about the various energy centers, and I was wondering if another way to express that answer would have to do with that concept of energy rising, and for the blue energy center there, that center of communication … it almost sounded like it was being activated. It sounded like experiences that people have talked to me about that have had kundalini experiences. Can you relate those two, or am I on the wrong track here?

I am Q'uo, and am aware of your query, my sister. The experience of the rising of the kundalini is one in which the feeling of energizing would occur throughout the centers of energy, from lower to higher. Thus, this experience was more localized and was properly a portion of this phenomenon. However, in this particular entity, the throat and chest region are of primary importance throughout the life experience, and therefore we would suggest that their activation has been of a more normal and natural progression, rather than the momentary experience of the kundalini energy rising.

Is there a further query, my sister?

Carla: No, thank you.

I am Q'uo, and again we thank you, my sister. We would ask if there would be a final query at this time?

Carla: No, I'm through.

I am Q'uo, and we would thank each once again for the great opportunity that has been extended to us in being allowed to join your circle of seeking this day. We are very grateful to be able to speak our humble words and opinions utilizing the instruments present. We would at this time take our leave of this instrument and this group, leaving each, as always, in the love and in the ineffable light of the one infinite Creator. We are known to you as those of Q'uo. Adonai, my friends. Adonai.

The Aaron/Q'uo Dialogues, Session 18
September 24, 1993

(This session was preceded by a period of tuning and meditation.)

Aaron: I am Aaron. I want to introduce you to this tuning process by asking you to participate with me in a brief guided meditation.

Please allow yourself to follow along without concern for whether you can or cannot do what I suggest. Our emphasis here is not on getting rid of anything within you, but simply on allowing the barriers of ego self to dissolve so that you may move into the divine aspect of yourself and hear from that place of center.

Begin by taking a few deep breaths and releasing … breathing in … There is nothing external to you. As far out as you can go into the universe, when you breathe in, you take that universe into that which you call self. When you exhale, you exhale that which you call self into the universe … breathing in and letting go, each exhalation dissolving the boundaries of self. Inhale and let go sending any resistance to taking the universe into your heart, sending any resistance that wants to hold on to being "somebody"; just letting it go … If anything holds on, it is okay. It will go. Nothing to do, just being. Breathing in and expanding outward with the exhalation flowing into the universe, then breathing the universe into yourself … open … the heart is weary of its isolation … open … allowing yourself to come into the essence of who you are, letting go of all the concepts of who you always thought you were, just allowing that pure, clear mind/heart to be what it always has been: Pure Awareness, Pure Soul.

As you drop your boundaries, feel the connection to the joy and suffering in the universe. Be aware of the rising aspiration in yourself to be a tool, to offer your energy as tool, for the alleviation of that suffering—not my suffering or your suffering, our suffering. The aspiration to be a source of energy, courage, love, faith, healing, for all beings; to manifest your energy in such a way that it promotes peace and happiness in the universe—this is the primary intention, moving out of the fearful, small self. In your own words, silently state your intention to serve the universe and all that dwells therein, to be a vehicle of Love. I will be quiet for a moment while you phrase this intention in the words of your own heart.

(Pause)

Given that aspiration and intention, the next question is, "How do I implement this?" You alone cannot implement it. You connected to all that is are empowered to implement joy, peace and harmony So the next step is to invite in whatever help there may be, each in your own way, invoking Jesus or the

Buddha, asking God's help. Silently voice your prayer that you may become an instrument for healing and love in this world—not for your own ego, but in service to all; not for your own glory, but that your service may be offered back to God in grateful thanks. For you are but a reflection of that divinity—divine in your own right, but taking your light from that most brilliant and perfect light, and with rejoicing, returning that light, ever brighter, ever clearer. I will pause again, then, so that you may voice your prayer in your own words.

(Pause)

All beings on human and spirit planes contain some mixture of positive and negative polarity. None is totally negative, nor are any but those most fully enlightened masters totally positive. We do not flee from the shadow in ourselves, but aspire to touch that shadow with love and thereby to grow. In the same way we do not flee from external negative energy, but aspire to touch it with love. If there be any being within this circle, human or discarnate, that is of negative polarity, of predominantly negative polarity, that wishes to hear these teachings, we welcome it. It may not speak through this instrument. It is welcome to listen and learn the pathways of service to all beings, the pathways of love.

At this point Barbara will be silent with herself for a few moments. Her own process here is to make the firm statement of what she stands for and values, and that none may channel through her unless they are fully harmonious with her highest values. She uses this process, although 95% of what she channels is this energy that I am, simply because it is an important statement which gives her confidence in what she receives and allows her to relax into the channeling. I will be quiet now and allow you each to meditate in your own way for two or three minutes.

(Pause)

Aaron: I am Aaron. Again, my greetings and love to you all. My brother/sister Q'uo suggests that I begin this session, and I will do so briefly and then turn the microphone to Q'uo. Our topic is, "What is the spiritual path and how do we live it?"

My dear ones, you have been on this spiritual path since the moment when you, as what I call a spark of God, first came into awareness and sensed a separation, illusory but seeming to be real—a separation from that which we might call God. There is nothing you can do that is not part of the spiritual path. There are only more skillful or less skillful ways to walk that path. By skillful I do not mean evil or good, simply ways that bring pain to yourself or others, or ways that help to free all beings from pain. When you "walk" this spiritual path (I put that word, walk, in quotation marks), perhaps what you are really asking is, "How do I become more aware that I am a being on a spiritual path? How do I live my life with deeper awareness?"

Each of you is like a pebble tossed into a giant, still sea, an infinite sea. Each time a pebble splashes, it touches everything around it and sends out waves that affect all the other pebbles. When you send out loving energy, your inter-reaction/interrelationship with the world is far different than when you send out hateful or fearful energy. And yet you are aware (and many of you have often heard me say), as long as you are human, you are going to have emotions. Fear is sometimes going to arise—anger, greed, jealousy … You cannot stop their arising, but you can change your relationship to what arises.

From my perspective, there is a vast difference between the being who feels fear as the foundation for anger or greed and then either becomes reactive and acts in anger or in greed, or becomes hateful to itself because those emotions have arisen; there is a vast difference between that and the being who sees fear arising, sees the anger or greed or other emotion that grows out of the fear and just relaxes and smiles at it and says, "Oh, you again. Here's jealousy. Here's desire. Here's rage." The difference in what I am speaking of here is in the ownership of what arises.

This is the illusion we keep getting caught in: that we are a self and we own this or that emotion, thought or sensation; and once you own it, you are stuck in it. Do you know the story of Brer Rabbit and the Tar Baby?[2] We have used this to illustrate something different, but tonight I want to use it to illustrate this ownership.

Brer Rabbit saw the Tar Baby, thought it was mocking him, so he punched it. He reacted to his anger and then he got stuck in it. He said, "Let me

---

[2] *The Complete Tales of Uncle Remus*, by Joel Chandler Harris (1848-1908). Boston: Houghton Mifflin, 1955.

go," and he punched it again. Two hands stuck! "Let's try a foot, two feet" … all his limbs stuck. Here is one very stuck rabbit! When you see an emotion arising or a thought, and there is aversion or attachment, and you grasp and try to hold on to it or kick and punch it to try to get rid of it, you begin to think that there is somebody who owns it. Then you are stuck in this concept.

This, too, is a part of your spiritual path. Even being stuck in it is an opportunity for learning, if there is awareness. But usually at that point there is so much fear and frustration predominating that awareness has dissolved.

It is never too late to come back. At any moment you can cut through that ownership and simply smile at yourself: "Here I am stuck in it again." Once more: "Oh, you again." Perhaps we could call this one, "Stuck in the Tar." A deep breath and a reminder: "This is not who I am; but I am human, and as long as I am human this is all going to keep arising. It is not given to me to fight with, but to learn from." Just relax and be with it.

Barbara spoke earlier this evening about the *Dzogchen* retreat and about *Rigpa*, or "luminous great perfection," which is just a fancy term for finding that space of the Divine in yourself and resting in it over and over and over. This is the essence of the spiritual path as taught by every religion that I have ever encountered in all of my many lifetimes. Some of them had it a bit distorted. Some of them were very clear about it. All of them aspired to that, to reaching that space of Pure Being.

We are not talking about specific religions here, but the spiritual path itself. The essence of that path is to learn how to come back again and again to this divine aspect of you, what I have called the angel aspect of you, to allow that to stabilize, to learn methods of recognizing that experience of angelness, of Pure Awareness. Until you recognize it, you can't do much about it.

Each of you is in that space far more often than you know, but because there is not awareness, it comes and goes without recognition. So, first you need to recognize that space within you. Then, you work to stabilize it, to be able to relate to the world more and more from that space of clarity and connection.

That, to me, is the spiritual path. As to, "How do we live it?"—that is what we will spend the weekend questioning. How do we live with our fear, our anger, our pain, our desires? How do we make space for all of that humanness in our hearts and find deep love for all of us as we exhibit that humanness? How do we let go of judgment? At the same time, we must be aware that while we aspire to let go of judgment, we are still responsible for our choices. We have here a relative reality and an ultimate reality. There is much that I wish to say about that, but will hold it until tomorrow.

At this point, I would like to pass the microphone to my brother/sister Q'uo. I use the term brother/sister because Q'uo does not offer itself as either feminine or masculine energy, but as a combination of both. I also am neither masculine nor feminine, but I have chosen to manifest my energy and put on a cloak of consciousness and being of that which was masculine.

All of you are a mixture of masculine and feminine. You are incarnated male or female bodies and more fully manifest the energy of that body; but you are all a mixture of both. Q'uo very beautifully balances that mixture, exhibiting the fullness of both the masculine and the feminine. And so I pass the microphone to my brother/sister/friend. That is all.

Q'uo: We are known to you as those of Q'uo. Greetings in the love and in the light of the One infinite Creator.

We thank the one known as Aaron for the masterful introduction, and would continue by noting that we are a complex made up of the thoughts and memory of what you would identify as male and female. We now study and serve as one. Our path to this point in our walk on the path of spiritual seeking has included your range of present incarnational experience. You are upon a path aiming towards an evolution of spirit, which you may intensify and speed up. Many among your people have no wish to learn more quickly the lessons of love; however, each of you does wish to assist that process of spiritual evolution of mind, as some call it.

For our part, we greatly and humbly thank each for calling us to your circle of seeking. For as we share our thoughts with you, we are learning and pursuing our chosen path of service; and your assistance both inspires us and employs us. We ask that each be continually aware that we are fallible. We make mistakes and would not ask that you hear us as the voice of authority. Take those thoughts which resonate within your heart and leave any others by the wayside, for we would not be a stumbling block for any.

So, as the one known as Aaron has said, you are here making choices. Let us examine this situation. It is our understanding that this, your density, is the density of those first self-aware; and in this self-aware state you begin to examine both your inner reality and the nature of your surroundings. Into the chaos of the untaught mind comes this illusion which you know as living. Colors, shapes, entities, relationships, shout out at the infant in incarnation; and the young years are full of the noise becoming signal, the chaos becoming increasingly ordered, the environment becoming internalized, the self painting the environment its own personal colors of meaning.

It is our opinion that the choices you face continue to be of a certain basic nature. Each choice has to do with polarizing or gaining a bias towards either that which is radiant, loving, freeing and expanding, or that which is attracting, pulling, grasping. We call this dynamic a choice of service to others or service to self, and assign the term *positive* to the service-to-others category, *negative* to service to self.

(The rest of Q'uo's statement did not record.)

Aaron: I am Aaron. There are a number of questions we will be investigating this weekend, but primarily it comes down to that which repeats itself over and over in your lives. To walk a spiritual path with awareness and love, one must be aware of when one has moved into fear and cutting off of love.

How do we find that awareness and deepen it? Fear builds walls around our hearts. How do we dissolve that fear? Where does faith come into it? When we have made the best decisions we can, thinking that we are acting out of love, and the results seem to boomerang and cause great pain for us, does that mean we acted out of fear without seeing it clearly or does it mean that we need to have even deeper faith? Sometimes it is one direction, one answer. Sometimes it is the other answer. How do we begin to differentiate that?

Is pain always a warning that we are doing something (I hesitate to use this word, but) wrong? Or is pain inevitable? Might there be pain even in wise choices at times? What is pain about in our lives? Is there ever going to be complete absence of pain in human incarnation or do we simply change our relationship to pain and end our war with it, certainly not inviting it in, but not hating it when it appears? I am not offering any answers here, just raising some of the questions. One can live one's life trying so hard not to harm others, but if one becomes a somebody trying hard to be harmless, does not that create its own kind of harm?

In a talk earlier this week, I gave an example of a situation that I have seen many times while in incarnation, where monks or nuns in monastic situations try to outdo one another at being nobody. Who can take the food last? Who can do the hardest work? You can make a career out of being a martyr and truly enhance this small ego self, solidify it.

So, it is not so much what you do. It might seem to be very kind that you always serve others and let others go first. What is the motivation for that? When you look, you will find there are multiple motivations. In every act, word, or thought, there are multiple motivations. You have an apple in your pocket and you realize that you are hungry and thirsty. Here is a red, juicy apple. You pull it out. Just as you are about to bite into it, there is a small child, big eyes, very thin, holding out its hand, "Please!" Your heart opens and you give the apple. As you give it, there is the small thought, "Didn't I do good? Did people see?" The giving of the apple is a pure, loving act. The accompanying thought grows out of a place of fear and wanting to be the good one. It is another aspect of somebody-ness.

So, we never act or speak or think fully out of love or out of fear. How do we get acquainted with our multiple motivations so that we may begin to understand our choices better, and thereby begin to choose more skillfully and lovingly for ourselves and for all beings? This, to me, is the focus of walking a spiritual path. And it is not only the resultant actions, words and thoughts, but the clarifying of motivation, the learning about how this small ego self does solidify, not being afraid of its solidification but using it each time it happens as a catalyst to remind oneself to move back into center, to move back into connection and into the Pure Mind, Pure Self.

We will explore all of this in depth through the weekend and also have time to answer your personal questions, speaking to your personal situations. There is sleepiness. It is late. I want to pass the microphone here to Q'uo. I thank you all for allowing me to share my thoughts with you tonight and very much look forward to our continued sharing through this weekend. My love to you all and I wish you a good night. That is all.

Q'uo: We are those of Q'uo and would echo the one known as Aaron's sentiments and would leave you with two thoughts.

Firstly, those who seek together to learn service to others shall, in each other, see how impossible it is to serve others without serving the self, for your actions are reflected; and as each serves each, each receives illumination. In your sister's heart is your self. In your brother's heart is your self. And you were not incarnated to be calm. Your choices are made in the midst of activity.

Secondly, there is for each outburst or outlay of your energy, the time to take in that food and drink of spirit that nourishes and rests. Begin to be more aware of these dynamics. See your self reflected, see love reflected and feel the outpouring and the in-gathering, one to another and all things whatsoever to the infinite One.

For this evening, we again thank each and bless each, leaving each in joy and in peace in the love and in the light of the One which is all. We are known to you as those of Q'uo. Adonai. Adonai.

L/L Research

L/L Research is a subsidiary of Rock Creek Research & Development Laboratories, Inc.

P.O. Box 5195
Louisville, KY 40255-0195

www.llresearch.org

Rock Creek is a non-profit corporation dedicated to discovering and sharing information which may aid in the spiritual evolution of humankind.

ABOUT THE CONTENTS OF THIS TRANSCRIPT: This telepathic channeling has been taken from transcriptions of the weekly study and meditation meetings of the Rock Creek Research & Development Laboratories and L/L Research. It is offered in the hope that it may be useful to you. As the Confederation entities always make a point of saying, please use your discrimination and judgment in assessing this material. If something rings true to you, fine. If something does not resonate, please leave it behind, for neither we nor those of the Confederation would wish to be a stumbling block for any.

CAVEAT: This transcript is being published by L/L Research in a not yet final form. It has, however, been edited and any obvious errors have been corrected. When it is in a final form, this caveat will be removed.

© 2009 L/L RESEARCH

The Aaron/Q'uo Dialogues, Session 19
September 25, 1993

(This session was preceded by a period of tuning and meditation.)

Q'uo: I am Q'uo. We greet you in the love and in the light of the one infinite Creator and thank each for the blessing of calling us to share in the blending of vibrations in this circle of working. We share our thoughts as we, too, travel upon the ever-unfolding way which is the path of spiritual pilgrimage.

We were saying that your density of existence is the density of a choice—one great choice upon which so much is based. We were describing this choice as that between radiant service and grasping or magnetic service: service to others and service to self. To discern this choice in each moment is a substantive portion of that learning which you incarnated to pursue. The other part of this learning is simply to continue offering praise and thanks. That is the music which gladdens your walking. The choice made once in full awareness is the beginning. Each choice made thereafter strengthens and deepens the energy which you may usefully accept and allow to move through you. You see, the energy of all things is love.

When the Creator chose to manifest creation, that thought which is the Creator was Love—but Love unknown and unknowing, unpotentiated by the free-will choice to generate manifestations of Love.

The first manifestation which this great original Thought generated was the photon, that which your scientists name a unit of light. All things whatsoever which can be sensed are manifestations created by successive quanta and rotations of light.

What you seek to do as you move through this school which is your illusion is to more and more faithfully approximate the vibration of this one great original Thought, which is Love. Those who choose the negative or service-to-self path are also choosing Love; however, it is a choice of path which bypasses the open heart, and therefore the energy or power which is created tends towards distinctions and control. This path of separation will eventually flow into a place where the negative choice becomes obviously inappropriate; and at that point, all entities which have chosen the negative path of seeking have the opportunity to reverse polarity and become again children of the open heart.

In your density, however, this choice is fresh and the negative path has its long and separate walk ahead of it. We realize that each within this group has chosen the path of love and service to others, and we may say that we feel that this path is the one which we prefer and ourselves have chosen. We feel it is more efficient and that it, in its use of power, is the desirable one; but we wish each to grasp that these choices are free. There is no final condemnation for any who seeks in any way, for that seeking will be gathered in ripe harvest in its own time.

This gives a foundation or a continuing of foundation, for much has been done already upon which we as sources talking to this group may metaphorically stand when we speak of the spiritual path and how to walk it. The context is infinity, brought to one single moment in manifestation in each consciousness now; and that now becomes now and now, again and again.

We would at this time transfer the speaking to the one known as Aaron. We are those of Q'uo.

Aaron: Good morning and my love to you all. As spirit I find much joy in every moment of my being. But I must say that a gathering such as this and the light that is being emitted from this circle bring deep joy to my heart, because I am committed as my most fundamental value to the alleviation of suffering in the universe, to bringing light where there has previously been darkness; and the light that you send out does indeed do that. So it is very wonderful to share with you and to rejoice in this blazing fire, the warmth and brilliance of it.

My brother/sister Q'uo is generally more poetic than I am. I must say that this dear friend inspires me to more poetic speech. Enough. Let us get back to basics. Q'uo spoke of the free-will choice each of you has. I wish to expand briefly here.

There is no such thing as absolute evil. There are those beings who are negatively polarized in service to self and act in love for that self. The selfishness of that motivation, let us say the self-centeredness of that motivation, may cause immense suffering for others, yet one must still acknowledge that this being is motivated by some form of love, however distorted that love may be. Such a being may indeed even graduate from the earth plane, carrying that negative distortion; but it cannot return to the One ultimately, cannot move through the higher densities beyond sixth density with that negative distortion. It becomes a dead end. So, it may carry its negative distortion to a very high level, but eventually it must change its polarity to proceed.

We have transcripts available that detail this process of reversal of polarity. Should that interest any of you, they can be found and Barbara can provide, so I will not speak of it in depth.[3]

The difference in path, then, seems to be that the path of service to others speaks of awareness of the suffering of all beings and the deeply heartfelt desire to alleviate suffering. The path of service to self ignores that suffering because it accentuates the separate self. It cannot ultimately carry one back to full unity with the Creator because there is still the delusion of separation. It is therefore a truly more difficult path. Can one begin to have compassion for beings who are set on that path rather than fear and hatred of them? Their negative distortion causes as much pain to them as to others.

Having made the decision to live one's life in service to others, one is constantly confronted by that fear in oneself which leads to grasping and aversion to self-service. Service to others and service to self are not mutually exclusive. This is a misunderstanding. Let us return to that imaginary being with the apple, whom we introduced last night. The apple is offered, seeing the child's hunger. But what if it were the only food that the apple holder had, and that apple holder had also not eaten for several days? Is that thought, "I also am hungry," an evil thought? We chop the apple in half and trust that further sustenance will be offered to each.

The self is also an other. You are part of this great scheme of things. To simply become a martyr and offer yourself with no respect for the needs of the self is to make needless sacrifice. Indeed, one must begin to respect the needs of the self while distinguishing which needs grow out of love and healthy respect, and which grow out of fear. That being who has had a full breakfast and the promise of a full lunch has no need to take half the apple. Can you hear the voice of fear that says, "What if I need it?" and simply note, "This is old mind speaking"? "In this present moment, I am not hungry and this child is hungry. In this present moment, I have no need of this food. I can give it freely." But mind goes back to those past experiences of hunger or deprivation of any sort, and that old-mind consciousness wants to hoard because of the very basic human fear, "Will my needs be met?"

---

[3] For more information, please contact the Deep Spring Center for Meditation and Spiritual Inquiry, 3003 Washtenaw Ave., Suite 2, Ann Arbor, MI, 48104, www.deepspring.org.

The person who lives its life in awareness will notice the arising of such thoughts and be able to identify what is the bare perception of this moment and what is old-mind habit. That same being, noticing that the desire to hold on to the apple is old-mind habit, that there is no present hunger or need—that same being will not scorn itself because that habitual reaction has arisen. It will see that reaction not as its own greed to be hated but as human fear which must be touched with compassion. So, it notices the old-mind habit arising in itself. It notices its movement toward contempt for that habit and it asks itself also to have compassion for the human with those fears, thus allowing space for it all to float. It then finds freedom to come back to the bare perception, to recognize in this moment, "There's no hunger. I can give this."

By bringing this level of awareness to each arising thought, emotion, and sensation, one begins to move away from the boundaries of old-mind habit, to live one's life in the present, in the now. It is only in this moment that one can live with love and wisdom.

What I want you to see here is that the choice of service to self/service to others is not clear-cut: "I'm generous!" or, "I'm selfish!" Rather, it is built on staying in this moment with a deep respect for all beings, knowing oneself to be part of this linked chain of beings, heart open to the needs of all, seeing fear as it arises and making the conscious effort not to live by the dictates of fear.

How to walk a spiritual path? This, to me, is the essence of it: to notice each dialogue with fear and have the courage to remove oneself from that dialogue, not hating one's fear, but also not owning one's fear nor being controlled by it. It takes much courage. As you work with this, you come to an intersection. You find that there is a, what I call, "horizontal practice of relative reality," living one's life skillfully and lovingly, moment by moment, but that there is an illusory self who is doing that skillful, loving living.

There is also a "vertical practice" which cuts through the illusion of self. Q'uo just spoke to you of this. When it is next my turn to speak I will elaborate on it, but first I would like to pass the microphone back to Q'uo, who would like to speak to us to elaborate on some of what I have just spoken of. That is all.

Q'uo: I am Q'uo, and greet each again in love and light.

As our beloved brother Aaron has so wisely pointed out, you are one of the other selves you serve. In fact, let us confuse you thoroughly and say you are the first other one whom you shall serve. And why is this? This is because, as the teacher known as Jesus has said, all the law is to love the Creator with all one's strength, heart, mind and soul and to love your neighbors as yourself.[4] If you do not love yourself, how can you truly love your neighbor?

Yes, each of you is all too aware of the missed steps, the erroneous conclusions, the impulses which do not do Love justice. Yes, you are completely unfinished. Is this a reason not to be in love with your self? Can your self, in all its distortions, depart one iota from the truth of Love? Yes, it may seem to, just as all whom you come in contact with may seem to. Yet the heart that loves knows that beneath, above and around all confusion, all missed steps, all seeming imperfection, lies the One—unblemished, unbroken, beautiful and perfect. Your nature is love.

The walking of the spiritual path is an opening of the universal Self within, to embrace more and more without distortion the heart of love in each entity and each moment. Your challenge is always to discern where the love is in this moment and to move—whether by attitude, thought or action—to support, encourage and enable that love. Giving that attempt your best effort shall occupy you well through this illusion which we term third density and through several densities to come, for we witness to our continuing pilgrimage through longer and more subtle illusions wherein the choice we made in third density is refined, first by attention to love, then by attention to wisdom, then by attention to the merging of love and wisdom.

These illusions to come are far different than your rough-and-tumble moment of choice. There is not the suffering, for there is not the veil of forgetting betwixt the conscious incarnate self and the deep Self that is aware that all harmonizes into unity. In your brave illusion, you face the dragons of darkness, rage, pain, war, starvation and all the dark and monstrous forms of dread, fear and ignorance because you cannot clearly remember that these illusions are only that. It is intended that you become confused. You

---

[4] Holy Bible, Matthew 22:37.

are supposed to be knocked completely off of your intellectual mountain. And in that momentous fall into the abyss, in midair, you pluck faith, undimmed by any objective proof that there is anything to be faithful to. You choose to live your love.

This is your choice—not that you sit upon a throne, view the evidence and choose, but that you become utterly aware that you cannot understand this illusion. And in releasing that desire and embracing only your heart's desire to love, you pluck faith from that dash through the middle air.

This wisdom of the heart to abide and hope and have faith without proof—this is the glory of third density. And we must say that much as we enjoy our continuing journeys, in looking at each of you and being with each and seeing the courage and commitment of each to seeking the truth, our hearts fondly cherish the memory of that striving, suffering and believing in Love against all the evidence. What a part of the journey you now are on. How exciting!

We would at this time bow to the one known as Aaron and offer the microphone. We are those of Q'uo.

Aaron: I am Aaron. As you rejoice in sharing deeply with your friends, so Q'uo and I rejoice in being able to share this teaching with one another. It is simply delight to sit back and rest. Not that I need the rest; I am not tired. But each of us expands what the other can offer, brings new perspectives to it. So, it is a joy for me to feel Q'uo's energy responding to that which I have said, to hand the microphone to my brother/sister for response and expansion, and then to take that expansion back and again enlarge it.

Q'uo spoke of the line of love and wisdom, which is precisely that horizontal and vertical line that I have mentioned, and that eventually you must come to combine the two, living at the intersection of that horizontal and vertical line, the center of the cross, the Christ Consciousness or Buddha Consciousness or Cosmic Awareness that is God.

I would like to briefly define my terms here so that when I use language, you fully grasp my meaning. Within consciousness there is still self-awareness, still some degree of personal thought and memory. Pure Awareness is quite different and moves beyond all consciousness. There is also a ground in between, where that which I call consciousness is still present but is not taken as "self" but known as tool of the incarnation.

Pure Awareness is that which sees consciousness and knows it. What we may call Christ or Buddha Consciousness is found here: Awareness aware of its divine nature and yet also aware of the tools of the incarnation, the self-conscious mind. The Christ Consciousness finds no less divinity in the incarnation than in the ultimate perfection.

While the human cannot ordinarily move beyond sixth-density thought (the consciousness of the Higher Self), your meditation can take you truly into the experience of seventh and even beginning eighth density, that borderline between the two where all concept is dissolved, where there is total dissolution of the body and the ego, where there is no longer any thought at all, just Pure Awareness, no consciousness. So, I differentiate these terms. I do not use them synonymously, consciousness and awareness. When I speak of Pure Awareness, it is that awareness beyond any conceptual thinking or any perception of self.

To live skillfully on this human plane, you need some degree of consciousness. This does not mean identification with the self that makes choices, but simple acknowledgment that the self is a tool and a necessary tool to the work of this plane. If you disown that self, learning cannot take place. So, there's a very fine line between allowing the experience of what seems to be self and knowing that the perceived self is illusion, useful illusion and tool of the incarnation.

All of the experiences that occur to that perceived self are also tools of the incarnation. Your physical sensations, your emotions, your thoughts—they are not burdens that you are asked to carry, they are gifts through which you may learn. One can learn to work very skillfully and lovingly with these gifts so that one is no longer reactive to emotions, no longer reactive to physical sensation. That being begins to live its life with great love, yet it may also experience deep pain if there is still identification with that which arises. The non-reactivity becomes a form of self-discipline and training, but there is not yet wisdom which sees that there is no ownership of that which arises.

One may also move into the wisdom vertical direction, focusing on a path of deepening wisdom through moment-to-moment mindfulness. Such mindfulness begins to penetrate the delusion of a separate self. It begins to know all arising as empty of self, as simply the recurrent patterns of conditioned mind.

Wisdom develops to understand the impermanence of all that arises. Ownership of that arising ceases. But without the love or compassion that grows out of acceptance of the human experience, such wisdom becomes sterile. Within such wisdom there can be desire to disassociate with the human catalyst. What you are learning, then, is to come to this meeting of the horizontal and vertical, this center of the cross, where compassion and wisdom meet.

I want to digress here a moment to speak about the words *love* and *compassion*. When we use the term love, we are not speaking of a maudlin kind of love with attachment, not a manipulative love or a grasping love, but pure love that opens itself to all that is. Love is a hard term to define. I am somehow more comfortable with the term compassion, which is an outgrowth of that openhearted love, but is more easily recognized, less easily distorted than is the term love. We can use them interchangeably as long as we understand what we mean by each: love and compassion.

There are many ways to work on the horizontal practices. Indeed, you all are doing that constantly in your lives as you attempt to live with more love and skill, as you attempt to live with non-harm to all else and as you process the emotions, thoughts and sensations that move through you and work on non-reactivity. We will talk more specifically about such horizontal practice, offering specific tools that speak to your personal situations.

I want to speak for a moment about the vertical practice. In essence, when you work with a horizontal practice, you are using mind to tame mind. Mind moves into a turmoil of fear and reactivity and you use the relative practices of faith, of devotion, of mindfulness, to quiet that tumultuous mind. When you move into the vertical practice, you use wisdom to cut through the delusion of self and tame the turmoil with wisdom, in a sense like cracking the shell of a nut and allowing that hard shell to fall open so the soft inner core is exposed.

Now I would speak to you of a practice that will help you move into that wisdom, and later this weekend we will talk about coming to that place where compassion and wisdom meet. There are two specific practices I would like to offer to you, one to be done frequently, constantly even, and one that you may do for a few minutes during your lunchtime break. First, as ongoing practice through the weekend, when thoughts, emotions, sensations, arise, I would like you to note their arising and to ask yourself whichever question is more useful to you: "Whose thought is this? Mine? Who am I?" or, "From where did this thought arise?" As you ask those questions and allow an honest answer to emerge, you are going to see that the answer is simply, "It arose from old-mind habit. I don't own this arising."

Let me give you an example. This morning at approximately 7:12, Barbara was sitting here meditating and had a thought, "Not many people are here yet. We're not started. We're going to run late"—a small contracting and sense of fear. She asked herself, "Where did this thought arise from?" And she could see clearly that it was just old-pattern marking her need to be in control as a way of protecting herself; need to allow things to be okay for others, not as a way of gaining approval for herself but due to wanting to create comfort for others. And she saw that was a response of fear, just a conditioned pattern. So, she came back to this moment and asked, "In this moment, is there any need for anything to be happening other than what's happening right now, 7:13, sitting and meditating?" with the awareness of how that fear had arisen, that she didn't own that fear. It is like a bubble that is popped by a sharp dart … *poof!* The fear is gone. In that moment one comes back to rest in Pure Awareness—not consciousness, awareness. For just that one moment, there is no "somebody" doing anything. The ego is totally dissolved. There is just resting in Pure Being. It may only last for a second until the next thought arises. Each thought becomes an opportunity to pop that bubble again and come back to Pure Awareness.

As one does this persistently, one lets go of the habit of thinking of oneself as somebody doing, shaping, fixing, and moves more into the true understanding that what one is, *is* this Pure Awareness connected to all that is. One finds the ability to rest in that space. One ceases identifying with the horizontal.

I am only going to take it that far here. As I said, I will talk this afternoon about the ways that you may combine this cutting through of delusion with the horizontal practices which relate to the relative reality of everyday living and which do require the self to participate.

The second practice I would like to offer is one that I ask you to do as homework during your lunch break. Do it with me now, but quickly, and then repeat it at your leisure. I want you to sit, preferably outdoors. Look at the lake or the trees or the sky. Meditating with your eyes open, send your awareness out. Breathe out and follow that breath as far as it goes. What happens to your breath when you breathe it out? Is there any boundary out there? What happens when it reaches the end of the atmosphere? Does it stop?

Sit and follow your breath. Looking at the sky might be most useful. Let it expand outward and outward and outward to infinity, beyond the ends of the universe ... nothing that stops it. Now breathe in. What are you breathing in? Is there a boundary beyond which you do not breathe in that substance? Visualize the in-breath also coming from beyond infinity moving into you, drawing in with each inhalation the core of all that is and breathing it back out into the universe, each exhalation a giant release ... *ahhh* ... releasing with an *ahhh* all boundaries of self ... breathing in ... Open your eyes and do this with me and with Barbara ... in ... *ahhh* ... sending it out ... in ... *ahhh* ... sending it out ... You may close your eyes again if you wish, each *ahhh* letting go of the boundaries of self, feeling one's merging with the universe.

Here we are talking of drawing the physical plane into yourself. After you have done that for a few minutes and really feel yourself moving into the universe and the universe moving into you physically, do the same with awareness. Where has awareness picked up false boundaries, non-existent boundaries, let us say, that you claim as "mine"? Send your awareness along with your breath out into the universe and breathe in again awareness, universal awareness, the deepest contact with all that is.

If in doing this exercise thoughts cease to arise, as they may, and you begin to move into a level of awareness of deep connection, simply rest in that connection. If thoughts arise again, ask the question, "Where did it arise from? Whose thought is it?" And as it self-destructs, self-liberates, *poof!* goes the balloon of thought. Rest again in that Pure Awareness, once again releasing the boundaries and expanding into the universe physically and in awareness, and allowing the universe to move into you. Please spend ten or fifteen minutes with this— longer if you like—over your lunch break, and I would very much appreciate hearing the results of this exercise.

Q'uo may have something that it wishes to add here. If not, I would like to open the floor to your questions and answers. That is all.

Questioner: How many densities are there?

Barbara: Aaron speaks of [eight] densities, each of which has seven subdivisions, each of which has seven sub-subdivisions and so on. He defines it loosely as eight densities and says that some people may find it different. For example, he is dividing fourth and fifth density. Some people may group them together.

Once we move past the need to incarnate and move into fourth density, we move into a group learning experience by which he does not mean a fixed group. There is a coming and going, still a free will. We're not drawn into something that we can't leave. But once we stop being reactive to our emotions and thoughts, we're ready for fourth-density group experience. In this group we're all telepathic, so the equanimity with our emotions and thoughts, which marks the end of third density, is a necessity for fourth. He uses the example: If right now we were all completely telepathic so that we all knew everything that each other was thinking, would this be okay? Have you had some thoughts this morning that you really don't want to share? Once we get to the point where we have such compassion for ourselves and such non-judgment of our thoughts and non-ownership of our thoughts, we also have that compassion toward others and we don't judge others' thoughts. Then we're ready to be in a fourth-density energy where there's total telepathic sharing. There's no embarrassment and judgment. We learn, then, not just from our own experience but from each other's experience, because experience can be shared totally.

As we move through the process of that fourth-density energy group, we begin to move out more on to our own, coming and going from the group. Sixth density moves beyond the capacities of those which came before ... deeper wisdom and compassion, and unconditional love. Seventh and eighth density—

again, some traditions lump them as one and others divide them into seventh and eighth densities.

How many of you here, from reading Aaron or other material, are familiar with this whole scheme of the densities? Put hands up high. How many of you don't know anything about this? Okay, then we're not going to go into it in detail. There's a chapter in the Aaron book[5] that you could read at lunchtime that delineates each of those densities and what each is about.

Carla: Just briefly, first density is the elements. Second density: things that can't move yet, like plants and animals that don't have self-awareness yet. They're turning to the light. The animal knows its master and wants to love it a little bit, but it is not aware of itself yet. Third density is self-awareness. Fourth density: the awareness of love. Fifth density: the awareness of wisdom. Sixth density: the awareness of wise compassion, compassionate wisdom, the merging of those two. Seventh density: Ra calls it the density of foreverness, where you finally take one last look back, turn your back on all that and start gaining spiritual mass, going back to the source. The eighth density is the octave, and it dissolves into timelessness and becomes the first density of the next creation. And that's the cosmology of it. So, the whole billions and billions of years until the big, central explosion of the central sun is just one creation, just one little heartbeat.

Questioner: Extraterrestrials, as in the movie *Cocoon*, have these light bodies. Where does the physical fit in, in these densities?

Jim: Supposedly, from what we gathered from Ra, each of our chakras or energy centers has a body with a physical nature that corresponds to that center. The yellow ray that we are inhabiting now has this biochemical body. Another body corresponds to the heart center. If you've been to a séance where ectoplasm is produced by the medium, it is seen as a smoky sort of substance that is used by entities to form the astral body, which is associated with the heart or the green ray. And each succeeding energy center has a finer and finer body as far as physical mass that we can see, but it is more and more densely packed with light. So, they're more dense as far as light goes, but less dense as far as our physical matter goes. But each of the centers has a body.

Questioner: Isn't physical matter just a slowed-down vibration of light? So, how can this be? Aren't you just saying that each body is a more rapid vibration?

Jim: Yes, that's basically correct, but it has more light in it, more vibratory brilliance, more rotational speed, more active light.

Carla: It is a heavy chemical body. And one of the things to think about is that if you heal the light body, the physical body also will be healed because it is a lower octave vibration. "As above, so below."[6]

Aaron: I am Aaron. You have many, many aspects. Repeated use of the single word *body* makes it difficult. Your language does not give adequate choice of words. You are familiar with the physical, emotional, mental and spirit bodies. You also have what we call a light body, which is the emotional, mental and spirit body separate from the physical body. The physical body is, in a sense, a reflection of the light body, or we might say a manifestation of the light body.

To further define the light body … there is a higher light body, which, in essence, is what you know as the soul, the Pure Spirit Body. The lower light body is a manifestation of the higher light body and includes the mental body. This is sometimes called the Higher Self. There are gradations in between and beyond. Those beyond bring in the emotional body. You might visualize, then, the purest light, which is the light simply of the spirit body in its interconnection with all that is. This light is absolutely pure, totally unblocked in any way.

Just the slightest bit below that is what I would call the light of Christ, Buddha or Cosmic Consciousness. It has just the barest, very barest tint to it, totally transparent, not blocking the pure light in any way, but shaded with just that smallest tint of self-awareness.

One step down, one large step down (there are gradations) comes the lower light body. For purpose of visualization here, I'd like you to picture the heart, which is the physical body's light center. Picture it as a ball, radiant with light. Within that ball, add black dots of the different emotions and

---

[5] For more information, please contact the Deep Spring Center for Meditation and Spiritual Inquiry, 3003 Washtenaw Ave., Suite 2, Ann Arbor, MI, 48104, www.deepspring.org.

[6] *The Kybalion*, Anonymous.

thoughts and physical sensations. Let us leave out physical sensations now. We are speaking of the lower light body and not the full human body, thoughts and emotions. There is still a mental and emotional body.

In the highest light body, there is nothing to deflect the light that shines out from you or the light that comes in … One moment please. I wish Barbara to draw something here.

Barbara: I am drawing a circle with the described flecks in it, demonstrating how those flecks block light from moving out from the center and in to the center. Our work in consciousness slowly allows this shadow to dissolve so that we move more and more (I am paraphrasing Aaron here), we move more and more into the living experience of this circle, free of those bits of shadow. Now, getting back to Aaron directly …

Aaron: The human body takes this one step further down because it adds the physical catalysts as well, and that which creates more shadow. If you take a being such as yourselves and put it in front of that perfect light, which I would call God, you see a sharp sense of shadow. If you take a being like myself, a sixth-density being, and put it in front of that perfect light, there will still be a distinction between that energy that I am and that perfect light. I am not fully merged into that perfect light. If you take a being such as the Christ or the Buddha and put the energy of those beings in front of that perfect light, they will be almost invisible, *almost* only because they choose to retain some degree of consciousness and have not yet fully moved into seventh density. I am not specifying, now, where these beings are in their evolution. A being that has moved into seventh or eighth density is not better than a being which chooses to remain at the borderline of seventh density so as to allow itself to be available to those of the lower densities, to allow its personal energy to be available. That is really a gift and sacrifice on the part of that being, holding back its own full merging with the light out of service to all beings and desire to offer itself as servant.

The distortions of the physical body are reflections of the distortions of the higher light bodies. Thus, as Carla pointed out, when you clarify the distortions in the higher light bodies, often there is physical healing.

There is disparity between the clarity of the higher light bodies and that of the physical body. You are here in physical form. Sometimes you create distortion for yourselves because you aspire to be something that you are not fully ready for. This is where you start to want to get rid of the heaviness of the physical or emotional bodies. You want to cling to being the Higher Self without having done the consciousness work to dissolve the shadow of the emotional and physical bodies. There must be harmony or you fragment yourself. You do not get rid of the emotions nor of any discomforting physical sensations. But as you find space for them and equanimity, non-reactivity to them, then you become able to work at the higher levels of light.

The frequency vibration of these bodies is different. They also must be in harmony, like the strings of a musical instrument. If the higher-level strings are perfectly in tune, but the heavier, coarser strings are out of tune, the instrument will play disharmoniously.

The physical body will be at a lower frequency than the higher light bodies. You tune it, not to bring it up to that high pitch but to make it harmonious to that high pitch, not by getting rid of the physical sensations but by letting go of fear of the physical sensations; and the same for the emotional body. Then you become a harmonious whole, and as that harmonious whole, the frequency vibration of the connected body begins to raise the frequency vibration of the whole. This can only be as clear as the frequency vibration of the lowest aspect of it. If one aspect is discordant, the whole is discordant.

So many of you have worked to clarify the energy of the mental and spirit bodies, but tend to want to disown the emotional and physical bodies. You work with the upper chakras and cast aside the work with the lower chakras, but it must come together.

There is more that could be said about this. Do you wish me to speak further, or is this sufficient? That is all.

Questioner: Today, while meditating and while Aaron and Q'uo were speaking, quite often I would go to a point where consciously I don't remember a lot that Q'uo and Aaron said. What can I do to keep that from happening, or is that supposed to happen?

Carla: I would say let it be. If you want to hear, you will hear, but you're getting it at a deeper level.

Questioner: Yes, I do feel that I got it. But I couldn't tell someone that Q'uo said this, this, and this.

Carla: I think that sometimes you get to a point where you protect yourself from bearing it all at once, and your heart is wise and it puts you in a place where you'll feed it in to where it will come up gradually and you can deal with it better. There's a lot said, a lot of points made, and a lot of work done. Some of us can't bear it.

Barbara: One of the things that we suggest to people is to acknowledge some of this "screening out." Sometimes Aaron puts people to sleep. Some of this is resistance. Instead of saying, "I've got to get rid of this resistance," can you just acknowledge it? "There's resistance here. Can I be gentle with myself about this resistance?" Allow it to emerge. "What's the resistance about?" you know. Don't think about it. Just acknowledge and let it work out. I want to give an example.

A couple of years ago, my son came home from college with a pile of literature about recycling; and I already recycle paper and bottles, but he wanted me to recycle everything. It wasn't a very big stack of literature, but I kept putting him off and saying, "I can't read it now." Finally, I became aware if I read it, then I was going to have to be responsible for it and I just wasn't ready to be that responsible. I felt like it was going to be a big burden, a lot of work. "I don't know if I can handle this. Keep it at a distance. I don't want to know about it yet. I'm not sure I'm ready to be that responsible."

We each need to work that through. If we really hear what they are saying and try to live our lives that way, it is asking us to be very responsible, and there's some fear: "Am I ready to be that responsible? What am I getting into here?"

We need to be very gentle with ourselves, not push ourselves beyond where we are, because we learn as we grow. We don't have to be anywhere but exactly where we are now, just moving at our own pace. There's no speed with which we do this. People get into trouble when they aren't honest with themselves. Some say, "Okay, I'm going to take all this in and I'm going to do it." And then, instead of becoming a work of love and kindness and gentleness to ourselves, it becomes just another kind of fear: "I'm going to get rid of that and I'm going to be this." But that's not honest.

Questioner: So, how do we clarify the lower chakras?

Barbara: I think Aaron and Q'uo will both be talking about that at length, but let me just say, in working with this "screening it out," the first step is simply being aware there's resistance: "Am I judging that resistance or trying to get rid of that resistance, or am I allowing myself to bring my heart to that resistance?" Do you see what I mean? The other thing that I'd like to suggest is, both Aaron and Q'uo—their energy is at a very high frequency vibration that's not completely in harmony with where many of us are. It is very tiring to experience that energy. There is sometimes just a sense of screening it out because there's so much energy coming in. We need to be very gentle to ourselves about that. Through the weekend, your ability to hear this and take it in more fully will increase. One specific thing that Aaron has sometimes suggested to people is simply opening your eyes, not to look at us as we're channeling, but a kind of unfocused looking that helps to allow more awareness.

Questioner: Yes. I did that today. It helped.

Barbara: On the question of how to clarify the lower chakras, Aaron is saying that's too big a subject to do before lunch.

Carla: I wanted to say thank you for one of the things that you all helped me to do: By listening and being in circles, I just get so much energy. I feel better when I channel than any other time, and I just really thank you for the beautiful sharing of this incredible energy that goes around the circle. Yum! And, as someone who came to a workshop recently said, "It's yummy!" ❖

The Aaron/Q'uo Dialogues, Session 20
September 25, 1993

(This session was preceded by a period of tuning and meditation.)

Barbara: Aaron and I are discussing which of us is going to lead this session. Aaron is suggesting he led the tuning last night. He would like me to share with you directly the process that I use, which is not with a guided meditation from him. It precedes opening my energy to him. As Carla pointed out this morning, this is simply my own process which I'm sharing with you. I'm not suggesting that you need to use it, just this is how I've learned to work with Aaron.

The first thing I do is to focus on my breath, simply settle my attention. This is not a matter of creating stillness. Sometimes there's stillness. Sometimes there's occurrence. Meditation is not to be mistaken for stillness, but for deep awareness and being in the moment with whatever arises in that moment—stillness or occurrence; simply coming to attention and choiceless awareness, coming to a place of center, where, if there's stillness, there is no grasping at that stillness. If there's turmoil and busy mind—thoughts arising, emotions arising—there's no aversion to that. It is coming to a deeper place in myself where I can watch all of this and move past. That place is still, a still point uninvolved in any outer stillness or occurrence. So, that's the first step for me. I'm going to be quiet now for a moment while I work with this and let you work with it, just focusing on the breath as we did in the meditations early this morning before breakfast.

When I'm in that space, the boundaries of self come down and I feel myself surrounded by energy, by spirit. At this point (usually not with words so much as wordlessly, but obviously to share it I need to use words), I offer a commitment of my energy, a statement of intention of my desire to be of service. If I notice any self-thought, of pride in that "being somebody doing something," I just notice that's part of it, that's the part of it that grows out of fear; and I don't condemn that in myself but I also don't build that up in myself. I ask for help in channeling clearly despite that human fear that is part of my make-up because I am human. I recognize that it is not a big part of my motivation. I don't focus on the negative in my motivation, on the fearful in my motivation. I focus on the loving and openhearted in my motivation.

So, I simply state clearly my intention. I want to offer my energy in the service of all beings. I want to offer my energy for the alleviation of suffering. Please use this energy in whatever way is most appropriate. I then state the continuing intention that I offer myself as an instrument through which spirit may speak. And I speak to whatever array of energy I feel out there, making the firm statement, "I will not allow anything to speak through me and use my voice which is non-harmonious to my own deepest values. I welcome any being that wants to be present to hear me, but it may not speak through me unless our values agree."

At this point I usually begin to feel Aaron's energy very strongly. I recognize it as Aaron's energy. When I'm simply talking to Aaron myself, we have a code that we use for a challenge. So, I abbreviate the challenge to that energy that asks it to identify itself. When I'm channeling with a group, I go through the full challenge to that energy.

At first I couldn't understand the reason for this because I said, "I know Aaron's energy," but then I became aware that a being that was negatively polarized to just the same degree that Aaron is positively polarized could feel very much like Aaron, the same wavelength of negative polarity that Aaron is positive polarity. Carla said to me a few times, "Challenge, challenge!" And I said, "I don't need to." And then once I experienced negative energy that felt like Aaron's, so I started to understand the wisdom of Carla's advice.

So, I offer a formal challenge to it; this, for me, being what I most firmly believe in. Each of us, in opening ourselves to spirit guidance, needs to use our own highest values and to challenge the energy—not only that which would formally speak through us in channeling, but that guidance from our own guides that we listen to—to challenge it by our own deepest values.

What I ask for myself is three challenges. First, "Are you that energy that I have come to know as Aaron, that identical energy?" I get a "yes" on that. "Do you come in service to the principle of love and service to all beings?" And finally I ask it, "Do you come as a disciple of Jesus Christ and the Buddha?" If I'm not channeling to a big group, I simply say three times, "Aaron?" and get a "yes" three times, so I don't always go through that procedure formally.

So, now I'm going to be quiet for a few moments while I work with this process of tuning that I use. I would ask you each to move through much the same process at your own pace, stating your intention that what you receive be of service to all beings and that as you lower your own boundaries and open yourselves to spirit you also challenge that spirit by your own highest values, which becomes a firm commitment of your own adherence to those values. A few minutes of silence now, and then we'll begin.

(Pause)

Aaron: I am Aaron. I call you angels in earthsuits. Your angelness is undeniable. This is who you truly are. With your incarnation, you have bound yourselves into these earthsuits, pulled closed the visor in the front which prevents clear seeing. Think of it as a coat of armor you have put on. Body armor would hamper the free movement of your limbs. And yet, in the society in which armor was necessary because of jousting and other such combat, the armor was both a burden and a tool, a necessary tool. Your earthsuits might by some be viewed as burden, but they are necessary to your learning. This earth is your schoolroom. And your body and emotions are the embodiments of the lessons you have come to learn, the tool through which you can learn.

The angel lives only in ultimate reality. It knows itself clearly for who it is. The being enclosed by the earthsuit can become so caught up in the tightness of that suit that it becomes its only reality. It forgets what it is like to live outside the suit.

My dear ones, here is where it gets tricky. What your incarnation asks of you is that you find the balance of both, fully expressing the angelness while in no way discarding or belittling the value of the earthsuit, paying attention to the earthsuit while aware that it is merely a covering that you put on—not owning it, but living it fully.

You are like actors in a play. When you come out onto the stage, if you look to the audience and say, "Oh, this is only a play. It doesn't matter," the audience is not going to get much from your lines offered with no sincerity. If you become so involved in the illusion of the play that you forget that it is a play, forget that there is an audience out there, you may turn your back to the audience or speak too softly for them to hear. The good actor must live its lines convincingly—live them, be them—while being fully aware simultaneously that this is a play, that when it walks offstage it no longer is the identity of that character. This is how the audience learns from a play. And you also are the audience, both actor and audience.

This is what your life asks of you: to live the illusion as full-heartedly as you can while still knowing this is illusion. Herein is the intersection of relative and ultimate reality, the intersection of the cross. You have one foot in relative reality, one foot in ultimate reality, and there is no separation between them. Some of you have understood that you have one foot on each side of this threshold, but you feel as if there were a wall, an infinite wall, dividing relative and ultimate reality so that you may only experience one at a time. It is very hard work to learn to blend them, to bring compassion and wisdom together. But that is what you are here to learn to do.

When we ask, "What is the spiritual path and how do we live it?" the spiritual path, for me, is one of awareness of the non-dual nature of relative and ultimate reality and compassion for the being who sometimes stumbles while trying to bring them together harmoniously; love and respect for these beings who keep brushing off the mud and moving on again, always learning a bit more about this balance and always learning a bit more about the desire to rest on one side or the other side of the balance; seeing the resistance to bringing them together because that requires such deep honesty and courage; and finding compassion for the being who cannot quite do it, but tries.

There is one very beautiful song from the play, *Man of La Mancha*.[7] I will not ask Barbara to sing it, as her voice is inadequate to the task. But one verse is the words, "To bear with unbearable sorrows, to go where the brave dare not go, to be willing to give when there's no more to give, to be willing to die so that honor and justice may live. And I know if I'll only be true to this glorious quest that my heart will lie peaceful and calm when I'm laid to my rest."[8] This is your path, a path of exquisite beauty. Honor yourselves for the humans you are, for the quest that you have undertaken and the extreme difficulty of it, and for the light not only at the end of the road, but the light that you emit with each step on this path.

I would like to change tracks now and move from the theoretical to the practical. Fine. We are looking for this balance of ultimate and relative reality, this balance of love and wisdom. How do we follow that quest in dealing with the very real and painful catalysts of our lives? I feel Q'uo wishing to speak. I do not know if Q'uo wishes to speak in answer to the question I have just raised, or wishes to add more that relates to the beginning of my afternoon talk here. I will simply pass the microphone to Q'uo for my brother/sister/friend to speak, and then we will move back to my own talk of the practical. That is all.

Carla: *(As a complement to Barbara's description of her tuning process, Carla's own process is provided.)* I begin in solitude by singing a hymn and continue with prayers, praying the prayer of Saint Francis and beseeching the Holy Spirit's presence. I invoke the archangels and all those whom they represent, who come from the world of spirit in the name of Jesus Christ, and ask them to help in maintaining the purity and safety of the circle and the contact. I then go through the process of looking into, and balancing, my chakra system of energies; and after balancing, I open up the energy system for potential channeling. Then I join the group, and continue tuning with the group. Before opening to a specific contact, I challenge the perceived contact in the name of Jesus Christ and ask that it say that Jesus is Lord. I repeat this challenge three times. If all three challenges are met, I open to channel.

(Pause)

Q'uo: We are those of Q'uo, and greet each in the love and in the light of the one infinite Creator. Greetings, blessings, love and peace. My fellow teacher Aaron kindly shares these teachings with us, and we stand humbly before this generosity.

Indeed, we wished to speak to the matter of how to conceive, if you will pardon the pun, of your physical, material selves being in the same physical vehicle with the infinite and eternal life form which you are. For you know that you are not your body, but were before the world had been and shall be long after it has been taken back into the unmanifest and unknown, which is infinite Intelligence that is the one great original Thought, which we label with the weak word Love, having no choice.

This instrument earlier this day spied an acorn, and picking it up, found half of it to fall away. The little pointed top fit nicely on the finger like a cap for a finger puppet. Consider the seed within this acorn's husk and the stature of its eventual manifestation. Can this tiny acorn conceive of holding such a seed? And each of you in your physical vehicles—fields after fields of energy held in articulated manifestation—to move as vehicles do through time

---

[7] Broadway musical of 1965, written by Dale Wasserman.

[8] "The Impossible Dream," music by M. Leigh and lyrics by J. Darion, 1965.

and space, delivering the precious load of consciousness that it may be buffeted by all manner of catalyst?

Within each of you is being born (as you choose to walk this spiritual path) the physical vehicle, if you will, of light that you shall grow to be. But now, within incarnation, this physical form of light is tiny, incredibly vulnerable and protected only by your sense of its being as you go about your everyday affairs. Each choice that you make strengthens this infant consciousness. Each of you is like Mary, mother to Jesus, in that you are birthing your spiritual self, and you shall carry this within you all your days within this incarnation. Each hurt, each abruptness which shocks, each sorrow, each feeling of solitude and longing for a more native country, causes this infant child within to cry, and you may stand confused.

How can you nurture this inner child of light? Each of you can, in every moment, imagine, dream and intend this nurturing; and with the energy of this intention, you touch that tiny light-being with the Mother's and Father's love, seeing you are not alone, "for I have touched Love." And all that you feel and care and reach for exists in abundance, abundance that shall wash over your sweet beingness. "Here, feel my love." And because you, in all your dirt and confusion, have intended and dreamt and imagined this love, this abundance—*this* becomes truth; and the nurturing of infinite Intelligence continues as the great work that rose beyond all of the seemingly independent sparks of consciousness and, in the end, feeds not only that spiritual self within but the more conscious everyday self that may feel so poorly equipped to nurture and love spiritually.

Your secret weapon always is the parents' eternal secret: simple, honest love. Love that questing spirit within and you nourish that which shall carry you into eternity.

We thank our brother Aaron for sensing this teaching impulse which came to us, and hand the microphone back to his teachings with our love. Greetings, my brother. How wonderful it is to be here with you in manifestation through these lovely children.

Aaron: I want to move into some of the specific questions that we so often hear, the main one being, "How do I know when I'm following a path of love or a path of fear?" If you only had one motivation, it would be easy to know. What confuses you is the multiple motivations. In the giving of that apple, 95% of the motivation was pure generosity—no ulterior motives, no desire to be savior to one another, no desire to be somebody who gives, just openhearted compassion to the suffering of another and a clear, heartfelt response. But 5% of the motivation or 7% or 3% or 10%, it doesn't matter, was the voice of fear—either the voice of fear that says, "What if I need it?" and then judges that fearful statement and says, "No, I should give," compounding the judgment, or the fear that wants to be somebody "good."

The difficulty, then, is sorting out these voices in yourself and learning to trust the sincerity of the loving motivation and not get into a dialogue with the negative part of the motivation, but simply acknowledge that it is there. If you deny it, then it becomes empowered. If you acknowledge it and smile to it and turn back to the positive part of the motivation, you deny power to your fear. I call this not getting into a dialogue with fear.

You begin, through attention, to see how that arising fear ensnares you and draws your attention away from the angelness of you. There are some very specific steps to working here. First is to know that in every human situation there is going to be multiple motivation. Like the ivory soap ad, it may be 99 and 99/100% pure, but it is not 100% pure. Your fear is not a burden given you for combat. It is the fertile soil upon which you may build compassion. It is the garbage that you turn into compost.

So, first there must be acknowledgment that there is multiple motivation. When you are faced with a choice, you look at what grows out of a loving and connected place and what grows out of fear. And second, while acknowledging the fear, you refuse to get caught in the story of it. This takes practice. You are never going to do it perfectly and that is okay. But with practice, the skill grows: "I know this is fear and I don't have to get sucked into it." The more you practice with this, the more you trust the impulses of your heart.

What happens when those impulses seem to lead you into pain? I want to tell the story of a friend here, while changing the facts sufficiently so as to render this being unrecognizable, although it is not someone who most of you know or perhaps who any of you know. We have here a friend who was in a marriage which had its ups and downs, as many marriages do. This was a second marriage for both partners. I'm going to refer to them as partners A and B so as to avoid any designation of the sex of either being.

There was both love and pain between A and B. B suggested to A that since B was living in the house A had previously owned before their partnership, it felt excluded because it now contributed to that home. It suggested changing the mortgage, changing the bank accounts, whatever. It does not matter what they would change, but changing it so as to share more equitably. A agreed to that with some hesitation, but A sincerely felt, "If I want to live my life in love and trust with this being, the first step is to trust it." So, A offered to B half of its possessions, let us say.

After the papers were signed, B turned around, not immediately but soon after, and betrayed A. It doesn't matter how. But there was real betrayal, which led to filing for divorce, leaving A feeling not only heartbroken by the betrayal of B but also in a drastic financial situation. A said, "What did I do wrong? I followed my heart. I trusted and all it led me to is betrayal." A very painful story.

Let us look at what really might have been happening here. My follow-up here is hypothetical. The personal reasons why this happened are not something you need to know. There are many possibilities and I would simply like to explore them with you on a hypothetical basis.

Why do seemingly bad things happen to people who are trying to follow the dictates of love? That is the question. First of all, yes, this is a very painful situation, very frightening to A, who would now be both alone and having lost much of its support of its money. Is that bad? What do bad and good mean? Painful, yes, but there is going to be pain in your lives. Is pain always bad? Is it ever completely avoidable? You have heard me say that pain shouts at you, "Pay attention!" Now, A thought it was paying attention, but perhaps it needs to pay closer attention. When one pays attention, one's learning is still not always pain-free. There is no guarantee of that. The question then becomes, "Can I take this devastation that's been handed to me and make some useful learning of it, rather than having it send me into deep bitterness?" Perhaps that is part of what the whole issue was about. I repeat that these are hypothetical answers, all of them possibly real, but we have stepped away from the actuality of A and B's situation here.

It is highly possible that A is being offered the opportunity to let go of having to make things happen a certain way, being offered the opportunity to trust not only the "good" but also the "bad" in its life. It is very hard when one must go through that, but if one lets go of trying to make it come out a certain way and relaxes into what is, then one can find love and healing even in the midst of pain.

Part of this might also be karmic. Perhaps very specifically in a past life, A had taken from B. This is only one of the ways karma works. It would not even have to be from B that A took. Perhaps A did not take physically from B, but only could not share. You say it seems like a very backwards way to learn sharing, to be punished for sharing, but perhaps A needs to take sharing beyond reward and punishment, to move to a place where sharing is not for reward, but only to share. Perhaps the past misunderstanding was that A held on to sharing for its rewards, and if it could not see possible rewards, it was reluctant to share. So, perhaps that is part of the karma.

I am reminded here of a story of a Zen priest. This is said to be a true story that happened in Asia sometime in the last twenty or thirty years. The police came to this being and said, "You have been accused of this wrongdoing. Come with us." And they took the priest to jail. They asked, "Can you prove your innocence? Where were you that night when this deed occurred?" And the priest said, "I was alone. I have no witness." The priest did not fight the accusation nor did it agree with it. At first it said, "I am innocent," but it did not fight. So, that priest went to jail, was imprisoned and penalized to serve with hard labor. Six years later another prisoner, who was dying, confessed to that crime. They came to the priest and they said, "You are innocent. Someone else has confessed. Why did you not stick to your innocence which you proclaimed at first?" The priest said, "Because when I meditated that first night in jail, I saw that I had done this crime in a past life and I had gotten away with it, and another had been put to death for my crime. Now I have paid in my own way and I am free. I have lived these six years in prison with much love, serving my fellow prisoners. I am free."

So, karma does enter into it. It is hard to understand that. You are not given the ability to clearly see your past lives. There must sometimes be much faith that even when life hands you difficult circumstances, you still can trust.

Another possibility between our A and B: Through A's ability to suffer this betrayal at the hands of B without moving into hatred of B, to allow B to feel his forgiveness, he is offering a very real service to B—opening a door. A may make it very clear, "What you did is totally inappropriate and I am very, very angry and hurt; nevertheless, I do not hate you."

To say no can be done with love. It does not have to be done with hate. Perhaps both A and B needed to learn these lessons, B being served by A's ability to work with this painful catalyst lovingly so that B might also learn and grow beyond its self-centeredness and fear.

Finally, A may be offered the opportunity to look at the multiple motivations in itself, that it shared its fortunes with B with a high degree of love and desire, aspiration to strengthen their relationship, but that there was also perhaps denial of any sense, "This being is not trustworthy"—denial of the fear in itself of letting go of a relationship with a non-trustworthy B.

So, one part of it is A's reluctance to be honest with itself about the realities in its situation, it is clinging to what love was offered rather than having the faith to say no. This is a hard one. So many of you have a hard time saying no with love. You aspire to be "spiritual," to be good and kind and loving, but sometimes you interpret that kindness to mean being a doormat to others. When you offer yourself as doormat, you are going to be walked on. Then rage builds in you and you erupt. And then you say, "Oh, I'm bad for having erupted," and you go back to doormat once again. But there is a place in between, when you have self-respect through faith in who you really are and in the loving-kindness of your heart, even while knowing that this is only part of what is there, that there is also fear and anger, jealousy and greed. But when you have faith in that segment of your heart that is loving and respect that in yourself, then you find respect for that which is loving in another. When you have compassionate non-judgment for that in yourself which is less than loving, you find compassionate non-judgment for that in others When you learn to say no kindly to yourself when the impulse is grounded in fear, then you learn to recognize that fearful impulse in others and say no to it with the same kindness. Living with non-harm to others does not mean never saying no; quite the contrary. It can be very harmful to another to allow them to use you as a doormat.

You must get this straightened out in yourselves by paying close attention to the multiple reasons for your choices, starting to see those motivations that are prompted by love and what part of it is prompted by fear, not hating yourself for the fear, but not being drawn into dialogue with that fear. This is what leads you not to be drawn into dialogue with another's fear, but to say no and to trust, "This is the least harmful thing I can do." Harming another by ownership is still harm. If you allow another to step on you, and hold your tongue, even if you are not hating them for doing that, you're still harming them. It is a very fine line.

A related question, one of choice of work is, "How do I know whether to stay with my present job, which is sometimes very painful to me, or when to move on to a new job? Am I copping out or am I being guided by love?" One might ask the same question in a rocky relationship. "How do I know when to stay with it? How do I know when to withdraw?" The same answer, my friends: When you start to allow yourself to experience the multiple motivations without needing to cling to being the "good" one nor to deny nor hate yourself for the places of fear, then you allow yourself to move into a deeper place of knowing in your heart, which very honestly weighs the balance and knows this choice is primarily motivated by love or by fear. It is never going to be clear-cut, which takes me one step further.

Please understand that there are only more or less skillful, more or less painful or joyful decisions. There is never a right or wrong decision. If you stay with the job or relationship and pain increases, you always have the right to leave. You ask yourself, "Am I still learning here or has the pain increased to the point where there's so much contraction of my energy that I can't learn?" If that is so, you forgive yourself for that humanness that creates that contraction and you let go of that work or relationship with the intention to look deeply at the places of fear when you are no longer so deeply stuck in it, and understand it, so you will not need to repeat it. If there is not that much contraction and pain and there is still much love and much joy in the work, and if you feel yourself learning in those situations, then you go on. There is no right or wrong.

There is much more that could be said about these questions which I would like to get into, but rather than working with hypothetical situations, we would like to hear your questions. I also sense that Q'uo may wish to speak before you get into your questions. What we will do here is pause for a brief break, come back and allow Q'uo to speak, if that is desired, or open to your questions. That is all.

(The session was paused for group meditation and tuning through story and song.)

Q'uo: We are those of Q'uo. Greetings once again in love and light.

We are happy to report that not only have Aaron and we spoken concerning the remainder of this session of working, but our instruments have also made their peace with our preferences, so all is well in hand. And this delights the one know as Carla, who enjoys arrangements.

We have looked at the walking of the spiritual path and seen that it is based upon the awareness that within the form which walks upon the surface of this sphere and dies and is no more, there exists a self which does not go down into the dust or in any way become corrupted, but which is infinite and eternal and unknowable, as the mystery of love shall always remain unknowable.

We have acknowledged that the beginning of this path may usefully be seen to be the first conscious choice of how to walk that path. Each here who hears our voice has committed the self to a pilgrimage of service to others on behalf of the one infinite Creator. We also have chosen this path, and this is why we have been called to your group at this time/space. We have suggested that beyond all questions of human motive, which keep intellects busy attempting to discern right, there is the actual center of this quest in the very body which is corrupt; for the consciousness which is Christ Consciousness, which is Buddha Body, dwells with a faithfulness that shall not cease, short of death.

In the midst of the physical vehicle which you know as your own body, no matter how its condition seems, it carries Christ within it. And this being, within which is your deeper Self, depends upon you to hope and dream and strive in faith amidst all difficulties and conditions whatsoever, to affirm this Self within, to proudly bear all the perceived errors of self as scars of a warrior who strives peacefully towards that inner Eden in which all physicality and confusion pass away. And the Christ within, well-launched from infanthood, may finally begin another voyage, another pilgrimage, in a lighter body within which this consciousness grows and has a larger weight compared to the physical body. You see, in all of your attempts to live, whatever you may think of them, they have been your best. How can any offer more than this?

Now then, we encourage each to feel the feet planted upon the path of pilgrimage. Yes, there are times when you may sit and drink in such beauty, whether it be of the eye or the heart, that you feel nourished and lovely and loving and well-equipped to do the walking towards the greater light. Yet, so much of any pilgrimage takes place when conditions do not seem favorable. And in these dry and desert times, it is central to pilgrimage that within your own processes of reasoning and consideration, you remember who you are, where you wish to go and how much you feel connected to this quixotic quest. It is when you are alone, without friends to encourage or understand, that the spirit within most needs your ragged, jagged faith—any scrap, any off-key rendition of the blues that still may praise the Creator within. Pilgrimages are difficult. But you would not find yourself upon this path if you did not hunger for that which gives meaning to difficulty. You wish to be wide awake and feel every stone, eat every mouthful of dust and sit at the end of any hopeless, empty day, rejoicing and giving thanks that you have been present at this miraculous disaster.

Of course, we can most well comfort each in these protected circumstances using channels such as this one and using the energy of each who seeks so that each helps each. But the testing and trying which tempers and encourages the growth of that spirit within is greatly fed by these difficult, desert moments or hours or days or, this instrument reminds us, years.

Sometimes, yes, each shall have losses, limitations and every discouragement. Indeed, each faces physical annihilation. One day this body shall be dust. None of this appeals or is easy to ponder, yet each of you shall walk along this path with the truth receding infinitely before you, never reached, always beckoning. And each day shall be new. Each situation, no matter how time-worn by repetition, shall be new if you choose to be fully the pilgrim. For you who wish to walk this path, wish nothing short of transformation. And one who successfully transforms oneself has virtually healed at least some portions of an older self, so that the new within has the opportunity and room to bud and flower and bloom in its turn, within.

The question, "How can one walk a spiritual path or have a spiritual vocation when one must labor at worldly concerns in order to provide food and shelter?" becomes less puzzling if you assign the value to labor that you assign to meditation, contemplation and all the good practices of the spiritual vocation.

We suggest to each that the spiritual vocation is to find love in the moment, every moment; and this makes no distinction between the worldly labor and the strictly spiritual practice. When an entity can gaze at the crowded day and see joy in the doing and Christ Consciousness in the very warp and woof of all labor, then a world opens up before that entity which is entirely drenched and marinated in Christ Consciousness.

This instrument has read the story of the nun who was asked how she could bear to wash the filthy, maggot-filled sores of infant children in your India which were soon to die, the odor and the look of putrefaction being so dreadful. The nun reportedly looked up at the questioner and said, "Oh, but this is the face of Jesus Christ. If I thought this was an Indian child, I could never do it."

My brothers and sisters, each of you is as this one. And no matter to what purpose you lend your hand, you touch Christ Consciousness. Do you doubt that there is this consciousness in one who does the taxes, goes to the grocery and attempts to park the car in a crowded lot with others jockeying for your place? If you do doubt, then praise and give thanksgiving to the one infinite Creator and go on anyway.

We shall speak to ways in which the spiritual vision may be tuned so as to be more fruitful in throwing out for your use tools and resources with which to meet Christ in the parking lot. But for now, we and those of Aaron, in the course of questioning, would like to address specific requests from you. We would open with the first query. Does any wish to question at this time?

Questioner: I've noticed in an experience that I had, and I've had it here today in listening to Q'uo, that as I get closer to God Consciousness I always feel a welling up of tears. I'm wondering why that is. They don't feel like bad tears.

Q'uo: I am Q'uo, and we agree that these are not bad tears. You have the sensibility to weep at the beauty, my brother. This beauty is called forth within you by words which you recognize, yet the beauty which brings your tears was within you all the time. Is there a further query, my brother?

Questioner: No. Thank you.

Q'uo: Is there another question?

Questioner: You indicated that all jobs are good. Aren't there jobs that are not so good, that are selfish and destructive rather than constructive, like developing atomic bombs or something?

Q'uo: The query about good and evil occupations assumes that one accepts good and evil occupations, yet we would suggest that each entity which strives to polarize towards service to others has the tendency to select a job for pay which is either helpful or not harmful. However, were a scientist put in the position of developing the atomic bomb, yet still this entity could invest every hope for positive use that it had, and with sadness accept such a development as a job. Given the circumstances in which the atomic bomb was developed, the intention of those who developed this was sad but firm commitment to stopping a war which was engulfing your sphere.

The worldly is seldom pure in its habiliments or circumstances. Good and evil are so plaited up and interwoven in the tapestry of living that it is almost impossible to do that which yields all positive and no negative. Those who have been given gifts must attempt to offer them with the very best of intention. And if there seems to develop negativity therefrom, then that pain and sorrow, too, must be taken into that place where forgiveness reigns, healing is real and the light does not waver. That place lies within each. It is a place as clear in location as Cleveland. You may not know its position within the body, but its position within your beingness is specific. It is your heart. And in that place there is no right and no wrong, but only love. Beyond all that occurs, all that dies, there is love A sorry race it is that each may run in terms of the outer appearances, yet each time that spirit within throws that metaphysical hand up and says, "Praise, love anyway. We'll work this out eventually, but now, praise and thanks that we are here to witness to love," that place is re-entered and the healing waters flow.

Does this answer the query, or is there a further query?

(Pause)

One final query, if there be one, then we would wish to transfer the podium, shall we say, to the one known as Aaron. Is there a final query to us at this time?

Questioner: I have a question. Is there any dharmic practice or service that you would recommend that would enhance, perhaps speed up, but at least keep one pointed on the path toward getting to this place in the heart?

Q'uo: Yes, my brother, there is. For each it is somewhat different. But perhaps you can see the slant when we say to you that the teacher known as Jesus, in attempting to describe its nature, said that it thanked entities who had fed it and clothed it and so forth. And when the confusion arose because entities had not fed Jesus, it explained, "Insofar as you have fed or clothed the least of these, you have fed and clothed me."[9]

There are entities starving. There are entities who are naked. There is always some soup to fix and hand to those who have no home. And for those who cannot achieve a sense of this healing place within by working upon the horizontal plane, there are those commitments of the spirit to pray and intercede and assist the consciousness of the planet upon which you dwell. For those who abide in love and thanksgiving, thinking prayerfully of the planet or the cause of peace, or any beau geste, any windmill which you may till at, the doing of this regularly, day after day, week upon week—this for those who do not see love in soup—shall furnish the love; for this, too, is food, a kind of food you might call manna or bread of heaven.

If you cook, offer soup. If you pray, offer prayers. And if you do neither, sit down in one place and give thanks and praise and then be quiet and feel the doors of the heart open. We do not suggest that this is easily accomplished, but only suggest that sometime in the rhythm of your own energies will be the time when all the waiting is over and you have that divine moment when Christ Consciousness thrills up your spine and through your very being; and for that instant, all is quite, quite clear. Ever after this first experience of the open heart, you then have this subjective memory which can shine within you, like the candle lit against all darkness, until your next moment within the open, full heart.

May we answer further, my brother?

Questioner: No. Thank you.

Q'uo: We thank you, my brother, and all here present. And we shall most happily speak with you again, but for now we would yield the floor in case any has queries which it wishes the one known as Aaron to answer. For now, we leave you in all that there is: the love that created everything and the light out of which all is created. We are those of Q'uo. Adonai.

Barbara: Aaron wants to speak for a few minutes before he opens the floor to questions.

Aaron: I am Aaron. I wish to briefly expand on a few things about which Q'uo spoke. First, before the floor was opened to your queries, my brother/sister spoke about living a life in faith. I want to pick up on this idea of faith.

One of the primary learnings of third density is faith. Sometimes your life hands you chaos, pain. The first impulse is to say, "What am I doing wrong?" or, "Why me?" It is very hard to have faith. I am not suggesting blind faith that takes whatever is handed you with no respect for yourself. This is the thinking that leads into "doormatism," if I may coin a word. This is not just blind acceptance which disempowers. Faith, on the contrary, *true* faith empowers because true faith comes from that part of you which cuts through the relative dualities of good and bad, right and wrong. True faith comes from that deeply connected core of your heart, and it is built on past experience of faith. It is built on wisdom, on looking back at this life and seeing that what you challenged with a bewildered, "Why?" turned out to have answers, turned out to be at times your greatest teacher. It is that grounded faith which grows out of connection and of love which enables you to deal with the bewilderment and occasional deep pain of your life, to cut through your war with

---

[9] *Holy Bible*, Matthew 25:40.

that pain and confusion and take the next step. Put as simply as I can, if life never challenged you by offering you that which was difficult, how would you strengthen these muscles of faith? How would you practice faith without the catalyst which asks that of you?

Taking this to another place, we will look at such a situation as the making of the atomic bomb. Of course it is possible that there were some, even likely that there were some involved in the making of that bomb who did so with hatred in their hearts and the desire to kill others for revenge. There were also those who acted in the service of love and caring for others as best they knew how. You may question their wisdom, but you may not question their intention. If one says to you, "I truly believe that I can best preserve peace and sanity in the world by creating a terrible weapon," their reasoning may be faulty, but their heartfelt motivation is to serve.

Is the bomb, in itself, good or bad? Is anything, in itself, good or bad? What grows out of it? There is a story of the man whose horse broke free of its barn and disappeared. The neighbors all said, "Oh, what bad luck!" The man shrugged and said, "Bad luck/good luck, who knows?" The neighbors shook their heads with bewilderment at his response. But the next day this mare came home leading a wild stallion, a strong and handsome animal. And the neighbors all said, "Oh, what good luck!" Again, the man shrugged, "Good luck/bad luck, who knows?" The next day the man's son was attempting to groom this horse and the horse kicked him, breaking his leg. And again the neighbors all said, "Oh, what bad luck!" And again the man shrugged, "Good luck/bad luck, who knows?" Later that week soldiers came rounding up young men in the area to become scripts for the army, and they took all the young men in the town except this one with the broken leg.

Good luck/bad luck. What does "good" or "bad" mean? What are the motivations? What grows out of it? I am not stating here that it is acceptable to go out and murder people and say, "Well, there's no such thing as bad." You do live with one foot in relative reality. If you harm others, you are responsible for that harm; and it is never all right in terms of relative reality. But nothing on your earth plane happens without a reason, and nothing is without its karmic consequences.

What was the motivation of those who created a bomb? No, the ends do not justify the means. It is not okay to kill people to create peace. You will have to decide for yourself, however, if it is okay to do certain work if your intention is pure.

What are we weighing here, the work itself or the motivation? There are times when the answer is clear. So one, for example, who goes out to hunt for sport—killing animals perhaps as a guide, leading others to this killing—it is clear that this is action that harms others. But sometimes it is not very clear. Most of your work does not directly point to harm. And we also might ask, "Harm for what?" There is honest disagreement. Do we cut down rain forests, thereby killing the life therein? If we do not cut it down, what do we use for fields to grow food?

I'm not suggesting an answer here. Of course, I have my own views; but they are merely my opinion. The question is, "What is the motivation?" And here, we come back to faith. One can work as hard as one can to follow the path which one personally sees as relieving suffering in the world, but one also must have faith that one cannot fix other people, that one cannot grab other people and shake them out of their views. If people need to do that which seems to be destructive, one must simultaneously work as hard as one can to alleviate the suffering that grows out of that destructive path and also have faith that things are unfolding as they need to. It is not given to you on the human plane to see all the answers with foresight.

We come back to this same question, "Can I look at the multiple motivations within me?" Perhaps the difficulty is being with another being's suffering. So I want to take that suffering away from them because it is so painful for me. I want to fix that. But in so wanting to fix them, I don't give them their free-will choice, nor do I give them permission to be who they are and to learn in their own way. Do I have the right to do that?

You can open a door for another, but you cannot push them through. You can suggest to another, "I think that this is a path that will lead to suffering." But you cannot insist on another's agreement with your view. Here is where you need faith that you must speak up and act without attachment to results, where appropriate. And then you must let it unfold as it will, doing what you can, and then resting and letting it open as it needs to.

A simple illustration here is the child that wants to touch a hot stove. You tell the child ten times, a hundred times, a thousand times, "No, it's hot!" But the child has no concept of hot. You don't simply shrug and say, "All right, touch the stove. See for yourself!" You continue to say, "No, it's hot!" But somewhere along the line, you know the child's going to touch that stove behind your back and learn for itself, "Yes, it's hot!"

You can open the door to another's learning, but you cannot know what the other needs most to learn. Perhaps those beings who built the atomic bomb and those who were involved in the bombing itself on both sides had lessons which you cannot begin to understand. We cannot judge others. That does not free us from responsibility for stating our viewpoint with love.

To shift tracks here, I would finally like to speak briefly to this last question of spiritual practice with one very specific suggestion, two actually: one all-encompassing and one specific. The all-encompassing: Whatever you do, do it with awareness; just that. Awareness is the key to all of your learning. The second: What is your own personal stumbling block? It will vary for each of you.

Awareness is the overall practice. There are many support practices which allow you to bring into your awareness the catalysts which give rise to that which you most need to practice. For the being, for example, who is very aware of the stumbling block of greed, of the fear, "Will my needs be met?" and the movement to hold on, to grasp—such a being might find it useful to move into a practice of always letting others go first, just to see what happens with that.

At a meditation retreat here last year, someone spoke of trying this: of seeing the fear in itself that it would not get what it needed to eat and of asking itself to always be last, to wait until everyone else had been served. In doing so, that being had need constantly to address that fear with awareness. And it also was given the opportunity to see that there was enough left. It began to see how much that fear was old-mind's habit and was not a fear borne out in the present moment. So, it began to find that it could let go, that it no longer needed to own and identify with that fear.

Jealousy: A practice here is to notice, with compassion for yourself, the arising of jealousy at others' good fortune; and then, very consciously, to allow the arising of gladness for them in yourself, to look as carefully as you can at that being's fear and pain, and at the arising of joy in what it had been given or accomplished. As you work consciously with such a practice, you find a very real joy in others' successes and happinesses. You allow a part of you that had been confined and not allowed expression to come out and express itself. And it allows for the disillusion of fear. You start to understand that another's gain does not mean your loss. You correct that misunderstanding.

Generosity: Another one, another part of holding on and fearing one's needs won't be met. If this is a predominant issue for you, another way to work with it is to practice giving. Start with very small things, seeing that another needs a fork or a napkin. You are not giving your own, you are just reaching and getting it for them. But it is a practice in giving. It starts to open your heart to how wonderful it feels to give and be attentive to others' needs. It starts to open your heart to that innate generosity of spirit. Then you increase the giving, not just of material things, but of your time and your energy. And you begin to learn that you do not lose anything when you give. Again, you correct the misunderstanding, not through forcing yourself with a "give till it hurts," quite the contrary: a gentle process whereby you learn that giving is joy.

I will not elucidate with each stumbling block that each of you may have. You have got the gist of it. There are a great many different spiritual practices. First you must identify the stumbling block and then you can find an appropriate practice that relates to it.

I would like to open the floor here to any questions that there may be. That is all.

Questioner: Aaron, do you have a practice for arrogance?

Aaron: I am Aaron. First we must look at, "What is arrogance?" Can you see that arrogance is simply the flip side of the coin of unworthiness? To be arrogant is to presume oneself "better than" or feel the need to express a superiority, and inversely, to put another down.

Do not concentrate on the arrogance. That is dialoguing with fear. Move your focus instead to the sense of unworthiness. When you see the impulse toward arrogant response arising in you, let it be a flashing red light saying, "Fear is here," and move that loving heart immediately to the fear. "In this moment, am I unworthy?" Your answer is going to be no. "Have I ever been unworthy at those times when I experienced an impulse toward arrogant response? No. It is simply the way that this mind/body construct has dealt with fear of being inadequate or unworthy. I don't need to do that." The spiritual practice that might then be derived from that is to allow the arising of arrogance to be a reminder to be compassionate to this illusory but seemingly real self that is experiencing fear.

The person who experiences that which seems arrogant in itself undoubtedly also frequently experiences arrogance in others. Here is where a valuable practice comes in, of seeing the arrogance in others as their fear. You may begin to work with a forgiveness meditation, really trying to see their fear manifesting that arrogant reaction. As you forgive them, you forgive yourself. Is that sufficient answer or have you further question?

Questioner: Can Aaron hear Q'uo, hear what Q'uo is saying? Is it communicated to you so you can pay due attention to Q'uo?

Aaron: I am Aaron. I hear Q'uo's thoughts but not Q'uo's words. In other words, I hear the thoughts, but do not know the choice of words with which Carla has framed those thoughts, because Carla is not thinking the thoughts. They are simply emerging.

Interestingly, last night at a point when the tape was being changed, Q'uo's thought was, "We now will pass the microphone to Aaron," so I told Barbara, "It is time to speak," but Q'uo had not yet said that. It was simply the thought. Thus, this instrument held back.

I can hear all of your thoughts. I will not tell Barbara those thoughts. Barbara is responsible for her deafness in ways that she understands. I am not saying she went out and punched a hole in her ear, but in very real ways she is karmically responsible for her deafness and responsible for the consequences of the isolation and limited communication that forces upon her. And I will not simply remove that burden from her. She must live with it. I understand that it then places a burden on others to communicate with her. Perhaps that is also part of the whole karmic cycle of it.

I will tell her when there is something that could be dangerous. For instance, in a car, at one point she had begun to move from the left lane into the right lane because there was a car behind her that wished to pass. As she began to pull into the right lane, the car that was behind her speeded up and started to pull beside her into that same right lane to pass her on the right, the driver driving erratically, angrily. He honked his horn, but of course Barbara did not hear that. Here I did step in, simply saying, "Left, left," and Barbara trusted my voice enough not to pull into the right lane but to swerve back left again, and the driver sped past.

So, I will help with that which she does not hear when it is a potentially life-threatening situation, but I will not step in to simply supply the ears she has lost. That is her responsibility. Does that answer your question?

(Inaudible)

Questioner: This morning Aaron was telling us about what happens when we die, and it was very interesting. And we said, "Let it wait until everyone can hear it," about the transition period and so forth.

Aaron: I am Aaron. This answer will take at least ten or fifteen minutes. May I suggest that it be my contribution to our fireside stories? Will that be acceptable to you? That is all.

Questioner: Do you mean you are going to tell ghost stories now? Wouldn't it be fun to hear some Christmas stories.

Barbara: Aaron says, "That's another kind of ghost story: Holy Ghost stories."

(Group laughter.)

Is there one other short question?

Questioner: Should we guard our socks when we go home?

Aaron: I am Aaron. It is my firm belief that socks are given to you in pairs for the sole reason of offering you the chance to practice at non-attachment and to practice offering other beings a free will. I have told you before that on our planes we take your cast-offs gladly and have no preference as to whether they match. Perhaps eventually we will be able to finally tell enlightened beings on this earth because they will randomly wear socks that match or do not match, with no great attachment. That is all.

(More group laughter.)

Questioner: Is that how we get lint in the dryer?

Aaron: I am Aaron. The lint in your dryer comes from the material of your clothes practicing dissolution of form. That is all.

(The session was paused for a period of group meditation, singing and poetry reading.)

Barbara: So many of us get trapped in that being spiritual, being good, means never saying no, never being angry, never having emotions. Aaron says that it is harder for those of us who are old souls, as all of us here are, because we so much aspire to purify our energy—an intention that works against us because even if there's a little bit of negativity in us, instead of just taking it in our stride as younger souls do, he says that the closer that we get to getting ready to graduate from the plane, the more perfectionistic we get. And that's one of the last lessons that we learn: finding love for our very fallible human selves.

Questioner: What kind of being is the Q'uo? Is it a sixth-density social memory complex? And for what purpose did it become one; that is, a joined group entity?

Carla: Before the Ra contact began, I was channeling mostly a fifth-density entity named Latwii. It was a social memory complex, fifth-density wisdom. I really liked Latwii. After Don died, I did not channel Ra anymore at Ra's request, and went back to channeling Latwii and others. I got a contact from Q'uo soon after that … six months. We thought, "Q'uo, what an odd name." A couple of years later we finally developed enough wit to ask who Q'uo was. And Q'uo said that they were a principle made up of Latwii and one of Latwii's teachers who was also one of our teachers by the name of Ra. I could no longer channel the narrow beam which required trance, but I could channel fifth density. And Latwii could talk to those of Ra and be somewhat better able to focus on the question than they were before. So, Q'uo is a sort of new, improved Latwii and Ra. The purpose of their contacting us is because we asked for it. The purpose of their joining was to contact us.

Questioner: Have they ever identified themselves as to where they're from?

Carla: No.

Questioner: Have you had much contact with Pleiadian entities?

Carla: I have worked with people who have been channeling the Pleiades. I have not accepted that contact.

Questioner: Have you turned it away?

Carla: Yes.

Questioner: Why? Is that a personal question?

Carla: No. It is a question having to do with my judgment that the contact is mixed.

Questioner: Yes. That fits with what we've heard about the Pleiades. There are different purposes at work coming from that system.

Questioner: Could someone speak to what they are? I've never heard of it.

Questioner: The Pleiadians are a star formation, aren't they?

Questioner: Yes! And it's one of the oldest civilizations in the galaxy. Aaron gave some talks about how a lot of our culture was seeded from the Pleiades and that a lot of us came from the Pleiades.

Carla: It's very strong energy, but it's also capable of a good bit of delusion.

Questioner: Can you pick and choose?

Carla: I don't think you can as well, once you accept contact. You're going to get what you get.

Barbara: Last spring Aaron talked about the Pleiades, but I have not yet seen the transcripts from that. Does anybody know what he said? Does anybody remember? Can you share a little bit with us?

Questioner: As I best recall, the Pleiadians were a very ancient civilization that was made up, not of one race, but of many different kinds of beings who came together—physical beings and non-physical beings like water beings, air beings, more ethereal beings. And they had a governing council made up of beings who were incarnate and discarnate. That council and those beings were aware of the distortions that were happening on Earth due to extraterrestrial contact with the Earth—negatively polarized contact. And there was a debate about whether or not to intervene.

So, some of the beings from the council (it is not a governing council but a voluntary council, like a service group) came to Earth. They came, not as incarnate beings, but as shape changers, which is a way of simulating incarnation here in the physical but being able to leave at will and not be subject to the karma here. So, they were hoping that by simulating the negatively polarized extraterrestrials, they could give a different message of love instead of a negative one of fear. But what they didn't realize was that by taking the form of these negative beings, they had to copy them so precisely that they had the capability to even emulate the emotional body to such an extent they could not separate from the negative polarity as well.

Thus, they fell into negativity because they also, despite their very good intentions, had a very small amount of mixed motivations or negativity within them. They were very loving beings with very good intentions, but they overestimated their own ability and their own need to learn from the negative half to understand negativity within them. So eventually many of them took incarnation. And as the years and incarnations went by, many of the lessons from their civilization became seed-points of our own great civilization. They were bringers of culture and light.

So, they came to teach, but also ended up coming to learn, and many are still here working out their karma. There is still contact going on from the Pleiades, as Aaron has told us, but there is still a debate about this contact and whether beings from other planets should actively intervene.

This was an echo of previous history in which the makers of Earth had seen the negative contact with their creations—the people of Earth—and they tried to protect them somehow, not trusting people's ability to learn from this negative contact. And this protectiveness by these beings who founded Earth became itself a negative catalyst; and further … yes! … it was the birth of fear on Earth!

This was long before the Pleiadians saw the contact of extraterrestrials, which was far more negative by then. So, now I think some of the contact that Carla is talking about is some of these beings come to do good, but not to intervene. There is a law or agreement not to come to Earth unless it is by incarnation. But what about those beings who do not follow the law? Do you enforce control or allow those beings to go ahead with breaking this law?

Barbara: Aaron says two things. He says, "Thank you!" to you. (I'm paraphrasing here.) He's saying that there is a force field of sorts around the Earth. They cannot use fear. They use love as the energy of this force field to prevent encroachment by negative energy. There's a force field of love which prevents highly negative energy from encroaching, because they're repelled by this force field. But energies such as the Pleiadians are not negatively polarized, simply, in Aaron's viewpoint, have misunderstanding that the end justifies the means, and thus have intervened rather than trusting and having faith in those on Earth to work it out on their own; but they are not repelled by the force field because they are positively polarized beings. That is all.

Questioner: Has anyone here read, *Bringer of the Dawn*?

Barbara: Yes, I have. And I asked Aaron about it and he said to read it very selectively. It is both clear and fear-based.

Questioner: It does tend to create fear in a major DNA change in another twenty years. That sounds pretty fearful. But there are some things in it that I think are interesting topics of discussion.

(The group offered topics for the next session.)

"How do we move into the space of being unselfconscious?"

"Do we connect with each other vibrationally, for the most part?"

"Is there reincarnation in groups? How does that work? How do we find each other?"

"Did Christ and Buddha "hang out" together?"

"It seems that unworthiness really goes deep, like it is genetically encoded, almost like a catalyst. Is it genetically encoded? What is the origin of unworthiness?"

"Is it better to take it slow or to try to complete this density in this lifetime?"

"Hopi prophesies?" ☘

The Aaron/Q'uo Dialogues, Session 21
September 26, 1993

(This session was preceded by a period of tuning and meditation.)

Aaron: I am Aaron. Good morning to you all. I want to share with you how much I enjoyed the spirited energy that rose from this room last night with your joyful gathering. Some of you forget that laughter is also a part of the spiritual path. We are asked please to open the shades. Laughter is one of the most effective ways—laughter, joy and lightness, the lightness that comes with deeply sharing your energy and opening your hearts to one another in playfulness.

There is no other plane that I know of where beings limit their playfulness, the natural playfulness of their light, as much as they do on the earth plane. It is part of your illusion of separation. So it was very beautiful to us, as your spirit friends, to feel and share in your joy.

There are a number of questions that were offered last night. While understanding the importance of each question to the seeker, it is of our mutual agreement, Q'uo and myself and also of those through whom we channel, that it is best to maintain the focus of the original question, "What is the spiritual path and how do we live it?"

Since our time is not unlimited in these particular sessions so that we cannot answer all the questions within each of your hearts, it feels most relevant to the entire group to limit ourselves to those questions which first drew you here, because we have by no means covered that topic. This does not mean that we do not value the other questions, but that we must answer them at a different space/time. Ones such as the one about dying and what happens after dying are easily answered on a Wednesday night.[10]

One thought in my mind is that in a future gathering, rather than starting with a specific focus, we could simply come together as curious seekers with questions. We can explore that route.

Q'uo and I would like first, then, to continue some of our discussion of, "What is the spiritual path and how do we live it?" coming back more to the question, "What is it?" and then to the second half, "How do we live it?"

Speaking to the particular distortions and confusions that offer themselves as catalyst in your lives, we come together here with a number of religious biases. I do not mean bias in a negative term, only in the sense of persuasions or beliefs. A bias might be considered a bend, a bend in the clear stream of light such as that bend that light makes when it hits the

---

[10] For more information, please contact the Deep Spring Center for Meditation and Spiritual Inquiry, 3003 Washtenaw Ave, Suite 2, Ann Arbor, MI, 48104, www.deepspring.org.

water, being bent by the mass of that water so it appears to the eye to have a crook in it. Your individual values, experiences and beliefs serve as deflector to the true light, so that the expression of that light becomes individuated into your own personal bias.

Your religious persuasions are not to be mistaken as synonymous with a spiritual path, rather they are the tools that you use to help you walk your path. There are hundreds of different religious beliefs in the world. We do not wish to favor some above others. They are all of value. Even those which have been viewed as negative in some way provide a value to the seeker.

Time limits us from speaking to the myriad religious persuasions of your many cultures, nor would that be relevant to you. We have here a group whose religious understandings are predominantly Judeo-Christian and Buddhist. There are those among you who have been influenced by the Hindu or Sufi, by Islam, by Native American cultures and beliefs. These are not any the less valuable.

The other reason why I choose to speak predominantly to, let us call it not even Judeo-Christian but Christian and Buddhist, is that the essences of these can be simplified into these qualities of mercy and wisdom. The beings who were the masters of these two faiths have become in your heart/minds the personifications of mercy and wisdom.

If we look into other beliefs, we will find other religious streams. We will find that those beliefs find some balance in these qualities of mercy and wisdom. Judaism, in its purest form, makes a very beautiful balance. Hinduism leans a bit more toward the qualities of love than of wisdom, as do the Sufi faiths The Native American traditions come to a beautiful balance.

While I speak of balance, be aware that a balance need not be 50/50. Each of you has been in incarnation so many times, you move into your religious bias because of what speaks most eloquently to your heart.

Mercy is one wing of the bird, wisdom is the other. Call it wisdom and compassion, wisdom and love. The bird cannot fly without two wings, but always one will be the stronger. Through the quality only of faith, one can find liberation. Through the quality only of precise and fine-tuned, awakened wisdom, one can find liberation. Could you see that bird struggling to fly with that one wing, the other wing at least held out for balance?

Your spiritual path lays before you the ways in which you find that personal balance. There is no right or wrong here. One cannot offer a recipe: 17% of this and 19% of that and 3% of this and so on. What do you start with? The stew that is too sour may need more sugar. The stew that is too sweet may need more lemon.

So, you must know yourself, know your strengths, relish those strengths and build on them, but not be afraid also to know the places of lack of strength and be willing to strengthen those muscles that are weak. The runner who works only on strengthening his muscles will lack wind in a race. The runner who works on his breath and lungpower and ignores the muscles will find the legs cramping and weak. And yet one runner may know the great strength of her legs and that it is what will put her ahead in the race, so she wisely strengthens her lungs so that they may endure through the race while the legs do the bumping and pushing.

What do you need to strengthen in yourselves? What are your weaknesses? It is always easier to strengthen that which feels most natural to you, that to which you are most deeply drawn. But I beseech you to look at your resistance to strengthening that which is more difficult to strengthen.

So, what are these paths of loving-kindness, mercy and compassion, and of wisdom? I spoke sometime this weekend about using mind to tame mind and using wisdom to tame mind. When I say mind here, remember that I do not mean the brain, but the mind/heart totality.

I want to speak here of stories of these two basic teachers and their teachings: the Buddha and the one who is known as Jesus. I have shared with you many stories from my own heart, from my personal memories of this being in that lifetime in which I was a poor shepherd and knew this being in the flesh, and the ways that he affected me deeply as teacher. Predominant in those memories were the stories of his deep loving-kindness to all beings, his deep sense of humility, his unwillingness to see another being suffer; and yet his deeds were tempered with wisdom.

I have shared the story with many of you of a visit to him soon after that being who was my wife had died and my heart was breaking. I was injured on the way and my leg was broken—that being who I was. I know that he had the ability to heal it, but in his wisdom he saw that my broken leg was not what needed healing. My heart was what needed healing. I was angry at him at first. I said, "I have to go home. I have children and sheep to be tended." "No," he said. "Your son can tend the sheep. Your neighbors and family can tend your children. You must stay here until you are healed." In my ignorance I thought he meant until my leg was healed, and it felt to me that he was withholding his healing. But I was forced to remain there for some months, being tended lovingly, carried from place to place, fed and my soul nourished until that deep grief within me had healed and I was ready to go home and be both mother and father to my family.

So, he was not maudlin in his mercy. It was tempered with wisdom. But he did heal because he could not bear to see another suffer when it was within his power to alleviate that suffering.

The balance to the story is a tale of the Buddha. This is not a personal memory, but a story that has been handed to me and is known in the literature of Buddhist stories. A woman's young child died, and she was heartbroken as it was her only son. The Buddha was camped nearby with his followers. And some said to her, "He can help." So she carried the child there and said, "Lord, can you revive him?" The Buddha looked at this dead baby and said to the woman only, "I can help you, but first you must go out and find [a certain kind of spice that was familiar in that country in India]. You must bring me a pinch of this spice." "Oh, that's easy," said the woman. "But," said the Buddha, "there is one thing. It must come from a household that has not known death."

The woman was cheered by the prospect that she could help this dead son, and she went and knocked on a door. "Can I have some of this kind of spice?" "Oh, of course," they said. "But," she said, "it must come from a home that has not known death." "We're sorry," they said, "our uncle died here last month." She knocked on the next door. "Of course, you may have the spice." "But it must come from a house that has not known death. Have you known death?" "Yes," said the woman sadly, "Our daughter died here last week" … "Have you known death?"

"Yes," the father died last year … "Yes," the grandmother died three years ago … "Yes," the infant died in childbirth … "Yes," the mother died in child birth … "Yes," the father drowned, and so on, door after door throughout the day until she finally understood: Death is part of the continuum of life. We cannot change what is. We must open our heart to it and continue to move on.

As dusk fell she returned to the Buddha, her tears dried, her heart open. She held her dead son one last time and bade farewell to him. And the Buddha helped her to bury him, cremate him as the case may be. This woman then ordained to become a Buddhist nun and a follower of the Buddha's, that through her new wisdom she might share with others.

What is "merciful" here? Was it any less merciful to help this woman find an end to her suffering through teaching her about the continuum of life and death and the suffering of holding on to that which cannot be held on to? Perhaps the child's birth and death were offered simply as a gift to the mother to help her move through this learning. Who are we to judge that?

What I want you to see is that the path of mercy contains wisdom and the path of wisdom contains mercy. And yet, each predominates in one direction or the other. Those of you who are drawn toward the Christ as your spiritual master are drawn more directly toward these teachings of loving-kindness and mercy and forgiveness. Those who are drawn more toward the Buddha as your spiritual master are drawn toward these teachings of wisdom tempered by mercy.

What does this mean in your own lives? Because each of you has strengths and weaknesses, it is easy to adhere to the strength and then hide the weakness, thus losing the opportunity to enrich yourselves and expand your path. Where there is firm adherence only to wisdom, not tempered by mercy and compassion, is there some fear of that mercy, some fear of letting your heart speak for you and following the whispered messages of that heart? Where there is attachment only to the teachings of the heart, is there some fear that if one moves into wisdom, one will also move into the dictates of the conceptual mind—an awareness that the brain cannot lead, that the brain is only a tool?

Perhaps you swing to the opposite extreme at times, that some who in past lives have misused the brain and followed its dictates while screening out the messages of the heart have now become so wary of doing that, that you have swung to the opposite extreme, and vice versa.

In the fullness of your being as human, you are offered this beautiful mind/heart combination. They are one, not two. Both deep wisdom and the ability to love are offered you. May I challenge you to find the appropriate balance for yourselves and to see where fear blocks that balance?

I want to expand this heart/mind, wisdom/compassion talk by speaking a bit further about the relative and ultimate practices and the coming to this intersection of them. This is not quite the same intersection as wisdom and love. All relative practices are not heart practices and all ultimate practices are not wisdom practices. They are both a mixture of the two. But I want to make sure that you understand what I mean by relative versus ultimate practices.

You are faced with great suffering throughout your world. Those of you who are aware and openhearted are attuned to the suffering around you and have deep desire to work to alleviate that suffering: the suffering of those who starve or are homeless or suffer great disease or hardship; the sufferings of the Earth—the polluted rivers and lakes, the dying forests, the species of plants and animals endangered and facing extinction. You know that you must keep your heart open to this suffering and work in whatever ways you can to alleviate suffering. And so you become involved in these relative practices, both spiritual practices such as meditation and prayer, and quasi-spiritual practices such as volunteering your time to help others. When I say "quasi," I do not mean that it is any less a spiritual practice, only that one moves inward and one extends the energy out into the world. They are both important. Unless one moves deeply into the meditative space where one recognizes the emptiness of self in the doing, the offering of one's energy, one can solidify self by one's very work to help others because there becomes a doer and a receiver. If I am helping you, we are separate. Can I serve you without trying to fix you, without any attachment to fixing you as long as we are separate?

It is the inward practices, especially meditation, which help cut through the solid *I*, which bring in the wisdom aspect that there is really no doer or receiver, that there is really nothing that needs to be done on the ultimate level. This cuts through and allows help to be given without helper or recipient.

Does not the helper benefit as much as the recipient? If I am starving and you give to me, of course you save my life, but what does my receiving your gift give to you? As long as you see yourself as the fixer, you solidify ego and prevent moving into the depth of wisdom. Or are you that being with deep wisdom and a closed heart that denies the reality of suffering on the relative plane. Can there be balance?

There are stories told in the Asian tradition where there is deep belief in karma, of children who fall off of a boat and they cannot swim. No one reaches out a hand to help them. The teaching is simply, "It is their karma." And they flounder and scream and drown. What kind of closed-hearted being can allow such suffering? What is the denial happening there?

Ultimately we are not responsible for one another, because there is no one another. We are all one. But the wisdom-mind also sees that we are all always responsible for this one; and if an extension of this one is drowning, then its own hand must reach out to save it. Wisdom must always be tempered by compassion. Compassion must always be deepened by wisdom.

What is your own bias here? In which directions do you most need to open yourselves in order to best live this center of the cross of wisdom, of compassion-mind, mercy, and love-mind and wisdom-mind, of relative reality and ultimate reality? Think of it as a cross with a small circle at the intersection. You may rest on the horizontal or vertical leg of the cross, but can you keep yourself within the circle?

I thank you for giving your thoughts to this, my dearest ones, and challenging yourselves as to how you may reside in that circle. I now pass the microphone to my brother/sister, beloved friend of Q'uo. That is all.

Q'uo: I am Q'uo. Greetings in the love and in the light of the one infinite Creator. It is a great blessing to be allowed to blend our vibrations with yours and to be asked to share our thoughts with you. As always, we ask that our words be subjected to your personal powers of discrimination, for we are in error often and would not present ourselves as any final authority, but only as those with relatively more experience.

As the one known as Aaron has said, it is well to come to a self-awareness of how one's inner makeup is configured. Whether the way of the heart more beckons or the way of wisdom, each may be taken. Each intersects with the other at every turn. The difference between them is that of the two sides of one coin; and of this coin, one cannot have too much. Yet every day the supply is newly infinite, fresh-minted in infinite Intelligence, sprinkled liberally into every waking consciousness by the graceful hand of Spirit.

Your need for this manna of love and wisdom is yours due to the circumstance of the veil which descends upon those in the third density, leaving each seeker in a relatively dark and subtly lit environment which has been called the shadow of death. Yet still, the spirit within remains moonlit and the spirit's walk is one wherein virtue must be scried out carefully, at length and with great patience. This is not unintended, but is specifically meant to be the case. For in the rough-and-tumble daily world in which you enjoy experiencing, innocent, sleeping youngsters still play, unawakened to the beauty and mystery of the call to faith and service.

There is a time which recurs cyclically within each seeker during which the seeker is plunged into a primary awareness of this moonlit landscape of the archetypical awakening mind, which is both mind and heart. These are desert times. During these times the bitterness may seem so great that there is no possibility of healing or redemption into innocence. Yet these are the desert sands which scour away that very bitterness which has plunged the seeker into this period. The going down into the darkness, the experience of spiritual death, of profound and sudden death, of slow and stealthy death—these are rich, not only in pain but in the fertility of new birth.

Enlightenment begins in this so-called dark night of the soul. And as you, the awakened seeker, move through this moonlit time, you drop away or begin the process of such precisely in order that your dearest wish may be followed. And as you emerge from this deep darkness, your new and transformed being is able to see more light, more beauty, more meaning and more of love. Then the sunlight is again yours, for you are a new and innocent child, and it is your time to gamble and romp and rejoice with your brothers and sisters. There is no one spiritual mood, no one best situation; but rather, the path wanders into the lightest and the most profoundly dark, into the most joy and increasing wisdom, and also into the most profound and sorrowful unknowing.

You have been forever and you shall be forever; and yet, not you, but Love that sent you—a spark of Love—out into materialization that you might experience and process that experience with your own peculiar and unique distortions, creating your unique beauty, your unique harvest of experience. How rich, then, is the Creator as It gathers more and more of experience into Itself, becoming more and more richly known to Itself. You cannot walk off of the spiritual path, for all experiences will be gratefully gathered by the one infinite Creator, who seeks to know Itself.

We would at this time turn the microphone to the one known as Aaron. We are those of Q'uo.

(The group paused and joined together in song.)

Aaron: I am Aaron. I want to attend now to some of the questions that were raised last night, questions especially referring to the catalysts of this earth plane and the question, "How do we walk this path with love?"

There are two different issues here. One is, "What is love and what is fear?" And having determined what is love, how do we choose love? What pushes us into the distortion of fear even though we recognize it as fear?

You cannot "should" yourself, force yourself, into taking the path of love when fear feels overwhelming. It is natural to the humans that you are to defend yourselves, and such defense is so often thought to be a movement of fear. But to act in care for the self may also be a movement of love. Thus the question is not *what* you do so much as, "What is the primary force behind those acts or words?" When you focus on the already present loving motivations, they will be reflected in the acts.

The ends do not justify the means of using force. If we are going to choose love, we must be consistent. Love is natural to you and becomes apparent when there is not fear. You do not need to create love in yourselves. It is already there. Fear blocks it. We do not look, then, at these two paths, fear and love, and say, "I will choose love," even though we quake with fear. Rather, we say, "What is this fear?" and attend to the fear lovingly so it dissolves, and then love is natural and open. I am not suggesting that it will not still take courage and determination, commitment and energy to choose love, but there is no force involved, just a loving aspiration.

You must, then, begin to see who you really are, that fear is an illusion, that you are Love by your very nature. When you penetrate through the illusion of fear, it self-destructs like a balloon popped by a dart, the dart of penetrating awareness which sees the illusion of fear each time it manifests and refuses steadfastly to be caught in a dialogue with fear; and yet does not disdain that fear but bows to it in respect for its presence, smiles to it but does not dwell in it.

So, how do we do this technically? There are so many possible areas that we could look at that we should need weeks to explore it all: relationships, work, all the various paths through which your life leads you.

I should prefer to look at basic emotions which distort your clear seeing along the paths of relationship—work, family, friendship, learning, religious following and so on—to look at two specific emotions which seem to offer the greatest degree of distortion and to talk about how you may more skillfully work with these.

Let me begin by saying that you have a wide gamut of emotions, but they can basically be broken down into fear and love. Within fear there are two basic kinds of fear: that you will be hurt and that your needs will not be met. The fear that you might be hurt brings up emotions of anger at that which might hurt you. This is a kind of defense. The fear that your needs may not be met brings up greed, sometimes seen as jealousy or grasping anger and desire, both offshoots of fear. Of course, there are many other emotions and they each can be fit into different places. Grief is a mixture of love and fear—a fear that your needs will not be met, that you will be hurt through this loss—and also a sense of deep sorrow which grows out of love for that which has been lost. Part of grief is not fear, but an expression of the depth of your love. It does not manifest itself in wishing to hold on, but it is an expression of the depth of joy that was there in the connection with that which seems to be lost. So, we want to be careful not to pigeon-hole too rigidly here, not to simply say, "This is love; this is fear." There is always a blending of the two.

Another kind of emotion, one that has been talked about here and about which we have written questions, is unworthiness. This is also some blending of fear and love. We were asked, "Is unworthiness genetic?" No. And yet, it is hereditary in a different way. It is, let us say, culturally conditioned and is especially prevalent in your society. Last year there was a gathering of western Buddhist teachers in India with the Dalai Lama. One of the teachers shared this story: The group was sitting around the table and one teacher asked, "What about those beings who despise themselves, who truly find themselves unworthy and inadequate?" (Remember these were all western teachers, the only easterners there being the Dalai Lama and his assistants.) The Dalai Lama was a bit puzzled. He said, "Do you mean people in mental hospitals?" The group of teachers turned and looked at one another, and the one who had asked the question said, "No, those who are sitting around this table."

Much of your sense of unworthiness is culturally conditioned. One would need to ask why; not only, "Why does it happen in this culture?" but, "Why did you choose to incarnate into a culture which is conditioned into the distortion of unworthiness?"

What is worthiness or unworthiness? You are divine. How could you possibly ever be unworthy? Unskillful at times, maybe, afraid or angry, a bit dull in your minds at times and creating illusory boundaries for yourself—but unworthy? Where does the story come from?

On the other hand, one might also ask, "If there is no such thing as unworthiness, is there such a thing as worthiness?" There is no duality. Can there be one without the other? Ultimately, there is no worthiness either. Worthiness is a meaningless concept because all beings are worthy. It is only your conceptual mind of duality which creates the concepts worthy and unworthy in balance to one another, and assigns yourself to one realm or the other and assigns other beings to one realm or the other, often assigning yourself to the unworthy category and everybody else to the worthy category.

How did you move into this pattern of distorted illusion, and why? Let us explore some of the reasons behind it as a way, perhaps, of providing some form of freedom from the ensnarement of the illusion.

Those of you who are old souls, which is true of all in this circle, have a very clear understanding of the Divine—of that perfect, unlimited light, which you may call the Eternal, the Absolute, or God, or Q'uo's term, the one infinite Creator. It does not matter what you call it. The name is but a label for that which cannot be limited by the labels we give it. We each have an understanding of what we mean by that which I prefer to simply label God.

In this dark night of the soul, we see the perfection of that energy and our own seemingly futile attempts to reflect that perfection. We despair. And out of that despair arises a sense of unworthiness. We despair that we can never fully merge with that light and love toward which we so deeply yearn. We despair of our own self-perceived limits and fear in our inability to transcend those limits so that a sense of unworthiness seems almost to become a necessary part of our path. Why?

Well, on the ultimate plane there is no worthy or unworthy and never was. On the relative plane, you must come to know your worthiness. And one of the best tools that can be offered to aid that learning is the pain of feeling unworthiness.

I am asking Barbara here if I may use her as somewhat of an example. At one time she spent some weeks at a meditation retreat in which she was looking at the residual feelings of unworthiness within herself. I asked her to use this analytic approach, which I introduced to you yesterday, when a thought arose. For example, simply seeing the being next to her immersed in meditation, the thought of her own unworthiness arose.

There were many senior dharma teachers at this retreat, by which I would mean highly experienced teachers in her tradition. So, the first few days as she sat next to these famous teachers, there arose in her mind a sense of comparing herself. And then she would look at that thought: "What is this thought? Where did it come from? From my old-mind patterns of unworthiness." And then I would ask her to ask herself, "In this moment, sitting here, all of us in this room, all seventy of us, is there anyone here who is unworthy? No. Am I unworthy? No. Have I ever been unworthy? No. Then what is this arising of a sense of unworthiness?" And in asking that question she could see that it was old-mind's way of handling a sense of separation or aloneness, perhaps an arising of anger because she couldn't hear or some other discomfort, and a way of old-mind's explaining it to itself. It was a way of dealing with her pain, a story of the mind which seemed to separate her from the direct experience of some pain. She could see that it had been more comfortable to simply put on the cloak "unworthy" than to look at the awareness of the pain. Unworthiness became an escape from that which was more painful to be with than the sense of unworthiness. It was very clear to her each time she looked that in that moment, looking with bare perception of the sense experiences of that moment, unworthiness was illusion. And yet, it yawned before her as a giant chasm.

As she looked, she could see into past lives and into this life the millions of times that she had enacted that process. She began to see it as a bare plain, just slightly inclined, onto which drops of rain fell. A drop of rain that could not soak into the ground ran off, creating the faintest scratch in the earth. The next drop of rain hitting in the vicinity of that scratch ran into the scratch, carving it a tiny bit deeper. Ten drops and you have an eighth of an inch of earth worn away … a thousand drops, a million drops: a river, and eventually the Grand Canyon.

But it is all illusion, an illusion heightened by each occasion of buying into the illusion. When it was clearly seen as illusion—that there has never been unworthiness, and in this moment there is not unworthiness and the process of clear seeing was not one of an hour or a day but of week after week of deep meditation, of constant mindfulness during the process of this retreat—suddenly something clicked into place: "This is all illusion. There has never been worthiness or unworthiness. I don't have to be caught in this anymore. It is just habit and has nothing to do with reality." Skillful or unskillful: That might have to do with reality. Patient or impatient, selfish or generous: Those may reflect the actual movements in our hearts, but were they unworthy?

You must work with this process over and over and over, each time cutting through the illusion of unworthiness, seeing how it has arisen. There must be a courageous readiness to deal with those emotions which unworthiness has masked. (I will get into that idea in a moment.) There must be a readiness to give up unworthiness, which means touching on the deeper pain that unworthiness has hidden. The reward is the awareness: There is no worthiness or unworthiness, there is only God.

What happened for Barbara, then, was that as wisdom cut through the illusion and as mercy tempered the pain that had led to grasping at the illusion, the thoughts of worthy and unworthy simply ceased to arise. The habit was broken.

I am not suggesting that she will never experience a sense of unworthiness again. But after she left that retreat, each time that sense of unworthiness has arisen, it has been clearly seen immediately as illusion, self-liberating … *pop!* goes the balloon, so that she is able to come back again to the clear perception that transcends worthiness and unworthiness, and then to ask, "What emotions have given rise to this illusion?" and to tend lovingly to those emotions.

Let us, then, look at what unworthiness does mask. There are many possibilities and I cannot cover the full range of them. I want to speak to two of the most common. One of the main catalysts that leads many of you into a sense of unworthiness is parental neglect or other abuse in your early childhoods. This does not need to be monumental abuse. Even the baby that is loved may be greeted by a grouchy parent at 3 a.m. The baby may feel the difference between that parent that greets it with love and dries it, feeds it, and that parent that stumbles in yawning, feeling a deep irritation because it is exhausted and its sleep is interrupted. The baby will feel the withholding of love at that time. Feeling the anger directed at it, the baby will often return a sense of anger.

So, we are not just talking about what you term abuse, but the distortion that occurs with the infant's or child's anger. The child is helpless and fully dependent on the adult. It needs to form a bond of love with that adult which parents it, singular or plural. It learns early that when it responds to the adult with anger, the adult, who was often less than fully cognizant of its own reactions, reacts with anger.

Back to the child: It needs to be loved. That is its overriding need. So, it quickly picks up the messages, "What can I do to be loved? If I play your game, you'll love me?" That game varies from family to family. In the worse cases, the child must allow itself to be a recipient of real abuse, and the only way it can do that is by denying its own rage. It learns that its own rage runs contrary to its overriding need to be loved. How does it deal with that rage? If the child is right and expresses that rage, it casts itself out of the boundaries of the adult's acceptance; therefore, the adult must be right.

Unworthiness becomes the tool by which a child suppresses the rage. It tells itself, "I deserved this abuse" because the alternative is unthinkable: "I did not deserve this abuse; therefore, this adult is wrong and I must contradict this adult, putting myself out of the reach of its acceptance and love." The child simply lacks the strength to do that.

So, unworthiness becomes the armor over the rage. Even in those cases of non-abuse, the same pattern is true, but it is harder to see. The child does feel rage toward that adult and it is usually not permitted the expression of that rage. It is told, "Your anger is bad." That is a pattern of your culture, the distortion of your culture.

When you are feeling unworthiness, then, a helpful tool for working with that unworthiness is to simply ask yourself, "What might I be feeling now if I wasn't feeling unworthy? Can I give myself permission to get in touch with that emotion? Can I forgive myself for feeling that emotion? I do not need to fling my rage at another and I do not need to deny it. If I was seriously abused and I feel rage at that, it is okay to feel that rage. It is not unspiritual. It is just feeling rage."

You cannot get rid of rage by denying its presence. The open admission of your emotions is the beginning of allowing yourself to transcend those emotions and cease your ownership and identification with them, to begin to view them simply as passing clouds which need no special reaction, only compassion for the pain they cause.

If you were not seriously abused, you may have learned unworthiness for other reasons. Perhaps you were raised by a very judgmental parent who always said, "This is bad; that is bad." Well, that is a kind of abuse, perhaps less serious than sexual molestation or hitting, but still is a kind of abuse. Or perhaps you were lovingly raised by a non-judgmental parent, but there was still rage and shame about that rage.

Another reason for the arising of a sense of unworthiness is that fear, "Will my needs be met?" teamed with the solidifying of the ego self, the arising of jealousy or greed, and the harsh self-judgment that arises when one experiences that jealousy or greed. This, too, has been learned from the adult who said, "You shouldn't be selfish. You should share." Is there anybody here who didn't hear that as a child? Yes, of course, it would be good if we could all share. But to enforce on the child, "You shouldn't be selfish," is to tell the child that its feelings are bad. How much better if the wise adult can tell the child, "I know you're afraid that your needs won't be met. I know you feel anger and fear about giving this." Then, the child can make the decision with support to move beyond its fear, without judging its own fear.

But this has not been the pattern of your culture. Again, why? Because you have all chosen this sense of unworthiness as a catalyst to your growth. You have all chosen birth into this culture and into its particular distortions. You choose the conditions for birth that will offer you the best opportunities for learning. You do not choose incarnative conditions for comfort and convenience. Yes, it is painful. So, what else is new? Are you here to learn or are you not here to learn? You are not incarnated to stop feeling emotions, but to find equanimity with those emotions and compassion for all beings who have emotions.

Instead of waging war with those incarnative experiences which you have moved into, can you begin to embrace them? They are not garbage to be gotten rid of. They are, perhaps, the waste products to be turned back into the soil and become the nutrients for growth; not garbage, but compost. How can you make your sense of unworthiness into compost instead of trying to throw it out? How can you transmute your anger so that it becomes the catalyst for compassion?

So, you have heard the parent or adult say over and over, "You should share. You should not be greedy." But greed arises. Desire arises. Here is where we again move to the tools of meditation and the nurturing of wisdom-mind, which begins to see how greed and desire arise, thereby cutting through the identification with greed or desire as "mine," allowing them to arise and dissolve without dwelling on them or owning them. This wisdom becomes one of the nutrients for the arising compassion for that human that keeps getting caught in patterns of greed or jealousy, so that you cease to hate yourself when those emotions arise. They cease to become a catalyst for unworthiness, but become a reminder for compassion.

I could speak to each of you in this room for an hour or more about how these principles apply to your specific situations. We, of course, do not have the time for that, nor is it necessary. You are each very capable of understanding it for yourselves. Please know how fully you are supported in this work. It is truly the work for which you took birth and will lead you to the healing for which you took birth. I would pass the microphone now to Q'uo. That is all.

Q'uo: We are those of Q'uo. Greetings once again in love and light. We ask your cooperation at this time.

(The group is asked to shout, "Ha! Ha! Ha!")

Group: Ha! Ha! Ha!

We thank each for the instant rise in energy.

How does this organ of reason you call the brain work, which you are so desiring to work to your spiritual benefit? We have described the birth of consciousness of light within as the little Christ child, nurtured in the manger of your heart. Now let us describe this same situation using other ways of description.

The analogy of the computer is also fruitful. You see, you are not one but two life forms which cooperate to offer this rich experience you call the incarnation. The first creature is your physical vehicle. This instinctually-driven creature is at one with all that there is, for it is a second-density being. Each cell within your physical vehicle vibrates with the love and light of the infinite One, and its instinctual desires are for all energies to harmonize.

The intellectual organ of this creature is driven by distinctions, the basic program being very much the 0:1 [of binary operations], the dynamics betwixt the characteristics. The mind which you could realize as biocomputer has its priorities. These priorities are fixed by the computer within, based upon experience. Of the complete range of catalyst which assaults the physical senses, perhaps 2% of these sense impressions are used first. These sense impressions which have been given priority have to do with survival, comfort and finally what may loosely be called preferences or happiness. As you gain experience, these priorities may settle and change somewhat; however, they remain logic-driven.

You carry within you what could be called an operating system which works only with expanded memory. Its programs are deeper than the programs of the biocomputer operating system of your second-density creature. Within the programs of this operating system lie archetypical structures which only flash into the normal biocomputer like the haunting, with a melody which can so easily be missed. Yet within this expanded operating system's programs lie truth and virtual reprogramming aids which do far more to reprioritize the biocomputer than all the earnest study and effort you can galvanize to life within your increasingly reluctant self.

Now, how to trigger (this instrument would say boot) this expanded operating system? Each of you knows the answer. It is triggered by your meditation and contemplation. The key is silence.

We ask each to become aware of the preciousness of the moments of silence you carve for yourself out of the all-too-preciously-short material you call time. It is self-loving, indeed, to create these moments of touching into that bottomless well of silent listening into which is poured light without measure and from which you may drink until you have no thirst.

The expanded memory's gift is at once unique and utterly intimate, expressing your deepest authenticity and completely impersonal, for just a tiny bit beneath the surface of your uniqueness lies your universality. This is the second life form that you now seek to nurture and which now seeks to nurture you, for even from the cradle this Christ child reaches out and loves you, for the Creator loves first. Your love of any entity, including the Creator, is a reflection—love reflected in love.

How this baby consciousness loves to love. Let the cradle of your heart, then, be made soft and your breathing deep as you rock this consciousness to more and more vigorous life within you. This is the being which marries, even melds with this second-density creature to produce that unique being—the human—which is both of the earth, born and dying, and of the universe, loved and loving forever. This unlikely combination is perfectly suited to beholding a life and assigning to the impressions received as you go through that life, increasingly meaningful values.

The biocomputer is very useful in going to the grocery, in attending to the errands, in becoming a scholar, in furnishing you with the knowledge necessary to begin and continue ways of making the living and taking care of personal responsibilities which you have chosen to undertake. At the same time, these sense impressions received by this biocomputer are also useful in expanded ways to one who has become aware of this expanded Christ Consciousness which has sprung into life within your flesh, so that you become also a spiritual animal complete. Even within the flesh this transcendence is utterly complete. And the energies which are finite to systems run by logic may become infinite as the larger system is more and more accessed, until it is up and fully running, fully integrated into the biocomputer.

In addition to the use of silence, we encourage each to examine the self for its gifts, whether they be of the arts or the sciences or any gift whatsoever. For all things may be used to spiritual good in those whose gifts are dedicated to the infinite One.

And lastly, as the expanded system becomes comfortable within and when things begin to be seen with new priorities, that long and level plain which is the routine day may begin increasingly to be perceived in more and more of an upraised and joyful posture until this level plain becomes full of the foothills and amazingly craggy mountains which are so interesting, and which so rest the weary eye. Going to the place of employment, working through the day, coming home to do the chores and put the weary self to rest may well be all of the room you need in which to create the accurate perception of heaven with all of its glorious houses and mansions.

Here is high romance as well as greatest difficulty. Here is light inexpressible as well as spiritual moonlight. And as you walk the paths of your days, you may move up and down the scales of perception with increasing ease as you begin to find the pure freedom of that logic which transcends distinction and partakes more and more of the values of love.

We would speak more upon this in the final session. For now, we leave this instrument in the love and in the light of the one infinite Creator.

L/L Research

L/L Research is a subsidiary of Rock Creek Research & Development Laboratories, Inc.

P.O. Box 5195
Louisville, KY 40255-0195

www.llresearch.org

Rock Creek is a non-profit corporation dedicated to discovering and sharing information which may aid in the spiritual evolution of humankind.

ABOUT THE CONTENTS OF THIS TRANSCRIPT: This telepathic channeling has been taken from transcriptions of the weekly study and meditation meetings of the Rock Creek Research & Development Laboratories and L/L Research. It is offered in the hope that it may be useful to you. As the Confederation entities always make a point of saying, please use your discrimination and judgment in assessing this material. If something rings true to you, fine. If something does not resonate, please leave it behind, for neither we nor those of the Confederation would wish to be a stumbling block for any.

CAVEAT: This transcript is being published by L/L Research in a not yet final form. It has, however, been edited and any obvious errors have been corrected. When it is in a final form, this caveat will be removed.

© 2009 L/L Research

The Aaron/Q'uo Dialogues, Session 22
September 26, 1993

(This session was preceded by a period of tuning and meditation.)

Barbara: I'm going to share my tuning process out loud and then invite you to join me in it, substituting whatever differences you want, to make it personally appropriate for you.

Moving attention to the breath, coming to center, to that level of awareness that is aware of all awareness itself … not caught in any of it, just watching it come and go, resting in that space of Pure Awareness … feeling this that I call myself connected to all that is, opening, expanding outward, dropping away boundaries, breathing myself out to all that is and inviting it back in to me … I offer my intention for the session: to manifest my energy as purely as I can in service to all beings for the alleviation of suffering and toward the liberation of all beings. I invite in that spirit which would like to speak through me in harmony with that intention.

Feeling Aaron's energy, I challenge it: "Are you that which I have come to know as Aaron?" "Yes." "Do you come with a principle of love in service to all beings?" "Yes." "Do you come as a disciple of that which is an embodiment of truth for me, which is that energy that I have come to know as Jesus, the Christ?" "Yes."

Aaron: I am Aaron. With that collecting of our energies and mutuality of motivation and commitment, I return the microphone to my brother/sister/friend Q'uo, who wishes to offer you some closing thoughts. Then Q'uo will return the microphone to me to answer some of your questions and offer my own closing. And finally we will join together in a very brief and simple Sufi dance. To Q'uo … That is all.

Q'uo: We are those of Q'uo. It is time now to greet you for the last time in this weekend of sessions of working in the love and in the light of the one infinite Creator.

We who are of the principle of Q'uo cannot express to you how grateful we are for this extended and exhilarating opportunity to share our humble thoughts with you. Your service to us is extreme, for as we teach you, we learn from how you hear us; and this represents our means of growing in love and service to the infinite Creator.

We of the confederation of angels and planets in the service of the infinite Creator have been called the brothers and sisters of sorrow, for we were inspired to come to this planetary influence because of the great cry of pain and sorrow which you had been sending out during especially these past two hundred years, and more especially the past fifty.

We have seen how your factories and technology have encouraged in your culture the opportunities for leisure, the blessing of time which is given beyond that time in which you must make your daily living. We have seen how this same factory and technology-driven cultural system has thrown up for you a culture which attempts always to distract and trivialize the day-to-day leisure. This is, indeed, in its own kind of balance. *(The last sentence of this paragraph did not record.)*

We do not condemn nor suggest that you condemn technology or factories, or your media programs, newspapers, magazines, fashion and all the culture based upon artificially produced renown, but we suggest to you that you are in possession of free will in all matters. We encourage you to make judicious use of all your time, all your space, all your relationships, leavening all earnestness with high spirits and the light of sarcasm, irony, puns and bad jokes. Be reckless with your laughter and generous with your sarcastic comments. The seemingly trivial moments of self-parody and parody of others are like yeast, lightening the whole of the texture of your living.

We hope that you may practice the art of the spiritual vocation, realizing that whatever you do in your living to create the energy of money may or may not be an obviously spiritual task, yet this is irrelevant to the living of the spiritual vocation. For within you is the heart's eye, the eye of that great consciousness which you are nurturing into strong and vigorous life during this incarnation. This eye sees with care and compassion, moistening the dry duty with the living waters of spiritual significance and context. The spiritual vocation is that which puts into a context all of one's experiences within incarnation.

Do not attempt to haul yourself into some discipline where you will be spiritual, but simply attempt in each present moment to be yourself and to respond as yourself, not being defeated by the thoughts of, "I should … I ought to …" but looking within for where the love is and finding that thread opening to more of that material within, so that you are constantly finding new springs in the topology of your mind.

The Creator lies before your face and in your face. You open your eyes and see the creation of the Father. You gaze in your fellow human's eyes and see the Creator. It is a wonderful masked ball. We hope you enjoy the many dances of life.

And lastly, we wish you to know with assurance beyond any doubt that we are with those who call to us, not to channel as through this instrument, for that would be an impingement, but to be as the carrier wave of love so that you need never be completely alone.

(The remainder of this session did not record.) ❧

Sunday Meditation
October 17, 1993

Group question: The question this afternoon comes from Session Number 41, *Book II* of *The Law of One*. We would simply like Q'uo to comment on any or all portions of this question.

QUESTIONER: In trying to build an understanding from the start, you might say, starting with intelligent infinity and getting to our present condition of being, I think that I should go back and investigate our sun since it is the sub-Logos that creates all that we experience in this particular planetary system.

Will you give me a description of our sun?

RA: I am Ra. This is a query which is not easily answered in your language, for the sun has various aspects in relation to intelligent infinity, to intelligent energy, and to each density of each planet, as you call these spheres. Moreover, these differences extend into the metaphysical or time/space part of your creation.

In relationship to intelligent infinity, the sun body is, equally with all parts of the infinite creation, part of that infinity.

In relation to the potentiated intelligent infinity which makes use of intelligent energy, it is the offspring, shall we say, of the Logos for a much larger number of sub-Logoi. The relationship is hierarchical in that the sub-Logos uses the intelligent energy in ways set forth by the Logos and uses its free will to co-create the, shall we say, full nuances of your densities as you experience them.

In relationship to the densities, the sun body may physically, as you would say, be seen to be a large body of gaseous elements undergoing the processes of fusion and radiating heat and light.

Metaphysically, the sun achieves a meaning to fourth through seventh density according to the growing abilities of entities in these densities to grasp the living creation and co-entity, or other-self, nature of this sun body. Thus by the sixth density the sun may be visited and inhabited by those dwelling in time/space and may even be partially created from moment to moment by the processes of sixth density entities in their evolution.

QUESTIONER: In your last statement did you mean that the sixth density entities are actually creating manifestations of the sun in their density? Could you explain what you meant by that?

RA: I am Ra. In this density some entities whose means of reproduction is fusion may choose to perform this portion of experience as part of the beingness of the sun body. Thus you may think of portions of the light that you receive as offspring of the generative expression of sixth-density love.

QUESTIONER: Then could you say that sixth-density entities are using that mechanism to be more closely co-creators with the infinite Creator?

RA: I am Ra. This is precisely correct as seen in the latter portions of sixth density seeking the experiences of the gateway density.

(Carla channeling)

We are those of Q'uo. Greetings in the love and in the light of the one infinite Creator. The pause which you have experienced before this contact has been somewhat more lengthy than our usual time of adjustment with this instrument. However, this instrument was also picking up other signals and there was time needed, as you would say, for straightening out the traffic jam.

We always try to mention these bits of detail concerning the mechanics of the channeling process in order that those who study it may become more nearly able to use the practices more and more skillfully. It is always well to take any amount of time needed by a channel in order for that channel to assure itself that it does indeed have the desired contact. We cannot overemphasize the centrality of this concern to the practice of channeling.

You wish to investigate further into the sun-body which we shall call "sun," as that is your appellation for it. And indeed, you may well find this sun-body to be provocative and interesting, for it quite obviously and literally is the light of the world. All that each of you thinks of as a life within the Earth plane thrives because of the sun, its radiant warmth, and the energies which it and its co-entities in creation have upon the world as seen, as you would say, and indeed upon each of you.

Let us move to the beginning where there is only intelligent energy created by free will, which creates unpotentiated love, which in turn, it being the first articulation of singular characteristic, out of this singular characteristic, creates one thing—the photon.

This photon is timeless and spaceless. It is unity and infinity. It does not have number. It is solid, that is, in its estate as light limitless, it is solid. All that there is, dwells in *(inaudible)* of that one original Thought. And at the level of this one great original Thought there is, eternally, the endless creation of light or what you call the photon.

We refrain from calling the first emanation of the sun-body light, for we wish to distinguish between the timeless, spaceless light which is limitless and a child of this light which is radiation of the light as you experience it upon your level of existence and as others experience it in theirs.

At the photon level, light is all that there is. This limitless light is the background created by Love before any articulated creation made from Light. This Light Everlasting, shall be as always, infinitely creating in an infinite and eternal present. At this level, light is a thought. That is, it is a perfect creation of a thought. It does not contain error but is a creature of utter Love containing the infinite intelligence without distortion.

Within the context of third-density lessons of love, this plane of light has little substance in reference to questions of moving from third to fourth density, learning the lessons of love. It is to the light which interests your peoples as an ideal is to a philosopher. Yet this is the environment, shall we say, within which the infinite Creator has being. This is for that mystery which is the Creator.

The way entities seeking to love the one Creator may visualize moving into the highest of all tabernacles, pure, limitless light, there is this place where light is still, for it completely fills all that there is. At this zero time/space intersection, there is the seed of all infinity and all eternity.

Once free will begins to operate and that great Logos begins its creation, the interest of seekers in investigating light often moves toward that radiation from the sun. Each already realizes that we have said before that the light which seems to radiate from your sun-body is that which has builded all that you see. All things are made of light—this instrument, the microphone which this instrument has about its neck, the clothes, the furniture, the Earth, the sky. These things all are created of light.

The characteristic of light to your plane is such that entities cannot see or often imagine how literally all things are made of light. This is in part due to the fact that the functions of light operating within your density cause the formations to lack obvious resemblance to that which is light. The operation of light and building structures is such that light appears as magnetism or electromagnetism or fields. We apologize for this instrument's lack of proper vocabulary.

Thus, when the intelligent light creates, it does indeed use light. However, this is seen as form, color, shading, size—characteristics measurable, visible and so forth. The objects are seen that they are in the way they are, that is, that they have the shape and form they have, [which] is known to be the result of each object having a field of energy that somehow keeps all together. In investigating questions concerning the use of alternative ways of healing, this point is well to remember.

A characteristic of light, which is indicative of the range of its metaphysical characteristics, is that light is inherently intelligent and, therefore, any amount of infinite light can grasp, as though it were an entity, the heartfelt communications made to it. This ranges from something as simple as the sun-body being aware when the radiation of the sun touches your skin and you praise the light and the love of the infinite One. You have communicated with the infinite Creator.

Entities who have followed sun worshipping practices have been known among your peoples for all of your history, the reason being that there is indeed that opportunity to converse with the, shall we say, as this instrument does, Lord of Light. And these conversations uplift the entity within. Again, when an entity goes into meditation and calls for the limitless light, and then remains in that light, basking in its glow, that entity is tabernacling with the one infinite Creator.

At this time we would have this entity open the meeting to questions.

Questioner: Could you tell me how the sixth-density reproductive function of creating light by what we see as fusion is accomplished and is there more there than what we see?

We are those of Q'uo. That which you see as radiation from the sun is an offspring of the mating by fusion practiced by some of sixth-density entities. You would more likely find accuracy in grasping that such who choose to become a portion of the sun-body to create offspring move to the center of that celestial body. The immediate offspring of this mating is more a "quality" than a "thing," more a tiny being than a measurable substance.

This tiny being, created as the Logos Itself has created, is a special class, shall we say, of light. Not all rays from the sun are the children of sixth-density love, however, that aspect of light which is healing is aided greatly by the working of the immediate offspring of those who choose to create their progeny by fusion within the sun. This is a sacrifice for the sixth-density entities in that they are not able then to enjoy the company and the living, shall we say, with their offspring. However, the offspring have the advantage of being only half way, shall we say, aware of free will. Thus, during their tenure within the sun-body, they may intelligently choose to drench the radiation, in general, which comes from the sun to those upon your sphere so that the maximum amount of healing energy moves into that sphere and into those locations wherein a prayer or pain has announced the existence of need for healing.

Is there another query, my brother?

Questioner: The rays of the sun provide light for the Earth which causes photosynthesis to happen in our second-density plants. It causes the cycle of rain and evaporation that continues to bring life. I'm wondering if these are some of the reasons that human beings from thousands of years in the past have worshipped the sun or have they also been aware of the metaphysical qualities of the sun as the reason for their worship?

We are those of Q'uo. In most cases, there is the sun worship because of the reasons you placed forth. In a few instances, some metaphysical material concerning the sun has been known in much distorted form, such as during the ancient Egyptian civilizations.

May we answer further, my brother?

Questioner: No, thank you very much. I appreciate everything you had to say.

Very well, my brother. Thank you for most interesting questions. Is there another query at this time?

Questioner: I was wondering, Q'uo, when our third-density fusion is achieved by scientists who manipulate matter to achieve it, is there a sixth-density entity involved in it? Can you comment on this phenomenon?

I am Q'uo. My brother, as you rest upon your seat within this domicile, you are immediately touching all densities. Every possibility lies directly at the zero point of your present moment. It is difficult to express in your language the fullness of creation. In a [man-]made fusion power [plant] there would be no more sixth-density entities than if that power plant were not there. However, there would be other beings, which also are children of light, sometimes called elementals, which enliven and particularize light and act as ambassadors, shall we say, to those upon whom light falls.

May we answer further, my brother?

Questioner: So what you are saying, if I grasp it in my thinking, is that thermonuclear fusion does not necessarily mean sixth-density beings are there as they choose to be in the sun. Is that correct?

We are Q'uo. It is correct that there would not be sixth-density mating within a thermonuclear fusion in a power plant. Nor would such be desirable, for some of the operations of entities living within fusion create in that fusion a perpetual motion machine, shall we say, in effect of an ever enlarging kind as seen within your relative mathematical picture. This would be extremely undesirable for one of your power plants, for it would blow up. Thusly, one would not wish to have that particular activity going on in a power plant.

Is there a further query, my brother?

Questioner: No.

We are those of Q'uo. We feel very full of gratitude that you have once again sat for a working with desire to seek and know the truth. We thank you for allowing us to speak our thoughts to you, knowing that you will subject them to your discriminative faculty. With you we feel the beauty of this occasion. The blending of vibrations is beautiful to us. And with reluctance, as always, we take our leave of you through this instrument, encouraging each to seek and keep the light touch, to hope and to dream in the love and in the light of the one infinite Creator. We are those of Q'uo. Adonai. Adonai. ✺

L/L Research

L/L Research is a subsidiary of Rock Creek Research & Development Laboratories, Inc.

P.O. Box 5195
Louisville, KY 40255-0195

www.llresearch.org

Rock Creek is a non-profit corporation dedicated to discovering and sharing information which may aid in the spiritual evolution of humankind.

ABOUT THE CONTENTS OF THIS TRANSCRIPT: This telepathic channeling has been taken from transcriptions of the weekly study and meditation meetings of the Rock Creek Research & Development Laboratories and L/L Research. It is offered in the hope that it may be useful to you. As the Confederation entities always make a point of saying, please use your discrimination and judgment in assessing this material. If something rings true to you, fine. If something does not resonate, please leave it behind, for neither we nor those of the Confederation would wish to be a stumbling block for any.

CAVEAT: This transcript is being published by L/L Research in a not yet final form. It has, however, been edited and any obvious errors have been corrected. When it is in a final form, this caveat will be removed.

© 2009 L/L Research

Sunday Meditation
October 31, 1993

Group question: The question this afternoon has to do with how the average spiritual seeker who works for a living from nine to five and who has other responsibilities and who feels quite rushed and pressed for time, how this person can find time and space for spiritual seeking and for making contact with that sense of unity and self that can sustain the rest of the week, or how the seeker finds the spiritual self in the week or in the meditation.

(Carla channeling)

I am with this instrument. I am Q'uo. Greetings in the love and the light of the one infinite Creator. It is a privilege and a blessing to speak with this group of beloved entities at this time/space. We are most grateful for the opportunity to share our thoughts with you and appreciate greatly this company and chance to blend our essence with your own. As always we ask for the privilege of being heard as brothers and sisters, not as those with any final authority. We always encourage each to discriminate carefully and take in only those thoughts and perceptions which feel to you to be your personal truths.

We come to this question with a wry smile upon our faces for we frankly envy you the confusion and struggle which form the background for your query. We are able to expend a nearly infinite amount of time and space with things which in your density would be considered ecclesiastical or philosophical but certainly metaphysical. There is not the necessity for busying ourselves with the gathering of assets which occupies so much of your peoples' time and energy. And to the degree that we do not go, as this instrument would say, out into the world we lack the context from which we might put into vibrant action those truths of the heart which sustain the spiritual life of us each and all. It is in your density, in your thick atmosphere of confusion which your illusion so richly furnishes which has the great privilege and the great teaching situation of forcing souls into direct confrontation with time and space and the appropriating of those things that is time and space either to show forth that which is in the heart or not to show forth that which is in the heart.

This may be hard to appreciate and we grasp that, however, from our biased point of view we look at the crowded time schedules of your peoples and we see the opportunity for great witnessing in that. We witness at all times and in all places, one might say is so, yet we have no choice, actually, for in our density our thoughts and experiences are very much, not precisely had in common but held in common, each witnessing to each with every moment. To your peoples is given the blindness, deafness and dumbness of the, what you would call, flesh. You cannot hear others' thoughts nor can you perceive the place within each other which you have in common which is the heart of common worship, shall we call it.

Without being able to say precisely why, your peoples have gathered together to express spiritual feelings since the beginning of your density as an instinct. Like all instincts, it is true. You do have every reason to gather at a time and place to express love, compassion, worship or whatever words you personally would choose to show forth your love of the mystery that is Deity and to anchor the outworking of this love within your environment.

Now, just such an occasion of common worship, shall we call it, is taking place and giving to us the opportunity to share thoughts. Let us express some of why this is efficacious or perceived by us to be so. It is within the context of your brothers and sisters that each seeker has his personal pilgrimage. No entity within third density is truly alone or isolated, spiritually speaking. This is foreign to your basic nature. The context for life as we understand it is social. When the purpose for gathering is the desire to express love and the desire to serve that occasion becomes a very big party in ways you cannot see. Many discarnate entities which this instrument would call angels flock to the planned site of this common gathering of spirit. This then strengthens and clarifies the energies which are coming to that occasion and enables those who do attend to feel differently. It is as though the simple room becomes the holy place, the empty church suddenly filled with invisible energy.

The first way, then, that entities who are too busy with things of the world, as this instrument would put it, the first way they can reclaim time and space for worship of the one infinite Creator and filling of the heart is by gathering. One alone who meditates and seeks is tremendously powerful. Two together are far more than their addition and three or more become the universe. It is difficult simply to express how the gathering of a precious few charges the occasion with such power. However, we assure you that as you sit and listen to these words you are in a vast and powerful company, witnessed each by many whose only hope is to strengthen the light and clarify the life within the combined energies of the group.

This entity is channeling at this time not in one of your usual religious places but in a small abode, a home, and yet this humble venue might as well be a cathedral, for it hosts a mighty company and indeed those who wish to experience common worship need not necessarily go to a place that has already been created or join where they may not feel welcome, for any small group can dedicate the treasure of time and position and begin to have such gatherings. The small gatherings do indeed gather and express an infinity of that which marks the uplifting or spiritual, that is, each feels the blessing of presence and intention and as these energies interweave there is spun a beautiful tower which stretches to your heavens which lifts all spirit within the charmed circle and as this energy is lifted to the infinite One the reflection of this energy rains down not just upon each present but upon all of the planetary energy into which each is grounded. So that the gathering together is not just for those present but indeed brings as witnesses all of those upon your planet who seek the one infinite Creator and lift their eyes to search [for] the light.

There are other ways in which that powerful treasure of time may be better spent but none is quite as powerful as the decision to set aside the time and the place to say, "First I will be here. First I will provide for my heart to touch its true home, to breath the air of things holy and innocent of the dirt of living."

Let us for the rest consider how time is used because a common meeting to worship is so powerful many times entities who so gather perhaps once within your week might feel that this one occasion will put into the energies of the spirit, mind and body enough to furnish good memories all the week. However, this is not normally the case. Normally, the morning does not automatically call the seeker to rivet its attention upon the Creator. Normally, the morning light calls the seeker to more mundane and daily considerations. What to be done? What to wear to do that which is to be done? Where to go in those clothes to do that which is to be done? How then to insert into this, shall we say, this running program of activities a time for stillness wherein that connection is remade with things holy and untouched by relativity and process?

There is the capability within each of you so to order the mind that a bell, shall we say, rings within every so often that says it is time to seek and know the infinite One. To make this occur within your mind there is the necessity for discipline. We suggest looking at the states of mind which you visit throughout the day, not an unusual day but the most normal and hectic of days and practice this looking at the self, listening to the self and ascertaining, gently but accurately, the most used states of mind. Find within this moving context of inner thought a comfortable place to insert the centering identification of self which is the marker for a location in time and space which is transformative, and when you have identified for yourself your subjective most favored state for inserting this centering then practice this repetitively.

The instructions are of necessity vague but we may be quite strict about this direction, that is, practice assiduously for this is the second way to move in mind into that identification of self in the context of seeking the one infinite Creator in all ways, in all things, which is the key to living the busy, hectic and seemingly confusing life of one who is active within third density and yet who has become able to remain within a spiritual context regardless of the physical location or the number of items which might be of necessity upon the mind of a daily and worldly nature.

There is much more that we can say upon this subject but for this working we feel this is enough material. We would circle about and close with that with which we opened, that is, our opinion that yours is a wonderful position to be in. It simply does not feel that way to you for you cannot see that which we can nor will you be able to discern the true nature of your condition. You simply must go on trust and faith and hope and that inspires all of us. We see you as love's witnesses within an illusion so thick that you do not feel each other's thoughts. This is something that we can only vaguely remember. For you to honor and love the infinite, original Logos and to so order your lives as to attempt to show forth your love and the Creator's love of you in all that you do is greatly inspirational to us for we know you are going on faith. You cannot see the beauty of your hopes, dreams and desires. You cannot know how successful you are.

It is our opinion that you in third density making the great choices between giving and receiving, between loving and risking, and being loved and not risking, we find your courage heartening and your hopes and desires and intentions beautiful and as each choice is made and that which blooms within unfolds yet one more petal we can only give thanks and rejoice. Please know that we are always with you, very willing to serve as one who meditates or as this instrument would say, prays with you, not in words but simply by our presence.

We thank you for your presence for together with you as we have focused upon this query we have been able to praise the one infinite Creator with a beauty and a joy that we could not have approached by ourselves. The blessing of humankind is humankind. The blessing of love is love and you are truer than you know or can ever know within your experience to the love which loved you first.

We would conclude this session through the one known as Jim. We are those of Q'uo, and leave this instrument in love and in light.

(Jim channeling)

I am Q'uo, and greet each again in love and in light through this instrument. At this time it is our privilege to ask if there may be any further queries to which we may speak.

Carla: I have two questions. Firstly, I would like to know your opinion on the possible effects that working as much as I expect I may have to this year for the church will have on my state of mind as a channel. Will being busier in the world mean that I need to do something different than I do usually in order to channel well? Will being busier affect that? Can you speak to that?

I am Q'uo, and am aware of your query, my sister. We can speak in general terms to suggest that as you are expending the energies of your mind, body and spirit complex in the increased energy required by experiencing the daily round of activities you will feel a certain need to feed yet another hunger and that hunger is the desire that each seeker has, to dwell with the One and to rest therein, that you may be nourished and supported in your life pattern. We would recommend that you keep your inner ear open that you may hear when the feeling for this nurturing is present and feed that hunger as it is asking to be fed. We can recommend only that you listen and feel as carefully as you work in the world of activity.

Is there a further query, my sister?

Carla: Yes, but I'd like to thank you for that answer because I think that's really straightforward and I am very much the kind of person that does do my work by thinking and feeling rather than thinking and knowing, so I appreciate that answer very much and I will …

Well, actually I have three questions because I just thought of another one, but along this same line, this week I have been more aware than usual of the people that depend on me to be a home to them. They're people that live all over the place and they have in common mostly that they are not particularly comfortable in the world and there is something about my nature that says to them, "This is a safe place," and I seem to function as a moving, living, walking-around home, in my being, in my having a big heart and I wonder—I can't be the only one and it can't just be women that do this. I know that some women and some men function as this kind of home.

Now, I was trying to think of a context for it and I couldn't, really. I know that it's like being a mother or a father, being a home. It's hard for me to know precisely what it is, but I do know if one of the people that needs me is thinking about something that's troubling them, whether it's S or whether it's N or whether it's D or who. Maybe this is a question for another time but as I get busier, still, when something like this, something like N's pain hits me this morning I have to respond. So I know that it works, regardless. That I guess that I have been concerned that getting busier I wouldn't be as good a home. Could you speak to that at all?

I am Q'uo, and am aware of your query, my sister. To some degree, we may speak, though we do not wish to influence your choices by speaking inappropriately. It is true that you have the quality of acceptance and freely given love that provides others with a safe haven and we are aware that there are many upon your plane who serve in this capacity. As you have surmised there are those of both of your biological sexes that offer themselves in this service as a result of their seeking …

(Side one of tape ends.)

(Jim channeling)

I am Q'uo, and am again with this instrument. It is more nearly the case that those of the female gender serve more frequently in this capacity for it is, in your culture, the female who provides the first and the most encompassing nurturing for the infant child. Thus, as you enter your round of activities you will find that the connections that you have formed with those who are within your care will be more apparent to you in those times where you are quiet in mind and body, those times of the beginning and the ending of your days. Thus you will find that there is a kind of communications center that will be functioning at these moments and the calls that are made will be felt more frequently and more intensely then.

Is there a further query, my sister?

Carla: Yes, Q'uo. It's been a concern of mine for some time that the one known as Jim and I are not making the absolute best use of these contacts that we have with you and that it would be even better to channel as equals, going back and forth the way Barbara and I do and I wondered … well, let me just say this, too. Also, the one known as Jim is channeling right now, this is … so it's not very easy to channel, I'm aware, but when the one known as Jim is being Jim the person he has a human opinion that I channel better and that is due to the fact that, culturally speaking, I have more use of more words and am more productive … I use more words to say things whereas I am aware, because I am not the one known as Jim, of the value of his seemingly brief and economical sentences.

It is my feeling that the very best use of the channel that we have would be going back and forth and using both of our energies to the fullest rather than mine, largely. Without your having to take sides, I wonder what you could say that would eliminate us both on this subject.

I am Q'uo, and am aware of your query, my sister and we shall attempt to speak through this instrument in some degree, though there is some resistance. This instrument has certain qualities that could be useful in the channeling process as they are being utilized at this time. The one known as Carla has the ability to receive information of a finer and more precisely tuned nature that is expansive and quite intricate in its detail. The one known as Jim finds it more easy to channel both the life energies and the contact energies in forms which are more concrete and usable, as you may say. Thus, each instrument has abilities which are pronounced and which give each certain—we search for the correct terminology—talents and abilities are best utilized here.

Thus, though it would be possible to utilize each instrument in an exchange of contacts as you have experienced with the one known as Barbara, it would affect the nature of our contact by giving it two flavors, shall we say. This is, of course, at your discretion and we seek always to serve as we are asked.

Is there a further query, my sister?

Carla: Can you give a value—relative value—to the channeling as we have it now and the channeling that we would have if we traded it back and forth?

I am Q'uo, and we are aware of your query, my sister. Again, we shall attempt to speak upon this topic without going past that point of encouraging a decision in one direction or the other.

Carla: I understand.

[I am Q'uo.] It would be as though one message were spoken in different languages or dialects, shall we say. Again, the choice is yours.

Is there a further query, my sister?

Questioner: Not at this time. Thank you. Thank you very much and then thank the one known as Jim for trying, really.

I am Q'uo, and we again thank you, my sister. Is there another query at this time?

(Pause)

I am Q'uo, and we would take this opportunity to thank each present for again allowing us to join your circle of working. We are most inspired by your efforts and your dedication to continue upon this journey even though the journey seems difficult and confusing a great deal of your time.

Carla: Can I ask one more question that I thought of late?

I am Q'uo, and we welcome your query, my sister.

Carla: Bless you, Q'uo. It occurred to me just when I was letting what you said sink in, how would you rate the work that Barbara and I have done together because certainly we are coming at subjects from different points of view, certainly, yet I have felt very, very good about the … doing it together.

I am Q'uo and we are aware of your query, my sister. We are pleased with the efforts you have made with the one known as Barbara and, indeed, are quite pleased with all efforts which you have made for they have been made with a whole heart. We do not seek to rate any effort above another.

Is there any final query, my sister?

Carla: No. Thank you very much.

I am Q'uo, and again we thank each for inviting us this day to join you. At this time we shall take our leave of this group and this instrument, leaving each as always in the love and in the ineffable light of the one infinite Creator. We are known to you as those of Q'uo. Adonai, my friends. Adonai. ☥

L/L Research

Sunday Meditation
November 14, 1993

Group question: The question this afternoon has to do with the concept of spiritual pride as it is balanced with an honest appreciation of your own efforts. We're all engaged in one kind of big effort, to earn money, to do a life's work, to complete a certain job or task and we were wondering just how much motivation one can hope for from appreciating your own efforts and where to balance the amount of appreciation with developing it into spiritual pride and being overly pleased with yourself and perhaps complacent and … who knows what else.

(Carla channeling)

Greetings in the love and in the light of the one infinite Creator. We are known to you as those of Q'uo. May we say what a privilege it is to be with this group at this session of working. We especially wish to greet the one known as G as this is the first time he has joined this particular group. We hope that our thoughts may helpfully inform and offer directions for further consideration. However, we as always wish to emphasize that we have opinions rather than the absolute truth. These opinions are earned, shall we say, by experience, however, we as each of you are pilgrims still seeking that mystery which we know not as it recedes ever before our approach.

Take those opinions which feel to you like the remembrance of that which was already half-known. Leave behind any thought which constitutes a stumbling block before your own discriminate—we correct this instrument—discrimination.

Let us begin focusing upon the query about spiritual pride and good works by looking at the various stories the teacher known to you as Jesus told concerning good works and money, the parable concerning the stewards who were given money to keep for the owner who was to be gone. This parable focuses upon the amount of energy put into using the gift rather than the amount of each gift in monetary value. The one with the five dollars made five dollars more and was considered equal to the one who had two dollars and made two dollars more. However, to the one who simply kept that wealth of spirit even that which that slave had was taken away.

So, we feel that the positive acceptance of spiritual responsibility is not only that which seems good but that which has great value. Nor would we encourage those who serve the Creator to, shall we say, slap down the rising feelings of joy in service. Given the amount of spiritual gifts which you have, the parable would suggest moving further, attempting more, striving to be even more full of service, using all that you have to offer, ever more of that which is the bloom and blossom of your own inner spiritual life.

The currency of the spiritual life, the money, is the energy with which the seeker is willing to accomplish the attempt of doing that which the seeker's unique spiritual gifts suggest for his proper vocation. One entity may have a dramatic spiritual gift, a gift of healing, for instance. Another may have the spiritual gift of nurturing and spend the life dwelling with the children and the spouse and extended family. That one who has healed in its—we correct this instrument—in the process of living the devotional life has done the excellent thing. However, this excellence lies equally with that entity who has the modest gift, that does not shine before the eyes of all men, if that entity offers heart and flesh in the attempt to give that which he has.

Again, as we gaze at the parable given by the one known as Jesus, the Christ …

(Pause of sixty seconds.)

… we see that the sheer amount of labor when using the spiritual gift is not in and of itself that which makes one effort greater or better than another. That is to say, that in the parable concerning the payment of money to those who had worked all day and those who had worked a half a day and those who worked only one hour, all gained the same amount for their seemingly uneven labors.

We suggest that there is no accuracy in maintaining that one entity has done more than another because the effort was longer or harder. Rather it is the moving into the work which stems directly from the spiritual gifts given to the seeker that the assessment of value considers. The one who moves into service with the prayer of being used in accordance with the Creator's will, whether this entity wash the dishes or found the nation, it is the equal desire to serve which has the equal value metaphysically.

Now, what we are suggesting is that one cannot judge one's effort by the amount of time it has taken, by its difficulty or any other way except insofar as the consideration remains focused upon the opening of the heart in service to the one Creator. This instrument is often fond of saying that one should take something in life very seriously, some great ideal or truth. However, this something should never be the self.

Consider with us then how one can approach that greatly desired knowledge of "What are my spiritual gifts and how may I offer them?" The process of meditation, over time, is helpful in familiarizing the self with who that self is on the deeper levels. The whole process of attempting to become formally open to listening to the silent will of the one Creator is that which works many deeper levels to increase the flow of subconscious material through the limen[11] of consciousness so that more and more the meditator becomes aware of deeper truths or deeper gifts within its own self so that more and more it becomes easier to recognize the opportunities for service along the lines of one's particular spiritual gifts.

Once one has gone through this process and begun a life of service or perhaps simply begun serving in hopes of finding a life of service, [one] may simply open the consciousness to the fullest extent, having within that spoken desire that is spoken to the self to serve, not as "I will" but as "the Creator wills." This stance or posture of keen desire and open willingness will in time always produce not one but often several ways of moving into more service. It is to the one focused all along on spiritual value or quality that the circumstances will become clear as a pattern for good works, as this instrument would call them. In other words, it helps greatly when seeking proper spiritual work to know consciously that you are looking for it.

And again we say, spiritual service is the substance of all of those exchanges betwixt people and people or people and ideas wherein the seeker does attempt to witness to that point of view which is that of the servant desiring only to be called forth into service.

Now, let us suppose that all have found their spiritual service. This never occurs but for this discussion let us assume that one need look no further. Shall each seeker then be satisfied with the quality of good works it has produced? Perhaps by mentally answering this query in the head one can see that somehow there is no proper answer to that query. Somehow if one attempts to put the value here or there in work done by those who are serving one has again missed the point.

Those who pat the back after accomplishing spiritual works are not harming themselves in terms of the

---

[11] limen: a threshold.

value of the work. The harm to the self has nothing to do with whether the work is good or not. The harm comes to the servant when it allows the work to be subjected to this reasoning process. Yes, it is incorrect and distinctly unhelpful for a spiritual seeker to be proud of its accomplishments but more, it is irrelevant. As each attempts to increase the polarity of one's service, one is always caught and stopped abruptly in one way or another when it attempts to quantisize [quantify] or qualify the particular value of any spiritual work. Better is it to release these considerations completely.

When one gazes within attempting to become a better servant think not of the greatness of accomplishment or the other characteristics concerning such. Simply continue to ask, "How may I serve?" for there is no entity given Brownie points, as this instrument would say. Each seeker works upon itself and no other regardless of the spiritual work. Strip all from the mind that would suggest otherwise. Naked are you. You cannot be clothed with righteousness. You are clothed, each of you, my children, by the light of your desire to abandon all except the desire to serve.

How then will you know when you have gotten it right, as this instrument would say? May we say that to each of you the moment when you are one with the work, or, to put it another way, when there is a feeling of complete freedom when doing that activity you hope will serve, then shall you be able, not to pat the self upon the back, but to turn and give thanks, for the feeling of complete liberty is at the heart of the state of mind which does often signify service well done.

Any pride whatsoever is, though understandable, not relevant to the spiritual walk which attempts to express the bias towards compassion more and more.

At this time we would deal with one detail and then would continue through the one known as Jim. The detail concerns that pause which occurred during this transmission. We feel that to point out what is occurring during the channeling process from our point of view may be helpful to those who attempt to understand this particular phenomenon. This instrument had moved too deeply into the trance state and the request needed to be made to move more into energetic alertness. When this instrument felt the difference in vibration it spent some of your time moving completely throughout the environment being sure that there was the appropriate protection of the place, the working, and those within the circle. Only then was this instrument prepared to move forward.

This process was important in achieving the appropriate—we search for the word here—this instrument's word is setup or arrangement. It was only after some period that the arrangement of connections between source and instrument was appropriately made.

We thank you for your patience during this pause. It is always the good idea for the instrument who feels some change in energy to investigate that change rather than attempting to override it and we thank you for your patience in allowing us to express these last thoughts.

We would at this time move to the one known as Jim for the conclusion of this session of working. We leave this instrument in love and light. We are those known to you as Q'uo.

(Jim channeling)

I am Q'uo, and greet each again in love and in light through this instrument. At this time it is our privilege to offer ourselves in the attempt to speak to any other queries which those present may have for us. Is there another query at this time?

Carla: If no one else has a question, I have one but it's not really on this subject. I wonder if you could comment, Q'uo, on the unusually strong feeling I had of being levitated during the time where I was waiting to find out what was wrong during that pause. The whole beginning of the channeling I felt like I was almost being lifted off my seat. If you could comment in any way, I'd be interested.

I am Q'uo, and am aware of your query, my sister. We find as the contact with your instrument and indeed with any instrument over a period of time continues that there are side effects, shall we say, that go with the prolonged intensive contact. That you feel the sensation of weightlessness is simply a portion of this process by which you give yourself over to serving as an instrument and move into that portion of your subconscious mind that is partaking of the time/space portion of your illusion more fully than is normal.

Thus you feel the sensation of levitation or of a floating that corresponds to a more malleable environment in which your physical laws have little impact. Is there another query, my sister?

Carla: Yes. Thank you for that answer, though. So, we're not supposed to slap ourselves on the back and say, "Good job, good job," OK? But encouraging and exhorting and empowering others is always, has always seemed a part of being a servant and it just seems to me that encouraging the self along those lines—I don't know, I guess maybe when you're encouraging others it's more obvious that you're really praising the Lord, shall we say. When you're patting yourself on the back perhaps you forget that you're basically praising the Creator. It certainly seems that someone should get the praise! Can you comment on that feeling? And I'm a little confused, I mean I do feel that it is a spiritual thing—definitely you're supposed to encourage people in their efforts, so why not yourself?

I am Q'uo, and am aware of your query, my sister. The encouragement, to be most effective in hitting the heart of the illusion and its opportunities, needs to be focused upon the one Creator as fully as one is able at any given moment, which is to say that as one is able to see the effort and the entities involved as the Creator and is able to give praise and thanksgiving for both then one is giving the highest encouragement. We realize that there are many steps to this point and encouragement may take any form and serve a useful purpose. We know that those here gathered wish to give the utmost in all efforts. Thus we give you the ideal, reminding each that one will always fall short. To accept whatever one can do is to give the encouragement that is appropriate.

Is there a further query, my sister?

Carla: No, Q'uo, there isn't. Thank you very much.

I am Q'uo. Again we thank you, my sister. Is there another query at this time?

Questioner: I have a question, Q'uo, and it is a sort of a personal question so *(inaudible)* could possibly to comment in any way that you feel appropriate, including not at all. I was just wondering about my difficulty to stay in meditation and concentrate that I was noticing lately. Is there a way that I can look at it to be fruitful or am I missing something just in seeing that it is difficult? How can I work with it somehow?

I am Q'uo, and am aware of your query, my brother. We would recommend that as any activity of the mind is noticed while you are pursuing the meditative state that you take one step backwards in your mind and observe the activity as a passing event, thus redefining your meditative position in a larger context so that you always are aware that you seek that metaphysical moment of unity while observing the activities of your mind. Thus, the larger perspective will allow you to move more in harmony with the moment of meditation which you seek. Is there a further query, my brother?

Questioner: When I think about meditation I think the effort going into it is important rather than the actual amount of time spent within the illusion, yet there is a period to be devoted to tuning so there, I assume, is some minimum, perhaps I could say, minimum time required to get in tune and then move into the moment. Can you comment *(inaudible)* that?

(Side one of tape ends.)

(Jim channeling)

I am Q'uo, and am again with this instrument. The most important portion of the meditative experience is cultivating the desire to meditate. This may be done in an instant. All other effort is an addition to this foundation effort. Thus, if you wish to tune or to practice any form of meditation after desiring to do so, you refine this desire and work with it in a specific fashion and this working may take any amount of your time. However, to desire to meditate can be done in an instant. Is there a further query, my brother?

Questioner: No, Q'uo, *(inaudible)* is … thank you for the answer. I appreciate your *(inaudible)*.

I am Q'uo, and we thank you, my brother, once again. Is there another query at this time?

Questioner: I guess not, Q'uo.

I am Q'uo, and we would take this opportunity to express our great gratitude to each present for asking for our presence in your circle of working this day. We feel very privileged to be able to share our opinions with you and, as always, ask that you remember that we share that which has been helpful to us and we hope that you will take only those concepts that are helpful to you, leaving all others behind.

We, at this time, shall take our leave of this group, leaving each as always in the love and in the ineffable light of the one infinite Creator. We are known to you as those of Q'uo. Adonai, my friends. Adonai. ✤

L/L Research

L/L Research is a subsidiary of Rock Creek Research & Development Laboratories, Inc.

P.O. Box 5195
Louisville, KY 40255-0195

www.llresearch.org

Rock Creek is a non-profit corporation dedicated to discovering and sharing information which may aid in the spiritual evolution of humankind.

ABOUT THE CONTENTS OF THIS TRANSCRIPT: This telepathic channeling has been taken from transcriptions of the weekly study and meditation meetings of the Rock Creek Research & Development Laboratories and L/L Research. It is offered in the hope that it may be useful to you. As the Confederation entities always make a point of saying, please use your discrimination and judgment in assessing this material. If something rings true to you, fine. If something does not resonate, please leave it behind, for neither we nor those of the Confederation would wish to be a stumbling block for any.

CAVEAT: This transcript is being published by L/L Research in a not yet final form. It has, however, been edited and any obvious errors have been corrected. When it is in a final form, this caveat will be removed.

© 2009 L/L Research

Sunday Meditation
November 21, 1993

Group question: The question this afternoon has to do with the forgetting process that each of us goes through as we enter an incarnation. Ra has suggested that lessons we learn here with the forgetting process in place carry so much more weight in our total beingness than lessons learned when the forgetting process is not in place—when we remember our total nature and the total unity of all creation. And we're wondering some about how the forgetting process works, how it is put into place, and then how our remembering takes place and the progress that we make in our lives that's due to a remembering of the purpose and the goals.

(Carla channeling)

We are known to you as those of Q'uo. Greetings in the love and the light of the one infinite Creator. It is a privilege and a blessing to join your group's meditation this day. We thank you and bless you for this request to share our thoughts with you, for in this request you aid us in performing that which we do to be of service to the one infinite Creator at this time. As always with those who have opinions, no matter how carefully held, it is well for each to discriminate in the thoughts chosen to take and use. We ask that only thoughts which are deemed helpful by you be retained. The rest may comfortably be left behind. Thank you for this courtesy.

We would say that there is an over-shadowing of this group at this time by the one known as Hatonn. This is in order that there be an appropriate confluence of vibratory patterns placed upon your taping machine. However, this entity has no desire to speak to this group at this time, but merely wishes that we express that they are with this group and also thank each for requesting Confederation presence.

Picture with us, if you will, a large mansion with many, many rooms as has been the style off and on for centuries. In this dwelling there are secret passageways and staircases, secret rooms and secret tunnels. A visitor might enter this immense dwelling and abide therein for a long time without ever being aware of the secret portion of the house. There would be, seemingly, all that was in the house to proclaim that this is all there is. Yet, this space would continue to exist on the other side of that secret door. That the visitor did not know the door was there would have no effect upon the door. It is in this kind of way that the forgetting process occurs.

When you picture an infant, newborn into the world of illusion, you see a tiny bundle of raw need and that tiny spark of life existing so purely and innocently; yet, this infant contains all of the space for its memories that it has ever had and ever will have. Some of these memories are from the many, many times of being incarnate in third-density physical vehicles; however, some of the content of this memory is that memory which is gained as a portion of essential beingness given from the original Thought, which is divine Love. The truth, shall we say, is ineluctably placed within each entity as a portion of the basic consciousness with which individual characters are injected, shall we say, to form that which one could call the soul or the whole entity.

Up until the breath is drawn for the first time, this newborn infant is a functioning portion of second-density, in many cases. The consciousness which is individually an entity's may well hover about the forming physical vehicle rather than take its seat within the physical vehicle, so that there is often no presence there except the physical vehicle within the mother. However, when the time of birth approaches, then must the entity which shall use this functioning physical vehicle go into the physical vehicle and form that bond betwixt lighter bodies and the physical body which bind the two together until the cessation of the physical body. This represents a true marriage, shall we say, of Earth and heaven, or of the elements of that which lives and dies and that which has not been born nor shall die—that which is forever the Mystery.

It may seem a cruel joke that such perfectly formed and pure infants must be taken from that consciousness of the truth in which inhabitants of second-density dwell. However, as the query itself notes, the advantages of functioning without these memories are great. To the conscious mind there is given what is more a shadow than a substance of the actual memories which are stored within the deep mind. It is as though the very workings of the most essential aspects of each personality were necessarily so ordered as to leave many hints and innuendoes suggesting that there is such a thing as a more ethical way to live or to decide between two things. This bare instinct for the right is that flag or token or suggestion that there is much more of a metaphysical or ethical nature which forms a system of deeper truth.

This deeper truth is protected from that quick and easy access by the conscious mind which entities are used to having in general. It is neatly and cleanly cached, not merely out of sight, but secreted and truly hidden, for there is extreme power which is released when the truth is claimed; and it is a worthy goal to seek and find more and more deep levels of truth. Were this truth not so well hidden, it would not have the power to move and offer transformation to that entity which perseveres in ceaseless asking and desiring of the Creator that more and more of truth be opened to one.

You dwell in a deep and convincing illusion—this you know. Each has already discovered some degree of personal power. Each desires and attempts to use that power rightly. As each continues that pilgrim's path, seeking always the higher truth, the higher compassion and wisdom, doors do open, and to the entity who watches and pays close attention, each and every situation can hold revelation. Yet, know that it is only insofar as one continues to apply those truths already learned that these doors do open.

The nature of seeking is such that many attempt to speed up the process of discovering truth far beyond that rate at which they may reasonably expect to learn and retain information. Therefore, we encourage each to allow for reflection and reiteration of lessons and truths, for the process of imbibing these heady waters of truth is much longer and more subtle than a simple model of the memory of an entity might suggest.

We suggest that each of you is a marvelously complex creature, and that many times when you may be most aggravated at the delays in learning lessons are the times when it would be far better simply to allow the waiting and the process of seating these growing perceptions of truth in the stable connection betwixt newly opened subconscious material and its emergence through the threshold of consciousness into the fully conscious mind.

It is as though these secret places within the mansion of your beingness are the treasure trove which the dragon guards in your mythology. The dragon is that portion of the universal Self which aids the self in staying whole and entire, for that which you seek—that great original Truth—is powerful enough to have created all that there now is, and is powerful enough to end all that there is. Contact with this energy is a thing which it is well to allow to occur in natural ways with no heightened expectations. In quietness and in peace shall truth be yours, which you have earned through desire purified through discipline, through emotion purified by wisdom.

Rather than moving forward from this point, we would pause and ask if there is a direction which any within this circle would have a desire to appoint.

Questioner: What would be your recommendation for the best way to aid this remembering process?

We are those of Q'uo. The door into that secret part of the mansion of your self has a key which opens it. This key is meditation, contemplation or prayer. These words suggest ways of expressing a relationship. We wish to use a term which points to that relationship, that truth within is to the self which functions daily as the bottom of a lake is to the bubble upon the surface. There is no actual touching of conscious mind to the ground of being, if you will.

When one meditates or in some way seeks to impress within the self its relationship to the one infinite Creator by whatever means, this intention to seek the Mystery triggers a kind of instinct within the conscious portion of the deep mind, thereby focusing energy and personal power around this mountaintop which has poked up from the subconscious into the conscious mind—that little peak which shows above the threshold of consciousness as the instinct for an ethical or moral right, or that little mountaintop which says that there must be a Creator. The act of meditation, then, not only works upon the mind and body to relax and open up the flow of energy, it also triggers a closer alignment of the self which is conscious with the fundamental or basic nature of that great mountain within the subconscious or deep mind which is the area which contains those deep and vast truths which have structured and formed all that there is.

You carry the blueprint of all things within, and the potential to activate any or all of this knowledge. That you are protected from burning yourself out in discovering these fiery truths beforetimes is to be expected in a universe where there is the possibility of advancing. The Creator has not hidden these truths in order to cause hardships, but in order to prevent premature awareness. Each entity is intended to open itself to transformation in this natural way, so that there shall be no loss of incarnation that is not necessary.

May we at this time request a further direction?

Questioner: No, that's very good. Thank you, Q'uo. I appreciate what you've had to say.

We are Q'uo, and we thank you, my brother. This instrument is asking us why we dally. We say to this instrument, "Relax." We rest in the harmony of this circle, reluctant to leave, yet, having fulfilled our function, we simply float within the vibratory patterns which are so beautiful to us in each of you.

We thank you again for requesting our service, and, reluctantly, we do at this time desire to leave this instrument. We leave each of you in the love and in the light of the one infinite Creator. We are known to you as those of the principle Q'uo. Adonai. Adonai. We leave you in love and in light.

(Carla channeling)

I Yadda. Hah! We take this instrument by surprise. She say love and light for you can speak. We greet you in love and in light. We look at your hopes and dreams and say to you, "Let no one discourage you." If someone seems to have authority yet discourages your efforts, then you must say, "He is not what he seems." Then to yourself you give encouragement. Perhaps there is not someone besides yourself to strengthen you, then you must stand on your two feet and encourage yourself. Be never faint of heart, and know always that energies such as ours are numerous.

We cluster about those who seek to hasten the day of perfect balance. Open the heart to that company which wishes to support you, and feel that wordless encouragement. We thank the one known as *(name)* for allowing us to share this thought, and now would leave. I am Yadda. I leave you in love and in light. Adonai. ✣

Sunday Meditation
November 28, 1993

(The tape begins in the middle of a reply to a question having to do with astrology.)

(Carla channeling)

[I am Q'uo.] … we seek at this time to do.

We are most happy to share our thoughts on astrology, with the disclaimer that our thoughts are to be heard as the thoughts of a friend, rather than those of an all-wise teacher, for we make errors. The request we have of you is that you simply leave behind any thought which does not seem worthwhile to you.

We give this instrument the picture of the world that lies in darkness. A kind of waiting, or anticipatory darkness such as the eve of a great holiday. The present period among those upon your sphere's surface at this time is an increasingly exciting one as there has been more and more of this consciousness among all of your world's peoples that some great event seems to be in the offing, so that the coming of the night is more acceptable.

It is into such a frame of consciousness, if you will, that we bring this discussion of astrology. This instrument wonders what we do, but we ask it to relax and go with us on this. There have been centuries in which it would not have aided most to look more closely into the archetypical mind. These centuries have passed for this third-density experience which you enjoy at this time. The end truly is near, if you will. Not physically, but more and more mentally and spiritually. There is that subconscious or unconscious awareness amongst your people that there are special reasons to look more deeply into natural phenomena and their possible effect upon the self, be it body, mind or spirit that is affected.

Astrology is a complex and detail driven technology, if you will, a system of ephemeral, mathematical constructs having to do with the configurations of heavenly bodies.

To the student who wishes to probe more deeply within the self to become more and more familiar with those uncharted regions of the self represented by the marker in consciousness which you would call sub-awareness, it [astrology] offers one way of learning more about the deeper mind. There is this sub-awareness that the deeper studies at this crux may be those which have fruitful results. On this level, let us say, the awareness of specific and personal detail is not that of which we speak at this time. Rather, the archetypical mind finds explication by the relationships of heavenly bodies to each other and to the planetary sphere upon which you presently enjoy incarnation.

At this level, much deep awareness can be encouraged by immersion in that complex set of relationships of star to star and star to the system of star and planets which you call home. On another level, the personal level, yield of useful information from continued study of and awareness of the progression of one's own—this instrument would use the word "chart"—is shall we say, a good way to develop both an instinct for influence and a relatively authentic feeling of control over the continuing life experiences which is so precious to you. To one entity, such a study would be work, a difficult chore done in order for the learning. To such a one, we would suggest investigating other avenues for learning more attuned to the environment and for aid in the feel of control over the life experience.

Astrology, then, is that for which some entities are well suited, others not. To the entity which feels positively or affirmatively concerning keeping up with the chart's progression for the self, astrology can bear that aid in consciousness which creates for the seeker a vantage point, consciousness which can act as a collecting area for the amassing of one's psychic self. The gift of being psychic or aware in non-physical ways is within all persons. The means of developing this gift are tremendously large, infinite, we would think. However, to a fairly large percentage of those now seeking to increase the rate of learning, spiritually speaking, a substantial number would, indeed, find in astrology that place from which to continue to learn how to gather more and different information from the environment, for the environment is illusory and more than that is an illusion with many sub-illusions which further color the catalyst which is retained for use by your minds.

Now let us speak more in general, for there is a point to be made as regards the use of systems created by the mind and observations of mankind. Insofar as any system is internally valid in its logic, that system may be to the entity which plumbs its depths that crutch or aid which acts as the collector for the abilities and gift of the seeker. In general, it is well to choose as a system, whether it may be astrology or numerology, the study of the eye or head or hand and we could list systems for a substantial length of your time. What avails then to the seeker as efficient tools is that very systematic nature, for the mind within incarnation has the instinct for the pattern.

Each entity in each experience is, in part, working internally to place the present moment into a context which will yield the maximum amount of information. This information is usually heavily biased towards comfort and well-being. However, the mind can be increasingly trained to retain catalyst which is presented to the mind which perhaps has little, if any, survival use but which does indeed aid in spiritual learning. And the way to become more able to do the work in consciousness is to persist in experiencing one system, be it of myth, science, philosophy or ethics or any system whatsoever which—we correct this instrument—to which the seeker is personally and individually drawn.

For you are, indeed, living on the eve of that which shall come to be. It is almost impossible to describe the nature of the shift of consciousness from basic third density to basic fourth density. This shift shall take you with it, if you dwell now on planet Earth. Therefore, we encourage the twin awarenesses that it is a great time to be watchful and that it is a good time to celebrate that which astrology or any "ology" might do, which is to aid in the development of that sharply tuned hunger for the truth that is revealed in the present moment.

How we do encourage each to more and more dwell and marinate the complete entity in the present moment. It may seem odd that the mind's structure is such that the entrance to the present movement is often roundabout, moving not through the invisible door into the fully accepted present, but rather going completely around the entire structure of living to surprise the present moment, only after the long walk has sharpened the appetite.

Astrology is, shall we say, the hors d'oeuvre which encourages an entity to more aptly fit the intellect to accept an increasing number of inferences. This ability to loosen the self from the physical and move into an abstract system of gazing at the self is key.

What you do in gazing at astrology is to sharpen the intellect's ability to let go enough so that the gifts which are called psychic may express themselves intelligibly to that mind which has been softened to accept increasing numbers of inferences, for that which you seek cannot be deduced or received.

Discuss what you will. You cannot bring instrumentation, as you know that, to bear on the nature, which is the original Thought of the one infinite Creator.

We would at this time declare with regret that this is the substance of our discussion at this time, unless there is a query which would take this line of reasoning further. Might any have the desire to proceed further at this time with this particular query?

(Pause)

In that case, we would close this particular session through the one known as Jim. We leave this instrument in love and light. We are known to you as Q'uo.

(Jim channeling)

I am Q'uo and greet each again in love and in light through this instrument. It is our privilege at this time to ask if there be any queries upon any other topic that we may attempt a response to.

Questioner: I have another question, Q'uo. Prior to the session the situation was discussed of helping ourselves. *(Inaudible)* to be at a disadvantage in our particular society and my observation was that the feelings that come to me during that Sunday were unexpected. I was wondering if there is any use for logical reasoning in trying to observe one's own reaction in giving aid or helping another, or if it is more useful for a seeker just to accept it as it is and sort of try to do the best every time that situation or event comes up. I wonder if you could comment on it?

I am Q'uo, and am aware of your query, my brother. The situation of which you speak is one in which you were offered the opportunity to be of service to another in a very direct and immediate fashion. This quality of immediacy is that which catches the seeker, shall we say, in an off-guard position, as you may put it. The spontaneous response of any entity to any stimulus is to act in this off-guarded moment in a pure and unpretentious fashion, to look at this experience as it has been completed, and to review one's reactions, thoughts and emotions is the archetypical path of the seeker for the examination of the life pattern is the seeking of truth. The illusion exists for your seeking and your learning. Thus we applaud the care taken in investigating one's responses to significant stimuli. The significance is chosen by each of you according to that which moves your inner rhythms, those patterns programmed previous to the incarnation. Thus is well to spend time daily reflecting upon the day as it has passed to note those experiences where there was movement in your own consciousness, those felt and [that] left behind a strength and a mark upon your memory.

May we speak in any further fashion, my brother?

Questioner: I will take it further by saying that when I agreed to help, I had some expectations in the way it would feel and it did not feel that way and so I would ask you what kind of experience does the seeker set himself up for with the approach he is giving it? Would you give some preconceived idea of what it might be like? What it should be like?

I am Q'uo, and am aware of your query. To have a preconceived idea as the to the outcome to any event is to confuse the perception of that event when it occurs. This provides additional catalyst to the seeker and it is not inappropriate to have these preconceptions, however, it may be noted to be inconvenient. It may also be noted by the seeker that there are a great many responses possible as a result of the giving of service and each response may be carefully noted and investigated so that the connection with giving without condition can be made.

Is there any further query, my brother?

Questioner: No, Q'uo. Thank you for that.

I am Q'uo, and we thank you once again, brother. Is there another query at this time?

Carla: Well this is personal, but I was talking with Jim the other day and we were wondering what had changed since the readings that I was given by Ra that have enabled me to [do] things that, at the time, I simply could not do. If this is not a subject you can speak upon, that's fine. If you cannot comment, great.

I am Q'uo. We first [must] ask if we spoke too soon?

Carla: Well, Q'uo, only because I always have something else to say, I was just going to say that, in general.

I am Q'uo. Still … *(laughter from group)* and we give this instrument the image of the steel door, locked carefully, and apologize for the lack of information. Is there any other query, my sister?

Carla: Would it aid my understanding of the energies at work in my life to meditate on this door?

I am Q'uo, and we would suggest that the query itself be the focus of meditation.

Carla: Very well. Thank you, Q'uo.

I am Q'uo, and again we thank you, my sister. Is there another query, at this time?

Carla: No, thank you.

I am Q'uo, and we thank each for your patience and most especially for your invitation to us for we are always filled with joy to receive it and to have the opportunity to blend our vibrations with yours. We are most grateful to walk with you this portion of your journey and assure each of you that there are many such as we who walk with you always and there are those who rejoice at your every step. We shall take this opportunity to leave this instrument and this circle of working, leaving each, as always, in love and light of the one infinite Creator. We are known to you as those of Q'uo. Adonai, my friends. Adonai. ✤

Sunday Meditation
December 12, 1993

Group question: The question this afternoon has to do with what the Confederation contacts that we speak with think about our continually asking basically the same sorts of question. We seem to need a lot of repetition concerning "being and doing" in our lives, controlling and allowing things to work for their own ends, or, basically, the lessons of love. And we're wondering how this all looks to the Confederation contacts as they observe our behavior, listen to our questions, and see our concerns—our sort of orbiting in small circles.

(Carla channeling)

We greet you in the love and in the light of the one infinite Creator. We are those of the principle known to you as Q'uo, and the love and light of the One with which we greet you is our way of expressing all that there is, so that in this greeting we have offered to you all that we have to offer in service. We are in service to your people to promulgate this one deeply held opinion of ours: that is, that there is but one great original Thought, that Thought called Love which is the Creator and the nature of all that there is, with light being that instrument with which the grand tapestry of your world scene is woven.

We come to answer your query concerning repetition. We were unaware that we ever do any other thing but iterate and reiterate the one simple truth, that all that there is is one thing, that thing being a mystery which recedes before us as we move in that which we hope is a positive evolutionary way. Therefore, we have a very favorable opinion of that which you conceive of as your repetitive queries.

The admonition, "Be ye perfect as your Father is perfect," is attributed to the teacher known to you as Jesus. We, too, encourage the attempt to be perfect, that is, be perfectly loving just as the infinite Creator is infinitely loving and purely loving. Yet, this instrument himself was a broken and imperfect entity within the veil of third-density incarnation. [However,] this teacher encouraged this drive towards perfection again and again. However, this teacher, in the ministry which expressed without words the nature of this entity's love, chose again and again to bestow that love, charity and wisdom upon those which any civilized culture would call imperfect—the tax collector, the prostitute, the halt and lame and those possessed—a veritable rogues' gallery of failed and sinful entities.

These profoundly imperfect entities were those to whom the one known as Jesus expended the most care, going after that one in the hundred which is lost, forgiving all for faith. To one who had faith, this entity was able to effect healing. Was any who was healed described as perfect or deserving? Not at all. We, too, encourage you to strive at your very highest level of effort to "fight the good fight," as this instrument would say, gazing upon the present moment and the future as the ever unfolding opportunity to become perfect. Yet, in this endeavor, we predict that the odds are great that you shall not perceive yourselves as being anywhere near to perfection.

This instrument earlier stated that she was in despair because she looked at the actions and thoughts of several different present moments, asking the self, "Is this the way you live in the Creator's presence?" May we point out that this entity was, in each instance, thinking of the Creator, with the relationship of the self to Creator inevitably and intrinsically characterized within the heart of self, so that there was no chance for the entity to be away from the Creator's presence.

In each and every self-perceived imperfection of thought and action, each of you, as you criticize yourselves, gaze at who is criticizing and who is criticized. These are both the self. The dialogue with self would not be possible were not the self composed of voices which include that voice which calls to remembrance.

When the seeker begins the conscious portion of its incarnational work in consciousness, all is unknown. The desire to learn is great, and the first lessons are transformational, as the conscious mind begins to deal with our opinions of how, within incarnation, entities might speed up the rate of their spiritual evolution. They are able to make large changes quickly. The meditation is placed in a kind of routine, and the entity begins experiencing fairly rapidly the results of that daily meditation. The world of nature is seen with brand new eyes which gaze upon the creation of the Father, seeing that which we, too, see: the euphonious harmony of all things in the visible world, vital, alive and praising the infinite Creator. The rhythms of life are seen in an entirely different way as the processes of meditation and contemplation go forward, and it begins to be a world in which there are things which the seeker can see to do, in the way of their service towards the Creator and others.

These things are noticeable changes. The difference it makes to the living a life based on faith is palpable, but the seeker moves onward, and each step takes the seeker into that new world in which things have not yet been constructed. Soon the changes within, meeting and reacting with the environment, begin to cause that which one might experience as a dying away of some of the self, the turning towards a different or transformed view of how the spiritual journey shall be run, and more and more as this process continues, the seeker finds itself torn loose from all that previously maintained equilibrium. The path moves onward, yet, the self is transforming and is not any longer a set character. The seeker begins to wish to have some kind of structure within which to seek, yet, that structure is constantly being torn down to some extent by the progression of the spiritual evolution which was desired.

Thusly, as this desire for spiritual evolution is progressively satisfied, just so it becomes that which is not familiar. And in the middle of this seemingly effortless meditational practice, one finds the self becoming very full of effort, attempting to digest and inwardly mark all that is taking place in a balanced and truthful way. The self becomes less known, for much is in motion. And as the question itself implies, the odds are good that quite often within the stretch of years of a seeker's conscious spiritual walk the self will be, again and again, rather frequently out of balance, or shall we rather say, perceiving the self as out of balance, and there is the wishing and hoping for more balance, for more skill in expressing the life in love and in service.

Perhaps our greatest message to you in this regard is: keep walking. Do not be disappointed in the self because there seems to be the repetition of message. This simply indicates where in a particular group or circle, the rubber, as this instrument would say, is hitting the road.

Shall you wish for a pure heart? Then, inevitably, shall you notice each and every impurity which you perceive in the self. Do you wish to be always the one who offers love? Just as strong as this desire is, so is the strength of your ability to notice unloving acts. And if your desire is to balance being and doing, then you shall surely notice, again and again, that you wish to be given more tools and resources to aid you in combating and working with the self as it is perceived by the self to be acting out of balance.

So those things which concern or worry, like this repetition, are not in our opinion negative, but rather merely indicative of where the energy is within each of you in the circle. Please consider how long this spiritual journey is, and how infinitely fine the distinctions and the enlightenments become as the Spirit progresses through the densities to gaze at the long view. Not only are you attempting within incarnation to balance the being and the doing, the resting and the acting, but there are millions and millions of your years ahead in which you shall only tighten and magnify the scope of that which you observe, looking always not at what has been gained, but at what there is to do. These lessons, shall we call them, go on forever, until time itself becomes meaningless and spiritual gravity takes over.

We ask, then, that the heart rest in a peace which does not come from settling differences or realizing truths. We hope for each of you a peace that is full of the striving of entities to rest in the Creator. That Creator is not still. The Creator in which you rest builds up and tears down all possible avenues. Dwell within the precinct of this peace. This peace is not still. This peace may be full of noise and full of prayer also, yet, this peace is simply the awareness of the Creator in direct relation to you, and in direct identity with the heart within, which contains that spark of pure Love which enlivens the whole.

You are mortal, experiencing incarnation within a heavy illusion. Those things you came here to learn you are indeed learning; but it takes your time, not simply one lifetime, but again and again called into incarnation to repeat and repeat that lesson not perfectly grasped as yet. If we felt that we should not repeat ourselves, my friends, we would soon be out of talk.

We are attempting to show to this instrument the image of the ice which forms on top of the pond or puddle. The sheet of ice across the top is solid to the touch. It is strong and holds weight. It is one shape only, and can only be changed by breaking and scattering its crystalline nature. Yet, below the ice is living water, the habitat of beings—fish and plant life thrive beneath the solid ice. This is as you in incarnation. The form which you have taken is crystalline in its own way, and marvelously wrought, and each entity has its own beauty and cleanness of form. This solid entity which greets you in the mirror shall be your physical identity until you leave both the illusion and that physical form behind. Yet, that solid entity is not the end of you, but merely the surface of your form. Within you are deep and living waters in which the flora and fauna, shall we say, of archetypical images which live in those deep waters may thrive and bloom. Does the physical form change because of this life which moves within? Usually not, yet this is your self, mostly unknown by you except that you can feel that pressure of vitality coming from the depths within and you can experience this depth and fullness of being.

The crystalline form will indeed need to be battered with that blunt instrument called repetition, a hundred or a thousand times before the dent is made—the form changes, the mental formation changes, the emotional changes—the work is slow, and you feel pokey and petty and tired of not quite getting it yet. We encourage and exhort each in the regular allowing of the definition of the self to be consciously altered by the bringing into remembrance and awareness that living, breathing, vital part of the deep self. Breathe deeply of that living water. Inhale it into the form which is the physical health. Consciously irrigate and marinate the self in these living waters of deep mind, then allow that consciousness to fade, so that you may, once again, take up the attempt daily, hourly, moment by moment, to live the life of faith, as witness. And in that witness, whether by expression or aura or any word or deed, may you celebrate that imperfection which is the perfect outworking of a life lived in faith and service.

Do you seem to need repetition? Very well then, my friends, repetition it is. And with each repetition, the total of Love does not expand but simply intensifies, so that as each lesson is repeated, new and deeper graspings and understandings are found. The entity has not been dealt, may we say, that can do the same thing twice—not in the world of spirit.

We ask each to lift the criticism that is implied in being aware that you are working towards an unattained goal. Feel each day both the perfection which is the true nature of all things, and the imperfection which is consciousness expressing through a medium. The medium of third-density is that which consciousness can do very little about, comparative—we correct this instrument—compared to its action upon other densities. Therefore, allow the self its nature, and be at peace with the repeated lessons.

We would at this time transfer this contact to the one known as Jim. We are those of Q'uo, and leave this instrument in love and in light.

(Jim channeling)

I am Q'uo, and greet each again in love and in light through this instrument. At this time may we ask if there might be any further queries for our consideration?

Carla: I didn't understand what he—what they meant, when they were talking about the deep mind. The images … It was just unclear to me about the deep mind, and the living, almost like beings in that deep mind, which are living. Somehow there was the suggestion that they're not precisely us, they're living like fish in the water of us in the deep mind. And I couldn't make anything out of that so I didn't express it. And I wonder if you could try again through Jim, because I was interested in that image but I couldn't express it well enough to use it.

I am Q'uo, and am aware of your query, my sister. And we would agree that this concept is one which is difficult to comprehend within your normal reference points of existence, for there is little of the deeper mind that your peoples choose to investigate beyond the individual subconscious. However, if an entity is successful in traveling to the roots of the mind beyond that that can be called the personal subconscious, there is the racial consciousness of its own kind, shall we say, and here there are experiences that have been gathered by those of the same racial heritage that affect the individual entities of that grouping …

(Side one of tape ends.)

(Jim channeling)

I am Q'uo, and am again with this instrument. We shall continue. Beyond the racial mind there is the planetary mind that is different than the racial mind on this particular planetary influence. For, as you are aware, many there are upon your planet that have had their beginnings elsewhere upon other planetary influences, so that there are various racial minds which compose your planetary mind. It is possible for a third-density planet to evolve with only its original second-density population progressing to the third, so that the racial and planetary minds are more alike if not identical.

Moving further into the roots of the tree of mind, we come to that portion which is called the archetypical mind. It is here that the blueprint for your evolutionary process is found, so that the influences that you experience from this source are of a fundamental nature, and provide insight and inspiration into your daily experience only in the form of echoes, hints and shadows. At the level of the archetypical mind there is the participation, both of the individual entity such as yourself and entities of quite another nature, though all are one in truth. The creative forces or intelligences that are responsible for this portion of the creation in its very essence are those which work upon the level of the archetypical mind, refining that cosmic mind of the one Creator in such and such a fashion, so that there is the possibility that the Creator may know Itself with greater variety and intensity than if the cosmic mind did not experience further refinement.

It is here, at this level, that we were speaking previously in suggesting that there are concepts that are basic to third-density experience which have their origin at this level of archetypes. And because of this similarity of lessons to be learned there is the seeming repetition of experience for the seeker of truth within your illusion. Thus, you draw from the same well waters that nourish your life-being and give it its flavor, its *élan*.

Is there a further query, my sister?

Carla: No, thank you. That was fascinating.

I am Q'uo, and we are grateful to you as well, my sister. Is there another query?

Carla: Not from me, Q'uo.

We are those of Q'uo, and are aware that we have spoken for a goodly portion of your time this day, and we are most grateful to each of you for inviting us to do so. We are overjoyed at this opportunity, and we can assure you that though it seems there is repetition upon repetition within your illusion, that the effort you make to greet each experience with love and with light is unique, and adds its own portion not only to your experience but to the experience of the one Creator. And each effort, each breath, and each thought that you take is treasured by those who observe and have responsibility for this progress as your teachers, your friends, and your guides, shall we say.

At this time, we shall take our leave of this instrument and this group, leaving each, as always, in the love and in the light of the one infinite Creator. We are known to you as those of Q'uo. Adonai, my friends. Adonai. ❧

Sunday Meditation
December 19, 1993

Group question: *(Inaudible) … (name)* concerning a dream he had, which he felt was an extremely enlightening dream. We will ask the questions in parts. The first one is: "Who are those who played the parts of my spirit mother and fathers?"

(Carla channeling)

I am Q'uo. Greetings in the love and in the light of the one infinite Creator. We are privileged to attend your session of working at this time and gratefully thank this group for calling us to share our opinions with you. It is our privilege and we are most heartily pleased and blessed by the company, asking only that our opinions be accepted as just that. So we ask each to consider what we offer, rejecting those things which do not immediately seem to aid in your particular spiritual journey, and if there remain any which do aid you, then we are most delighted.

We speak this day concerning the interpretation of a dream. Such is often the platform upon which information necessary to a spiritual seeker is offered, the dream state being marvelously outfitted and equipped to handle complex and shifting values and concerns which are being considered by the seeker on many levels, some conscious and most subconscious. This dream state, then, is marvelously wrought for maximal lading or layering of information. To one who is not yet working with the dream state, dreams may seem ephemeral, nonsensical and useless. However, to the seeker who spends the care and attention to prepare for remembering and considering dreams this resource of the mind is a stout friend and a wise teacher to the conscious self, expressing in rich detail the tapestry of deep energies which move through the self within the incarnation.

The denizens of dreams have various identities when gazed at from various points of advantage. In a very real sense, and perhaps one of the most important, all figures within a dream are the self. This seems confusing at first glance, for if all figures in a dream are the self, then where is the dynamic which expresses thought and carries instruction? Yet the self is a large entity, an entity of a level or order of complexity which is difficult to express. Within each self there exist the pre-traces or foreshadowings of all potential possible states of mind, all feelings and emotions, indeed, all situations.

In a dream in which all entities are the self, then, the interpreter of the dream is looking at the characters of the dream with the hope of penetrating the symbol or figure or motif which the figure represents. In this regard, it is helpful to have some familiarity with the archetypical mind in one of those disciplines, such as the tarot, which attempt with some degree of success to capture the complex and many-layered values and colors of this tapestry of the self.

When one gazes at a mother, within the dream, looking for the archetypical match for this particular entity one may perhaps find some degree of success holding each archetype in mind and allowing the dream figure to be matched to it. The figure of mother contains, shall we say, the essence or heart of the dynamic called female. Those incarnate—we correct this instrument—incarnated in physical vehicles which are female contain the world within them, for to their wombs and through their wombs all must come who come into manifestation.

The female is the doorway through which all life essences stream. Within the heart of the father, then, is that which acknowledges the high position or ruling standard of the feminine. Before that door, that gateway, all men kneel, all give homage. Toward the female, then, is felt an irresistible love, often experienced as a darker or more convoluted love bearing in its folds the pain of that within the male which is not alive as is the female.

Thus, we encourage the one known as *(name)* in its consideration of the various female archetypes to illuminate this search for self and further to illuminate that within the self which now stops searching.

(Pause of thirty seconds.)

The three images of father—that which is rough, that which is strong, that which is wily—are not mutually exclusive images, yet what, archetypically speaking, within the male is rough, is wily? What depths do these words suggest? What divisions within the self do the unification of these three characteristics foreshadow? We suggest consideration of the mind, the physical vehicle and the spiritual self, moving always back from the detail to the essence, from complexity of detail towards unity of wedded understanding.

To the student which has achieved comes the clear dream which points both to the completion of one season of the self and to the moment of beginning, the next season of the self. In what way, then, does the incarnation, as its events lie in the present moment, provide resonances with this dream of mother and of fathers? These considerations may well produce further queries.

May we answer further at this time?

Jim: The second part of the question is: "What of an helpful or clarifying nature could be said regarding my spirit mother's answer to my question about the constancy of my experience of being?"

Carla: Could you read that again?

(Repeated)

(Carla channeling)

The metamorphosis that occurs in some life forms is far more striking than transformation within the third-density consciousness. When the tadpole becomes a frog, there has been quite an obvious change. When the pupa becomes a butterfly, there is an obvious change, but when a seeker has unwittingly fulfilled an archetypical task, the transformation is not obvious or even visible, necessarily.

Further, this transformation takes place at two very different levels of being. In one level, the subconscious level, time/space holds sway and there is no veil, so that clarity of color and detail is seen. However, the portion of the personhood, shall we say, which is conscious is like that of the iceberg. The conscious self is often tempted to think of itself as it sees itself in the mirror as the whole self. However, most of that which makes a seeker that particular and unique seeker lies forever hidden, and as an entity continues to do work in consciousness, great magnitudes of change are seen below the threshold of consciousness and rainbows of colors detail this marvelous melodrama of evolving selfhood, while above the threshold of consciousness the changes are muted and the desire to see these changes, be it ever so keen, must make itself comfortable working largely with the palest and dimmest of hues compared to the richness of color in the time/space portions of consciousness which lie below the veil.

Thusly, it is well that there be in a seeker attempting to learn new ways the willingness to accept upon—we correct this instrument—on faith alone that the work done faithfully and persistently is indeed creating new selfhood below the veil of forgetting, even though that which appears within the conscious experience may not at all times have the brilliance and clarity which is instinctively felt as the work of seeking revolves and moves the seeker in its orbit of evolution.

It may be seen, then, that on one level a state once experienced becomes the basic state and further evolution holds this value as its ground value. On the conscious level, however, the value which is stable subconsciously seems to be anything but stable as the conscious entity working within this shadowed valley of existence which is your normal waking consciousness must work to understand what it can amid the ever changing emotional mind-sets which bias most entities' web of perceptions according to those defenses and adjustments which have fed into the increasingly eccentric and individualistic web of characteristics which is the evolving personality of the conscious self.

Thusly, there is always change, but the fruits of these changes, the completion motifs of cycles within incarnation, though steady and stable within the deep self, will not seem stable at all within the conscious life. How to evaluate oneself with regard to this holding of the steady state? We encourage any seeker with this kind of query simply to lay it aside, for the least among your peoples can judge the self but the greatest among you cannot judge wisely. Therefore, we encourage the lack of the taking of the spiritual temperature and also the releasing of the opinion concerning which state it would be best to be in.

Certainly one wishes to always run the straight race with a pure and full-hearted effort. Yet we suggest that the running of this race is in itself that satisfaction which truly endures. The grasping or holding on to that which has occurred, we suggest, is not necessary, for such clear dreamings generally signal the ending or completion of one cycle of learning and the momentary or new entry into the next cycle which shall be the next lesson of love.

The entity which began the cycle, now ended, is no longer that which calls itself *(name)* and now that this cycle begins, to turn back and reach for these experiences felt within the dream queried about is just a holding on to that which is rather a signal, a fairly complex signal, which suggests without specific delineation the nature of what may be called the initiation which has been gone through.

May we ask if there is a further query?

Jim: The third portion asks: "How did the nature of my question to my spirit mother constrain the form that her answer took?"

Carla: Could you read that again?

(Repeated)

(Carla channeling)

I am Q'uo. This instrument is not aware of the content of this particular part of the dream, so we shall have the difficulty of working without this instrument's awareness of what we refer to within our words. Therefore, this response is less than complete.

Let us consider the archetype of the two women, one of the negative polarity and one of the positive polarity. The central figure which is male has his hands crossed across the breast holding in each hand one of the women's. The moment comes when the choice between these two women, between that which they represent in all of its richness, must be made. The particular energy which goes into that moment of choice constrains or configures the shape of that level or way which opens before the male which has made the choice. Therefore, we suggest a consideration of this archetype known to this instrument as The Choice, one of the tarot images.

May we ask if there is a further query?

Jim: The fourth portion asks: "Why did the experience occur in the dream state instead of during waking hours?"

We encourage the one known as *(name)* to rejoice, for the dream which has been given is of a certain level or kind in which what may be called reality or ground of reality is enhanced so that there is a reality to the dream which is greater than the waking reality.

In actuality, the subconscious is always far more fully conscious than the waking entity. So the, shall we say, syntax and vocabulary which in …

(Side one of tape ends.)

(Carla channeling)

… which informs these images is of an order impossible to contain within the waking state. Were this material to be given with this degree of clarity within the waking state the consensus reality which the self depends upon would tend to be greatly shaken, the energy of this harvest being that which the waking self could not bear.

Thusly, were this same information to be given in a waking vision, there would of necessity be some bias within the self which would form the pattern for the translation of these bright images into the grays, the pearl, off-white and tan of human experience as you know it, all the shades of gray and tan, the colors of shadow, rather than substance. Yet that which is so gray seems to the physical eye quite bright. Imagine the impact of that which would make the colors of your sky and your sea, your land and your earth, seem drab. Such brightness pierces the eye and blinds it. Thusly, the dream is skillfully knitted up for the self by the self in the way which allows the self to remain sturdily within the incarnational set of biases which define the perceptions of self to self at the moment.

Is there another query?

Jim: The last portion asks: "My own opinion on how to best appreciate this experience is to continue to meditate on the observations and items of experience that depended from it. What else, either in my considerations or actions, might be beneficial in this same quest?"

We are those of Q'uo, and we suggest, first of all, that the skill which is able to move forward from such a dream-vision is encouraged, for to stay with the lesson, which is today, tomorrow and tomorrow and tomorrow is that energy which is baffling the natural flow of ongoing experience. Thusly, in the most general sense, it is well for the mind to open the hand, as it were, metaphorically speaking, to release from any bondage or prison that great gift which has been given to the self by the self. This self will continue to supply to the conscious mind that material which ennobles and illuminates the experiences now causing catalyst or material for the self to push and wrestle against and learn from.

It is more efficient to cooperate with that ongoing flow, to open the self forward and gaze into the present moment and the near future, having faith that that which has been harvested and accomplished within is safe and cannot be denied or stolen from the self.

In terms of those studies which move positively from this recorded group of images called the dream, we again suggest pondering and musing over the archetypical male and female roles played by each, whether reluctantly or gladly, throughout the incarnative experience.

Let us pull back then, and gaze at this experience. What is it to be male? What is it to be female? What power lies within the female? To what, within woman, does man bend the knee, and rightly so? And what within the present experience mimics these archetypical images in quality or feeling?

May we ask if there are any queries from those present?

Jim: None from me, Q'uo. Thank you very much.

We thank you, my brothers.

As we take our leave of each for this working we rejoice with you that you are able to pursue that spiritual quest which is every man's with joy and faith. We applaud the courage it takes to persist beyond any limitations in intending and desiring with a whole heart to learn the truth, to witness to the light and to live serving in love for love's sake.

When dreams occur there is a glamour cast over the experience. The dream is fantastic, immediate, the speaking a reality beyond that which you may see with the physical eyes. Yet this waking world into which we speak at this time is the place where, as this instrument would say, the rubber hits the road. This frustrating, confusing, chaotic, ongoing experience which entities rush through, calling it life only if it is thought about, this is the ground upon which lessons are learned, love is taken in and given out and all of worth is collected through the webs of perception.

When studying something like the dream about which the queries were asked, always keep in mind that respect which one has for a teacher, no matter how difficult. This illusion is your teacher. Your ability to learn is enhanced by information such as is within this dream but this information always turns back into the waking self, pointing the way for further service, defining the nature of passages of seasons within the learning self.

Above all things, respect the incarnational self. Respect and offer homage to the intransigent and often negatively seeming face of everyday life. The mind turned towards the present moment with respect and charity is that mind which is ever closer to the veil of forgetting. That which accepts and reaches for the conscious life with gusto, though that gusto were for seemingly petty and everyday life, expresses great wisdom. You need not cling to any information but allow the information to travel as it will, occurring and recurring, and when recurred, thought about.

Yet, what does the entity hope for from the physical incarnation but the opportunity to make and remake the choice of how to serve?

Unbind the mind always and ask it freely to ramble. Then each day do some reflective considering of the flavor of the day's perceptions. By such means the material of the day is seated and works down into the roots of mind. The unexamined in life is far less likely to be used by the subconscious to teach the conscious self, so look to the perceptions. How are the biases of the seeker that you are in mind affecting the priorities which order the perceptions which are allowed into the conscious mind? Look always, when reflecting upon experience, towards ways to improve that gathering of perceptions so that there is better information given to the self which makes the choices. And always, as always, we encourage the steady, persistent, daily meditative times, be they short or long, for these meditations seat and stabilize learning and open the door into the silence which births the creation.

We leave you in this silence, above all things. It is made of the love of the one infinite Creator. And we leave you in the builded and constructed universe, which is all light. We are those of Q'uo. Adonai. Adonai. 2

Year 1994
January 2, 1994 to December 25, 1994

Sunday Meditation
January 2, 1994

Group question: The question today is from N. The first part is about the cycles. Since "as above, so below," only by understanding the universe, cosmos, celestial bodies and finding correlations with the activities of the mind, the human body, cells, tissues and molecules, atoms and subatomic particles, down to the etheric body, can we comprehend the whole. Could you comment on the correlation between cycles and the relationship to the human body?

(Carla channeling)

We are those of Q'uo. Greetings in the love and in the light of the one infinite Creator. We feel pleasure that we have been called to this session of working in order to share our thoughts with you. Thank you for this honor. Please, as always, take what is meaningful from our opinions, discarding the rest.

The physical makeup of your visible universe is most impressive, the systems, seeming rigidly hierarchical until there is a closer look, at which time anomalies begin to mount. The part of the crystallized creation which is withheld is great. This withholding is not in order that visibility be restricted, rather the withholding is due to the lack of sufficient sight, or opportunity for sight. In other words, neither the third density physical vehicles nor the consciousness inhabiting these physical vehicles is at your present equipped with receptors capable of assimilating the amount of data which exists.

We say this because the attempt to match perceived cyclical hierarchies is made non-useful by this fact. It is indeed so that that which exists, as you say, above, is indeed reflected in that which is, as you have said, below. However, that which is above is other than can be conjured or mentally figured out. That energy which created all that there is may be seen to be the center of all that there is. This field of love is of a nature which is reproduced and is the stuff of all levels of vibration which stem therefrom.

This nature is an essence or a fullness of field. The energy is saturated, that is, there is fullness of love. You seek in understanding cycles to better understand healing. However it is an understanding, shall we say, of fields and of the amount of saturation or fullness of love in the fields, in field strength, shall we say, that aids in the efficacy of healing. That is, the more saturated the awareness of love is the more fullness of health there is.

To work on the influences of heavenly objects, as you call these, is instead to do fairly subtle work in the area of the archetypical mind. The influences upon these archetypes from celestial objects varies according to the native ground or earth of a particular entity and the study of these correspondences yields a wealth of detailed information in each individual which undertakes such study.

This touches only tangentially upon healing information in that it is so that in working with the archetypes and their relationships there is much opportunity for the skilled student to take fire from a newly perceived gracefulness of relationship that clarifies in some way the student's thinking or, as you so often say, understanding.

May we ask if there is a further query?

Jim: A minor harvest cycle is related to the solar year which is the amount of time it takes our sun to go around the zodiac, about 25,000 years. The master cycle is said to be 75,000 years. Is there a star around which our sun or solar system moves that is the center of this 75,000 year cycle and, if so, can you tell us is it Alcyone or some other star?

We are those of Q'uo. While it is so that the numbers 25,000 and the turning of sun about solar system—we correct this instrument—Earth around solar system are similar, there is not the importance placed upon the connection between these two similar numbers. The timing, shall we say, of cycles of spiritual living or advancement are as they are because of quite sensitive factors involving the energies of the group of entities moving through third density. In other words, since your Earth sphere has certain populations of entities from various planetary influences the timing of these cycles of spiritual evolution is set in such and such a mold. As the group populations' biases collectively are altered through what you know as time the timing of the cycles also evolves.

The setting of these cycles is ever liquid and is regulated quite, quite precisely according to every single entity and thought of each entity. This energetic whole has a nascent life which expresses its times of blooming and learning in such and such a way while stars wheel above in the heavens according to your physical sight, the constellations of thought and intention infinitesimally added until a towering largeness and fullness of information has been assimilated. This living entity expresses as a field and this entity's expressions create the exact timing of the cycles of learning.

The cycles of learning have only tangentially, again, to do with the concerns of healing which we believe we understand these questions to be directed to. It is difficult to express how this perfectly logical seeming set of correspondences actually has an effect because the archetypical mind is most deep and for that reason most difficult to penetrate. We are happy to work upon the metaphysical implications of cycles concerning the archetypical mind, however, it is our feeling that this is not germane to a study of healing except as a rather advanced and subtle portion of healing which has to do with abstract or mental body healing at certain levels. We would suggest working from other assumptions than the assumption that cycles of spiritual learning are correlated with the cycles concerning healing.

Is there a further query?

Jim: He also mentions a 206,000 year cycle and he would like to know if there is any relationship between this 206,000 year cycle and Arcturus or Aldebaran and if there is a metaphysical significance to this cycle.

We are those of Q'uo. We do not find the comparisons listed to be useful.

Is there a further query?

Jim: Yes. He would also like to know if there is any significance in a 26 million year cycle and if it has any relationship to a specific star or location.

We are those of Q'uo. And again we do not find a significance to the 26 million year cycle. Perhaps we could suggest that the center of the universe is the center of each entity's heart. The open heart of the great Self which each self is is that center which is a unity. All of the portions of the Creator, shall we say rather misleadingly, seem to themselves to be in time and space each unique, each separate and each apart. Yet, in truth, the center of the constellations is the open heart. All measurement, all numbering, all ways of detailing and patterning the observed creation fall to dust before the open heart. Love is of a certain nature. The fullness, breadth, depth and height of the nature of love is both revealed and concealed by its visibility and ready accessibility for each self contains this center without distortion within the open heart.

It is both blessing and curse that those who seek so longingly and yearn so profoundly for scientific information to aid in being of service must have their hopes thwarted by the illusive and ever receding face of spiritual knowledge, for this knowledge is not that which has to do with the kind of measuring which is used to calculate the hierarchies of the observable, physical universe, but love moves and its traces dwell within all things. The keys to healing echo the ways or nature of love itself.

We find that to speak further at this juncture is to infringe upon the free development of the awareness which would ask further queries upon this healing subject and consequently we feel that to speak further at this working is not appropriate. We thank this instrument for bearing with us while we attempted to use some concepts which stretched the instrument's ability to understand, if we may again use this term. We also thank the questioner and encourage study and further queries on this interesting subject. Our hearts are full of a love and desire to be of service, as always, and we are most thankful for the energy and desire and longing to be of service that this group expresses with these queries. It is truly a privilege to be able to blend our energies with your own and we cannot thank you enough.

Is there any other query at this time?

Jim: Not from me, Q'uo. That was very good. I'm sure he appreciates that a good deal. Thank you.

We are those of Q'uo, and we greatly appreciate your kind words. May we close by simply spending a few moments stating the wonder, the marvelous wonder of hope when hope is not logical. The wonder, the miraculous wonder of faith, when the faith is not logical. May we encourage each to live in hope and in faith, forgetting not one iota of the darkness perceived but knowing that no darkness eradicates light. Live, then, in light, for [inwardly] you may always be standing beneath the bright sun.

As your spirit basks in its intelligent warmth the body is most positively effected. So may the time of cold and darkness be for you lighted within by the sun of hope and faith. We leave you rejoicing in this faith, in the love and the light of the one infinite Creator.

We are known to you as those of the principle Q'uo. Adonai. Adonai. ☥

L/L Research

L/L Research is a subsidiary of Rock Creek Research & Development Laboratories, Inc.

P.O. Box 5195
Louisville, KY 40255-0195

www.llresearch.org

Rock Creek is a non-profit corporation dedicated to discovering and sharing information which may aid in the spiritual evolution of humankind.

ABOUT THE CONTENTS OF THIS TRANSCRIPT: This telepathic channeling has been taken from transcriptions of the weekly study and meditation meetings of the Rock Creek Research & Development Laboratories and L/L Research. It is offered in the hope that it may be useful to you. As the Confederation entities always make a point of saying, please use your discrimination and judgment in assessing this material. If something rings true to you, fine. If something does not resonate, please leave it behind, for neither we nor those of the Confederation would wish to be a stumbling block for any.

CAVEAT: This transcript is being published by L/L Research in a not yet final form. It has, however, been edited and any obvious errors have been corrected. When it is in a final form, this caveat will be removed.

© 2009 L/L Research

Sunday Meditation
January 16, 1994

Group question: The question this week has to do with how we accept change and the attitude that we can best utilize to meet change. Then we would also like some information on what it is exactly that changes. What is this sense of ourselves that changes and uses various tools like the mind, dreams, archetypical mind and whatever to change?

(Carla channeling)

Greetings from the love and the light of the infinite Creator. We are those of Q'uo, and we are privileged to bless you in the love and the light of the infinite One. We thank each for calling us to your meeting this afternoon and cannot adequately express our feelings of honor, for it is privilege indeed to be able to blend our vibrations with your own and to share our humble opinions with you. As always, we remind each that we are fallible beings prone to error. We need to request that each choose those opinions which seem to resonate within the unique web of energies which are your evolving self and to lay the rest aside, for we would not be a stumbling block before any.

This concept of change is interesting. Imagine if you will the unity and infinity which characterize the creation and all within it. That which is various is infinitely various. That which is infinite is made of one thing. Where, then, is the change? Where the manyness? Each entity focuses within itself every energy within the unified creation. Within each unique and infinitely precious soul lies all that there is.

Thusly, the changes and chances of incarnation take place against a grand backdrop. You now see this backdrop as though it were the universe; you cannot see the stage beneath your feet for it seems to be Earth, nor can you see the self within each character that you play, nor can you see each character that you choose not to play, for you are of tho[se]—we correct this instrument—within the train which spends its speed into gathering twilight, the cars filled with light, the travelers talking and drinking and eating and sleeping and gazing out the windows at the passing scenery.

How much of this landscape that you see have you made yours? This image is intended to funnel your conceptual mind into a configuration within which you may see that the incarnated experience which to you seems greatly various and changeable is in a more light-filled illusion—which is your metaphysical counterpart at this space/time—straight as an arrow. The change you perceive is just that: perception of change, not change. You are on the incarnational train. It is not a local. It does not stop until you disembark. The concept of destiny is *(inaudible)* to most who chase under its heavy hand. Yet, we say to you that this *(inaudible)* destiny is your greatest ally. This train which shall keep you on track regardless of what scenery you view will ride through its destination well in mind, all the curves, and mountains, valleys and great chasms that seem to toss and fling you through life are the scenery of your spirit's learning, the visual aids of the great college which is your incarnation.

To focus upon change is skillful for the one who works to accelerate the rate of spiritual evolution, but we greatly encourage each to couch this focus upon change within the larger picture in which you may see that there is a strong and substantial reason to trust and have perfect faith in destiny.

You have put yourself on this train. This trip is planned by you. You did not ask yourself to be happy or sad, to do well or to do poorly, not at all. You asked yourself to experience this exact incarnation. This is your responsibility, to experience as fully as possible each moment—to be hungry for food, that food being all that you can pay your attention to.

Therefore, the first thing we would say about change and the entity changing is, remember that the changes are apparent as great and sweeping *(inaudible)* changes in direction, but in a more true sense you are simply moving from car to car on that train of destiny. You are beyond all changes secure, safe and held with the greatest tenderness by the love of the infinite One. When all overwhelms you it is well to remember that you need do nothing but rest in those arms. As change occurs the disoriented and torn consciousness which is often experienced can be most unsettling, yet there is always beyond the unsettling emotions the comfort which you may claim, that comfort of the one who loves, the one [whose] love is greatly *(inaudible)* of you. Love created you and love loves you.

This resting and abiding certainty can heal the most tattered spirit, but the gaze must be shifted away from the torn and bleeding circumstances, relationship or whatever is perceived as changing and making vulnerable and afraid that self which is your conscious self. To attempt to get a true grounding from the other passengers, shall we say, is not to invoke the higher or more overarching energies, rather, to turn to the infinite Creator for solace and comfort is the effective action, for consider that each entity who you interact with is also on that train which his destiny has chosen.

Let us now gaze at who it is that changes, and who it is that records or witnesses change. Imagine the self standing in the desert at night. The entity you [are] imagining reaches one hand to *(inaudible)* sky. Moving finally from this *(inaudible)* attitude this figure begins to dance, and as this figure dances and spins, the stars above begin to whirl *(inaudible)* until all of creation is drawn star by star into the self. This figure, then, has all within, all of star, all of space, all of emotion, all of life, all within. This is the entity which witnesses change. You see the manifestation of yourself, it seems to have dimension, to be the daughter of time and space, or the son of time and space.

We say to you that in actuality all that you have experienced as rock, as tree, as human, as what you call angel, as sun, as Creator, all of these things are the witness that flings the hand to beckon the stars. All that moves moves and has being in an instant and within this instant the millions and millions of years of a whole creation beginning, *(inaudible)*, and ending has taken place. You now experience the instant before the Creator coalesces once again. Time is an illusion, space is an illusion. The witness knows at some level the depth of this illusion, and through all change it keeps its feet steadily upon the desert floor. There is that within you which has such power that you could not image or believe this selfhood to be yours.

You ask how to meet change? We say to you the second thing that is you do not have to meet change. You have only to remember who you are. You are the witness; pay attention. Remember the desert floor and the out-flung hand, remember the stars spinning into your consciousness and meet change with love, for you have nothing to fear. You commanded this change.

The third and final thing we would say about change is most skillfully taught by the one known as Jesus. This teacher said to worry not about what to eat or what to wear or what things to say, for food and clothing and words will all be supplied as the destiny kindly arranges one day at the time, as this instrument is fond of saying. Yesterday's change is moving away behind you, tomorrow's change is not imagined. You need only focus upon the present moment as you perceive it.

The impulse of the manifestation of yourself which is human has the instinct to grasp and hold those things which are perceived as being needed. There is the stretching and the reaching for enough to withstand what might occur. Yet change does not happen well to entities which are holding on to anything. What if in this instant the gravity you experience was reversed. Would you do a somersault or would you fall all over yourselves while explaining that this was impossible. How much of change is painful because it is resisted? There is in the makeup which you have supplied yourselves with a great tool; as always, we mention this tool, that being meditation. The levels upon which are lived the life are several. You see, to unite the spirit, the mind, and the body to promote that unity which appears as health, that health may be greatly aided by the frequent remembrance of the ground of being during meditation, even if it is only for a second. The various pieces of self are knitted up in that opening to the presence within that loved you before you ever hoped to love it. How precious each of you is.

It is as though within the meditation, regardless of how scattered it seems, there is a pure and distilled waterfall of light which irrigates and illumines cell by cell the body, mind and spirit. It is like being rinsed and polished to relax into that presence which is holy. And do not simply confine the self to one kind or form of meditation, for various experiences request various kinds of coherent illumination or meditation. Sometimes you may wish to contemplate a certain eye-catching thought or question, sometimes the meditation may be very active, the sacred dance, the sacred song. Sometime the true need is for the self to rail and complain bitterly to the infinite Creator, to say, "This does not seem to be a lesson in love at all. This hurts, this is painful, and I don't like it." Complaining is allowed, my children, complaining is encouraged. Too much is made of the wonderfulness of the infinite Creator and not enough said about the intimate love of this love itself that engages you in conversation and responds caringly and intricately to the way you speak your experience and tell your story to [it].

We encourage each, especially in times of dislocating change, to tell your story either mentally or out loud to the infinite One. The infinite One is never happier than when being addressed, and you, in addressing the infinite One, receive reflections you cannot imagine, reflections of the highest of truth and beauty. Each of you is waiting to flower and bloom from moment to moment. To most ably assist the self in [blooming] through change we encourage each to remember who you truly are. Remember the true magnitude of your infinite self. Remember the impossibility of ever judging a circumstance or combination of feelings in any accurate way, and shed the responsibility for that. You are responsible only as you will yourself to pay attention to that which is before the eyes and then to address that situation, curious to find the most love within the self and the most appropriate way to share that love—first with the infinite One and then with the self and others, looking in times of change for ways to love and ways to be love, and accepting all with a brave heart.

(Inaudible) in the deeper and deepening consciousness of the witness self that watches all change yet remains the self within the rock, the self within the Creator and all points between. Then may you be tossed about by experience only a little, only to the extent that you accept with a high and courageous heart. We feel you cry out in this change's occurrence. We feel the pain within the voices that ask "Why?" and we do not wish to be cold-hearted. Yet, it is the perception of the animal within that change is dangerous, and that mind which is the mind of the second-density animal which carries your consciousness about in this lifetime resists and demands a cessation of change, for it does not have faith, is not self-conscious. Its instinct rule and its intellect rationalizes instinct. Yet, you are not this life-form but another. You are consciousness, and you have accepted partnership with this entity which walks and talks and moves about.

It is not wise to be driven by this animal or its very capable mind. Retain the awareness of that consciousness that does not resist destiny, and school yourself as far as possible to create the response to stimulus which is positive and says, "Yes, I will accept this change and will be sustained in it by the presence of love." Call upon your own faith, feel strongly the hope which abides, and attempt to remember that all those changes have to do with lessons about loving. You are experiencing manyness; you seek infinity. You are experiencing concern and questioning doubt and worry. Bring in, too, remembrance, love. All things will pass away except love. You are love, you just don't know it yet. Give yourself and the illusion time.

We would at this time leave this instrument and transfer to the entity known as Jim. We thank this instrument and leave it in love and in light. We are those of Q'uo.

(Jim channeling)

I am Q'uo, and greet each again in love and in light. It is our privilege at this time to ask if there may be any further queries for us from those within this group. Are there any further queries at this time?

Carla: I just—I have one question. Is there something within women that is fundamentally different than men, in that woman seem to want so much more than men … comfort. Is that part of the archetypical nature of woman, that they wish for reassurance more, comfort, reassurance, hugs, approval, that kind of thing, or is it training?

I am Q'uo, and I am aware of your query, my sister. This is a query which reaches deeply within the nature of the biological female within your third-density culture, and indeed beyond and before as well. We shall speak briefly and rely upon further queries for specificity.

The female of your peoples is that entity through which the force of life manifests itself, and knowing this both consciously and subconsciously the female nurtures that life force in every way possible, seeking as all mothers to guarantee the circumstances of the birth and rearing of that life force in manifestation. Thus, the female is more disposed to seek and preserve those situations which shall enhance its abilities to give the life force manifestation through its being as are all such *(inaudible)* or distortions within your illusion. This distortion also has those echoes and ramifications that attend to each individual female's interpretation, both that which is conscious and that which is subconscious, so that the desire to nurture the life force may occasionally express itself as the desire for the more comfortable environment that will allow it to do that which is its destiny.

Is there a further query, my sister?

Carla: No, thank you, Q'uo.

I am Q'uo, and we thank you, my sister. Is there another query?

E: I have one related to the male/female difference, that is, given that females are inherently more nurturing than man, why is it that all major cultures on this planet are dominated by males?

I am Q'uo, and I am aware of your query, my brother. Again, we do not wish to oversimplify that upon which we speak but we may in brief reply that the male of your peoples is an entity that has its part to play in the preserving and the enhancing of the life force as it manifests in succeeding generations. Thus, as the male finds itself physically superior in most cases, it has the task in symbolic form, if not always in practical form, of finding those shelters and food sources that it shall provide for the family, that is the means by which the evolution of the species is accomplished.

As we mentioned previously, this protective aspect of the female nature to provide safe surroundings for its young has the distortion that can be personally expressed; so does the male have the personal and somewhat more profound distortion of taking that nature of providing physical sustenance and distorting it in a fashion which allows the preeminence of the male to be expressed. Thus, each function of male and female, and indeed of any entity, may be echoed in various portions of the environment that is created by the interaction of individuals and groups. Thus, the physical strength may be overemphasized to such a degree that the male claims physical dominance, or a dominance in any number of avenues. This quality is one which sets up the dynamic tension, shall we say, that works many times in [retrograde] nature, as the male does not always see how it may relate in a more civilized sense with those about it, both the male and the female.

The tendency to view the self as superior because of looking at one quality only is a common feature of many of your peoples. Thus, there are individuals who judge themselves well because of mental brilliance, because of physical strength, because of creations of one kind or another for which they give themselves credit. These are means by which distortions maybe noted and may be set up for balancing, shall we say.

There have been other times upon your planetary influence when the male was not in all cultures in the position which it finds itself at this time. However, you may note that the cycles of relationship move and change and there is much of this change evident now within various cultures at this time, moving as always from the pioneer individuals, shall we say, to those about it, and spreading as the ripple effect to others as well.

Is there a further query, my brother?

E: No, thank you. That was very helpful.

I am Q'uo, and we thank you, my brother. Is there another query?

Carla: No, Q'uo. Thank you.

I am Q'uo, and we seem to have exhausted the queries at this time. We are hopeful that we have not exhausted your patience as well. We are most grateful for your invitation to join your circle of seeking and we rejoice with you at every stop upon the journey, for indeed we and many others walk with you, perhaps unseen but forming a goodly company nonetheless. We shall at this time take our leave of this instrument and this group, leaving each, as always, in the love and in the ineffable light of the one infinite Creator. We are known to you as those of Q'uo. Adonai, my friends. Adonai. ☙

L/L Research

Sunday Meditation
January 23, 1994

Group question: The question this afternoon has to do with the phenomenon that we've noticed over the years—a number of people have read the *Law of One* books and have become interested enough in the information to want to come visit us, and have indeed done so for a period of days, or even just a few hours, so that as time goes on we collect a growing family of very close and harmonious spiritual seekers, all of whom are focused around the *Law of One* information, and when they're here they feel like there is some sort of transformative experience, of some kind, in differing degrees of intensity, I guess you'd say, and we're kind of wondering just how this works.

We know that we don't do anything in particular—we just live our lives here and people come and feel very much akin to everything that's going on and become a member of a family. How does this work? Do you have any comments on this for our group and for any group that seeks to be of service to others?

(Carla channeling)

I am Q'uo. Greetings in the love and in the light of the one infinite Creator. We are most privileged to come to your circle of seeking this evening to share with you our thoughts concerning your question. We thank each for the gift of presence and the further gift of direction to our remarks. We enjoy being able to address a certain topic or question and thank each for taking the care in shaping your query that you do. As always, we ask each to take from our opinions those that seem to have that personal ring of truth and let the balance go, for we are fallible and prone to error.

As we focus upon this question of what it is that is occurring with entities making the pilgrimages to your dwelling, we find we need go no further than the present moment to begin the discussion. At this present moment there is a small group gathered expressly to seek along lines of spiritual inquiry. To this modest gathering have—we correct this instrument—has come myriads of what you would term inner planes and outer planes entities, which flock to those places where light is being generated by natives, shall we say, of your sphere in order both to join in the joy of the experience and to lend their limitless light to the light which, by your seeking together, you have also begun to create yourselves.

In this present moment, then, your small group has fulfilled that for which a group would exist—that is, that there has been aid given to those who are in this circle, for each entity alone could be prayerful, or meditative, and certainly do much beautiful work in consciousness. However, when the small group gathers, the one and one and one become more than two or three, they become, indeed, the entirety of creation. And to that universe, so well represented by so few, comes the one infinite Creator in the active or energetic mode.

If we were to ask any of those present how well they could attract the love and the caring of the infinite One, perhaps the answer would seem to be along lines of hard personal spiritual work, prayer and fasting, or some difficult task, such as the silence over an extended period. Yet we say to you that when even the smallest group gathers, seeking the Creator, the Creator is immediately present, and listens carefully to the requests made by seekers.

A light center, then, fulfills that quoted from the one known as Jesus: "When two or three are gathered together in my name, there I am in the midst of them." To this small group, then, of the one known as R, the one known as Jim and the one known as Carla, come countless hosts, some which you would call angels, others which you might call extraterrestrials. All who seek to add to the lightening of this sphere—all these come and lend their aid, seeking, as you seek, the presence of the eternal within the finite—that magic point of flame where spirit touches matter and the creation is forever altered by that light.

When entities such as yourselves decide to live lives of devotion and service, there are many, many avenues for how to proceed—we correct this instrument—avenues along which one may proceed. The organizational questions seem important, and indeed to some extent they are, for in the, shall we say, legal skeleton of such a group as yours, it is well to align the legal organization along lines of ethical and general impeccability.

But there is much more to the organization than the framework on paper. There is that living edifice which walks upon two legs. Each of those which associates itself with such an organization is also that which is always intended to be most clean and without lie. With these requirements carefully met insofar as humanly possible, the organization then has simply to abide.

The power of abiding is deep, and its roots lie solidly within the archetypical. We are aware that you seek more information along this archetypical line of query, and would say that in grasping just how the entity called L/L works one may see the archetype being called upon. The way of this group has been to sacrifice this or that within the personal lives of those who began it in order to create the sure and certain time when the meditation, the study, the questioning might be trusted and counted upon to occur. Even within the physical dwelling which houses both the personal and the organizational portions of the existence of the ones known as Jim and Carla [there] have been sacrifices, the former living room becoming office and so forth.

Each having done what was necessary in order to bring L/L into manifestation, each now may simply abide. We look to the archetype of the Hanged Man. This is your archetype. Into manifestation you offer the self and all the life, knowing that it literally turns one upside down. This you accepted, and so it comes into manifestation with plenty and bounty as its characteristics.

Insofar as these sacrifices of time and money and talent have been given purely, and indeed we do find this to be so, just to that extent this nexus of spiritual light and energy may then be used as that beacon to which other spiritual seekers may set their course.

Now switch with us from the point of view of the lighthouse to the point of view of those who seek to come to that place of light. Those who set sail upon a spiritual journey or pilgrimage sail in trackless blackness. The winds blow the thin cloud before the moon, and the spiritual sea is never quiet. Where is the North Star for those who sail so? To most no direction is found, no star may guide. For most there is only the faintest of directions which can be counted upon.

Yet when an entity seeking in this sea manages to come across the work of a positively oriented organization, such as yours, there is the aid or push from what we might call kind destiny. It is as though the sailor, having known surely that there is no direction to be found, settles itself down upon the dock and simply says, "All right. I know there [is] no outer answer, no visible direction. This is all of me, all that I am. I lay it before my Creator. Yield to me in your good time the star of hope. Show me a way." This prayer does not have to be aloud or in words, but it must be heartfelt and single-minded.

To one who holds up this hope, the star of hope does appear, and sometimes that star has the label "L/L." And destiny has kindly given a direction.

What do entities who find L/L, and come, find when they arrive? Perhaps now you may see that while outwardly they find simply the one known as

Jim and the one known as Carla and a living room office, yet inwardly there is the certainty which comes from experiencing the tides and ways of destiny, that herein lies the infinite and the eternal, touching into manifestation.

We are aware that the ones known as Jim and Carla are amazed at the fire that is ignited when seekers find L/L. Yet they may put aside amaze and likewise put aside that inner guilt from feeling that they are not worthy, insofar as all are unworthy—that is, prone to error. Certainly each contains much error. Insofar as entities perceiving them without error, we suggest the concern be removed, for as entities see the ones known as Jim and Carla they see not Jim and Carla, for these entities have gotten themselves out of the way and it is the spirit within, the Creator present within, which is seen.

When entities create a place with a physical address which has as its only and heartfelt purpose the aiding of spiritually oriented seekers seeking the one Creator …

(Pause)

We are sorry for this pause. The one known as Carla went to sleep. We are those of Q'uo, and are with this instrument.

We are with this instrument. However, we are having some difficulty bringing this instrument to a working level of consciousness, and we were very close to the end of that which we had for you this day before asking for queries, therefore we would go ahead and transfer this contact to the one known as Jim in hopes that this entity is somewhat more alert than the one known as Carla, who is somewhat fatigued.

We would at this time transfer. We are those of Q'uo, and thank this instrument.

(Jim channeling)

I am Q'uo, and greet each again in love and in light through this instrument. Thus it is that [for] each entity which comes through the doors that are opened to L/L Research there is the fulfilling of the destiny for the one. And those who find this experience with those of L/L are those whose vibrational destinies, shall we say, resonate in harmony for the experience that is shared, each thus teacher to each, learning as the preparations have allowed, providing opportunities for further experience.

We who speak with those who gather feel the greatest of honor, for we know that the love and light of the one Creator which we are privileged to share is that which attracts all, and as each entity on the path of seeking moves from light to light, there is the growing union with all light everywhere. Thus does each seeker and each group provide light for the great unveiling of unity that all consciousness partakes in.

At this time we would ask if there might be any further query to which we may speak?

Carla: Q'uo, when people come here, quite frequently I end up listening and sharing and doing some teaching, and I wonder, is there a way that I could improve my listening ability or my openness to offering right counsel, because these people give an enormous, and really kind of a scary, amount of authority to people like me and Jim, and of course we really try to be really careful about what we say, but you can just be who you are and do the best you can, and I certainly feel there is room for improvement here. Do you have any suggestions or comments?

I am Q'uo, and am aware of your query, my sister. We would not wish to play the mechanic and tinker with various portions of this finely tuned engine, but would simply recommend that you do as you have done, that is, to live as you are and to take advantage of those opportunities to witness or share as they arise. There is no need to be concerned about what will be said or how it shall be spoken, for there is the flow of energy that is apparent to each, and as the life is lived more in accord with the flow of experiential energies that are all about, then those opportunities that are appropriate for sharing present themselves as surely as does the leaf to the light.

We would ask if there is any further query, my sister?

Carla: Not at this time, Q'uo, thank you.

I am Q'uo, and again we thank you, my sister. Is there another query at this time?

R: I have a query, Q'uo, that concerns something that is on my mind when I come and join the circle, and that is that I wish to bring in as much love and light to the circle, with—and minimize the flaws, so to speak, that come from my personality. So my question is if you can comment on how to improve on it, or if it is something that I need not worry about.

I am Q'uo, and am aware of your query, my brother. Again, we would simply recommend that you do as you have done, for it has been well done, and that is to join in the circle of seeking with as happy a heart and as clear a mind as is possible, and we find that each within this circle is diligent in this regard. Thus, removing worry or concern for improvement is the only suggestion we can make at this time.

Is there a further query, my brother?

R: No, Q'uo, that is all I have. Thank you.

I am Q'uo, and we thank you, my brother. We would ask if there is a final query.

Carla: I do have one query, and it is just—I have been hearing more and more people getting AIDS, and as we pray for AIDS, and as we pray for aid for people who have AIDS, is there one image or one kind of healing that we could yearn for, because it's just—it's just a horrible problem. So many of the most kindly and beautiful souls that I know—earnest, seeking souls being just laid completely down to the earth and just killed by this.

I am Q'uo, and am aware of your query, my sister. We can only recommend that prayer for courage, for strength of faith, and for the purpose of the life well lived in the opening of the heart be offered, for all within your illusion shall find its end, and each will walk through the door of that you call death, and for each, the experience completed will be that which was the destiny of the incarnation, and each shall look upon that experience as that which is most cherished. Pray for the happy heart to come soon, for soon it shall come, indeed.

We would at this time thank each again for inviting our presence. We are full of joy at each such opportunity and give thanks to the One for the blessings of your queries and your desire to seek that truth which we seek, too.

At this time we shall take our leave of this instrument and this group, rejoicing with each step and with each word spoken, leaving each in the love and in the light of the one infinite Creator. We are those of Q'uo. Adonai, my friends. Adonai. ☙

L/L Research

Sunday Meditation
January 30, 1994

Group question: The question this afternoon has to do with facing the truth, telling the truth and feeling a balancing or release of limitations of fears, and we're wondering how the facing of fears, the telling of truth, affects our growth either mentally, emotionally, spiritually or physically. It is said, "Know the truth and it will set you free." How exactly does this work in our daily lives as we're trying to recognize the truth and tell the truth?

(Carla channeling)

We are those of Q'uo. Greetings in the love and in the light of the one infinite Creator. It is our pleasure and privilege to join your circle of seeking this evening. We bless and thank each of you for calling us to your group to share our thoughts and opinions with you. As always, we ask that our words be listened to as you would listen to any friend, taking that which seemed to you to be helpful and leaving the rest behind, for we do not claim infallibility, but rather assure you that we are far from perfected. There is much for us to learn. We are as you, those who seek the truth.

Perhaps that is where we shall start to discuss the concept of healing by the truth. This instrument's mind is furnished with much detail concerning the practice of the religion which you call Christianity. Consequently, we find the nearest example available to us is often, when working with this instrument, one which comes from the scripture which you call the Holy Bible. In this particular instance, the scene within which truth is sought is that scene of the one known as Jesus' trial, scourging and crucifixion. While the process of the trial was working itself out, the civil authority having to do with the one known as Jesus—the one known as Pilate—pondered long that which the one known as Jesus offered and this entity's comment was, "What is truth?" This entity could not find within the true statements made by each entity an overriding truth which would create choice. Consequently, this entity walked away from the debate giving control over to others rather than answering that question.

One truth seemingly obvious was the sincerity and the ultimate dignity of the one known as Jesus. The one known as Pilate wrote a sign for this entity as this entity suffered and died. The sign read, "The King of the Jews." This was Pilate's truth. Those who wished this entity stopped, if not killed, saw that this entity known as Jesus had the capacity to rouse his countrymen to civil rebellion. They feared that this entity would indeed ascend to an Earthly throne, disturbing greatly the peace and tranquility of the empire of Rome.

The one known as Jesus also possessed a truth. The scope of this entity's truth was overarching a truth of another level of beingness and witnessing to the truth. For the one known as Jesus, the truth of its being was not applicable to the world of temporal affairs. Yet to witness to this truth that was otherworldly, this entity saw virtue and value and truth in the sacrifice of all Earthly energy and this entity moved willingly and deliberately towards that cross upon which it was indeed crucified. This truth was that for this entity, there was a freedom. That freedom was complete service. This entity felt that it was given the job of so dying and then showing itself to bear life that the world would come by this truth to its own truth and ultimate freedom.

To find the truth in this story is impossible, for there were several levels of true feeling, true fact, true intention. The truth is most slippery. It recedes from the attempt to pin it down, for that which you experience is not truth. That which you experience within your own consciousness is seldom truth. Truth is living and truth alters constantly in its appearance as the processes of perception circle the concept of truth, looking for a way to settle upon a complete surety of truth.

Now, let us pull back to a position where we examine simply what brought each here. Each feels within an identity and that identity is felt by each to be authentic and true. Each comes to this circle of seeking hoping to encounter the truest part of the self, for within the energies of a group lie tremendous power, that power of hope and intention of desire and yearning. We come to share our perception that all things are one, and that one thing is love.

The love that created all that there is is a concept, an original Thought of such a powerful nature as is unimaginable. This articulated thought or logos called love has a vibration. This vibration is the truth, for it is all that there is and each of you is at heart that vibration and that vibration alone. The rest is illusion.

We speak to groups like this simply encouraging each to more and more attempt to vibrate in accordance with the one original Vibration, and as the vibratory level rises from the sea of confusion which is the life experience, it partakes more and more of vibration closer to that one original Thought.

Each of you is not the God in some conscious sense but love, and you hunger for the freedom of your true nature and seek to move into more and more close vibratory similarity to that true vibration or nature which is love. When the truth is a vibration, perhaps it can be seen that the truth is a very difficult concept about which to speak, for after one says the simple truth, so called, that there is a vibration which each intuits within and seeks and hungers for, after this each entity moves out of the original concept into manifestation.

Before your incarnational experience begins, already you are isolated from the truth because you have self-consciousness as a spirit or entity with a soul. Before you entered your mother's womb, already you were a stranger to truth, hungering to return to that vibratory configuration in which truth is known but the self is lost. And then, illusion already completely surrounding and filling you, you entered into a heavy chemical body, a physical vehicle which moves your consciousness around and generously supplies that consciousness with that which the senses pick up and report to the brain. Each impression is a true one, yet each impression is biased by your perception of it.

You have perhaps heard the old adage that no two witness' report an accident the same. What is truth? Yet you seek and experience a growing amount of truth. The energies within you bring that present moment in a cyclical manner so that each entity will have its cycles, times when—we correct this instrument—within which they are more well suited to do work in consciousness attempting to find a higher truth and times when it is better to simply shower the self with compassion, for compassion is a truth regardless of the object of that expression of self.

We encourage each to loosen and free this concept of truth from any rigid limitations, for the seeker on this journey towards truth walks with much aid. Each seeker has cooperation and support from the world which is unseen. There are guides and essences which live in order to serve the seeker and to further that seeker's search, so that instead of there being the truth here and then the truth further on, lesson one and lesson two, rather there is a process whereby each step the pilgrim takes has a point of balance which is graceful and skillful. The seeker then simply attempts to sense where that beam lies, how that ray falls, that ray of light unseen, for it lies directly down the middle of the spiritual path.

We would encourage you to think of the levels of truth as you go through your moments, your hours, your days and your years. There is the light and the momentary truth. The fact, the schedules and processes of your worldly life contain vast numbers of these facts, these simple truths. "The garbage is picked up on Monday. I am supposed to be at work at 9 a.m. The Superbowl is today." These are truths. They are not truths which in any way better equip you to live according to spiritual principles. There is no healing in them, yet they are the truth.

At a deeper level, there is a true self. That true self within has its vagrant moods and there is emotional truth in hewing with fidelity to these inner moods. It is excellent practice to know what is going on within, to be as aware as possible of the deeper energies, the emotions which underlie the experiences. Without judging the self, there is great healing in simply acknowledging the nature of the self as it is self-perceived. The acceptance of the emotional makeup of the self is very freeing if it is wholehearted, for there is great difficulty in altering that nature if it is not first completely accepted, yet the truth for which each seeker yearns is that truth which cannot be accessible, not by words, not by converse, but only by the inner experiencing of things far too inimitable to be available for description.

The hunger within the seeker is to see the face of the infinite One, and there is no face for that infinite intelligence, rather that face is your own, and that face is the entity next to you and that face is the face of nature. Everything that you see both displays and completely obscures that face of deity. Spiritual seeking is a process in which the attempt is made and made and made again to be honest with the self, to submit the self to the disciplines which strip away illusion, how the seeker strives to clear the mind, to become more authentic, to become more self-aware, to confront the self where it is hiding from the self.

You speak in your query of fears in attempting to speak truth to those fears, yet we suggest that these fears are also a truth and fear is not something to be rooted out before its time. Each of you has an infinite amount of time in which to seek and find the one infinite Creator. You have no need to rush. The Creator will not leave. The creation may fade away, yet you and the Creator shall seek each other until, in the glory of final awareness, the self is given away so that that separate self might become a portion of the only portion that there is in reality: intelligent infinity or love.

Now let us come back from the ethers to the self struggling to know more of the truth, struggling to face the fears that hold the self captive. We spoke earlier of compassion being a truth. It is well to equip the self with the awareness that compassion is always truth. When entities such as you attempt to be, as you call it, "too nice," yet in this attempt is truth. It is not a truth that makes you feel good, for in expressing compassion, you are allowing the other to see only the truth of love in its unabridged form. You become a witness to the truth that nothing matters as much as loving.

Over against this truth is another truth that is involved with where you are as an entity in your cycle of expressing and not expressing. If you are in a strong and powerful place in your spiritual cycles, it is possible that manifesting the truth of compassion is more satisfying to you than expressing your emotional feelings. At a weaker or more transparent part of this cycle, it is actually harmful to you as an entity—or we could perhaps say self-sacrificing—to express compassion, for there is the emotional lack of ability to give up the truth of another color which would be the truth of the emotions which may have the need to express seemingly negative information. Therefore, it is not always skillful to be compassionate. It is well to know the self well enough to see when compassion alone is the truth to tell and when instead it would be more skillful to speak seemingly selfishly but honestly in expressing the limitations and the needs of the self.

The truth, it is said, shall set you free. This was in your query. How does it set you free? We hope that you may see that there are levels of truth. The more deep or profound truths set the spirit free at a more profound level. The use of the intelligence is encouraged in the attempt to accurately estimate the capacity of the self to be at any one level of the truth. For instance, in the one known as Jesus, this entity's truth was at the profound level which moves beyond all fear of death or dissolution. The truth this entity saw was that it could embrace the grave and willingly go down into it because the entity's true nature was the Creator and this entity's true place was eternity. This is your highest truth also, but you will note that the one known as Jesus did not go to his death before the various levels of truth of all others so coagulated and combined as to be that time destiny had provided for the one known as Jesus to in one moment express that truth.

Each of you do well to open your sensing mechanisms and look to your perceptions. Certainly it is well to seek that truth which lies in and beyond the fears of each, but more than that, know yourselves as pilgrims which have many, many levels and be not harsh with yourself when you find yourself expressing that which you perceive is not entirely true. For the freedom truth promises is involved in that release from trying, seeking and making things happen. The truth, in a way, is a process. That process is one in which we often encourage each to come to the place of ultimate quiet within, that all the worlds tears and hopes and untruths and fears may at last cease and a door open within. Across that threshold each walks into the silence of the heart. Within that silence lies all that there is and it is all holy. Each of you now stands on holy ground. The truth of your being is within your silent heart. Listen each day if you can to that silence. Within that silence a silent voice speaks love to you. This is truth. All your fears shall fetch up against this rock and flow away.

We would at this time thank this instrument for its service, and transfer this contact to the one known as Jim. We leave this instrument in love and light. We are those of Q'uo.

(Jim channeling)

I am Q'uo, and greet each again in love and in light. At this time we would offer ourselves in the attempt to speak to any further queries which those present may have for us. Is there a query at this time?

Questioner: I am still interested in the physical manifestation in our bodies of the … perhaps the tension that's produced by this seeking of the truth, or the time when you're searching for the truth. Can you speak to that further?

I am Q'uo, and am aware of your query, my sister. We shall attempt to do so. As an entity perceives the life experience moving through it and before and around it, it has those means of dealing with this basic element of life that you would call the belief system. This is a means of containing that which is perceived as truth but which has been in some ways distorted by the very attempt to perceive it and define it in such and such a way so that it will be useful to the entity as it grows. Such distortions are necessary in order to be able to utilize the life experience in a certain fashion that is congruent with what you would call preincarnative choices or lessons.

Thus, as a means of setting the stage, shall we say, each entity defines, confines and refines the truth so that the opportunities it desires are likely to be presented. To hold that which is true, that which is love without end and with complete compassion in a confined or compacted way that you would call your own illusion, the stage upon which you move, is to invoke or require a certain amount of what you have called tension—mental, emotional, physical and spiritual attention, shall we say. The belief system that has been chosen, then, confines in a, shall we say, intense or restrictive fashion, that which is limitless, that which has no bounds. This takes an effort on all levels of energy; this effort you perceive as tension. This is why a great feeling of relief and release is experienced by those who are able to extend or in some cases remove the boundaries of definition upon that which is love.

Thus, your physical vehicle takes upon itself various conformations that are symbolic representation of mental belief boundaries. There are possible an infinite number of bodily responses that you would see as a disease of some form that are a result of the mental configuration. As the mind/body/spirit complex that each entity is makes choices to move in other belief directions there is often the release of the tension, the configuration of the body corresponding to that release of the mind, the emotions as well. Thus, you see in many cases that the change of belief system or component of that system affects the actual configuration of the physical vehicle.

Is there a further query, my sister?

Questioner: No, thank you.

I am Q'uo, and we thank you, my sister. Is there another query?

Questioner: D had a question that I was interested in, and it had to do with when you have experienced a feeling of release—a place where you have gotten at a truth and seen a true, purified version of what held you in thrall in times past, and you've seen that and you've experienced that—how can you complete this release so as to finish most appropriately that energy and really, really release that whole complex of held tension that has really sort of been an untruth …

Questioner: Actually, also, after listening to what you have just said, I'm beginning to question as to whether or not the intensity was the actual holding onto a belief system and perhaps it wasn't even a releasing but it was, rather, a battle of wills between the mental belief system still holding on to something and another kind of truth attempting to come through, and perhaps that was really inappropriate tension felt as opposed to healing tension that would have been released.

Questioner: Can you make anything of that … can you comment?

I am Q'uo, and we have sufficient information for a response, we believe. We give this instrument the image of a stream full of rocks of various sizes which divert the flow of water according to the size and the placement of the rock. The freeing of one's belief system, the removing of the boundaries, is much like removing of the rocks one by one from the stream so that the full force of the water's flow may be felt without distortion.

Thus, when one moves in consciousness to alter the beliefs, one allows the intelligent energy that is love and life itself to move in a less restricted fashion which is more freely able to express the power of love to transform. Thus, the release can be seen as a harmonizing effort that allows energy to be more available to the entity to be—we correct this instrument—to be consciously used. The seating of this release or healing may best be accomplished by observing in the meditative state the condition as it was, the nature of the distortion, the removal of same and the giving of thanksgiving to the one Creator for the opportunity to more fully experience and express the energy of love.

Is there a further query, my sisters?

Questioner: Not for my part, thank you.

Carla: I'm still a little confused here. I still can't determine whether or not there are a couple of boulders in that stream, and although I may be consciously attempting to allow that stream to flow, there is an unwillingness to allow that due to the belief system, and although I can go and meditate on such a situation, I'm just a little confused about how to go about that because I don't quite understand if what has occurred was a healing process or was the exact opposite, in which case I need to know which it were, so that if it were the exact opposite I would be able to go about healing that in another way than I attempted to do so with Jim earlier. I would be …

maybe less tense on my physical vehicle. Can you comment in any way without infringing?

I am Q'uo, and we may speak in a general fashion to suggest that the experience which you describe is one which heals, that is the facing of fear, the recognition of truth. There is the removal of restriction which is a portion of the realignment of mental beliefs; as each pebble is removed from the stream there is the healing, as you would call it, however, it must be recognized that each pebble, rock or boulder allows water to move around in such a fashion as to carve, shall we say, a certain groove within the entity's mind/body/spirit complex that is in accordance with preincarnative choice so that the analogy which you mentioned earlier holds true: if one can experience great pain carved by much experience in the life pattern, then one can also experience its opposite, the great joy as well. Each entity has come to incarnation to be able to move from chosen parameters to other chosen parameters. The parameters for each incarnation include greater and greater opportunity for experiencing and expressing love. However, there must be the distortion of that which is whole into that which is many for the many to be able to choose the path back to the One.

Is there a further query, my sister?

Carla: The only other thing I was just curious about was what happens energetically when your physical vehicle does go through such a jolting thing? How does the energy as it is pulsing and raging through your physical vehicle—what does that do? Does it kind of vibrate off, what has been held in? Can you describe the process energetically, speaking of what happens when what has otherwise been termed as a healing crisis comes through? We experience the trauma in order to be able to release it. Can you explain that process briefly in an energetic way?

I am Q'uo, and we shall attempt this, my sister. As the energy is allowed to flow more freely, the vehicle that is physical and the vehicle that is mental and emotional as well tends to vibrate more harmoniously, that is to say, there are less discordant vibrations. It is as though a loose nut or bolt within your automobile has been tightened so that there is less jarring vibration upon the road.

Is there a further query, my sister?

Questioner: Then what is the jarring that is experienced—is that a result of releasing? Why do we feel the exact opposite of what you have described has occurred? To the human physical vehicle, it feels like uncontrollable vibration … it feels as if this is fully electric and cannot … or is that the potential for being able to hold that kind of energy? I just feel the opposite of what you have just said is occurring.

I am Q'uo, and am aware of your query, my sister. The process by which the physical vehicle comes into greater harmony and less jarring vibrations is one in which the mental configuration which has been holding that which we have called love or truth in a confined manner, allows that truth now to flow by removing the boundary. The boundary belief is that which has been, shall we say, out of place in the true alignment of energy and has been holding the energy of love in a difficult position, shall we say. To release that energy requires that which held that energy—the mind and emotional components—to fall into a new alignment.

This falling into place, even though it is from that which is less harmonious to that which is more harmonious with energy flow, yet is a jar to the system which was held in such and such a fashion; however, the energy of love will eventually allow this new configuration to express itself in a more harmonious fashion which then is the new steady state of the mind/body/spirit complex.

Is there a further query, my sister?

Carla: No, thank you.

I am Q'uo, and we thank you again, my sister. Is there another query at this time?

Carla: One other thing, and it may be irrelevant and you can certainly say if it is. R and I were attempting to do some healing work and we only had a concern that what we were attempting to do might have been insignificant, or invalid or transient or just not worthy of our attempts, and we were wondering if you could comment on the purpose or if there is validity to uniting through dreamwork purposefully to be able to rebalance and heal more with the power with two as opposed to one individually. And whether or not that reverberated out in any direction other than just the two working on that, if there was any purpose or any reason that we should see continuing in that direction?

I am Q'uo, and am aware of your query, my sister. We find that the desire to be of service to others through the healing process is one which has great merit within your illusion. The task which you have set for yourselves is one which is difficult enough and which requires the mastery of many skills, is one which through the practice through these skills will reverberate to other areas of your incarnation and perhaps others as well. The practice of each of these skills will require the intensive dedication of effort. This, in the service of others, is quite helpful in the polarizing process and in the disciplining of the personality in particular.

Is there another query, my sister?

Carla: I guess we picked a tough nuts thing to do, huh, R? I don't think so, not for me.

I am Q'uo. Again we thank you, my sister. Is there another query at this time?

Questioner: Are you aware of my discomfort at this time?

I am Q'uo, and we are not specifically aware of your discomfort, however, if there is discomfort in the perception of our vibration we would ask that you mentally alert us to this fact so that we might change our approach to your vibrational field.

Questioner: I feel like I am the one that has to change because I am resisting out of fear.

I am Q'uo. We would ask if there is some fear to which we may speak or some way that we might be of service? Could you speak more of your fear?

Questioner: Well, I've had this really hard time hanging on to myself, like I feel like I am being lured away and I was wondering if there was someone like you that was trying to speak through me?

I am Q'uo, and am aware of your query, my sister. We have not attempted to speak through your instrument nor are we aware of other entities attempting that as well, however, we are aware that you are a sensitive instrument which is open to impression and we perceive that you have felt our vibration in a more accentuated manner than most entities are able to perceive. We would recommend that the request be made that we reduce the amount of the conditioning vibration which we make available to those who sit in the circle of working with us.

Questioner: So I need to tell you guys to turn it down a little?

I am Q'uo, and this is basically correct.

Questioner: Okay. I am really uncomfortable. You spoke earlier about beings who we can't see but who help us. You said that there are those [who] are only [here] to serve. Is that what you do?

I am Q'uo, and am aware of your question, my sister. The entities which serve the third-density population of your planet as guides are those who are much like yourselves in many cases except that at this time they are not incarnate and have chosen a means of service that is the guide, the teacher, the helper, the unseen hand that aids in the helpful coincidences, shall we say, within each entity's life pattern.

We are those which come from elsewhere other than your own planetary sphere who answer the call of many upon your planet for information pertaining to the nature of the creation, the one original Thought that we see as the one Creator. Thus, we answer a call and serve as we are asked in the name of the one Creator.

Is there a further query, my sister?

Questioner: Do you ever get bored?

(Carla begins laughing.)

Carla: I'm sorry … *(chuckles).*

I am Q'uo, and we may assure you, my sister, that the creation is varied enough that we find no opportunity for boredom, as you would call it. We are overjoyed at the opportunity to observe the one Creator in the process of knowing Itself in as many ways as any entity could possibly imagine. We see the one Creation as a great field of energy playing with energy.

Is there a final query at this time?

Questioner: Can you hear us thinking our questions or do we have to speak them?

I am Q'uo, and we ask that entities verbalize queries so that we do not infringe upon free will by, as you would say, reading the thoughts.

Is there a final query?

Carla: I would ask as a final query that you give suggestions on ways to put one's mind at ease when one does feel somehow invaded by energies which seem to want to invade—even if that perception is incorrect, there is still stress. Could you just suggest some resources for when that would occur, how she would perceive?

I am Q'uo, and am aware of your query, my sister. If any entity feels that it is being, as you would say, invaded or overtaken by any other entity of an unseen nature, that the one feeling invasion request the entity invading to leave, and that this request be made in the name of that concept, entity or quality which the entity being invaded holds most dear in the life pattern, be that the quality of love, of truth, of service or an entity such as in the name of Jesus the Christ, the name of the Buddha or the name of any saint or angel that an entity may feel affinity, for that if this request is given with the whole heart that the entity invading will be required to leave, and then the entity giving the request would be advised to circle the self in light and in love so that the shield of light and love might be in place.

At this time …

Carla: Wait, Q'uo! Could we stop for a sec'? I really need to drag this back to this point. I just had this question that was bothering me. Just stepping back to the chakras, and the experience that you had described which was the releasing of the mental belief system, which is the yellow ray, as I believe. How come the upper portion of the body was what went through the "trauma," as opposed to the lower rays which were being adjusted? Why would the vibration be from, say, the heart up, as opposed to … from what was felt from the heart up, not from the lower rays? They seemed to be rather relaxed.

I am Q'uo, and am aware of your query, my sister. However, we must apologize for being unable to answer, for we find that the answer would be an infringement upon your own choice-making ability and responsibility. We do not wish to do that work which we find you have set for yourself.

Carla: I gotcha. Thanks anyway.

I am Q'uo, and we thank you once again, my sister. We find that we must leave this group and this instrument at this time, for we have spoken overly long and have wearied many here, and we apologize for the length of our discourse but we are overjoyed at the opportunity to be with you and to feel the intensity of your desire to seek that which you call the truth. We seek with you that same truth, and walk as brothers and sisters, offering a hand when asked and offering love at all times. We are known to you as those of Q'uo, and leave each in the love and in the light of the one infinite Creator. Adonai, my friends. Adonai. ✥

L/L Research

L/L Research is a subsidiary of Rock Creek Research & Development Laboratories, Inc.

P.O. Box 5195
Louisville, KY 40255-0195

www.llresearch.org

Rock Creek is a non-profit corporation dedicated to discovering and sharing information which may aid in the spiritual evolution of humankind.

ABOUT THE CONTENTS OF THIS TRANSCRIPT: This telepathic channeling has been taken from transcriptions of the weekly study and meditation meetings of the Rock Creek Research & Development Laboratories and L/L Research. It is offered in the hope that it may be useful to you. As the Confederation entities always make a point of saying, please use your discrimination and judgment in assessing this material. If something rings true to you, fine. If something does not resonate, please leave it behind, for neither we nor those of the Confederation would wish to be a stumbling block for any.

CAVEAT: This transcript is being published by L/L Research in a not yet final form. It has, however, been edited and any obvious errors have been corrected. When it is in a final form, this caveat will be removed.

© 2009 L/L Research

Sunday Meditation
February 6, 1994

Group question: The question this afternoon is from N and it's concerning healing disease. The basic statement is that it appears that illness or disease, not chosen pre-incarnationally, are the last resources of evolution for the processing of catalyst during incarnation. This basic imbalance is addressed by the healing modalities in one or both of two ways that depend on the degree of Christ awareness possessed by the one to be healed.

Then N lists two different possibilities: the one to be healed may be aware that the illusion has presented the disease as a means of showing a deeper imbalance that can be healed, with the one to be healed working on him or herself and receiving assistance from a healer. The basic change would take place mentally with the realignment of beliefs.

There is also another chance for healing by a person that is not aware of the relationship of disease to the spiritual journey and in this case the one to be healed would go to an allopathic healer and surgery or medication or some sort of an allopathic treatment would be given and it would seem that this removes from the one to be healed the chance to grow, the opportunity being removed by the allopathic treatment.

The first question, of four that will address this area, is, "How does the learning occur, the unbalance addressed and the catalyst processed in the unaware person?"

(Carla channeling)

We are those of Q'uo. Greetings in the love and the light of the one infinite Creator. It is a privilege and a pleasure to commune with this group. We thank each for calling us to your presence to share our thoughts with you on healing. Please be aware at all times that we give not dogma nor doctrine but rather opinion and thoughts to consider. Those which help any, each is free to choose. Any thoughts or concepts in which the receiver is not interested may quickly be placed aside for each shall recognize his own personal truth. Therefore, we leave these opinions to your discretionary use.

In addressing the stated question we find we would make introductory remarks. This step is taken because there are assumptions within the introductory paragraphs which we find to be other than our own understanding. Consequently, we will back up, as it were, from the stated inquiry and later ask that that query be read again, if this is satisfactory to this circle.

Jim: Yes, that's fine.

We are those of Q'uo. Very well, then.

It is a distinct privilege to be able to view the light of your sun using this instrument's eyes which, needless to report, perceive much differently that other physical vehicles belonging to other densities. In such a beautiful, glowing creation it is difficult from a long distance to realize how much of the total of an incarnational experience is involved with issues of healing. Indeed, healing is a much misunderstood concept for healing and cures are not the same. Furthermore, the term of healer suggests a definition which is incorrect. That is, the healer does not do anything. The healer does not heal. The healer presents to the one requesting healing an opportunity.

In healing which has been termed psychic healing or absent healing or many other noninvasive healing procedures, the opportunity which is tendered to an entity is created from the crystallization of the healer's personality, shall we say, so that the healer becomes the equivalent of the healing chamber within the Great Pyramid. When surgery or chemicals are used by a healer this represents a physically objective means, visible to the eye, touchable by the hand, of offering the self-same healing opportunity. In every case the actual healing is a process which involves the unmanifested self.

Therefore, to the healer, we would always suggest the surrendering of that personal agenda which is natural for any healer upon viewing an illness or the physical evidence of an illness. It is so easy to feel that one shall do this and that and it shall operate in a healing modality. Actually, it is well to remain humble as a healer for the healer works upon its own self and in no case does the healer heal.

The strong and invasive avenues of affecting bodily health do in most cases affect the physical vehicle of the patient in the way expected by the healer. However, these are means of curing or masking the symptoms of ill health. They work to make a body function differently and, hopefully, more normally. In no case can a curing by invasive means function as a healing of the imbalance which the ill health is addressing. It is well to make a careful distinction, therefore, between the objectively provable change in health between before a pill was taken or an operative procedure applied and afterwards. This remains in the precinct of curing a physical condition.

Thusly, at all times, the one who wishes healing makes good use of the service rendered by a physician or healer but remains completely responsible for its own processes of healing. To the healer, therefore, all patients are the same. The processes of actual healing are in each case the same. This is hard to see for healing modalities range from the work done in thought by spiritual practitioners to the most obviously invasive and life changing healing modalities of your allopathic practitioners. Yet, in all cases, the healer offers an opportunity and in all cases the healing is the choice and the business of the patient.

It may indeed aid in the attitude of healers who find themselves frustrated by seemingly uncooperative patients to realize that the patient's seemingly nonsensical complaints do make more sense when the struggle of the entity to heal itself, which is going on beneath the threshold of the conscious mind, is actually taking place. There are often strong unconscious motivations which drive a patient to alter and often worsen the medical picture. This is not the healer's concern and the failure to groom the patient so that it does all that it should is often not a battle the true healer wishes to win. When given the choice between a cure and a healing, which would each choose as patient? Which would each choose as a healer serving the infinite One? To whom, or to what agency lies the responsibility for asking these questions?

We would at this time request the first query.

Jim: The first query concerns, "How does the learning occur, and how are the unbalances addressed and catalyst processed in the unaware person?" It seems that you've spoken to this topic which means that we could ask the second question about, "Does the healer who's aware of the spiritual aspects of healing incur any karmic debts? Does the healer who is not aware of the spiritual aspects incur any karmic debts by helping with the healing process?"

We are those of Q'uo. There is no karma involved in the work of healing, per se, for the healer works upon itself, attempting so to balance and empower its personality, if you will, in such a stable and open condition that the opportunity can be offered to the patient for healing. The concern of the physician, then, is with its own spiritual situation. We refer not to the mood of the day or to surface frequencies concerning subjectively perceived spiritual states. One may be, as this instrument would say, in the desert, where the spiritual topography is alien and mystifying or it may be in the most exalted of subjectively perceived spiritual states. To the healer which is mature and therefore efficacious, this will make no difference for the healer who is mature has become aware that the Creator is always present, that the power of the unnamable mystery is always infinite and that this power exists in every location, at every time and under any and all conditions. In other words, the healer learns to tap into that which lies beneath the experiences of the desert or the oasis. That deep level is as a sea which once tapped into offers the absolute inner subjective surety that faith is real and hope exists to save. The healer, in other words, turns from all appearances within itself before it turns away from the appearances presented in the patient.

Karma is a phrase [which is overused] by those meaning various things by it to the point that we feel it may be helpful to state our grasp of this concept. We see karma as a kind of spiritual momentum, [where] unbalanced acts concerning another, and unforgiven by the self and perhaps by the other as well, remain in motion in an entity's incarnational experience. Energies which have not been balanced on the level karma was incurred, or above that level, are carried over into another incarnational experience. This, then, provides for distortion of that experience in such a way as to provide for the entity the opportunity to balance this energy, to stop the momentum of this imbalance. The …

(A loud crash of something toppling over is heard.)

(Laughter)

Carla: OK. OK. A little bit of retuning here.

(Singing)

(Carla channeling)

I am Q'uo, and am with this instrument again. We actually did not leave this instrument, however, the instrument's ears seemed to be much disturbed by the noises of your feline playmates. Therefore, we are glad to make a fresh start, as it were.

We were saying that perhaps it can be seen, then, that there is no karma between healer and healed. The actual predictable difficulty or incorrectness of perception for healers is that it is easy to forget that the healer is actually working upon the self. Then the healer takes responsibility where there was none.

Now, in the matter of curing, the healer applies the skill, whether it be with the surgeon's scalpel or with the specialist's detailed knowledge and pharmacopoeia. To cure conditions the healer which chooses also to cure has the responsibility to apply this curing as sensitively and well [as possible]. There still, however, is no karma between the healer and the one who is cured, for the healer has but altered some personal circumstances of the entity needing healing. Another opportunity will replace the opportunity for healing which seemed to be taken away when the condition of the patient was cured.

Thusly, the healer simply needs to do that curing work it chooses to do in a spirit of joy. Joy that there is some way to reduce suffering. Joy in being of service, but not joy at changing a patient's experience for the patient itself will change its experience in response to its own inner agenda. It is well for the healer which is an allopathic practitioner, then, to speak to this when the healer finds it helpful, that is, stating that these are ways in which the condition presented can be controlled or altered to some extent but that the true work of healing will come from the patient as it deals with its new circumstances.

Is there another query?

Jim: I believe you've just spoken to whether or not the healer abridges the free will of the patient so I guess we can move to the last one and that is, "If the person seeking healing dies are these imbalances that it dies of worked on in the astral plane or is another incarnation necessary or how effective can the person do healing after the incarnation is over?"

We are Q'uo. There is healing which takes place outside of the environment of the physical incarnation, however, that healing is on a level of metaphysical wholeness and does not address physical, mental or emotional conditions as experienced while the entity was alive. Between incarnations, within the form-maker body, the spirit or soul will undergo much healing, not of the—we correct this instrument—not of this condition or that condition, rather inter-incarnational healings address the process within which the entity, shall we say, looks through the book of self, missing no pages, and then reintegrates the substantial significant self in a way which more accurately and lovingly places the various distortions and patterns within the unique entity, gradually preparing that entity for its next incarnation. It is within physical incarnation, not outside of it, that questions raised or imbalances, shall we say, within a previous incarnation are taken up again.

The work of inter-incarnational healing, that is, the healings between incarnations, is, indeed, most necessary and does constitute a vast array of healing modalities. However, these do not shine through to those within incarnational experience unless the entities deliberately pursue the creation within incarnation of a, shall we say, window whereby the entity within incarnation can climb, shall we say, into a special place which has access to the higher self, as the form-maker body does between incarnations. This can be done in some cases by what this instrument calls regressive hypnosis.

My brother, is this the last query?

Jim: I believe that was it, Q'uo. We appreciate your responses and I'm sure N does as well. Thank you very much.

Thank you for your thanks. Is there a query which any would make which has come as a result of that which we have offered at this time of working?

Jim: Not from me, Q'uo. Thank you very much, once again.

We are Q'uo, and thank each for the kind words. We would speak finally requesting the continuation of queries concerning this area. We realize the difficulties involved in asking questions from a distance and because of this instrument's thoughts shared fully with us earlier we know that the one known as N is full of regret that it cannot put these queries to us in person. We would address this.

Within this instrument's mind are many stories from her holy work called the Bible. There are many, many instances within this work in which healing occurs. The one known as Elijah demonstrated the extent to which a healer will go to express a literal understanding of healing …

(Side one of tape ends.)

(Carla channeling)

… asked to heal one who was dead, lay upon the body of the patient, hand to hand, foot to foot, mouth to mouth, literally breathing life into the patient. The one known as Jesus healed even when it was not aware it had been asked. We refer to the incident where a woman who was ill touched the hem of the one known as Jesus' robe and was healed. The one known as Jesus knew healing had taken place for it felt the power go forth. It did not intend this personally. It was an instrument through which healing came.

We would ask simply that the healer to whom we now speak, the one known as N, if this entity would find it desirable to allow the concerns, and there are many, to recede on a daily basis, perhaps there is energy for a good meditation, perhaps there is not. We ask in this latter case, then, that the one known as N simply begin to contemplate a few concepts. Primary among these concepts is the practice of the simple presence of the infinite One. How can one practice this presence without the meditating? In the case where meditation has become difficult or impossible to the self as it perceives the situation we would suggest some physical means, however momentary, of dwelling within the creation of the Father. Contemplate the sun, which gives so generously that life and light which is so welcomed as the springtime nears. Stand beneath the tree which is generating itself from light and offering oxygen to its companion upon the earth plane, the human and all animals, while all animals move about their business, breathing out just that which trees and plant life need, your carbon dioxide. Observe the way in which events fall, seeming, when looking back upon them, so right, so inevitable. Gaze about the self to find any arrhythmic or out of place detail in the creation of the Father. Is there any except that which man has imposed upon the creation of the Father?

The nature of faith is that it is what one claims it is. Questioning faith is useful only in the context of a life in faith where the seeker has become able to posit faith as the promise that never becomes a lie, regardless of all appearances. Thusly, faith is often quite incomprehensible. However, faith is served by the simple act of will, the refusal to stop believing. We commend this to the attention of all seekers. The simple assertion of a life in faith creates, when persistently invoked, the life in faith. Harder and more rewarding work for the spiritual seeker cannot be conceived.

May each, while crashing upon the craggy reefs of doubt and disbelief, confusion and inner anguish, stand firm on one thing: that is, love. You may call it faith or love or truth or, as this instrument often does, Christ, but the claiming of this precious thing is a most creative choice.

We leave this instrument reluctantly. We so enjoy these workings, so enjoy the converse with each dear entity. We bless each, thank each and leave each as always in the love and the ineffable light of the one infinite Creator. We are known to you as those of the principle of Q'uo. Adonai. Adonai.

Carla: If you don't mind waiting just a little bit more, there's a lot of pressure here. Is that all right? I think there may be … OK, thank you.

(Carla channeling)

I am Hatonn. Greetings in the love and in the light of the one infinite Creator. We wish to thank the one known as Carla for being aware of our presence for this instrument is somewhat fatigued as is its nature and practice within this particular incarnation and could easily have missed our request. We have no need to speak at length at this time, however, we are aware of the call of the one known as N. We simply wish to confirm this entity's knowledge that it has our constant company when we are so requested, not to give answers but to aid in what this instrument would call practicing the presence of the one infinite Creator.

This is all we wished to communicate and would therefore leave this instrument and this group, thanking each and praising and thanking the infinite Creator. May each comfort himself with the knowledge that all desire and seeking for that vibratory level which is the love of the one infinite Creator is felt and does indeed change the inner balance. Therefore, we do encourage a steadfast desire for love, truth and a life of service. No matter what the outer appearance, these thoughts result in the desired inner changes.

We leave you in love and in light. We are Hatonn. Adonai vasu. ☙

L/L Research is a subsidiary of Rock Creek Research & Development Laboratories, Inc.

P.O. Box 5195
Louisville, KY 40255-0195

www.llresearch.org

Rock Creek is a non-profit corporation dedicated to discovering and sharing information which may aid in the spiritual evolution of humankind.

ABOUT THE CONTENTS OF THIS TRANSCRIPT: This telepathic channeling has been taken from transcriptions of the weekly study and meditation meetings of the Rock Creek Research & Development Laboratories and L/L Research. It is offered in the hope that it may be useful to you. As the Confederation entities always make a point of saying, please use your discrimination and judgment in assessing this material. If something rings true to you, fine. If something does not resonate, please leave it behind, for neither we nor those of the Confederation would wish to be a stumbling block for any.

CAVEAT: This transcript is being published by L/L Research in a not yet final form. It has, however, been edited and any obvious errors have been corrected. When it is in a final form, this caveat will be removed.

© 2009 L/L Research

Sunday Meditation
February 13, 1994

Group question: The question this afternoon is from N and it is, "How would Q'uo go about designing a healing strategy that would encompass all of the needs of third-density entities if Q'uo were itself a third-density entity, here with that purpose in mind?"

(Carla channeling)

We are those of Q'uo. Greetings in the love and in the light of the infinite One. We are most pleased and privileged to be called to your circle for this working and would thank each who has come to this opportunity for the sharing of thoughts.

Your query addresses the concept of healing in a provocative way in that the question asks what we, that is, we of another density, would do within your third density in order to best maximize universal healing. It is one thing to be where we are, looking upon the Earth scene and philosophizing concerning the prospects of improving that world scene according to our views. It is quite another to be within that third density which you now enjoy, for not we, with our experience, but you, with your limitations and challenges, are the ones called to service at this particular juncture.

Were we you, we also would be equally limited. Let us rephrase and say that were each of you to be able to have access to that portion of your totality of self which vibrates within our range of vibrations in our density you, then, would find yourself completely unable to take those understandings and attempt to affix them into the net of third-density illusion reality. Perhaps the best way to say that is there is always the 20/20 vision of hindsight, yet it is to those who have no hindsight but only the situation as it appears who act. It is you who are called to act and to serve, you with all of your self-perceived limitations.

The Creator encapsulates Itself within each, so the true self that you are is in one sense beyond any limitation, beyond any distortion, beyond any impurity. Within each of you does lie truth, does lie healing, does lie grace, beauty and justice. And we would have to say that were we one of you or many of you, we would, as do you, feel profoundly confused by the illusion of third density. You have no easy task, you who seek to serve. So one response to your query is that your fine, hard-earned understanding does not translate into a master plan for third-density healing. Only those who are within third density have the right to attempt to create such conditions as universal healing.

We see the concept of healing or health having to do fundamentally with not the physical vehicle nor simply with the mind or mental vehicle but, rather, we see healing as that which creates a broader or deeper faith, for what is health but the just proportion or balance of energies within the individual self. Health is not simply a matter of sickness and curing sickness. Health has to do with the balance of energies within the self so that the self is tuned, shall we say, as much as can be achieved by the seeker to a continuing awareness of the self as a child of the infinite Creator. Healing begins with the realization that love and loving constitute wellness.

More than any one method of medical treatment the philosophical, metaphysical or religious paths of service offer a way to teach those who wish to learn how to call inwardly and move toward that inner room wherein the heart of silence speaks its blessed and hallowed chant: love praising love, love thanking love, love having any emotion whatever to love. The soul which seeks persistently this inner sanctuary, the mercy seat of the heart, is as the one who chooses to go into the grand hall and to set the table for a sumptuous banquet. To the human eye the banquet hall may not exist. To the heart within, beating in faith, the hall shall fill to overflowing and the feast shall take place.

The over-arching energy which heals is accessed through faith. Then what each seeker does with that open channel of love and faith is very much dependent upon that seeker's particular journey. Many are the ways to teach faith. Each who is a parent teaches, by the way it deals with its children, the ways of faith and blessed indeed is that child whose parents have retained a strong sense of the importance of living faithfully. Blessed indeed is that child who learns not only to value knowledge, wisdom and power but also to value the ways of faith and the ways of service.

Those within your churches who preach according to some religious system have great opportunity to teach in healing ways. Indeed, when one discovers any path of service one may see that this too is a way to bear witness to the forces and energies of wellness or healing. Let us gaze at the simple concept of wellness or health here, for it is our perception that the third density is not intended to be universally healed. The perceived imperfections of the illusion are innumerable and it is a virtue of third density illusion that it continues rough, unfinished and unhealed. These are the conditions which promote rapidity of learning. The real health of the soul is not risked by the third-density conditions, whatever they be. It is necessary and desirable, in terms of the opportunity to grow and to go forward upon the journey of seeking, that the physical conditions, mental conditions, and emotional conditions experienced be perceived as broken.

This is a difficult concept to grasp. Why would the Creator allow, much less determine, that suffering on a continual basis be part of the excellent and beautiful plan for spiritual seeking? This does not have an obvious answer, yet we feel it is true. The virtues of your environment contain none greater than that virtue of predictable imperfection and limitation. What the Creator has in mind, we feel, is not an increase in health of the body or of the mind or of the emotion but rather a continuing possibility for improvement in the balancing and aligning of mind, body, emotions and spirit.

Health, then, can be seen to be within third density that state in which the entity—and each is unique—has achieved a stable balance within the self so that each energy has space for clarity and focus, much as you would see a color become more pure so one could envision the energies of the entity becoming more true, more just in balance and proportion, one to the other. This point of balance is unique for each unique entity.

Were we to attempt to teach perfection, that concept might, in one powerful moment, dismiss all illusion. However, we cannot move into your perceived reality and hook perfection out of the sea of confusion like a fish, nor would we be doing the Creator's work to attempt to lift any bodily into perfection. We count ourselves most blessed if we are simply able to suggest to even one entity that a stubborn focus upon infinite perfection will take the energies as they are and will, through time, produce for that entity such visions and clues concerning balance as are necessary for that individual's progress.

How does this relate to a concerted attempt to put in[to] manifestation the ideal healing environment? This question is a large one. We would suggest that there is no higher standard than that which is implicit in this question. It is to—we correct this instrument—it is a call to a great adventure to seek with great energy to materialize such an environment. This environment shall be visualized more and more frequently as your time moves forward for many entities now have become aware, both of the many, many ways of affecting cures and healing and also of the supreme place that faith has within an entity's individual health. These two concepts are ones we would suggest for contemplation.

We would wish to allow this response to be received by the one known as N before responding further, if that is acceptable to those within this circle. We pause for communication.

Jim: That's fine with us, Q'uo. Thank you.

Very well, my brother. Then we would ask if there is a query upon the material given or another line of questioning at this time.

Jim: I have no other questions myself, Q'uo. I appreciate what you've said.

We are those of Q'uo and we thank you, my brother. We are not quite ready to leave this delightful gathering and would speak a bit further but did not wish to move forward in that which we specifically gave in answer to the opening question.

We would speak to this entity's question, for we are aware, of course, when a channel such as this one questions whether it is still being of service. We encourage each to ask questions such as this. It is not wise to be smug or to feel that one has gotten the final answer. It is quite healthy, shall we say, for this question to come up when the world does not beat a path to your door, when meetings are small, when, as we see in this instrument's thinking, that physical parameters are unmet, such as money for the publications, it is perfectly logical to question one's path of service.

We then must say where is the heart of service, for you? Where is love, for you? Where are your gifts? Which gifts do you wish to use? When seeking answers to questions concerning service we encourage the exploration of one's own gifts for each entity moves into the third-density illusion with all of its woes and wonders with a certain package of gifts, a certain combination of virtues and darker virtues, which you call vices, and out of this broken and seeking existence blooms forth all of the beauty and generous harmony of that same entity's blossom of selfhood.

So we ask the instrument to take the time in the following days to contemplate its gifts and to seek an inner feeling of certitude concerning the service which is desired to [be given] so that the service may once again be made calm and unruffled by self-doubts. Always, it is not the outer appearance which determines the success of employing one's gifts but, rather, one must simply move as one feels to move, always being aware that the service is service to love, in love, for love, by means of love alone.

We would encourage each to lift the heart, lift the mind, lift the viewpoint, just as the sun seems to lift the flower bud, lift the grasses and the leaf. Attempt to give yourselves the freedom within to turn to …

(Side one of tape ends.)

(Carla channeling)

… [towards] the light, as that light is most deeply and purely perceived.

To sharpen these perceptions, again we say, spend time contemplating. Certainly it is good to have the meetings together, for those who seek together band together in a way which improves the hearing, shall we say, of all involved and creates a much improved atmosphere for seeking, but more than this, spend the time alone seeking, whether in prayer, meditation or in the joy, the laughter and the fellowship. Spend time praising and rejoicing.

Why rejoice? Why give thanks and praise? Because the greatest energy of all is always the same: love is always the over-mastering power and creator. No matter what the experience, praise, joy and thanks are appropriate. When one can, even for a moment, see and feel the truth of the turning to love above all things then shall healing truly multiply.

We would at this time leave this instrument and this group, apologizing for the lack of satisfactory answers. However, we are dealing, when we deal with healing modalities, in an area in which, through this instrument at this time, the information we may share is, and will continue to be, of a nature more abstract than practical. However, we would not wish to employ this instrument differently. And there you are—a situation.

As we close, we would say to the one known as N, that portion of us which is Latwii greets and blesses the one known as N and thanks the one known as N for enjoying our jokes.

We would leave you in the love and in the light of the one infinite Creator. Adonai. Adonai. We are those of Q'uo. ✣

Sunday Meditation
March 13, 1994

Group question: This afternoon our question is: "How is it that the Creator steps down His, or Her, or Its conscious being in order to occupy a physical body and utilize the various rays of the bodies and have an incarnation?"

(Carla channeling)

We are those of Q'uo. Greetings in the love and in the light of the infinite One. We cherish this opportunity to share our vibrations and our thoughts with you. It is a privilege to be able to respond to your call and we most thankfully do so. As always, we ask that each use his personal discrimination in hearing our opinion, releasing that which is not part of your personal truth at this time and taking only that which has touched a sympathetic chord within you.

You ask this day how the Creator has stepped down its selfhood in, and to experience as, a third-density entity. The shortest and most bluntly accurate answer to the query is that the Creator has not stepped down this selfhood in anywise, in any density, or circumstance. The truth is the Creator; the rest is illusion.

All that you strive to comprehend, you already know. All that you strive to be, you already are. However, free will so dances with each entity in this Creatorhood. Thus each entity becomes unique within illusion and the oddity and peculiarity through illusion is valuable. However, let us move back to the point that the Creator is manifest in you and in all whom you see. Similarly, as regards healing. The healing is already perfected. Insofar as the entity wishing can lay hold of the vibrations which are those chosen to the original Vibration, just to that extent has the individual opened the self to a new reality with illusion.

The vibration of selfhood is seldom grasped. The basic vibration of a self, or entity, is the vibration which is identical to the vibration of love. This overlaid by the range of vibrations presently enjoyed and [which] contains undertones begins the history, shall we say, of accumulated vibratory processes. An entity, then, is as powerful metaphysically as the degree of awareness of the original Vibration which it can lay hold of and sustain an intimate relationship with.

It is difficult, we know, to even contemplate or ideate the situation in which you, in all of the glorious imperfection of hastening life, are yet the Creator. This truth is basic and many paths to the Creator posit this in one way or another.

Each within third density is conscious of himself. This self-consciousness is a great prize. The awareness of self is at one and the same time a great burden. Prize and burden. Self-consciousness opens the door to entities working consciously upon the self to the end of becoming more wise, more secure, more filled with charity and many other human reasons. This self-consciousness is a kind of anguish, the looking in the mirror. It is the great tool of third density.

If an entity should be able to within manifestation to focus fully within the consciousness of self this hypothetical individual would feel the full force of godhead or creatorship. Needless to say, few there are who have even touched that quality of self-awareness while in manifestation.

Indeed, the plight of humans dealing with their creatorship is much like that of the swimmers in the ocean which is a mile deep. That of which the swimmer is aware barely even scratches the surface of the sea. And so it is with consciousness that all the highs and lows of thought encompass merely the surface of selfhood, for that surface is the surface whose depths cry out in praise of the one infinite Creator.

Does the Creator, then, praise Itself? Yes, this is so. All of creation sings a hymn of praise and thanks. This is the vibration of being; this is your nature. Insofar as one may lay hold on this truth and allow it to be described within, some learning shall occur.

In other terms, for we are aware that this query was asked for various reasons, the identity or vibration of love at the moment of creation was given all of the densities and sub-densities, those coming into being in an inevitable pattern representing the settled view of the infinite intelligence which regarded the creation prior to your own. Thusly each of you walks a trail which was improved and embellished by selves walking before and in the unimaginable time when time has stopped and started again, another creation shall experience the Creator with densities and sub-densities now improved, because of the experiences of selves at this time, in this creation.

We would wish to speak of an experience this instrument had earlier in this day. The situation was grave. A soul lay close to dying. The priest with that soul was reading the prayers of ministry to the sick. With each prayer and affirmation, the sick man became calmer, but he could not hear well, so the priest raised his voice, reading the Twenty-third Psalm.

"The Lord is my shepherd. I shall not want." The patient became comfortable and as the last verse was spoken, "Surely, goodness and mercy shall follow you, all the days of your life and you shall dwell in the house of the Lord, forever."

The man simply stopped breathing. It was a good death. This entity knew that he was in the house of the Lord, forever, and fear had no more place within him and the healing took place, instantly. It was a healing death.

Insofar as each of you is aware that you dwell in the house of the Lord, forever, so also have you encountered and taken in a great truth.

The mind is far more powerful than any other force within your experience. What you know or think you [know] creates your illusion. Therefore, it is well to know what you know, to build only what you personally have experienced and know from an organic and involved viewpoint. For the deepest part of what you know is what you are, not what you do or say.

In this situation where there is illness and the heart cries for healing, the healing is that intangible process where the mind becomes aware of a more powerful field of energy than that expressed by the sickness. The physician may work upon the mechanical and chemical aspects of a body, tinkering with the mechanism and oiling the dry spots, as it were, but the actual state of that body is quenched by what the entity knows, or is.

To put it another way, the highest energy an entity can access either consciously or unconsciously determines how much the ills of flesh shall move according to the rules of manifestation, in general.

The more sure awareness an entity has of the illusory nature of an illness, then the less this illness can actually create in the way of sickness. If there is a basic key to healing as opposed to curing, it is this: the awareness of the entity moves to that place where that entity feels sure this is reality, where that energy is when the entity states to itself, "This is who I am." This is, indeed, who that entity is, where that entity will move, what limitation this will attend for learning and what suffering it shall enjoy as it learns.

Each of you controls the degree of healing within by that which you know, that which you are, that which you desire, those three things. We encourage each to make a practice of knowing the Creator in self. The Creator is all. We encourage each to be that loving vibration first, and words and actions second.

We encourage each to desire only the most high truth, to desire far beyond that which can be stated or imagined, for as you seek, your thirst is expressed in the outstretched call of soul to all that resonates with it. So is attracted to that entity ministers of light, shall we say, drawn to you justly and appropriately in accordance with that [for] which you have desire. Therefore, lift your desires even higher. Seek to know that true and real vibration which is your identity. He who can vibrate with this desire is moving as quickly as possible along the trail of the pilgrim.

We would stop at this time and ask if there is any query, now that we have given this much material?

Jim: Not from me, Q'uo. I appreciate very much what you said. There is a lot to think about there.

Questioner: I don't have a question, Q'uo.

We thank you, my brothers. We are unwilling to speak further upon this topic until there has been the mulling over and perhaps the direction taken for further querying. Therefore, we shall leave the subject. Before we leave the instrument, however, we would simply say a few words.

This instrument has **no** *(emphasized)* idea what we would have to say, so we shall have to ask this instrument to quit thinking, or we shall not be able to speak.

(Pause)

We ask each to breathe deeply. Take three or four breaths.

(Pause while this is done.)

My brothers and sister, we would speak with you concerning relaxation. Each of you is a keen and careful student of the mystery of life and eternity. You are concerned, metaphysically, to know and to understand, to grasp and to accelerate your learning, spiritually. Further, each of you is a careful and studious worker, always attempting to do the best. In relationships with people, each attempts always to give the best. This is all admirable and we do not fault this, however, it is a common and understandable error of the earnest and idealistic entity so to enmire the self within the strictures of desire and learning the heart forgets how to skip, the mind, to sing. All entities need and crave not only the metaphysical truths, but also the immediate experiences which in their authenticity outrank the highest understanding.

We ask each in the days and weeks to come, to deliberate—we correct this instrument—to be deliberate about releasing the self into an immediate appreciation of the environment of your earth. To breathe in and breathe out, knowing that partnership with all living things. To feel the heart lift because the sun is golden, or the moon serene and beautiful. Even within the dwelling that earth and health and energy may be instantaneously pulled upward into the body and the body's awareness by the direction of the will.

Each entity has their feet upon the floor. We ask each entity—we correct this instrument—we ask each entity whose foot is on the floor to think that foot into contact with earth. Can you feel that energy now coming in the soles of the feet? It is your surety that this is possible that makes this possible.

You do not have to be amongst the trees and the grasses to get the energy of the earth to strengthen you, but you must be able to, by your will, assert that relationship and send out that attraction of desire. It is not wise to attempt to be too serious. It is wise to be the fool and be foolish regularly. For there is truth not just in the earnest and serious things of metaphysics, there is also much truth in the playful, in the energetic fun.

Therefore, we ask each please to attempt to open the self to lightness, merriment, fun, relaxation and the deep breathing that expands the mind, the soul, and the point of view. Hurry not. Cease rushing. Spend more time being. These things we encourage this circle, for the circle is very serious *(humorously)*.

Balance in all things, my dear ones. We thank each for this delightful opportunity and would, at this time, transfer the contact to the one known as Jim. We are those of Q'uo.

(Jim channeling)

I am Q'uo, and greet each again in love and in light through this instrument. We would ask if there are any queries remaining upon any mind before we take our leave of this group?

Carla: Well, yes, I do. Are you aware of the situation of which I talked earlier, about a woman at church that I simply cannot talk to because she's not respecting the truth?

I am Q'uo, and we are aware of this information through this instrument's memory. Is there a query, my sister?

Carla: Yes, Q'uo. I just simply ask if you have any comments, or suggestions for this situation, where there is a disagreement between people. Not because there is an actual disagreement, but because one of the two simply will not look at the truth and clings to the point which divides. I feel frustrated because I cannot resolve this situation, but at the same time, I realized I have to respect her and allow her to carry on as she needs to, but it is causing me hurt.

I am Q'uo, and am aware of your query, my sister. We give this instrument an image of a fulcrum point that may represent the truth. All entities move about this point. The relationship between any two entities may be seen as that straight line which you would call the "teeter-totter" or "see-saw" upon your playground for your children.

Each entity will find itself in a relationship with another moving about that which is the truth. In some relationships, the entity may find itself closer to the truth.

(Side one of tape ends).

(Jim channeling)

I am Q'uo, and we shall continue. However, each entity must move in that fashion which brings it into closest harmony with the concept of love and acceptance, for it is not clearly known within your illusion where this point of truth resides, though each sees it with what seems to be a clear eye. Thus, it is not truth or wisdom which is of importance within your illusion, for they are concepts which are beyond your illusion. It is instead that which accepts the Creator in all faces and then does what it will in the face of love and with the motivation of love.

Is there a further query, my sister?

Carla: A kind of confused one, yes. You say simply act in love, and I think it is wonderful advice. It's very hard for me to see where that love takes me. There's something that I have to call politics involving this woman's ability to talk to people and I hear back around from other people that she has said this and people are believing her. And part of me wants to continue to say nothing and take the high road and I just don't know where the most helpful action lies, not in just context of myself but in context of this organization that I'm trying to help. You see the question that I'm asking, and I simply don't know how to value the truth, whether speaking the truth at this point is helpful or not. Is speaking the truth a loving thing to do? Is not defending yourself still a loving thing to do if people would be helped if they heard your side? I'm just really stuck. I'm having trouble making decisions.

I am Q'uo, and am aware of your query, my sister. Because of this confusion and because of the importance of your decision in your own evolutionary journey, we must not infringe upon this choice and can only suggest that when you have prayed or meditated yourself to a point of loving acceptance, then the choice will become more apparent.

May we answer any other query, my sister?

Carla: No, Q'uo. Thank you for that.

I am Q'uo, and we thank you, my sister. Is there any other query at this time?

Carla: Would you take a short question about something that I don't know anything about and that is these "rays of incarnation"? I've heard about them twice. Do you feel that this is a fruitful subject for further exploration?

I am Q'uo, and am aware of your query, my sister. We would recommend that these queries having to do with so-called "rays of color and manifestation" be more carefully considered and organized, for their present form is somewhat chaotic, shall we say, for there are many ways of looking at the bodies and centers of energy and their manifestation within your illusion for you are entities of a complex nature. That of mind, body and spirit and the relationship between each as well as the nature of each are manifested in various ways and are described by your peoples in far more [detail].

May we ask if there is a final query at this time?

Carla: I'm done.

I am Q'uo, and we thank each once again for the privilege of your company and your call. We are honored to join you and to share our humble opinions with you and we ask that each remember that opinion is that which we share. Take the concepts and words which have value to you and leave behind those that do not.

We are know to you as those of Q'uo. At this time we shall take our leave of this instrument and this group, leaving each in the love and in the ineffable light of the one infinite Creator. Adonai, my friends. Adonai. ✺

L/L Research

L/L Research is a subsidiary of Rock Creek Research & Development Laboratories, Inc.

P.O. Box 5195
Louisville, KY 40255-0195

www.llresearch.org

Rock Creek is a non-profit corporation dedicated to discovering and sharing information which may aid in the spiritual evolution of humankind.

ABOUT THE CONTENTS OF THIS TRANSCRIPT: This telepathic channeling has been taken from transcriptions of the weekly study and meditation meetings of the Rock Creek Research & Development Laboratories and L/L Research. It is offered in the hope that it may be useful to you. As the Confederation entities always make a point of saying, please use your discrimination and judgment in assessing this material. If something rings true to you, fine. If something does not resonate, please leave it behind, for neither we nor those of the Confederation would wish to be a stumbling block for any.

CAVEAT: This transcript is being published by L/L Research in a not yet final form. It has, however, been edited and any obvious errors have been corrected. When it is in a final form, this caveat will be removed.

© 2009 L/L RESEARCH

Sunday Meditation
March 27, 1994

Group question: …information about the nature of our spiritual seeking in general and perhaps the role that those such as Q'uo have to play in that seeking and how you are a service to us and how we might be of service to each other in this seeking.

(Carla channeling)

Greetings in the love and in the light of the one infinite Creator. We are those of Hatonn. We thank each for calling us to your group this day. It is a privilege and a blessing to join in your meditation and to blend our vibrations with yours.

We are those who come to your peoples at this time in hopes of being of service by providing information and opinion concerning spiritual evolution. It is our understanding that this present period which you now enjoy is part of a season of harvest or completion upon your Earth world. In this time of transition to a more densely lit illusion there is great opportunity, we feel, for entities who are seeking to accelerate their process of spiritual evolution to do so. We are those who wish to assist, as we may, those who request our opinion and presence.

We are those of the Confederation of Planets in the Service of the Infinite Creator. Institutions equivalent in general nature to ours among your peoples might include the Peace Corps or those who work with Vista in the inner city. Not missionaries, not religions do we present in ourselves but, rather, counselors attempting to inform those who request our service of our understanding of the basic nature of the creation, the Creator and each seeker's place within this cosmology or world view.

In many, many ways through the years which we have spent speaking to your peoples, we offer again and again a very simple message: the Creator, we feel, is of a nature which is unified which may be summed up by a vibratory level. This vibration we call love. The Creator, to us, is a mystery. We know, or feel we know, that the Creator is indeed the Creator, that this Creator is possessed of an infinite intelligence. This infinite intelligence is expressed in that vibration which is love. Each entity also has a vibration, indeed a complex of vibratory levels harmonizing to make your unique signature or pattern of vibration.

The teaching we offer is this: as each seeker moves its vibratory complex closer and closer to the vibration of love, so does the infinite self within each seeker begin to sound its true note and identity. Thusly, as it is written in your holy work, one might say as did the teacher known to you as Jesus, "Be perfect, even as your Father is perfect." That this is an unreachable goal within the illusions we both experience is undoubtedly so. However, as the seeker sharpens its desire for and its hunger for more harmonious vibratory patterns, as this seeker then persists stubbornly in seeking again and again to move the personal vibratory complex closer to the pure vibration of love, so does desire create the perfect work within.

In any human terms these attempts to be as the Deity are useless. In the metaphysical world, where intention and desire are as real as a chair or a person, such seeking is effective and as the seeker persists in seeking this vibration the seeker begins to experience more and more spiritually-based coincidence or synchronicity which acts as a kind of feedback, letting the seeker know that it is cooperating with its destiny and has begun to accelerate the rate of its spiritual evolution.

We come not to move people away from paths of seeking which are satisfying to the entity. We wish to place no stumbling block before any. However, in many cases among your peoples those who seek most fervently are themselves alienated from the traditional, cultural, religious systems. To those entities we present a general and non-dogmatic way of looking at creation, the Creator and each seeker's place within that creation. By doing this we hope to be of service, by affording those who may need a home, spiritually speaking, such a home. We hope for no church nor do we hope for any power within your world, rather, we simply make ourselves available through channels such as this one in order to present that alternative for those who may find it useful.

It is our understanding that each who sits within this circle existed in perfect potentiation before the world you know as Earth was formed. Each unique spark of love, each entity, was already loved and cared for before all that you see as the creation came to be, for the essence of each of you is a thought. The manifestation of that thought, your flesh and blood, bone and sinew, is as a garment. You clothe yourselves for your few years of incarnation in this flesh and wear it until you have truly worn it out and then, like a garment, it is laid aside and that unique spark of love which is you moves onward and where you move onward to is dependent upon how you have dealt with those issues which you chose for your own learning within this incarnative experience. You are love and you seek love, yet this love is biased and distorted in many, many crazy ways. Crazy, we say, like the images in the fun house of mirrors at a carnival.

Why would the Creator place each entity within such a heavy and crazy illusion? What is the point behind all of this manifestation which seems to offer suffering, loss and limitation at least as often as it offers those things which you think are good? We see each of you in a very, very long view. To us, you belong to infinity, for we see each of you as eternal. We also see that the great glory and purpose of your experience is that you shall suffer as you learn and in that suffering you shall be transformed.

Now, not all of your peoples wish to hear our words and this is entirely acceptable. Many there are who do not yet wish to take control of their own spiritual evolution. They do not yet desire the responsibility of considering the possibility that it does make a very real difference how one chooses to be and to act. To those entities we bow with respect and say, "Sleep on." But we say to those who are awake, "Watch and pray for you know not the hour when that which is yet to come shall arrive."

Now we quote again the teacher known to you as Jesus. This entity spoke of a wedding feast. To this feast were invited the high and the mighty, the comfortable and the well-off. Yet one must have business here and another there and so the wedding feast had empty places. Therefore, the father sent out people to comb the neighborhood for anyone on the street to come to the feast. There is a feast and we do invite each to come. That feast is love and each of you may be more and more one who dwells in the presence of that divine love.

In terms of the practical—for this instrument requested mentally that we be more practical—we suggest a commitment of some of your time and attention to the process of seeking the one infinite Creator. This commitment of time need not be a great one but, rather, it needs to be regular. We suggest to each what you might call silent prayer or meditation. Now, there is much good in prayers of thanksgiving, praise and intercession. There is much good in speaking to the infinite One, to having a relationship with this infinite intelligence. Yet does not a part of any relationship depend upon listening? Just so, we suggest that each seeker spend some time each day, if it be only a few moments, actively practicing the listening to that still, small voice which your Bible speaks of. For the Creator speaks not with thunder or disaster or great noise but rather the Creator speaks in silence. For there are no words which may carry the energy of the infinite One.

Therefore, the infinite One's relationship to you is one of being, is one of presence. We encourage each to spend a few moments each day practicing the presence of the infinite Creator, simply allowing the self to realize that the ground upon which he sits is holy ground, for the Creator is everywhere and all things come within that holy orbit.

When we speak of love we do not speak of the love of friends or the romantic love of men and women. Indeed, we realize that this word, love, is itself confusing for it means so many different emotions, not one of which has the power or purity of the one infinite Creator's love. This love is as a creative thought and energy which has literally manifested all that there is. The nature of the universe is love which affects light in ways which build all that is manifest. You gaze at a creation builded entirely of light governed by love. When we greet you in the love and in the light of the infinite Creator we ground ourselves and you in all that there is.

We would at this time stop and ask if there are questions at this time. We are those of Hatonn.

(Thirty second pause.)

We are those of Hatonn, and would then go forward.

Questioner: I have a question, Hatonn. I have a question concerning communicating with others, those that we are meeting in everyday life and sharing with them the world of seeking and our feeling about it in such a way as not to infringe upon their free will. I wish if you would comment about talking about what is important for me, for example, with somebody else who doesn't ask. Do I wait until they express desire to hear or what is a harmonious way to go about doing this, spreading the light?

We are those of Hatonn, and grasp your query. Service is one of the more difficult things to accomplish well. The attempt to be of spiritual service to another, we feel, must depend in the first or primary place upon the free will of the individual to be served. It is well to wait until an entity asks you for your service before you attempt to render this service for if that which you have to say has not been requested in some way it is very likely that it will be considered irrelevant by the one whom you seek to serve. More than that, it may constitute a stumbling block for the entity you wish to help. This is sometimes frustrating for it is as though you see a child who will burn itself on a hot stove, yet the child must learn just that way what "hot" means, and if you see an entity bowed down with grief or trouble and you feel this entity could be helped by your opinion we encourage you, then, to see that you have, by offering what is not requested, confused and baffled energies that need to be felt as harmonious and sympathetic.

The service that is rendered by overtly speaking is easy to understand rationally and therefore it looks like the best way to serve. However, it is hard to underestimate—we correct this instrument—it is hard to overestimate the effect that a silent witness may have. There is a witness which each gives by the way it lives, by the way it moves through the being and the doing of everyday living. If you are practicing the presence of the one infinite Creator, if you are living in faith rather than seeking and scrabbling for proof, if you have hope and trust and love and a smile, these things will speak for you, without your doing anything and this silent witness may bless without invading for it is primary that each entity freely choose that which it chooses for the choice made is so very important.

What choice would that be but the choice of how to love? There are two ways of expressing more and more love. One is the way of the sun, the radiant energy of free giving. In this way of accelerating the process of spiritual evolution the seeker attempts at each point of choice to make the choice which is of the higher amount of service to others, feeling that in each face which it sees is the face and nature of the Creator.

The other way of accelerating and progressing spiritually is to take all the light around and attempt to hold it to the self. This way of being and learning has various names among your peoples, such as the left-hand path. We often call it the path of service to self. When you see an entity relating to those around it depending upon what use they might be to it then you see an entity operating along the lines of service to self. Perhaps one might call entities such as this negative or selfish and perhaps one might call entities who are following the path of service to others those who seek along the positive path, but these are simply names.

The entities who are still asleep to spiritual seeking dwell in the middle of a great arc of energy. For them the energy remains at the bottom of the energy well for they are not creating or amassing power by how they live …

(Side one of tape ends.)

(Carla channeling)

… are of the Confederation are seeking along the lines of service to others and we come to those who are seeking along this positive path.

We are very willing to aid and if you wish us to aid in your meditations you have but to mentally request our presence. When we are with a meditating entity we do not give messages or attempt contact. We simply move into the meditative vibration, sharing with the seeker in this meditation. It is as though someone else was singing along with you: the note is more firm and steady. This is the benefit we offer, that your meditations might be somewhat deeper. We are pleased to do this if you wish and would not infringe upon you unless you ask.

We have thrown a lot of ideas out this day and before we leave we would again ask if there are any queries.

Questioner: I have another question. I don't … I wonder if you would comment on a particular feeling that sometimes I experience but perhaps others also feel it, and that is during meditation when the energies are shared sometimes I feel some energy running up inside that is pleasant and yet it often brings tears into my eyes, it feels like a great wave of emotions sweeping over me and then it fades, and I wonder if that is a conditioning wave or if it simply indicates some blockages, energy blockages, in whoever feels this during meditation, such as this one.

We are those of Hatonn. We believe that the experience of which you speak is that of an entity dimly sensing that which is beautiful beyond description, the love between two seekers. This love is close in vibration to divine love for the love of those who together seek is completely selfless. The goal for both in such a relationship is each to aid and encourage the other in spiritual seeking. This partakes of the nature of love itself. Thusly, there is the great feeling of emotion because of the beauty which is sensed. May we answer you further, my brother?

Questioner: No, thank you, Hatonn. That answers my question.

We are those of Hatonn. We are grateful to you also, my brother. Each time this love is shared back and forth it blesses infinitely, does it not? Is there a final question at this time?

(Twenty second pause.)

We thank each for allowing us to share our opinions. Take only those words which have meaning for you and leave the rest behind, for we are not authorities but those who come in friendship and love. We love you and bless each of you and thank you for the great honor of speaking. At this time we take our leave of you, rejoicing merrily in the love and the infinite light of the one infinite Creator. Adonai. Adonai. ♣

L/L Research

L/L Research is a subsidiary of Rock Creek Research & Development Laboratories, Inc.

P.O. Box 5195
Louisville, KY 40255-0195

www.llresearch.org

Rock Creek is a non-profit corporation dedicated to discovering and sharing information which may aid in the spiritual evolution of humankind.

ABOUT THE CONTENTS OF THIS TRANSCRIPT: This telepathic channeling has been taken from transcriptions of the weekly study and meditation meetings of the Rock Creek Research & Development Laboratories and L/L Research. It is offered in the hope that it may be useful to you. As the Confederation entities always make a point of saying, please use your discrimination and judgment in assessing this material. If something rings true to you, fine. If something does not resonate, please leave it behind, for neither we nor those of the Confederation would wish to be a stumbling block for any.

CAVEAT: This transcript is being published by L/L Research in a not yet final form. It has, however, been edited and any obvious errors have been corrected. When it is in a final form, this caveat will be removed.

© 2009 L/L Research

Sunday Meditation
April 3, 1994

Group question: N has asked us to ask for specific and particular information on the topic of the rays, the energy centers, and the bodies associated with the energy centers. We are aware of the difficulty Q'uo has in giving such information if it infringes upon people's free will, and we would like to ask what Q'uo could tell N or what direction Q'uo could point N in since he is a healer with a great desire to be of service to others? How can N get more expansive responses from Q'uo?

(Carla channeling)

Greetings in the love and in the light of the one infinite Creator. We are those of the principle of Q'uo, and we thankfully bless each for asking us to share our thoughts on healing. It is this instrument's day of rejoicing. The Eastertide, as it is called, the time when the ultimate healing, the resurrection of that which is dead into new life takes place within this mythical system of faith. It is most appropriate, for a question upon healing is at base a question about death, transformation and resurrection.

That which is considered among your peoples, as we have said before, is far more often the curing of a condition. This in no way breaks into the storehouse, the treasure house, where each soul's totality of living is recorded and saved. Rather, it manipulates a manifestation. To focus upon the healing systems is most efficacious for the medical practitioners, and the detailed information which is collected by the various processes of medical investigation are also most efficacious at altering the manifestation, the clothing of flesh that the human body, so-called, is in essence.

For us to move into a mode of expressing or assigning various phases of medical practice associated with various items within the body, or your so called subtle bodies, is simply more of the same. However, we continue to be most eager to serve. This is an interesting subject and a fruitful one. We cannot be those who shape another's answers for them or learn for them, for that would be infringement upon free will. However, perhaps since the query was asking us to express any comments we might have, perhaps we may be able to find some solid ground upon which to get a firm stance. We shall attempt to bridge the gap between where we, as this instrument would say, are coming from and where the one known as N comes from.

It is our perception that healing takes place when the integrity of the field which is the soul or spirit—that is, the essence of an entity—is maximized. This maximum integrity of field occurs at an unique position within the nexus of the various bodies, wherever within that nexus that that one entity is at that one particular time. Not only is each entity unique but each entity is continuously changing between vibrations. Rare is the individual in third density that can attain and maintain maximum integrity or health, even for a moment. Those who come the closest are those whose balance is seen by others, perhaps, to be above the ordinary.

We use the term, balance, to convey a situation in which the various energy centers of the physical, mental, emotional and so forth bodies are at a state where there is a clear strength or center and a comfort in the, shall we say, fit of the energy distribution. An entity which is in this kind of balance may be thought to have attained a high degree of wellness or health. When entities become ill, the physical aspects of this situation are more clear or evident than other portions of the situation causing illness. When work is done upon the physical body, then, the manifestation may change. However, if the entity has not had the process encouraged wherein that entity moves towards balance then the physician has done work only skin deep.

Now, we realize that the modest aim of most medical practitioners in your society is to do precisely that—to cause the mechanism to work properly once more. It may seem that we continually retreat from talking about healing because we are continually retreating from changing the physical manifestation of illness. When we wish to consider healing we then must orient ourselves and you to whom we are attempting to share some of these thoughts to a new emphasis, that emphasis being upon the essence of a person, as you would call it.

We do not distinguish in a way that makes psychiatrists more able to cure than the surgeon or the general practitioner. No, indeed, for the outpourings of the mental/emotional complex within an entity within incarnation are of much the same detailed and non-unique kind as physical symptomology. It is not mind or emotion or body that is healed in healing work, but, rather, the entity, whole and full of integrity. You hear of the phrase, "integrated personality." This perhaps catches a notion of that to which we point as a starting place.

What psychologists and psychiatrists may mean by a well integrated personality is along the lines of symptomology. That is, the ego this and the id that. However, it does fasten upon the concept that all the various parts of the mental/emotional complex of thoughts form a kind of energy grid, a pattern of usual associations which have been used in concert enough that the entity has become comfortable and in balance as a personality with this particular way of expressing.

What the healer does in healing is provide, on some level, catalyst which will alert the higher self of the entity to be healed. The more powerful and effective the healing the closer to the heart of essence of self that the healer shall come. In other words, the more effective the healer, the more accurate the touch upon the point of balance is, that is, the healer meets the entity to be healed where that entity to be healed is not yet. Healing comes from a new perspective, not from moving about to find one which is already pursued.

How can the healer do this? Each healer works differently. For some there is the healing touch. For some the healing word. For some the skill of various of your resources such as the gems, the massage, the—we cannot give this concept to this instrument well—the plumb line, shall we say. This is not the correct term … that which dangles from the held string and moves eccentrically—the dowsing, shall we say. These skills vary from healer to healer. What each healer has in common is a gift which the healer simply shares with the one to be healed. The work is done, not by the healer, but by that entity to be healed's own self which, because of the catalyst of the healer, has the opportunity to select in an integrated fashion a more balanced configuration of energies.

In each case this configuration and its change is unique. The human animal, shall we say, is wired eccentrically. By this we mean to indicate that each entity has an unique pattern, not simply to the physical body, but to all bodies. Each wiring system functions a little differently from any other; some to the extent of functioning backwards. Consequently, the strength of healing is the strength of the field within which the healer and the one to be healed rest during that time when the interaction between the two essences creates that moment which allows new choice.

We thank the one known as N for continuing to hope and to have faith that there is a better, more universal way to heal. We are glad to continue to work with this entity. However, we would express that we simply refrain from certain levels of specificity, for when an instrument such as this one seeks repetitively to attain specific material when the same query is asked several times and there is not the new awareness to the questioning, when this situation exists there is in the relationship of questioner to the truth of, shall we say, the hangman and the one to be hanged.

(Carla stops channeling and challenges what was just channeled.)

(Carla channeling)

I am Q'uo. We thank this instrument. We are having some difficulty with this information. There is some interest in this particular session and we have good contact but it is to be noted that when the specificity of information is requested, especially more than once, there develops a kind of specious interest which attracts those who would mimic our thoughts long enough to detune the channel. If the one who is channeling continually accepts such assignments and within its own self continues to ask for this information we are then unable to continue holding to a truly protected channel. And the general course of such is that we lose that particular channel who has been turned to other uses by those who seek other than as we do; that is, those who are interested in service to self.

This is not particularly easy to understand. And we would be glad to work with these questions as long as necessary. However, we applaud this group's awareness of this particular pitfall and we encourage this group to continue in its fidelity and its willingness to fail, if failure is the higher truth to witness to.

Are there any queries at this time?

(Pause)

I am Q'uo. To the one known as N may we say that the ones of Hatonn greet you. We thank our brother again for the purity of its interest and we hope we may aid. We have so enjoyed this quiet hour with each of you. May we bless each once more and thank each for the level of desire and purity of intent. We leave you only in voice, in the love and in the light of the one infinite Creator. We are those of Q'uo. Adonai. Adonai.

L/L Research

L/L Research is a subsidiary of Rock Creek Research & Development Laboratories, Inc.

P.O. Box 5195
Louisville, KY 40255-0195

www.llresearch.org

Rock Creek is a non-profit corporation dedicated to discovering and sharing information which may aid in the spiritual evolution of humankind.

ABOUT THE CONTENTS OF THIS TRANSCRIPT: This telepathic channeling has been taken from transcriptions of the weekly study and meditation meetings of the Rock Creek Research & Development Laboratories and L/L Research. It is offered in the hope that it may be useful to you. As the Confederation entities always make a point of saying, please use your discrimination and judgment in assessing this material. If something rings true to you, fine. If something does not resonate, please leave it behind, for neither we nor those of the Confederation would wish to be a stumbling block for any.

CAVEAT: This transcript is being published by L/L Research in a not yet final form. It has, however, been edited and any obvious errors have been corrected. When it is in a final form, this caveat will be removed.

© 2009 L/L Research

Sunday Meditation
April 10, 1994

Group question: The question today has to do with communication, and what is it that we really communicate when we are speaking with each other. We live in an illusion. We experience the catalyst to help us grow. And we're wondering … beyond the words of small talk, and the intentions and the emotions and the concepts and the way we say things, there seems to be something else of a deeper nature that is communicated when we really communicate. And we're wondering what it is that is communicated, and how this works through the various forms and means of communication that we use.

(Carla channeling)

Greetings in the love and in the light of the one infinite Creator. We are those of Q'uo, and we are most grateful to have been called to your session of working this afternoon. The topic is communication, and since we are communicating on communication, perhaps we have a theme this particular session.

Think back, if you will, to your experiences as trees, rocks, sunlight. In all of these states of beingness you have experienced the essence of the infinite Creator without reaching for any word or, indeed, any thing. The first and second densities are certainly filled with sound, however, there is little conversation. It is in the third density when the self becomes self-conscious, that the desire to communicate is born as a basic instinct and urge. Even the little child new to manifestation seeks for the sound of the parent, which communicates. The tiny infant has the instinct to select and prefer the sound vibrations made by the mother and the father, those figures who give sustenance and improve comfort. Already, before the infant becomes aware that words carry specific messages, this third-density entity instinctually is reaching for that sound, hoping for that comfort—the human voice. Beyond all meanings of words, the human voice sings its way through life. Although few hear the music of spoken words, yet, nevertheless, they do have tune and cadences. Subtle though these patterns may be, they carry the breath—the air which is breathed in and exhaled.

The essence of manifested third-density life is breath. This breath is that which signals the aliveness of the present moment. One who is able to breathe is that one who is alive now. The breath of life is deeply intertwined with the spirit, both the spirit within and that spirit which strengthens. In a way, each time the human voice is heard, the tune is that of the infinite Creator Whose property alone it is to give life.

This is the density wherein entities such as yourselves appear like flowers to bloom, blossom, bear fruit, wither and die. During this natural process which is instinctual to your flesh, the life within focuses upon the lessons of love which third density brings. These lessons are those given by each to each, shared back and forth across the seemingly uncrossable chasms betwixt entities.

It is in this density that each has the opportunity to make the choice between service to self and service to others, and in the process of creating that first choice and then deepening that choice with successive ones, the human voice is everywhere.

Each entity spends much breath upon its own self, perhaps talking out loud even to the self, or if not, certainly carrying on internal conversation. In the attempt to discover the true point of balance that lies patiently within each and every human situation, if we may call it that, there is a kind of solitude native to third density that is never before and never afterwards experienced with the same intensity. That solitude, that feeling of aloneness, is due to the veil of forgetting having been dropped, so that those within your density simply cannot recall the unity betwixt the self and all others. This is the density where teachers are more and more important—those who are able to use their breath to speak support, comfort and challenge to those whom they would aid.

What is that essence which the human voice, then, carries? It is the essence of love. Each voice you hear is the voice of the one infinite Creator, experienced through distortion upon distortion, yet, nevertheless, unmistakably alive, clear and vivid. Each voice is the voice of the one infinite Mystery.

To relate to others within your density is often a difficult matter because the voice of the infinite Creator is a spontaneous one, whereas within your illusion it seems that, in many cases, events conspire to remove spontaneity. Then, the manners and the rights and rituals of words take over. The spontaneity drops away and the politeness, the courtesy, the cultural amenities take over. Yet, even with these meaningless conversations there is the vital essence of love carried within those sound vibrations, for love is not that which can be experienced directly. For the most part there is an indirect experience, the sensor web of the perception making choice upon choice concerning what is heard and what is said; yet, faith and fellowship can be carried along the most meaningless conversation.

Fellow feeling is most valuable in a world in which each cannot know that another is a safe person to be next to. The darkness of the veil has dropped upon you, and though you can remember dimly how it was not to have to explain, not to have to do aught else except simply exist to be in full communication, still, those dim memories do not serve to carry one through the seemingly endless meetings and cycles of meetings and greetings that go on within your everyday existences.

Know that the human voice has great power. Know that when you vibrate your voice and speak, you are expressing beneath the words the essence of life as you are experiencing it. That is, you are expressing your breath—that which, when it is gone from your physical vehicle, shall signal your absence. How precious that breath! How short the time to use it well. Know that when you hear the human voice, you hear the infinite Creator in all of Its love. Remember when you speak that the essence of that sound you make needs to be the love of the infinite Creator. Your breath specifically expresses that love. What shapes shall you place your sound vibrations into, then, to harmonize with that tune which is love? May your speaking be a blessing. May you be blessed by an overwhelming number of voices of love, for, truly, all you meet are love.

Do we need to say that often this love is in deep disguise? Therefore, may you always have the patience to wend your way through the dry and brittle valleys of difficult communication-clearing. May you have the faith to continue communicating past anger, past tears, until the words you speak are shapes that again harmonize with love.

We would close this meeting through the one known as Jim. We thank this instrument. We are those of Q'uo.

(Jim channeling)

I am Q'uo, and greet each again in love and in light. At this time we would ask if there are any queries to which we may speak—those thoughts upon your minds which have arisen during our speaking.

Questioner: I have a question for Q'uo. I wanted to ask, as we attempt to be of service to others, can we help others communicate? Can we help them with improving their communication … not really having a good grasp of it ourselves?

I am Q'uo, and am aware of your query, my brother. As you speak and exchange experience with those about you, you are aiding in every aspect of each entity's evolution, for there is no other thing that can be done. All experience is the Creator experiencing Itself. Thus, you may partake more and more fully in this identity as the Creator as you are able to engage more of your own being in that which you experience.

We realize that you ask about ways to serve others, and appreciate the dedication that you express. We wish to give you the comfort of knowledge that tells you that you aid others well by each activity you undertake, for there are indeed no mistakes. And we encourage each to continue to seek the deepest level of communication with the self and with all other selves. Thus, you consciously move yourselves in the direction of your realized unification.

Is there another query, my brother?

Questioner: Yes, I would ask you if … I'll say the question this way: as you, as I, as someone who attempts to be of service tries to communicate with another, is it possible to do this by just opening yourself inside to the unspoken words and questions of the other person, and perhaps say no words and yet still communicate your desire to help, just by listening? Are there any … do you have to actually speak the words, because of free will, to be of service? Is that a clear question?

I am Q'uo, and am indeed aware of your query, my brother. We would take those words which you have spoken well—the concept of opening the self to the desire to serve—and suggest that this is a foundation stone upon which your service to others may be built, and indeed in some instances this may be the only activity necessary. However, in most of your endeavors with other selves you will find it is also helpful to offer one's self when the need is seen in a more outward fashion. However, the beginning of any service is that opening of the heart to the concept of service and to the desire to serve.

Is there another query, my brother?

Questioner: No, thank you, but that is all for me and *(inaudible)*.

I am Q'uo, and we thank you once again, my brother. Is there another query?

Questioner: Yes, I have one. Aside from the physical communication human beings have, is there something deeper that goes between two people when they're talking? Aside from … I know you spoke of the love, or breath … Are there other energies that are being communicated during conversation?

I am Q'uo, and am aware of your query, my brother. Indeed, at the heart of each communication and all experience there is a portion of the Creator which seeks Itself. Thus, there is the yearning between those portions of the One which have traveled outward from the One, traveling through the One, seeking the One, and becoming again that which is One, while realizing that there has always been only One.

Is there any other query, my brother?

Questioner: No, not at this time. I think I'll give that one some thought.

Carla: So, each conversation is a love song. Is that what you're saying? The yearning to … The voice is actually that expression of not having made it back to unity yet, and there's a yearning. Is that right?

I am Q'uo, and you are quite eloquently correct, my sister. Is there another query?

Carla: No, but thank you. That was a great thought there.

I am Q'uo, and we agree that there is no greater thought than that which posits the song of the Creator as the great chant of the Universe.

Is there a final query at this time?

Questioner: I'll just say that I wish to communicate that you have communicated *(inaudible)* to this group *(inaudible)* Confederation. Thank you very much.

Questioner: Thank you, Q'uo.

I am Q'uo, and we again give our great gratitude to each present for sharing with us your seeking, your questions, and your sense of unity. We appreciate your effort immensely, and walk with you upon this journey, rejoicing with each step, each experience, each exchange.

We shall take our leave of your group only in an illusory fashion at this time, for in truth, we shall always walk with you. We are known to you as those of Q'uo, and we leave each in the love and in the light of the one infinite Creator. Adonai. ✧

Sunday Meditation
May 1, 1994

Group question: A question about relationships this afternoon. We have noticed that people in relationships that seem to have the best time, to stay together the longest, and who enjoy each other the most are people who don't let the little oddities of their partner's behavior bother them all that much. Some people can actually get so upset over these little things that they divorce, and I guess that a lot of divorces come from the cumulative experience of a lot of little things that one can't stand about the other. We are wondering what kind of transformation has to take place within the self for a person to move from where the little oddities in their partner's behavior no longer bother one, and in fact become a lovable part of the other person's image, and how does one move from the rejection of another to the acceptance of another and how does this happen within the self?

(Carla channeling)

We are those of Q'uo. Greetings in the love and in the light of the one infinite Creator. It is a blessing and a privilege to greet you on this day of transition from your cold to your warmer season. We thank each for calling us to your circle of seeking, and we share our humble thoughts with you most thankfully, asking only that you listen to our thoughts keeping that which seems of worth and truth to you and disregarding the remainder, for while we wish to be of service, we do not wish to become a stumbling block for any. Therefore, we ask that you invoke your own discrimination, for you will recognize that truth which is for you.

A query concerning relationships is always most welcome to us for the essence of third-density learn/teaching and teach/learning is that there are other selves, to which one must relate in choosing the manner of that relationship with others. The choice of polarity becomes first recognized and then made. The third-density physical vehicle was designed to function only in what you may call the family. By oneself one cannot reproduce and create new life. Without other selves working in cooperation, your own self will be unable to create a meeting of all needs. The essence of what you may call human is an absolute need for relationships with other selves.

Now, we have often pointed out that the other self in its interaction with you acts as a kind of a reflective surface or a mirror, reflecting back to you your own image, for that to which you are drawn or from which you are repelled in others is a somewhat distorted image of that within the self which has not come to the light of self-perception.

Thusly, when one sees that which is good in another, one does well to contemplate this positive reaction to discover that which one may by reflection of the nature of the self and the self-perceived virtues. Similarly, when one is disturbed by another, one does well to reflect upon this event to discover what it is within the hidden self that the self perceives as wanting, unworthy or in error. Yet these descriptions would almost create the image of the self as actually separate, a "Monet" if you will. Within a universe created completely of mirrors this is not the case, although the work one does is upon oneself, if it be excellent work. Yet still in the process of working upon the self, other selves offer the opportunity for service, the service which you offer to another and the service which you offer to another by being needy and needing that from another which will help you. It is as important to be able to receive love and kindnesses it is to offer love and charity.

So the other self is the self yet not the self. The reactions to the other self are the business of the self. That which is proactive, not responsive but creative with regard to another self is often that service which you may best offer that particular other self. We speak always about love. Our message continues to be simple, to the point of confounding the wise. We ask you to open to the love of the infinite Creator; we ask you to become aware of the presence of this love as the center of the life; we ask you that you work towards creating within the self a channel for that infinite love so that this highest truth may be attested to by the solid witness of your being.

Now, could you accomplish this, you would be dwelling within the fourth density at this time. It is expected and appreciated that the nature of learning is the attempt and often the failure to manifest the infinite love of the infinite Creator. This is not the sort of test wherein one must study, memorize and accomplish a right answer. Living as a witness to an infinite Love is the kind of test that occurs when one is being observed but not stimulated by a teacher. The teacher rather watches as the spontaneous and natural rhythms of life are created and expressed moment by moment throughout the incarnation.

The watcher of your life is your own self in its higher manifestation, and at the end of this test, upon the dissolution of the bond between physical and spiritual self, this higher self shall dwell with you, gazing through the record of the days and years of this incarnation. There will be the center of the balance of this particular incarnation perceived. Its perception will be accurate and precise. As the spiritual self walks what has been called the steps of light, those who stop at a certain level shall be within third density again, those who stop and feel comfortable at a somewhat fuller light shall be those who take up higher density lessons for the next incarnation.

Therefore, one cannot maintain a mentality of a spiritual homework beyond a certain point, for the homework is for a test that will not be held within your lifetime. You see, the self seldom has any very accurate notion of its own essential issues, needs and excellences. Rather, the self tends to perceive the self in a fairly distorted pattern because the self is so hidden from the conscious mind, and because the self within the flesh cannot truly see the self within, there is that veil drawn.

So, to begin to be able to make the transformation about which your query spoke one must first begin to allow the judgment of the self concerning the self to fade away and become unimportant, for there is no possibility of accurate judgment of the self by the self. It is well to examine the life as much as is possible but only in that [it] enables one to see into the uppermost layers of selfhood. Certainly this is valuable, however, it does not make you a judge. When one is able to lay self-judgment aside and instead to take up the solitude and the dust of the spiritual path taken on faith then is one beginning to be able to dwell and abide with others in a creative and living way.

Each self carries a great and terrible burden, that is, the self-perceived difficulties and errors and mischief which the self has seen the self think, speak and do. No other entity who dwells with you will ever be able to share this burden with you, for even if you were able to talk, confessing every sin you could think of, every error you could remember, yet still would the self feel that such was not truly enough to wash clean human frailty. This is an accurate perception. You did not come into this incarnation to get everything right but to be a witness to love and light. You are not going to become right or better or finished but will remain one who seems to sow seeds in the wind.

The phrase, "casting one's bread upon the waters" comes from your holy work, the Bible, and that is what each self is intended to do, to cast the love and light and being a witness unto the ever moving, ever disappearing waters of life. Indeed, one may rejoice and offer thanks when one is simply giving away love and light, for within this image in your Bible it is pointed out that if one achieves a true release of gifts, a lack of holding them in memory, then does the Law of Plenty move into action and the self becomes conscious of receiving one hundred and one thousand times the blessing back upon those moving waters of life.

So, to become able to make the transformation from tolerating another to celebrating another—to use this instrument's phrase—the first step is to become detached from self-judgment and unattached to one's thoughts, words and deeds. In that you do them, think them as well as you can and then forget them and move onward to the next creative moment. Each entity vibrates within a certain range, this basic vibration is as a—we correct this instrument—each entity is an unique vibratory signature. It vibrates as it is, completely whole and completely clear no matter what muddle you may feel you are in. That basic vibration is completely identifiable as you and only you. This vibration, this basic signature is that which you are attempting to affect by the way you live your life and the lessons—we correct this instrument—the way you live your life and the way you concern yourself and deal with the lessons of love you encounter along the King's Highway, as this instrument would put it.

By choosing again and again to serve others, by choosing to seek the Creator in the self, in others, in creation, and in the center of the being, you attempt to affect the narrowing of the gap between your vibratory signature and the basic pure vibration which created all things, that infinite Creator's Thought or Logos of Love.

So you have a relative vibration, that is, relative to the Creator. A great many incarnations are consumed in the slow and inevitable progression and narrowing of that gap betwixt the self and the All Self. This vibration may be seen to be that which is of love and of fear, these are the two basic dynamics within the vibratory levels. To be simplistic we would say that there is always some ratio of fear to love, however the greater the love, the greater the life, the greater the fear, the greater the death, for that which is alive, creative and moving is of love, and that which is judging and defending and inwardly focusing beyond a certain point is of death.

When one attempts to learn tolerance of another one is attempting to be able to accept another in complete love and lack of judgment. To the extent that this is accomplished there is a great benefit to the self, to the other self, and to the Creator. When one finds that one must engage in judging, in defending against and so forth, then one is dealing with emotions which may be identified with the death, or the forces of death.

We speak now of death not in the sense of your living things which bloom and die, but rather we are speaking of that which is of the Creator and that which is separate from the Creator. That is, all things are of the Creator but within your illusion and, indeed, in many illusions beyond your own the—we correct this instrument—there is an apparent choice between energies which move to a fuller life and energies which separate one from life.

There is a great and intensive battle within for your attention from both your deeper self and from the energies which surround you. Constantly you move within a spiritual atmosphere which is flowing and continuous, which never stops in its movements, and which is greatly affected by desire and intention. It is within this intuitively perceived sea of being that you swim, shall we say, or sail, either towards the unity of love which is the Creator or towards that archipelago of perceived self and other selves which is the seascape of the service-to-self entity who perceives the self apart from all by choice, and controlling all for the best good.

The battle is fought for the heart of the self and sometimes a seeker may begin to think that he has more than one self within him, so full of contradictions does the wandering vagaries of selfhood seem. Thusly, to move from tolerance to celebration of others, the first challenge is to begin to perceive the self within this larger view which does not judge but rather uses energy in a positive and creative manner, in self-acceptance, self-forgiveness and self-[em]powerment. To keep faith, continue in hope and do all such good works as open before the eyes.

When this has been perceived as a goal towards which to move, then it is that the self becomes able to extend this charity to other selves. We would offer the model of the way things are that the one known as Jesus offered when this entity described the situation where the sower sows a crop which another shall harvest. When this crop of love and positive desire is sown with a glad and merry heart it then becomes more and more possible to begin to see through the veil, to perceive for the first time the extent to which others sow for you to reap. How rich each is in the harvest given by others to the self, and how much richer shall the self be as it learns more and more to sow those seeds of love and virtue with a careless and generous hand, not waiting for the self to applaud but moving on, practicing the presence of love.

Lift the eyes from the page of life and you shall see far more between the lines.

At this time, we would ask if there are continuing queries upon this interesting subject?

Questioner: Not from me Q'uo, but I really enjoyed what you had to say, thank you very much.

We thank you, my brother. This has been a very good group.

Questioner: No question from me Q'uo, I just enjoyed … *(inaudible)*.

We humbly thank you, my brother.

How we love you! How beautiful you are to us! We see you wanting so much to cherish each other. Cherish yourselves, and then turn the eyes towards the infinite One, and your instinct shall more and more be that which does celebrate others, that which does have charity and wisdom towards others. These are natural ways. You are simply relearning them. Never doubt that behind the veil of suffering and limitation lies a land where love is visible. But hold fast to that faith and let it be the rock upon which you stand, with arms open to receive love … and hearts open to give it. May you truly celebrate and enable each other as you walk along the King's Highway.

We thank each again for the joy of your company and the beauty of your shining hope. We leave you in the love and in the light of the one infinite Creator. Adonai. Adonai. ✤

L/L Research

L/L Research is a subsidiary of Rock Creek Research & Development Laboratories, Inc.

P.O. Box 5195
Louisville, KY 40255-0195

www.llresearch.org

Rock Creek is a non-profit corporation dedicated to discovering and sharing information which may aid in the spiritual evolution of humankind.

ABOUT THE CONTENTS OF THIS TRANSCRIPT: This telepathic channeling has been taken from transcriptions of the weekly study and meditation meetings of the Rock Creek Research & Development Laboratories and L/L Research. It is offered in the hope that it may be useful to you. As the Confederation entities always make a point of saying, please use your discrimination and judgment in assessing this material. If something rings true to you, fine. If something does not resonate, please leave it behind, for neither we nor those of the Confederation would wish to be a stumbling block for any.

CAVEAT: This transcript is being published by L/L Research in a not yet final form. It has, however, been edited and any obvious errors have been corrected. When it is in a final form, this caveat will be removed.

© 2009 L/L Research

Sunday Meditation
May 22, 1994

Group question: The question this afternoon has to do with wanderers. What does Q'uo have to say to those who have discovered that they are wanderers to be of service to others and what would Q'uo have to say to those wanderers who have not discovered that they are wanderers?

(Carla channeling)

We are Q'uo. Greetings in the love and in the light of the one infinite Creator. We thank you for calling us to your circle of seeking. It is our great privilege to share our thoughts with you on the subject of wanderers. As we speak, please feel free to take those thoughts which appeal and leave others behind, for we are not without error and would not wish to be a stumbling block in your path.

We are aware that this instrument has been much concerned with this subject. We would express to this instrument that it would aid the contact were the instrument to completely release the fear of contributing too much to the channeling. This is not a problem from our point of view, and the releasing of worrying would relax the instrument and improve the contact. We also would say, before we continue with this subject, that the one known as Hatonn is with this group this particular day as there is a desire for this entity's basic vibrations which will be imprinted upon the tape.

When the term "wanderer" is used the basic meaning of this word is that one is traveling without reference to a goal or destination. There is, implicit in this term, a feeling or emotional/mental mindset of aloneness, restlessness, shared solitude, and indifferent scenery. The winds blow cold and harshly for the wanderer. The sun beats down mercilessly for the wanderer. Few there are who use that term who feel that it is desirable to be a wandering spirit. All of the third-density instinct is towards putting down the roots, securing the home, and protecting the home and family. The wanderer is uprooted when gazed at in the cultural context that you enjoy upon your sphere. Therefore, it is natural that this term be chosen as descriptive of those who have come into the Earth's sphere of influence and incarnated to become as one with all citizens of your Earth.

So, at the heart of being a wanderer is that feeling of dislocation, of being in the world but not of the world in which you find yourselves. Because this situation seems full of discomfort many who have wandered here are simply miserable without finding any comfort. To respond to that need for comforting some who have responded have leaned in their discussions heavily towards comforting wanderers by encouraging a sense of separation from native Earth humans. We do not encourage this line of thought because each wanderer, in coming into your Earth's sphere of influence, took upon it the responsibility of citizenship of this Earth. As much as any other native inhabitant, wanderers will be expected to walk the steps of light when this incarnational experience is at an end, and, just as much as any native inhabitant of Earth, if the steps are walked to a point of comfort within third density the wanderer shall not return to its home vibratory nexus but, rather, shall continue in third density until graduation is achieved.

Therefore, we greatly encourage all wanderers to take up the burden of a dual existence, for that is precisely why you have put yourselves to this task. As difficult and disagreeable as it sometimes is to live with this double vibratory pattern, this difficulty is worthwhile and one hundred times worthwhile, for the basic vocation of every wanderer is to bear witness to the light and the love of the one infinite Creator. Therefore, the life may be seen to be full of everyday matters, yet offer ample time and space for the spiritual vocation to which wanderers have called themselves, that of bearing witness.

And how does a wanderer bear this witness? It might seem that witnesses are best when they are expressing by words that witness to which they hew, yet this actually is not so. Rather, wanderers may best bear witness by being most fully themselves, for it is the basic vibratory complex carried in the violet ray by each wanderer that is witness by its very essence. Therefore, the wanderer's job in everyday affairs is to keep the channel of selfhood and essence clean, clear and pellucid. This is in many ways a passive spiritual vocation. It is easier to make the mistake of attempting to speak this witness and not being understood or of service than to refrain from some activity and, therefore, fail to bear witness.

The planetary consciousness is drinking in your essence. It is lightening the planetary vibration and is acting as an ameliorator of birth pangs within the planet itself and within the great congregation of entities which now approach your millennium. Inconvenient and difficult times beckon. Within these confusing times the silent witness of being shall more and more be needed as the planet reaches for a new point of balance.

We encourage each so to arrange the daily habits that the center of being is given respect and pride of place within the daily life. As always, we suggest a daily meditation, a turning in and out of season towards that infinity which is the inarticulated love of the one infinite Creator. The challenge for each wanderer is to be able to dwell in this particular illusion, to enter fully into the processes of becoming a transformation yet remain at the center of being, consciously turning again and again to love itself.

To those who feel somewhat dislocated and alienated by the outward environment but who have not yet decided for sure that they are wanderers we say to each that it is well to act as if you are a wanderer, for that which wanderers came here to do is that which all may help by attempting to do. For at heart, all are wanderers. We, as well as you. All have wandered from that inarticulated love which is the one infinite Creator. We have wandered through many, many creations and have experienced manifestation upon manifestation. Within each place we have found eventually the one infinite Creator, and as we have found the Creator we have felt that homecoming. Yet as soon as that is felt the new challenge arises, the new day dawns, a new lesson is to be learned, and once again the restless wandering begins within.

May each wanderer find comfort in the knowledge that it cannot help contributing positively to the planetary vibration. Even with what seems to be gross mismanagement of time and energy, yet still in that very basic alienated mindset there dwells that vibration which is fuller with light. This very alienation is simply a surface symptom of a deep and spiritual gift. Comfort yourself when the heart is heavy and the feelings bruised with the knowledge that you are being of service. You are doing that which you came to do. You may find ways to do it better, but you are not failing no matter what it seems like.

In the great circle of creation we salute each brave soul who has chosen this sacrificial honor. The one known as Brother Philip has said, "The crown shall weigh heavy upon the head, yet you shall wear it and you shall serve under it." May this be most truly so for each.

We would, at this time, ask if there are any queries.

(Pause)

We thank you. The ones of Hatonn wished only to place the basic vibration upon the tape in order that comfort may be given to one who hears.

We once again thank each for gathering to seek within spirituality for that ultimate reality which beckons. How confusing it is to have chosen to become manifestations of love. At the point at which we all are it seems very strange that we as Creator chose to become co-creators, moving in and out of illusion after illusion. Yet that which is infinite calls for more and more and each carries that eternal stillness and the eternal free will within. The combination creates that which is just and right and good. Yes, you shall suffer, but this suffering is infinitely worthwhile.

We leave this instrument and this group in the love and in the light of the one infinite Creator. We are known to you as those of Q'uo. Adonai. Adonai, vasu.

(Carla channeling)

I Yadda. This instrument wishes to challenge and not trust the vibration, so we must stop and challenge. We accept this instrument's anal retentiveness, as she would say, understanding that she is in earnest in the attempt to receive only positive information. We, too, say of wanderers, "Go to it, and stop complaining." You came to work, so work! Where is the joy unless you sink your teeth into the vibration of your Earth? Feel that strength within and stop namby-pambying. We exhort you—have fun!

We leave this instrument in the love and light of the Creator. We thank this instrument for allowing us to bare our barbaric "yawp." We leave you in the love and light of the infinite One once again. I Yadda. ❧

Sunday Meditation
May 29, 1994

Group question: The question today has to do with healing. Many of the newer and more holistic means of healing deal with the body that has to be healed, the mind and the emotional system that has an effect upon the body, and then each one attempts to deal also with the spiritual aspect, which has ascendancy over both the emotional and the physical realms. We are wondering how a healer who is using any particular holistic method to heal might aid the patient to engage the spiritual aspect of the healing so that the healing has a better chance of being successful and so that the roots of the problems are dealt with. Could you give us some information on that?

(Carla channeling)

We are those of Q'uo. Greetings in the love and in the light of the one infinite Creator. It is indeed a privilege to be called to your circle of seeking and we humbly thank each for offering us the honor of sharing our vibrations and our opinions with you. As always, we request that those thoughts which seem helpful to each be retained and that those which do not appear helpful at this particular occasion be released, for we are prone to error, being those who journey with you, but perhaps a few steps further in that infinite journey. With this understood we may speak freely.

The difficulty in speaking about spiritual healing and cleansing is the difficulty common to all attempts to put faith into words. Whereas physical and mental, emotional—we correct this instrument—emotional problems have a large vocabulary of closely fitting words to work with, the issues of spirit must depend upon words such as love and faith which have no objective referent that is at one's hand to pin down and to create as a fully meaningful term. Words like faith indeed do refer to a real thing, but that reality is at best approximately symbolized by language, for the level of this truth is beyond the reach of words created as tools in dealing with one's environment.

The entity who is attempting a life lived in faith is perhaps the closest one might come to a fully meaningful symbol of faith. A person who is attempting to love is perhaps the soulful expression of love itself. When that verb which is the seeker seeks to attain the objective of spiritual health, then, there is no set of words that can bring about healing, for the health of spirit is at once always within that entity seeking help, regardless of the outer appearance. However, this health is also most suggestive when there is attained within the seeker the releasing and balancing of all energies which can be felt, and then the simple willing belief of a believer who believes not in the words of faith, but who believes that faith is the appropriate energetic balance.

This is difficult for us to give this instrument but we would ask each to picture the entity who rides upon the bicycle or the entity who flies the airplane. When the various moments of motion are moving harmoniously, the balance is effortless. To achieve an approximate balance, however, for the newly—we correct this instrument—for the new practitioner is very difficult. The beginner does not know what true balance feels like and has not the ready instinct usually for that point of balance. So it is when a seeker begins to reinvent the life so that the life becomes a life lived in faith.

Structurally speaking, there are two clear portions to working upon spiritual healing or health. The first energy which needs to be worked with by the entity and by a healer who wishes to assist is that portion of the self which could perhaps be seen as muddied or roiled in terms of energetic patterns. The torque of spiritual disease is such that the unhealthy entity that one could say knotted or twisted and then held in that pattern by the energies which wish to untangle that unhealth, but yet each attempt to untangle just (close) the knot tighter.

This darkness, shall we say, is a darkness which is in the midst of the light which is also perceived as darkness. Therefore, there is no vision within which can tell what of the shadow world of spirit is of health and which is that of disease. Therefore, in the combing out of these tangles the dependency must be not upon precise visualization, but rather upon the willingness of that seeker to lay down all judgment of both disease and health, or of both the darkness which is knotted and that great darkness of spirit which is the rightful realm of the healthy and balanced spiritual seeker.

The right ways of working to release these tightly held points of disease are those which heavily move into symbol, both the use of symbols and the general willingness to work with parallel healing modes, with the realization that the cleansing of the mode used is specifically intended and desired to be reflected within the patterns of energy of the individual as spiritual counterparts. So that perhaps an entity seeking to release old mind and old unhealth of spirit might put the self upon some sort of fast or diet, this being specifically stated within and repeated often as one form of cleansing which is reflected into the spirit; as the parallel of the body is cleansed, so the paralleled spirit also becomes more cleansed and less full of substance.

As a healer wishing to aid this process, one may work within one's experience and thought to achieve methods found by one particular healer to be efficacious. These might include, for instance, the aiding of that patient to achieve a more suggestible state, or hypnosis. In this state, then, the healer may take the entity to a point between incarnations where the higher self is [a] voice available to and able to respond to questioner and questions so that the healer might gently request the higher self be asked by the patient if this entity is indeed ready to experience healing. In other words, is that lesson for which this distortion was necessary now learned; if not, may there be some thought upon this. Thusly, that entity's higher self may give impressions and words within the hearing and control of that patient.

Alternately, a healer might choose, when a hypnotic state was achieved, simply to speak in terms of lessening fear by means of extending the range of the viewpoint. This entity recalls the story told her of a patient whose ulcers were life-threatening. In hypnosis this entity was told that the entity sat on the side of a large planet, a ball whirling in space. The scope of time, the reaches of spaces were piped into the inner world of this entity. Those [concerns which] seared and burned within could more and more be seen to be of less import because of the widening of the viewpoint from this moment and this place to an infinite sweep of time and space.

Another entity might wish to use the conscious technique, that is, the patient remaining conscious of the tones sung or the prayers offered. In doing these chantings or singings or sharing energy in some other way, the healer and the patient are together seeking to release the disease by these energetic displacements, not of thoughts but of tones and so forth which have for the healer the ability to carry prayer, the energy of prayer. For what is a prayer? When one wishes to aid the spiritually ill one truly needs to be able to speak of prayer in a way which is flexible, but yet which holds for the healer that ring of authority which indicates experience, which the healer does have. So perhaps it is well to look at prayer.

But this moves into the second portion of the material we hope to share at this working. Before we leave the first there is a bit more to be said. What is this knotting that indicates that the shuttle of spirit is not in good working order? The simplest term is fear. The spiritually ill entity has moved into an isolation, a place alone within which the entity is unforgiven and unnurtured. This isolation is crushing and once entered is very difficult to see, much less to work with. So, the energies of the healer pour like a blessing over this wounded spirit, lessening the isolation. However it is an infringement on the free will of the spirit being healed to substitute one's own faith for the faith of the patient, so the healer who wishes to be of benefit must work on itself, offering, too, itself those energies of forgiveness and wholeness. And in this offering to self, opening and sharing this purifies emotion of an at-one-ment with the patient.

Simply to say, "All things are love and love casts out fear," is in almost all cases inadequate. Perhaps one entity might hear and understand in a moment of realization that truly love casts out fear, but to the ailing spirit, such encouragement usually is received as if it simply constituted another pressure which was painful, the feelings of inadequacy and helplessness continuing and perhaps even growing. It is well to be humble and silent before or in the face of the temptation to overstate or speak too much. However, there are an infinite number of ways to create within the self of the healer that dynamic balance to forgiveness and love which may far better speak to the spiritually ill.

This instrument is concerned that it is not picking up all that we are offering, but we ask this instrument to quit being so picky and move on please. We are teasing this instrument.

Once that fear that isolates and anguishes the patient has been addressed, once the way has been to some extent cleared, then the healer moves to the darkness of spiritual hell, still in that place of mystery where faith is born, but now is free because of having addressed and bid farewell to fear. Into this environment may prayer come.

The one known as D has offered the information that although the spiritual illness can now be to some extent determined or found, yet there has not been a corresponding mode of healing with the exception of prayer. Again this is because the spirit, while acting as a shuttle for energies into the physical and mental and emotional bodies, is not in direct contact with energies within the instinctual body and mental frame of individuals upon planet Earth, but rather can be reached roundabout, or so it seems to those within third density. The praying seems roundabout because one is praying to forces or essences within the world of spirit. And then that energy which lies without the sphere of Earth is persuaded to enter into the tangle to breathe balance into it. However, in actuality prayer is the most direct way of healing, for true healing is the restoration of all energies to their rightful balance.

But how to pray and how to aid patients in praying? Firstly, we would suggest that it be told to patients who are interested in helping themselves in this wise, concerning the physical place where he or she might pray, where in a specific environment shall the prayers be, how long shall they be given, of what shall they consist, thereby aiding the seeker in its growing ability to visualize this as a real and efficacious healing mode. For those among your peoples, for the most part, do not have the daily prayers, do not have the praying without ceasing, and if neither the daily repetition of prayer, or the constancy of prayer are things which the patient is familiar with then the suggestion to pray leaves the patient in a vulnerable position, feeling alone and inadequate. Thusly, the healer aids by making a place in time and space where the outer form might be observed. Thusly can a healer move the patient into that mental and emotional feeling of "I can do this."

It is seemingly merely working with details to get down to basics to decide which chair to use or what time of day to make for prayer time, yet these down-to-earth details truly do aid in the formation of faith. Now, prayer could be said to be that tune which, though unheard, is the tune of hope. Prayer can be said to be that inner flower which bears the scent of love. Prayer can be talked about indirectly by speaking of the beauty of a poem or a rose. Prayer is a form of communication whose object is one with its subject. The prayer, in reaching to the infinite Creator, reaches within. The self talking to the greater Self, this is the structure which seen from the outside may be said to constitute the house of prayer. The actuality is that that seemingly far away source of unity which love itself is, lies within, so the journey of prayer is a journey from self to the greater Self within, then circling back to form the unending circle between prayer and prayer, that is between the one who prays and the object of prayer.

It is not that we are saying that people pray to themselves, rather we are saying that …

(Side one of tape ends.)

(Carla channeling)

… to which people pray lies within, for as the illusions of manifestation are progressively cast aside, that which is uncovered is already holy ground, and that far away Creator of one who fears is in reality that imminent presence which is the internal truth of all, shut away from the heart's awareness by that door which the seeker is always able to open but has not discovered the way to, or the key for it.

Thusly, it is well for the healer to speak some words concerning this practice of the infinite presence of that one great original Thought, that logos which is love and which is the One infinite Creator. In your Holy Bible it is written that the one known as Jesus states, "I am come that you may have life and have it more abundantly." This abundance of life is that which is the healthy spirit. When you have been able to, as healer, to place within the seeker's hands these basic concepts, then the healer's job is done insofar as communication with the seeker. From this point onward the healer may pray and know that presence within and offer this state of prayer to the infinite Creator on behalf of the patient, and the seeker who is the patient may begin to create for itself a life which is transformed. But this transformation shall come not visibly, not plainly, but rather from inside out.

There is much which might be added upon this interesting subject, however, we are aware that we have talked overlong, and at this time we would move on in this session by transferring this contact to the one known as Jim. We thank this instrument and leave it in love and in light. We are those of Q'uo.

(Jim channeling)

I am Q'uo, and am with this instrument. I greet each again in love and in light. At this time we would ask if there are any queries which have arisen in the minds of those present to which we may speak?

Carla: When you are talking about prayer, is it just that any prayer will do? I mean if people know certain prayers, for example the prayers of St. Francis of Assisi, or is it more … what you are trying to say is this energy of knowing that all is one. I mean, I am not really getting what you are saying that prayer really consists in so that you could tell somebody else how to do it. Where am I going wrong here?

I am Q'uo, and am aware of your query, my sister. The quality which the prayer most beneficially offers the one to be healed is the avenue through which to express the heart, and the heartfelt desire to be healed, this, then, expressed in a manner which for this entity allows the most open and clear expression to be healed. For some it may be that prayers which exist in your literature are most helpful. For others it may be that the prayer of the moment is the one which is most helpful. Thus, it is not important whether or not the prayer is structured in such and such a fashion, rather it is important that the prayer provide an avenue for the heart to be expressed.

Is there a further query, my sister?

Carla: Well, and also not just for the seeker, but if the healer wants to pray, is prayer just totally unique for each person, that that person would then feel the clearest contact with love? I mean, is basically what you are saying is whatever the person can do to express that faith in unity … like silence for some people might be the best prayer? I guess I am getting hung up on the word.

I am Q'uo, and we would respond by suggesting that for the healer it may be more efficacious if this entity who regularly seeks to aid in healing constructs a prayer, a ritual which allows it to express those qualities which it feels are important in this process, or it may be that the entity serving as the healer is one who feels that the spontaneous prayer of the moment is efficacious. For the healer it is often helpful to ritualize the prayer since it is often used. But again the needs of the moments and the nature of the healer will determine this.

Is there a further query, my sister?

Carla: Not at this time, thanks.

I am Q'uo, and we thank you, my sister. Is there another query?

Questioner: You spoke of dealing with the person's fear. Do you mean the fear of letting the disease actually go, because they've had it, or what did you mean by dealing with the fear that the person actually has, because I know it is important.

I am Q'uo, and am aware of your query, my brother. An entity seeking healing is seeking relief from a pattern of thought and belief which brings it disease of one nature or another. To face the situation that is internal to the entity is often difficult for the entity, for the pattern of thought and behavior that has resulted in the disease is one which has, until the point of healing, remained for the most part hidden and a mystery.

As the desire to be healed grows within the entity and more especially as the entity seeks the healing, the entity actually in the metaphysical turns to face the problem, the structure of thinking, in full light. This is often painful or fearful for the entity seeking healing, for the experiences which have been a portion of the entity's formation of the diseased patterns of thought are often traumatic and to face this once again in light is for many a fearsome proposition.

The healer may aid the one seeking healing in the facing of the fear by reminding each who seeks healing that the healing is a natural process for a disease which is also a portion of a natural process of growth, that the entity is not alone, that many have gone before it and have been healed of that which ails it, that far many more walk with it unseen to aid the healing. In these ways and many others may the healer aid the one facing the fear and seeking the healing.

Is there a further query, my brother?

Questioner: Not at this time.

Carla: Is it possible that the reason that we are getting a lot of spiritual disease is because a lot of people are here from other vibrations, other densities, wanderers coming to help planet Earth, and they just bring spiritual difficulty into this illusion as they get born because their vibrations are just fighting with our vibrations? Is that part of it? Are people being born with spiritual disease all ready to kick in because of that vibratory mismatch?

I am Q'uo, and we believe we grasp your query. Please query further if we have not. The spiritual unease of which you speak is often the result of precisely the situation which you have described, that of entities who have journeyed to this sphere for the purpose of aiding its birth, shall we say, into a new level of vibration. The blending of vibrations that are more harmonious with the vibrations of your planetary sphere as it suffers some difficulty in the birthing often causes a jangling to the spiritual complex which is likened to the feeling a traveler has in a distant land of not being a portion of that population. The healing that is of the body and the mental and the emotional complexes is for many entities more a product of the utilization of this density's vibrations for the working out of an incarnational pattern which had its roots in many lifetimes previous.

Thus, the healing of such entities is that which often is accomplished by means which are similar to that which is offered to the one seeking spiritual healing as well, for all healing must have the foundation set in the etheric or form-making body which is that more closely aligned with the spiritual complex of any entity.

Is there a further query, my sister?

Carla: So what you are saying is that you are in prayer, you are reaching and saying let this higher truth eliminate my condition, basically.

I am Q'uo, and am aware of your query, my sister. You are basically correct in your assumption. The prayer serves as a means whereby the earthbound portion of the entity's personality addresses that portion which may be called the higher self, the form-maker, the etheric body, which then will respond to the heartfelt prayer by opening the waters of the spirit that they may wash the entity clean in one area or another according to the purity of the desire to be healed and the efficaciousness of the ability of the one serving as healer to aid in the opening of this pathway.

Is there a further query, my sister?

Carla: Just one, and that is I really feel that a lot of people are very sincere about asking for healings, spiritual healing, and they don't receive what they consider to be spiritual healings. So there seems to be something really desiring something, but does not always fire right, does not always come out right … What is there? What is the difference between one who thinks that he desires that just totally, desperately wants to healed, yet is just knotting it up, and the person that truly does desire and doesn't knot it up but is releasing the knot. It is really critical.

I am Q'uo, and we believe we grasp your query, my sister. There are many explanations for why entities who seem to seek wholeheartedly their healing do not receive that which they seek. Oftentimes there is simple desire without previous work that has the purpose of uncovering the roots of disease. There is the need for each entity to seek the basic understanding of the distortion that is to be healed.

Carla: And that's why the change in diet or something that goes along the lines of cleansing you suggested first before you talked about prayer? OK. Thank you.

[I am Q'uo.] We wish to add in addition to this that this seeking to illuminate the self according to the causes of the disease may indeed be expressed in a number of ways—the change of diet, the change of behavior, the looking at a situation in a new attitude, or any other means by which an entity may seek illumination of the distortion. There is also the need for each entity, no matter how desirous it is to be healed or illuminated it has become concerning its distortion, to realize that the primary attitude that underlies all attempts at healing or seeking healing is the attitude of "Thy will be done."

When there is no healing one must look at what opportunities are presented as a result of the seeking of healing and the seeming lack of healing. The will of the Creator that moves through each entity's life pattern is that which always presents to the entity that which is most efficacious to its present growth. Whether that includes healing of distortion or continuation of distortion, there are opportunities available for praising and giving thanksgiving to the one Creator and these opportunities are that which the entity might look to, who has sought and seemingly not received the healing.

Is there a further query, my sister?

Carla: So, are you saying that if the person acts as if the lines of healing are opened, that the person generates faith by this action?

I am Q'uo, and you are correct, my sister. The quality of faith balanced by the exercise of will are the rod and the staff which can comfort the seeker. By continuing to exercise faith and will that opportunities are available for the seeker to grow, to serve and to know the Creator then such opportunities are indeed available.

Carla: OK. So you are praying not to heal anything but just to give praise and thanksgiving and to offer the self in any way that you can to do the Creator's will. That's the basic plan?

I am Q'uo, and this is correct, my sister. Whether the entity seeks knowledge through one practice or another, seeks healing through one means or another, the entity, in order to be most in harmony with its own life pattern, must needs seek these things that it might be of greater service to the one Creator. Thus, the entity says, "Whatever Thy will be for me at this time, that is my will as well."

Is there a further query, my sister?

Carla: No, thank you.

I am Q'uo, and we thank you, my sister. Is there a final query at this time?

(Pause)

I am Q'uo, and we would take this opportunity to thank those present for inviting our presence to your circle of seeking this day. It has been a great honor and privilege to blend our vibrations with yours and to walk with you upon your journey of seeking. We would remind each that we are but your brothers and sisters who walk this same dusty path with you, and we have gladly and joyfully shared our opinions with you. Remember, please, that we share opinion.

At this time we shall take our leave of this instrument, leaving each in the love and the light of the one infinite Creator. We are known to you as those of Q'uo. Adonai, my friends. Adonai.

L/L Research

L/L Research is a subsidiary of Rock Creek Research & Development Laboratories, Inc.

P.O. Box 5195
Louisville, KY 40255-0195

www.llresearch.org

Rock Creek is a non-profit corporation dedicated to discovering and sharing information which may aid in the spiritual evolution of humankind.

ABOUT THE CONTENTS OF THIS TRANSCRIPT: This telepathic channeling has been taken from transcriptions of the weekly study and meditation meetings of the Rock Creek Research & Development Laboratories and L/L Research. It is offered in the hope that it may be useful to you. As the Confederation entities always make a point of saying, please use your discrimination and judgment in assessing this material. If something rings true to you, fine. If something does not resonate, please leave it behind, for neither we nor those of the Confederation would wish to be a stumbling block for any.

CAVEAT: This transcript is being published by L/L Research in a not yet final form. It has, however, been edited and any obvious errors have been corrected. When it is in a final form, this caveat will be removed.

© 2009 L/L Research

Special Meditation
June 12, 1994

(Round robin channeling.)

(Carla channeling)

I am Q'uo. Greetings in the love and in the light of the one infinite Creator. We thank you for the privilege of being asked to offer our opinions at this session of working. This humble service that we provide is a sharing of what small understanding we have. We ask each seeker to realize that we do make errors and are not final authorities. Therefore, we ask that each who hears choose for himself those truths which he has found and disregard the remainder, for we offer thoughts which are of aid to the various entities within the circle and each may find her own truths there. Always, that which does not seem right to you, please know that for you it is indeed not right. Your own power of discrimination will aid you as you seek to remember that truth which you have temporarily forgotten.

Each member of this circle has come to this moment as the culmination of years and years of seeking. Always the present moment is the intersection of enormous energies and possibilities. Each has suffered and experienced that anguish which lies beyond suffering, and therefore each comes to this present moment full of grief, sadness and well-earned wisdom, and each comes to this circle seeking still the highest good, the absolute which lies beyond the chances and changes of the mortal life.

Were any entity here present to express in depth the nature of his own suffering, she would astound the remainder of the circle. In an illusion life is experienced. In an illusion seekers must craft as best they can their ship and their direction, and each within this circle has gifts to give of support, understanding and silent companionship. Greetings, brothers and sisters of love and light. Each has earned this title. We would now transfer. We are those of Q'uo.

(Jim channeling)

I am Q'uo, and greet each again through this instrument. As brothers and sisters of love and light you are also brothers and sisters of sorrow, for as you serve the light by giving of your love you find those whose need is that you tend their sorrow. There are those whose experience of the one Creator is not as filled with light as is yours and who, as a result, move in somewhat erratic patterns and experience the difficulties of moving in darkness, propelled only by faith and will in whatever degree. The very being of those who seek the One, yet who know not precisely how to find the One is as a call to those whose hearts are listening. Thus, you move in your experience and your attention to those who give the call for whatever it is that you may have to offer. Oftentimes it is but a listening ear, the gentle touch, the shared tears that one can offer. Yet each offering is given wholly and freely as that which is yours to give.

We would transfer at this time.

(S channeling)

I am Q'uo, and we are with this instrument. Even as it happens that one is upon a happy chance able to offer solace to a fellow traveler, so does it occur that one's fellow travelers are able to offer a gift to one in return. Sometimes this gift is of the nature of solace, sometimes it is of the nature of catalyst of a different kind, sometimes gentle words meet with words less than gentle and when this occurs it is often enough to cause one who would serve to recoil in pain and in horror at the realization that one's own gift has not been received in the spirit in which it was intended. We would speak to the question of what one who has intended to serve might do in response to a service which is rather, we might say, more darkly rendered. For it is our understanding that all service is mutual in the sense that the legacy of the attempt shall remain with all parties until such time as a clarity of response has been achieved by all.

And so it does come to pass that once one's attempt has been put forth whatever is received in return becomes the new focus of the service effort. And it often is the case that one who has received in return a painful reply may need to do a kind of work that is work upon the self rather than work in immediate or obvious relation to the other. This we would assure you is work that is still of the nature of serving others, for indeed it has two characteristics that are notable in this respect. The first is that a self that has become displaced [decentered] is not a self that can sally forth with its hands offered in service. But, secondly, there is a more subtle point which is to be noted, and that is that one who has truly and earnestly offered themselves in service and received in return a pained reply has this pain now as a gift to be worked through, and it is indeed a gift that one gives not only to the person from whom the person has received this gift but to the entire planet that one takes gratefully the gift which has been given to one and works assiduously and patiently to balance this gift and often surprising and often difficult energy.

At this time we would transfer this contact.

(Carla channeling)

We are Q'uo, and are now with this instrument. Words are necessary within the illusion you now enjoy. Yet words are quite limited in their ability to convey spiritual truth. Hence it is that we stumble about speaking of one entity offering gifts to another as though the universe were created of individual, unlike things, each entity an island universe. The spiritual truth lies in the direction of the obliteration of distinctions betwixt subject and object. Consequently, when the work is done upon the self the work is also done in an universal sense, which redounds to the lightening of planetary consciousness.

It is always a temptation to be of service to others and consider such active and overt instances of service the superior or, indeed, the only type of service. However, there is a much deeper and much simpler avenue of service available to each and that is, as each is undoubtedly aware, the entering into the silence which contains the voice of the infinite Creator. This unheard voice, this unfelt footstep into our hearts is the silent witness of light and love. As each seeker moves into that silence which lies beyond all words it enters holy ground indeed. And each moment in which you are able to practice this silence will be a strengthening and informing moment.

We would transfer this contact at this time. We are Q'uo.

(Jim channeling)

I am Q'uo, and am with this instrument. As you enter into that silence which is beyond words you move into an area in which there are many benefits for your being and your efforts, for there is the rejuvenation of the being which occurs in the center of the heart and the time spent there is cleansed of those minor worries and details that tend to tie your feet and hands with the small knots of details during the day. In this silence you find again the center of self and its connection to the great Self. This practicing of the presence realigns your energy centers and meridians so that the universal love of the one Creator may move in a more harmonious pattern through your centers and become that energy that you expend in your efforts to learn and to serve.

As you experience the centering effect of the presence of the One you also will discover that this peace is that power which then begins to more and more find a place within your daily round of activities, having an effect that is of an harmonious nature; that is, allowing you to blend your vibrations with the intelligent energy and also allows you more the ability to blend your vibrations with that work and those entities that are within your daily reach of experience. We heartily recommend daily practices of meditation in order that you may find a place that sustains you as you serve others. This place is truly holy ground and it is most sacred in that it is the temple within the physical experience. To this temple, then, retire frequently for there is great sustenance within that will aid your being within the experience of teaching, of learning, of serving, and accepting the love and light of the one infinite Creator.

We would transfer at this time.

(S channeling)

I am Q'uo, and I am now with this instrument. The practice of the daily meditation is in relation to worldly activity something of a retreat. It is where one goes for that kind of nourishment which is not of this world, and we cannot stress enough the importance of allowing this world to be imbued with a coloration which reflects all that is holy in the life of the spirit. There is a warm welcome that always awaits within the inner temple, and yet over and over again one finds within this inner temple doorways leading out, and, my brothers and my sisters, it is given to you as those who have volunteered to undergo this experience and this density that is the third that you shall go forth and that you shall bare your breast to this world. There is not a plan which we can recommend that will solve all problems you encounter here. There is not a solution which can be bought, studied, practiced and perfected. There is, however, available to you this one constant resource, and that is your intent to heal, to be healed, and to allow the effect of your healing to radiate outwards. This requires a kind of vulnerability which runs counter to practically everything one learns of the necessity for self-defense within the world.

The world does seem such a dangerous place and it does seem folly to expose one to it with the fullness of intent we are recommending. But it is just this folly which is at the core of the creation itself, for in the creation the Creator has exposed Itself in a way which is inconceivable and utterly unpredictable. Within the chaos of a seething creation the one steady factor is the intent. Your intent is a power which accrues to you as your birthright in the Creator, and it is through your intent that you participate, for better or for worse, in the drama that is the creation.

When your intent, as we can assure you it will, vacillates and loses itself in the many divergents and confusions of daily life, this is not something for which you need to stand judged but it is something of which it behooves you to be reconciled, and—tirelessly, meticulous, assiduously—to draw this intent back into that safe room where it may be looked at and it may be allowed to undergo that process of self-adjustment which it will undergo if it is allowed to do so.

This is what we would recommend for those who would seek communion with that part of their being which is of a higher and more spiritual nature so that this communion may be taken as the source of an inspired offering when one does again turn back towards the world of illusion which always seems to present an unexpected face.

We are those of Q'uo, and would at this time transfer this contact.

(Carla channeling)

We are Q'uo. So there comes to be a familiar rhythm to the centering process, the turning within to touch the awareness of the sacramental nature of the creation, then the turning outwards to a world which awaits that centered gaze. It is in the minds of most seekers to request of oneself the perfect offering of service, the perfect meditation, the perfected realized awareness. Yet we say to you that you are equally effective when you do not know whether you are centered, when you do not know how to serve, for the striving to know is in itself a holy business and the world recognizes love and compassion whether or not that compassion is couched in what you would consider to be your most skillful efforts.

Indeed, the living of a devotional life is the simplest thing in the world, shall we say, for love may be given every which way and it may be received in every which way. The most stumbling attempt is still love. The most error-filled attempt is still full of light. The mistakes are simply mistakes. They do not change the nature of your gift. In your holy works the prophet known to this instrument as Isaiah cried out to his Lord, "How can I go forth for you? I am a person of unclean lips and my people are a people of unclean lips." But the Creator speaks to this entity and to each by saying, "I need a witness."

The appropriate response, then, to this realization of the need for the Creator to have witnesses is that of the one known as Isaiah, "Here am I. Send me, Lord. Send me." May each of you continue to have the courage to offer this precious witness.

At this time we would ask if there remain any queries of a somewhat shorter nature that we might attempt an answer to at this time?

R: Can you comment on my tendency to drift in and out of what you are saying? Is this normal, or is this just me?

We are those of Q'uo. My brother, it is typical of the human condition to vary from moment to moment in the skill to concentrate. The conditions which provide the instruments with the appropriate calm needed to continue to focus upon the channeling process create an atmosphere in which it is easy simply to move into a deeper state of meditation where words simply sound like rain upon the roof, pleasant and lulling. The consciousness itself, that which is truly you, has picked up all that was needed.

However, it may perhaps be restated for your conscious mind in the following few days as things rising from the mind within the waking hours or through dreams within those hours in which your physical body rests. Consequently, when you perceived that you might have missed a point or two it is skillful to pay closer attention to the dreams and bright ideas which seem to come up spontaneously, for by those further channels within yourself you offer the truths to yourself which you may have missed this particular session.

May we answer further, my brother?

R: Thank you. Can I help the instruments in the circle do what they are doing?

We are those of Q'uo. You are correct in assuming that you may be of maximum help in offering energy to the circle. When every hair is pointed to receive the next glorious word which we may endeavor to get through this channel, perhaps you may see from our sarcasm that we feel that the true service is not in being the perfect circle participant, but it continues to reside rather in your being most truly and authentically yourself, with all your dirt, with all the imperfections of attention and composition of attitudes. Demands come upon you within the illusion from all directions to conform, to move hither and yon by appropriate means. The culture has many demands. Love has but one. All you can give is acceptable.

It is well, then, to strive to be your best, but far better, when you feel you have not given your absolute best, to realize the value of that which you have given and to take any thought which may be self-critical and turn it so that the other side of that thought shows, that side wherein you take to yourself the self within which feels imperfect and allow the love of the infinite Creator to flow through you into this spiritual child, for each of you within this illusion is a spiritual infant.

The awakened spirit makes many cries, yet it needs so much given to it, like any infant. Is the infant's job, then, to be wise? We suggest rather that it is your job as the caretaker of your own consciousness always to offer mercy, kindness and unconditional love as you perceive it in all conditions and situations, as best as you can. The imperfection you perceive is literally true, yet it hides the infinite perfection which lies beyond appearance.

May we answer you further, my brother?

R: No, thank you.

We appreciate you as well, my brother, and we thank you.

B: Thank you for being my friend for all these years. How can I help others that I love better?

We are those of Q'uo. We shall attempt to speak to your needs, my sister.

Picture, if you will, the star-studded sky with its unimaginable numbers of points of love and light which shine infinitely forth, and know that the brothers and sisters of sorrow are as these stars. And each entity is as a star. When the desire to serve is felt within and a channel is opened to the infinite Creator by means of praise and thanksgiving to that infinite One then it is that this infinite mystery may flow through you, and as a star shines out into the infinite reaches of the one infinite and unified Creation there is no time or space. There is no size of large or small. Each speck of consciousness contains the Creator. Therefore, the wish to serve followed by the dedication to the mystery which is the one great original Thought, that Creator whose name is Love, know and take comfort in this truth as we understand it: you are effective. As you desire to serve, so do you serve. That soul whom you touch may never know you, may never be on the same continent as you, yet that universal love which you channel forth in that silent witnessing finds its target, for it is called and it goes where it is called. You have only to sit and know the truth that all is love.

That infinite intelligence will take that energy which you breathe forth and will touch the hearts who are in pain. Know this truth and rest in it, just as we hope to serve by our words yet we know that we cannot serve beyond a certain point person-to-person. To be our most deeply effective we move into meditation, into that silence where the Creator is felt.

May we answer you further, my sister?

B: No, thank you very much.

We are those of Q'uo, and we thank each very much for this great privilege. Your vibrations are most beautiful. We encourage each in love and in light, and thusly do we leave you in that mystery which is the one infinite Creator. We are those of a humble service. Adonai. Adonai. We are Q'uo. ✣

L/L Research

L/L Research is a subsidiary of Rock Creek Research & Development Laboratories, Inc.

P.O. Box 5195
Louisville, KY 40255-0195

www.llresearch.org

Rock Creek is a non-profit corporation dedicated to discovering and sharing information which may aid in the spiritual evolution of humankind.

ABOUT THE CONTENTS OF THIS TRANSCRIPT: This telepathic channeling has been taken from transcriptions of the weekly study and meditation meetings of the Rock Creek Research & Development Laboratories and L/L Research. It is offered in the hope that it may be useful to you. As the Confederation entities always make a point of saying, please use your discrimination and judgment in assessing this material. If something rings true to you, fine. If something does not resonate, please leave it behind, for neither we nor those of the Confederation would wish to be a stumbling block for any.

CAVEAT: This transcript is being published by L/L Research in a not yet final form. It has, however, been edited and any obvious errors have been corrected. When it is in a final form, this caveat will be removed.

© 2009 L/L Research

Sunday Meditation
June 19, 1994

Group question: One way of progressing on the service-to-others path is by biasing our balance and then balancing our biases. These biases are brought to our attention by our perception of events and offer catalyst for processing. Eventually one profits by seeing the Creator in all and radiating love and acceptance in that reality. It appears that the construct of the mind is of such a nature that processing painful catalysts are engraved in the subconscious in a much firmer and more definite fashion than those learned by experiencing joy or happiness. Why did a loving Creator allow the constructs that learn more effectively with pain rather than with joy?

(Carla channeling)

I am Q'uo. Greetings in the love and in the light of the one infinite Creator. We are those of Q'uo. We greet you with joy as you rest in meditation this day to speak with you concerning joy and sorrow, gain and loss, illusion and truth. It is, as always, a distinct privilege to share your meditation, to blend our energies with your own, and to join you in the circle of seeking for this working. As always, examine our concepts with the ear for the recognition of personal truth. Lay any thoughts which do not seem appropriate for you to one side. For this we thank you.

The nature of third density is primarily dictated by the lessons which have been prepared for each seeker to walk with. And for the goal towards which these lessons point, that basic nature of your illusion is division into opposites, for yours is the density of choice. Yours is an illusion rich in either/or. The raw material which you bring to this illusion is itself duple. On the one hand, you bring to these lessons a physical, mental, emotional complex of great instinctual beauty, symmetry and harmony. The physical vehicle of third density is unimaginably rich in sense perceptions. At all times the inner eye is filled with an enormous variety of sense perceptions. These are instinctually prioritized and held in an instinctual state of balance. This is that second-density creature which has accepted the role of carrying your consciousness about for this incarnative experience.

In return for all of the unimaginable wealth of sensations and perceptions the physical body asks in return that it be tended, and this tending is established as a large and pivotal activity throughout third-density experience. The right use of this instinctual vehicle constantly remains an issue to the seeker.

To this density has been brought also the infinite, eternal, creative consciousness which is within the Creator and which, as you hear these words, is experiencing that which the instinctual body offers and then perhaps having the awareness to reprioritize the wealth of sense perceptions made available by the instinctual body. Thusly, your very physical situation holds a dichotomy which may be seen to be peculiarly vulnerable to choices. The beginning of third density rests in the either/or of spiritual or physical, eternal or time-bound. At this level one does not view good or evil, positive or negative. Rather, one is viewing the temporary as opposed to the eternal.

The Creator—that creative principle of Love in which all reside—rests within the infinite intelligence of unpotentiated love. However, each individualized spark of this love experiences time, space, and within your density, choices, whereas the truth rests always in peace. The seeker of truth, time and space-bound within the physical incarnation, must place one foot ahead of the other, moment by moment, day by day, revolving about that truth which lies imminent within each moment, constantly having the opportunity to gaze into the present moment in such a way that sense perceptions are reprioritized in order to maximize the effectiveness [of] the choices available in that moment.

Always, there is the choice between that which lies upon the surface and that which lies beneath, beyond and through the surface unto the deepest profundity of awareness. We have often said that the journey of the seeker is one from the head to the heart. When the perceptions of the moment are evaluated by one drifting upon the surface of the moment there is fairly constantly the making of choices which maximize comfort. We do not imply that there is something wrong with comfort. We simply point out that comfort or happiness is neither joy or sorrow, but simply comfort. That which most entities call joy is actually no more than a surface degree of comfort and ease within which one may rest and enjoy the illusion. With this we find absolutely nothing amiss. It is only that the state of mind which is comfortable runs directly counter to that state of mind in which the seeker may make choices.

It is not that sorrow, loss and limitation are the only [effective] means of learning the lessons of love and polarizing towards the infinite Creator's vibration, but, rather, that few indeed are the entities which are willing, in the absence of pain, to do the intensive work which is needed to attain an acceleration of the polarization process using joy as catalyst.

Here is how to be joyful. Upon the arising, turn to the infinite One and instant by instant turn again to the infinite One, again and again, in all things giving thanks, in all conditions rejoicing. Turn again to the infinite One and rest in that peace which truly the world does not know. Joy is a living energy as powerful and as effective a teacher as sorrow. However, it demands of the seeker a self-imposed discipline of the personality which looks beyond ease and comfort and energizes and exhorts the self again and again unceasingly to rejoice, give praise and offer thanksgiving to the infinite One.

One of your teachers known as Joel Goldsmith has called this joyful path "practicing the presence of the one infinite Creator." The path of joy is equally as effective as the path of sorrow. Yet, if the seeker is truly upon the path of joy there is the same degree of creative unrest in this process that there is while undergoing the catalyst of losses, limitations and grief. This is the road not taken, the path of joy. If you would be good at this path, learn to be dissatisfied with happiness and count all things as loss except turning again to praise and give thanks to the one infinite Creator. If the intensity of desire can be maintained while there is an absence of negative catalyst, then the negative catalyst is not necessary. You may see that, indeed, few there are who are able to walk this particular path to the infinite One.

The path of sorrow, then, is that path which nearly all experience nearly all the time within incarnation. Misery, anger, grief—all the uncomfortable emotional and mental states—create a necessity for seeking some means of relief. The limitations are there because the nature of the choice is such that the surface illusion can be seen by the seeker to be an illusion. And it is through the growing discomfort of catalyst, of loss and limitation, that the wayward spirit is finally alert to the need for discipline.

That which needs to be grasped may perhaps be seen to be held in the concept of sacrifice. The seeker is born into a world which offers great riches. These riches are apparent: health, possessions, power. All that which is seen, however, is the illusion. If the world thinks well of something, it is almost sure to be that which is illusory. So, how then to get the attention? How to make the self work, spiritually speaking? The infant comes into the world in a state of unrestrained joy. This is the path upon which entities begin. Often before the entity has opened the eyes to the physical world that joy has been compromised. Certainly within the first year or two of incarnation that native joy will be compromised, and the entity plunges into the myriad catalysts of this rich illusion which you now enjoy. As one watches the growing child one can see this joy more and more compromised by circumstance.

Where are the teachers of the path of joy? Why is this path [not] more used? There is a simple answer; that being that the path of joy is the path of the adept and to the adept all things are loss, except the infinite Creator and serving that love which is the Creator. All things whatever may be counted as loss except that service. It is for this that each has come into this incarnation, to learn this path. This shining goal waits for each and becomes the path of fourth density. But third density still is being processed by each. This joy is still to be experienced fully except in many moments for each seeker where there is the click of sliding into that presence which is electric, which is the Creator within.

So, we welcome you to this path of sorrow, loss and limitation. We encourage each to practice the path of joy, to practice the presence of the one infinite Creator. But we say to you that most of you shall, again and again, fall away from joy into comfort, happiness and eventual sorrow. And we say that it is well that these sorrows then occur, for this is that which teaches at this particular stage of awareness. The primary choice, we say again, is toward the absolute, the infinite and eternal as opposed to all things temporary and illusory.

We encourage each seeker to practice this joy as much as possible within the framework of an authentically lived life which grapples with the sorrows of an incarnation. Encourage and exhort each other to practice the presence in all ways which are meet and appropriate, one to another. Encourage the self, whenever the mind may turn to awareness of self, to turn again and again to that center within in which all things reside, abide and have their being. Give thanks always and for every blessing, including the most unimaginable loss and pain. Rejoice in hardship and suffering. And let your heart be glad in life, in death. Then you shall not be troubled with sorrow. But, dear ones, if you cannot achieve this state of vibration, know that this is no more than what was expected for third density. You now walk in a shadow land where nothing is what it seems. Within each atom of this shadow land resides an infinite, absolute reality. The journey takes no time, no space. The answers lie within. Do not begrudge your sorrows their place, for the path of joy does await.

At this time, we would transfer this contact to the one known as Jim. We thank this instrument as we leave it. We are those of Q'uo.

(Jim channeling)

I am Q'uo, and greet each again in love and in light through this instrument. At this time we would ask if we may speak to any further queries which those present may find value in the asking. Is there another query at this time?

R: Could you restate the comment that "all things are loss which are part of the illusion"? Could you say that again?

I am Q'uo, and am aware of your query, my brother. When we say that all things are loss we mean that there will come a time when all things that are made shall not be made, for the creation of things evolves and changes until there is another vibratory pattern that replaces the old. In each incarnation there is the experience gained that is reserved or kept according to its quality and kind rather than the details of the makeup of the experience being kept. Thus, distillations of your incarnational experiences become that soul essence that is you as you progress through the octaves of light. That essence remains and is eternal, whereas the forms that were utilized to provide experience that is later distilled to essence, these all fade away.

Is there a further query, my brother?

R: No, thank you.

We thank you, my brother, and we would also thank the one known as N for providing the focus for our working this day. We are with this entity in meditation, upon request, as we are with all entities who request our presence in the meditative state. We are happy to blend our vibrations there and to aid in the deepening of your meditation.

At this time we would take our leave of this instrument and this group, leaving each, as always, in the love and in the light of the infinite Creator. We are those of Q'uo. Adonai, my friends. Adonai. ✤

L/L Research

L/L Research is a subsidiary of Rock Creek Research & Development Laboratories, Inc.

P.O. Box 5195
Louisville, KY 40255-0195

www.llresearch.org

Rock Creek is a non-profit corporation dedicated to discovering and sharing information which may aid in the spiritual evolution of humankind.

ABOUT THE CONTENTS OF THIS TRANSCRIPT: This telepathic channeling has been taken from transcriptions of the weekly study and meditation meetings of the Rock Creek Research & Development Laboratories and L/L Research. It is offered in the hope that it may be useful to you. As the Confederation entities always make a point of saying, please use your discrimination and judgment in assessing this material. If something rings true to you, fine. If something does not resonate, please leave it behind, for neither we nor those of the Confederation would wish to be a stumbling block for any.

CAVEAT: This transcript is being published by L/L Research in a not yet final form. It has, however, been edited and any obvious errors have been corrected. When it is in a final form, this caveat will be removed.

© 2009 L/L Research

Sunday Meditation
June 26, 1994

Group question: The question this afternoon is from N, and after listening to a lot of our tapes, he says that it looks to him like there are three selves in incarnation: the higher self, the incarnational self and the illusional self, which he describes as basically the genetic material biased by the culture, and he would like to have a discourse on these three selves, and their relationship to each other, and I think we might want to correct the incarnational self and the illusional self as being sort of aspects of the same self, and we might want to add the soul that exists before the incarnation. If Q'uo would like to add any other selves, or subtract, we would be happy to listen, and … that's it!

(Carla channeling)

Greetings. We are those of the Confederation of Planets in the Service of the Infinite Creator. We are known to you as those of Q'uo. Greetings in the love and in the light of the one infinite Creator. May we thank each for calling us to your circle of seeking this working. We are humbly pleased to have the opportunity of sharing concepts with you concerning your question.

As always, we request that each who hears or reads may identify for the self those things which we have to offer to that self, for each entity has its own set of personal truths which speak to that place where that one spirit is at this particular moment. Therefore, take that which is of use at this moment and leave the rest behind.

When you ask us to speak concerning the various selves of a third-density human you ask us to take on a story of movement in well conceived and fastidiously executed patterns which describe what could be seen as an elliptical or circular process, in which tremendous amounts of time and space fall away from the present moment for incredible stretches of time and space. The relatively short period of the third-density cycle is preceded by tremendously long, unimaginably lengthy terms of space and time. And, similarly, after this third density experience, the continuing refining of choices made in this density are the agenda for millions of years of learning and service.

The first self, of course, is the great Self which is the one original Thought, love itself, that infinite and creative principle from whose riches all who are self-aware have drawn not only the outer trappings of Creatorhood, but indeed the inmost essence of the infinite Creator. This great Self has no way to communicate Its essence. Consequently, in the fullness of free will, there comes that time of creativity wherein an octave of creation is begun with the sending forth of that which is one, that it might take upon itself the partnership with manifestation which is the very fabric of space and time.

Out of space and time, then, is created by light all that may be called so, and all that may be used by the self to move forward in that lengthy journey away from that great source of all that there is into more and more thickness of illusion, until that great Earth plane which you now experience is reached and the stuff of earth, air, wind and fire becomes self-aware and self-determining.

Thusly, the first self is your true self, and that is the great Self. However, since the experience of self as the great Self is not available to most within third density, the examination of it is in this context unnecessary. Certainly, when that which you now perceive as self is born, when that impregnating of consciousness with self-awareness occurs, and the seeker as a new, self-aware consciousness—we correct this instrument—point or spark of consciousness enters the first of many incarnations within third density, that new self represents all of the instinctual selfhood of the creature which is the physical vehicle for humankind, and as the process of living, feeling, and sensing and experiencing begins, various distortions come to be within that selfhood in a repetitive manner, so that at the beginning of each birth, there is a self-entering birth which has already been biased and distorted in a lasting way by previous choices made during previous incarnations.

Each incarnation, then, is not only an opportunity to learn lessons of love, it is further an opportunity to emphasize those biases found within the self which are considered by the self to be positive or helpful. The self also has the opportunity to look again at each and every distortion which is preincarnative, which seems to have sprung from birth, rather than from incarnational experience, and to decide differently, thus loosening the framework of thinking and ideation, and reshaping it in small or large degree.

Thusly, there is the opportunity, as a conscious being within incarnation, to use the consciousness that has been attained to look at the self, to look at the harvest of self anew and to have such an openness of mind that it will be possible for the self to work effectively upon the self.

Now, the eternal or spiritual self, to use a general term, is only to a very small extent differing from that self which the query called the illusional self. The difference, however, seems quite large to the self-aware being, for it seems that there is an enormous chasm between the infinite self and the self within incarnation. However, there is the continuing difficulty of the subject observing itself. Selfhood tends to keep the self from seeing clearly into its own nature. Thusly, each entity may be of service to others by reflecting honestly and clearly for others that which is being received. Others have the gift to give you of this reflection.

Thus, we always encourage the listening ear and the understanding heart when entities are attempting to communicate, especially concerning relationships. For it is the gift of each to each that in communication a more objective or unbiased viewpoint might be had by all. Each has gifts of this kind to give, and each has much to receive, even from those who seem to be negatively impressed and critical. Open the ears always when this occurs, for perhaps truth may lie there, and perhaps freedom might come from a new perception of this truth.

For with each other's help the incarnational self attempts more and more to conform its vibrational pattern to that one original pattern of great Selfhood. This is the object, to match the vibrational characteristics of the one infinite Creator. All of self-perceived selfhood is an illusion. All of creation is an illusion. There is nothing here. There is nothing there. There is only everything, and it takes up no time, nor space.

So, the distinction betwixt the self between incarnations and the self during incarnations is in fact a subcategory. An even smaller difference exists betwixt these two. But in terms of the work of incarnation, the difference is, of course, most telling. The times of meditation which we encourage are those opportunities wherein the self within incarnation is able to link up with those selves before, those lives before, and that self which more and more has become articulated through the continuing process of reincarnation. That self's great desire is to move back into unpotentiated great Selfhood.

So, as incarnational beings, as incarnational selves, we relate to the self between incarnations as one who knows no secrets would relate to the twin, shall we say, or the fellow who knows all the secrets. So much within an incarnation, especially toward the end of a cycle, is already determined by the great weight of previous choice, that [the] memories of all that has gone before almost have more confusion to offer than riches to consider. However, we encourage the use of both meditative periods and sleeping and dreaming to more and more easily link into the self that exists between incarnations. While it is not the great Self, being a biased entity, it does nevertheless have much of wisdom which it aids entities to link up with within incarnation.

It is not so much the knowledge of what has happened in past lives that helps as it is the seating and grounding of the self from the part which blooms in incarnation down to the roots of that being which lie within that portion of your consciousness which carries all memory of previous lifetimes and other deep awarenesses such as the archetypical.

So we would encourage a model in which the incarnational human may be seen to be the bloom that arises and shall return to the elements which are used to create the personhood and walk it about on two legs. This blooming of self is related to its roots which feed and nourish it. That root is the abiding self, not yet the great Self, but that unfinished but heavily biased self which has learned, and relearned, and relearned many lessons already. There are things within this bloom which the roots wished to extirpate from the entire plant. There are ways of blooming which the roots hoped would become clear to this particular bloom, and that root of being roots down through all the illusion of all the incarnative selves and all the incarnations and becomes all that there is.

At this time we would transfer this contact to the one known as Jim. We thank this instrument as we leave it. We are those of Q'uo.

(Jim channeling)

I am Q'uo, and greet each again in love and in light. It is our privilege to greet each through this instrument and to ask if at this time there may be any further queries to which we may speak this working period.

Carla: Do you have any suggestions as to how someone who would like to work on the bloom, who would like to make some changes in the way the self expresses, could go about using the relationship between the self and the higher self, or the between incarnations self—beyond meditation?

I am Q'uo, and am aware of your query, my sister. We feel that the entity which is able to accept that which is the self in all of its detailed analysis and enumeration is one which has, shall we say, the leg up on the incarnation, for the energy of the incarnation is that which expresses itself as the seeker. The seeker who wishes to change some portion of itself is one which wishes to approximate the ideal, in most cases, more closely. We would suggest that rather than feeling that there is the possibility of changing the stripes, shall we say, that greater freedom comes to those who are able to accept the self with equanimity and to work as a full-blooded self, shall we say—that entity which realizes more of that which it is as a result of accepting that which it is. This provides a truer range of expression, for it builds upon that which is solid.

If one attempts to manufacture a change which has no foundation, the change will not weather the storms of everyday experience that beat about one in a certain sense and cause a reverberation, shall we say, in those expressions of the self which are temporary and which are of the fleeting moment, as it were.

Is there another query, my sister?

Carla: I have one more. When one is trying to counsel or teach and to give an accurate and objective reflection of what something that someone else is doing [that] seems to have the patterns, is there any resource the teacher can call on to make sure that teacher is not … to make sure that that teacher is being an accurate mirror?

I am Q'uo, and am aware of your query, my sister. The same discrimination that we suggest exercising is that which will determine the feeling tone of another's teaching. That which reminds one of that which one knows deep within the heart of being is the discrimination which is necessary for the choice making.

Is there another query, my sister?

Carla: No, Q'uo, thank you very much.

I am Q'uo, and we thank you very much as well, my sister. Is there another query at this time?

Questioner: I do not have a query, Q'uo, but I do want to take this opportunity and thank through you to all the brothers and sisters of the Confederation, because I seem to draw inspiration

[from] the various subjects channeled through this group and it helps me to stay on course.

I am Q'uo, and we appreciate your gratitude and the opportunity to be of service to you. We would thank you for allowing us to speak to your queries and concerns and would like to add that we feel you are doing well and we are inspired by your efforts as well.

We are those of Q'uo and at this time we shall take our leave of this instrument and this group, leaving each, as always, in the love and in the light of the one infinite Creator. Adonai, my friends. Adonai. ✣

Special Meditation
July 14, 1994

Group question: The question this morning has to do with the difference between the Tree of Life, mentioned in Genesis of the Bible, and the Tree of Knowledge, that is also mentioned in Genesis. We would like to know what part these play in our spiritual evolution and any information Q'uo could give us about them.

(Carla channeling)

We are those of Q'uo. Greetings in the love and in the light of the one infinite Creator. We are most privileged to be called to your group for this working and wish especially to greet the one known as S. All of those within the principle of Q'uo send many greetings.

As always, we ask that our thoughts be treated not as those of authority, but rather those of a fellow seeker.

When one is investigating the resonances of racial symbology or ethnic symbology, one must be prepared to treat the symbol or symbols involved upon more than one level. Both the Tree of Life mosaic, or figure, and the Tree of Knowledge figure are masterpieces of condensed, yet articulated, concept. The dynamic betwixt these two is an integral part of their nature. These symbols open far better to the heart of the mystic than to the tongue or pen of the intellectual or scholar. However, insofar as words can attempt to explicate these symbols, we are glad to comment.

The Tree of Life is a cabalistic configuration which, in general, describes a universe or cosmology wherein only the tiniest or end part of reality, as such, is in any way visible while the seeker is within the valley of birth and death, that is, in the body of flesh. The great preponderance of this reality is firmly rooted within the concept of heaven or ultimate reality. Within this figure, this tree may be seen to be then upside down as far as mortal eyes might behold, that tip of the tree being the entire physical universe as seen by mortal eyes. The unity of this symbol is preserved through the creation of a harmonious array of dynamics which can loosely be called male and female or positive and negative. Within this system, then, all is harmonized into a unity, so that even that tiny tip of reality which is the physical universe has, as in a holograph, a complete idea of reality. Each tiny spark of this limitless reality, then, contains the pattern of the whole and unity is preserved throughout the figure's dynamic system of archetypes.

Over against this figure is brought to bear another complex conceptual figure which is thoroughly divided, clearly delineated, just as the figure either/or is clearly delineated. Within this figure is the concept of eternal brokenness. This figure sees differences and claims this difference. It sees the *either* and the *or* as having no resolution in harmony. Thus, this Tree of Knowledge is a figure betokening that activity within the time/space portion of the incarnate seeker which demands to know which of two things is preferable. This is the figure encouraging entities to make choices between opposites.

Within this system it is expected and desired that the seeker play judge and decide, or deem, what is appropriate and what is not—hot over cold, or cold over hot, light against darkness, attraction against radiance, and so forth. The "evil" then, which is seen within this figure by one defending the Tree of Life, is the implicit suggestion within this figure that seekers can relate to dynamic opposites only by choice. This truth is, shall we say, one which effects only the third-density experience, that experience which is of life lived beyond that veil of forgetting.

In this human state of forgetting, then, the figure of the Tree of Knowledge holds sway and entities must indeed play God, choosing right from wrong, choosing positive from negative, making those choices which define and increase polarity towards the goal of graduation from this universe steeped in illusion, in which there is an operant—either/or.

If the entity were, then, to move beyond the illusion of incarnate third-density life still thinking that it must choose, then, indeed, the Tree of Life would be shaken, for this overriding symbol holds the true nature of reality, if we may misuse this term. Perhaps we may say that the lesson here is that as the Tree of Knowledge figure suggests, seekers do indeed have a quest for truth, that truth which does choose, yet within these choices, there needs to be within the entity's heart that portion which praises, gives thanks and blesses that mystery which lies behind and beyond all that seems and configures all that there truly is.

When a seeker goes too far with the knowledge of good and evil and begins to attack and fragment the basic unity of all things, then that entity must needs, either by personal choice or by catalytic action, be made humble once again and aware of the overarching unity of all that is.

The difficulty humankind has in accepting the limits of its knowledge is amazing to us. There is much pride within the hearts of your peoples who feel that all things may be known. This pride is fatal, for within the life of the spirit all that seems so in the world is indeed far otherwise.

The many, many spiritual writings of your peoples continually suggest that strength lies in weakness, wisdom lies in lack of knowledge, and so forth. The Tree of Knowledge is that tree, that figure, that attitude, towards the living of a life which gets the seeker started upon the road towards the acceleration of spiritual evolution. However, when that seeker has indeed begun to walk upon that dusty path, and when it has gained experience along this path, then it is that the seeker does well to remove that figure from the mind and replace it with the Tree of Life. The choices possible to make within an incarnation having to do with polarity are rather quickly done, in that it becomes easier and easier to adjudge the polarity of various responses to certain catalyst.

Beyond these choices, however, lies the true ground wherein work in consciousness is done and into that ground it is unacceptable to bring this consciousness that is divided. Once upon the service-to-others path, then, it augers well for the seeker if he chooses to observe creation as the Tree of Life suggests, the "as above, so below" of ultimate reality being implicit in this cosmology that is seen, as well as that which is unseen.

We would pause at this point to inquire if there are queries from the material which has been given. We are those of Q'uo.

S: Is it correct to assume that the Tree of Knowledge is—that we interpret [it as]—the intellect, the symbol for the intellect to get the seeker started in this density, and that the Tree of Life is the subconscious? That is, one follows the path on the Tree of Knowledge and then chooses the deeper symbols of that intellectual choice, so the seeker moves from the intellect through the subconscious in the deeper regions of the heart—and the Tree of Life is reality and the Tree of Knowledge is the illusion.

We are those of Q'uo. My sister, this is quite correct. The Tree of Knowledge is, shall we say, the necessary evil and it is the place of those beginning the path of spiritual seeking to focus upon differences and make those great ethical or moral choices for the soul's health and for further learning. Just as you said, when the seeker is established upon that path, then it is that the time comes when the seeker acknowledges its lack of understanding and accepts, instead of demanding clarity, that vision given to the heart alone, in which the whole of the infinite creation is felt to be imminent, though noumenal, in every instant of perceived consciousness.

May we answer further, my sister?

S: How does one balance becoming split—or is it simply that one of the initiative stages between living or seeking as completely as possible the Tree of Life—while it is still necessary to function in the world which we acknowledge. That is where I find, and perhaps then it's just something that all seekers have to go through, as an initiative of living two distinct lives, not only physically but spiritually.

We are those of Q'uo and, my sister, indeed this is a working which continues throughout third density and into fourth and even the fifth density. The dynamic betwixt that which is manifest and that which is ultimately real is acute and continuing. Perhaps the concept of one who lives on two levels at once may be helpful. In many things there is an inner and an outer reality or way of being. The outer practices of most of the world's religious systems are often divided into those prayers and services shared with all of the people and those prayers and services offered only by, shall we say, clergy or those of the religious life. It is the burden and the glory of those who do live a religious, spiritual or devotional life to live on two levels at once, for the level of the outer world is, indeed, the either/or of service to self or service to others and the dynamics of that life are unforgiving. Yet still, within these outer appearances lies an inner reality which only the heart of humankind can know or experience.

The joy within this illusion you experience flows most freely when it is consciously accepted and visualized within each daily period that these levels are not contradicting each other but rather are the inner and the outer layers of that which is being experienced. When—we correct this instrument—whenever it is perceived that the seeker has focused overmuch upon the Tree of Knowledge then the seeker does well to pause momentarily in order to remember that inner reality, that inner universe and open a shuttle from that inner universe through the seeker's own part so that while the seeker is dealing in a practical and intellectually appropriate way with either/or dynamics, yet still that seeker's heart is open because of that vivid memory and remembrance, which is renewed each moment, of the overriding and overarching reality within, which illumines, transfigures and reconfigures the whole.

This is most difficult work and we commend each for striving to reconcile the depths of the illusion and its dynamics with the undergirding reality, so-called.

Is there a final query at this time?

S: Just one. You know of the symbol of the Tree of Life that I have at home, the Indian rug. Is it—or can I transfer the archetypes of either the tarot cards or the kabbalah to this Tree or will I need to adjust them more subjectively?

We are those of Q'uo. The figures are such that you may use them as they are. You also might find that you begin to wish that you could create your own system of relationships and interconnectiveness and leave that Indian, or any other version, to another. It is of aid to the seeker to work with these archetypes regardless of the designed interrelationships. Therefore, we encourage students of the archetypes to have the feeling of freedom to reconfigure according to the personal experience and truths of each seeker.

We, again, thank each for calling us to your session this morning. It is, as always, a most blessed chance for us to be with you and to mingle our vibrations with your own. We leave each with the utmost of love and light in the one infinite Creator. We are those of Q'uo. Adonai. Adonai vasu. We are Q'uo. ♣

L/L Research

L/L Research is a subsidiary of Rock Creek Research & Development Laboratories, Inc.

P.O. Box 5195
Louisville, KY 40255-0195

www.llresearch.org

Rock Creek is a non-profit corporation dedicated to discovering and sharing information which may aid in the spiritual evolution of humankind.

ABOUT THE CONTENTS OF THIS TRANSCRIPT: This telepathic channeling has been taken from transcriptions of the weekly study and meditation meetings of the Rock Creek Research & Development Laboratories and L/L Research. It is offered in the hope that it may be useful to you. As the Confederation entities always make a point of saying, please use your discrimination and judgment in assessing this material. If something rings true to you, fine. If something does not resonate, please leave it behind, for neither we nor those of the Confederation would wish to be a stumbling block for any.

CAVEAT: This transcript is being published by L/L Research in a not yet final form. It has, however, been edited and any obvious errors have been corrected. When it is in a final form, this caveat will be removed.

© 2009 L/L Research

Sunday Meditation
September 11, 1994

Group question: In our world today it seems like most people are overstimulated with information and distractions and busyness. How can the seeker who wishes to remember the Creator do so in this kind of world today? How can we remember our harmony, our unity, and our place in the world and in the Creator?

(Carla channeling)

Greetings in the love and the light of the one infinite Creator. We are those of Q'uo. It is a privilege indeed to share in this meditation with you and to be called to your group to discuss the subject of having time enough for the infinite Creator. We thank and bless each of you for having the desire to seek the truth and we bless each in the spiritual journey which we share with you as those brothers and sisters who have perhaps walked a bit longer on this path, but who are still pilgrims. We are not authorities, and we ask each seeker to test our words or any words against that discriminative faculty which is every seeker's and encourage each seeker to leave behind those thoughts of ours which do not seem useful and take those thoughts that seem to have a resonance within. We thank each seeker for exercising this discrimination. Each seeker's truth lies within, awaiting the rediscovery, the remembering. When your truth does come to you, this is how it feels, as if you had remembered that which had slipped your mind.

The speed at which things become old has a profound impact upon the intelligence of those who are witnesses of this phenomenon. In your far distant past things became dated and obsolete at a snail's pace, for it took great reaches of time mechanically to explore, to come across new and strange ways. As the technology of humankind's creation was first added to the experience of living, the globe began to shrink. Geographical distances were suddenly able to be traveled, not at the pace of the wind-driven sail, or the sturdy horse and wagon, but with motorized travel over water and land. Things began to change at a quicker pace.

Now, as each of you experiences incarnation that which is new becomes old quickly. In the atmosphere of constant change there is not the rest and relaxation available from the surroundings. The environment has become geared to the handling of constant-seeming progress, and within your culture this situation is seen to be as most beneficial. The age of information has arrived amongst your people. The seeker now routinely is aware of an enormous array of situations around the globe, aware of fires and earthquakes in far-flung places, aware of wars and rumors of war from near and far, aware of the suffering and starvation of displaced nations of peoples—aware, aware and aware.

Now that we have flattened this instrument with the horror of the present day we shall attempt to give some pointers as to how, in this very trivia-ridden existence, it is not only possible but inevitable that the infinite Creator shall be discovered at the very heart of this tight-wound world. Each who hears these words has a universe of its own. In each seeker's universe the center lies deeply within, opening like a flower to a melange of sense perceptions, infinitely rich and varied, infinitely full, infinitely profound.

Within this web of sense perceptions, within this inner universe, seemingly the self is at the center and events impinge upon that self from without. The telephone rings. The mail lands upon the desk. The door opens to bring more concerns, more things into the environment. Each seeker alone is not trapped but certainly encouraged to remain within that perceptive web, seeking the infinite One as best it can.

However, the Creator's plan for your particular illusion contains one essential adjustment to this personal world view. That adjustment is in the perceptual shape of the realization from the inside rather than from the outside that others, other selves besides the self, are those who are able to express lucidly and clearly the presence of the infinite Creator. At first the seeker is involved in the perceptions having to do with seeing the self without regard to others. As this attempt deepens, the seeker begins to collect the memories of those entities which said just the most helpful, the most correct thing in order to open the door within the heart which invites the Creator in. And we find that we become for others that same witness to the light. Perhaps we, ourselves, might not feel like the mirror of the infinite Creator, yet another may find within what we say that encouragement and support that turns the seeker's heart to remembrance.

The role of the seeker is often seen as an isolated, lonely role, and in many ways it is. The quest for truth places each seeker in that wilderness of spirit in which the testing and tempering of the spirit may most fruitfully take place. In this instrument's mind is the old refrain, "You have to walk that lonesome valley by yourself. No one else will walk it for you. You must walk it by yourself." This remains true. However, as the seeking moves forward, as we said, others seem to appear at just the right moment to offer to you that realization for which you hunger. So each becomes to each a teacher, a supporter, a strengthener.

Realizing that each person you see bears this precious gift of presence, the seeker may then begin to practice regarding those who come before the eyes as that instrument of the infinite Creator that they truly are, showing to you the deepest truths of creation implicit in the connection between self and other self. Imagine each of you upon the globe, each within the infinite reaches of its own universe, yet each able to reach across that chasm created by space and time and illusion and touch heart to heart and hope to hope, each seeker strengthening the other.

We have a simple message and we repeat it endlessly. The goal of the seeker is, shall we say, a vibration or a state of being which is the vibration of the Creator Itself, the one great original Thought or Logos which is Love. Each seeker attempts to form that vibration of self more and more like that vibration which is infinite love. Each movement towards that primal vibration of being is a step out of the sea of confusion which the everyday illusion offers. And as each seeker attempts to correct the many, many distortions of its own vibratory patterns, the greatest gifts that the Creator has to give are those paintings on the path which intend service to the infinite Creator and to all of those upon the planet within which you dwell.

So a great resource, then, for the seeker intending to become less fettered in time is the readiness to listen to and to admit the words, the expressions and the actions of others. For you were not incarnated for yourself alone. That which has been prepared for you involves other entities inevitably. The lessons of third density revolve about other selves. This is the time of choice for each emerging, unique consciousness, and each lesson which enables the seeker to make those choices more deftly and accurately involve relationship with others.

Perhaps the simplest way to attempt to remember that entities are first spiritual is to practice gazing at another person and seeing for a split second the reality of that entity, for that entity is the one infinite Creator with a few rough edges that a millennium or three might work a little more magic upon. Each of you is as a hologram of the infinite One. This is the deepest realization. Yet at the point at which that realization is accepted, at that point the seeker no longer carves out great boundaries between the self and other selves. The seeker fully open to the possibilities of third density knows the great value of other entities.

The second way in which the mind may be, shall we say, encouraged to find that awareness of the Creator is the meditation, the contemplation, the prayer. We are aware that each does attempt to spend time with the infinite Creator within the daily round. We commend each for this effort and encourage its continuance. It is as though there were a hunger within which nothing within the illusion can satisfy. Those who are not on a spiritual path, those who are happy with life as it is, gaze at the seeker in amazement wondering why, in the midst of a happy life, this seeker must spend so much time and energy upon that which does not even make the entity more happy. For certainly the spiritual quest does do many things, but it certainly shall not make you happy.

To explain to this non-seeking person the reason for discontent is difficult, yet to one to whom this spiritual hunger has been awakened lies the responsibility of foraging for something to eat spiritually, some wisdom or intelligence that informs. Where to find such information? My children, it will not surprise you to hear us say that it is not in the noise of your culture but, rather, in the silence of your meditations. That listening within which meditation encourages is the activity which allows food and drink to come to that spiritual self within. The more times during your daily routine that you can find a way to work in just a moment or two of meditation, this is a helpful thing.

This instrument, for instance, has worked in a school where the bell marks the changing of the period, and when that bell sounded the instrument's effort was, for one split instant, remembered. Each of you has within the day certain repeated experiences, the ringing of the bell, the ringing of the telephone, the marking of the hour by a chiming clock. Whatever it is that you find within the environment to use as a key or trigger, we suggest that the seeker target this and train the self to use these found moments to turn once again to the infinite perfection of the mystery that is love.

The third thing that shall teach each more and more to dwell in the presence of the infinite One is time itself, for as the experience of the incarnation mounts there comes that point wherein the seeker has experienced enough time to have become somewhat desensitized to that mechanism within which rings the tocsin[12] of alarm. As the incarnation becomes full, it is not that maturity overtakes the seeker but rather that the entity becomes able to care less about those things which it cannot affect. To one who is relatively unmoved by his own imperfections, to one who has begun to accept the imperfect self, is given a state of inner peace which is a healing gift. Beyond all other lessons, finally the seeker in third density grasps and accepts its own lack of perceived perfection, seeing the myriads of issues the world offers for consideration. The entity which has accepted and forgiven the self for being human has a greatly enhanced opportunity to remember the infinite One and practice Its presence.

Those who come to third density plunge from innocence into confusion. Within the brightly colored illusion which time and space have given, the seeker moves to find that infinite love which is at its heart, moving always within utter chaos and confusion. The seeker must choose its own way. We urge each to hold out the hand more and more to life as it is on the surface, to embrace the multiplicity of the tales, the boisterous comings and goings which seem to distract and fritter away the time. For it is not that the time has sped up, rather it is that the nature that beholds that time at this moment in the ending of an old age and the beginning of a new one is more transparent to catalyst and stimuli. Each begins to see the vainness and emptiness of surface life, and each becomes more and more willing to let go of the demands to be such and such a way.

(Side one of tape ends.)

(Carla channeling)

… that things are so changed, but rather in wonder that we have done as well as we have.

Each of you is so courageous, my children. Gazing at illusion, stubbornly you know that there is an infinite love. Oh, you who are of this stubborn faith, we bless and embrace each. As you attempt more and more to practice the presence of the infinite One use these tools as they help you. Use each other and grasp that that is appropriate. Joyfully seize those moments that you can turn for even an instant to contemplation. Rejoice in and encourage each other, for each shall show the Creator. The only question is what aspect of that Creator shall you choose to give as gift to the infinite spirits all about

---

[12] tocsin: a bell used to sound an alarm.

you? And when the time comes when the emotions and nerves are tired and worn by suffering, rest back in the strength of heart that lies within one who has suffered and affirm the perfection that shall never be sensed by the self for the self, but which is the higher truth for each.

As always, we again encourage each to lay aside any thought of ours that is not useful. We are most happy that we have had this opportunity to be with you. How we have looked forward to this event. We would like to transfer the contact to the one known as Jim at this time. We leave this instrument in love and in light. We are those of Q'uo.

(Jim channeling)

I am Q'uo, and I greet each again in love and in light through this instrument. At this time it is our privilege to ask if there might be any further queries to which we might respond. Is there another query at this time?

Carla: I have put aside channeling for the last two months because I felt I needed a break. It's good to be back. Could you evaluate taking a break? Is there a better or best way to remain fluent in the channeling work while the actual channeling practice is being given a rest?

I am Q'uo, and am aware of your query, my sister. We are unaware of any technique by which an instrument might maintain the fluency while resting from the practice. However, we are very well aware of entities' needs for the variety of experience that taking a break from one's work will provide. We are aware of how intense the experience which entities such as yourselves encounter each day, and we do recommend that you do take those times of rest and peace which allow you to become reinvigorated, as the newness of your experience becomes, shall we say, seated in your pattern and is then able to alter the flow of energy in a fashion which becomes refreshing rather than becoming more of a weight to bear.

Is there a further query, my sister?

Carla: No, thank you. I always yearn for a closer connection to a spiritual life and it seems that we always fall short of what we desire in that regard. And you are saying that we always have that connection and we just need to open to it. Could you comment on that?

I am Q'uo. It is that feeling of falling short that is both the blessing and the curse of the seeker, my sister. For the desire to move even closer and move in more purity in the work that you do is that which allows the progress in the work, yet can also become the source of the over-critical self. Thus, we salute the desire to increase one's purity and purpose of work. Yet we suggest the gentle hand as the estimation and criticism is given to one's work by oneself.

Is there another query, my sister?

Carla: No, thank you.

We thank you, my sister. Is there another query at this time?

(Pause)

I am Q'uo, and we thank you all for your kind words. Since there is no further query we shall take this opportunity to express our great gratitude for allowing our presence in your circle of seeking. We would, again, ask that you take only those words which we have spoken which ring of truth to you, leaving behind all others. We do not wish to become a stumbling block to any but would walk with each upon the journey in whatever way is possible, for together we seek and reveal to each other the one Creator. At this time we shall take our leave of this group and this instrument, leaving each as always in the love and the light of the one infinite Creator. We are known to you as those of Q'uo. Adonai. Adonai. ☙

Sunday Meditation
September 18, 1994

Group question: The question today has to do with the concepts of anger and sorrow since they seem to be so common to our experience. We're wondering if there's any good way of opening ourselves and allowing the processes of anger and sorrow to pass through, to be broken by the experience and to be healed so that afterwards, we are stronger or wiser or more loving or will somehow benefit from having had this experience. Could you talk to us about anger and sorrow?

(Carla channeling)

Greetings in the love and in the light of the one infinite Creator. We are those known to you as Q'uo. And we offer this circle our thanks and blessing for allowing us to blend our vibrations with your own. And to be called to share our opinions with you on the subject of dealing with trouble and woe.

As always, we respectfully ask that each who hears these words employ discrimination, accepting only those thoughts which ring true to you and allowing all others to pass by, for we would not wish to create a stumbling block by sharing our mere opinion. We, like you, make mistakes and share with you as fellow seekers after truth, not as those who are in authority.

In order to speak of this subject we must back up and begin from the general standpoint, looking at the whole being and its purpose as seeker in experiencing incarnation in this third density of yours at this particular time. As it is the latter portion of the cycles before the phenomenon this instrument calls the coming of the New Age, all—we correct this instrument—many of those who are seeking at this time are those who have by seniority of vibration been given the opportunity of incarnating at a time when both the positive polarity and the negative polarity are attempting to increase the intensity of their distortions toward service to self, for positive entities and service—we correct this instrument—service to others for the positive entities and service to self for the negatively polarizing entities.

In this environment both the positive and the negative of polarization shall naturally seem more extreme and so it is that within your culture at this time there are many whose seeking of the truth is outstanding and whose efforts to learn the lessons of love are substantial and persistent. At the same time, those involved in seeking negative polarization are attempting in a marked manner to create negatively-polarizing situations, which may express the utmost in negative orientation. Consequently, there are legions of those who think nothing of stealing, or killing, some for a holy reason, supposedly, but many for no reason except the attraction of power.

It is against this backdrop in your history that the seeking for truth now goes on upon your sphere.

The rules, shall we say, have not changed but the experience is more intense for all upon your sphere. We, therefore, have the ability to speak to this circle and say that each within this circle has won through to the present incarnation by virtue of much labors of love, shall we say, done prior to the present incarnational experience. Therefore, each feels fairly strongly that the seeking of the spirit, the seeking of the heart, the seeking for a greater understanding of love, is properly the center of the incarnation. Each is attempting to live according to the positive path and attempting to polarize positively. Therefore, we do not have to coax any to do the work necessary to continue working on that polarization. Each has some grasp of why he or she is here—to learn the lessons love has to teach.

The questions that remain are more along the lines of wondering why it must be so confusing to seek the truth, why the Creator so often seems hidden within a situation. To sum up many thoughts—why does it have to be so hard, for the heart remembers perfect ease and harmony. Contradicting all experiences within the incarnation there lies the heartfelt feeling that the normal way to live is not available in this incarnation. The memory stubbornly persists that harmonization between people is second nature, and we say to you that, indeed, except for third density experience, harmonization betwixt any two entities is not just possible, but to some extent in positive polarity, inevitable.

The question then becomes, "Why did I leave that pleasant estate to come into this intensely difficult environment equipped only with the limited and confused biases which all seem to fall wide of the truth, so-called. What is the great goal seen that made me come here?"

Perhaps you already have the answer. You came here because you wished a challenge and because you wished to serve. The challenge for each is unique to each and was set by you before this incarnational experience. Each entity wished to take particular courses over again in the school of life, as this instrument would call it. Each wished to drive home one way of learning to love.

Now, each also wished to be of service and that is another topic. We speak now of that entity who came here to your orb, not because it was pleasant, but because it was difficult, confused, and very dark in many cases. And because each wished to immerse the self within this difficult and baffling set of conditions so that the lesson would be enduring, deep and thorough. Each wanted to work very hard. Now, before an incarnation the self remembers that incarnations are more difficult than they seem beforehand, but just as the student remembers the joy of learning and forgets some of the agony of change involved in learning and adopting amended ideas, so each has an element of surprise and even betrayal. Each argues to some extent with the judgment of that higher self that chose these lessons.

In addition to the services which each came to offer, there are, indeed, tools which one may use to work with one's own grief, anger, disappointment and rage. The first tool is the one around which we have been throwing up a structure of words to rather enclose. That reason is a stubborn faith that you came here to work, so now, let us work. The first tool, we are saying, to use when you are working with negative emotions, is simply remembering who you are and why you came here, why you are here now. For there is, in each case, good reason for you to be precisely where you are. As the one known as Ra has said, there may be surprises, however there are no mistakes.

The knowledge that you, yourself, judged these lessons possible to be learned can be a cheerful knowledge to recall. Not only would the Creator not offer you more than you could bear, also neither would you, yourself, before this experience place yourself in that kind of situation. Therefore, if you are to be overwhelmed by these negative experiences, we encourage the allowing of this being overwhelmed. If there are the tears, cry them—cry them all and respect each drop, respect and love those mute expressions of grief, anger, sorrow and rage. Accept the excesses of feeling that shake and seemingly hurt you. Know that these feelings are justified, that these feelings are protected, that there is time for these feelings to express. And work with the self to encourage the eventual completion of expression of the feelings involved.

We encourage each to nurture the self through these difficult times, allowing and even encouraging those tears, the raised voice, the angry motions, all the silly, childish, acting-out that is involved in being overcome by emotion. For within this opaque, deep illusion, there is no other way to complete and then balance negative emotions. The only way through the feelings of negative emotion is directly into the midst of them.

So, attempt, if you would be good to yourself, not to turn and run from painful feelings, but rather to choose a time to nurture the self and within that nurturing time alone look at, accept, and offer respect to the bruises, the hurt feelings, the pain that is going on. For these emotions, when accepted and respected, can scour and scrub much material that is ready to be taken off of one's shoulders, emotionally speaking, and rinse those ripened, matured evidences of pain away. In many ways, sorrow and its tears, anger and its loud voices, are healing to the troubled soul. The anger, the sorrow, these are not things to fear; they are experiences to go through in the way that is most true and real for each.

The second tool, which may be used when these feelings are seen, is the turning to the one infinite Creator, for these feelings are taking place in an infinite creation. Within this infinite creation there is one thing that is true. That thing is love. Love expressing as truth, as beauty, as goodness, love expressing as mystery. It is not necessary, you see, to remain in the sea of confusion, paddling about in the frail *barque* of flesh that is your own upon this infinite voyage. Once the reality within the illusion is addressed, once the sorrow and anger have been owned, accepted, respected and the entity within all that feeling nurtured, then is there wisdom in turning to praise and thanksgiving of the one infinite Creator, to turning once again to love.

And this is not done in a way which denies all that seems imperfect, but merely setting those painful emotions into the most true version of a universe which you can find, and that is, that infinity of space and time against which the troubles of a day begin to seem somewhat small. For, within the self lies all that there is. The portion of the self dealing with the surface emotions within a particular incarnation is most small. It does not belie the agony felt to place it against the backdrop of infinity and see that it does not take up the entire creation, but that there is a deeper and surrounding environment which goes beyond space and time and of which each is more a native than this present Earth. Each is a citizen of infinite and eternal creation, moving into praise and thanksgiving, readjust[ing] the point of view, biasing it towards truth and polarizing it towards service.

When the object of anger or sorrow is another, there is a type of meditation or experience this instrument would call prayer, in which prayers are offered for the entity which has been catalyst for this sorrow or anger. Praying for that entity which has harmed you also reorients the deeper mind and biases the deeper mind more towards truth.

The last of the tools we shall speak of this day is the tool of the one Self. When the mind can settle upon the unity of each self with all other selves, then it can more readily be seen that each entity outside of the self is simply a mirror reflecting your self back to you. Those things which anger you are angering you about yourself within some portion of your inner, larger, self. The sorrow felt for others is sorrow felt for the self. It only seems to involve others. Taken upon the surface, this statement seems patently false. However, in the deeper sense, and certainly in the sense of working spiritually with emotions, it is true, as far as we know, that all that you see is your Self. You are in common with all that there is.

The one known as J, whom we greet for the first time today, has spoken concerning these issues and we wish to encourage this instrument to go right on with that thinking, for we feel there is much merit therein. Allow these common experiences their rhythm and their time.

We would at this time transfer this contact to the one known as Jim, for we find that this instrument is somewhat fatigued. We will leave this instrument at this time in thanks, love and light. We are those of Q'uo.

(Jim channeling)

I am Q'uo, and greet each again in love and in light through this instrument. At this time, it is our privilege to ask if there might be any further queries to which we may speak. Is there a query at this time?

Carla: I'd like to make a quick one. I abruptly lost the contact and when it came back it just said to go to you. I wonder what happened, or is that beyond the …

I am Q'uo, and am aware of your query, my sister. We felt that we had utilized your instrument to the fullest extent, given your physical weariness, and had spoken the greater portion of our message which was, as usual, of some length. Thus, we felt it was well to make our usual break in the working by transferring our contact to this instrument so that your instrument might rest and those other selves in the circle listening might have the opportunity to query with specificity any point not understood or ask concerning any other area. Thus it was convenient all around, shall we say, for the transfer to take place at this time.

Is there another query, my sister?

Carla: No, that's very well, I just do not usually have such an abrupt leaving. Thank you very much.

I am Q'uo, and we thank you, my sister. Is there another query?

Questioner: When dealing with others who express their anger for me, or directed to me, other than prayer for that person, is there any—the question has to do with other people's anger and other people's sorrow, that seems so overwhelming to them, that to share what I understand, hurts, rather than helps, and, other than prayer, is there anything that can be done with those people, for those people?

Also, I'd like to ask about the idea of beings being of the Earth, and how to best utilize that, how to get to a growth, a growing through. Is that enough?

I am Q'uo, and we are aware of your query, my sister, and shall endeavor to speak to this topic.

The process of growth is one in which all entities participate. Whether one experiences the anger of another or of the self, the experience is of anger and the spontaneous response instead of, shall we say, the studied response is most helpful to all concerned as this process continues, for the spontaneous response is that which is nearest to matching the ability of an entity to give or receive [the] love in a particular moment.

Whether there is difficulty or ease in this process will depend upon the entity's previous experience at learning to give and receive the love of the moment and of the heart. Thus, as you mirror each other's emotions you mirror that which is within yourself as well, for not only are you all seekers of the same truth, you are seekers who experience much the same catalyst of pain and of sorrow in making the great journey which you call seeking the truth.

Thus, to do that which is within your heart is that which is most helpful at the moment and who can say what that will be before the moment comes. Trust always that inner feeling, that heartfelt movement, that moves through you as you experience the catalyst of your incarnation. Share these emotions with those about you who have shared their experiences with you. Thus, you are seekers of a like mind who seek together and have, as a group, far more opportunity of progressing than would each of you individually.

Is there are further query, my sister?

Questioner: No, thank you, Q'uo. Thank you.

I am Q'uo, and we thank you, my sister. Is there another query?

P: I have a question. I want to ask if you could explain about the process of setting boundaries, how to do it in our *(inaudible)*, different relationships, friendship involved, etc.

I am Q'uo, and we believe that we grasp your query, my sister. If we are incorrect, please requery.

We do not necessarily feel that there is the practice of boundary setting that is what we could recommend, shall we say. For we are aware that there is a portion of your mental health profession that feels that boundaries are of necessity for each individual and in some cases there may be the situation where the boundary is …

(Side one of tape ends.)

(Jim channeling)

I am Q'uo, and am again with this instrument. We shall continue.

It is well to remember that all is, indeed, one being with many perspectives in experience. Thus, if an individual feels that there is the need for a boundary or a definition in a relationship which does not presently exist, then it is the honor and duty of that individual to speak with clarity to those with which it is in relationship and to speak those thoughts that are heart-felt concerning the definition and nature of this relationship.

This is the great work of this illusion in which you move at this time—to come into relationships with those about you, to communicate concerning the shared experience, and to be willing to work again and again with all of the catalyst that appears, with the inevitable misunderstandings and miscommunications that are the grist, shall we say, for the mill of your life experience.

Thus, it is the decision of the seeker, indeed of each seeker at all times, to find those balances of relationship that are most meaningful and to work in a clear and compassionate sense in order to share with others in relationship this perspective that will hopefully enhance the overall experience of relationship.

Is there a further query, my sister?

P: No, thank you.

I am Q'uo, and we thank you, my sister. Is there another query at this time?

Carla: I don't precisely get angry, but there are times when—I mean I do get angry—but what I'm talking about, what I'm asking about is—it's a time when I click over into a program having to do with my father, and to some extent, my mother, having to do with having to defend myself and explain myself, and nothing ever quite being acceptable. No one in my life now does this to me, but sometimes, if I feel as if it's happening to me, I'll go right into that old program and it's not real, it's not responding to the situation that's actually—now, I don't know how to break into that programming. Is that a question unto itself?

I am Q'uo, and am aware of your query, my sister. Again, we would suggest more of the working with the spontaneous eruption of emotions than would we suggest the breaking into this programming, as you have called it, in order to stop its movement. Though many programs, responses, emotions and inclinations are difficult, painful and confusing, it is well to allow oneself to be in the midst of these emotions for their duration in order to experience the fullness of their effect, for all experience has the potential to change or to transform the being which experiences. It can become confusing if an entity looks at its behavior as that which always needs correcting. It is far more helpful to look at the behavior as that which shall be experienced at the moment of its inception, allowed to run its course, then looked upon and analyzed at a later time with the objective eye that may be able to glean from the experience that which is available for the learning.

Is there a further query, my sister?

Carla: Yes, let me work with it just a little bit. There's a part of me, when that happens, that there's a witness to it—just watches it. Is there some skill involved in leaning more into the witness, while allowing the program to run? Is this witnessing a helpful part of the self, at that time?

I am Q'uo, and am aware of your query, my sister. The faculty of the witness is a portion of the process of experience which is later to mature, shall we say, for each entity is the witness of all previous selves and behaviors and can look with an objective eye more at this time than at the time of the experiences occurring.

Thus, as you are able to become a witness to your current experience, you are able to observe it more for the movement of energy and the patterns created, than be moved by it and become unaware of the direction of movement. It is helpful to be able to see these energies in motion, yet it is not that which one strives to achieve. It is that which one becomes, as a natural part of the process of learning to accept one's destiny, shall we say, or to work with one's catalyst in a clear and open-hearted fashion.

Thus, we again recommend the allowing of the experience to unfold as it will, including the experience of the witness.

Is there a further query, my sister?

Carla: No, Q'uo. Thank you very much. I'm *(inaudible)*.

I am Q'uo, and again, we thank you, my sister. Is there another query, at this time?

Questioner: I have a query. I've heard that I'm too analytical, and how does that fit in with the emotions? I had another question that I can't think of, but maybe it will come back. But the analyzing, the intellectual, perhaps, interpretation of—attempt to process and understand the emotion is what I think is meant by "too analytical," and how does that balance out?

I am Q'uo, and am aware of your query, my sister. The intellectual ability to review or to analyze previous experience is that faculty which is much like the surgeon's scalpel, in that it seeks those portions of experience that are valuable and need to be preserved and removes from them those portions of the experience which are of little or no value, so that there is, from each experience, a certain harvest that allows one to improve, shall we say, the balance of mind, body and spirit. This balance is that which each works towards and makes an attempt to equal or live up to, shall we say, the personal ideals or standards of excellence—that which one believes in.

The analytical ability allows one to compare the experience of the day with the ideals of the life. Thus, it is best to utilize the analytical mind at a time that is set aside for such, rather than attempting to apply the intellect at each moment of experience, when one is in the midst of it, shall we say. Thus, the analytical ability balances the emotional experience by gleaning from it that which is helpful for the overall balance of the being.

Is there another query, my sister?

Questioner: No, thank you.

I am Q'uo, and again we thank you, my sister. Is there a final query at this time?

R: Thank you for answering my unspoken query, Q'uo.

I am Q'uo, and we are grateful, my brother, to be able to serve in any way that we can.

At this time we shall again thank this group for inviting our presence. We are most filled with joy at each opportunity to blend our vibrations with your own. We assure each that we walk with you on this journey and that no entity walks alone, for each has those friends, teachers and guides that walk with it as do those brothers and sisters within your own illusion walk with each in spirit.

We are known to you as those of Q'uo and we shall take our leave of this group at this time, leaving each, as always, in the love and in the light of the one infinite Creator. Adonai, my friends. Adonai. ✤

L/L Research

The Aaron/Q'uo Dialogues, Session 23
September 23, 1994

(This session was preceded by a period of tuning and meditation.)

Group question: What is the true definition of a wanderer?

Aaron: I am Aaron. My greetings and love to you all. I would simply like to ask you that as a group you offer the intention that the work of this group is for the benefit of all beings.

Each of you has your own areas of pain. It is fine that a part of this motivation is to alleviate your own pain. But it is important that you not become stuck there. Thinking of all beings who wander in darkness and confusion, may the work of this group be a lantern in that darkness, helping all beings to find their way. May each of your energy help to brighten that light. That is all.

(Pause)

I am Aaron. It has been decided that I will begin. We begin with the question, "What is a wanderer?" I heard you ask before: "If I am of a higher density and come back to Earth, what is my role there? Am I both teacher and learner? Why am I demoting myself or accepting demotion?" My dear ones, it isn't demotion. Let us get this concept straight: You are in an open-classroom school. Each of you begins as what I call a spark of God, just a small bit of that energy and light moving into self-awareness. I will not explain how you move into self-awareness; simply, it happens. You begin to perceive the illusion that this self that is aware is separate from that of which it is aware … God is out *there*! … and thus begins your journey. The only way out is through, through the illusion of separation. This illusion is not a burden that you must carry, but a gift. Would you remain that small spark forever or would you blossom into a brilliant sun in your own right? The passage must involve a journey.

That first self-awareness is part of the gift. At some point awareness notices itself being aware, and with that first notice there is a shift, something which feels itself to be aware. At that point awareness chooses a direction in which to begin evolution. I emphasize *begin*, because nothing is ever fixed. You do not move into a path and stay on that one limited path until eighth density. There is always choice. Some of you will choose material planes and some will choose non-material planes. I will explain later in this weekend some of the factors in that choice. For now, it is sufficient that there is a choice.

There are innumerable planes, both material and non-material. In some planes you have only spirit and mental body. In other planes there may also be emotional and, if it is a material plane, physical body. The earth plane is the only present material plane that has a foundation of positive energy and love, and in which all four bodies are brought together. As such, it is a very powerful experience.

Time is not the factor that leads one into the emphatic learning experience of the earth plane, but a deep aspiration to learn. Some beings choose to move into that earth plane immediately. Others, for one reason or another, are led in different directions. Again, later in the weekend we will talk about some of the material and some of the non-material planes where beings evolve.

What is a wanderer on the earth plane? As simply as I can put it, it is a being that has begun its evolution on a plane other than the earth plane and at some point in its learning has made the decision to incarnate on Earth. It may have been in a physical form before on other material planes or it may have only existed previously on non-material planes.

To say material and non-material, in itself, is a bit confusing. Light is energy, so one tends to think of the light planes as non-material; but all material substance is made up of bits of energy, molecules of energy. What we are speaking of here is simply the degree of tightness of cohesion of those molecules. At a certain point we call it solid and move into the illusion of that solidity.

You are not solid. You only think you are solid. It is the illusion that establishes material body. Thus, the difference between material plane and light plane is less in the form itself than in your belief that the form is what you are. All of you are simply energy and light with enough density of molecules that you may become convinced of your form. At a certain level, the physical body and the emotional body are illusion. They are the gift of the incarnation.

Moving into Earth incarnation, you become actors in a play. The actor that walks onto the stage unprepared says to the audience of which it is also a part, "This is illusion; just a play, not real life." That actor deprives the audience of the opportunity of learning from the script, from the play. The actor must believe in the play if the audience is to feel the meaning with its heart, yet that actor must not be lost in the illusion to the point that it turns its back to the audience and forgets that it is a character in the play.

This balance between relative and ultimate reality is what allows the deepest learning on the earth plane. Some beings incarnate here become lost in the relative, blind to ultimate reality. Others find it very difficult to stay in the body and live the relative-plane experience. Wanderers have an edge here because you have lived, dwelt is a more accurate word, on other planes on which there was no veil of illusion. Many wanderers, then, are able to penetrate both realities. The difficulty you find, many of you, is that there is some aversion to the illusion, some attachment to resting in that ultimate reality, which is so spacious and joyful.

A helpful tool to learning to more fully enter the incarnation is to understand why you came. Each being that moves to the earth plane is both teacher and learner. This is true of every being, not just the wanderer but also those who move directly from that first self-awareness into the earth plane. Even those small sparks are teachers, which I will explain at a later time.

The wanderer is not set apart, then, in being both teacher and learner. This is true for every being. What more clearly sets the wanderer apart is the clarity that it has entered the illusion. This clarity may manifest simply as awareness: "I came here for a reason. I don't know what it is, but I came for a reason." Eventually, every being breaks through this veil, wanderer and non-wanderer alike, and awakens to the spiritual truth of its being.

The wanderer moves into the incarnation, bringing with it potent tools to pierce the illusion. It is far less likely to be lost in forgetting. It is far more likely to feel a sense of frustration and confusion: "Who am I, and why am I here?"

I said that every wanderer—every being, but we speak here of wanderers—is both teacher and learner. I also said at the start that this whole process of evolution, these eight densities, is an ungraded classroom. On the earth plane there is clear distinction between first, second and third density. At present, when you graduate from third density you cease to incarnate on the earth plane. This will be changing and is something we will speak of further this weekend.

There are some planes where third-density experience is minimal. The lessons for each plane remain the same. The foundations of faith and love support the learning of wisdom and compassion in fourth and fifth density, but they are not necessary to that learning. The process can be reversed. Some of you, for example, at some period evolved on a non-material plane in which there was essentially an open classroom: third, fourth, fifth grade. The material was learned in whatever order one was ready to learn. There is no upper limit to how much faith, how much love, wisdom or compassion can be learned. This school offers these lessons; that school offers those lessons. If you wish to study music and your school has no orchestra, you join the band or choir. You may still wish to go somewhere else to learn to play the violin.

Thus, some of you evolved on planes where you moved into deeper lessons of wisdom and compassion before fully penetrating the lessons of faith and love. You learned much that could be gift to the earth plane, each with your own special skills. Feeling stuck in some way, you made the decision to more fully enter the illusion through human incarnation. Another way to phrase this is that your karma drew you here. Because you learned to play in a band and sing in a choir does not put you ahead of your neighbor. You learning the violin, you simply have a different background. You have highly refined certain skills and understandings. There is still much that you need to learn or you would not be here. There are very few beings in the history of the Earth's evolution who have incarnated only to serve; and even those few, of course, have also learned. The difference—I think of such a one as Jesus here—is that this teacher did not need to come to the earth plane for its own evolution. Being here, of course he learned.

I would suggest a figure of 98.6% of wanderers need to incarnate for their own learning … please rephrase that … need to understand something for their own learning, and choose the earth plane as catalyst for that understanding. That 1.4% is those beings which are fully evolved, usually into high sixth density, and incarnate simply with the desire to serve and in order to return with fourth- and fifth-density beings. They do not need to incarnate as they are past the need to incarnate. For those who come back as wanderers, the third-density lessons could be learned elsewhere; but because there is something they could teach on this plane and they could learn the lessons as well, they might as well come here.

The sixth density has completely shed the emotional body and is not attached to the mental body. It understands the mental body to be a tool. This is the being that has no need of the teachings of the incarnative experience, but will wisely make use of the teaching when offered that opportunity.

Those that come as wanderers are most likely to be of third or fifth density. Fourth density is occupied with its group learning experiences and less likely to move back into incarnation, although it may occasionally choose to do so. Most wanderers are third and fifth density. The lower sixth-density wanderer has shed the emotional body but it may still have some attachment to the mental body. This being will be helped to release this attachment through its incarnative experience. Only the upper sixth-density energy is completely free of the illusion of ownership of the mental body, and makes the skillful and loving decision to incarnate solely as servant. As I said above, it will also learn.

I want to emphasize, then, the wanderer may be highly evolved in some areas—an outstanding French horn player with great understanding of musical theory—but he or she still must learn the correct hand position to hold the bow or place the fingers on the violin. What he or she brings to the incarnation is that advanced skill for which a need is perceived. For example, a wanderer of our acquaintance who is in his first human incarnation is what you might term a computer wizard. He is offering skills and understandings gained on other planes for which it was clear the Earth was ready. There are two ways to bring those teachings to Earth. One is channeling. One is for a being to incarnate into human form and teach it. Neither way is better than the other.

I have no need to return in incarnation to the earth plane. This is not to say I would not learn in incarnation; but I have no need, so I teach through an instrument. This friend of whom I speak was drawn to the idea of incarnation because it was clear that he had lessons that could well be learned on this plane. He has incarnated now, rather than fifty years ago, because now the earth plane is ready for what he offers.

In summary, a wanderer is a being who has evolved on other planes up to a certain point of high second density or beyond. Beings below that level of density are not yet evolved enough to make the decision to move into the earth plane. Wanderers are beings of high second density or beyond—third, fourth, fifth, sixth—who make the decision to move into the illusion of earth plane to teach and to learn. That they thus choose indicates that they are spiritually awakened, not fully so but enough to choose. Regardless of what density they have been, as soon as they move into incarnation they are third density and they are fully human. They may think they do not wish to be third density and here on Earth, once they wake up here to the fact of their decision; but some higher wisdom within them has agreed to it. Whatever skills they may have had, whatever wisdom and understanding, there are still compelling reasons why they have chosen incarnation; there are necessary areas of learning. We have barely touched the surface. I lay this before you as background.

I wish at this point to pass the microphone, as it were, to my brother/sister/friend of Q'uo, that it may offer its continued thoughts on what I have presented. As always, it is great joy to share this teaching. That is all.

Q'uo: We are those of Q'uo. Greetings and blessings to each in the love and in the light of the one infinite Creator.

May we thank each for calling us to your group. The privilege of blending our vibrations with your own as this circle sits in meditation is great. We encourage each to discriminate in choosing those thoughts which may seem to be of interest and value to you. These thoughts and opinions are our service and our gift to you. We make many errors and are not infallible. Consequently, it is well that each lay aside those thoughts of ours which are not recognized as a portion of your personal truth, for we would not be a stumbling block to you in your seeking.

This instrument knows a song, *I Wonder As I Wander*[13], and each of you has wandered into this precise situation, wondering, seeking, hoping, yearning for love, for truth, for beauty, for peace. We, too, have wandered. We seek with fervent hope the truth receding before us always, infinitely.

Each age, each culture has its wandering spirits. Within the framework of your present civilization, the scope of wanderers may be seen to have been extended, as the consciousness of the vast universe as native land and home becomes more and more a portion of the cultural ethos or setting of mind.

Once the wanderer was one who literally walked, being upon a path of seeking, moving from one wise teacher to another. Within your present experience the wandering is often that only of the mind, of the heart, and not of the weary feet.

As the days of your millennium grow most short, the seeking and hungering for truth has increased, activating a great process of transformative birthing. Each who seeks may now rest in the knowledge that he is no longer alone, for many awaken now to wonder. And in that wondering, in that searching—first intrigued, then fascinated and finally transformed—the nascent seeker of truth arises from the peaceful condition of acceptance of consensus reality, shakes the dust of sleep from foot and eye and starts the journey, the wandering, the leaving of one home which is no longer home. Upon this dusty path lie, oh, so many marvelous and frightening events. Adventure is the companion of the wanderer. Joy and sorrow aplenty rest within its quiver.

What is the definition of *wanderer*? Beneath all specific details, the wanderer is one upon a journey without an ending, seeking a home in a land where there is no home, sailing upon a sea which has no port, no land, but only infinite voyaging. Upon this sea, this ocean, the rudder that stabilizes and steers the ship is the spirit within. Within this inner heart or spirit lies home. How to move through this vast ocean of sense experience skillfully is always hidden within the very air you breathe, within that which you hear and sense and think. To the seeker who pays attention come myriad clues and cues. Listen! Hark! The call has gone out.

There are many beings with each of you, hoping and wishing to serve by strengthening each servant of the light. When each goes into that inner sanctum in prayer, in meditation, in contemplation, we ask each to rest in the knowledge that those who seek to serve the infinite Creator wait to support and nurture by sharing vibrations within meditation, by sharing that seeker's own meditative energies. We have no complex scheme to offer you so that you may know more about yourselves. We are here as companions in this wandering. We, too, seek and hope and wander still.

We thank this instrument and this group for asking for our service. We look forward to working with your queries throughout this series of sessions. We salute our brother Aaron, and once again bless each

---

[13] Appalachian folk song; music and lyrics collected by John Jacob Niles, 1933.

of you. How we love you, you who are in the fog, in the mist, wondering, "Is any of this worthwhile? What is this for?" Thank you most heartily for your attention.

We leave each of you in the love and in the light of the infinite Creator. We are known to you as those of the principle of Q'uo. Adonai.

Aaron: I am Aaron. It would help this instrument if the fabric which covers the monitor would be placed over the monitor. Thank you. I will be brief. Time is an illusion but your energy is not. The spiritual energy and love that you bring to this session is very high, but the physical bodies are tired. I wish only to offer a metaphor suggested by Q'uo's speaking of the mist that beclouds your journey.

Last month Barbara spent several days on a canoe trip in a very remote wilderness chain of lakes. In early morning's light, she emerged from her tent each morning and found the lake covered with such a dense mist that one could not see beyond eight or ten feet. These were big lakes: eight miles long, a mile across. She found much joy paddling out into the mist where she sat in her canoe and meditated, drifting in that opacity. There was no sense of direction. Since she had only visual balance, even up and down lost meaning except for her weight sitting in the bottom of that canoe. There were no visual cues at all. She experimented, first paddling out into the lake with some vigor, then stopping and sitting, looking around and seeing the slight arisings of fear when all was obscured around her. She knew she was safe. There were no motor boats on this lake to run her over. If for some reason the fog did not lift, she could call out for help and one of her sons would come in another canoe. She knew she was safe. She found it wonderful to rest in this illusion of total obscuration. She found much parallel to the illusion of incarnation, the sense, "I don't know where I'm going. Can that be okay? Can I just rest here and enjoy the wonder of watching the mist rise off the water?"

As the canoe drifted in total silence, occasionally it drifted into the field of a loon, duck or goose, as there were many waterfowl on this lake. Since Barbara does not hear, she had no auditory warning that their presence was immediate until they entered that ten-foot circle around her and she could see them. At first there were fears: "What if I drift into something?" Slowly fear was relaxed: "I am safe. I don't need to see far ahead or far behind. In this moment I am safe, and the wonders of the universe will unfold right here in this small circle of vision." What intense joy she felt as fear relaxed and she allowed herself to be fully present in this small circle where the illusion was penetrated, where the water and mist met.

She found that each morning as the sun rose (and it took several hours before it got high enough), it burned off the mist and the circle of clarity expanded. She watched herself grasping at that clarity at first, wanting the mist to rise, wanting to be able to see. And then she found as days passed, she let go of that desire, found that she could be present with the mist without hurrying it away. Can you hurry it? Can you force the sun to rise? When the sun finally got high enough, the mist burned off quickly. Within a quarter hour of your time, the horizon expanded all the way to the shore, mist still dwelling at the treetops but the lake now visible.

I ask you each to draw this metaphor into your own lives. Part of your incarnation is agreement to this veil. It is wonderful that you come here to seek answers for yourselves and all beings. I deeply honor you for that. But I ask you to ask yourselves, can you metaphorically sit in the bottom of this canoe and trust that the mist will rise when it is ready? I ask you to trust your lives, not struggling in fear, within the illusion that is meant to teach you.

You also wish to penetrate the illusion but not to deny the illusion. This relative reality *is* illusion. Those of you who are wanderers tend to want to deny that illusion, to return to shore, to return home with a clarity; but you entered the illusion with your free will, and with great wisdom you opened your heart to the illusion and asked to become teachers and learners in that illusion. Trust that illusion, my dear ones.

I echo here Q'uo's statement: I am not infallible. What I offer you comes from my heart, and I offer it in loving service. If it in any way is not harmonious with your own deepest truth, please put it aside. My deepest love to each of you, and my gratitude that you have joined together for this teaching, learning and sharing.

May I ask you, whatever meditation you may enter tonight or in the morning, will you visualize yourself in that canoe literally? Note the arising of fear as your canoe moves away from land and you cannot see. Sit there in the bottom of that canoe, arms and paddle at rest, allowing whatever drifts into your presence to be there, neither grasping nor pushing away. Sit with the simple reflection: How can I more fully open my energy to the incarnation, complete with its illusion? That is all. I return you to Q'uo, should Q'uo wish to speak.

(Q'uo recognized the group's fatigue and the session was ended.)

The Aaron/Q'uo Dialogues, Session 24
September 24, 1994

(This session was preceded by a period of tuning and meditation.)

Group question: What can a wanderer do if he or she wants to remember lessons? Are there preplanned services? Is there a difference between lessons for a wanderer and third-density entities? How do we connect to the earth and ground ourselves, instead of only using our higher energy centers?

Q'uo: We are those of the principle of Q'uo. Greetings in the love and in the light of the one infinite Creator.

We are most privileged to be with you this morning, and have enjoyed those humorous and yet profound considerations which your group has offered. Truly, for those who seek to serve, the way becomes far less severe and difficult when there are companions upon that dusty path. To serve together is to serve far more ably and effectively than each one separately. This instinct towards cooperation which we see developing within your numbers—this is an art and a skill which is key in the creation of the enhanced being, offered within what is so often called the New Age.

Fourth density is not separated from third by a great chasm, but merely by the resistance of third-density entities when faced with the need to become a part of a unified and euphonious group. Know that each of you is most valuable in your unique way; and if there is never the opportunity to function steadily with a group, yet still, the service provided by living a life of faith is infinite in value. Yet when the opportunity arises to serve the Creator as a portion of a circle or group, we encourage each to seize that chance with glee.

We find the term *wanderer* to be one which has many layers of meaning. Certainly those who are upon the earth plane having come from other earths, other densities, have wandered far, yet consider how each entity in incarnation has come not from Earth but from that mystery which lies behind all appearances and substances. The earth cannot breed spirits, but can merely offer a home to the spirits' physical, mental and emotional bodies during the processes of incarnation. O dear souls, each of you has a native land far from the earth plane. This home lies beyond space, beyond time; and each is indeed a wanderer. For most entities there is a degree of comfort, a great ability to enjoy and feel at home within the earth experience. Those who call themselves wanderers or are drawn to that term are those whose natures are such that the present environment of third density simply does not feel comfortable or native.

Let us look at the shape of a wanderer's story. There is the rising into an awakened awareness of difference from the normal run of people. Often, within early childhood even, there is for the wandering spirit a feeling in the heart that, "I do not belong here," and so the wanderer sets out upon a trek; whither, she knows not; why, he cannot perhaps say. "What shall I take? What shall I leave? What are the rules of the road?" each questing spirit wonders. The answers fade and evade precise capture, yet always the inner nature calls the wandering spirit onward into the unknown, ruthlessly asking the personality who seeks to lay previous structures aside to become uncomfortable and discordant in emotion, upset and overwhelmed with change and transformation; and all the goods of the earth plane fly away. The traveler has no luggage. Sore, weary, puzzled, the wanderer may sit by the side of that road oftentimes. Finally, with all resources spent, with no end in sight, the wanderer turns—no longer reaching, having given up—and then is the moment when it becomes so clear, so apparent, that the wanderer is incredulous: "How could I have missed this signpost?" This signpost points inward.

It is so necessary to move outwardly, to wander and travel and reach in order to hone the desire, in order to temper the personality. Yet at the end of each trail there is the bare signpost: "Go within … go within … Enter thine own heart and know for the first time that you are at home and one with all that there is, that there was and that there will be."

As our esteemed and beloved brother Aaron and we speak concerning various aspects of the experience of discomfort and alienation, isolation and hunger, yet always keep within the heart our reassurance that you truly are at home within. The road to infinity, to greater reality, to opened awareness of love—these are the gifts within each being. To them you shall always come at the end of the day's sorrow and struggle. There is joy. There is comfort. There, within, may each tear be dried. And from that hearth of home and love and wisdom you may wake refreshed to move into the dance of divine play which you experience as life.

We would at this time offer the microphone to the one known as Aaron. We are those of Q'uo, and leave this instrument in love and in light.

Aaron: I am Aaron. My love to each of you.

What is the difference between the experience of the wanderer coming to the earth plane and the third-density being who has evolved fully on the earth plane? Is there any difference beside that recognition that you have been someplace else and the seeking of that someplace else as my brother/sister/friend Q'uo has just described it? For all of you, that someplace else is carried within you always. For all of you that are evolved fully through the earth plane or have passed through other planes, a keynote in your evolution is to come to discover that you need not seek home, that it is within; God is within, not the entirety of that unlimited light and energy, but your own personal piece of it.

Picture a child's drawing of a sun: a round disk, glowing and gold. The child puts assorted triangles on that disk. That is its drawing of sunbeams. One may say that the sunbeam projects from the sun. Take that sunbeam with its pointed tip and push it inward. Is there anything there which is not of the same nature as the sun? Wanderer or non-wanderer, once you discover your true nature is divine and never separate from all that is, then you are ready to live on any plane with love and wisdom, with compassion. The earth plane offers all beings the opportunity to discover their true nature.

Each being on any plane has its own particular skills and experiences that it brings to the next moment. I ask you here to enter into an envisioning with me. Let us visualize a somewhat primitive farming culture: people living in great harmony with the land, creating the food that they need out of the earth, and feeding themselves and each other. There is not chemical understanding of such subtleties as crop rotation; but there is a feeling for the earth, a sensitivity to the vibrations that the earth emits, so that the earth is treated as companion and not as slave in the venture of creating food.

This culture finds itself in some trouble at some point because there is a lack of rain. Within this extended drought, crops are bad, people are starving. Word of this drought comes to one in an advanced technological culture across the sea. This one desires to serve and also feels that he or she could benefit by learning the ways of this culture that works in harmony with the earth. This one is disturbed, perhaps, by the ways its peers treat the earth as slave rather than as companion and co-creator. This one sets out, then, on its boat with a plan in mind: "I will teach them the technology to bring water to their fields, and I will learn how they live in harmony with the earth." This one comes from a highly advanced technology where combating drought is simply a matter of harnessing power, pumping water through conduits. It cannot bring thousands of miles of conduit with it. It cannot bring electricity with it, nor atomic power. So, it arrives barehanded with an understanding of how this may be done, but without the tools. It must fully enter the culture it has come to, fully accept the culture's limits:

"What if I see an image that those within the culture do not have?" it wonders. It knows that it is possible to bring water to these fields. How does it do this in a manner consistent with the culture's knowledge and values? But it knows that it can be done! To do this work it must fully immerse itself in the culture. It must pay attention: "We cannot make copper pipes. What will we do?" In paying attention, it notices some of the vegetation in the forests, that some of them can be hollowed and connected. It notices the windmills whose power can be harnessed to draw the water up into the fields.

In a sense, this is what a wanderer must do. Before your incarnation you have clarity: "Here's the job ahead. I will help to teach this." What would be a simple matter on the astral plane changes vastly when you enter the illusion. To teach what you came to teach, you first must fully ground yourself in the illusion, must accept your humanness.

For this being we have used as example, in finding that the earth does provide everything that is needed, that it did not need the technology to create copper pipes, it comes to a deeper respect and harmony with the earth. What could better teach it what it came to learn about working in partnership with the earth? When you separate yourself from your experience—dismissing the earth as mundane, disinteresting even when you are reluctant to work with the lower chakras, to work with the emotions and survival that are part of the earth plane—you cannot learn. If you cannot learn, you cannot teach. It is as simple as that. You must fully enter the illusion.

We began with the question, "What differentiates the wanderer's experience from the experience of that being which has evolved fully on that plane?" Let us re-enter the metaphor: A traveler from across the sea may move through these forests, watching, looking for something to carry water, but be unaware of the nature of this particular tree, that it is hollow. If he keeps his quest to himself, the conduit may never be discovered. When he tells his friend who has dwelt in this place, "I search for that which can carry water," and draws a pipe, then his friend may say, "Ah hah, *this* tree!" and cut one down and show him: "Do you see the hollow space within? We can connect them up." This is a matter of cooperation. The wanderer does not come to the earth plane and simply hand information to the earth plane on a silver tray. The wanderer must come in cooperation with the earth and all that lives there.

Those of third-density earth who have evolved fully through the earth plane have their own deep skills and understandings. The wanderer may bring skills, insights and energy from another place. Pooled together, learning grows; and within the experience of that pooling-it-together, prior boundaries fall away. To work together you must look at the fears that arise as you let go of your separation. To look at those fears and begin to evolve beyond them is the essential process of your growth. It all comes together perfectly.

No matter how advanced this wanderer (perhaps it was sixth density, had great wisdom, great compassion), it still must learn as well as teach. To learn, it must fully enter the illusion with one aspect of awareness, while knowing with the other that it is entering an illusion and that this illusion is not to be taken as the sole reality. I spoke of this yesterday with a stage metaphor and will not repeat it here.

Perhaps the greatest pain for the wanderer is the pain of fully entering the illusion. It wants to maintain its separateness because it has the misunderstanding that in clinging to who it was on some other plane, it is strengthened or more wise. I am not suggesting that it does not want to get its feet dirty on the earth plane so much as that there is a sense of fear of losing its clarity, as when an actor steps out on the stage and is so deeply moved by this part that he or she is afraid to give itself fully to that part for fear its heart will break.

I wish to return you here to Q'uo. Thank you for your loving presence and attention. That is all.

Q'uo: We are those of Q'uo, and we thank the one known as Aaron.

Yes, each has the sorrow as well as the joy, the heartbreak as well as the elation of romance. Each, often, may wonder whether there is profit in relationships. We say to you that our opinion is, it is for relationship and all that this discipline teaches that you have come into the earth plane.

Each gaze within now. Look at the energies of what this instrument calls chakras: red, orange, yellow, green, blue, indigo, violet. Can you feel the difference in these energies' balance within your being from the configuration that they were in when each arrived at this gathering? Perhaps each may see that the accepted presence of each to each has been the support necessary to come into a new and more harmonized configuration of energies; not merely the higher centers, not only those gifts of heart, of communication and of work in consciousness, but also and equally those energies of survival, of self-to-self and of relationships one to another. Rejoice, then, in that golden net which grows daily upon your planet's surface as those seeking to lighten the consciousness of the planet called Earth reach out to new entities, forming networks of networks which, in turn, may reach out to find more and more threads of this wonderful net to weave together until all of the sphere upon which you enjoy life is wrapped and sheathed in an embrace of love and acceptance.

This planetary consciousness and its creation are the primary vocation of each spiritual seeker. There are many possible ministries or vocations which may seem more vital or important in the eyes of the world. The wanderer may look at a healer and feel insignificant in comparison, for she may not have a gift of healing or of speaking or teaching. He may only be able to be who he is, yet this one ability becomes paramount, this one ability to exist whole and complete within the cradle of the present moment.

We would move aside to welcome back the one known as Aaron into this discourse, with most great pleasure, my friend. We are those of Q'uo.

Barbara: Before Aaron talks I just want to say I am in awe of and very much enjoying feeling the shift of energy, reading this on the computer screen from Q'uo and feeling the thought in their mind from Q'uo, "Do you want to talk about this?" and Aaron's, "Yes," and the shift of energy. It's beautiful.

Aaron: I am Aaron. Q'uo just spoke of the evolution of a planetary consciousness as primary vocation to all seekers. This does not mean that the evolution of planetary consciousness is more important than the evolution of individual consciousness, but they are a part of each other. This earth was created with highly positive vibrational frequency. Its foundation—the foundation of the earth, the soil itself, this first-density energy—is permeated with love.

As Q'uo stated, there is no barrier between the third and fourth densities. As you find more spaciousness around the judgments and opinions of the emotional body, as you find equanimity within yourself when fear, anger or greed arise, and a lack of judgment of others when such states arise in others, then you lower your barriers. With the barriers lowered and judgment falling away, you are ready to enter the fourth-density experience.

Earth is in process of becoming a fourth-density planet. There are those of more negative polarity who would wish to see it become a negative fourth-density space. I lay aside for now an explanation of what negative fourth-density experience would be like. Should you wish, we will talk about it at a later time. Simply put, as each of you does this work within yourselves, as each of you opens to the infinite potential of your being and shares that without grasping for self-inflation, each of you creates the deeper possibility of the Earth evolving more smoothly, more harmoniously, into positively polarized fourth density. Yes, this will be a space where beings are telepathic. We have talked about what that means in terms of one to another, but you will also be telepathic with the vegetables you eat, with the trees that you cut down for lumber for your home. There must be full communication both of each being's need and each being's desire to serve others, without any disdain for its need but with respect of that essence.

The beginning of a fourth-density Earth does not mean there will be no more fear. You are still going to have emotional bodies. You are still going to need to work with fear; rather, there will be a spaciousness around fear, a sense of compassion that allows fear to be touched with loving-kindness rather than judgment which would seek to shut it out.

You are learning at many levels. This one I spoke of before was not only finding ways for the more primitive culture to bring water to its fields. At another level it was learning and teaching respect for the environment, and full communication with and participation in the environment as partnership.

Those of you who are come to Earth with some technical skill to share—and healing skills, deep wisdom, deep loving-kindness—that is what you may share on one level. On a deeper level, you bring this energy which helps all beings to lower their boundaries, to come to the direct experience of God within each, animate or inanimate, and to live in loving reverence of the God in all that is.

The force that will be generated on an earth that has moved to this degree of highly positively polarized energy will exert tremendous influence throughout the entire universe—a source of immense energy, of love. While you ask yourself, then, "How can I be a better healer or teacher, a better mechanic, a better friend?" do not neglect to ask yourself, "How does the learning of these skills help me learn more fully to love? If I keep myself separate in any way from the incarnation, in what ways is that a disservice to this deepest aspiration to bring love and light where there has previously been fear and darkness?" When you ask the right questions, my friends, you will find the answers appear in your heart and the strength to act upon those answers, the clarity of your path.

I pass the microphone here to Q'uo, with much joy in this sharing. That is all.

Q'uo: We would at this time thank the one known as Aaron. We are Q'uo, and greet each once again in love and in light. This greeting is not merely a courtesy. We repeat and repeat it because it is our humble understanding that this is all that there truly is: Love, the one great original Thought or Logos that created all and creates infinitely; and light—love made visible—which has built all that is manifest in all densities of the infinite creation. In this love and in this light we open the communication for queries. Are there any questions to which we may offer a thought in an abbreviated manner at this time?

Questioner: Q'uo, if I might ask, you spoke of the archetypical pattern of the hero's journey. Is that a pattern that is found reserved for a more initiatory level of experience or is it a pattern that can be found in our daily lives as well?

Q'uo: We are those of Q'uo, and we feel that this circle of experience, this moving outward and returning inward, is a cycle or circle which may be found in many, many ways, as in the circle of the seasons: the sprouting of new life in spring; its flowering and blooming in the heat of summer; the maturing and ripening and gathering of the great autumn harvest; and the time of bare trees and brown grass, the time when all life sleeps, rests and reconstitutes the vital energies by acceptance of the limitations of the darkness, the innerness, the contraction of the cold and the winter when all seems dead or dying.

Once the circle is seen the first time, it appears again and again to the seeker who has eyes that may see and heart that may understand. The seeker's work shall always be given to the circle and will often seem to be a loss, gaining nothing for that seeker. Yet this offering comes to another who offers to another; and in the fullness of the circle, that seeker who first gave until he was poor shall become one who has received tenfold, a hundredfold and a thousandfold.

May we answer you further, my brother?

Questioner: Thank you, Q'uo. May I ask you what you can comment on the idea of the holy breath?

Q'uo: We are those of Q'uo. In one of your holy works it is said that man's life is but a breath. So it is when a spirit leaves the plane of physical existence. Your doctors call the event of death an expiring. This, perhaps, may be seen to be humorous, as your culture most often says that subscriptions to magazines expire and we realize that you are more than your present current issue. However, it is so that the incarnation seen before and after is a breath, a moment, one glorious intense moment when the soul has the opportunity to choose to serve the infinite Creator with all the heart, all the strength, all the mind, all the self. Beyond this moment there is no need for breath. Within this moment of incarnation breath is all, so breathe in life and breathe out life deeply, gratefully, lovingly; and the devil take the hindmost.

May we answer further, my brother?

Questioner: No. Thank you very much, Q'uo.

Q'uo: Is there another query at this time?

Questioner: I have a question. What sort of initiatory experiences are wanderers likely to have?

Q'uo: Ah, my sister, initiation. How painful. How awkward. Anyone who has gone through puberty knows the anguish of initiation. In fact, your peoples would do better with this initiation of the physical body if they allowed the suffering involved to be ritualized so that each who became adult experienced sharp and keenly that pain of piercing. It is not considered a good idea to abuse the body, yet those who are considered savages, who ritually cut or pierce the chest or some portion of the anatomy while becoming the man or the full-grown woman, are far more able to know and accept the burden of responsibility and suffering that go with full adulthood.[14]

Initiation, in general, is the occasion of sleeplessness and inner disquiet. The self seems to have become *other* somehow. The way seems lost and there is no light. There is within each initiation a fire that burns, a source that hollows the pipe as it passes through. Initiation is anguish, yet at its end lies the beginning. So, when the self becomes full of this anguish, we ask each to meet that anguish with resolve and good nature. The gift of faith is that it does not have to make any sense. When one decides to live in faith, one can be silly, one can be foolish, one can say, "I haven't slept. I can't eat. My head hurts from all the confusion; but thanks be to the infinite One and all praise for this anguish, for this pain, for this teaching, for this time." Does this make sense? No. Is this fun? No. Is this necessary? Yes. Will you be glad when it is ended? Oh my, yes.

We ask each to be sensitive to each other's times of awakening and birthing of Self. Reach out the hand to the grumpy bear. Reach out the heart to the nagging pain of complaint. Accept the variant behavior of one who suffers, for you see as in a mirror that side of yourself which you shall, and you may count on this, one day be inflicting upon your environment.

The more you desire to seek and serve, the less comfortable your life shall be. We offer no softening comfort except that it is just the acceptance of this hardship, emotionally and spiritually speaking, that finally opens the tempered soul to a joy and a peace that is not in any way happy but only purely joyful, so that you are companioned with joy and can truly give thanks and praise with awareness that this is the deeper ground of being, this is the truth of being. May we answer further?

Questioner: This is the truth.

Q'uo: Is there a final query at this time?

Questioner: Is the mirror the answer to finding the other wanderer? And what is going on there?

Q'uo: We are those of Q'uo. My sister, you are most perceptive. This is so. You are the gift you give to each other. How infinitely precious.

We shall rejoin you, Aaron and ourselves, soon, and look forward to that with joy and happiness; for we, too, enjoy happiness as well as the truth of joy. For now we leave each in love, light, blessing and peace. We are those of the principle known to you as Q'uo. Adonai. Adonai.

(The group sings.)

Barbara: This is Barbara, and at Aaron's suggestion I want to tell a very brief story that my son told me. At a church gathering, a young parent stood up and told this story: She was expecting a baby, and her three-year-old said, "When the baby is born, can I have some time alone with it?" And the parents said, "Well, we'll see." And she kept asking. They talked to the pediatrician and the pediatrician said, "It certainly seems important to her for some reason. I would try to monitor what goes on for safety, but give her time alone with the baby." So the baby was born, and after a few weeks the little girl asked again and they said yes. They left her alone in the room with the baby. They closed the door but they had turned on a walkie-talkie so they could hear, and they went and sat in the living room. They heard the little girl say to the baby, "What is it like to be with God? I'm already forgetting." ❧

---

[14] Clarification of context is pending, with regard to balanced participation in ritual practices as a path to maturity.

L/L Research

L/L Research is a subsidiary of Rock Creek Research & Development Laboratories, Inc.

P.O. Box 5195
Louisville, KY 40255-0195

www.llresearch.org

Rock Creek is a non-profit corporation dedicated to discovering and sharing information which may aid in the spiritual evolution of humankind.

ABOUT THE CONTENTS OF THIS TRANSCRIPT: This telepathic channeling has been taken from transcriptions of the weekly study and meditation meetings of the Rock Creek Research & Development Laboratories and L/L Research. It is offered in the hope that it may be useful to you. As the Confederation entities always make a point of saying, please use your discrimination and judgment in assessing this material. If something rings true to you, fine. If something does not resonate, please leave it behind, for neither we nor those of the Confederation would wish to be a stumbling block for any.

CAVEAT: This transcript is being published by L/L Research in a not yet final form. It has, however, been edited and any obvious errors have been corrected. When it is in a final form, this caveat will be removed.

© 2009 L/L RESEARCH

The Aaron/Q'uo Dialogues, Session 25
September 24, 1994

(This session was preceded by a period of tuning and meditation.)

Group question: Everyone seems to want to go deeply into how to do the work that we have come to do, as it pertains to wanderers especially. Do wanderers have more issues of forgiveness, for example? And perhaps tomorrow, if not today, we would like to know how we can take the energy that we have as a group here, back with us to our homes and continue that work there. We are interested in how we gather our information as individuals and use it, together and at home.

Aaron: I am Aaron. Regardless of where you came from, many of your reasons for being incarnate are the same: to learn deeper compassion, deeper love; to move beyond judgment; to move beyond attachment to your opinions and to the small ego self and come more fully into the group consciousness; and as one mentioned earlier today, to learn forgiveness. The learning of these things takes you into working with the many catalysts of your life: with loss, with relationships, with work. Q'uo and I would like to know how much you would like us to go into these questions.

"How do I do the work I came to do?" This has been the subject of many other of our meetings with Q'uo as well as of our ongoing teaching. It is never a waste to repeat it. And yet, you are here to focus on questions pertaining to wanderers. Please decide amongst yourselves how much you want to stay with that narrower focus and how much you want to move into this question of, "How do I do the work I came to do?" That is all.

(The group engaged in further discussion and tuning.)

Aaron: I am Aaron. You have joined me here, coming out of the sunshine of a brilliant day. I enjoy seeing that the sunshine that you carry in is in your own hearts.

You ask, "How do I do the work I came to do?" and, "What differentiates the work of the wanderer from another?" Each of you has come with different work, but related. And there is one area of work that is true for all beings: You are here to learn to love more fully; you are here to move beyond judgment and beyond the illusion of your limits and of separation into self and other.

When you move into fourth density, all beings will be fully telepathic. Are you ready for that? A question I often ask is this: If everyone in this room were fully telepathic, not just during the session but all day, would that be okay with you? Or have you had thoughts about which there might be some sense of shame? Have others had thoughts about which you might feel some judgment or some threat?

You are not incarnate to get rid of the emotional body but to learn equanimity with the emotional body. When there is a sense of spaciousness that sees how emotions arise when certain conditions are present for their arising and how those emotions pass away, you no longer need to dwell on those emotions. You no longer fear them, so there is no need to deny them nor to be reactive to them. When you have learned that degree of non-judgment, you may move deeper into the learnings of compassion because the open and non-judgmental heart can truly hear your own and another's pain.

What does compassion mean when there has been no judgment? Some of you have moved into the higher densities before coming to third-density earth. Supposedly you learned compassion. Now you come into the earth plane and find heavy emotions arising, which lead to judgment of one sort and another—to fear, to the desire to protect. My dear ones, can you see that this arising of judgment is not something to be met with disdain and hatred, but to be embraced and used as catalyst for learning?

The wise gardener does not cut away the dead growth from its garden and throw it in the garbage, but turns it into the soil and uses it as nutrient for new growth. You do not want to throw away your emotions but to make space for them, that you may move deeper into love and into compassion. This work, of course, is true for all beings of third density. The question is, "How do I work with judgment and the various emotions carried by fear?" Here is where there is a distinction, not only for the wanderer but for any "old soul"; but it is experienced certainly differently by the wanderer.

Many of you suffer from what I call old-soul syndrome. When you are a young soul, you excuse yourself for treading on others' toes. You shrug and say, "Well, everybody does it." As an older soul, you so deeply aspire to oneness with God, so deeply are motivated by the desire to come home. You have the erroneous idea that to do so means you must be perfect. Every arising that does not manifest itself as loving-kindness must be demolished; and so you become more and more judgmental to yourselves, more perfectionist, more judgmental to others.

As with every catalyst on the earth plane, this increasing judgment and push toward self-perfectionism is both painful and useful. When there is minor discomfort, you squirm a little. When you begin to feel yourself bashed by that proverbial "four by four," you finally need to pay attention. The very pain of your self-and-other judgment pushes you to pay attention. It is only then that you become truly ready to see that what you have viewed as imperfection is another side of the perfection of your being. This does not mean that you practice greed, reactivity, anger toward others; but when these arise within you, you begin to treat them differently—not with that hard-heartedness which would drive them out so that you can be perfect, but with a kind acknowledgment, "Here is human fear manifesting itself again. I offer it my love." It is this constant practice of offering love to that which you have judged negative which frees you.

I said that this old-soul syndrome creates more discomfort for wanderers. This is because many of you have memories of being largely free of the emotional body. It was not there so you could not use it as a tool for learning, but you also did not have to worry about it. Some part of you wants to deny this emotional body of yours: "Let's throw it in the garbage and go back where we came from!" The beauty of the incarnative experience is that you cannot do that. You must attend to it and you must learn to attend to it with love. The being who has moved solely through the earth plane has memories of being on the astral plane between lifetimes, but still with an attendant emotional body. It may suffer this old-soul syndrome, heeding its judgments, striving ever for more and more perfection, and finding itself feeling deeply unworthy because it cannot express that perfection that it wishes to express. But it is not haunted by memories of being free of the emotional body.

This is not a problem for you as wanderers. There are no problems, only situations that ask your loving attention. For those who have aversion to the emotional body and to the arisings of the emotional body, and have attachment to being free of that so you can feel more "perfect," I ask you simply this: Can you begin to offer some mercy to this spirit essence that you are, which has so courageously entered into an illusion of form and emotion so as to learn? Instead of saying, "It's too hard. When I saw the ground I didn't realize it was going to get muddy when it rained. Now I'm knee deep in mud. I want to go home where there is no mud." Instead, can you just know, "Yes, here there is mud. That means I'm going to be muddy. Can I allow that to be okay?

My deepest truth is not expressed by being clean of mud, but by the deeply loving and courageous ways that I work with the mud I am given."

Later in this session I would like to hear your specific questions: "How do I work with the mud I am given? Is it different for wanderers or non-wanderers? How do I open myself to my emotions? How do I learn non-judgment?" Whatever your questions may be. We could spend a session on each of these areas. We do not have that time. So we would like to know of what is the area of greatest interest for you.

At this time I pass the microphone to my dear friend of Q'uo. That is all.

Q'uo: We are those of Q'uo. Greetings once again in the love and in the light of the one infinite Creator.

We shall continue our brother Aaron's discourse upon mud. You see, wanderers gaze with a more jaundiced eye at that mud because it is not as familiar and it seems unnecessary to that witness within. If the wanderer is fourth density, the mud will tend to be along the lines of what is right and what is wrong, what is moral and what will help. There is a kind of desire to battle the forces of negativity. When the wanderer has come into the cycle of reincarnations from fifth density, the mud is likely to tend towards sticking in the area of life dealing with intimacy, for the wisdom density has the hard-won opinion that the war of good and evil is not necessary. Whereas the fourth-density wanderer will speak in terms of relationship, the fifth-density wanderer will speak in terms of self and Creator, certainly a relationship beyond all others but not a relationship easily practiced upon the family and acquaintances one meets at first glance. If the wanderer is sixth-density, the likelihood tends to be that both of these areas: the right/wrong issue which so often polarizes relationships between entities, and the issue of lack of ability to allow intimacy. These energies of compassion and wisdom are being balanced in sixth density. So the wanderer who comes to the third density to aid brings through the veil of forgetting unrealistic expectation, both in the areas of relationship with others and relationship with the Creator.

Now, the wanderer is also a convert in that the wanderer did not have to come to this party. The wanderer chose to come here, so that entity who is a wanderer has outsized, larger-than-life feelings that she came here to serve, that he must find the service, whether the scope and direction of this service is in finding the Creator in other people or finding the intimacy of family with the self and the Creator. These desires will be exaggerated beyond that which is normal for those who "have to be at this party, have to pass this test—*now*." The wanderer, indeed, is in a precarious situation until he can lay down his armor, his differences, his pains; and grievances that bind her to her body, her situation, with ribbons of "should" and "must" which tie us in knots.

So the first step in constructing a life in this alien camp is the creation of a safe place where you can lay all your burdens down, even if you have to prostrate yourself on the floor where you can weep until you are dry, where you can ask and wait until you have an answer or until you die. When this place exists only within, then it is more difficult to do the work. It is desirable that there also be a physical location for this safe and sanctified place. Some feel the need to lean upon the truth found in beauty. These entities will vibrate most harmonically and resonantly with a place in which there is ritual, whether it be the ritual of a tea ceremony; the ritual of creating a bonsai plant; the ritual of meditation, prayer and contemplation; or the spare ritual of *zazen*, the sitting or walking, merely that: sitting, walking … For some this is quite sufficient to alter and transform into that being which is self-forgiven.

This entity has a high opinion of one close to her who merely gardens. Whereas this entity's needs place her within an elaborate community of worshipers of the myth of the Christ known as Jesus, whereas this entity spends time and energy treating that congregation of brothers and sisters as the Christ, this gardener accomplishes all and more by turning the earth, by gazing at the sky, by being one with each flower and each planting, by feeling the changing needs of this kingdom created of tree and shrub and stone and water, which has become a builded entity holding personality, purpose and passion.

There is no best way; but the wanderer has, along with the many aggravations of being unfit for the climate of Earth, many, many wonderful things which are treats not often given to the natives. There is within wanderers a sharper ability to grasp the truth when it is felt; therefore, once the wanderer has developed a safe place and is using it conscientiously and regularly, the potential for true self-healing is actually greater than for the native who has not yet experienced anything "better" than the current world scene.

Once this sacred, private and inviolable space has been created, there is much self-to-self work to accomplish. The tools for learning more about the self include the study of dreams, the keeping of a journal in which the thoughts of the day are faithfully recorded, the seeking out and giving time and energy to what this instrument would call birds of a feather; for as the wanderer reaches out to help another, as that other expresses its tale of suffering, who is helped more, the sufferer who hears a little comfort or the healer who is given the great gift of hearing, of being heard, of being able to be present with such a precious gift as the confidences exchanged? It is no mystery why those who are willing to teach, learn twice as much; for when that hand is stretched out and the ear is opened, the invaluable and incalculable treasure of trust and faith is given. What beauty there is in this. What strength we can draw from each other. For all beings suffer, wanderers as much or more than most. Yet those who wander, those who wonder, are also those who receive.

The asking that is so vital comes naturally to a wandering soul. She is uncomfortable; she must speak up. He is lost; he must ask direction. There is the tool called "practicing the presence" which is most helpful to some. In this practice, the wanderer may simply move through each moment without attempting to solve or to understand as much as to witness, and to remain with that witness no matter how the picture might change; for the center is again and again called into being by this practice. When there is joy, the wanderer may speak of it to the infinite One. When there is sorrow, the wanderer may speak of it to the infinite One. Anything whatsoever may be experienced, and the response being praise and thanks to the Creator remains relevant for each and every possible situation.

The edge the wanderer has is this very discomfort coupled with the typical, enlarged certainty that this is not the way it has to be; this is not necessary. The wanderer can pull from its subconscious those gifts allowed through the veil of forgetting, the heightened sensitivity that so often erupts as allergies and food sensitivities, asthma and other illness. These manifestations are the shadow and flip side, as it were, of the ability of the wanderer to trust that remembrance of a life made of light in more harmonious configurations of energy betwixt beings who are more obviously beings of light.

We would at this time pass the microphone back to our brother Aaron. We leave this instrument for the present in love and in light. We are Q'uo.

Aaron: I am Aaron. Q'uo has just spoken to you of the importance of finding a clear place to rest in the deepest truth of who you are and has pointed out that there are many paths to that clarity.

There are two aspects to your incarnative work. First is the work with that which you perceive as shadow arising in yourself: the angers; the desires; fear and all of its manifestations and the judgments about those manifestations. The greatest gift of the physical plane is that you must learn to work skillfully with this arising. No matter how much you may wish to deny anger or greed, you cannot do so. To deny it is to bury it and torment yourself to prevent its re-arising someplace else. To act it out is not a viable option past a certain place in your spiritual path. You forget that you have a third choice, which is to find a spacious presence with this difficult energy, neither denying it nor manifesting it further. You see it as a result and bring attention to the causes, to fear itself and to the delusion of separation, but with compassion for the human who knows fear, who is caught in the illusion.

There are many ways of working with this discomforting arising. They all have one thing in common: opening the heart. Eventually you may become quite skilled at making space for that which arises in the emotions, at making space for physical sensations and thoughts as well, without reactivity or fear of any of these.

You are still caught in the illusion. You are busy being somebody who possesses sensations, emotions and thoughts … being somebody who works skillfully with them. Eventually you must let go of the illusion without denying the illusion its place as learning catalyst. You must come to know who you truly are when you are not somebody who is being busy learning to be skillful. This opening to your true being is the second aspect of your work.

I want to show you something here, something that your eyes can take in. Would somebody please hand Barbara an unwrinkled sheet of paper, and may I have your visual attention for a moment?

We have here a perfect, unwrinkled sheet of paper. Look at it. This is symbolic of the perfection of your natural state. I ask Barbara to crumple it, then uncrumple it. Wrinkled, yes?

Questioner: Yes.

Aaron: Wrinkled. Let us call them wrinkles of anger, of greed, of jealousy, of impatience, all the familiar wrinkles of your lives. Can you see that the perfect, unwrinkled sheet still exists? It is right here. Where would it go? Your perfection is not something that you find when all the wrinkles are gone. Your perfection is something that is constantly within you—your divinity. Look once more before you settle back down and be sure that you can see the perfect, unwrinkled sheet that lies within the wrinkled sheet.

There is a balance in your work: working to learn to deal skillfully with the wrinkles and learning to rest in that divine perfection which is what you truly are. Those who are not wanderers tend to work hard at dealing with the wrinkles, but it is harder for them to recognize their innate perfection. Those who are wanderers find it easier at times to rest in the innate perfection, and want to take an iron and cross out, uncrease, all of the wrinkles and pretend that they did not exist. Both exist. Relative reality exists within ultimate reality. You are perfect; you have always been perfect; and there are wrinkles …

A very helpful practice for many, then, is to use whatever practices are useful in learning to work with the wrinkles without reactivity, and simultaneously to find what Q'uo has just spoken of: that safe place where one may rest in one's own deepest truth, where one may know its intimate connection with the Divine. From this space you have a different perspective. You relax and open to those wrinkles as the compost of the incarnation. What is compost, but composed literally of shit, of garbage, and yet containing the needed elements to support new growth? When you are certain of this, you no longer have need to get rid of it. You no longer fear it or push it aside because you think it will stink, but become more able to embrace it with a merciful presence.

You must not hide in ultimate reality and fear the physical, emotional and mental wrinkles of the incarnation, which is the temptation for a wanderer. Another way of phrasing this would be to say that you must work with the lower chakras and not just the upper. You have a clear sense, many of you, of yourselves as spirit even if you cannot fully acknowledge your own divinity because you see the flaws in the human manifestation. At least intellectually you recognize your perfection. Come down to earth; ground yourselves; play in the mud. Forget that your mother told you, "You are bad," because your hands were muddy and you must scrub them clean. You are not bad or unworthy. You are gardeners, and a gardener does get muddy. But the gardener also remembers that its purpose is not simply to turn the soil or make mud pies but to grow the greatest blossoms of creation.

I do not wish to repeat here, what on the one hand would take weeks to teach and secondly has already been taught. Past transcripts, both loose pages and books, are available that would talk of these teachings of balance, of relative and ultimate reality and of the energy and meditation practices you may do to help you move more fully into both relative and ultimate reality.[15]

I want to pass the microphone back to Q'uo, and when it comes back to me again I would like to hear your specific questions. My friend of Q'uo has that to add which will enhance this teaching. That is all.

Q'uo: We are Q'uo. Greetings again in love and in light.

Indeed, we call each wanderer away from perfection, away from ultimate reality. We call each wanderer to service on behalf of the people and the planet of Earth. You have suffered much, sacrificed all memory and lived through many years in a strange and foreign land. You had to want badly to come here. Your intention before coming into the earth plane was clear: to lend your vibrations to the lightening of the consciousness of planet Earth at its birthing into that fourth density which moves steadily through the process of fecundity, growth within the womb and manifestation. How upset you would be to discover, after an entire laborious incarnation, that you had spent your time complaining about not being a native and expressing disappointment in the quality of people and concepts.

---

[15] For more information, please contact the Deep Spring Center for Meditation and Spiritual Inquiry, www.deepspring.org, 3003 Washtenaw Ave, Suite 2, Ann Arbor, MI, 48104.

Dear ones, you came to be servants of Earth. You came to lay all aside and give yourself fully to the cause of love. You came to suffer and to manifest throughout your suffering your faith and persistent devotion concerning the Creator and those other selves which you know are the Creator. Your biggest stumbling block is that veil of forgetting which causes you to repine at these discomforts rather than rolling up the sleeves and pitching in to a very unsanitary, untidy, but wholly natural process of growth.

No natural function is tidy or clean. Think of the act of love: sperm lubricant, strange postures … Was there ever a less dignified, more earthy way to create the opportunity for a human soul to come into this sacred earth? How could it have been made more low, more basic, more messy? Think of birth: the open, yawning gate of the womb; the spread legs; the pain; the blood; the water; the worrisome, mumbling medical personnel. Where is there dignity, cleanliness or neatness in birth? Consider death if you can—the getting old, the failing health, the vomit, the urine, the excrement—all going wrong until you praise the Lord for a good dump and thrill at relative ill health because you are still alive. This is the world you came to change. You cannot do it if you think you are doing it. Your only hope of being of service, as you meant so wholeheartedly to be, is to embrace this messy, untidy life with each and every portion taken in, accepted and known.

You are servants. This will weigh heavily upon you, for you feel as those somewhat superior, for you have faith in better things, you can see further. Give these gifts away … learn humility … ask for suffering … ask to be the last one served … go hungry … cry … Allow the pain of living to be real, acceptable, even lovely. Get dirty with this boisterous, bubbling, infinitely energetic process of breathing in and breathing out, seeking always to serve love within situations, truth within falsity and people, regardless of how they present themselves. Await the order, the command, from those you came to be slaves unto. Bow before these commands and lean your shoulders to the work.

What is your work? The first work for a wanderer is to engage in the process of life as it is. When you attempt this beginning, again and again you shall fail. This is how you shall learn. Rejoice at each perceived failure. Rejoice at your failings. Rejoice at that portion of you that would kill, that would steal, that would rape or at least have as many as possible, if not by force, by seduction.[16] When the pride falls, rejoice the most; for truth, beauty, justice and mercy are learned only in the dust. Suffer, and praise the infinite Mystery for the opportunity; and when you can do nothing but give up, rejoice, for now you have the idea. Now you are onto something good.

We have such love for each of you. How noble are your aspirations. Know that we are here for you, that our presence is ready to support, to comfort and to accompany any who call upon us. We will not speak words, we will not attempt to be obviously there. But lean into the silence and the solitude when you have called upon us, and feel our love, our total and complete support; for each of you is the infinite One, experiencing and harvesting for the Mystery which created us all. Harvesters of Earth, brothers and sisters of sorrow, place the crown upon your head, then throw it and you into the dirt and do your best. *That* is perfection.

We would at this time transfer the cynosure to the one known as Aaron. We leave this instrument and this beloved group in the love and the infinite light of the one Creator. Adonai. Adonai. We are Q'uo.

Aaron: I am Aaron. Q'uo has just suggested the importance of learning humility, of learning to embrace the mess of incarnation. While you embrace that mess you must also not deny that there is pain in it. How do you learn to embrace that which is painful? Ask to be served last, Q'uo suggested. What do you do with the voice that says, "What about me? If I am last, will my needs be met?" You must not throw away fear, but allow it to dissolve when it is ready. It is the very arising of this fear which is the compost for growth.

We are left, then, with the major question: What do any of you do, wanderer or not, with the threatening experiences of the incarnation? I am not going to seek to answer that at this time in a generalized way. I would prefer to hear your specific questions

---

[16] Clarification of context is pending, with regard to rejoicing in using such portions of being as catalyst for loving thought and action. It may also be helpful to reference Aaron's second address in Session 20, dated September 25, 1993, concerning the question, "How do I know when I'm following a path of love or a path of fear?" and including the statement, "Your fear is not a burden given you for combat. It is the fertile soil upon which you may build compassion. It is the garbage that you turn into compost."

addressed to me or to Q'uo, or simply tossed out at random to whichever of us would choose to answer. Are there questions? That is all.

Questioner: I have two questions. My first question has to do with the frustration of wanderers regarding the veil of forgetting of the subconscious memories of greater unity and of the apparent separation experienced on Earth (in other words, how we humans tend to treat each other), and of course the need for compassion and understanding. So, any comments about that and also any instructions in particular Q'uo might have or perhaps Aaron on penetrating the veil as much as possible: what we do to remember what we are here for or seek guidance.

My second question relates to the material that Barbara brought, a question I've always thought about because I identify very strongly with that (some of that information was channeled to me directly); and that is on how wanderers are trapped in earthly karma. We have talked here about how we're volunteers, but some of us also get the sensation of doing time. And it might be useful to know what common things such as spiritual pride tend to entrap us, how to work with them and how to support one another in that feeling of entrapment, which I personally find to be a very strong experience. Thank you.

Questioner: Is this directed to Aaron or Q'uo or either?

Questioner: Either and both.

Aaron: I am Aaron. The veil is also a gift of the incarnation. You do not want to become lost in the forgetting; but do not forget, my friend, that you are here to learn faith. If the veil is entirely torn aside so that there is absolute clarity of who you are and why you are here, then your work on this plane becomes more a work of determination and willpower rather than the learning of faith which was your intention. Thus, the veil serves a purpose. Your quest is to punch holes in it, not to tear it aside. You may learn to punch holes in it by paying more attention to those moments when you are truly resting in a space of egolessness, a space of deepest connection and Pure Awareness. Each of you has moments of this: the times when you are listening to a symphony and there ceases to be symphony and listener, no self or object, just symphony happening. You see the sunset; and suddenly there is nobody watching that sunset, just Pure Awareness with the barrier of subject/object fallen away.

To use a simple example, if you wake up and your stomach hurts, you notice that experience of discomfort; but when you awaken pain free, you fail to notice the natural space of no pain. Similarly, you do not notice when you rest in Pure Awareness, which is the natural state of your being. You notice when you are shunted off into a separate self, because it is painful. The practice, then, involves paying attention to these arisings of Pure Awareness and connectedness. As you more frequently recognize this space of total connection, you begin to allow that experience to stabilize. You come to a deeper, ongoing awareness of who you are. When you are not busy being somebody else—being the doer, the observer, the wanderer, the friend or lover—who are you?

There are many practices that can be done to come to rest more fully in that space of Pure Awareness. Two of the simplest that I know, I will teach you quickly. We will not take the time to practice them here in this room, but you may wish to try them on your own after our session. The first is a breath exercise. Breathe in … breathe out … in … out … in … out … Begin to notice that there is a pause between the inhale and the exhale, and again between the exhale and the inhale. Just a *(Clap!)* small break when the first part of the breath is complete and the next part has not yet begun. When you are breathing in, you are moving into the future. When you are breathing out, you are letting go and looking for the next breath. This space between the breath, often called an aperture in the breath, is *(Clap!)* now. Try it just for a moment here. In … *(Clap!)* … pause … out … *(Clap!)* … pause … I am emphasizing the pauses. You'll find that one is more comfortable for you than the other between inhale and exhale, or exhale and inhale. I suggest that you not try to notice and rest in both, but only one, whichever feels more natural. Let's try it this way for one minute. In … pause … out … in … pause … out … Do not hold the breath so long that it becomes a strain. Just enough pause to be fully in this moment.

(Pause)

When you are experiencing that within relative reality which is discomforting to you, try this breathing. This is not to escape from relative reality but to make more space for it by allowing yourself that shift of weight, balanced between relative and ultimate, coming back more fully to that Pure Awareness which never has borne a veil.

The other practice I would have you try is a very joyful one. Go and lie on the grass or on a porch or terrace where you can see the trees and the sky. Breathe in, breathing in the infinite space that surrounds you, feeling yourself filled with all that is. Breathe out and allow your energy to expand outward. Feel the borders of self that you have set and just gently relax. You are not trying to expand outward. You are *allowing* the experience of that natural outward expandedness, which is a deeper truth, simply letting go of borders, moving into the infiniteness of the sky. These are simply tools that can help reconnect you to a deeper truth of who you are. From that place of truth, as it stabilizes, you are more able to punch holes in the veil.

Do you wish further elaboration on this question from either of us, or is this sufficient? That is all.

Questioner: I have a question, which I offer to either Aaron or Q'uo. In the earlier portion of this life it seemed to me that doing something of value was the primary purpose of existence in this body. Over the decades I have shifted my opinion to where I believe that it is relationships that are, in fact, the treasure of this life. My question is, is this a factor of maturity or age, or have I simply stumbled onto what is already so?

Aaron: May I? I am Aaron. May I reply quite briefly here and then pass this to Q'uo who also has an answer?

Questioner: Please.

Aaron: I would raise this question, my friend. Is there any difference between doing something of value and establishing relationship?

Questioner: Doing connotes the creation …

Aaron: To establish relationship and enter into it fully is to let go of your boundaries and fully merge your heart in beingness with others. It seems to me that what you have learned is the real value of opening the heart, that this is the greatest gift. I pass you here to my friend Q'uo. That is all.

Q'uo: We are with this instrument. We are those of Q'uo. We believe we may say a bit upon this point. The seasons of the year have much in common with the seasons of an incarnation. The early creations of mind and brawn—will and steel and thought—are often used with most efficacy by the younger, less experienced entity who does not yet know that life is vain, work is empty and all passing in an instant. Knowledge of this kind greatly cuts into that "eager beaver" mentality necessary for creating whatever dam or distortion might seem desirable.

In the summer of a life, the being expresses the epitomes of youth—the physical beauties, the keen sensing, the indefatigable energy, the beauty of form, the excellence of learning—like flowers. The summer's children, embracing each other and life, create the seeds and in the blossom create the bait which catches the forces of procreation, inner creation and creation with others.

The prime of life is an autumn season where the entity reaps, harvests, winnows and then goes back to the threshing floor, seeking yet again until all has been harvested that was seeded in the youth of years, leaving the winter of life a seeming cold and undesirable time. Yet to the mature entity this is the time of realized being, the time when the sense of proportion is most informed, the time when the most plain and skeletal truths may be seen, shared and preserved. The winter is the ripening of doing into being, the ripening of solitude into willingness to go in any direction to form bridges between the self and anyone who wishes to learn from and give to the entity. All of these seasons have their wisdom. They all have their drawbacks as well.

There is a good partnership in most entities betwixt the inevitable lessons of time and those lessons learned about love which are special to just you. This great gift of self is most easily seen when the fire of ambition has been quenched by achievement, when the unbalance of ambition has been balanced by inevitable loss, so that each choice—in season or out—is, in a sense, precisely equal to all other configurations of thought or priority. The genius of all seasons is the inner awareness that this, too, is the Creator. May we answer further, my brother?

Questioner: No. I thank you both very much.

Q'uo: We thank you very much, dear brother.

Questioner: I would like to ask Aaron if he could speak on the practice of dissolving that he mentioned, using the emotional judgment as an example.

Aaron: I am Aaron. I hear your question.

Emotional judgments will arise. It is a necessary element of the incarnation. These will be judgments of good and bad, right and wrong, wanting and aversion. These judgments do not arise by chance. Consciousness moves into contact with an object or with a thought. It finds that thought or object pleasant or unpleasant. The quality of pleasantness or unpleasantness is not inherent in the object or thought, but is contained in the relative relationship with that which has arisen. For a simple example, to plunge into a cold lake on a hot summer day is quite pleasant. To plunge into the same water in midwinter is quite unpleasant. It is not the object that changes but your relationship with that object. When attention is brought to each stage of this process, you will find that while the emotional judgment may still arise, all identification with it begins to dissolve. Then you no longer become caught in the stories of these judgments but see them simply as passing, conditioned objects.

Questioner: Does Q'uo have a response to that … because I have a question.

Aaron: I would speak a bit further. The move from pleasant/unpleasant to like/dislike is common. If you watch carefully you can begin to observe how your energy reaches out to grasp and hold on to that which is pleasant and to push away that which is unpleasant. There is nothing wrong with this. It is very natural to you. If, in that grasping and aversion you are pulled out of the present moment and into old-mind condition, then you are no longer free to respond directly to the object, thought or emotion with which you have been presented. For example, if as a child you often experienced rejection by your peers, if you were in a situation where you came into a coffee shop and saw friends sitting at a table together, you walked to the table and they said hello but did not invite you to sit down, old-mind conditioning might move you into gear, into a sense of being rejected. Anger may arise, judgment at that anger may arise and you become ensnared in all of these heavy emotions.

Using various relative reality practices, one can begin to see how those emotions arose without need to deny the emotion, nor need to be reactive to it. Nevertheless, the emotion still has arisen and it contracts your energy field. The first part is to be able to recognize the arising and to know this is old baggage: "I don't have to carry it around anymore. I don't have to be reactive to it or discomforted by it." Seeing clearly this is old baggage, one can do practices such as the in-pause-out breath, something to bring you back into a space of Pure Awareness, a space of resting in your divinity. From this space you see the contractions of your energy field as the illusion that they are.

Each of you has a light body that is perfect. We spoke earlier of a child's drawing of the sun and the projecting sunbeams. The light body template is and always has been perfect and undistorted. The distortions in your energy field are these wrinkles in the sheet of paper. They exist in relative reality. They have never existed in ultimate reality; therefore, you are given the combined work of handling those distortions skillfully on the relative plane by acknowledging aversion, seeing any desire to be rid of them because they are discomforting, and knowing this is all illusion. You must come back, not hide in ultimate reality, nor to deny the pain of the relative experience but simply to recognize, "This is old-mind condition. In this moment I am not being rejected, and even if I am I need not fear it." You do not get rid of the illusion of contraction of the energy field. You simply release that which is clearly no longer needed. On the relative plane you recognize old baggage and then you make the skillful decision to come back to that truth of who you are, to reconnect with the perfect light body, to release that contraction from the energy field so it may no longer create the illusion of distortion.

You have been practicing the distortions over and over and over. Releasing the illusion of distortion is not the work of an instant, but a continued practice. As a continued practice, it must be done cautiously; there is no getting rid of the distortion. If there is aversion to the distortion, then one must move back into their relative practice, finding mercy for that being that is feeling the pain of rejection, for example. But when there is clear seeing, "This is old-mind, just old habit, and I don't need to carry it around," then you release it. There are many practices that are useful here. They all center on releasing of boundaries, expanding energy outward, coming back into that place of your own divinity and perfection.

I would offer one more image to help clarify some confusion in the group. I'd like you to visualize a perfect, brilliant light shining on a piece of paper. Let us call the light the perfect light body template for your being. Let us call the piece of paper the physical body. If you take a sheet of cellophane similar to the sheet of paper we crumpled, clear cellophane, and hold it in front of that light, the perfect light will still fall on the sheet of paper. It will not appear distorted. If you wrinkle the cellophane and hold it in front of the light, the wrinkles will manifest on the sheet of paper. Then you think, "Oh, I've got to get rid of the wrinkles," and you begin to try to unwrinkle the sheet of paper; but the sheet of paper never had wrinkles. The wrinkles are an illusion of the incarnative process. Finally, you turn your attention to the cellophane, try to iron the wrinkles out of the cellophane. Eventually you come to the truth: "The perfect, unwrinkled sheet of paper is still there. What I am seeing on the white paper of the physical body is simply the illusion of wrinkle. Attending to it skillfully on the relative plane, I must look at the light of the incarnation and find the perfect, unwrinkled sheet of paper and allow my identity to rest there." Then the distortions which are no longer practiced will go, just as the wrinkles will fall out of a piece of cloth when it is left alone. But if you keep picking up that cloth and giving energy to the wrinkles, they will become more solid. This is the teaching in capsule form. I would be glad to expand on it if you have questions. People are becoming tired. If there is a brief question now, we will attend to it.

Questioner: This may be a real simple question, and if it is I would appreciate it if it were agreed upon just for the sake of the group. I just wanted either a clarification or a correction of my understanding of emotion. And I was wondering if Aaron could give a brief description of emotion. Is emotion strictly the relation of one's reaction either positively or negatively to an object? And is it strictly a tool, or are there other qualities in emotions that are helpful, possibly, to our awakening to our distortions?

Aaron: I am Aaron. I hear your question. Each of you has an emotional body distinct from the physical or mental bodies. All three bodies are connected to what we would call consciousness, which I will not attempt to define in this brief explanation. When there is a physical or mental catalyst which is perceived by the small ego self as something that will enhance or diminish, help or harm, there may be a contraction of the energy field toward or against that catalyst. The experience of this contraction, not the contraction itself but the relationship to the contraction, is what I mean by emotion. Does that sufficiently answer your question or would you like me to speak further? That is all.

Questioner: I may need to think on that.

Barbara: Aaron asks if there are any questions to be considered later.

Questioner: Okay. First of all I have a question on the table still that didn't get answered about "stuckness"; and I'd like to hear from Q'uo. And even more so I'd like to hear from Q'uo about the harvest: What will happen? What we can do to help people prepare, if anything, and maybe some more technicalities and specifics about that. That was your question also?

(Group comments that is will be a good session tomorrow.)

Questioner: I think my last question is personal, but I'm interested in the phenomenon of physical contact with our brothers. Maybe I can formulate a question more specifically tomorrow.

Questioner: I might have one for tomorrow: A commentary from both Q'uo's point of view and Aaron's on what is actually going on when a group such as ours gathers that is not visible—interactions between and among the group.

Carla: And I have a final consideration. It's not a question or an answer, but it's a consideration; and that is that because of the schedule of L/L, we will be having a meditation at four o'clock tomorrow afternoon in addition to the session in the morning. Probably Barbara will have to leave, I don't know. But you all are welcome to stay. Barbara of course, if she stays, will co-teach as channel with me and Jim. So, if things don't get wrapped up and if you are going to be here longer, panic not. We will be glad to dedicate the four o'clock session to working further with questions that you came with and don't want to leave unanswered in some way.

Questioner: Well, I've got one from out in left field. In Santa Fe we get all the strange and wonderful ideas like changes to the DNA, that there's some evolution going on in the DNA, that kind of thing. I want to hear about that and see if that's true; and how that might come in with the harvest question.

Questioner: DNA/RNA … you can modify it to DNA/RNA.

Questioner: Yeah, what kind of modifications; and what we could do about it, if anything.

Barbara: Aaron would like to say something very briefly.

Aaron: I am Aaron. One of the questions just raised is, "What's happening here under the surface, beyond these sessions?" Each of your vibrational frequencies has raised considerably since you came yesterday because of the nature of these sessions and your own inner work. Rejoice in that energy. Share it joyfully, and please be as aware as possible. None of you are here by chance. Allow each to be catalyst and serve you as you serve each other.

Catalyst is both joyful and painful. Embrace both the joy and the pain. My conjecture is that there will be far more joy than pain in your presence with one another, but that others' questions and issues may raise some pain in yourselves. Embrace this opportunity for deeper learning. With this in mind, much later this evening I would like to offer a brief ten- or fifteen-minute guided meditation before bedtime for any who would like to participate. It may be a loving-kindness or forgiveness meditation. It may be one of letting go of boundaries. I will wait through the evening to feel the energy I am receiving from you and note what would be of most use. If none of you choose to participate that is fine. Any who would like to are welcome.

Once again, I thank you *(Clap!)*

Questioner: What timing!

Aaron: … the movement of love that has brought you to this gathering and enabled you to participate; and my deepest joy, that—the sharing between Q'uo and myself and all of you. That is all.

(The group paused and engaged in song.)

Aaron: I am Aaron. I have been reading your energy tonight. I have the idea of two distinctly different kinds of meditation. One, to generate a deeper sense of loving-kindness toward yourself and all beings. The other, to work with the boundaries that arise within you. While I see the value of either to most of you, I think we will work with the falling away of boundaries, as it is more directly relevant to what we have talked about today.

Visualize yourself walking through lovely woods. You come to a small clearing where there are wildflowers growing, and just beyond the clearing, a stream. To the opposite side from the clearing there is a rocky wall, a cliffside of ten or twelve feet. As you contemplate the beauty of this scene, suddenly someone across the stream starts throwing rocks at you. The first whacks you on the shoulder and you turn and look to see a large, menacing person. You have noticed there is a cave in this cliffside, so you retreat into it. This is an unusual cave, more like a bowl—a soft, lined container. It is very dimly lit, enough so it is not total darkness, but not what you would consider light. It is shaped like a large balloon. The mouth has the quality that when you push it aside, it remains as open as you desire it to be until you take your touch away; and then it contracts, closing completely—a magic cave. Allow yourself to enter. Feel its softness. Feel the sense of safety within. You can hear the rocks still bouncing off the walls, but nothing can harm you. After some time, the rocks stop. Minutes, hours, years, centuries, pass.

I said this is a magical cave. You are fed. There is air. Your needs are met. You are enclosed. You spend eons dreaming in this softness. Finally the light comes to your awareness. A very dim light within this cocoon touches memories of a brilliance you had known. There arises the desire to remember and re-experience that brilliance. Tentatively you reach out to the mouth of this cocoon, remembering how the walls will expand with your touch and hold that expansion, but with the magical quality that as soon as you say, "Close," it snaps shut. Reach out from this place of utter safety. Touch that doorway and allow it to open just the smallest amount. Allow light to stream in. It is springtime. Allow the sweet smell of the air to enter. How long has it been since you have opened yourself to that freshness? What made you close yourself off here in the first place? There is the dim memory of danger. What if that being with his rocks is still there? But it has been an eternity.

Acknowledging any fear or resistance, ask yourself if you can open this doorway just a bit further and come out into the light and the fresh air, not moving out of your safe spot but allowing an opening big enough that you can truly look out. Here is the meadow, just as you remembered it, filled with wildflowers. There is the bubbling stream with small waterfalls over rocks and lovely pools where one could sit. The trees sway in the breeze and are alive with songbirds and their own whispered melody of the wind. You are safe. Open the armor just a bit more.

Can you see how terrifying it would be if someone were to slice into this cocoon with a magic sword, cutting it in half so it fell apart? You would be free but you would be in terror. It would be a violence to you. One is not freed by being forced into freedom, but by choosing freedom when one sees that the armor which was chosen for its safety is no longer needed. We honor that armor. It served a purpose; but we recognize, "I do not need this anymore. Whatever illusion of danger there was from which I sought safety, it no longer exists. I am safe."

The memory of the man with rocks does not die easily. The dim memories of the many horrors you have experienced through your many lifetimes does not die easily. You are not attempting to rid yourself of those memories, but to allow them to take their place as part of the catalyst that has brought you to where you are today. The armor served its purpose; now it is old habit. I am going to be silent for a few minutes. What I would like you to do is to enlarge this opening as much as you feel comfortable. Remember, a light touch of your hands will ask it to grow bigger. Simply the thought, "Close," will lead it to snap shut, and you will be enclosed and safe again. Here you can experiment; you can look into your fear in a safe way. You do not need to emerge completely. You may choose to open the doorway enough that you may sit in it, like a doorway, knowing that you are still within. Or you may find that you are ready to come out and smell the flowers, to play in the pools of the stream.

With great gentleness and kindness, allow yourself to move out of this armor and to be touched directly by the world around you. There is no right or wrong way to do this. Simply emerge as far as is comfortable and investigate the nature of the fears which hold you back. We will be silent now for five minutes.

(Pause)

As you open to the world beyond your armor, you become aware that there are others emerging, each from their own armored shell. At first you may startle at the presence of others' energy and want to withdraw. If there is any sense of needing a shelter, allow yourself to withdraw a bit until you feel safe. See that the others do not threaten you, that this is old habit which wants to pull itself back in. Then you can simply acknowledge old habit, old conditioning: "I do not need to do this anymore." Touch the walls and come out again. As your armor falls away, you will find it natural to make contact with others. If it is appropriate to your own emergence from your shell, reach out your hands, feet, whatever limb can make contact to one or more neighbors—those sitting beside you in this room. Very carefully and mindfully, see how it feels to allow yourself to be fully vulnerable and open to another's energy field and to release your own energy field out to them. I ask you to do this now quite literally, if you feel it appropriate, reaching out hands or feet so that you contact at least one other person. Gently explore the nature of this opening. Know that there is no force; you may retreat at any time. This practice is to help you experience the nature of that armor as old baggage, to more fully experience the nature of the presence and that you are safe and may continue without your armor, without the illusion of limits and boundaries.

You may wish to drop the hand you touch and then take it again, to feel how it feels to separate yourself from the other's energy and then rejoin. I will be quiet for one minute.

(Pause)

It is quite late, so we will end this meditation here; but I would like you to carry this practice with you to bed and through tomorrow. Each time you feel threatened, notice the contraction of your energy field and the way that pulls you back into a sense of armoring, perhaps seeing two people talking together and feeling rejected by them or hearing something which threatens you and asks you to look deeper at fear. Watch each contraction and the way you pull into your armor and then ask yourself, "Is this old habit? Can I allow these boundaries to reopen? Can I allow myself again to emerge? And again and again …?"

May all beings everywhere come to know their infinite nature and their limitlessness. May all beings everywhere emerge from their self-made prisons and find the true freedom of their connection with all that is. May that knowledge of your freedom and infinite perfection bring you home. I love you all and bid you a good night. That is all. ☙

The Aaron/Q'uo Dialogues, Session 26
September 25, 1994

(This session was preceded by a period of tuning and meditation.)

Group questions: Should we begin with all or one of the questions that we came up with at the end of the session yesterday? The feeling is to put all the questions on the screen and let Aaron and Q'uo speak to them as they will.

M would like to hear from Q'uo about the quality of the harvest, what will happen then and what we can do to help to prepare for it, if anything.

There is information about DNA/RNA changes that are occurring, and we would like to know if there is information on this topic that would be helpful to know.

What is actually going on when a group such as ours gathers that is not visible, as interactions among and between everyone in the group? How do we use that energy when we go home to continue to grow and serve?

Q'uo: We are known to you as those of Q'uo. Greetings in the love and in the light of the one infinite Creator.

Upon this morning dedicated by your peoples as a Sabbath, we embrace each in holy joy and thank you for calling us to you in these sessions. You have made it possible for us to offer the service that is ours to give. There is no greater help to us than that precious call for information. Without this we could not serve in the way we have chosen to offer service. It is only in the work of serving you that we may learn those lessons which are before us as a people at this time. Therefore, we most humbly thank each for the enormous service you have done for us.

As each relaxes about the circle, we ask each to pause and simply look within, asking to see in some symbolic, mental visualization your energy nexus. How do the harmonics, resonances and balances of this present moment compare with that system of energetic displacement with which you came to these sessions of working? We suspect that each may see the brightening, regularizing and balancing of energies far beyond the system of energy with which each entered this environment.

Each entity is as the radio. There is the ability to vibrate at various speeds and levels of rotation or vibration to send out to other receivers, and there is the receiver which may take in those vibrations sent by other senders. When a group such as this converges for a united desire, the energy available to each in the group skyrockets exponentially because each is as the flower turning to the sun. Each basks in the others' radiant warmth. Now we realize this work is done for the most part without conscious intent; however, the conscious awareness of this process is not necessary in order that this adjustment process occur.

Now, to each entity there have come the new faces, the new personalities. There has been the opening to that first meeting of the mind and heart. In the natural way of third-density beings there has been the instinctual movement toward groupings, these groupings shifting and further harmonization taking place as each spirit deepens the lines of communication with the various other entities so that over the period of these few rich hours of companionship and heartfelt love, a community supporting each has evolved, complete with stories to tell of laughter and of tears. For wanderers, this gathering of like souls is especially poignant because of the extended spiritual families or clans which make up the chosen groupings of entities into community in higher densities. When each departs this crystallized, new entity of light, each may carry within the memory of the heart, this supporting and enabling group ethos or spirit.

You wish to know how to use this incalculable, priceless gift. Firstly, we ask each to gaze often into this memory, for there is comfort and validation in this group, each for the others. This simple remembering is potent and is one occasion which maximizes the development of faith; for each has the faith for the others, each falls down in faith when the gaze turns inward. Therefore, this community of seeking, devotion and faith that has been born here may withstand the plangent, painful doubts and fears that will come to each. Further, when this memory is seen as that crystallized gem of offered and accepted love which it is, that gem may be scried as the seer's glass; and within its light the Creator itself lives, accessible in that intimate, personal way in which family members all have the same remembrance of loving parents, loving father, loving mother. So, each may see the memory both as invaluable in itself and as a clear glass in which each may become transparent to the one great original Thought, which is Love.

Now, each has its own network of friends who also walk upon a path of faith, attempting to live a life of devotion to the Creator. Thusly, each may link this group with others. In this way, that golden net of which we have spoken is more and more finished, the strands covering more and more of the globe's inner spheres. This is a time of beginnings, the dawning of a new millennium. In this new day, your riches shall be each other. How much you have to give each other, my friends! Yourself, you cannot save; another must reach the hand. Yet, what you are not able to do for yourself, trust and know that you—imperfect, broken and sorrowing—yes, you, just you, only you, can do great service for others. Just, merely, only you, as you are, are of infinite, infinite value to each other. This is the way of salvation for all peoples: love reflected in love until your entire environment moves as though to one great music, even the flowers and trees swaying to that dawning, enhanced consciousness which is coming gradually even now to each questing spirit.

We would at this time, turn the microphone to our beloved brother, the one known as Aaron. We are those of Q'uo.

Aaron: My greetings and love to you all. I am Aaron. My beloved brother/sister of Q'uo has spoken of the ways you may draw your energy together to deepen love and faith as you reside within this illusion. That foundation of love becomes a strong source to draw upon as you work with the sufferings of the third-density experience.

I wish to speak to these sufferings a bit more specifically, especially as they occur for wanderers. Each of you is unique. I do not wish to categorize you and in that way minimize your pain. What I describe here, then, is a map, and you will need to fill in the details yourselves; but I offer the map as guidance through your confusion.

I see three basic areas where wanderers find themselves struggling. The first is the physical distortion. When you enter a density which is disharmonious to your own frequency vibration, it is not only discordant with the physical body's frequency vibration, but often has the illusion of discordancy with the emotional and mental bodies' frequency vibrations. Each of your four bodies has its own specific frequency vibration. You can retune, but must also acknowledge the heavier vibrations of the physical and emotional bodies and not try to force a higher resonance before the human is ready.

The second area of distortion comes here. Rather than trust your situation, you may use grasping and force of judgment to attempt to penetrate the veil. The third area of your discomfort lies just on the other side of that veil: "Home; I want to go home." You cannot say it more simply or poignantly than that. Let us speak to these three areas and begin to look at how the discomfort itself may become tool for learning and enrich your readiness to serve on this spaceship we call Earth.

I said that each of these bodies resonates to its own frequency vibration. When you strum one string of a stringed instrument, sometimes the nearby strings will vibrate as well. While each has its own vibrational frequency, the harmonics involved set up accompanying patterns of vibration. Many wanderers come into the incarnation out of tune with the vibrational frequency of third-density earth. The feeling is as if you were a giant violin string wanting to sing out your music to the world, but every time the string that you are begins to vibrate, something clamps down on it, preventing the fullness of that vibration. The more you fight against that which stills your string, the greater the illusion of discordancy. The hand that touches the string and string itself can come into harmonious interaction. The earth plane and the physical vibrational frequency of the wanderer can come into greater harmony when one relaxes into the environment in which you've incarnated.

It is common for wanderers to suffer from allergies/asthma, reacting to both the natural substances of the earth and the distortions of those substances. I do not suggest that such allergic reactions are mental. Certainly, it is the physical body that is finding disharmony; but part of the disharmony comes from your fight with the incarnation.

I want to go into some specific detail here. There is not specific vocabulary to discuss this. Let us use metaphor. I return to that example I gave yesterday. We have the perfect light, the perfect light body template, shining down on a white sheet of paper, which is the physical body. Let us adapt a term that we will call *sub light body*. This is not sub "dash" light but sub light body, slightly lower than the light body. Let us envision here a piece of perfect cellophane. The light that shines through onto the paper of the physical body is perfect. When you wrinkle the cellophane and unfold it, the reflection of those wrinkles shows up on the piece of paper. When you identify with the wrinkles and start to believe they are real on the piece of paper, you act in certain ways as if they were real. When you remember that the perfect, unwrinkled sheet lies within the wrinkled sheet, your attitude toward the reflected wrinkles on the lower page, which represents physical body, will change. You look at the wrinkle and you say, "It's there, or appears to be, but I don't have to act as if it's real." When you can dwell more fully in the ultimate reality, what happens is that your energy field does not contract around each wrinkle. There is spaciousness around what has arisen.

Let us bring this picture back to the situation of the wanderer with physical-body discordancy on the earth plane. The light body template is always perfect and in full harmony with all that is. Here sitting in this room is the ever-perfect physical body which carries an experience of distortion. Focus on that pain or discordancy, seeing it literally as a reflection of a wrinkle in that sheet of paper: the painful back, the stomach problem, allergies, whatever it may be. I am not suggesting that it is not real within the relative reality in which you dwell. If your stomach or back hurts, your stomach or back hurts. If there is allergy and watering of the eyes, that is happening; you are experiencing it. But it is not the only reality. A higher reality is the innate perfection which is also there.

We move into the same two steps I discussed yesterday, acknowledging the real, uncomfortable experience and finding openheartedness for the discomfort, that there is no longer such strong aversion, no longer such fear of it. The pain and/or aversion themselves are part of all that is. Do not create a duality here.

The second part is to move back into this perfect light body template. Instead of allowing the physical body to reflect the discordancy which mental and emotional bodies have created, and in which you have pain, come back to your perfection and rest in it. In a sense it is a kind of wordless affirmation. You are not denying the relative plane of reality, but choosing to more fully ground yourself in the ultimate reality of who you are.

No, you will not wipe away all your physical ills with this practice. They are gifts of the incarnation. Through your own pain on the earth plane, you learn a deep sensitivity and compassion for the pain of all who suffer. You are meant to fully experience this as third-density human. So this practice is not going to get rid of all physical distortion, but it will considerably lessen the intensity with which you experience it. All you need to do is to sit for a few minutes in meditation when this physical distortion feels strong, send deep compassion to the human which is suffering its stuffed nose or back pain, and then allow yourself to connect to the light body template and relax into the perfection of your being. Remember, the light body template is not disharmonious to this density. You create the body disharmony through the contractions which arise out of your struggle with the heavy density experience. When you relax and rest in the spaciousness of the ultimate, the disharmony resolves.

Work with the emotional and mental bodies is much the same. I will not repeat the details of the practice. When I look at you I see light literally streaming down from this light body template, light that surrounds you not just as your aura but as the entire energy expression. The silver cord is a metaphor for what I see. Of course, it is not a silver cord in ultimate reality, but there is this seeming silver cord that connects through all the energy chakras of the physical body up through the sub light body and into the light body, and through that perfect light body into that which is the source of the light body. Here is that child's sun and triangular sunbeam of which I spoke yesterday. The energy comes from the sun through the sunbeam, through the reflection of the sunbeam, which we called the sub light body, and down into the physical body. The energy field radiates out, not just from the light body and physical body but from this whole connected cord.

When your energy is open and relaxed there is no hard edge to it. Picture it as billions of dancing molecules of light, denser toward the cord of the physical structure, more disbursed as it moves out. The energy of that which you contact moves in because there is no skin, no edge. When you freeze up inside, as wanderers especially are prone to do, this has a different vibrational frequency and it is going to hurt. You put a shell or hard edge around your being and move into an illusion of separation. But my dear ones, how can you help but smack into the various illusions of this plane when you create a hard edge against which they will smack? We keep letting go of that edge, then. First, you must see that you've built it. Each time you feel the edges, you ask yourself to let them down. Then you will no longer feel the physical, emotional and mental densities of the earth as a hand clamping down over your string that wants to vibrate. You will begin to experience them as sister strings; perhaps no longer a violin, but a base and a cello. But you can begin to vibrate in harmony with them. First, you must allow them in.

Finally, we come to the deepest pain of many wanderers: "I want to go home. I feel so alone, so isolated, so abandoned. I want to go home." I said yesterday—Friday, pardon—that all wanderers, 98.6% of you, come equally to serve and to learn. We cannot specify and say this and that and that are what each wants to learn. You are each unique; however, a common chord in your learning relates to that of which I spoke yesterday. I called it old-soul syndrome. It is not something that applies only to wanderers; but because wanderers generally are old souls, we find that it does apply very deeply to most wanderers: "God seems to be out there and it is perfect. I am here, separate from that divine energy and I am imperfect. I can't go home until I become perfect." That is the misunderstanding. You strive to become perfect instead of simply looking deeper into yourself and understanding that you are and always have been perfect. What you seek is not out there, it is right here in your own heart. The Divine is no place else … please correct that … the Divine is every place, but needs to be sought no place else than right here. This is the greatest misunderstanding and threshold to the greatest gift this incarnation can offer you: to begin to know your own divinity.

If you were already perfect you would not need to be here in relative terms. The relative human is never going to be perfect. The light body template of which you are a seemingly imperfect reflection is and always has been perfect. That light body template is none other than a projection of the Divine, in which sunbeams beam back into the sun. There is nothing there that is not of the same nature as the sun.

You are trapped in the illusion of the wrinkles. That is not a problem. It is your catalyst for remembering your divinity. Allow it to teach you. When you finally understand who you are, you understand that you have always been home. How could you leave that which fills you always? How could you have ever been separate from that? What a joyful moment it is when you understand what you truly are. The healing of that delusion of separation and flaw fulfills the learning for which you came into form and frees you to offer your energy with a greater focus and greater clarity to the service that you came to perform.

I pass the microphone at this time on to my brother/sister Q'uo, with much joy in this sharing and the way we may elaborate on each other's thoughts. That is all.

Q'uo: We are Q'uo. My brothers and sisters of sorrow, long ago as you measure time, we and others came among you. When we left, we had salted the way within your planet's inner worlds the fair fruit of our peoples, those who loved so deeply and heard the cries of Earth so clearly that they were willing to sacrifice present pleasantness for the difficult and painful, challenging and worthwhile mission, if you will, of sowing within your peoples' awareness those seeds of harmonic understanding or awareness that might hopefully assist those of your sphere and the sphere itself, your beloved planet Earth, to weather the crossing of that channel of birth that looked as though it would be a difficult earth. Now the time ripens, the fields of the Earth's spirits are white with harvest. Now the harvest of Earth begins.

Wanderers, sorrow's own folk, you have come here to serve. We call you all to service now. Take up your crown of thorns. Lift the burden of your humanity and walk forth unafraid. We encourage each to trust destiny. Your basic vocation is devotion. Work with your moments of conscious awareness in your own way, at your own speed, taking rest and comfort as you need that refreshment. Allow each morning's light to form within you its own agenda for your day and your night; and study patience, for in addition to this great central vocation that even now regularizes your planet and its steadying light, you will come into, grow into those apparent and overt services that have been prepared for you.

To many, the service of devotion is the complete service required. If this is occurring within your life, come to an informed understanding of the value of being, for it is because your ground of being is remarkable that this lonely job of keeping the lighthouse burning has been given you. Tend, then, to this light within, hollowing the self through anguish, pain and initiation until you are transparent to the light. This may be your destiny: to act as radiator and regulator of the light of planet Earth. To others shall come ministries, as this instrument would call them. Those who begin to develop as channels of some form of healing, move along the path of your gifts. Look always to the true shape of the gifts within.

Perhaps, in addition to being the light that shines upon the hill, you may also have what the world and the illusion know as vocations. Entities such as this instrument, the one known as Jim and the one known as Barbara have developed such vocations; and there seems, perhaps, a glamour or desirable charisma emanating from these services. Yet in truth, these entities are but channels. The glamour, the charisma, exists within the channel, the space which these entities have created by their faith. When such an opportunity arrives for you, you may embrace it, being completely unworthy in your own eyes; for in such service the actual job requirement is willingness to sit with that light that has been given, reaching not, striving never, but ready to accept the souls given into their care. Never accept the opinion of others when praise is given, but always know and offer credit to that which has flowed through your channel. This is so difficult: to remain open and accepting when it appears that you are successful in helping. What a difficult trap to avoid, yet each shall keep the other's balance through communication and mutual support. Each may encourage each to true humility, true servanthood.

You have sacrificed much for this opportunity to serve. Take, seize, grasp this opportunity, not to rush forward with it but to sit embracing it, asking it: "Change me as I must alter to do the will of the infinite One. Humble me; comfort me; give me companions along my way. Give me persistence, stubbornness and courage. Let me love insult and misunderstanding. Let me embrace criticism and shame. Let me become empty." These are the prayers of the brothers and sisters of sorrow. These are prayers of tears and joy beyond all knowing.

We would at this time transfer the microphone to the one known as Aaron. We are Q'uo.

Aaron: I am Aaron. I want to speak to this term *harvest* and what it means. This is a word that is often used. Perhaps you flinch at the term and your energy quails because the word implies force to you, that someone goes out into a field and harvests the grain and fruit to take it for its own, as if the grain or fruit were being used or manipulated. Think of the small energy that moved into that stalk of wheat, into that apple or bean. When energy moves into that which is used on this plane as food for others, its greatest will, at whatever level it is conscious, is to learn how to offer its energy to others and become part of the greatness which is universal consciousness. When you pick an apple from a tree and express gratitude for the nourishment and sweetness of that fruit, that honors the apple's greatest joy: to serve. Its free will is not being violated by being plucked to be eaten. If it did not want to be eaten it would have invented blemishes of one sort or another that would make it unappealing. The richer it appears, the more vibrant its energy field, the more it wishes to offer itself and make itself attractive.

Just so, the evolving human that has become ready to move beyond this density becomes vibrant in its desire to be a tool of the Divine. It becomes radiant in its selflessness. Its greatest wish is to be of service and, as my brother/sister Q'uo just said, to allow its will to be offered to the greater will of the Infinite: "Not my will, but thine be done[17]; not for my glory, but for thine. It only comes through me. I am simply a channel."

Think you of this. Barbara, here, is a channel. She channels this energy that you have come to know as Aaron. Do you not think that I am also a channel? What I offer you does not originate with me. I offer you divine wisdom and tell you nothing that you do not already know in the depths of your own divine wisdom. I am a channel. I am empty. When you come to this, what Q'uo has referred to as harvest, it is not that your being is snatched up with no accord to your own will, but that the greatest gift that you can offer is to allow your energy and light to evolve to the point that you are ready to move beyond the limits that you've previously believed, to be "harvested" into the next step of your evolution.

It may help you to think of it with this image. Within each being is an intense light, unlimited in its power. Around each being are many layers of shielding, like an onion; but place that intense light in the center of the onion. With each giving up of fear, with each bit of clarity of the truth of that inner light, layers of the so-called onion fall away; you become translucent. At a certain point you emit so much light that you are ready for the so-called harvest, to move into another plane where further layers may fall away. With higher densities, more and more layers of shielding and separation fall away until finally that brilliant and intense inner core is exposed and offered into the service of the Infinite, of God.

What is this harvest about on the earth plane? I spoke yesterday of the move of Earth from third to fourth density. In fourth density you are part of an energy group, not forced into that and not fixed in your placement, but desirous of that deepening contact. In a sense, the connection between you this weekend is rehearsal for fourth density. When you let your barriers down and allow yourself to be both more telepathic with each other and very open in your energy fields, with thinned shielding, you are practicing for fourth-density experience. The illusions of separation will fall away.

Fourth-density Earth may appear not much different in some outward aspects. There will be seas and mountains and forests. Yet, there will be a new understanding of the deepest interconnection of all that is, both upon the Earth and outward from the Earth. You will be co-creators with the soil in the creation of your crops. If you choose to eat solid food rather than to dwell simply on the light and energy, that which you eat will be thanked graciously; and as Q'uo thanked you for the opportunity you give him to serve, your food will thank you for its opportunity to serve by nourishing your body. You will understand your codependence on others in a positive sense. You will not be ashamed of that which arises in you. Since there will be no shame over the arisings of the emotional body nor any need to fling those emotions on others, you will deeply share your joys and sorrows much as fourth-density energy does now. Fourth-density energy now is fully telepathic within its group. The learning of compassion is so profound because you fully experience the unshielded emotions of another: its pains, its sorrows, its joys. You no longer are limited to learning from your own experience but become able to learn from everyone's experience; and because you no longer guard your own experience out of shame, you offer it to others for a source for their learning. This is what Earth is in process of becoming.

People ask me: "Is this really going to happen? What about the arising negativity I see on the earth plane?" My dear ones, if you fear and hate that negativity, you simply add to it, and it will become the source of your own stagnation. This is much as a child learns lessons in school and asks, "Am I ready to go on?" If he or she does not study for an examination and does not pass the test, he may not go on. The focus is not on progression but on understanding.

---

[17] *Holy Bible*, Luke 22:42.

The work must be reviewed until it is understood. There is no time pressure. If you continue to return fear to fear and hatred to hatred, you have not understood and the work will be repeated until it is understood. The Earth will continue to offer you catalyst. When enough of you understand the lessons and can return kindness and love to fear, can allow fear to become a catalyst for compassion rather than hate, then you will be ready to shed the illusion and move into fourth density.

Many of you will continue on fourth-density Earth. Others will move back to non-material planes from which you came and find whatever other ways you may choose to serve and to learn. The radiant fruit that you have become will find its next place in the universe, its next place to serve, to grow and to love. I would like here to pass the microphone back to Q'uo. That is all.

Q'uo: We are Q'uo. The time has come for us to bid each dear spirit here farewell. We cannot express our humble thanks sufficiently for calling us to you to share our opinion with you. Our most deep wisdom, my friends, remains: Love the Creator; know that the Creator loves you and brought you into being to delight itself; dance as the child of the stars that you are and always know that the key is to love one another, to share each other's joy, to bear each other's burden of sorrow, to bring each other home. We of Q'uo leave each in the love and in the light of the one infinite Mystery which created all that there is in unity and harmony. Adonai. Adonai. Adonai vasu borragus.

Aaron: I am Aaron. I would like to close by teaching you a very simple meditation practice, drawn from the Tibetan Buddhist tradition, which may be used to open up your own hearts and to more deeply offer your energy and service to another. It has two parts. I am going to teach them to you one at a time and then we'll put it together.

Feel yourselves seated in a cylinder of light. Breathe in, feeling that light enter through the crown chakra and coming down to the heart center. As you breathe out, feel that light stabilizing within you, filling you. Breathe in, visualizing some person or place of suffering. It may be used with a friend, or perhaps when you are watching your television and see the victims of war or famine. It is best to hold one image in your mind here and not to scatter your energy. So you have breathed in that light, breathed out and let it fill you, especially moving into the heart center, breathed in and visualized suffering. Breathing out, allow that light to move out, directed to that place of suffering. That is part one. Let us practice it several times. Breathing in the light … exhale, feeling the light expand within you … breathe in, visualizing the person or place of suffering … breathe out, sending that light out to suffering … breath in light … exhale, expand the light … inhale, visualizing the suffering … exhale, sending the light out … inhale light … exhale … inhale … send the light out.

Now we add the second part. After you've sent that light out to the one who is suffering, visualize that suffering as a heavy, black, tar-like mass. Breathe in, allowing yourself to breathe that heaviness into your heart. Breathe in … exhale, feeling the weight of it … breathe in, opening your heart and awareness to God … breathe out, releasing that heaviness … just let it go … breathe in light … exhale, expanding light … inhale, visualizing the suffering … exhale, sending the light to that place of suffering. Visualizing that suffering as a heavy, black mass … breathing, feeling the weight of suffering in your heart … breathe in intention to release … breathe out and release. That is it. I ask that we do it for two or three minutes. I ask that you do it at your own pace.

(Pause)

This practice may be done at double the speed, simply breathing in light with the inhalation, sending it out, breathing in the suffering and darkness with the next inhalation and releasing it; or it may be done at half the speed with a full inhale and exhale for each step. Suit the speed to your own temperament. It may also be done with yourself as subject and object when you are in much pain. You may become a channel of light, bringing light into your heart, and a channel of release of your suffering, reminding yourself through the offer to take that suffering from yourself and release it. It is a way of expressing your energy, of truly becoming that servant of light; and expressing your willingness not to hold onto that light in service to self but to offer it out to where there is pain; and your willingness not to bar yourself and separate yourself from pain but to be a channel through which that suffering of the world may be released.

I thank each of you for calling us to speak with you this weekend. I thank each of you for the beautiful being that you are. Each of you I see as a rose opening into the sunshine, with each new day or each new incarnation of your being more fully expressing your glory. Please know how deeply you are loved by beings of all planes and that you are never alone, but are surrounded by loving energy which would assist and nourish you on your path. That is all.

Carla: I want every single one of you to know how privileged we are to have had you this weekend. It is such a blessing to us that you are here. This is what we are here for and it really feels wonderful. If there are times in the future when you need to come back, don't think twice, just give us a call to let us know you're coming. We know you will bring your healing with you when you come; and we are always here to welcome you and answer any questions we can about the mechanics of living, while you have the healing that you came to have. We hope you shall keep in touch with us, whatever happens to you, because we love every one of you very much. Thanks for your company. It's wonderful to suffer with such great people. Perhaps Barbara would like to say a word or two.

Barbara: Just, thank you.

Questioner: I don't know how my, and I'm sure shared by others, sense of gratitude can be expressed to Carla, you and Jim, and Barbara for coming as well, but thank you for holding this space and time apart that we might come and sit together with you and listen and be filled. Thank you so much.

Group: *(Sings)* "Love one another, love one another, as I love you. Care for each other, care for each other, as I care for you. And bear each other's burden and share each other's joy. Love one another, love one another and bring each other home."[18]

---

[18] Reference is pending.

L/L Research

L/L Research is a subsidiary of Rock Creek Research & Development Laboratories, Inc.

P.O. Box 5195
Louisville, KY 40255-0195

www.llresearch.org

Rock Creek is a non-profit corporation dedicated to discovering and sharing information which may aid in the spiritual evolution of humankind.

ABOUT THE CONTENTS OF THIS TRANSCRIPT: This telepathic channeling has been taken from transcriptions of the weekly study and meditation meetings of the Rock Creek Research & Development Laboratories and L/L Research. It is offered in the hope that it may be useful to you. As the Confederation entities always make a point of saying, please use your discrimination and judgment in assessing this material. If something rings true to you, fine. If something does not resonate, please leave it behind, for neither we nor those of the Confederation would wish to be a stumbling block for any.

CAVEAT: This transcript is being published by L/L Research in a not yet final form. It has, however, been edited and any obvious errors have been corrected. When it is in a final form, this caveat will be removed.

© 2009 L/L Research

Sunday Meditation
September 25, 1994

Group question: The question this afternoon has to deal with the comparison of the concept of the wanderer, an entity from a more harmonious illusion, moving into this one to be of service to those here, and the Fool, the twenty-second archetype, which walks off the cliff with the eyes covered and with seemingly a lot of danger on all sides, and we would like to know if there is a way that you could compare these two, if they have relationships and if there is some information that might be helpful for us to consider in applying to our daily lives as we wander about and appear to be fools.

(Jim channeling)

I am Q'uo and I greet [each of] you in the love and in the light of the one infinite Creator. We are most pleased to be with this circle once again and are honored that you have called for our assistance in your seeking of that which you call the truth.

We again would remind each that we are but your brothers and sisters who have walked, perhaps a bit further upon the trail which you yourselves walk and we share with you our journey with joy but with the realization that we are fallible journeyers and we have made missteps and wish that you would assess all that we say with your own eye of discrimination, taking that which has value to you and leaving that behind which does not.

This instrument asked for tears. They are that which the heart feels when the seeker opens itself completely to those about it. It is painful, my friends, to feel with a whole heart in your illusion for there is much that seems dangerous and threatening and yet, when the seeker looks within its own heart and finds that there is love there that is a gift of the one Creator, the seeker is filled with joy to give that which has been found if but the fear to open can be overcome. There is much in your illusion, my friends, which causes you to believe that it is well to remain closed to those emotions which are available to those who live a full and open life and who are willing to share the essence of their being with their brothers and their sisters about them.

You each move, as the one known as Aaron remarked, in a kind of shelled existence, where it is more nearly the accepted practice to remain behind the shell and to send out feelers, shall we say, from time to time, testing to see if it is yet safe enough to open the heart a little further to another.

We would at this time transfer this contact to the one known as Carla.

(Carla channeling)

We are those of Q'uo, and greet you again through this instrument.

There are so many obstacles within to this opening, so many sensible voices within, encouraging caution, suggesting the wisdom of silence, offering support for being discrete, being the observer, being wise. Your culture is not the culture to appreciate the wanderer or fool, for it values the shell, the discretion, the distance kept between. Why would the culture, created by spiritual beings, come to be such a deadening influence? Why does not this culture of yours support spiritual fools?

There is the strength of the world to consider. That strength is that it is safer and more pleasant to remain within the shell. It is easier to govern entities who are complacent and willing to be led by mass communication media. Woe betide the entity who reaches adulthood still choosing to be inwardly alive to new possibilities, for the culture is geared toward efficient working. This efficient working is far easier to make reliably present when entities follow like sheep. That is the strength of the illusion: that it is set up to discourage folly. The parents tell their children not to be foolish but to look ahead, to know the right people, to get in the right situation. The consideration is towards security and against risk.

We would transfer.

(Jim channeling)

I am Q'uo, and am again with this instrument. The risk, my friends—what is it that is risked? As each seeker moves through the daily round of activities the path of least resistance, shall we say, is that gliding upon the surface of things in a more functional manner than would be expected from one who seeks the truth. The surface appearance, or personality, is that which has been builded over the course of the incarnation and which has as its portions of self those elements taken from family, friends, teachers and the community at large which expects the conformation of the entity to equal that which is generally accepted.

Thus, the same palette of colors is offered all and the seeker who chooses the newer colors, the differing aspects of self to express, the point of view that disagrees, the action that moves the self from the crowd, the choices that are not understood, cause the seeker to place itself in a position of being ridiculed by those about it—the ridicule, or threat of it, being the means by which compliance is gained.

Thus, the seeker risks that which it comes to know as the self but which is but the veneer of personality. To break through that veneer is a great risk for there is no sure knowledge, it would seem, of who exists behind the veneer. And if it should be suggested to any seeker that the entity there may be different than expectations, then there is the fear of ridicule and reprisal.

Each entity, then, seeks to break through this veneer by discovering what exists behind it. In the search for the self, the seeker finds this self in all others about it when it is able to open its heart and break through that veneer to the love which is the self. By opening more and more to those about it the seeker discovers that the self within is full of variety, the creative energy of love expressing itself in myriad ways, each of which is a glorification of the one Creator.

Thus, as the attempt to break through this veneer and to seek the heart of love is carried on by more and more of the seekers within your planetary influence, the difficulties faced by these seekers rises as a crescendo of pain from the heart that wishes to beat freely and this pain is a call that is heard throughout all creation. There are those who hear such calls and who wish to serve, realizing that as they give that love of their own being to another in service to that other, do they also find more of that love within their own being. Thus, they move to the source of the call for assistance and offer themselves with a whole heart.

We shall transfer at this time.

(Carla channeling)

We are Q'uo. The veneer, the shell, feels at first of security, the master, and the growth within is comfortable. When the time comes for the entity within to burst that veneer, to break the shell, to, in a real sense, be born, the difficulty of breaking that shell can be great. The structure of a shell is purposely designed to be resistant to breakage. Direct assault may well not work. The new entity within, which could be considered to be that spiritual self, born not of man and woman, but of the questing heart, is so feeble, so new, so tiny, so fragile, it cannot break the shell of its own accord. The most joyous sound in this entity's world, then, is the tap, tap, tapping from without, which occurs because there are those who listen for those cries and who come to aid the birthing process.

Perhaps the most difficult part of attempting to become that fool of spirit who opens all, accepts all, gives all, and wills all, is that there is not enough of self. The self which is attempting to nurture this spiritual child within becomes exhausted and it is so tempting to turn the back upon that very real, heartfelt desire to become spirit's fool, to be able to claim the true nationality, the true citizenship of self, as not this world, not this illusion, but an illusion known only to that spiritual child within, that foolish, untaught, instinctual child who cannot express clearly, for it has no words.

The self which interfaces with the outer world continues to find little aid from the very outer world which seems to support it and all within the culture. The challenge, then, is so to develop patterns within of deliberate exposure to that spiritual environment sought by the child within, that little by little, inch by inch, the spiritual child may grow and may begin to speak to the bumbling, fumbling idiot of the society whose personality interfaces with that outer world, for the will of the self is to grow and the hunger for that growth, once discovered, places that foolish child within on a path from which it cannot waver, no matter how tempting it seems to stop and turn and deny all of foolish spirit.

We would transfer.

(Jim channeling)

I am Q'uo, and am again with this instrument. This young spirit is the seed of a new being, that being which lies waiting within each and which through the nurturing is able to grow stronger in the sense of itself as it ventures forth from the safe grounds of its beginnings and moves as a voyager onto the uncertain seas, knowing that there will be challenges, yet wishing with all its being to move forward and explore all possible sense of self that calls it forward for the Self of the one Creator everywhere seeks the union with all other portions of this one great Self, that is Itself a voyager, an explorer, through each portion of Its creation.

Thus, it is only natural that other portions of this same Self would hear the call for assistance in this process of discovery, this journey onto the uncertain seas. Those that you have called wanderers, then, are those which have moved far enough along this journey of discovery to understand that the call for assistance is a call from another portion of itself. Thus, the answer is automatic. The wanderer journeys forth and enters into the illusion from which the call has emanated, taking upon itself the cloak of third-density humanity, and walking with uncertain feet within your dusty illusion, with only the desire to offer the self to the Creator seen in all other selves, walking as does any other entity within your illusion, walking as does each seeker which attempts to learn the lessons of love.

So often, my friends, as you know well, these lessons of love contain much which does not seem loving, for in this way is the seeker given the opportunity to strengthen its ability to love, for what value is there in loving that which is lovable? Do not all do so? No, my friends, you will be given those opportunities which are filled with uncertainty, with pain, with confusion, with doubt, and if you can love here, then, have you done something that will make its mark within your soul being.

This is the challenge of each seeker, this is the challenge of the wanderer: to love that which is painful, confusing, fearful—that which is difficult in every way that you can imagine and in many that you cannot.

We shall transfer at this time.

(Carla channeling)

We are those of Q'uo. Within that glowing sense of spiritual self does lie a divine folly. Its first and hardest choice of entities to love is the Earth-bound personality of self, that second-density creature that carries consciousness about for you, your body and that mind that was furnished with that body, the bio-computer, if you will, which thinks in either/or terms, yes or no, hot or cold, good or bad, right or wrong. Consciousness has little to say to this self, this surface of self, for there is the strong feeling within, quixotic as it may be, that this is not the correct solution, that there is more to the creation than either/or, that the creation is both/and rather than either/or.

It is the journey of a lifetime for the spiritual self within to take as it seeks love and seeks to give love, failing at first almost always to be able to have love for the obviously imperfect surface self. The spiritual self within looks for companionship, someone who is more bright, more illumined, more spiritual, someone to relate to upon that journey which is inevitable once taken, that it be a lifetime walk with destiny. And it attempts to embrace first one, then another entity as friend or mate or working partner and each time the entity finds one to love and one who loves it, all is thought to be well, for that surface self is so easily convinced that the outer appearance is satisfactory and enough, yet always the spiritual self will begin to see the cracks in the surface—the wrinkles that Aaron talked about—and one after another, other people disappoint. One feels let down, abandoned, unsatisfied, betrayed and looks further and moves through that dance once again. For the mirror insists upon reflecting the self and each other entity whom the wanderer meets is the wanderer itself, precisely angled to catch and reflect the light to offer a better image, a clearer reflection of self.

The mind is finally overcome; it knows at last it cannot understand and at this point, at this point finally, when it lets go, when it gives up, when it walks into mid-air, then, and only then, do the scales fall from the eyes, and for a little while, the pressure of that decision, the release of that drop into the abyss of unknowing, forces open the heart's knowing eyes and the air is suddenly filled with angels, love bursting from each beaming countenance, hands beneath and around, supporting, loving, holding, keeping safe, yes, in mid-air, keeping safe.

Nothing is as it seems. To be wise, it is most wise to be foolish for love.

We would transfer.

(Jim channeling)

I am Q'uo, and am again with this instrument. At this time we would offer ourselves in speaking to any further queries which those present may find value in the asking. Is there a query at this time?

I: Q'uo, you have spoken in such a way as to already intertwine the image of the wanderer with that of the Fool and the archetype. Are there any other resonances that you could speak about at this time between those two images, seeming so similar?

I am Q'uo, and am aware of your query, my brother.

This process of seeking which we have described in our previous words is one which is universal for all third-density entities which live within the illusion of the separation of conscious and sub-conscious mind. To penetrate the veil of forgetting enough to love without expectation of return is a process which has steps, or as you know them, the archetypical images, that reflect the seeker's journey.

We have been speaking this day of the choice that is represented by the twenty-second archetype, known as the Fool. The entire process of seeking within your third-density illusion is one in which you become that fool. It is a process which contains the, as your Bible has called it, the valley of the shadow of death. There is in this process a rod and a staff which comforts those who walk through the valley of the shadow of death. These are the will and the faith components that ring throughout each archetypical image and are as the guiding star, for the faith that this process will end well must be fueled by the will to persevere. Thus, there is the threat of the falling to one's death, the being eaten alive by the illusion, the inability to see the danger about one, for it is all about one in darkness, it would seem.

Thus, the image of the Fool is well suited to your illusion and is given as that motto by which each might look for inspiration and illumination of the heart. We speak of the heart for there the love of the Creator may be found and experienced for the self and for all other selves as the self which is the seeker continues to place itself in positions similar to the walking from the cliff, willing to be vulnerable and to give without expectation of return.

Thus, you see this image again and again invoked by the seeker in the daily round of activities and, indeed, within this circle of seeking, as you have begun your meditation, each placed the self in that position to share openly with all others gathered here that the effort of seeking might be enhanced by the open-hearted sharing of what was in each heart.

This archetype is the most active archetype, shall we say. Though it is the last to be mastered, it is the first to be called and the one to be called most often, my friends.

Is there another query, my brother?

I: Yes, Q'uo. I have considered the archetype of the two lovers, also one imbued with this idea of choosing the two paths, and would like to ask your comments on its difference from the twenty-second archetype and its similarities, as I have had little success in commenting on that to myself.

I am Q'uo, and am aware of your query, my brother.

The archetype known as The Lovers is the archetype which, as you have correctly surmised, best illustrates the choice of your illusion: the path of radiance, which shines the love and light of the one Creator freely to all, or the path of the magnetic attraction that seeks the love of others to use for the self. When this choice has been made, then we see the twenty-second archetype, the Fool, being fully invoked, the seeker, then, having made its choice, becoming available for the opening of the self to love in the complete sense—that is, to give love as a response to all catalyst.

Thus, the Two Lovers present the choice; the Fool journeys on, having made that choice.

Is there another query, my brother?

I: Thank you, Q'uo, no, not at this time.

I am Q'uo, and we thank you once again, my brother.

Is there another query?

(Pause)

I am Q'uo, and we feel that we have exhausted this group with information this day and we apologize, in one sense, for overloading the seekers of truth with too much of a good thing. We are most grateful to have been able to join this group this weekend and this session of seeking. It has been, as it always is, a great privilege and joy for us to work with your hearts and your desires and your great seeking for light and love. We are most pleased to be with your group on its journey.

At this time, we shall take our leave of this instrument, leaving each in the love and in the light of the one infinite Creator. We are known to you as those of Q'uo. Adonai, my friends. Adonai.

Sunday Meditation
October 2, 1994

Group question: The question this afternoon has to deal with the energy centers and how we can balance the activation and the energy that moves through the centers, whether it be red, orange, yellow, green, blue, indigo or violet. We would like some information on how we can use the experiences that we feel at those centers in our daily meditations to balance that experience and to help the energy move through in a more normal fashion without distorting it by our own personal wishes.

(Carla channeling)

We greet you in the love and in the light of the one infinite Creator. We are most happy to be called to your circle of seeking at this time, and thank and bless each entity whose vibrations are so beautiful. It is a true joy to mingle our vibrations with your own, and we do join you in that meditation circle. We are offering our opinion on the question that you have asked, though we wish always to remind each that we have only an opinion. We do not grasp the ultimate and absolute truth, but rather are as you, those who seek the truth and who follow this desire with a full and dedicated heart.

Thus, we ask each entity to use his or her discrimination with these words or with any, for that which is your personal truth shall be recognized by you at the time that you hear it and you shall feel as though you had just remembered something that you already knew.

The balancing of energy within the mind and body and spirit of an entity is not the work of one week or one year or one lifetime, but is a process that is as natural a function as growing up physically, going through puberty, opening to the forces of insemination, pregnancy and birth, and being, in good time, shut down gradually from these energies as the spirit moves on through the incarnational process. The balancing of energies is then an on-going concern, an on-going process, one which we would not expect to end but rather we would expect from our own experience that this process moves on infinitely until such time as the spirit chooses simply to release and relinquish these concerns. At that point the self is becoming the Creator and moving back into that great, unknowing, unconscious well of infinite intelligence which is the infinite Creator.

In terms, then, of actually working day by day to balance the energies within at their optimum is not to solve a problem but rather to allow a natural function to be molded to some extent by either the opinion of the self as to what that balance should be or by the dedication of the self in whatever capacities might be required in order that the will of the Creator be accomplished for this one entity. As the one known as Carla was suggesting earlier, the goal in balancing is certainly not to attempt to climb that ladder of energy into the treetops of the highest spiritual seeking, but rather to observe without judgment those energies which exist at the present moment, to look with compassion upon this inevitably imperfectly balanced configuration of energies, and without blaming or causing grief to the self by judgment suggest to those energies those activities which might more closely bring the desired confirmation of energy—we correct this instrument—energies into the lucid focus which is always the hope of one sensitive to these energies.

This is not a simple or short project. However, the beginning is one word long and that word is "accept." The first job of one who comes to work in consciousness is to accept the 360 degrees of selfhood. This 360 degrees of complete humanity is also a 360 degrees of complete divinity. The energies of each are necessary to the other at this time and this space. This intersection is your selfhood. Thusly, you are accepting yourself as you murder, steal, lie, commit adultery, take holy things in vain, and all the other heinous crimes connected with grocery shopping, doing chores, and living the day to day life. There is much catalyst for anger, irritation, even rage, in the bumping up against other entities which mirror back to the self the self's dark side.

How painful it is to see that dark side of self, yet when this is seen, should the heart not rejoice, for this is a portion of a perfection. That perfection is shrouded in mystery. Why it is perfection to have both the virtue and the vice is a question forever unanswered except by internalized experience. It is difficult, indeed, to accept the whole self, to love and nurture that very self none other, none better, or wiser, or sweeter, but that self at that moment. The acceptance of self by self is perhaps the most difficult, and yet the most fundamental work in consciousness one can do, and you shall do it time and time again for there is no lack of opportunity to gaze into the mirror of other selves and see the criminal mind at work.

Forgiving the self, accepting that self, in its imperfection and error as perceived by the self, is difficult precisely because the self knows what it is thinking at all times. The public speech often does not reflect the inner thoughts, yet these thoughts are, metaphysically speaking, real, valid and, as this instrument would say, "out there." Simply because they are not spoken, much is preserved of harmony for other entities. However, within the self, there is much work to do to humble that self that does not want to have a dark side to the point that in all humility the self may say, "Dear, dear self, I do accept you and I want to nurture you and love you and comfort you." This acceptance of self by self is absolutely fundamental to work in consciousness and you shall be working on this one always, for the truth recedes infinitely directly in front of the gaze of the seeker.

When the self-acceptance has been addressed for the moment, then there is a kind of housekeeping that can be done that is quite helpful in the short run, and is a good habit to get into. This uses the ability to visualize, which we find in this group is exceptionally good, except for this instrument, therefore we shall instruct this instrument as well as the rest. We apologize for any extra time.

For this instrument it is well to visualize the chakras as a roll of candy, a roll of Lifesavers. This is a familiar visual aid, and the seven colors, then, would be visualized—red, orange, yellow, green, blue, indigo, violet. For those with more experienced visualization ability—we correct this instrument—more developed visualization ability the visualization may become much more subtle, involving brightness, degree of rotation, a degree of color, and whatever other subtleties come to the consciousness of the one visualizing.

The goal, firstly, is to simply become in touch with what is occurring in that energetic system at the moment. There is the recommended time of silence before beginning this work to quiet the waking mind and to awaken the sleeping subconscious, for the intuition plays a great roll in visualization, and it is well to request that the mental ground be cleared and a degree of awareness be reached concerning the work being done. The dedication of the self in any work with consciousness to the service of the one infinite Creator is recommended.

Firstly, then, one wishes to simply see into that system of energetic displacements, to see the energies as they are. Then, imbalances as perceived may be addressed, either mentally or verbally, asking a sluggish energy to rotate, a clotted color to brighten and elucidate, to ask an overactive center to become more congruent in energy level with the other energies. This visualization can be done not once but several times during a diurnal period if there is the need to pursue this concern, for this is a short term solution to the problem of feeling temporarily out of balance, and is a resource for the worker in consciousness.

Now, notice that we have not encouraged an actual change in the energy system, but, rather, an adjustment of one energy to another to bring the system more into a comfortable balance as it is. Once this practice has become comfortable then there are, indeed, ways in which one may further work to improve and energize the entire system, but this work is not done chakra by chakra. The work which informs this energy system and improves it is work on the whole self, for it is always the balance of energies which expresses the nature of the self, rather than the most active or most developed energy center. Consequently, work such as the silent meditation, the prayer, and the contemplation, works which address the whole self, these are the more advanced and productive techniques for further developing that energy system and encouraging its degree of evolution.

For, dear ones, beyond the perceived experiences of the energy of the self there lies beyond perception the infinite Creator expressing through the self. The ground of being, which the energy system informs, is fed by time spent with the infinite One, whether in meditation or in the rush of everyday life. Know yourself to be whole, to be complete, and to be unified beyond all harmonization. This knowledge, this faith of wholeness creates the atmosphere within which the evolution of the spirit is accelerated. The result of this meditation, or prayer, or contemplation, may manifest in many ways: healing, loving, a channeling such as this instrument. There are so many gifts, most of them quite unappreciated, such as the mothering, the parenting in general, the chores, the cooking, the cleaning, the driving. Each activity done by the whole self becomes a devotion, and the practicing of the presence of the infinite Creator becomes constant.

To this end do those within this density of the flesh seek to come. To this end, to this choice, to love and serve were each born. This very incarnation is the one into which each was born to seek the infinite Creator. All is ready for the present moment. May each open the heart and say, "Yes," in whatever way is most true to the self.

We would at this time transfer this contact to the one known as Jim, realizing that we have barely scratched the surface of this interesting topic, but realizing also that, as this instrument has reminded us, we speak sometimes too long. Thank each—we correct this instrument—we thank each for allowing us to ramble on.

We are those of Q'uo, and would transfer at this time.

(Jim channeling)

I am Q'uo, and greet each again in love and in light. It is our privilege at this time to offer ourselves in the attempt to speak to any further queries which those present may have for us. Is there a query at this time?

Questioner: I have one.

I am Q'uo, and we would be happy to speak to your query, my sister.

Questioner: Why—when … Why did I get a sort of a heat rush, and get sort of dizzy *(inaudible)* …

I am Q'uo, and we are aware of your query, and will attempt to speak in a general fashion concerning this experience of the heat rushing through your physical vehicle.

The heat is a byproduct, shall we say, of the energies with which you work as you are offering yourself, or attempting to offer yourself, as that known as a healer. These rushes of energy will not only appear at the opportunity for offering yourself as a healer, but will from time to time be experienced even when there is no opportunity to serve as a healer present before you. This is much like the testing and clearing of the system that is your mind/body/spirit complex. Thus, you have these pulses, and may expect more in your future as you are, shall we say, fine tuning your vehicle for the service that is yours to offer.

Thus, we would recommend no concern that is necessary for this experience. It is a portion of that which is to come. Is there a further query, my sister?

Questioner: I wondered why I got so dizzy when it happened.

I am Q'uo, and am aware of your query, my sister. As your physical vehicle becomes aligned with these healing energies you will find that the dizzying effect leaves slowly. However, at this time the physical vehicle is, shall we say, at the limit of its ability to experience and express these energies. Thus, the byproduct of such is, again, the dizzying effect and the heating effect. Is there a further query, my sister?

Questioner: No, thank you very much.

I am Q'uo, and we thank you, my sister. Is there another query at this time?

Carla: I'd like to follow up on hers, by asking is this analogous in a healing channel to conditioning in the kind of channeling that we do, 'cause I can relate to that better if I understand that that's the same kind of thing.

I am Q'uo, and am aware of your query, my sister. This is a good analogy for each is, indeed, an instrument through which energies move and each vehicle that has been offered in service needs the tuning, the conditioning, the preparation for the greater service that is to follow, so you may expect that this will continue, and is an effect about which there is no need for concern, but is simply a portion of that process of offering the self as an instrument for service to others. Is there a further query, my sister?

Carla: No, thank you.

I am Q'uo, and we thank you once again, my sister. Is there another query?

P: I have a personal question. I've been noticing an energy in my throat chakra and—for a while—and it feels like a blockage at times. Would you be able to speak about this?

I am Q'uo, and am aware of your query, my sister. We find that due to our desire not to infringe upon your own free will that we can only affirm that which you have assumed, that the energies of the blue-ray center are those which have some need for expression within your own experience at this time. For us to specify the nature of this expression, or with whom it may occur, would be, in our opinion, inappropriate and we must apologize for leaving this portion of the mystery to your own discrimination.

Is there a further query, my sister?

P: No, thank you.

I am Q'uo, and we thank you, my sister. Is there another query?

(Pause)

I am Q'uo, and we feel that we have exhausted the queries for the nonce, and we would at this time take this opportunity to once again thank each present for the great honor of being invited to join your circle of seeking. We are always overjoyed with this opportunity for we are allowed at these times to move more closely with you upon your journeys and to experience that which you experience through your questions, your comments, your concerns. This allows us to see the action of the one Creator knowing Itself through Its many portions in a way which we are not usually privy to. It is a valiant effort that you make in accomplishing your daily round of activities, remembering the one Creator as you move each foot in front of the other. We know, my brothers and sisters, that this is not an easy task, for the illusion in which you move has been so constructed to obscure the unity and love which binds all things and which is an easy reminder for those such as ourselves. We realize that this experience of the third-density illusion is one which is most confusion—we correct this instrument—most confusing to many of your peoples, for it works so well, does it not, my friends, to hide the one Creator where one would not think of looking—into the eyes of a friend, a stranger, a situation which seems most out of harmony. Yet, there the Creator also resides, my friends, waiting for your seeking, waiting to reach a hand as you reach yours, waiting to respond to each moment, to each breath. We commend your persistence and take courage from your efforts.

At this time we shall take our leave of this instrument and this group, leaving each, as always, in the love and in the light of the one infinite Creator. We are known to you as those of Q'uo. Adonai, my friends. Adonai. ✺

L/L Research

L/L Research is a subsidiary of Rock Creek Research & Development Laboratories, Inc.

P.O. Box 5195
Louisville, KY 40255-0195

www.llresearch.org

Rock Creek is a non-profit corporation dedicated to discovering and sharing information which may aid in the spiritual evolution of humankind.

ABOUT THE CONTENTS OF THIS TRANSCRIPT: This telepathic channeling has been taken from transcriptions of the weekly study and meditation meetings of the Rock Creek Research & Development Laboratories and L/L Research. It is offered in the hope that it may be useful to you. As the Confederation entities always make a point of saying, please use your discrimination and judgment in assessing this material. If something rings true to you, fine. If something does not resonate, please leave it behind, for neither we nor those of the Confederation would wish to be a stumbling block for any.

CAVEAT: This transcript is being published by L/L Research in a not yet final form. It has, however, been edited and any obvious errors have been corrected. When it is in a final form, this caveat will be removed.

© 2009 L/L Research

Sunday Meditation
October 16, 1994

Group question: The question today has to do with the concept of pride. We've been talking about being honest in relationships and how we behave and how we sometimes build a persona, whether it's used positively or negatively. It seems to be used in the way we feel like we will get what we want out of a relationship or communication, whether it is a harmonious experience or being honest or maybe telling a little fib and just letting that go. Our pride seems to be the motivating force behind a lot of the things we do and why we do them and we would like some indication as to perhaps the description of pride, how it arises, if it has any beneficial uses, if pride has a balance to it that we can come in contact with in our daily lives.

(Carla channeling)

Greetings to you in the love and in the light of the one infinite Creator. We are those of Q'uo. May we say how privileged we are to be called to your group this day. We bless and thank each for seeking and for attempting to discover that which is called the truth. We also seek that illusive perfection and are your comrades on the way. Therefore we ask that each listen to our thoughts, retaining only those which have use for you in particular.

To gaze at the pride within an entity is to gaze upon that portion of the self that has been created by the self for the purpose of self-defense. That is, one who has pride has attempted to discover a good, right or noble way to think or behave or speak. Then one adopts the mask that is most efficient, most in line with the desired making of an impression on others. It is as though a man with a modest garden were to put a wall twenty feet high about the garden, certainly more than the garden needs in order to be a protected plot.

The one known as Jesus pointed out that when the spiritual seeker attempts to do everything right in order to become worthy of the kingdom of what this instrument calls heaven—we shall start that sentence again—when a person attempts to reach what this instrument calls heaven by piling up and accumulating good deeds and appropriate attitudes, that path is the center of the emotion or emotional imbalance which can be seen as pride. In the person of pride there is the unspoken assumption that there is one right way. And that by *(inaudible)* to that right way, the self may maintain the attitude of pride, an attitude which functions as an armor against the encroaching world so that the self may hide behind its good works and appropriate attitudes and not uncover that truth which each entity within third density, becoming more conscious of the self, becomes aware of, and that is that there is no possible way to become worthy of the nature which the Creator has shared with each and every entity within the limitless creation.

Now, why is pride considered such an inappropriate emotion or imbalance or distortion for the spiritual seeker? The seeker within the spiritual or metaphysical world is creating itself, nurturing itself within just as the physical self is born with flesh and blood, so the spiritual self may be seen to be born within the consciousness of the seeker when that first choice to seek and to serve is made. The beginner is humble knowing that it is a beginner. This attitude tends quickly to wear off for many seekers and the balance of inquiry and contemplation is overset by each choice which moves away from inquiry and answers new questions with old answers. For the truth or the ideal is actually far more subtle than one truth, one ideal. There are currents and movements within truth which the seeker moves into and out of repeatedly throughout the process of receiving essential input and choosing the portions of that input that the self shall react to in first priority.

If you would characterize pride in a simple way, it could perhaps be seen to represent the Earth itself and the kingdom upon it which humankind has built. In this model or way or parable of seeing pride, the world becomes a worldly, corrupted and imperfect world, whereas the world of the spiritual is seen as that which is better, non-material, a higher way. Spiritual pride may be measured by how far from the everyday experience the seeker has placed itself, by which we mean that if an entity decides it cannot worship or seek or meditate or learn spiritually in the everyday world, then to that extent the entity is dealing with spiritual pride. For the energies that are metaphysical are energies that move as the wind into any situation and burn like fire, tempering and refining in the very crux and heat of the everyday.

Now, we are not saying that those who choose to be solitary or within religious orders and seek spiritually are all filled with pride. We simply say that insofar as an entity seeks, eschewing and looking down upon the world without it, and feeling scorn for that everyday world, to that extent the entity is dealing with a false image or idea or paradigm of what spiritual seeking is about. For the service-to-others seeker the path of seeking lies squarely through servitude and servant ministry. The more of humility and the less of grandeur that seems to adhere to a position or line of investigation, the greater chance that line of investigation has of being a good and appropriate model to follow.

The teacher known as Jesus offered a simple parable which may aid this discussion. This entity pointed out that there was a wealthy man who was very, very careful to say all of his prayers, to cover himself with ashes in the public streets, to show the depth of a religious penitent. This sort of man, then, was seen as one who would say to himself, "I am glad I am not as other men are, thieves and robbers. I have two fast days a week. I give much money to the temple." Then there was another man beside this proud man who only knelt upon the ground and said, "Lord have mercy on me." The one known as Jesus then asked, "Which of these two men went home justified?"

Dear ones, we know that you know the answer. That entity who asked for mercy had a clear and honest awareness of its position, spiritually speaking. For any of the infinite Creator's creatures, the honest evaluation of self shall inevitably include a request for mercy, for there is no way an entity within illusion can build perfection. This is not a goal that we would recommend to any. The striving for perfection is seen by many, and certainly this instrument, to be an important goad, urging the self always onward to a more wholehearted effort, a more total attempt to be perfect. We suggest that a little of this thinking will be adequate. In other words, it is acceptable and wise to keep the ideal in mind, to aim for. However, to give the self the hard time if that perfection is not reached, or to give oneself the patting upon the back if the self perceives perfection has been reached, these are not the ways that shall produce learning.

We find that there is a true desire within each to relate the self back into the society in a way that produces more love, more compassion, more understanding, to make the world a better place. While this is certainly a good attitude, the center or middle way that this entity spoke of earlier must move back into that place where the self is seen as a servant and the question is, "Not my will here, but Thine needs to be known. So Creator, what is Your will for me?" Then if the impulse or inspiration moves to small or great success, neither matters, for the attempt given in wholehearted and single-minded effort is the total and sum of that which metaphysically matters.

To bleach the pride from this attempt to strive towards perfection, simply remove the editor and judge of the self from the picture so that you are free to do your best and then let that be good and sufficient. The pride will take you back many times looking for how the perfection could have been more closely approached. These deliberations are seldom fruitful, for the self shall not build a stairway to heaven by any good works or appropriate attitudes or systems of knowledge and understanding, but, rather, all that you shall judge of yourself after this experience will be held within that basic vibration or thought which is yourself. No works shall you take with you, nor thought, nor attitude, nor behavior, but that vibration that is you, integrated, unified, harmonious and whole. You cannot, by any knowledge or work, no matter how good, affect this vibration. You can only empty the self as often as you can, hoping always to become as the window through which all may see the Creator and all may feel Its love.

You cannot be proud or embarrassed about that vibration because you cannot get at it. You can only work on those things which are beginning, just beginning their descent into the roots of mind. You can only fuss around with responses. It is that sum total that is never seen in your illusion which shall be sum and substance of who you are always forever. It is that which is you. And what is there to be proud or not proud of in something you cannot ever, ever see?

We encourage each to take up the dance of life, dancing around judgment, moving away from vanity and glory and pride, seeking to serve, seeking to be servant. For every entity whom you meet is love itself, and, if you speak always to angels unawares, let your heart be humble, your hands be empty, your heart at rest that you may seek to love, and reach the hand to touch, and lift the heart to share love.

We would at this time transfer this contact to the one known as Jim. We leave this instrument in love and in light. We are those of the principle known to you as Q'uo.

(Jim channeling)

I am Q'uo, and greet each again in love and in light through this instrument. At this time we would offer ourselves in the attempt to speak to any further queries which those present may have for us. Is there a query at this time?

(Pause)

I am Q'uo, and we are satisfied that we have for the [nonce] spoken that which those present need to hear, and we are most grateful to be able to join your group at your invitation. We remind each of you that we are available for aiding the deepening of your meditations during your week, as you call it. A simple mental request is all that is necessary for us to join you in the presence of the one Creator. We, of course, will not speak at that time, but will blend our vibrations with yours that your meditation might be deeper and hopefully richer as well.

At this time we shall take our leave of this group, leaving each, as always, in the love and in the light of the one infinite Creator. We are known to you as those of Q'uo. Adonai, my friends. Adonai. ☥

L/L Research

L/L Research is a subsidiary of Rock Creek Research & Development Laboratories, Inc.

P.O. Box 5195
Louisville, KY 40255-0195

www.llresearch.org

Rock Creek is a non-profit corporation dedicated to discovering and sharing information which may aid in the spiritual evolution of humankind.

ABOUT THE CONTENTS OF THIS TRANSCRIPT: This telepathic channeling has been taken from transcriptions of the weekly study and meditation meetings of the Rock Creek Research & Development Laboratories and L/L Research. It is offered in the hope that it may be useful to you. As the Confederation entities always make a point of saying, please use your discrimination and judgment in assessing this material. If something rings true to you, fine. If something does not resonate, please leave it behind, for neither we nor those of the Confederation would wish to be a stumbling block for any.

CAVEAT: This transcript is being published by L/L Research in a not yet final form. It has, however, been edited and any obvious errors have been corrected. When it is in a final form, this caveat will be removed.

© 2009 L/L Research

Sunday Meditation
October 23, 1994

Group question: Our question this afternoon has to do with the situation that so many of us find ourselves in from time to time where we have a disagreement with someone else and even though we give our very best effort at communicating clearly, being compassionate, and of doing everything that we can think of to bring everyone into harmony, these efforts seem to do nothing other than throw kerosene on the fire. It seems like the negativity and hostility seem to have a life of their own. It seems like one can do nothing to affect the situation, and we are wondering if there is something that can be done. Is there an attitude of mind, of heart, of spirit that we can invoke at these times? Is there some deeper lesson or process going on that we don't really have any idea about? Are we destined to be victims in these situations, or is there something that we can do to bring harmony to the other person, ourselves, and to the situation as a whole?

(Carla channeling)

We are those of Q'uo. Greetings in the love and in the light of the one infinite Creator. It is our privilege and blessing to be sharing this circle of seeking at this time. Your afternoon sun shines so beautifully on this pretty autumn day, and we relish the sights that we see because of our interactions with you. Your planet is most fair.

We thank you for this privilege, and request of each only that you listen with an honest heart, leaving behind any of our thoughts or opinions that do not ring true for you, for we are not infallible, but, rather, travelers upon the Pilgrim's path, as are you.

To begin a discussion of anger within your density one might well move backwards in your historical time to the time when the physical vehicles which carry you about were developing to be opportunities for consciousness of third density but had not yet achieved that third-density link and were completely instinctually second-density beings. You would call these the animal and it is that physical vehicle which transports you and gives you sensual input that is the source of what you call anger, and the source, too, of negative emotion in general.

This animal that carries your consciousness about is a proud and rather noble animal in that it attempts social cooperation. It forms lasting attachments in mating. It cares deeply for its young. This great ape, the featherless biped, makes decisions for its survival. When occurrences overset the plans made for survival the reactions are in place instinctually to alert the mind of this animal that it needs to act. We wish to be sure you grasp the difference between that portion of mind that is the mind of the animal within as separate from and distinct from that consciousness that you truly are. The brain of this animal is a fine one, skilled in making choices. The apparatus for thinking is built around these choices and their prioritizing. This mind begins and ends. It copes with the living it does.

Immersed in this web of flesh, this field of instinctual consciousness, is an eternal awareness. Sitting as the bird in the cage, the awareness that you are and that you will be in ten thousand or ten million years sits rather placidly, for the most part rather unaware of the extent of its confinement in the world of sensual input. This awareness attempts to express its true nature. The awareness that is you shall always attempt to express its true nature. However, this nature has no anger, has no fear, and is free.

Contrariwise, the mind of the body has instincts towards anger which exist because they are needed, or so that animal within is certain. The instincts, those instantaneous responses, ungoverned by logical, reasonable awareness, work usually quite well, landing the seeking pilgrim repeatedly off the beaten track of devotion and lovely thoughts, taking that awareness and flinging it aside in the rush to defend territory. For that animal which you are, which carries your awareness about, is territorial. It measures and sifts. "This is good." "This is mine." "That is bad." "That is not mine." "That should be mine." "That will be mine because I deserve it."

There the anger comes in—the hunger for possession, the hunger for safety, the desire to defend. The search for peace, dear ones, is a search for true identity. Who are you? Are you that limited mind that must protect against unseen danger with the same gusto that was used to defend the self from a predator? Or are you that awareness that gazes unblinking on the human scene, knowing all things as love?

The difficulty is that these two kinds of mentation, this double mind, is supposed to be working together to create maximum confusion. You are supposed to be baffled; you are supposed to be confused; you are supposed to feel that there is almost no hope. This is planned in order that you may do work in consciousness. The great spiritual drives, the great religions [of] your kind, revolve about suffering. Your Eastern strain of religions looks at suffering and, as this instrument has thought recently, says it is not real. The Western tradition looks at the suffering and flings the self upon the cross so that others might not suffer. Both of these paths work for those to whom they are suited.

Each path will have to deal with this issue of suffering. In dealing with the self and the self's anger we encourage each seeker to be patient and to realize and re-seat within the deep mind, over and over again, the dichotomy betwixt the temporal and the eternal. Have mercy upon yourselves for your anger, for indeed that which you see is the mirror, the anger directed at you is within you, like the werewolf baying at the moon that only comes out when the moon is full. Know and accept this part of the dark side of self. There is a price to life. That price often is that one wishes to prolong life, and, therefore, attempts to control all elements so that life is safe, secure and protected. See this within the self. Love this self which has so little time to live, and when it is seen in another, attempt that same degree of understanding. See the fear, the true desire to protect, in the negative emotions of others, for however distorted these emotions are, they are distortions of love.

The energy within anger is so close to the positive extreme of freeing the self that it actually tends to feel good to be angry, for it is in this kind of fire that life is created. The creative principle of love is also the destroying principle of death. Passion has its inevitable counterpoint in tragedy. Life and death go together as concepts. Anger is the other side of the coin of love within limitation.

Let us, then, move back in concept, moving away from the particular, seeing the fear, the suffering, all the negative emotions. See them within the context of life abundant, yielding its harvest of wisdom and compassion to those who simply persist at gazing at that which goes before the eye, comes before the ear, arrives at the nose or the skin. For the creature that you are is most special. We encourage each again and again to touch into this space where love may be felt in the silence, where comfort moves deeply within, opening the heart, relaxing the grip of circumstance. Move away from the particular often within your days and nights, moving in mind to the more profound ground of your being, that eternal, undying awareness beyond all distortions. It is love. You are love. This is the deeper truth.

We would at this time transfer this contact to the one known as Jim. We are those known as Q'uo, and leave this instrument in love and in light.

(Jim channeling)

I am Q'uo, and greet each again in love and in light. We would, at this time, offer ourselves in the attempt to speak to any further queries which those present may have for us. Is there another query at this time?

S: I am wondering if people who come to this planet who have what we call disabilities—what is their special place, and what is their purpose on this planet?

I am Q'uo, and am aware of your query, my sister. It is not an easy task to move within your illusion of third density and to be able to love under the circumstances which one finds here with so much mystery surrounding the basic qualities of your life patterns and interactions betwixt peoples. Yet, one may look at this illusion as one would look at a school which has many grades and many course offerings, all with the purpose of enhancing the student's abilities to give and to receive this most precious quality of love.

Each entity, before the incarnation, will set about reviewing those lessons which have been learned and those which await the learning according to previous incarnational experiences. As each entity is unique, and as the interrelationships enhance this uniqueness, it is difficult to generalize in every situation and yet be accurate. But we can assure you that each entity which incarnates has some, what you would call, a disability—that is, a difficulty or blockage in the free flowing experience of love.

Many have blockages that are from previous incarnational experiences and are expressed in the present incarnational experience and are expressed as a distortion of one kind or another. Each distortion, whether it be of the physical, the mental, the emotional or the spiritual complex has as its purpose the allowing of the learning of love. When love has been absent in some facet of the entity's life pattern the opportunity for adding it to the reservoir of information is usually programmed as a, shall we say, a difficulty or blockage, a distortion in some facet of the being that serves much as the sand for the oyster which will eventually produce the pearl, yet with some irritation in the process, shall we say.

The process of learning to love is one which will oftentimes be experienced in a difficult manner, a traumatic manner, a manner which is intense and rich with opportunity for growth. Only when this type of intensity has been experienced can that which has been learned from it carry a weight in the totality of the being that will enhance that being's total nature. Thus, to learn is to experience a kind of pain, for one is enlarging a portion of the self in a manner much like giving birth for your entities within this illusion. The process of the birth is filled with pain, yet the joy which comes from the birth of a new entity is great; so it is with each entity within your illusion as each continually gives birth to a new portion of the self.

In order for this entire process to make its mark, shall we say, upon the soul, upon the total being, there needs to be the exertion of great effort. Those with what you have called a disability of a physical, mental, emotional, and in some cases, a spiritual nature have increased the degree of difficulty, shall we say, for that learning process. This increased degree of difficulty has as its reward an increased level of learning to love and of allowing others to learn to give love to the self.

Thus, if you look at this illusion as the laboratory in which the student seeks to put to the test those ideals which it holds dear prior to the incarnation one may then see all that occurs within the incarnation as the conducting of the experiment to see if love can be found in this situation, in that situation, in even that situation. For there is an infinity of possibility and opportunity that awaits each entity within the mystery of this particular illusion, for as you seem so separated from each other, from the Creator, from the environment, from those principles of love, truth and beauty and all other principles that are valuable to you, feel yourself isolated, alone and perhaps at times unable to make sense of all that is about you and much that is within you, yet just this dilemma, just this confusion, doubt, anguish and pain is that quality of angst that shall push, provoke and prod you further. These are the ways that the soul has to remind itself in the incarnation that there is yet more to do, and each portion of the incarnation offers the opportunity to give and to receive this precious quality of love, and each circumstance that one finds one's self with is yet another opportunity to give or to receive or perhaps to give and to receive love.

Is there another query, my sister?

S: No, thank you very much for answering that.

I am most grateful for your query, my sister. Is there another query at this time?

A: Can the sensual or animal being be the total person where the spiritual part is not recognized?

I am Q'uo, and am aware of your query, my sister. The nature of the animal which we spoke about earlier which carries each of you about so faithfully is indeed one which has the senses which are rich in their ability to perceive and to bring information into the brain/mind organism in order that the entity may learn, may choose, may grow, and may be able to offer itself eventually as a servant of the one Creator, and, indeed, may realize itself to be the one Creator at some point in its evolutionary path.

The various qualities that compose each entity are always available for utilization of this process of growth. One may see the self and all other selves as being what we have heard described as the 360 degree entity, that is, with all potential, all abilities latently available. As an entity pursues an incarnation with a certain set of lessons revolving about the central quality of love it is possible for an entity to focus upon any set of abilities or even to focus upon one particular quality in preference to all others and for the time of that focus to seem as though it has no other dimensions. This is an intensive form of practice for an entity and will aid an entity in balancing an area which has perhaps been less than fully utilized in its previous experiences.

It may seem to the entity itself and to those which observe it that it has perhaps become overly stimulated or interested in some facet of its being, whether it be the sensual nature of the animal that is each entity's beginning or basic self within this illusion. It is possible for entities to move so far into a portion of the self that it becomes blinded to other portions of its self. However, we see the cycles of your lives moving endlessly as a spiral through time and space and can assure each that there is ample opportunity for the balancing of all distortions and the experiencing of the self as a true 360 degree being, which is another way of saying experiencing the self as the Creator.

Is there another query, my sister?

Questioner: *(Inaudible).*

Is there another query at this time?

R: In the moment when you feel the anger pulsing through you, is there anything that you can do to benefit from the anger or to deal with it?

I am Q'uo, and am aware of your query, my brother. It is our suggestion that as you experience all of the emotions including anger which are available to you that you allow them to spontaneously …

(Side one of tape ends.)

(Jim channeling)

… Only if the expression of your anger has the possibility of injuring another person would we recommend that you damp it down, shall we say. Far better is it to experience the emotions as they occur and then to work with them later in your meditative times, balancing the anger with the love that naturally replaces it when one sees the object of the anger as the other self and as the Creator as well.

It is well at that time to investigate the complete ramifications of the situation which brought about the anger and to use the mental faculties then. To do so at the time of the experiencing of the anger is to confuse the process that is moving through you and is to pull the reins too tightly upon the animal upon which you ride. Far better, as we have said, to do this analysis at a later time which, as the process continues, may allow you to find more harmonious means of relating to the entity for which you experienced the anger previously.

The efforts to rectify difficult situations can oftentimes lead to breakthrough experiences with the other self as hearts open honestly to each other. That this does not occur often makes the desire for it all the greater in those who wish to give and to receive love within your illusion. The constant desire and effort made in this direction is that which builds within you the metaphysical or spiritual power which is much like the power of any battery which stores energy. As you increase the positive polarization the battery has the ability to do more work.

This is so in conscious[ness] as you intend, and intend, and intend and work without stint to attempt to find love within the self, within others, and within the situations that you share. That you shall feel that you fail most of the time is not of central importance. Of central importance is that you continue to try.

Is there another query, my brother?

R: No. Thank you.

I am Q'uo, and we thank you, my brother. Is there a final query at this time?

(Pause)

I am Q'uo, and as we observe we have exhausted both the queries and some of the physical vehicles present from sitting overly long, we shall, at this time, thank each once again for inviting our presence. We are most grateful for your invitation and for your dedication to learning. We walk with you upon your path and rejoice at the opportunity of sharing our opinions with you. We shall take our leave of this instrument and this group, leaving each in the love and the light of the one infinite Creator. We are known to you as those of Q'uo. Adonai, my friends. Adonai.

L/L Research

L/L Research is a subsidiary of Rock Creek Research & Development Laboratories, Inc.

P.O. Box 5195
Louisville, KY 40255-0195

www.llresearch.org

Rock Creek is a non-profit corporation dedicated to discovering and sharing information which may aid in the spiritual evolution of humankind.

ABOUT THE CONTENTS OF THIS TRANSCRIPT: This telepathic channeling has been taken from transcriptions of the weekly study and meditation meetings of the Rock Creek Research & Development Laboratories and L/L Research. It is offered in the hope that it may be useful to you. As the Confederation entities always make a point of saying, please use your discrimination and judgment in assessing this material. If something rings true to you, fine. If something does not resonate, please leave it behind, for neither we nor those of the Confederation would wish to be a stumbling block for any.

CAVEAT: This transcript is being published by L/L Research in a not yet final form. It has, however, been edited and any obvious errors have been corrected. When it is in a final form, this caveat will be removed.

© 2009 L/L Research

Sunday Meditation
October 30, 1994

Group question: We are going to take pot luck on our question this afternoon with the feeling that all of the conversation we've had previously concerning how people with 180 degree opposite realities and interpretations from ours in our experience can help us to look within for a direction for our own seeking that is neither too stubbornly consistent with our own thinking in spite of other people's opinions and which would take other people's opinions too much into account so that we are constantly changing our course. We would be interested in hearing what Q'uo has to say about this and the other topics that we talked about this afternoon.

(Carla channeling)

We are those of Q'uo. Greetings in the love and in the light of the one infinite Creator. We apologize for the delay, but this instrument was challenging a spirit which eventually had to leave. We commend this instrument for its care. Accepting that particular vibration was well not done.

The vibratory complex of this entity was very like a well known and familiar contact. However, this spirit was of the service-to-self polarity. This describes the kind of difficulty each seeking spirit has in attempting to learn from other selves who, as you were speaking of earlier this afternoon, show a façade of behavior which seems to vibrate in a positive manner. The actual vibratory complex of one service to self seems on the surface to be robust and strong, full of energy, and when a negative [spirit] wishes it so, the imitation, shall we say, of that familiar light vibration is almost precisely as positive energy on the surface.

The challenging of spirits, then, is a process of digging deeper within the self to find that ground of being which rings so true within the self that that which does not ring true within and below the surface of that spirit's façade is detected and isolated so that it can be sensibly decided whether or not to accept that particular spirit. This is not the work done quickly, and we confirm this instrument's suspicion that it shall be learning for as long as it continues to avail itself of the opportunity to do that which is called channeling.

Each entity, each self that you meet is just such a spirit as that which was discerned accurately by this instrument, and each of you, each in your way, is capable of the same challenging of spirits dealing with those other selves with whom you interact day by day. The truth of an individual is a unified vibratory complex, a state of being. The exterior of this state of beingness might be seen as a ball or orb. Now, this orb has the surface and that within. The surface tends to be regular and unblemished. Within that sphere of being, however, the various internal connections made by choices chosen and re-chosen over a period of time will come to differ in various ways from the seeming truth of that smooth-surfaced orb.

Now, the way in which the seeker attempts to grow may be seen in one way to be simply a matter of the seeker looking at the vibratory complex which is the Creator or intelligent infinity brought into manifestation, so that the goal of each seeker is to so act and think that the vibratory complex which is the truth of that seeker becomes more and more like the vibration of love, the Logos, the great original Thought Itself. The spirit within seeks and yearns for deity, unity and rest. This completely natural process of spiritual evolution moves on instinct within the life of the seeker so that there is a ground of being within which becomes slowly, gradually awakened as that attempt to move closer to the love and wisdom of the infinite One is followed persistently.

Now, if a seeker finds that it is experiencing turmoil and difficulty with several entities at once or over a period of time then it is that the entity does need to gaze into that mirror and ask why this image so painful to see keeps recurring. However, in those remarks made previous to this session of working, it was said between each in the group that these were occurrences within the life path [were] remarkable for their rarity, that it was remarkable that such and such occurred. When this rare occurrence happens and it is not often repeated, then the seeker may relax that question within, "Is this my vibratory complex which I am perceiving?"

However, even though the seeker looks into the mirror and sees no true reflection, yet, still that too, for all its rarity, is part and parcel of the self, and it is well to open consciously to the task of accepting and reintegrating into the full self, that shadowed, darkened portion of self which can be seen to be grossly distorted so that the mirroring effect is that of the carnival fun house, or "house of mirrors," where you may be two feet tall and four feet wide in one mirror and ten feet tall in the next.

However, these entities have gifts to give. They are people, as you, suffering as you. That suffering has overwhelmed them, just as suffering overwhelms all entities in your illusion from time to time. We see that none has chosen in the personal experiences under discussion to seek revenge or to correct or judge the other. This is well. However, more than this also may be done. Refraining from judgment is well, but there is still that suffering that has come to your attention. Given this information, the seeker then has the honor of responding to that suffering. It may be the response of one who holds the entity in the mind to send light to it. It may be that the personal style of the seeker is such that prayers within each daily offering might be included for that suffering soul, but whatever the way chosen to nurture, support and tend that entity in thought, in silence, in that which is divine within each, this is the work of consciousness with regard to others.

The challenge always is to see distortion without being distorted by it to the extent that balanced action becomes impossible. It is the work of many years, as this instrument would measure time, indeed, the work of many incarnations to begin to respond to the suffering that is given to the self as though the self were responsible for that suffering. That presents the prime challenge, for the self wants to correct that misperception, "Oh, no, I am innocent." However, in such an entity's mind the ways of thinking and behaving have become hardened or crystallized and that entity is a prisoner within those distortions just as each imprisons or frees itself again and again simply by how it chooses to think. It is well to see that each entity creates its own prison and chooses its own freedom. The prison walls are felt when they limit and hold an entity where it wishes not to be limited or held. To one who is blaming others much is lost of sense. To one who works rather with the constant attempt at new or non-crystallized mind the limits are not immediately there or obviously there. So the more the seeker refrains from distortions in making judgments, the more freedom that seeker creates for the self.

As the seeker working with service-to-others polarity develops, many, many opportunities are given that test, teach and help to develop the values and choices that seeker has made. Distortion [is] to some extent due to the illusory quality of the face of reality within your incarnative experience. All is distortion seen from the viewpoint of intelligent infinity. It is not then necessarily a bad thing to be distorted, it being impossible to avoid. The wise seeker, however, attempts so to make choices that it does not become boxed in and bound up with judgment and opinion which more and more hides the eye from the full range of present and continuing change.

In sum, we would encourage each to seek within always that Creator's perfect original Thought, to seek that state of being which is deity, and to find within that relationship the energy which moves one to seek more, to hope more, to offer the self with less reserve to the work which is prepared by the infinite One for each day of the incarnation. Moving upon that plumb line of connection with the Creator, the seeker finds it increasingly easy to be persistent in practice, in seeking the good, the true, the beautiful, in seeking to express love. As the seeker becomes more loving it may find it must work upon receiving love, and then when an entity such as you have spoken of comes to you to share its suffering with you, you might not need to pull away from this distortion, for you have not the fear that blinds you from seeing this suffering spirit.

In your heart hug this suffering soul and bless it as it moves along its life path, for much sorrow and suffering shall be for that entity, and by its choices it is more and more isolated. Let your heart become softer and softer, more and more open and willing to love when the surface picture is no longer beautiful, good or true, for just as within the self who attempts to make the impression, the surface is gleaming but the interior may not be. With the unhappy soul who screams and abuses, even that surface has become marred, yet within there lies in perfection the one infinite Creator, and the truth of this entity remains deity. As you love, as you serve, look always to that infinite, original Thought which is love and see the life fall into place.

May you love each other in good and in evil times. May you redeem each other by forgiving, and may you allow suffering to occur with your sympathy, for these are the sorrows of one who is growing and learning, and from these mean beginnings shall come great heights of learning and service. Nothing is truly as that which it seems, for there is one truth beyond all appearance and that truth which unifies all can be seen by none in fullness. Yet, as you seek and seek again, over and over and over, so shall you become free.

This instrument has a prayer within her church with the phrase, "in whose service is perfect freedom." My friends, as you seek always to serve that highest truth within know that each seemingly slavish action, each act of humility, is that which increases freedom. Find that simplicity as you move in the dance of your days and your life.

We would, at this time, transfer this contact to the one known as Jim. We leave this instrument in love and in light. We are those of Q'uo.

(Jim channeling)

I am Q'uo, and greet each again in love and in light through this instrument. We are honored at this time to be able to ask if there is any other query to which we may speak as a portion of our service with you this day. Is there another query at this time?

P: I wonder if you could give me any insight as to what I have been experiencing for the past three years in my relationship with my ex-husband?

I am Q'uo, and we would need a more specific type of query in order to respond in a fashion which does not infringe upon one's free will. We are not free, by our own decision, to pluck those concerns of most importance from your mind and from your heart without your first delineating them yourself. Is there a more specific manner in which you may phrase this query?

P: No. I think I will think about it. Thank you.

I am Q'uo. And we are grateful, my sister, even in the general form which we may make a small response to, since it is so general. However, the broad nature of the response may not satisfy and thus may bring forth a more specific query.

The nature of any relationship is a placing in dynamic tension, shall we say, of two different points of view that have enough points of agreement in common that there is the attraction, one to the other, for the purpose of further illumination of that which is mysterious. The points of commonality, then, which form the basis of the initial attraction are the first areas to be explored in any relationship and are those areas which shall begin the process of providing catalyst as each entity moves from that which is known to that which is unknown within the self and within the relationship. As this movement continues for each entity, other areas of the self and of the relationship become available to the light of shared consciousness. As these other areas are explored and are added to the catalyst-producing process, the relationship is continually altered and there are changes in the perception of the other self for each entity, and in the relationship itself as well. As this process continues, it is the question of the strength of the original attraction, those areas of commonality, that will determine whether there is the continuing growth of that acceptance of common ground, shall we say, within each entity.

As this process continues there develops the quality of harmony or the quality of disharmony depending upon the basic areas of agreement and the primary desire of each entity to be able to open the self enough to each other so that each entity is offered the opportunity to accept not only one's own self but the other's self as well as a part of the growing self of the relationship and the growing desire of each entity to place that relationship self before the smaller self.

As you can surmise from this model of relationship that we have constructed, there are numerous opportunities for each entity to reject either a portion of the self that is one's own or a portion of the self belonging to the other or a portion of the greater self being created by both.

The desire of each entity to truly be in relationship and be willing and able to undergo this process becomes the true strength of the relationship.

(Side one of tape ends.)

(Jim channeling)

We shall continue, with thanks to the one known as P for the assistance with the recording device.

To continue—each entity will have continuing opportunities to choose to give that which the relationship needs at the moment, or to continue to hoard for the self that which is felt to be needed.

This is a dynamic which all entities partake in as they join in groupings with other selves. This is the illusion of third density where the social self is explored as an extension of the smaller self that exists within the family structure, and, indeed, with the individual self that exists within its own perceptions. The continual expansion of the self outward is a preparation for the process of becoming what you have called the social memory complex, where each entity, although quite distinct and individual in its expression and experiences, willingly blends the vibrations of its soul self with others of its own kind or desire for seeking.

Thus, the relationships which you experience within your own illusion are preparation for that which is to come as well as a continuation of the process which has been ongoing for this entire third-density illusion, that of the development of the self to the point it is willing and able to become a greater self.

Is there a further query, my sister?

P: This is not a question. To restate what you said—to transform our smaller identities into larger ones to become ready to establish a social memory complex. Is that right?

I am Q'uo, and this is quite correct, my sister. Although it is also well to make note of the individual process of growth that occurs in any relationship due to the mirroring effect, there is also the opportunity for the self to expand into a greater and greater self.

Is there a further query, my sister?

P: No, thank you.

Is there another query?

(Pause)

I am Q'uo, and we are most grateful for your invitation to us once again, and we cannot thank you enough for the honor and joy of blending our vibrations with yours as you seek your own paths of truth and light, my brothers and sisters.

We would, at this time, take our leave of this instrument and this group, leaving each, as always, in the love and in [the] light of the one infinite Creator. We are known to you as those of Q'uo. Adonai, my friends. Adonai. ✦

L/L Research

L/L Research is a subsidiary of Rock Creek Research & Development Laboratories, Inc.

P.O. Box 5195
Louisville, KY 40255-0195

www.llresearch.org

Rock Creek is a non-profit corporation dedicated to discovering and sharing information which may aid in the spiritual evolution of humankind.

ABOUT THE CONTENTS OF THIS TRANSCRIPT: This telepathic channeling has been taken from transcriptions of the weekly study and meditation meetings of the Rock Creek Research & Development Laboratories and L/L Research. It is offered in the hope that it may be useful to you. As the Confederation entities always make a point of saying, please use your discrimination and judgment in assessing this material. If something rings true to you, fine. If something does not resonate, please leave it behind, for neither we nor those of the Confederation would wish to be a stumbling block for any.

CAVEAT: This transcript is being published by L/L Research in a not yet final form. It has, however, been edited and any obvious errors have been corrected. When it is in a final form, this caveat will be removed.

© 2009 L/L Research

Sunday Meditation
November 6, 1994

Group question: The question this afternoon has to do with healing. We would like to know what are the prerequisites for healing, when is healing appropriate for an entity, when would healing not be appropriate for an entity to experience, and just anything in general that you can tell us about the healing process and how we can partake in it.

(Carla channeling)

We are those of Q'uo. Greetings in the love and in the light of the infinite Creator. It is a blessing to be called to your circle of seeking, and we thank each who joins this circle for the privilege of being asked to share our opinions with you on this subject of healing, reminding each, as always, that we are fallible and prone to error. Therefore, we request that each person listen with discrimination, rejecting those things which do not seem fruitful for you, and retaining only those truths which have the quality of being remembered rather than being strange, for those truths which are yours are as those memories which are awakened.

As we gaze at the substantial subject of healing we find that perhaps the first item on our agenda is the crystallization of a common grasp of the term "healing," for not all who are cured are healed, and not all who are healed are cured of any indisposing illness or condition. When a cure is effected there is a clear and physical process involved: a diagnosis of pathology is made; harsh chemicals are often given; the physical body sometimes is cut into and adjustments made to the various processes of the physical vehicle. The patient, then, is pronounced cured, for that illness has been vanquished, or that condition has been fixed, as a mechanic would fix a car.

A healing, on the other hand, is a state of balance within the entity. Illnesses and conditions are sometimes evidence of imbalance, blockage or weakness. At other times that illness or condition which is not cured is, on the other hand, balanced. This is true of those who carry an illness or condition in order to learn a lesson concerning love, and many there are who do choose some indisposing condition, not for the joy of it, but for the precise kind of suffering which shall ensue.

Next, we would gaze at the fear which your people understandably express concerning illness, severe illness, and death itself. As this instrument is most familiar with those teachings of the one known as Jesus, we would move now into some of this teacher's sayings. Most people know these sayings as the "beatitudes." "Blessed are the poor in heart." "Blessed are they who are reviled or persecuted," and so forth. Each blessed entity is blessed because of its suffering. When illness comes, suffering does also come, yet it is from the suffering that the blessing is received.

So, where does this great fear come from concerning these illnesses and this ill health? Certainly, it is easy to see where a great deal of fear is engendered. One need only gaze at the passing of the seasons to see that the seasons of decay and death are within each living entity. As each was born, so each shall pass from this illusion. However, the physical vehicle does not wish to decay or to die. There is a deep and primal instinct towards the continuance of living, the prolongation of the breath. That is a necessary portion of the physical instinctual net of reactions and responses to stimuli. Although this is instinctual, it need not be the attitude which a seeker might choose to work with within the daily life, for the entity that each seeker is is infinitely more than the physical vehicle.

The forces of finity and limitation are here for very good purposes, but they work upon the consciousness of a being that is eternal and unlimited, either by space or by time. This consciousness and awareness which each has in common is that which endures as though there were no space or time, but only infinity and eternity. This being which each seeker is is a being of pure love, that primal and original energy which created all that there is. When this awareness, which is the deepest portion of your identity, is first housed within the physical vehicle which carries you about, the limitation and frustration of being in that heavy chemical vehicle is immense.

The awareness of the total being, then, begins the incarnation on bad terms with the physical body. The awareness that you are could not make its arms and legs move or its tongue speak for such a long, long time, and, indeed, the awareness never seems to completely embrace the physical vehicle. This distance which is perceived between the self and the ills of the body is an imbalanced perception, and we encourage each in the daily meditation and contemplation which each may offer to the Creator to do work which more and more creates that bond of unity between consciousness and physical vehicle. Much of illness is due to the disrespect paid to the physical body as that which is not holy.

So, if the physical vehicle has the aches, the pains, then we suggest and encourage giving this situation respect and attention. This attention may be simply seeing the physical vehicle as the perfect mechanism, which it is. It may be sending light to those portions of the physical body which are perceived as hurting or ill. Each seeker may find its own way of coming more and more into loving relationship with the physical body, but it is work which will aid in the balance or health of the body, mind and spirit together.

We can give no clear or provable way to determine whether or not an illness or condition is ready to be dropped from the experience of the awareness. Consequently, the seeker must pursue this question for itself, for it is a fairly important question. If the seeker has no idea what the illness may be working upon it may ask for the clear dream, or it may go to the hypnotherapist, and ask the higher self to give a reading on whether or not that illness or condition has done its condign work and is ready to be dropped. Once the seeker has decided for itself that the illness is ready to be dropped, then it may choose the manner of its healing.

For some few entities the only healing necessary is the seating of the realization of why the illness had virtue and was needed. Perhaps the seeker feels that the lesson has been learned. Then the seeker becomes ready for the next step in healing which is to gaze carefully into health and wellness, seeing if the self is ready to take responsibility for the work of living which is given to each healthy entity. For there are times when the lesson has been learned but the healing will not prevail because the seeker is not ready to take up that lesson which full mobility and lack of limitation shall surely offer.

We ask each to see the subtlety of the process of healing. Each entity responds to different stimuli. One entity might be healed because of another entity which was able to create the atmosphere within which the seeker could indeed take responsibility. Much of the therapist of psychologists and psychiatrists is involved in bringing such material before the seeker and aiding in the grasping of this material. Some there are who will find changing the diet to be helpful, for others this would not have the effect. Each entity has an unique balance. Each entity, then, shall need to find its unique healing. What works for another may not work for you.

The energies within the physical, mental, emotional and spiritual bodies are infinitely, carefully, lovingly arranged so as to express a central vibration which is the essential self manifesting at this space and time. The higher healings, then, will more and more pinpoint that essence, that essential vibration, and find ways of increasing the harmony with which that vibration may move. The best of the techniques for opening this essential nature and clarifying it remain meditation, contemplation, prayer, and as this group was speaking before, the remembering of that context of sacredness within which all of what is known as life and all that is known as death involve. All is sacred. That which your feet rest upon this moment is holy ground.

Pause to feel the breath that moves in, the breath that moves out. The health begins with the breathing deeply in and deeply out, and feeling the peace of breathing in and breathing out, for no matter what an entity may do, it shall breathe in and breathe out. No matter how complex the life of the mind and emotions becomes the physical vehicle expresses the infinite Creator by the living breath—in and out. You breathe into you the love of the infinite Creator and breathe out of you all that is tired, old and ready to leave. So you take in health with each inhalation, and express the detritus of imbalance with each and every exhalation. Healing is not a process which stops. Rather, each entity is constantly in a state of healing, balancing and strengthening that energy web which is your essence.

At this time we would transfer this contact to the one known as Jim. This is indeed a substantial subject, and we have not exhausted it by any means. However, this instrument is beginning to give us signals that we need to move on. Therefore, we leave this instrument in love and in light and with thanks. We now transfer to the one known as Jim. We are those of Q'uo.

(Jim channeling)

I am Q'uo, and greet each again in love and in light through this instrument. It is our honor at this time to offer ourselves in the attempt to speak to any further queries which those present may find valuable in the asking. Is there another query at this time?

P: I have a question. I would like to ask, how can you help a person who you perceive may need healing without infringing upon their free will?

I am Q'uo, and am aware of your query, my sister. Many times in the history of this particular planetary sphere have those of Confederation origin asked that same query, for there have been many, many instances where there were groupings of your peoples who were much in need of healing, yet we were not asked by them to offer healing. Thus, we have found in our own experience that to send these entities love and light and the wishes for the regaining of the whole balance is the most that we can do without infringing upon an entity's free will, for in order to be of service to an entity in an overt manner one must be invited by that entity to attempt to serve.

To attempt to serve without invitation is not a service, in our humble opinion. Thus, even though the desire may be great to reach out the hand in service to another, without the invitation it is only possible to send these entities love and light for the use that they may have for it, whatever that use may be.

Is there another query, my sister?

P: No, thank you, Q'uo.

I am Q'uo, and we thank you, my sister. Is there another query?

Questioner: I have a question. If the individual finds this balance, and, will they be open to healing?

I am Q'uo, and we believe that we grasp your query, my sister. If an entity is able to find a balance within itself in an area which has been imbalanced, then this finding of wholeness becomes the foundation stone upon which the healing of the entity is built, for it is true for each entity that as wholeness, unity and perfection are realized deep within the self, then that which is in need of healing is indeed healed.

An entity may seek the healing process from any number of sources, yet there shall be no healing until the entity itself—through the catalyst of others, perhaps—finds this wholeness and this perfection. Thus, the healing follows the finding of this wholeness.

Is there another query, my sister?

Questioner: Yes. *(Inaudible)* speak of regarding this wholeness, or feeling of wholeness. Are there any other tools?

I am Q'uo, and am aware of your query, my sister. There are many tools, as you have put it, that are available to an entity for the finding of the wholeness within. There are, for example, the uses of meditation, contemplation, the prayerful attitude, which are most helpful in preparing the entity for healing. There is the examined life, shall we say, that looks at the need for healing and sees many behaviors, perceptions, thoughts and attitudes, which flow from the distorted being that is in need of healing. These behaviors and attitudes may be worked upon by the conscientious seeker to bring them into a balanced state. The entity may seek the healing catalysis from one of your medical profession that may utilize any number of healing modalities that themselves become tools for the healing to occur.

The entity, in the long run, shall we say, will rely upon an inner faith that will take form in whatever manner has meaning to the entity. This faith will then provide a channel, or a doorway, through which the healing efforts of others may move into the life pattern of the one to be healed. Thus, you may find that there are many, many tools available to an entity seeking healing, yet the attitude of this entity and its ability to exercise its own faith, coupled with the entity's work in consciousness focused upon its own patterns of thought and behavior, are those tools which are most efficacious in this healing process.

Is there another query, my sister?

Questioner: No, thank you very much.

I am Q'uo, and we thank you, my sister. Is there another query?

Questioner: Yes. There are people that seek to help and heal others, yet the reception is not there, especially among the *(inaudible)*. How much effort and energy does one put in to reaching out when one sees and realizes that they are pushing you away. It's done out of love and concern for these individuals. What *(inaudible)* to do?

I am Q'uo, and am aware of your query, my brother. When the healing and loving efforts offered to another are not accepted, it is well, then, to leave the door open to such entities that they will know that they are welcome always to move through that door and to accept that which is offered. More than this is not possible to accomplish without the infringement upon the free will of another, for it is necessary for entities to seek in order to find. It is not usually possible to find for another that which it does not seek. Thus, to remain open in the heart, to remain open in the offering, and to continue to give that of love from your heart to the other's heart without expectation of return is the most that can be done. This is difficult for many who seek to be of service, especially to those that are loved dearly, yet it is that which must be accepted, for the free will of each entity is of paramount importance. For any progress to be made, the steps must be taken by each entity for the self.

Is there another query, my brother?

Questioner: No, thank you very much.

I am Q'uo, and we thank you, my brother. Is there another query?

Questioner: Yes, I have one more question. What *(inaudible)* an entity to be a healer—would perform healing?

I am Q'uo, and am aware of your query, my sister. In order for an entity to serve as an healer it is necessary in most cases for the entity to have worked enough upon the self within the energy centers or chakras that its centers of energy are in enough balance that the energies that may be used for healing can move through them with minimal distortion. These healing energies, then, are utilized as a means by which the one to be healed's auric field will be temporarily interrupted in order to allow the older, more distorted pattern of thought to be replaced by a newer, more harmonious pattern of thought that will allow the healing to occur. This is the process, whether the entity needing the healing seeks such from one of your orthodox medical professionals or from an entity that offers the healing catalyst from the more metaphysical background, or modality, of healing. It is necessary for the healer, then, to be able to assist in the interruption of the older patterns of thought that exist within the aura of the one to be healed.

(Tape ends.)

L/L Research

L/L Research is a subsidiary of Rock Creek Research & Development Laboratories, Inc.

P.O. Box 5195
Louisville, KY 40255-0195

www.llresearch.org

Rock Creek is a non-profit corporation dedicated to discovering and sharing information which may aid in the spiritual evolution of humankind.

ABOUT THE CONTENTS OF THIS TRANSCRIPT: This telepathic channeling has been taken from transcriptions of the weekly study and meditation meetings of the Rock Creek Research & Development Laboratories and L/L Research. It is offered in the hope that it may be useful to you. As the Confederation entities always make a point of saying, please use your discrimination and judgment in assessing this material. If something rings true to you, fine. If something does not resonate, please leave it behind, for neither we nor those of the Confederation would wish to be a stumbling block for any.

CAVEAT: This transcript is being published by L/L Research in a not yet final form. It has, however, been edited and any obvious errors have been corrected. When it is in a final form, this caveat will be removed.

© 2009 L/L Research

Sunday Meditation
November 13, 1994

Group question: The question today has to do with the attitude that might be most helpful when in our daily round of activities we find ourselves in the position of having to change our plans and having to surrender to a new set of circumstances. We wonder if there is a value to this being out of balance, to this learning by trial by fire, if there is a way that we can adjust our perception or responses and our thinking to help this process go more smoothly. Is it helpful if it does that? What can we do to help ourselves in such a situation?

(Carla channeling)

We are those of Q'uo. Greetings in the love and in the light of the infinite Creator. How pleased we are that you have called us to your meeting this day. It is a privilege to be asked to share our humble opinions with this circle of seeking and we greet and bless each who has thought this day to seek the truth, for surely there is no greater desire, no better hope than the seeking of that truth which is not transient, for years and millennia pass, yet above all space and time the truth remains perfect, whole and utter. All else, all in manifestation is illusion. But, oh, what an illusion. And into this illusion come entities across the timeless into this particular coordinate system. What unimaginably long journeys has each spark of consciousness traveled and, oh, how long the journey ahead still lies waiting.

You wished this day to ponder ways to deal skillfully with the untoward catalyst of the daily life. May we say that we also work with this catalyst, that higher densities as you call them remain nonetheless the native land of impatience and frustration, for we too seek the truth, and yet that truth recedes in front of us infinitely, so that we always are reaching and never grasping. Yet we suggest to you that this reaching has independent merit, that is, a merit independent of an outcome.

Now, as we share these thoughts may we please ask each to use discrimination as each hears these concepts, for we would not constitute a stumbling block for any. Therefore, if that which we say seems good to you then you are most welcome to these thoughts. If, on the other hand, anything which we say does not ring true then leave that thought behind, for this is not your truth. Always we urge each seeker to safeguard its own powers of discrimination when listening to any opinion, no matter how authoritative it may seem, for truth has two faces. One is hidden, the other is an illusion. You dwell now with an illusion, yet when you leave this illusion, no matter how many truths you can name, yet still the truth itself shall not be in these things, but [merely] the shadow which the truth invisible and eternal creates. Beyond all imagining lies that mystery, that collector of paradoxes, that is the one great original Thought, Love or Logos.

Move as we pretend that we are living one of your days. Come with us into your third-density illusion. The morning dawns, and the seeker awakes. Shall it remember the Creator this morning? The day stretches ahead unsullied, pristine, without any flaw apparent to the eye. Those with the orderly minds immediately begin sorting through those duties and chores which are first to do upon the usual long, long list of things to do. A structure begins to take shape within the mind. Then the seeker moves into the quick paced rush of full morning and broad noon and by early afternoon the schedule has been first changed, then changed radically, and then perhaps discarded entirely.

Another seeker, one who does not have the orderly mind, awakens in the morning with the dawn. Does it remember the Creator? This entity moves into the day, its mind responsive to that chore and duty that first comes to greet the eye. This entity begins to work with that concern until a second item catches the eye, and for this careless one the day is quickly spent in moving between this and that chore or pleasure doing a little of this and a little of that.

We say to you that each of these ways is a skillful way to move through the day. The Earthly personality that you are should indeed follow its nature. If one is orderly, then make the list; if one enjoys freedom, seeing it not as chaos but as the liberty to do that which feels right, this entity has at the end of the day completed perhaps the same amount of the orderly one. Yet have they thought of the Creator today?

We now ask each to seek within the self. As you awoke, what thought you? Did you think of the Creator first or last or in the middle? You seek skills and resources for learning better to flow with the catalyst as it is presented to you, and there are certainly many ways in which the self may remind the self that it truly wishes to transform its stale, stiff and seemingly deadening over-regularity. Yet, beyond all these skills lies a basic attitude which, once grasped and persistently returned to, shall substantially transform each experience which occurs within the consciousness of the one who remembers. You see, beyond any logical, linear plan for improving the flow of events lies a simple attitude that contains more wisdom than all learning placed together. That wisdom is a point of view which includes as its primary relationship a real, living, conversational relationship with the one infinite Creator.

The key phrase that addresses the whole ray of questions concerning right use of time, energy and talent, is that which the teacher known to you as Jesus stated: "Not my will, but thine." You see, you and your consciousness are as the tip of a great iceberg. Your self, that profound and illimitable self that you truly are, has only a small amount of selfhood showing. That selfhood is wrapped within your personality, or your ego, if you will. It is not supposed to show, for indeed that true self is to you a goal towards which you strive in consciousness, for when your consciousness is awakened fully, then you shall see that you have held the truth safely within your deep mind all of your existence. Moreover, this silent wisdom, that spark of love within, moves into and transforms pain, suffering, misunderstanding and each and every negative emotion. It is as though the seeker dug within the earth of selfhood, making the garden of self broken [up] into smaller and smaller clumps of self, until the self has become broken up completely and lies ready and fallow for the seeds of new transformation.

The earth within you, your sticks and stones of expectation, must be broken up so that good seed may be planted in the soil of your lives. This plowing of the self in order to plant new awareness is painful. It feels as though the self were being torn down like an old house, and that old self is being torn down. Yet we have a promise, and that is that that which is being torn down shall seem to you in the future not a self. When service to others is attempted, you serve not only that personality but primarily you serve the Creator self within that is the truth of that entity. Therefore, pour yourselves out in service to others, worrying not whether you have succeeded, but only working toward more purity of desire to serve.

Above all let not your heart be troubled. This is under your conscious control, if you choose to claim the mastery over the self. Work when you can towards that point of balance, within which you are able to see clearly, not removing yourselves from the thick of things, but rather bringing into the thick of things that sacred aspect, that relationship with the Creator within. An attitude is only one word, yet this attitude is the key to the spiritual devotional life, for all things are sacred to the one who has the eyes to see, the ears to hear, and the heart to understand.

We would continue this channeling through the one known as Jim. We would leave this instrument in love and in light. We are those of Q'uo.

(Jim channeling)

I am Q'uo, and greet each again in love and in light through this instrument. It is our privilege to be with this group this day and we are most grateful to be invited to enjoin you in your seeking for truth. At this time we would ask if there might be any other queries that those present would have for us.

E: I'd like to ask if it is possible to stay with another by leaving this incarnation when they do.

I am Q'uo, and I am aware of your query, my brother. We are aware of many of your peoples who do this very thing. The process of evolving in mind, in body, and in spirit is a process that is much aided by grouping of entries undertaking this effort together so that there is the sharing of many, many life experiences that together are able to offer the appropriate circumstances for pursuing the balances that each entity is desirous of achieving. It is often helpful for such grouping of entities to exchange the positions within your illusion that have been shared in previous incarnational experiences, so that in one experience there is the assuming of the identity of perhaps a sibling to another, and in a further incarnation, these entities shall perhaps be friends or mates, or be related in another fashion that has meaning to each that is relative to previous experience and also to the present objective of learning.

Indeed, we find that it is more nearly the common case for clans or groups of like-minded entities to move together through the third-density illusion and those which follow it. Oftentimes these groupings will enlarge themselves as further contact is made with other entities that will enhance this process for each grouping. It is well for those entities comprising the groupings to be able to rely upon fellow travelers, shall we say, to provide the appropriate assistance, catalyst, challenges and support for this process of discovering the heart of love within each entity and to enhance the expression of this love in each succeeding incarnation.

Is there a further query, my brother?

E: No.

I am Q'uo. Is there another query at this time?

P: Yes, I would to ask about the point of surrender. How to know when to remain in control and when to surrender?

I am Q'uo, and I am aware of your query, my sister. We feel it is an important point that one be aware that though one might give great value and effort to the quality of control, that it is not possible to retain control in the ultimate sense within your illusion, for there is the necessity to offer oneself to the moment of inspiration. This is to say that surrender in the fullest sense will prove to be a far, far better friend than any ability to control events or entities about one. It is even difficult, my sister to be in control …

(Side one of tape ends.)

(Jim channeling)

I am Q'uo, and am again with this instrument. Again we would thank the one known as P for the assistance with the recording device.

The surrender of the self at each opportunity is far more helpful than attempting control, though we do understand the need to feel that one has a definite effect upon the surroundings and the situations that one finds oneself in. However, it is more helpful to examine and experience the spontaneous responses to each situation, rather than to construct the desired outcome and then attempt to cause the situation to fit into this desired outcome.

The reason that surrender has far more value to the seeker than does control is that in surrender to the spontaneity of the heart one may get a truer reading, shall we say, as to the true nature of that portion of the self that one is attempting to balance. As one allows the spontaneity and love within to express itself outwardly to others, one is able to feel and experience a fuller and truer representation of one's position, shall we say, upon any particular point that might be of any importance to the self, this being the greater self or the soul which inserts a personality into each illusion and experience.

Thus, though each might feel that a certain amount of control is necessary in order to give coherence to one's experience, we would suggest that one always be open to the surrender of the moment as the moment requires. In this way one moves more in harmony with those lessons and balances which are being pursued for the purpose of the evolution.

Is there a further query, my sister?

P: No, thank you, Q'uo.

I am Q'uo, and I thank you, my sister. Is there another query?

R: I don't have a question, but I want to thank you for being a source of inspiration to me. Again you did it.

I am Q'uo, and we are grateful to you as well, my brother, for the response to that opinion which we have offered. We are grateful to have been of service and can assure you that you have served us just as certainly. Is there another query at this time?

(Pause)

I am Q'uo, and as we observe the exhaustion of the queries we shall again …

(The last page of the transcript is missing.)

L/L Research

L/L Research is a subsidiary of Rock Creek Research & Development Laboratories, Inc.

P.O. Box 5195
Louisville, KY 40255-0195

www.llresearch.org

Rock Creek is a non-profit corporation dedicated to discovering and sharing information which may aid in the spiritual evolution of humankind.

ABOUT THE CONTENTS OF THIS TRANSCRIPT: This telepathic channeling has been taken from transcriptions of the weekly study and meditation meetings of the Rock Creek Research & Development Laboratories and L/L Research. It is offered in the hope that it may be useful to you. As the Confederation entities always make a point of saying, please use your discrimination and judgment in assessing this material. If something rings true to you, fine. If something does not resonate, please leave it behind, for neither we nor those of the Confederation would wish to be a stumbling block for any.

CAVEAT: This transcript is being published by L/L Research in a not yet final form. It has, however, been edited and any obvious errors have been corrected. When it is in a final form, this caveat will be removed.

© 2009 L/L Research

Sunday Meditation
November 20, 1994

Group question: Realizing that each person comes into an incarnation with sort of a plan of lessons to learn and services to offer, we are wondering if it is possible to do what could be called the "healing of the incarnation," which would be doing everything that you had planned to do and then going on to "Plan B" since you had accomplished "Plan A." Is it possible to heal the incarnation to the point that you are able to simple improvise from that point on and put frosting on the cake, shall we say? We would like whatever information you could give us on the healing of the incarnation.

(Carla channeling)

We are those of Q'uo. Greetings in the love and in the light of the one infinite Creator. As always, it is a pleasure and a privilege to speak to you. We thank each for calling us to this circle and ask only that our thoughts be considered. Certainly those that do not seem correct may well be left behind, for our service is to offer our thoughts and our opinions and to do this is truly a pleasure, for it is our way of polarizing at this time.

As you speak of healing we feel that you speak of balance. The healing of an incarnation, then, is the genuine crystallization of the fruits of an incarnation at a given point that has created [such] a depth of equanimity within the spirit that it becomes free to create further harmony in ways that, until the incarnation is seen as being in balance, are impossible.

For instance, if one has created the hoped for actions within an incarnation but has been unable to balance relationships created or taken up again in the process of offering the service to the creation, there will not be the clarity of perspective necessary in order to effectuate further healing. For many entities, then, the incarnation shall not be healed within the incarnation because there has been created within the seeker no firm rock, depending solely upon the relationship with the Creator, upon which that balance might be viewed clearly. For you see, you cannot precisely cause the self to come into a balanced perspective.

Work in consciousness is work without an object. However, [it is] this work, done in the bits and pieces, which creates the miracle of continuing consensus reality among your people. The confusion which reigns universally within your density is simply too thick to penetrate. The mind attempts to create balance within the self and certainly there is work which the mind can do, and do well, which adds to the balance which may be achieved by a seeker.

However, although it feels, when one is ideating and thinking about balance and about healing, that this process should be able to be done mentally, for it is seemingly quite logical, however, this is only apparently so. Deeper and closer to the truth lie ocean depths of bias and prejudice which function subconsciously as a natural portion of the process the spirit is going through within the incarnation, but on the metaphysical or time/space level or dimension. There is no mental access to these subconscious processes which have far more to do with the archetypes of selfhood than with any conscious logical or developed line of reasoning. Therefore, one is relatively helpless to heal one's own incarnation consciously.

However, there is a clear and lucid path towards aiding one's self in the balancing of an incarnation. That way is the way of faith. The most vivid blossoms along that path are those of self-forgiveness, forgiveness of the Creator and forgiveness of all those whom the heart has held in thrall with anger. Once these dusty cobwebs of past negative emotion are swept from that subconscious place then forgiveness may blossom and then the seeker discovers almost by reflex that the circumstances of the incarnation have been transformed. The first few epiphanies or times of transformation within a seeker's experience are those which free portions of the self so that various energies are sequentially set free within the individual, clearing the channel on a higher and higher level.

Entities who work with healing the incarnation are those which have gone through those times of testing which may be seen to be partial and, therefore, have come to a place where the next time of transformation is that one which was the final transformation within the life or incarnation which has to do with oneself only, and at this time of final transformation, or initiation, the whole self, the whole life becomes soft and malleable, if the seeker is at that time perfectly willing to forgive all.

Therefore, the way of faith being followed, in due time the healing of the incarnation becomes a gift given to the self by the subconscious levels of self, aided by what this instrument would call the Holy Spirit and what we often call the higher self.

As the energy is very low in this circle, we shall limit our remarks to these very few, thanking each again for calling us to this circle. We would open the meeting to queries before we leave. And, in pursuit of this, would transfer to the instrument known as Jim. We are those of Q'uo, and leave this instrument in love and in light.

(Jim channeling)

I am Q'uo, and greet each again in love and in light through this instrument. May we ask if there are any further queries at this time?

E: I want to know how two people can prepare to leave this incarnation together. I want to know what spiritual preparations two people can make to leave this incarnation together.

I am Q'uo, and we are aware of your query, my brother, but as it is one which requires a great deal of consideration in order to answer properly, we may only speak with some notations and thoughts which we hope might be of service to you.

We do not expect to be thorough in this particular area, for it is the work of each entity within this illusion to progress along a certain path of seeking and of service that has been chosen for its excellence in balancing those weaker areas within the total mind/body/spirit complex of each entity. There are many entities within your illusion who are so well attuned to the mate, shall we say, for want of a better term, that the paths coincide to a large degree and may even end at the same time as each exits the illusion together.

However, it is more nearly the case for seekers within this illusion to pursue paths that, though they may join for a great portion of the illusion, may also find individual points of departure, for within the larger frame of reference, looking at this illusion as a small portion of the experience that is available to mind/body/spirit complexes, the actual timing of the departure from the illusion is seen as relatively unimportant, the important portion of the incarnation being those efforts to find the talents which have been inlaid and perhaps hidden, to find those services which are in the provenance of the seeker's abilities and talents, to find those lessons that have been secreted in various latent potentials and meetings with others that are incarnating for the purpose of the meetings and the catalysts that can depend therefrom.

However, there are many entities who are so well attuned, each to the other, in pairs or in larger numberings, that there is the melding of the seeking and the serving to the degree that the incarnational patterns become more or less congruent, including the departure from the illusion itself.

We would recommend to all seekers that in order to make, shall we say, the grand and completed exit, that there be the attempt within each portion of the consciousness to give what can be given, to forgive all, and to seek to learn all that is within the possibility of the incarnation. This is not a simple exercise, for it requires the constant attention and the attending to the moment to the degree that one is fully able to realize the possibilities of each moment in seeking and in serving and in reflection, to learn that which can be crystallized as the seed or fruit of each effort at seeking and at serving.

May we ask if there is a more specific avenue that you would wish us to speak upon, my brother?

E: No, thank you.

I am Q'uo, and we thank you, my brother. Is there another query at this time?

(Pause)

I am Q'uo, and we appreciate your words and your heartfelt gratitude, and are on our equivalent of the little rock as we begin to say our farewells to this group. We realize that there is an energy deficit at this time, for there has been the expenditure of much energy this past—what you would call—week, as many have given the experiences and efforts towards making one from a distance feel at home and feel nurtured. This is a good effort, my friends, and we can recommend to you that you always see each other as the dear friend from afar that appreciates the love and support of its close friends and family.

Each of you is a portion of a greater family that moves within the illusion at this time, helping those that need help, inspiring those that are weary, and lending assistance to those who walk with difficulty. This is a grand illusion and a grand journey that you are upon, my friends. There are many adventures that await you and many moments that may disappoint you, but you may always take comfort in knowing that the love of the one Creator resides in full in each and but requires the smallest of need or inspiration to be kindled into flame.

We can tell you from our own experience that there is no greater joy than to share the flame of love of the one Creator with those kindred souls that walk with you upon this dusty path. We take great pleasure and feel a great privilege to be some of those who walk with you. There are many, my friends. There are many.

At this time we shall take our leave of this group, thanking each for inviting our presence. We are those of Q'uo, and leave each in the love and in the light of the one infinite Creator. ✣

L/L Research

L/L Research is a subsidiary of Rock Creek Research & Development Laboratories, Inc.

P.O. Box 5195
Louisville, KY 40255-0195

www.llresearch.org

Rock Creek is a non-profit corporation dedicated to discovering and sharing information which may aid in the spiritual evolution of humankind.

ABOUT THE CONTENTS OF THIS TRANSCRIPT: This telepathic channeling has been taken from transcriptions of the weekly study and meditation meetings of the Rock Creek Research & Development Laboratories and L/L Research. It is offered in the hope that it may be useful to you. As the Confederation entities always make a point of saying, please use your discrimination and judgment in assessing this material. If something rings true to you, fine. If something does not resonate, please leave it behind, for neither we nor those of the Confederation would wish to be a stumbling block for any.

CAVEAT: This transcript is being published by L/L Research in a not yet final form. It has, however, been edited and any obvious errors have been corrected. When it is in a final form, this caveat will be removed.

© 2009 L/L Research

Sunday Meditation
November 27, 1994

Group question: We're going to take pot luck this afternoon. We have no particular question. We'll see what Q'uo has to say from what all the information was that we had to offer beforehand.

(Carla channeling)

We are those of Q'uo. Greetings to each in the love and in the light of the one infinite Creator. It is, as always, a great blessing to be called to this circle of seeking. We bless and thank each who has so desired to seek the truth that this circle has been formed. We especially greet and bless the one known as D, who is new to this particular group. It is a privilege and a pleasure for us to offer our opinions and thoughts. We ask that each seeker evaluate these thoughts for himself, for many are the personal truths within each entity, and that which does not ring true to an individual may easily be left behind. We are not authorities and we are fallible. Therefore, we call each to discriminate for the self.

We are those which have been known to your people as the Confederation of Planets in the Service of the One Infinite Creator. Our desire and purpose for being within your planes is communication, for there is, shall we say, a great call upon your planet at this time for truth. More and more of your planet's peoples are crying out within, seeking a truth that they cannot find, for all the places which are traditionally considered as sources for spiritual food have, in one way or another, been spoiled and made unpleasant as paths of seeking, and consequently the seeker must seek without the structure created by another and must instead create that structure within which the seeker feels best positioned to accelerate the pace of his own spiritual evolution.

What we have to offer such seekers is at base, as this instrument said earlier, a very, very simple truth. It is in that truth that we greet you, and in that same truth that we leave you each time we visit with your sessions of working. This thought that we bring is a living, creative and vital force which also encompasses the powers of darkness and death. This force, this one great original Thought, this Logos, is Love. Your word "love" does not in any way fulfill a satisfactory position as a symbol for that which we speak of. However, love is the closest which your language has to describe the nature of the Creator. This Love, this Logos, is that which has created all that is.

In untold amounts of what you call time, each of you has gradually developed as a consciousness, and all that has come before has fallen in such a way that you are experiencing the dance of living, the incarnational experience, together at this precise time and place. Each has walked a crooked path to be in this circle this day. The seeking has largely been isolating, lonely, alienating and difficult. Yet within each seeker's breast, we are quite aware, the hardships have not been counted. The suffering has been accepted, either gladly or with complete resignation.

From this circle each shall again move into what seems to be the ocean without direction. Love creates, love is, and each is that love. Yet, you are that love clothed in flesh. Your heavy, chemical, physical vehicle ensheaths that which is light, created of love in such a way that you may walk about within the illusion that is your third density. You gaze about at your second-density friends—the trees, the birds, the grass—and you can see in these simple things clear and lucid examples of love. The trees offer to the seeker the oxygen which aids that seeker. The seeker itself is offering carbon dioxide to the trees, a food they need to eat. All within this second density tends toward the perfect order. Not that it is neat or tidy, but that it is in balance.

Now, you exist within the sheathing of your physical body, a flower opening toward the sun. You came into incarnation from the seed and as you blossom, so shall you surely perish from this illusion. And that which was earth shall again become earth. Yet the spirit within flies free, both within incarnation and on each side of that parentheses in eternity which is your lifetime.

And if you are creatures of love and light, then what shall you do to fulfill the truth of your being? This instrument has worked for the last several of your years to bring itself into the physical condition necessary that it may do physical work within this incarnation. The hunger within, that desire which controls, was that which it was taught, that which the culture teaches: to become worthy is to work. Many among your peoples are moved into the situation of labor not simply for that which is salary, but also to fulfill the desire to seem to be worthy, busy and productive. We have been glad to see this instrument moving towards a more natural attitude towards right vocation.

Each within this circle searches for that right vocation, but we say to you, and we know this is not at all original, that the first vocation of each of you, by your very nature, is the vocation of living a life of devotion and faith. In this way, the deepest portion of your true nature is also the basic portion of the outer experience. When this attitude of mind, this bias or prejudice, shall we say, is realized within as a true desire, that which is within you of love has, for the first time, a voice. That voice is a voice which speaks in silence.

Consequently, we encourage each seeker to devise for itself that ritual or period of time which feels most appropriate to each individual seeker for a spiritual practice. We always encourage each to include in that practice a period of silent meditation. If this can be done daily, we encourage each to make that commitment, and turn each diurnal period to that silence within, for within the heart of self, within that vast creation which lies within your consciousness, there is a holy of holies, and within that room waits the Creator. The door is guarded and locked against intruders, and yes, you yourself are an intruder to yourself if you attempt to storm that door, to wring something out of truth. The key to that door is silent meditation. It may take five minutes, it may take years. However, there comes the time when the seeker knows that the door has been opened, for within that entity the incarnational experience becomes transformed.

Within this transformation lies a tremendous degree of surrender, and because this surrendering feels like dying, the path of the seeker is often perceived by the self as difficult, painful and awkward. However, we encourage each to consider that there is a natural tendency to resist change. Within each cell of the body and brain there is a tendency towards holding on to the status quo. The spiritually directed life lacks not in joy, however, it does increase suffering as it increases the rate of change within the entity.

Consequently, we ask each who wishes to know the truth, wishes to find true vocation, wishes to truly serve, to gaze unblinking at the cost of walking this dusty seeker's path, for it shall cost all that you are and all that you have to become that truth which you are seeking. We say to you that as far as we know you cannot know the truth; you can only become true.

As each hews as best as he can to the seeking of that one great original Thought, we ask each to realize that each may teach each, each may support and encourage each other. Truly, the seeker's path is lonely. The hard choices made must be made alone. Yet, how much empowering strength does the fellow traveler give the weary pilgrim?

You each have chosen to be seeking within this incarnation. A destiny awaits you. Your choice of how to fulfill it is always your own, and upon that fathomless, directionless sea of consciousness there remains much confusion. Yet, the love within others shines to light your way, and the light which moves through you from the infinite One is a lighthouse to others. Your being, your essential self, is your main service to the one Creator and to all of those upon your planet.

As you enter this silence again and again, as you seek and seek again, you hollow out within yourself an ever smoother channel for light, for love, for the Creator, so that what is seen is not you but the Creator which shines through, and when those moments occur in which the self realizes that it has been that lighthouse, then indeed does that entity finally feel the joy of right vocation.

You dwell in a sea of confusion, whose chief characteristics are distraction and sorrow. Yet overarching all the tawdry precincts of your Earth world lie shining—we find we do not have this word within this instrument's vocabulary, so we shall remake our sentence. This instrument is thanking us for doing that. Know that that which overarches your world is more deeply true than that illusion which you now perceive with your senses. We would indeed liken the truth which overarches and surrounds your illusion to that program within a computer which controls programs which are subprograms to it.

There is within the deep mind of each of you an archetypical self which often is objectified by your people as the Holy Spirit, or the guide, or the inner teacher. There are many names for this source of wisdom and compassion. When a seeker is able to access this program, then it may do much good work in reordering the priorities with which sense impressions are received. So when there is that time in which the seeker enters meditation and listens to that silent voice within, much is occurring which acts as does yeast within the life experience. Small though that yeast may be within, shall we say, the loaf of life, yet it does create a complete transformation of the dough, and you too are made of a malleable material, which can indeed become [instinct] and honeycombed with life and light.

At this time, having given all of these thoughts to you, we shall transfer to the instrument known as Jim, to continue this contact. We are those of Q'uo, and leave this instrument in love and in light.

(Jim channeling)

I am Q'uo, and greet each again in love and in light through this instrument. At this time we would ask if there might be any further queries which those present may have for us. Is there a query at this time?

Questioner: How does a human break through the wall of fear that we all have in order to do new things? The wall of fear which demands security, false security, since human life is so fragile anyway?

I am Q'uo, and am aware of your query, my brother. We find that much of the existence which your peoples experience, especially at this time in your cultural evolution, is filled with fear of one kind or another. This fear, as you have described it, is that which keeps the mind and the spirit confined in smaller quarters than are normal to these complexes when they are fully functioning. The fear that each entity feels within the life pattern may be likened unto the weight that one who builds the muscles of the physical vehicle would lift in order to strengthen those muscles. One may see this fear as a kind of barrier that increases the value of free choice and action as it is attempted by those who choose to either ignore the fear and go forward, or to accept the fear and to work with it nevertheless.

It is a basic human quality that is derived from the fight or flight mechanism, as we observe your peoples to have called it, and it has its effect in each entity's life, for there is much of your existence that is comprised of building a safe surrounding in which one may move quietly, without the bother of fear. To break forth into that which lies beyond the safe environment is the challenge of each entity in each daily round of activities. However, we find there are many who choose not to accept such a challenge, and choose rather to remain within the safe confines so constructed for the safety.

This is acceptable to each entity insofar as this is necessary for a certain portion of time, until what we may call a ripening within the entity occurs. This ripening may have as its potentier—we correct this instrument—may have as its potentiator any of a number of sources, be they curiosity, boredom, fearlessness, the desire for more or whatever may be the stimulus that provokes or pushes the entity forward. We observe that this quality of breaking forth is that which must come from within each entity's existence, though it may be in some cases inspired by another. Yet each must for the self decide to take a chance to surrender the description of the safe environment, to surrender the self to the unknown, to give of the self to a higher principle that will offer an avenue of expansion of that concept of the self which one has held dearly for so long.

This decision, this movement towards breaking the boundaries of fear, is that necessary ingredient that will allow the doughty seeker to go forth regardless of fears, in spite of that which has held one in place for as long as one has been held. Thus, it is a decision made by the entity itself to try that which has not been tried and to venture forth, to accept whatever comes, to see that the environment is that which responds to fearlessness, shall we say. That as one does go forth, there is a kind of momentum of exploration that tends to align the experiences awaiting one in such a fashion as to offer to the seeker those treasures and fruits of the journey as one can only begin to imagine before the making the first step. Thus, there must be a willingness to be foolish, shall we say, a willingness to surrender, and a certain spark of adventure that takes one out of one's ordinary self.

The timing for such experience is that which is the mystery of being for each, for one cannot push forever against the river. One cannot speed the process for another or for the self. One can only intend, and attempt, and try, and go forth with as much faith in the process and in the self as possible. And add to the faith the will to persevere against the disturbances and distractions that hinder such efforts.

Is there a further query, my brother?

Questioner: No.

I am Q'uo. Is there another query at this time?

Questioner: Yes, I have a question. Would you please comment on the use of sexual energy for a spiritual seeker, by oneself or with a partner?

I am Q'uo, and am aware of your query, my sister. We must preface our response with the notation that this is a large field of inquiry, and we can only make the barest beginning for an answer at this time. However, we may suggest that the sexual energy exchanges between the mated pair are one of the most powerful means of advancing the spiritual journey that is known to your peoples, for as each seeker is able to clear each ascending center or chakra of energy, there is therein released the energy that has been holding the consciousness in a certain place, and this freed energy then can allow each seeker to move the level and quality of perceptions higher and higher within the centers of energy until each is able, either individually or together, to move into the brow center, the indigo ray as we have heard it described by this group, and is able to experience the one Creator in full and without distortion.

This holy experience has been called by many names in various of your peoples' cultures: the enlightenment experience, the samadhi, the [akensho], the nirvana, etc. The overall effect of the sexual energy transfers is to so align the energy centers of each entity as to create an harmonic resonance between them that serves as a kind of generator of energy that pulses one forward so that the physical orgasm that is experienced then releases the mental orgasm, which then frees the spirit to serve as a shuttle and a connector to the experience of the one Creator.

Is there a further query, my sister?

Questioner: No, thank you.

I am Q'uo, and we thank you, my sister. Is there another query?

(Tape ends.)

L/L Research

Sunday Meditation
December 11, 1994

Group question: The question this afternoon has to do with the so-called mirroring effect, where if you notice a feature, characteristic or behavior of another person that you do not like and you dislike the person for that behavior, what really is happening is that you are disliking some behavior or portion of yourself that is reflected back to you in the other person's behavior. This could be an indication to you of an area where you have some work to do in acceptance of yourself, and what we are wondering is as you are more and more able to accept yourself for various types of previously unacceptable behavior that you have seen in yourself and in others, do you then begin to see others and the rest of the world and are able to accept yourself and others more easily. But is there a point beyond which you are observing correctly and the behavior is truly repugnant or that which deserves criticism and stands objectively by itself? How does one look at the self with this mirroring effect in mind when determining what is acceptable and what is not? We would appreciate any information that you could give us on this mirroring effect.

(Carla channeling)

We are known to you as Q'uo. Greetings and blessings to each in the love and in the light of the one infinite Creator. We are most honored and privileged to be called to speak with this circle. We thank you for the beauty of your vibrations, for the dedication of yourselves to service and seeking the truth. We thank you most of all because we are those who have offered themselves in service by this communication as those upon your sphere begin more and more to awaken and find the heart hungry for truth and wholeness in a broken world, in a crumbling religious group of systems, in a fragmenting cultural nexus. We join many other energies and essences in our concern for your people, for there is an agony of the spirit that moves outward from those who are seeking, as do the ripples of the wave moving in time from one continent to another. So these ripples of distress came to our ears and we responded with this effort at continued communication through instruments such as this one.

We have only one truth to offer, one thought. All the rest is embellishment and various ways of discussing that thought and its implications. This thought is that which is a Logos, a Thought so creative and so primary that it forms that which is both Creator and created. That one great original Thought is Love. Within the system of organized religion that you call Christianity there are the words, "In the beginning was the Word." This is the Word of which we speak. That word that created all was and is and shall be love, yet love as you understand it is most pale and weak compared to that vital love which both creates and destroys.

Within this love are all things visible and invisible. Each consciousness listening to these words is a complex which is love and which manifests in various forms of love. Many are the distortions of that love, yet the energy within them, no matter how great the distortion, is that of love. Often in the attempts to progress either emotionally, mentally, physically or spiritually various things are attempted, tested and tried to see whether they be resources or be found wanting. And so as the seeking soul moves through the moment by moment living out of that love which is all that there is, many structures are tried within which the experience of living makes more sense.

The query this evening concerns one such structure. Within this structure which is not original to us but [is] an amiable portion of the perennial philosophy [that] that which meets the physical senses is to be seen as the reflection of self, your medical doctors consider that various people are seen by the self to be, as the one known as Jim said in his query, projecting onto others that which is actually within. This can be taken too far quite handily, and we would suggest a tempering of the ease with which generalities are made, for indeed all possible actions, motives and ideas whatsoever are a portion of each consciousness which hears these words. All things are one. The self seems to be separate and seems to have a certain personality. This is largely an illusion, the illusion having been created so that the consciousnesses within it could do work and thereby progress spiritually. Within this illusion other entities shall almost always seem to be other, for it is only within the intimacy of intense catalyst, the love-making or the shared creative experience or the laughter that ends in tears, that hearts become so close as to perceive their actual unity, one with the other.

It is not necessary for progressing spiritually that there be the continual focus upon the judgment of how the self is doing, and we find in the attitude of seeing all that comes before one as the mirror that generalization which has moved beyond its heart into that rarefied area which logicians are pleased with but the heart does not find useful.

Let us redirect our thoughts to see where this mirroring effect might be the best tool to use for the aid of the self. In the working of self with self it is frequently useful to take that which sticks within the mind like a burr, that which will not stop bothering the mind, and examine it. Gaze at it as if it were a mineral mined out of your soil to be gazed at and evaluated for its purity, its type of mineral, and so forth. Just this kind of eye may see a fairly accurate version of that mirroring effect if the mirror is not seen to be too large.

In other words, when there is an entity which has, over a period of time, continually created aggravation as catalyst for you then it is well to gaze at that feeling complex regarding that entity with the eye to see where the true source of pain and fear is that is creating the need within to make the separating judgment, for one cannot truly judge another or the self. However, it is a portion of the seeker's life work to attempt to discriminate for the self, avoiding judgment in the pejorative sense if possible, but focusing carefully to attempt to draw the inner picture which has the least distortion in it. However, when one experiences the reactions within to that which a stranger or a passerby might do one is doing work where there is no work to do. For the truth, whatever that mysterious word is, is not within the chances of desire-driven destiny.

We attempt to give this instrument a concept which it is having difficulty putting into words. If you may allow us a pause. We are those of Q'uo.

(Pause)

We show this instrument a bright and shining hall. The aspect of this hall is grand and mirrors line both sides and both ends. Into this stage in the dress of the costume ball walk ladies and gentlemen in their finery. The conversation is brilliant. The lights glitter, and images repeat themselves endlessly, depending upon this location within this hall of mirrors upon which one stands. Where lies the truth in this gathering? In the flat images within the mirror? In the conversation? In the clothing so grand and lovely? We suggest a turning from all mirrors that seem to reflect and let the discrimination within you choose that time in which you shall invoke the simile or the parable of the mirror.

Choose carefully that time in which you are involved in judgment of others or of self and keep within logical bounds and intuitive baby steps the tendency to destroy that within you which is unfinished by creating harsh or over-generalized judgment. The desire to judge remains compelling throughout the experience of your third density. The ability to judge correctly is not given to any which draws the breath.

There is no spiritual use in judgment. When that desire to judge comes upon you, attempt to see it for that which it is, the small self within incarnation attempting to put into order the chaos of perceived stimuli. Release, when possible, that desire to control which has you judging, and turn instead within to that fire which burns at the heart, at the holy of holies, locked within you by silence.

When you can be silent enough to enter that heart, there lies the truth that can only be expressed by the living. Let that journey begin each time the effort is made to look at the self in the mirror of a projected opinion. Yet, always, turn at the end of such logical discourse to that which is underlying and overarching all logical considerations: the infinite love of the one infinite Creator. Intelligent infinity calls each locus of consciousness to live vividly, to open the heart and to choose the manner of living to begin to seek to be of service. We ask each to be gentle with the self while attempting to seek the truth within, to be gentle with others as they mirror to you some portion of the universal self out of which pot all soup is drawn, that is, each variety which comes in the physical can you call the body.

My dear ones, that which is within you is impossible to express yet we feel that each has experienced that essence of self which merges with all and becomes the created and the Creator. Always, at the end of such discourse, turn to the Creator which tabernacles within you and within all. Warm your hands at the flame of this source, for beyond all attempts to grasp the truth there is that consciousness which is the truth, and into its silence you may dip. It is yours to choose when and how, whether it be the contemplation, meditation or prayer. Take the time within each day, if it be only thirty seconds, to turn to the truth which lies within and which all that is without merely suggests, and open the self to the being that is that which you seek, but with no words.

(Tape ends.)

L/L Research

L/L Research is a subsidiary of Rock Creek Research & Development Laboratories, Inc.

P.O. Box 5195
Louisville, KY 40255-0195

www.llresearch.org

Rock Creek is a non-profit corporation dedicated to discovering and sharing information which may aid in the spiritual evolution of humankind.

ABOUT THE CONTENTS OF THIS TRANSCRIPT: This telepathic channeling has been taken from transcriptions of the weekly study and meditation meetings of the Rock Creek Research & Development Laboratories and L/L Research. It is offered in the hope that it may be useful to you. As the Confederation entities always make a point of saying, please use your discrimination and judgment in assessing this material. If something rings true to you, fine. If something does not resonate, please leave it behind, for neither we nor those of the Confederation would wish to be a stumbling block for any.

CAVEAT: This transcript is being published by L/L Research in a not yet final form. It has, however, been edited and any obvious errors have been corrected. When it is in a final form, this caveat will be removed.

© 2009 L/L Research

Sunday Meditation
December 25, 1994

Group question: Today we are going to take pot luck. We have been talking about relationships, communication, understanding and [epiphany]. And we will see what Q'uo has to say to all of that.

(Carla channeling)

We are those of Q'uo. Greetings in the love and in the light of the one infinite Creator. We thank and bless each within the circle for gathering to seek together and for calling us to you by your desire to know the truth. Although we ourselves do not know any absolute truths, we believe we do have opinions that may function as a resource for those who may wish to consider them. As always, however, we ask that any thoughts of ours which jar or distress the *(inaudible)* of any seeker be immediately placed aside and left behind, for we are not here as authorities, but rather as those who share the path with you.

Much of the discussion previous to this session of working contained the joy and sorrow of each, and in that shared breath of conversation there is the immediate presence of the one infinite Creator, working always as the spirit of love to harmonize, realign and reposition this or that aspect of the mind, body or spirit in its complex form and with its interrelating energy fields. Perhaps you may have even felt tension released as concerns perhaps not even your own were discussed in a sympathetic and supportive atmosphere. Whatever the interactions between any two entities, the sweetness within the stream of moment by moment living is dependent greatly upon the selves' ability to open the heart both to giving and to the receiving of information, communications and shared emotions such as affection, love or appreciation.

It may seem, indeed, that some things never need to be said. Yet, if there is a kindly opinion, a good thought, or that which occurs in the impulse of the moment which seems fair and loving to be shared, let that be shared, for when the breath is expanded in speech concerning the desire to love, to understand, to support, or to strengthen another, that energy is as the healing that moves between the words, between the lines, between the thought, conceptions and intellectualizations of the rational mind.

Language, indeed, could be well dispensed with were it not for the need to communicate, for that which most deeply uncovers and cleanses the self is most often not the rational, logical or common sense, but rather that speech or action which is intuited by that portion of the self which dreams and receives information from the subconscious, for that portion of the self which is visible is but the tip of a very large iceberg which is completely submerged beneath the surface of that water's edge which is the alignment of the deeper mind, or subconscious mind.

There is a particular energy which creates certain combinations of feeling which are fairly recognizable to help to inform the seeker as to when he has accessed this well of true emotions, that is, emotions which have undergone refining and purification. Trust that feeling which says this feels right, and do not overstretch the rational mind's burden with requests that all be rationally seen or logically arranged, for often that which is the saving and healing key within one's impulse is that which cannot be explained except by the feeling that there is indeed such a thing as intuition and that this faculty can be honed.

In speaking of attempting to converse and communicate on ever clearer and deeper levels we speak truly, yet we wish also to point out that anything which can be said in words is not the truth, indeed, our very concepts [of] that which is below the veil in your density are not the truth. They are true, but we continue to feel that there is an absolute truth which we may experience but never ever understand or control.

Therefore, the process of living a life of the open heart in service to others creates situation after situation in which the seeker is moving to the rhythm of a drum it itself does not fully comprehend. There is a special art to being willing and able to trust the flow of experience. This instrument's mind immediately says "No, 'the flow of catalysts.'" However, we are speaking of how you learn at this moment, but rather how you can open the heart and in that state communicate one with another. It is impossible to convince any one that the spiritual search is real, or true, or desirable or that the faith in the goodness and the rightness of the creation as it is can be explained. Always the seeker must rest in the security of mid-air. The seeker who dares to venture greatly simply walks over that archetypical cliff into the abyss of unknown things. Is there then the sensation of falling? Indeed not. But that leap must be made first, before any knowledge has been gained by experience.

Imagine then, if you will, the feet planted firmly upon the earth. Yet ahead of you lies the infinity that you have come so far and sacrificed so much to behold, to study, to begin the attempt to grasp, to understand. How precious is this realm of shadow and confusion which each has been speaking of and laughing about, for it is these very shadows that enclose the Creator, and were one to move into the brightest day, one would not find truth. Truth is not attainable from the position which each now occupies. It can be intrinsically experienced, but it cannot be known, held or told.

Indeed, this instrument has frequently experienced the light in its undiluted form. Yet when this entity moves back into the everyday mode or frame of mind, by no exercise of its skill with word can it generate an explanation of what has been experienced, or a description of it, or any way whatsoever to translate that primary personal experience into a teaching tool for others. Each entity is indeed its own teacher in terms of experiencing truth. Yet that feeling of having experienced and lived a truth has occurred to each within this circle of seeking and, indeed, to almost all of those who at this time, if you will, feel that they are awakening to a deeper truth about who they are and where that pilgrimage that they then take up shall lead.

Treasure each and every experience of this kind that has been given to you as a gift. Remember these moments, for many are the times when only the memory of faith is available to the conscious mind. Yet that sweet memory is so over-arching and so transcendent that the one instant of union with the divine is infinitely more than enough to justify a lifetime of faith, sacrifice and service.

Each has treasures within that cannot be seen by the inner or outer eyes. These gifts open to the pilgrim who sets itself to watch and pray and trust in that which it does not understand, yet recognizes as spiritual food and drink. When such a moment comes, then the possibilities multiply, and in that heady experience of light or love there is the opportunity to sow for the future self those seeds of desire which shall best aid that seeker in its long, indeed, its endless journey.

Be mindful, therefore, in remembrance when such a moment occurs. If it is possible even for a moment, stop, and give thanks and praise and ask the self to remember, for in that experience is truth. And as those moments slowly accumulate and the memory becomes thickened and fertile, enriched by memory, the pilgrim self gains those small bits of sense of truth or confidence that support and sustain the persistent, unflagging orientation towards seeking the deepest desires within that spiritual self within which must speak through the veil.

This is slow and subtle work. However, this is only the beginning of a very long process of refinement. The rough materials lie within; many, many permutations are possible, and as the experiences revolve, as the self revolves in its cycles, there is the increasing capacity to perceive within the self.

Those patterns which speak to the individual's path and those resources which shall be of the most aid upon that path, these aids can be written, they can be those teachers which speak or embody wisdom or compassion. All possible experiences are fallow, with treasures to be mined, to be found in the roots which underlie those blossoms of experience which the conscious mind perceives. Can the beholder of a beautiful tulip or iris see that homely bulb or seed which has created the blossom? Never. For that root lies deep within the dark and rich soil. And light and warmth had acted upon that which you cannot see in order to put forth the shoots of manifestation and the bud of experience. Realize that that which you consciously perceive is but a clue, a hint or an [inkling] of that substance which lies within the ground of being, perfect in every way and absolute in its union with the Creator and the utter totality of creation.

We realize we are speaking a bit longer than this instrument would appreciate. Yet there is within that heart of darkness which you now experience upon your planet a great deal of riches. This is a very magical time, a time when that spirit which is the true life of all is seen to be naked, stripped and bare. Just as the trees without their clothing of leaves look skeletal, standing in their rarefied beauty severe and stark against the winter sky, these are times within the self as well for moving into the roots and ground of being. There is that within you which is the seed of new life. Huddle yourself to support and love and cherish that self that is being born each moment. Bide impatience, release expectation and know for this little time of darkness and shorter day that there is a condign and worthwhile function which the darkness and inclement weather create an enhanced possibility for the seeker to enjoy. Flow into that darkness, move into the solidity of earth and cold and contraction, and allow the rest, the sleeping, the rekindling slowly of hope, desire and courage for that which is to come, for days there shall indeed be, and all too soon, when that which you have stored up in the winter shall be called upon in the day. May your winter thoughts be sweet, for spring is soon to be with you.

We shall at this time transfer this contact to the one known as Jim. We are those of Q'uo and leave this instrument with thanks in love and light.

(Jim channeling)

I am Q'uo, and greet each again in love and in light. At this time we would ask if there are further queries to which we may speak.

R: I have a question, Q'uo. I just wondered if it is correct to say that when we sit here in the circle, and I in particular try to open up to your energies, that if it is agreeable at some level that you help release some blockages or tensions within me. I was thinking about it because I noticed I have a very runny nose this time, that did not come until we started. I don't know if I am seeing things or if there is something to it. I noticed at other times too, I come up with emotions and tears. You don't have to answer that, but if you can I'd be interested to hear what you have to say.

P: I would also like to add to this. I was wondering about the thoughts and images that come to one's mind, hearing these channeling meditations and how they are related to the teachings.

I am Q'uo, and we believe we grasp your queries, my friends. We shall attempt our response, please re-query if we do not speak to your true question.

As we are able to utilize the instruments in this contact, we also share our conditioning vibration with each entity present in the circle of seeking. This conditioning vibration has its purpose, the deepening of the meditative state that each has achieved. This meditative state has various components for each entity that are unique to each entity. If there is within the seeker present in this circle a desire to move into those areas which would release the energies held in place by what we would call the spiritual inertia, then the conditioning vibration aids in this process as well.

Thus, one may feel a greater fluidity in the thinking, the feeling, and the willingness to receive new insight. If there is a concern that may be captured in an image, or a thought, then the conditioning vibration will aid in this process as well. We do not set out in any meditation to invade any entity's thoughts or emotions, for this we see as an infringement upon the free will of the entity. However, if the entity wishes to use the energies at its disposal, including our conditioning vibration, for any particular purpose, then the conditioning vibration shall allow the entity to do this much as your magnifying glass will aid you in enlarging the print upon a page.

May we speak further to either?

R: I will expand in the second direction and that is … Let me put it this way, when I am in a meditation I assume that as I try to open up to your energy or the particular entity that comes through either of the instruments that if there is a real intent to add and open up, I assume that it may enhance the contact somehow. I wonder though if this helps the instruments that are actually channeling to be more stable, or whether that is really a function of the particular instrument in tuning. And I don't know if you can really say anything about it because this sort of affects the contact, but I am just curious if this is the right feeling about it.

I am Q'uo, and I am aware of your query, my brother. Indeed, your intentions are most helpful in this contact, for it is the desire of each entity for our words and contact that aids such an occurring. This is most helpful, and we thank each for this desire to hear our words and to seek our service, for by such desire and intention we are invited and a place is made for us in your beingness.

Is there another query, my brother?

R: No, I guess not. The desire was a Christmas present for you.

I am Q'uo, and we thank you, my brother, for your delicious present of desire.

Is there another query?

P: I have a question. It's a thought in my mind. Actually I didn't talk about it during our conversation prior to the channeling. The thoughts are about the usage of narcotics, drugs. I have been thinking of maybe taking LSD, and wanted to know what Q'uo could comment on the usage of such substances, and how it would be of help for a seeker in opening windows of mind?

I am Q'uo, and am aware of your query, my sister. We find that we are limited to a large extent in the response which we may give, for we do not wish to influence another in a course of action which may have ramifications within the seeking. We may suggest that whatever ingestion of chemical substances an entity may consider, it is necessary for any seeker to have a great desire for the seeking of light and to prepare for this most carefully, for any substance which speeds up the normal process of perception for an entity also carries with it the greater responsibility for that entity to use the occasion for an opportunity for seeking the light, for there are many entities and energies that are made available at such an opportunity that the seeker must be most fastidious in the preparing of the self for this experience.

Is there another query, my sister?

P: No, thanks very much for your comments.

I am Q'uo, and we thank you, my sister. Is there another query?

Carla: Not for me Q'uo. Just thank you and Merry Christmas.

I am Q'uo, we greatly appreciate the warm wishes of this season of renewal, that we feel offered to us not only by the one known as Carla, but by each in this circle. We are quite aware that each views this particular season in an unique fashion, and we see also that each offers us the purest of blessings and good wishes that are associated with this season. We are aware that the time of the birth of Christ has various meanings to various entities, and we can assure each that there is a Christ within each that responds to this time within each entity that occurs, whether it be at your Christmas time or at any other time during your year. There is the babe within that awaits the birthing; there is the attending of this babe by those portions of the self that are wise and which bring gifts to this young self that is being born. We see within …

(Tape ends.)

Year 1995
January 15, 1994 to July 6, 1995

L/L Research

Sunday Meditation
January 15, 1995

Group question: We have been sitting and talking about things we have been affected by in our past, things we are looking forward to in the future and planning for, and adjusting our present according to, and realizing the value of all these things. We are just wondering if there might be some way of focusing more on the present moment and what it really means to be here right now, emotionally, mentally, physically and spiritually.

(Carla channeling)

I am Hatonn. Greetings in the love and in the light of the infinite Creator. May we thank you for calling us to this circle of seeking. It is a great pleasure to once again experience the blending of our vibrations with your own and we feel most blessed to be sharing in this meditation. As we offer our opinions, we ask that each entity take what seems good and discard those thoughts that do not seem appropriate, for we offer our opinions and are your error-prone friends along the path, rather than any absolute authority.

It has been some time since we spoke through this channel and we enjoy that also. To stay in the present moment is to stay in eternity, for the fully realized present has infinite depth, and breadth, and height. To be present in that moment, in a full sense, is possible to third-density experience, but highly improbable, for the aim of third density is towards creating a sea of confusion within which entities may exercise their free will in choosing the manner of spending time and attention. So if you feel again and again that you are spiritually lacking because of dwelling upon the past or hoping overmuch for the future, step back from judgment of the self and remember that you did not create this illusion so that you could best it, defeat it, or win from it the prize of perfect conformation to that infinite present moment. Rather, you came to, shall we [say,] the party, in order to be intoxicated with life, and to stray from the path that is straight, drawn instinctively by those interests and biases which you brought with you in such a way that the dilemmas of reconfiguring and re-aiming the path might be set up just precisely in that way which shall instruct, reform and teach most accurately, pointedly and profoundly.

As you stray and [wander] the weather of the emotions blows through the experience of the self by the self. There are times when it seems possible to become fully aware, centered and present. There are often times when the self perceives its nature as hopelessly foolish, scattered and inefficient. The full gambit of these judgments of self by self may be upon the surface true and may seem helpful, however, beneath these surface experiences of self that portion of the self which does indeed dwell eternally within that present moment is alive and well within you. You cannot escape the perfection out of which you were created and into which you now are maturing.

Have we confused you, my brothers and sisters? We do not mean to confuse, but rather to put into a perspective this quest for righteousness or right thinking. These attempts are indeed important. It is well to strive towards the ideals of being present and practicing the presence of the infinite Creator. It simply needs to be pointed out that this, like other states of conscious existence, is that which is upon the surface of the personality of the life experience, whereas the work of an incarnation redounds to the very depth of the self, to the roots of mind, the last thirsty roots of consciousness that reach into that which is deity.

You see, your nature is such that the striving, the activity of an incarnation, remains in a sense frivolous or unimportant, the many self-judgments being not only frivolous but inaccurate and inappropriate. We suggest that each encourage those thoughts which refrain from judgment and discourage the self in its desires to castigate and rebuke the self for its shallowness, its lack of appropriate awareness of the present moment. This we say in order that those many times when the self is perceived as being out of harmony with eternity, that the judgment will be not chosen, but rather a shrug, a laugh at the human condition, and a turning once more to thanksgiving and naked praise for the infinite One which fills the days, the moments, the years and the life with such beauty that it is beyond description.

Now having said this, we do encourage each student to muse often within that sacred tabernacle within, to sit mentally and emotionally down within that holy ground of being, where lies truth and eternal things; to sit with bare attention, knowing that silence which speaks of the mighty presence that is both Creator, creation and created. For these are moments out of time, out of space, and rather eternal and infinite. These moments of practicing the presence of the Creator may be keyed according to your individual needs and circumstances. This instrument has often used the ringing of the telephone or the sounding of a bell, heard from a neighboring church, to remind the self to turn to offering thanksgiving and praise. This reminder aids and in each life experience there is a structure of habitual use of time, wherein there are predictable moments, which might be best laid aside for a quick visit to eternity. This does not have to be formal or long. Indeed, it can be, if you chose, most frequent.

You see, when seekers speak of living within the present moment, they are attempting to describe within the illusion and using [as] the tools of the illusion that which does not take part within the illusion. When entities are struggling for a personal healing, when they are in some kind of therapy, there may be suggested another structure within which one may attempt to discipline the personality and the habits of the mind and emotions.

Whatever the language, the student of truth is basically looking for ways to stop thinking, and instead allow the nakedness of pure attention. Feel for a moment that incredibly powerful love that is the Creator. Sense this love within you as the sun warming the heart, radiating throughout the physical vehicle. Within the curtain of flesh lies deity, and that vessel that you are is being hollowed out to receive ever more fully that love which is all that there is, which wraps up eternity and infinity in a tiny ball, and, throwing it, creates the universe.

We would leave you at this time in the love and the light of the Creator. We are with you in eternity and bid you joy of your party. May you seek most purely, forgive most completely, and love each other with all your heart.

We are those of Hatonn. Adonai vasu borragus. ☙

L/L Research

L/L Research is a subsidiary of Rock Creek Research & Development Laboratories, Inc.

P.O. Box 5195
Louisville, KY 40255-0195

www.llresearch.org

Rock Creek is a non-profit corporation dedicated to discovering and sharing information which may aid in the spiritual evolution of humankind.

ABOUT THE CONTENTS OF THIS TRANSCRIPT: This telepathic channeling has been taken from transcriptions of the weekly study and meditation meetings of the Rock Creek Research & Development Laboratories and L/L Research. It is offered in the hope that it may be useful to you. As the Confederation entities always make a point of saying, please use your discrimination and judgment in assessing this material. If something rings true to you, fine. If something does not resonate, please leave it behind, for neither we nor those of the Confederation would wish to be a stumbling block for any.

CAVEAT: This transcript is being published by L/L Research in a not yet final form. It has, however, been edited and any obvious errors have been corrected. When it is in a final form, this caveat will be removed.

© 2009 L/L Research

Sunday Meditation
January 22, 1995

Group question: The question this afternoon has to do with the incarnation into various races and cultures on this planet. We are wondering if people tend to incarnate into only one race or culture and move as a unit or group within that race or culture and maintain their identities from incarnation to incarnation as members of a particular race or culture or tribe, or if people are more likely to incarnate across racial or cultural boundaries and have a multitude of different types of experiences, and if this experience is what the soul experiences. Does the soul experience many different kinds of racial, tribal or cultural incarnations, or does the soul have identification with particular races or cultures?

(Carla channeling)

We are those of Q'uo. Greetings in the love and the light of the one infinite Creator. Our thanks to this circle of seekers for calling us to your session this day. We are most beholden and thankful for you who seek and by your seeking serve, for we have no ultimate answers but, rather, are partners with you in refining those questions which lie ultimately shrouded for both of us in mystery. It is the continued focus upon these questions that create the vibration that is purified desire and the truth that is purified emotion.

This day you would seek knowledge of how the spirit moves through the incarnative process with regard to what populations it may choose to be a portion of, and you ask that which has not a difficult answer, but, rather, a clear but complex answer. Thusly, we shall need to work at several levels, not that one is deeper or more spiritual than another but that there are various facets of relationship which we shall view with you.

The first portion of the discussion will revolve about the basic spirit or what you would call soul. Each spirit is in essence the same, for each spirit is a mobilized, potentiated phase of infinity, or an infinite nature, or self. This basic self is one, and this is true across lines of race, nation, planet, galaxy and creation. Each seeming monad or unit or spirit or soul is an holographic representation of one original unified Thought, Logos or Force. That we have given the name of Love. Each is Love. Each was always Love. Each shall always be Love.

The creation began and shall end. Your galaxy began and shall sooner end. Your star system began and yet sooner shall end. Your planets began and shall end. And each entity began its manifestation and shall shed it ere soon. That which seems different and unique is an illusion. It is easier to speak this unity than to communicate that unity. However, we shall pause for a moment that each may sink into love, and we shall attempt to aid in that feeling that you may in some small wise find this feeling within that is unity. We are those of Q'uo.

(Pause)

We are those of Q'uo. Feel that wind of spirit that has allowed you the creation of your unique personality. Personality can be seen to be shallow, that creature of one incarnation. However, the more basic personality is the child of many, many incarnations. And so as with all that is manifest, you as an unique personality first found life a thing of reality by virtue of being slowly more and more aware of, not yourself, but your surroundings. And the process of individuation began.

Imagine that you, spirit just born, sprung from the Creator's fertile love, sailed through many, many universes and saw many, many beautiful stars, constellations, vibrations of beingness and through many, many densities, many, many experiences you moved that infant soul until there was a choice, a preference, a bias. This star, this constellation, this planet. And one day you were water, or earth, or rock, or rain, or wind, or sand. And your incarnations had begun. Was this unity then forgotten? Not in the deep mind. This essential unity remains that truth which for all, moving through the densities, cannot be denied, for it is felt within as a heart's truth. It is not that you are like others—rather, you are all that there is. This is your foundation. This is that plinth upon which you build that creation which turns stone to statue and form to life. This is the rock upon which you may stand. You are one.

The second way which we wish to look at this question is that way of naming. We need not go through that process by which you have come to third density. You may simply accept, if you will, for the purpose of this working, that you did indeed rise in consciousness through various forms in first and in second density; that is, as elements and as plants and as animals and then came to the dawn of third-density experience. Once again, you may have wandered far from sun to sun, looking for third density. Or you may have chosen this particular planet to begin third density with. Choices are possible, not conscious ones as you know them, but rather like calling like.

However you chose, the planetary influence and the racial influence with which you began the long process of learning through incarnations remains that which has had the first biasing effect presenting the first catalyst giving you that turning of the archetypical mind's themes and biases which are most deeply rooted within. For the Logos expressing as your sun body touches each planet differently, and, indeed, each portion of a planet somewhat differently, so that large masses of entities which are of a single racial origin or national origin may be more probably biased similarly than those whose minds contain etchings of another set of planetary, racial or other influences.

Thusly, there is, to some extent, the experiencing of like calling like that expresses within the conscious mind as a feeling of comfort and of being at home with certain people; that is, with certain national groups of people or certain religious or spiritual groups of entities. Within these large divisions those within the same body of influences begin the work of learning what love truly is. And in doing this together, over many lifetimes, ways are created, and over more and more time, embellished upon and strengthened so that each culture, shall we call it, with its characteristic ways of dealing with ever eternal situations common to all of humankind, become more and more handy to the mind and useful to the commonsense, everyday spirit.

Just as national or spiritual groups of entities tend to speak one language or a language in a characteristic sense, so do different cultures have unspoken language and ways of communicating which do not travel well. The one known as P, for instance, spoke to this group concerning an American who does not take the hint and stop being a nuisance, for this entity, brought up within a culture which simply shuts the door and does not answer the communication by telephone or by mail, has no innate ability and certainly no desire to leap across the cultural divide which separates this entity from one who has been reared within a culture in which hospitality is an holy thing, and the bad company must needs figure out by hint and the tone of words that he has overstepped the bounds of courtesy.

Thusly, entities do indeed often incarnate again and again within one planetary and one racial or spiritual group.

Thirdly, the thrust of the question, we believe, centers about whether there is a spiritual value of one culture against or relative to the spiritual value of another. And so we must ask you to, again, wipe the mind clear. Now, each of you within this circle has experienced incarnation with a substantial percentage of incarnations upon one third-density planet, and within that planetary influence one nation, spiritual, or other group of that kind. However, in the fullness of time, as entities grow, as they wake up, spiritually speaking, and discover that there is much more to know about love than has been understood, shall we say, by any one group these entities naturally choose to begin the process of gleaning from other cultures, other nations, and other spiritual groups those subtleties of insight, those inner structures that lie behind the spoken word and conceived thought, each of which educates and trains the mind in certain patterns. Each pattern has its place and is its equally valuable teacher. Just as the physical entity which you now experience yourself as wishes to travel and broaden the understanding of what humankind is, so the soul or spirit chooses again and again to travel in other shoes, other bodies, other races, creeds and color, for each has something to offer.

To be humble in one culture educates. To be humble in another culture offers a completely different education. To be proud in one society is one kind of distortion of self unlike pride seen from the subtly but crystallinely different colorations of another culture's way of pride. We ask you then in this third way of seeing to imagine, if you will, the vast extent of time and space within which the soul first becomes familiar with one family at a time. Then, after many, many incarnations, one larger family, one national or spiritual group, and then one begins to travel, choosing those situations which shall fill out and energize that awareness gleaned so far. For in all of these learnings, in all of these environments, the spirit within expresses its essence in a desire for a return to the awareness of unity which was life and shall again be life without manifestation. The manifest spirit yearns endlessly for that zero within which all is one, for that and only that is the true nature of all who may hear or read these words. There is one original Thought. Each of you is that. Each of you has wandered far. Each of you seeks with grace and rhythm to complete the journey so long ago begun and perfectly encapsulated within each incarnation as that spiritual hunger within which always seeks the source of life, the truth of being.

As the harvest approaches, you well may find yourself within a family which cuts across all lines, for, again, like calls like. Certainly those who are wanderers are one such group. Those who have wandered from different planets to this one may seem obviously different from each other as they have incarnated in various races and so forth. Yet that bond of shared experience, shared hunger and the biases that lie beneath words create spiritually oriented families which are service oriented and offer service instinctively, not only to each other but always there is the desire, however well or ill nurtured, to reach the hand of service to any other who may be served. It is in these often unusually varied groups such as your own that the heart of the lessons of love may begin again to become unified, as each soul now has sufficient experience in seeking the truth of self and the way of service to find commonalities that move beyond race, religion, nation and culture, and instead find residence in a common foundation of self within which that deep mind which is the archetypical mind of self has had sufficient experience in combining self with other selves across all boundaries that the unity beneath all distortions is dimly sensed.

Yet even the dimmest of inklings of this underlying unity act like the explosion or the fireworks, tossing the entity experiencing this unity into a kind of excitement that only the experience of love itself can engender. And once this underlying unity is sensed personally the days of the personality that you now think yourself to be are numbered. The soul which has awakened to the truths that lie beyond the archetypes now has the energy to work through those rich sources within of wisdom and of truth, now has the sufficient reason to attempt to penetrate each and every archetype, becoming one who can assume characteristics which are archetypical in a cleanly pure way, finding within these time-worn structures not only the elegance of internal logic within these systems but also the doors which shall open when one comes at last to a realization that is at the end of each and every archetype or leitmotif.

For instance, in many, many experiences of grief it is an experience and then an experience, and so forth. The experiences add up. They are as they are; but in a course of a million incarnations, at some point the pure and undiluted tone which is grief within you sounds, and suddenly you have experienced for the first time a true grief, a grief which lights up grief incandescently. This tone sounds through all of the infinite creation and is a thing of utmost beauty, and this rich experience retires within that soul the need to experiment with grief, for it has been purely experienced and is no longer that which must be studied.

Is there a spiritual connotation, then, to races? All races have great spiritual treasurers to share, both what you would call positively and negatively. In all things, however, the spirit of each remains equal, and thus all cultures, all nations, all groups are equal. All contain the same love. You shall experience that which you choose to until nothing calls you into flesh.

We would at this time urge you to gaze gently upon all beings and to give to each your best attempt at service, not weighing one against another, yet at the same time we do encourage you to follow the heart, for when like does find like then learning may be swifter for both. And the group which learns together becomes a blessing not only to itself and to its members but as it reaches out from that home within a certain and sure blessing to humankind.

At this time we would transfer to the one known as Jim. We are those of Q'uo, and leave this instrument in love and in light.

(Jim channeling)

I am Q'uo, and greet each again in love and in light. We are privileged at this time to offer ourselves in the attempt to speak to any further queries which those present might have for us. Is there a further query?

P: Yes, I would like to ask a question which was put to me by another person. The question is about a situation where a person feels very strongly what we may call love or a certain attraction to another entity but that person doesn't have the same feelings. Could you shed some insight about that situation, what it may mean how the two entities help each other to reach a certain level of harmony?

I am Q'uo, and believe we have the gist of your query, my sister. Please query further if we do not satisfy you.

If entities have a desire to experience love to the best of their understanding of this concept then the desire will be to give love without expectation of return, for that which is love is that which gives rather than that which takes, though it is true that love, when fully experienced, is that which both gives and receives. However, the concept which you have spoken of here is that which is felt by one and not another, and in this case there is the participation in what is felt to be love by one and not the other. Therefore, the one who feels the love, if it be love indeed, then this entity would desire to give to the other that which the other wished and this entity would seek, then, to know the desires of the other, and, once having ascertained what these desires were, would bend every effort to satisfy these desires.

For entities to truly know love it is necessary to surrender whatever idea the self may have as regards the nature of love and then to be moved by the power of love. In most cases, in our opinion, upon your planet at this time entities perceive only portions of love, those portions which are more to their own desires and definitions, those aspects of love which are more likely to feed their self-identified needs, and, therefore, the experience of love is only partial. If one wishes to truly be of service to another by loving another one must determine what service is desired by the one loved.

Is there another query, my sister?

P: Not at this time. Thank you.

I am Q'uo. And we thank you, my sister. Is there another query?

Carla: I would like to follow it just a little further. If the person who doesn't love wishes to serve the person who loves, the surface impulse is to say that the way to serve that person is to allow that person to love you, allow that person to fulfill his desire. Now, practically, I feel this is a wrong answer, but I don't know how to untangle free will and service and just how to put it clearly. Could you comment in a way that clarifies?

I am Q'uo, and though we are aware of your query, my sister, we also agree that in the situation in which you are describing there is some complexity and lack of clarity which makes a clear and definite answer difficult, for there are circumstances within your culture which require certain behaviors and commitments that put a kind of boundary on love so that love may be experienced more purely by those who are entered into the mated relationship that you call marriage. Thus, love is not freely given to all, but finds the need to be given in such and such a manner within boundaries which entities have agreed to.

Thus, in a mated relationship when an entity moves beyond the boundary to share what is perceived as love with a person other than the mate, then it is that the difficulties and confusions arise, for it is not the accepted practice within most of your cultures for entities to share the full ramifications of love with any but the mate. So it is a situation in which each entity must use the personal and most profound, shall we say, moral standard to judge what is acceptable to be shared of love with one who is not the mate.

We find that the purest form of love which requires no return or action of any kind may be shared with all, for this is the love of the Creator within the heart of each for every other portion of the Creator that is recognized. However, when entities find a need to make conditions and requirements and desire certain returns from their expression of love to another that is not within the mated relationship then we have the confusions of which we spoke. In this instance we cannot give direct advice, for this is, in our opinion, an infringement upon free will. But we can suggest that entities that are in a relationship with another look deep within the heart to see where love resides for another and find within the self the small voice that is speaking the known truth, shall we say, for each entity knows beyond all rationalization what is love, what is its truest expression within each situation. And, while recognizing all cultural boundaries, will be able to affect this true loving, even if the true loving is to reject a portion of that which is offered from another.

Is there a further query, my sister?

Carla: I'm just working on this one point and if you will forgive me I would like to go a little further. Is that all right?

I am Q'uo, and we are quite ready to speak to any query, my sister.

Carla: Thank you. The way it feels to me reminds me of when Don was asking Ra how he could serve our fifth-density negative friend. He wanted to find some way to be of service to this friend who wanted to stop our communications with Ra, and Ra couldn't get through to him that the very essence of the service that he wanted was to stop the contact. Besides stopping the contact there was no other service from Don that he actually wanted. It just feels like this situation is one where what the teacher wants infringes on P's free will and is a desire for an object rather than the love of a person, because in getting what he would want he is walking all over the truth and asking P to be untrue to the feelings within her which say this is not the one. I just don't know any good way to line it out in a simple way, but it feels like the same kind of situation. If you would comment on that to any extent I think that's the end of my thoughts on the subject. Thank you.

I am Q'uo, and we would agree that this subject is one which requires a good deal of thought. Indeed, this is our recommendation that the meditative state is the means by which the true voice of each may be heard and the most appropriate expression of love experienced. We realize that there is a certain purity to the naiveté that the one known as Don expressed in the queries to Ra concerning serving the negatively oriented entity, and there is a certain purity and naiveté in the situation in which you speak, if the one known as P would receive the offerings of love from the entity that is in question. However, there is also the need to respond to the cultural practices that we have mentioned and the need to seek within for the deepest form of service, for all services are not equal.

This was the point that those of Ra were attempting to make to the one known as Don. What is the deepest service? To simply open the self to receiving love from any entity that would offer it in any form that the entity would offer it, or is there the need to consider other ramifications? Is the highest form of service to allow an entity to break its word to another? Is the highest form of service to simply reject another entity? Is there the need to find another means by which love may be expressed? These are queries which we know each has considered this day, and these are queries which we may not answer for you, for there is value in finding answers for yourself that we would not take from you.

Thus, we must bate our answers as we have, but we may recommend to each the value of seeking within meditation the answers for the self from the self, for we assure you that they are there within your very heart, and though the answer may be difficult to put into experience and into action there is value in so doing.

Is there another query at this time?

(No further queries. Thanks from all expressed.)

We are those of Q'uo, and we add our thanks to the pot. We are most grateful, my friends, for your invitation to us this day. We know that the struggle to be human and to move in flesh is not easy. We salute your valiant efforts, and we remind each of you that there are truly no mistakes. There are only opportunities to learn and to know the Creator. Undertake each opportunity with the full gusto of the life that moves through you and which brings the energy of the Creator into your being as you pass through your daily round of activities.

We would, at this time, take our leave of this group and this instrument, thanking each once again for the opportunity of sharing our opinions with you. We are known to you as those of Q'uo, and leave each of you in the love and in the light of the one infinite Creator. Adonai, my friends. Adonai. ♣

Sunday Meditation
January 29, 1995

Group question: The question this week comes from N and has to do with the concepts of service and love. It is his observation that the basis of all creation is to serve, one portion of the Creator serving another, and that the substance of the creation is love, everything is made out of love, the creative energy of the Creator. Now, N feels in our daily lives that service is more obvious and instinctual. We are able to recognize our opportunities to serve as they come about. We just see what needs to be done and do it. Love, however, seems to be of the nature of that which needs to be worked on. It takes will or an effort to do it and we are never really sure of how well we are doing it. Whereas with service we are aware of what we have done and can at least be sure that something was accomplished. In loving, it is not so obvious, and we would like Q'uo's comments upon N's observations.

(Carla channeling)

We are those of the principle of Q'uo. Greetings in the love and in the light of the one infinite Creator. We apologize for the length of time that the challenging process took, but this is always necessary work which needs to be done meticulously and we attempt never to fail to mention this when it applies. We thank the one known as Carla for pursuing this process until satisfied. The discernment was necessary, in our opinion.

We are called to your group by your musings upon love and service. We thank you for this call, this opportunity to share our humble thoughts with you. As always, we encourage each to use his discrimination at all times and with each thought we may offer you, for we would never wish to put a stumbling block in your path. Therefore, discard those thoughts which do not shine with a kind of recognition within your perceptions.

Discussing love is our favorite occupation. No subject rings with the purity of that primary Logos, that mystery, the great original thought of Love. Here the mystery begins and here there shall be its embrace when all distortions cease. Love the beginning, and Love the doom, or ending. Before we embark upon words which shall surely fail to create full truth we pause to worship that mystery. We are those of Q'uo.

(Pause of thirty seconds.)

We are those of Q'uo, and are once again with this instrument. We greatly appreciate sharing your vibrations at this time.

It can certainly be seen to be evident and true that service is easier to attempt than love. True, also, is it that the boundaries between qualities pertaining to the divine shall always be weak, for love is, and is all that there is. Thusly, service is the visible manifestation of the invisible and primal love. Let us work first, then, with service.

The questioner labors diligently within, what this instrument calls, one of the helping professions, being a medical doctor. It seems obvious that those who come before the gaze have need of a certain sort of help that is then gladly given. However, serving in the clear and everyday ways people relate to each other within their professions there lies a vast territory of very complex and shadowed landscape wherein discerning true service remains an attempt made by the follower of mazes and puzzles. It is sometimes very difficult to discern right service and the efforts of a seeker to move beyond the limits set by the culture so that solutions to questions concerning true service may be found, for what is the service in a given situation wherein two souls wend their way, moved by destiny? That destiny is inward and its ways are felt only by the seeker herself, not the one who attempts to help from without.

Or there is often that entity who asks for service but for whom such service may well not be good to give. Those sensitive to this dynamic wherein service finds its nature in truth have a goodly work to do, for what is the service of an entity but that gift of love which has been his to give?

The one known as Paul the Apostle suggested that in terms of service one might well think of the body which has many members: the stomach aids by being a stomach, the ears by being ears, and so forth. So each entity has his gifts to share. Yet, if each offers a different gift how infinite must the body of love be! Then, is service visible love? Is the service of an entity to share its gifts? Indeed, that is so, but there is the level beyond this wherein the seeker realizes that the purest service is the realized or illumined being, that joyful self that has been nurtured and allowed to bloom in the light of faith. This is love. This is service, to be. Then, the entity may share each gift, yet knowing that the breath that fills the service with meaning and value is love.

Now let us return to love. We agree with you, my brother, that the ways of love are ways of mystery. This mystery is the nature of all manifestation driven to its point of entrance into manifestation. Examined physical phenomena end in mystery. Metaphysical concepts may be followed far, but always end in mystery. Unknowing is the *sigil motto* of the spiritual warrior. Yet love feels a certain way, touches and transforms each entity in ways which tell that entity of the overwhelming and primary strength and force of that invisible quality.

Within your density true love has no voice, yet there are many voices which strive to express love. Each seeker is that which is love, yet which is creating sound and motion constantly striving to discover that which it is.

Turn the gaze inward, and gaze steadfastly at that which the one known as William Yeats called the "rag and bone shop of the heart," one of this instrument's favorite lines of poetry. Gaze at that illusion, that imperfection perceived, that undeniable self. You look at love. Continue always to seek love, how to express love, and how to be of service. Know these efforts as the often subtle arts that they are. Respect right use of power in being of service, in attempting to manifest love, and develop always little by little, step by step that place within which is engraved with the print of your feet, that place wherein holy things reside. Know this sanctuary daily. No moment of visiting this holy of holies is in vain. To all who are weary we extend the encouragement of the fellow traveler. Within the suffering does always lie perfect blooming and fresh the one infinite Creator whose nature and being is love.

We thank this instrument and leave it in love and in light and transfer to the one known as Jim. We are those of Q'uo.

(Jim channeling)

I am Q'uo, and greet each again in love and in light. At this time we would offer ourselves for the further querying, if there are any further queries.

P: Carla is having a hard time dealing with physical and mental/emotional challenges. I wonder if there is anything that can be done to help the instrument? Thank you.

[I am Q'uo.] We find that this particular entity is not a stranger to that which she experiences at this time and indeed from time to time periodically. Whenever an entity feels the weight of the incarnation upon the shoulders and is able to bear such weight in good humor, [with] faith for the effort and the next opportunity, then an entity has become aware of more of the nature of the incarnative state, for too often are the senses dulled to that which is of importance, being the central focus of an incarnation. Entities are easily distracted and incarnations are often used less than optimally by such avoidance of the catalyst placed for the progress preincarnatively.

Thus, we offer this preamble as a kind of recognition that [it] is a worthwhile achievement for a seeker to recognize that [that] which is of importance in the incarnation, whether there be great difficulty associated with it or not, is an achievement in the spiritual discrimination necessary for development of the personality, metaphysically speaking.

Thus, for the entity itself we cannot speak any more helpfully than to commend the recognition and discrimination and the faith-filled perception accompanying these recognitions. There is always assistance that it is possible to offer another in prayer and in meditation, for the prayers of each entity are as the rays of the sun to the growing flower.

Is there any further query, my sister?

P: No, thank you.

Is there another query?

(Pause)

I am Q'uo, and we are aware of the fatigue that is present at this time, and we would use this opportunity to thank each for making a great effort to join this circle of seeking, for we know that it was not particularly easy for a number of those present. We are always thrilled at this opportunity to join your gathering, for we are able to be with you in a way that is most satisfying to us in that we blend our hearts and minds with you as we speak with you and listen to you. In this way we have our beingness in your illusion, and we thank you for the invitation at each opportunity.

At this time we shall take our leave of this group, leaving each in the love and in the light of the one infinite Creator. We are known to you as those of Q'uo. Adonai, my friends. Adonai.

(Carla channels Nona in song only.)

Special Meditation
February 5, 1995

Group question: How do we recognize what we are supposed to learn from our catalyst? Can you recommend any techniques or procedures that we could use to learn from our catalyst?

(Carla channeling)

We are those of Q'uo. Greetings in the love and in the light of the one infinite Creator. We are most thankful for your call to us, and, indeed, we hope that we might share our thoughts with you in a helpful way. If any thoughts which we offer are not pleasing, we encourage you to lay those thoughts aside, for we speak not with ultimate authority but as your brothers and sisters within the beautiful path of spacious existence which lies open to those who seek the spirit within each moment, the life within each instant, the eternity within the now.

To speak concerning catalyst, it is well to gaze first at the way in which the physical, mental and emotional relationships of persons to others or to themselves are designed, for there is a logic to the moving forces of destiny which lies far beneath that literal logic which distills questions to a proof of an answer. The truths of the seeker are not usually clear, for the mystery that is at the base of all systems inevitably becomes the view in front of the face of one who gazes deeply enough into that which is occurring at any given time and space. This arrangement of logical alternatives cannot be pinned down because each incarnation has a basic plan in terms of areas of learning to love or learning to accept love, and these goals are fairly clear to the seeker who has persisted in inner work for any length of time.

The means of going after these goals, however, is usually very much a free will choice so that there is not one right or correct response to incoming catalyst. The attitude of the seeker in this wise might, perhaps, be skillful to choose the far-seeing eye when gazing at a situation in which there is catalyst, not moving upon impulse, not concluding quickly concerning issues, but, rather, remaining serene in the sure and certain knowledge that your destiny will provide continual opportunities to follow through with the lessons that you have identified for your own self.

Now, what consists of catalyst? To what characteristic should the seeker look to identify it? We might suggest that the experience of discomfort, whether it be physical, emotional, mental or spiritual, is a hallmark of catalyst, for catalyst, by definition, will create changes although it, itself, is not altered. Therefore, when the seeker finds itself fretting, worrying and hesitating concerning an issue the student simply steps back and takes note that there is this discomfort. Therefore, there is catalyst.

The next question within the mind of the seeker is, "How shall I respond to this discomfort? Shall I attempt to alleviate my distress? Shall I preserve patience and see what happens?" Again, there is no one answer, for that wind of life within which blows about the inner heart and cleanses the atmosphere of the spirit has a blessed and intimate connection with the discomfort caused by catalyst. There is an instinct deep within that connects in a graceful and grace-filled way with situations in which discomfort is a symptom of the transformation for which the catalyst was supplied in the first place.

There is the model of the world which sees questions and answers in neat compartments. This model of the world works well within your culture. However, it does not work at all well when the seeker is prosecuting that long, long process of seeking to find the heart of self and, therefore, the heart of catalyst.

Perhaps the shortest way of expressing or suggesting a way of dealing with catalyst is to say that each experience is a new one. The type of catalyst becomes ever easier to identify as the seeker continues with the dogged patience which is the hallmark of spiritual health. Eventually the link between the spirit within—which this instrument often calls grace—and the heart of discomfort begins to be perceived ever more flowingly and less rigidly until the happy state becomes possible wherein the seeker is upheld simply by doing the dance of life, and then gazes at all that moves him or her with a trustful and cheerful eye.

For suffering and pain, while being necessary concomitants to learning the lessons of love, do not need to be clung to or held within the mind, emotion, body or spirit. A child playing upon the seashore goes through many instances of temporary discomfort. The sun is too hot. The pail is washed out to sea. The shovel gets broken. The child swallows salt water. To the child these events mean very little, for this young spirit is still being surprised by life itself. That spirit of newness, that allowing of catalyst to move you as if it were the first experience, is a key to finding your own balance within the processes of change and transformation.

Using catalyst is something the seeker cannot avoid. This illusion of yours is created to make evasion of catalyst impossible and full use of catalyst improbable. This illusion leans upon imperfection and forces the mind and the emotions to gaze at that which is not perfect in appearance. This false worldview is designed to be that backdrop against which the common life with its suffering may become a life incandescent with the seeker's joyful acceptance and eagerness to pursue the processes of change.

So we would suggest that you be eager and hungry for those processes of change. Recognize discomfort as the hallmark of inner work being done, and recollect at all times that this work is not mental. You may think and muse endlessly concerning catalyst, but the way that catalyst is seated in the experiences of the seeker is, for the greater part, functioning within the deep mind of which you are not conscious. The key, then, in this regard is allowing time to pass until the heart feels and senses truth. It cannot be rushed. It cannot be figured out. Although these processes do aid in a growing grasp of the incarnational pattern that you have, they cannot take that essence that is you to a more truthful or genuine expression of self. You are not here to understand and know the self beyond a certain point. You are not here to become perfect. You are here within an illusion which forces you to seek beyond the limits of that which is visible or knowable.

The hungry man has a sore stomach and when the seeker awakens to the call to walk the path of pilgrimage there is that overriding hunger and the spiritual appetite is keen. Treasure this discomfort. Allow it to continue. Allow the self to see the self with a bit of distance and let that editor or critic of the self reassure and remind the everyday mentality that when one is following the spirit surprises often occur, and the one thing to keep watch on is where the attention is placed, for there is that place within, that inner sanctum sanctorum, wherein that which is holy rests. Moving into this space is that which is the wisest of all resources to choose, for in the end all the catalyst can do is offer you opportunities to learn your own nature and to begin, just begin, to grasp infinite love, eternal life, beingness forever.

And we encourage each to find the light touch, to share the laughter and the silliness of such idealistic and spiritual goals. There is rich humor in every fiber of your density. The less you blink, the less you are overcome by the seriousness of situations, the more humor you shall find, for the Creator is most playful. So allow that spirit within to romp and play, and, above all things, to reach out to others as they ask, as you can serve. For the love you bear each other is that fruit which the other cannot create and love is the great gift, the inner and deeper truth of all being and all relationship.

We would at this time transfer this contact to the one known as Jim. We leave this instrument in love and in light. We are those of Q'uo.

(Jim channeling)

I am Q'uo, and greet each again in love and in light. We are privileged to offer ourselves at this time to those who may have further queries for us, and we would ask if there might be a further query at this time?

R: I wonder if you could talk some about accepting the darker part of the self?

I am Q'uo, and am aware of your query, my brother. You are many things which you are not aware of, for you are indeed all things. This is the great mystery of creation. We worship with you this mystery, my brother, and can only shed a limited amount of light upon this topic, for the Creator which has set all energy into motion and has pleased Itself by giving fields of energy which are called entities free will to choose the manner of their being and the way in which they express this being as a manifestation of that being.

We are aware that each seeker feels an affinity for entities that are other than the self or seemingly so, and especially feels affinity for entities which suffer. Each seeker also wishes to accept those portions of the self which are suffering and which may be hidden in their origin. We can only say to you, my brother, that as you move through the various influences in your life pattern you will find that there is a new way of looking at yourself that is developed by the processing of catalyst. There are discoveries that one makes when one finds oneself in new circumstances. There are abilities called forth, perhaps for the first time, or in a more accentuated form of manifestation that a new set of stimuli will request or evoke.

As you continue to process the catalyst that forms various patterns in your life you will find that there is more to yourself than first imagined. In this way you can begin to see the circle of your being, shall we say, that of which you are aware of consciously and dimly aware of in your deeper mind. This circle is lighted by your consciousness and your attention to it. It increases its circumference with new experiences. That you are unable to imagine what it would be like to dwell in terrible darkness and delusion, that of the murderer, that of the thief, and so forth, is only testament to the present circle of your being that it includes certain experiences and does not seem to include others.

Yet, we can assure you that as you explore more and more of this beingness—the beingness of the one Creator—in incarnation after incarnation and density after density, you will have covered a great deal more of this total being than you are now aware of. You shall set for yourself in various of your incarnations and portions thereof a variety of parameters, expressions of energy, intersections of entities, and you shall immerse yourself in the moving tides of your kinds' history.

In this infinite march of the One to the One, by the many portions of the One there is available the infinity of opportunity that is the Creator. At various times you shall choose hither and yon and shall choose widely disparate selections of opportunities that will teach in a variety of ways that which you seek. Thus, though your present experience may seem small we assure you this is so that you can focus more clearly and sharply your attention upon those lessons which are currently before you and not dissipate your precious conscious working focus on many and sundry issues.

Thus, if you are well focused the experience of the current incarnation is also in a sharp focus or distinction that allows for efficient working. Other incarnations shall focus in other areas, my brother.

Is there another query?

R: What you are saying is that I should feel through my heart and focus on what is in front of me and work on that while allowing all of the other mystery that I cannot grasp to work as it will? Could you comment on that please?

I am Q'uo, and we feel that you have a basic grasp of that which we have attempted to share, though we would amplify in a small way by suggesting that the feeling through your heart of the acceptance of that which is is another way of stating the concept of faith, which is a great enabler …

(Side one of tape ends.)

(Jim channeling)

I am Q'uo, and am again with this instrument. You must have faith, my brother, that you are well placed within the one Creator, at the very center, for there is no other being or place to be, and if you walked quite literally in the shoes of your fellow seekers, you would walk as do they for reasons that are well or poorly understood, that have results that are more or less helpful, seen in a relative sense, with the cause and ultimate effect of all thoughts and actions being rooted in that great mystery that is the one Creator. And that as you do indeed walk in each shoe of every brother and sister that you know and do not know, you do indeed walk where only the Creator treads.

Is there another query, my brother?

R: No, thank you, Q'uo. That gives me a lot to think about from a different angle.

I am Q'uo, and we thank you, my brother. Is there another query?

P: I would like to ask if there is another reason for existence besides the Creator knowing Itself?

I am Q'uo, and though we are aware of the query which you have asked we are not aware of any other reason or indication that the Creator might have for this experience which we all share, though we do not say such a reason could not exist. As far as we have plumbed this great and infinite mystery the only reason we have found for this experience is that it is our portion of the one Creator's pattern of beingness, that is that we should become that which is and should find a greater and greater expression of ourselves to be the same as the Creator's self.

Is there any further query, my sister?

P: Yes, could you clarify the notion of time? When you talk about the concept of becoming it suggests a forward moving direction oriented in time. On the other hand, we are told that everything exists at the same time. Could you comment on this aspect of creation?

I am Q'uo, and am aware of your query, my sister. We utilize the terms that are most easily understood—if we might use that misnomer—within your illusion, for to speak the ultimate truth would not only be impossible in words, but would be confusing in practice, for as you have correctly surmised it is true that all does exist in a simultaneous fashion in regards to time. However, within your illusion the focus of consciousness has been constructed in such a precise manner that the illusion that you experience does its work in what seems to be a linear progression of time and experience. However, that is not just within this illusion but is a portion of the greater experience of all that is that has been, shall we say, been segmented or focused upon in such a way that it seems that your life patterns move on after the other and in a sequential manner within each, whereas in truth there is the greater self that is your higher self that exists at this time with a complete expression of that which you are, that which you shall become, that which you have been, together with other expressions of your self as well. These you are. These you move toward. These are a portion of the great paradox and mystery of creation.

Is there a final query at this time?

P: How is it possible in our present experience of third density, with our five senses, the simultaneous existence of time … How can we experience it in our lives, that we exist at all times?

I am Q'uo, and am aware of your query, my sister. The great veil of forgetting which each passes through upon the entry into this illusion insures that this far-seeing ability that recognizes all time as simultaneous is that which awaits discovery only in those moments of grace, shall we say, which present themselves to you at various points within the incarnation as a kind of implication, shall we say, of that which truly is a guidepost or sign along the way. Many such experiences are achieved in the meditative state, the fasting, the prayer, the dream in which the future or the past or both are blended with the present. Thusly, the door to the greater experience is only cracked a tiny bit within your illusion so that your focus remains carefully placed upon those lessons which you choose for each incarnation.

Is there a further query, my sister?

P: No, thank you.

I am Q'uo, and again we thank you, my sister. We thank each present for allowing us to share our opinions with you again. It has been our great privilege to join in your circle this day and we are always hopeful that we have been able to share with you some small portion of our thoughts that might be of service to you in your journey with each other and with the one Creator. We walk with you and give praise and thanksgiving for each step.

At this time we shall take our leave of this group, leaving each, as always, in the love and in the light of the one infinite Creator. We are those of Q'uo. Adonai. ❦

Sunday Meditation

February 12, 1995

Group question: We would like to know why suffering is necessary, and, in light [of the fact] that so many people in the world suffer so much, how is it that suffering is a service either to the people who suffer or to the Creator who watches the suffering as part of Itself?

(Carla channeling)

We are those of Q'uo. Greetings in the love and in the light of the one infinite Creator. We are grateful for your call to us. As always, we answer this call as your brothers and sisters of the path. We are fallible and make errors. Therefore, we ask that each listen and chose those thoughts of ours which appeal, leaving the rest behind. Always we would ask those who appreciate our council to use and value the personal discrimination within. This is not easy to do when the seeking is for a mystery and a purity that seem impossible to reach without help from outside. However, both past and future are within you, and no amount of reaching from without or outside of the self can ever be equivalent to those truths which are realized internally through the process of discovery.

We consider ourselves blessed to be able to function as those who remind you of truths you already know. We do not bring news. That is, we have nothing new to astound you with. We are simple, and our message is simple. To achieve the simplicity of nature we now have has taken a great deal of work or suffering or experience, whatever name you wish to call it. The truth that we see is that the process of spiritual evolution is slow beyond your wildest imagination. Yet, this work remains fascinating. And we do not regret one iota of the time and energy we have spent in reaching this place. Nor do we quail before the challenges we now face, for we are eager to learn and hungry for that source which is our and your all in all.

In speaking with you about suffering, we would begin by looking at what we just said. It took us a long, long time and a great deal of careful work—work of the mind, work of the heart, and work of the intuition—to achieve the awareness which we now enjoy. We have removed brick by brick the walls between us who are of Q'uo. We have removed before that brick by brick the walls within ourselves which kept us from allowing ourselves the surcease of that suffering which we so needed to experience. Suffering is a word biased substantially in the negative sense. When one suffers one is considered to be bearing pain, difficulty, and trouble. Yet to suffer is actually to allow, and what is allowed in suffering is fear. Any experience may be suffered or allowed to occur, yet it is the experience which is not resisted which brings a lack of suffering.

We do not speak of the suffering of hunger and nakedness and imprisonment when we say that suffering is a choice. In those cases also suffering is indeed a choice, but we would deal at this moment with the normal suffering, day by day, which strikes at the heart of most entitys' life experience: the suffering of a self which is resisting the flow of that which is occurring in front of the eyes, the suffering between people, the suffering at a job, or doing some work, the suffering because of what one does not have, the suffering because of that which one has and cannot be rid of. These are a measure of the resistance the seeker has, usually subconsciously, to the drift of that destiny which always lies before one, which one spins out as does the spider its web from the nexus within which experience is recorded.

Let us look at the suffering of the rock. First, it becomes rock by being cast out of the fiery molten core which is beneath that which is rock upon your planetary sphere, flung into space, tossed away by that which was its home. It now thrusts upwards through an atmosphere of air. Nothing is as it was, and through your time this rock is worn, slowly and steadily, eroded, pitted, roughened and crevassed until little bits of earth cling to its surface, and gradually it is covered by earth which then grows plants whose roots reach down into the rock, breaking it, further wearing it away until perhaps this rock is upheaved by another burst of molten energy, becoming broken, falling down in splinters and shards, rolling perhaps into the bed of some stream and washing, century by century, until it has become a million pebbles, a billion grains of sand. The rock has a long life; from its first identity as rock until its last dissolution, it is constantly worn away, broken and re-broken that earth may come to it, that it may support growth and blooming, and that it may eventually dissolve.

Because the rock has no self-consciousness, it does not suffer. It experiences. It is not that rock accepts the erosion which eventually dissolves it. It is that its nature is as it is and that which occurs is that which occurs.

For the animal, the life is that which is, for, again, there is no self-consciousness except that which is implanted within it by its human caretakers. If it has the cut or the lame paw it simply has this. It endures it without suffering. It experiences the pain, the discomfort, but it does not suffer, for it does not reflect within itself but rather seeks the sleep which frees it to dream of days when it was chasing game and being that which it is as a young one.

However, within third density lies that great gift and that great burden of self-consciousness. You, also, as the rock, as the animal, from the first moment of being thrust out into the atmosphere to that last moment when breath expires, experience and suffer through every change, every new discovery, every phase and stage of development, both physical, mental, emotional and spiritual, and insofar as the experience is not resisted and is entered into faithfully, there is not the suffering. Few there are among your peoples who have achieved a lack of fear sufficient to claim no suffering from fire, torture, sudden death, or a million smaller mishaps of circumstance. For the great millions suffering is a fact. The resistance to discomfort and pain on whatever level is instinctive. The creature seeks comfort. This is an instinct.

This instrument was reading this morning concerning those who chose not to suffer less but to increase suffering in order to pay homage and worship to the one infinite Creator, for these ascetic individuals, often called saints among your peoples, felt such great love of the one infinite Creator that the desire was to ignore any and all impulses of the body which kept the soul from thinking on the one infinite Creator. We do not say that these saints are correct in the lengths to which they take an embracing of suffering. This was their path. It worked for them. We do not suggest it for any except those for whom it is desirable.

However, we do encourage each seeker to gaze without fear at the troubles of the day. When resistance is felt, when the suffering occurs, this is a puzzle for later contemplation, not to stop the flow of suffering but rather to allow a portion of the self to observe it so that it may be accurately remembered. When there is a distinct lack of suffering it is well also to take note of that which constitutes the enjoyment experienced, for there is much to learn about the self from the simple reactions or responses which the self has to various stimuli. The path to self-knowledge is one in which reflection and contemplation upon one's own inner workings does bear a substantial part.

Why is suffering necessary? We would change this question to "Why is experience necessary?" For as we have said suffering is not necessary, even for those who starve, for those who are naked, suffering is not necessary. The experience, the pain, be it ever so deep, does not necessarily bring suffering. For entities to turn and embrace their troubles it requires much, much learning, much grasping of the true nature of experience. The experiencing is necessary because you have chosen to manifest and to manifest one must accept space and time in a structure which creates a process through time or through space and in that process through time and space the reason for manifestation develops itself, which is to say that as each experience is processed within choices are made which advance the uniqueness of that entity's identity. These experiences are as necessary as the text books of your classrooms. There must be some way of learning the lessons which are given in the school of life, for your incarnation is, indeed, a school, and it is a school which you enter in each incarnation with great hopes of achievement. Yet when the semester begins the work is hard, painful and inconvenient, and it is only natural for the student to protest that inevitable grind of one project after another after another. Is there no end to learning? No, indeed, there is not.

This school of incarnation is most generous in offering as much experience as you wish to take on and as deep a probing into the nature of it as the seeker has the resources to mount. The Creator wishes to experience Itself. Insofar as each of you suffers, so the Creator experiences as suffering. The Creator is most grateful for these experiences and does not judge or condemn an entity for having a hard time with the subject. It appreciates the effort. It appreciates the experience.

In truth, we might say that the goal of the suffering seeker is not the end to suffering but, rather, an increased or enhanced sense of the sanctity, the hallowed nature of these processes of learning, of changing, of evolving through experience. Each seeker chooses the degree to which it shall suffer as it resists or does not resist the beckoning call of its own destiny. Each is co-creator of that destiny. Each has chosen the classes it is in in this school of incarnation. Therefore, all is well, metaphysically speaking, whatever the suffering looks like, for it is simply a portion of experience allowed to be suffering through the resistance and fear of the changing that the learning creates.

When one steps back and thinks again of the rock, one sees that if the rock were self-conscious it would suffer, for it is blown into manifestation and eroded and perhaps blown again into smaller and smaller pieces until it is ground down completely and disappears into sand and dirt and elements.

The nature of living is that it is fullest in the first instant of life and is steadily eroded until its end in death. It arises. It falls away. That is the nature of incarnation. Seen from this standpoint it may be clearer why suffering is the common lot. Each arises on the Earth scene full of a life and the nature of that life's manifestation is that the coin of time, the treasure of attention, is spent and eventually the personality is completely bankrupt and out of time, out of treasure, out of lessons, and out of school. And the incarnation ends. Loss upon loss, limitation upon limitation until that final expulsion of breath and the ceasing of existence within third density.

The Creator does not need your suffering. The Creator wishes your experience, and if suffering is involved the Creator may gladly take that also, for that is your truth. It is accepted without judgment. It is loved. It is blessed. It is not desired. All that is desired is that the unique spark which is yourself do as it pleases to find out to the deepest level possible what that essence of self is. The journey of discovery lies within and it is a long voyage.

We would, at this time, transfer this contact to the one known as Jim, as this entity runs low on energy. We leave this instrument with thanks, and in love and in light. We are those of Q'uo.

(Jim channeling)

I am Q'uo, and greet each again in love and in light through this instrument. We have felt a great deal of sympathy for those of your peoples who must move through this third-density illusion fraught with so much that causes suffering, for we know from our own experience the difficulties that are inherent within your illusion. There is no obvious unity which binds all entities in a supportive community upon which to call for most of your peoples. There is instead the seeming fragmentation of all that is unified into the manyness of a creation which seems most of the time to be at odds with itself. We feel a great deal of sympathy for those who are in the midst of famine, of disease, of loneliness, and of that dryness of spirit that turns to bitterness in the view of life. Yet, we are comforted in our feeling of sympathy by knowing that each of these experiences shall make a mark upon each entity which is one stroke of the artist's brush upon an eternal canvas of complete harmony.

There is the offering of each entity laid at the feet of the Creator by the very nature of the illusion, that which begins and ends, that which you call the life and the death, and each entity shall give over to the Creator the harvest of each incarnation which shall allow the Creator to experience that which has been experience by the entity and so enrich the Creator by the choices made and the joys and sorrows known.

At this time we would offer ourselves in the answering of further queries which those present might have for us. Is there a query at this time?

P: Concerning the truth, absolute and relative truth. Most of the time what we experience seems to be of relative truth. What is the relation of relative truth to absolute truth?

I am Q'uo, and am aware of your query, my sister. In this great octave of experience which we all share there is that which can be seen as the ultimate or absolute truth and that which is relative, and we would utilize the portion of the deep mind which is called the archetypical mind as an illustration of that which is, for this octave, an absolute truth, for it is the architecture of the process of evolution. It is the journey upon which we each find ourselves moving upon. It is that which we all shall fulfill, each in our own way, which is that which we would call that relative truth.

As we move through this pattern of expression of the one Creator we do so in a way which is a function of our unique choices, a way which is a function of memory and experience. The archetypical mind is not affected or changed in any way whatsoever by memory or by experience of any entity moving within its patterns and opportunities. Thus, each entity provides an—we search for the correct word—interpretation of this journey which is relative to all other entity's choices. Yet the architecture of the Logos, that source of Love, is absolute. In truth, there is one great Absolute as far as we are aware and that is the unity of all things and all entities, for even the archetypical mind is that which is expressed by an infinite number of logoi throughout the one creation.

Is there another query?

P: We as individuals seem to be the builders of the archetypical mind, so aren't we the builders of absolute truth?

I am Q'uo, and am aware of your query, my sister. In the deepest sense, that which recognizes each entity as the Creator, this is so. But in the sense of entities which move through the illusion as portions of the Creator this would not be so, for there is no choice which you can make as an individual entity that changes any portion of the archetypical mind. This is given by the Logos. You may choose an infinite number of manners to move through this mind, but it is ever and always the same.

Is there another query, my sister?

P: No, thank you.

I am Q'uo, and we thank you once again, my sister. Is there another query at this time?

R: I am curious. What makes you sometimes come up with a little joke in the end? Is it the energy that we put together at that moment?

I am Q'uo, and am aware of your query, my brother. We are those who have blended vibrations of those of Ra and those of Latwii. Each of these social memory complexes have an appreciation of that which you call humor. This group is well aware of the humor of those of Latwii. Humor, as we are able to see it, is the view of a situation with a sense of proportion about it. As one looks at the entirety of a situation that may, from one point of view, may seem difficult and distressing, may when seen from its entirety or when the entity experiencing it is seen in a more full view there is often the opportunity to balance the situation by seeing another characteristic which, when taken in comparison characteristic, adds a sense of comic relief, shall we say. The difficulty is relieved by the larger view, and we feel that humor is an excellent means of restoring the larger view to entities who are perhaps a bit over-stressed by one portion of a picture.

Is there another query, my brother?

R: No, thanks. I appreciate that.

I am Q'uo, and we thank you, my brother. Is there another query at this time?

(Pause)

I am Q'uo, and since we observe a lull in the querying at this time, we shall assume that we have, for the nonce, spoken to those areas of concern and we are grateful to each entity for presenting us with these opportunities to share with you that which is our experience and our opinions. We are most happy to do so and can always count on this group to query in a thoughtful and profound manner.

We shall at this time take our leave of this instrument and this group, leaving each, as always, in the love and in the light of the one infinite Creator. We are known to you as those of Q'uo. Adonai, my friends. Adonai. ✣

Sunday Meditation
February 19, 1995

Group question: The question this week has to do with the "Who am I?" question that each seeker asks. We are wondering about the incarnational personality as a focus as to who each seeker might be. The incarnational personality, of course, has connections with the soul identity that has been through many incarnations and has connections with the one Creator as a portion of that Creator. We are wondering if you could tell us something about the incarnational self, who that self is, and use it as a vehicle for evolution.

(Carla channeling)

We are those of Q'uo. Greetings in the love and in the light of the one infinite Creator. We are most pleased to have been called to your group this day. There are also those energies about which you know as those of Hatonn. However, as this instrument ascertained, the energies of Hatonn are simply to be placed upon the circle of seeking and in a very subtle sense upon that tape recording device which records these words. That carrier wave, shall we say, of meditative quiet and stillness is an helpful one, and those who listen to such a recording such as this one may be offered that silent gift. In addition, we shared a joke with this instrument which caused the challenging process a little longer to deal with. We are always hoping that this instrument will not be too earnest about her challenging, so when she asked us if we came in the name of the one known as Jesus we said, "Oh yes, we stop in the name of love." But this instrument would not accept that. However, to our minds the one known as Jesus is the one known as Love, for this entity managed during incarnation to express that energy in its fullness.

As always, when speaking with a group, we request that our words be taken with a grain of salt and that the personal discrimination be used. We do indeed thank this group, and deeply, for sharing these moments with us and allowing us to share with you what humble service that we may offer at this time.

The question of self-identity is indeed the signal question of a density devoted to the exploration of self-consciousness. The other experiences gained in first and second density, as powerful and all-encompassing as they have been, are as a simply elementary school class compared to the complexities of self-discovery and self-perception. Being aware of the self being is in many ways confusing. There is confusion because of each entity viewing itself through the passing kaleidoscope of circumstance and event about which one spins one's life's threads.

The child, that young soul whose mind is infinite and eternal but whose body is clumsy and small, must determine what of his body makes him who he is and what not of his body but of the mind or of the emotions. This is most puzzling and the questioning begins for each entity as that soul becomes enough aware of itself within its little world that the focus becomes inward.

Those of young ages are frequently viewed by their parents and teachers as those who do not have native wisdom or the ability to think upon abstractions at the age of pre-school, as this instrument would call the years of four and five. Yet by this age the larger part of your people are philosophers in their own small way, picking up questions of life, death and being and looking seriously and probingly at them for clues as to identity and that ineffable and indescribable sense of belonging that is yearned for but not entirely felt with those identities which the world sees and passes so to the young self.

Each year, indeed, each season, which adds to the child's life its burden of days, yields also a crazy quilt of perception and misperception, accurately perceived and inaccurately perceived memory and the drifting of memory and thought through those inner seasons which color perception so profoundly, usually without being themselves perceived. The burdens that the child has taken up often become invisible yet still are burdens carried, yet carried not within the conscious mind but stowed safely as in a ship's hold for the long voyage which shall occur before that self is able or ready to open the cargo doors and work with that burden which has laid patiently awaiting such a visit since the childhood.

These hidden storage areas of the self are hidden for good reason. The self is a living entity in a way which transcends current definitions of life, for there is not the embodiment or the gross manifestation in many forms of vivid life which entities upon your sphere tend to attach life to. The life within, as has been pointed out by this group, moves through incarnations, one upon the next, in a journey unimaginably larger than the journey through incarnation. Yet that journeying and questing self that is infinite and eternal is only taken in full realization and seated or embedded within that infinite self through the processes within incarnation through which the mind comes to be more and more acquainted with the self.

Therefore, sitting down and taking the pen and writing upon paper those things known about the self, and those things logically assumed and attempting to infer identity in some mental way—this process is not useful, for the self is not built with the logic of the mind. That self which is the deepest self is a distortion of love and the heart as it opens simply becomes more and more able to resonate to the pure emotions which are that unique distortion of love which is each entity. Thusly, one better feels and intuits one's way towards a deeper understanding of the identity of the self than work with the logic and the mind can ever produce.

These are subtle matters. And using words is a clumsy option when working in this area, yet we do not have a choice other than these words, so if you will forgive us and this instrument who must, in a way, translate our concepts, we shall continue attempting to throw some light upon this very central subject.

When the entity that each is comes into incarnation it is aware ahead of that time that it will lose its way; it will not remember that way; and it will need to wake up in the life in order to begin that journey of self-discovery. Those such as this circle now present were awakened by the call of that nature which as each grew it uncovered within its self. So each has gone through several generations of thought concerning self-identity and has discarded many self-identities, finding them too limited and not enough evocative of self-perceived spiritual advancement or evolution. It is good to have started this searching, this pilgrimage, for as entities seek the light, as they are drawn to love, they are also seeking their identity.

The ideals and philosophical arrangements which work to create a more spiritually aware life experience must hang in mystery and in veiling much that the self would know yet cannot know within incarnation. There is no use in incarnations if the work done within incarnation is over and if the puzzle, shall we say, is completely and perfectly solved for an entity, then this entity has just transcended third density and will soon depart from this planet and its physical third-density existence.

It is a prerequisite, shall we say, of incarnation or the continuance of incarnation that the person be working to discover truth, the truth of self, the truth of love—the truth, however that entity describes or phrases it. When school is out the Creator simply allows that entity to move on. So the one sure thing about entities within incarnation upon your planet at this time is that they are imperfectly known to themselves. This, then, being a prerequisite for life as you know it may be counted a good thing by some although one would not expect a universal "yes."

It does, however, seem to most entities somewhat unfair, in that the deck is stacked against being able to know the truth that is so hungrily sought. Yet we say to you that the spirit within incarnation that is still seeking is that spirit that has the right to manifest within the illusion those gifts that may help that illusion. No on upon your sphere, native or wanderer, is fully realized. Each entity is upon that journey, and so are we, and for us, as larger truths have appeared, things have fallen away and new mysteries have appeared. So it has been also for you and so shall it continue to be.

One may gaze at this identity at the level of its programming and see a very mechanical aspect to self-identity and by this we mean that there exists within the melding made between consciousness and the biocomputer of your brain those ways of perceiving which have been chosen throughout incarnation so far, which have re-written and distorted the way and the priority with which incoming sense data is received and processed. Thusly, on one important level the seeker may find its identity to be an amalgam of those programs which run when the self is presented with sense data. A simplistic example of this would be the cliché which this instrument is aware of concerning the glass of water being half full to the optimist and half empty to the pessimist. By such judgments the self accretes a system for judging incoming perceptions, and it decides and makes choices concerning this incoming data based upon choices previously made which have biased the incoming perceptions before they have arisen to the conscious mind.

So that it is very fruitful to move back into inner work gazing at those things which grab the attention throughout each day, and working with that harvest of daily knowledge of self by observing and contemplating what has been observed. Much healing might be done by the entity who goes back into those early experiences which biased the program, discovering those centers of pain, anger, disappointment or whatever negative complex of emotions caused that crystallization which distorted the programming in the first place. And we encourage those efforts to know the self by working with the memory and with the dreams which may offer memories which have been forgotten.
However, it is equally helpful to surrender all knowledge of self as being utterly irrelevant to the self that wishes to become one with the one infinite Creator, who wishes only to lose itself in that presence, who seeks to tabernacle with the infinite love that is the one Creator.

Each entity has an identity. Looked at from the highest level each entity is an illusion. And as the densities mount towards the end of an octave those self-realized entities which were so full of emotion in earlier densities and who experienced such ideal states of compassion and wisdom find themselves releasing layer after layer of illusion until in the final gesture of individual personality the self is released into all that there is by desire. We cannot at this point in our own learning imagine what it is like to yearn so for the infinite One that the personality is completely released, but this does in the end occur, as far as we know.

Theoretically, then, if one took no thought at any time and simply stayed comfortable when in incarnation and avoided worry it might be possible never to be concerned with self-knowledge, simply choosing to love the Creator. No entity has as yet taken this shortcut, however, since the physical senses in any density are such as to give the individual clear subjective proof of existence and self-awareness.

Perhaps the best way to advise a seeker to look at the incarnational personality is to suggest that each allow the self the freedom of semi-permeable boundaries, allow the self to go deeply within, encourage the self to move deftly and deeply within the self as the opportunities, the moment come to each. This is not something one can do with a schedule. These moments of clarity come when they will, and we simply urge each to appreciate them and to yield to them when they come, for these are good opportunities to learn. And when the self is not in such a state we encourage each to allow the questions to rest, for self-discovery is a process which needs time. It is not something which is grasped in a crystallized and gestalt way, but, rather, lies too deep for such experiences. And as long as the self is allowed its natural freedom to be profound at one mood and shallow at another, to be light one day and heavy another, and so forth, this is the best way to study the self. It is a matter of catching it unawares. One cannot gaze forever at the self with profit. One must look away and become spontaneous.

There is that balance between the work and the rest which fuels and feeds the work which we would encourage each to keep in mind. The mundane tasks of everyday life may not reveal the self to the self, and certainly one is not what one does. Yet washing the dishes, teaching, or any activity whatsoever may one moment may mean nothing and another moment reveal profound truth. So the wise seeker is one who is alert to those moments when the present moment ceases being a moment in time and reveals the infinity of depth and width and breadth that is the truth of each present moment, for the present moment is the only one which exists and all present moments exist simultaneously. Do not be surprised to find realization occurring in the midst of the smallest and most routine chore, for the inner mountain tops of experience are not those which seem high in the outer world but rather those which have there being and their altitude deep within the self.

As we said, this is a difficult subject, for the truth of personality is a shifting one, yet we honor it greatly, for from it has come all that has been needed by us to evolve to where we are now, and we feel secure in saying that for each entity. This is also tending to be true, that within the everyday and ordinary daily existence lies not one way but many ways to pursue self-discovery. No truth you find of your nature shall ever be complete within incarnation, for there is not the amount of material available to the waking self.

However, we have offered enough for a beginning and welcome future queries at a later session. We would at this time transfer this contact to the one known as Jim. We are those of Q'uo, and leave this instrument in love and in light.

(Jim channeling)

I am Q'uo, and greet each again through this instrument in love and in light. We would like to thank the one known as Carla for allowing us to speak our thoughts through her this afternoon, for we know she suffers some discomfort.

At this time we would ask if those present might have another query to which we might provide a small answer?

P: How does the process of individuation differ from the process of separation that the service-to-self entity would practice?

I am Q'uo, and am aware of your query, my sister. The entity which has chosen the service-to-self path will in the process individualize itself as you have mentioned in a fashion that will utilize the intelligent energy gift of the one Creator in a manner which sets entities and events about it in the influence or control of this entity. Thus, the energy that it receives on a daily basis and from moment to moment is utilized in a fashion which causes others to serve this self.

The entity which has chosen to proceed on the evolutionary path in the positive sense utilizes the same daily gift of intelligent energy in a fashion which attempts to share this energy with others and to seek with them the mystery of creation and its subtleties. Thus, the use of energy by each polarity is opposite. The individualization process for each polarity is that process in which the seeker will utilize the intelligent energy of the Creator in a fashion which either reveals the unity of creation in some degree for the positive entity or which reveals the power of the entity which has chosen the negative path.

Is there a further query, my sister?

P: No, thank you.

I am Q'uo, and we thank you, my sister. Is there another query?

Carla: I want to follow up on P's question. How is the person who is self-aware different from the person who is serving the self as a choice of polarity?

I am Q'uo, and am aware of your query, my sister. We shall attempt to clarify. The entity which is self-aware, whether it is on the negative path or the positive path, is an entity which is seeking to utilize the energy of the one Creator in a manner which reveals more of itself to itself. If this entity who is becoming more self-aware has chosen the negative path then the use of this energy to become self-aware is utilized in a fashion which tends to cause others to serve it, thus bringing them under the control in more or less degree of this entity. If this entity which is becoming more self-aware has chosen the positive path, it shall further refine the use of the intelligent energy of the one Creator in a manner which reveals the Creator to those about it and thus offers this energy as a kind of gift to others.

Is there another query, my sister?

Carla: No, thank you.

I am Q'uo, and we again thank you, my sister. Is there another query at this time?

P: I wonder if the archetypes have an effect in shaping national identities of a large number of people and have an effect in shaping history and how nations interact?

I am Q'uo, and we believe that we grasp your query, my sister. The archetypical mind of the one Creator represented in this portion of the creation by your local logos has an effect upon all experience within the illusion that is, shall we say, in its care. There is the calling upon archetypical influences in each instance in which entities interact. In most cases this calling is not done consciously. However, the nature of the relationships and the choices which are made by all entities within them determine the kind of influence which is called upon by the very energy expenditure that is made in each relationship. The effectiveness of the calling upon archetypical concepts and influences is increased by the more and more conscious and willed calling upon these archetypes.

There are few who do this in a conscious fashion, for most of your peoples pass through their incarnational patterns without becoming aware of the basic architecture of the great Mind of which they are but a small portion. Yet each entity in its daily round of activities does move in a fashion which, by the expenditure of energy—its nature, intensity, purity and so forth—does call upon larger and larger influences that may redound to the very nature of the archetypical mind itself, for the nature of your creation is one in which there is a simple structure, a relationship to the Creator which is logical and all-pervasive and which resonates when a small portion of its being is set in motion by its own free will choice in a certain fashion.

If you can see the experiences that you share with each other being likened to a song, a great chorus, if you will, each note of the interrelationship sets up an harmonic response from larger and larger or, shall we say, more and more basic portions of the one creation, the most basic in many ways being the archetypical mind, the most basic in a fundamental sense being the universal mind of the one Creator.

Is there another query, my sister?

P: When a nature engages in war what kind of archetype is it fulfilling and does it need to do that in order to grow? How can they help themselves to find peace?

I am Q'uo, and though we are aware of your query, my sister, it is of such a large nature that we could not begin to answer it, for there is much complexity within the process of evolution for each individual entity and each group entity and the historical relationships that are built over thousands of years of experience. Yet you may rest assured that all archetypes are available and utilized in some fashion in this entire process. It is most helpful in the study of archetypical imagery and influence, in our opinion, for it to be reserved for the individual entities that are the seekers of truth. This is not to say that any entity would be excluded from this group but that the archetypical mind is most effectively seen and utilized by individuals in their own incarnational experiences.

Is there a further query, my sister?

P: No. Thanks so much.

I am Q'uo, and again we thank you, my sister. Is there a final query at this time?

Carla: Might we ask that query again as a main question?

I am Q'uo, and we are of the opinion, my sister, that the query concerning the relationship of the archetypical mind to the movement of nations is a query which asks too much explanation for how the archetypical mind would move through each entity within a country that has had generations of entities moving through its borders and within its influence. Thus, we would suggest that queries concerning the archetypical mind be reserved for the experience of individual entities and how the influences of the deeper levels of mind might be brought to bear within that sharper focus.

Is there a further query, my sister?

Carla: No.

I am Q'uo, and we would ask if there is a final query at this time?

(Pause)

I am Q'uo, and as it appears that we have exhausted the queries for the nonce we shall take this opportunity to express our complete gratitude at having been invited to join your group. We feel that we have been blessed with a great honor and we are always glad to respond to the call of this group, for when we walk with you we are enriched in our own journey as well.

We shall, then, at this time take our leave of this group. As always, we leave each in the love and in the ineffable light of the one infinite Creator. We are known to you as those of Q'uo. Adonai, my friends. Adonai. ☙

Sunday Meditation
February 26, 1995

Group question: We would like to know about the formation of the social memory complex on planet Earth. Does our technology such as television, computers with internet, radio, music, etc., aid any as training wheels in the formation of our social memory complex? And are there more subtle and efficient ways that this formation of our social memory complex is accomplished in our everyday lives?

(Carla channeling)

We are those of Hatonn, and greet all in the love and the light of the infinite Creator. We come but briefly to speak through this instrument those words of care, of affection and support that may perhaps be appreciated by those who seek with such hunger that truth which lies in that far country of truths not yet known. We encourage each to take courage, to care for each other and always to know that if our carrier wave is desired to aid in your meditations we are glad to come if you mentally request our presence. We would not intrude but are glad to respond to a request for our presence.

We appreciate this instrument's willingness to separate our call from the ones known to you as Q'uo and would express our great pleasure at coming into the visible or manifested portion of your illusion to experience with you for some of your moments the joy at blending our vibrations with our own. We thank you and this instrument and leave you in the infinite love and light of the infinite Creator. We are those of Hatonn. Adonai.

(Carla channeling)

We are those known to you as the principle of Q'uo, and we greet each in the love and in the light of the one infinite Creator. We thank each for inviting us to join you in this working on this day of new growth and new hope as the light lengthens each day and the atmosphere becomes slowly warmer and your planet stirs its roots in search of new food and reaches its leafy arms to the life-giving light. We find your cycle of seasons most beautiful in each stage and most evocative of the lessons of life and death which revolve about love and learning about love inevitably.

As always, we ask each to use his and her own discrimination to test those things which we say by the standards of your own heart so that our contributions may be your resources and never your stumbling blocks. Those ideas that we have that do not fit in with that that you know of as truth we ask you to leave behind. And we greatly appreciate your doing this with us and with any words which you may hear, for the true authority on truth is the heart of any self which has begun the process of becoming known to itself.

This day your question is one which is difficult to get, shall we say, organized with as the concept of social memory complex as the ultimate computer is at the same time a wonderful metaphor for what the social memory complex has as its resources and at the same time a guide which is easily misread, in that the social memory complex is of a transcendentally different nature from that of the computer, no matter how complete the information upon it. Let us look first at the metaphor of the global intelligence which is made available through the internet, as this instrument calls the rapidly expanding system whereby mass quantities of information are made available to masses of people.

No longer does the seeker of information need to spend large amounts of time physically moving from place to place, searching out materials to study. More and more those who wish information simply turn on their computers and access the information desired either through the internet or through what this instrument would call software which may be placed upon the memory of the computer, especially as those completely familiar with computers become able to use them with skill. The model of the computer with its global connections certainly is a promising and substantial metaphor for the golden net of love which the social memory complex is.

Now, that very description of a social memory complex may easily uncover the element lacking in the metaphor of the computer internet, for this computer, no matter how complete its store of information, cannot express the concepts which move into emotion; those shadowy concepts which are so deeply a part of truth cannot be carried by that which is not living, for there is no logic to emotion. There is no expression outside of words, numbers and other symbolic notations which can be carried with the structure of the computer. Rather, the nature of the social memory complex is one of less intellect and more—we confess we find no words in this instrument's vocabulary to express fully the dynamic between the mind's intelligence and its way of organizing material and the heart's intelligence and its way of organizing and prioritizing the same material.

The computer, then, has no heart. The seeker may well find the heart within to be more like the computer, yet as the seeker moves along its path, more and more, catalyst shall come which gives the seeker opportunities to move from head to heart.

This is a necessary step: the relinquishing of knowing, the surrender to unknowing, and the acceptance of truths which are felt and known in every cell instead of those truths which are learned, memorized and repeated.

The social memory complex, then, is a net that is as alive as are those which have contributed to that infinitely great network of connections from person to person to person. When a member of a social memory complex wishes to know something then that intelligence or information is indeed accessed, as this instrument would say, yet it is accessed through the heart, through a knowing which is like instinct once it has been awakened within. This insight or intuition as a way of knowing is that which the computer, no matter how sophisticated, cannot replicate.

However, much can be learned about the self and about the process of spiritual evolution by paying attention to the ways in which those about each of you are more and more beginning to relate to each other. There is an eagerness and an openness about such grand global concepts as the internet, which offer a kind of hope and promise which is most salubrious at this time for those among your people who wish to make connections and have begun to awaken to their true position. That is, that they are not truly native to the soil which they trod, but are, instead, beings of quite another kind than it would appear to the naked eye.

What we see occurring is a two-way dynamic in which environment entities have constant stimulation which may lead to awakening. The desire of entities to conform and to be distracted moves as a negative influence which tends to break down the process of reaching out and making fearless connections with those about one. Insofar as the mass media of your culture focuses upon the portion of human activity, shall we say, that carries a heavy, negative emotional charge—such as the war, the murder, the rape, and so forth—there is that which builds fear and raises walls betwixt entities. However, the same mass media also contains much that is yeasty with hope for those who are hoping to find some place to belong, some place that does not feel alien. And with the greatly enhanced capacities of entities to make connections with one another that the age of information—as this instrument calls it—brings, these same mass media are gratefully applauded harbingers of the capacity of entities to make these connections, to strengthen that golden netting of love manifested in light that will become internalized in time. And, therefore, that are the parents in a real way of the social memory complex.

Much shall occur within your culture which may seem full of strife as the peoples upon your sphere are rocked to their foundations by the change in consciousness which is even now occurring. The service which entities provide who do actively use the resources at hand to make connections shall be those which help this planet in its birthing process. We simply caution each that in making these connections no outcome be held in thought, no limitation placed upon the possibilities of any connection.

Those who wish the most sometimes to aid a culture or society or world are drawn by their concern into rigid conceptual structures concerning ways and means of arriving at the goal desired. We would encourage each who wishes to press forward along this path of making connections to continue seeking that intuition and sense of the heart rather than making great plans and carrying out this or that campaign conceived irrespective of connections made spontaneously. For the social memory complex shall be builded one relationship at a time, just as when entities seek peace as a nation they must first seek peace within the self. The great desire to see the global self emerge is most productive when that vision does not lead to impersonally conceived and organized attempts to contact everyone.

We encourage each to continue to trust that connections that need to be made shall be made as they come to a ripeness and a readiness. Trust and faith are those resources which shall see good use here, for the instinct of those who breathe and know that their incarnation is short is to plunge ahead, to take the bull by the horns, as the saying goes, and to move as quickly as humanly possible towards a desired end. However, the deepest desires of the human heart are those which cannot be shoved, pushed or prodded. Rather, the skillful seeker and worker in light is he who is able to surrender to the rhythms of his own destiny and to act in such a way as to magnify those internal connections in the heart and mind which keep the seeker from beginning to direct the flow of events according to some preconceived plan.

For those who are destined to create the larger catalysts of this birthing time are those who shall not be able to do aught else. Do not, then, be concerned that you are not doing enough to press forward in the path of evolution for this planet, for there is a rhythm to these affairs and all seems to be going well. The rhythm seems strong and the planet is slowly but surely awakening to its true nature. Each and every day can extend that circle of relationships if it is desired simply by leaving the private dwelling and moving among the people of your planet. Simply place the self in the way of relationship when the opportunity is there, and when that results in a new connection, rejoice. When the day does not bring new connections, rejoice. There is no strain to the tempo of spiritual evolution.

We see this instrument wonders why we speak about seemingly a side issue of computers and other mass media. However, as we said in the beginning this is kind of a sideways question, for the computer model is so like the social memory complex in some ways. Yet, perhaps we have been able to express the dynamic involved. The social memory complex lives and has the soul. No collection of facts or expression of them has that same quality of being organic and alive.

We encourage each to continue making those connections that each is already consciously attempting to make. Your culture is really speeding up. We encourage each to enjoy this often uncomfortable process of transformation and to remain open to the connections that are destined to be offered to each. See each with the eyes of love and the connections shall be true.

We would transfer this contact at this time to the one known as Jim. We thank this instrument, and leave it in love and in light. We are those of Q'uo.

(Jim channeling)

I am Q'uo, and am again with this group, greeting each in love and in light through this instrument. We would at this time ask if we might speak to any further queries which those present might have for us?

P: I would like to ask about the timing of the transformation from the third to the fourth density and the format of that. Ra had spoken about this transformation, saying in the first stages that third density could not coexist with fourth density. Could you comment on these two concepts?

I am Q'uo, and we believe that we grasp your query, my sister. The transformation of this planetary influence into that grouping of entities which is called the social memory complex of fourth density is a work in progress, shall we say. There are many signposts available. As to the beginning stages of the fourth density, past the period of transformation we can see that this is likely to occur within the next few hundred of your years at the most, a time which is but a twinkling from our perspective. And from the point of view of those within your density this is a time which is variable according to choices being made now by each entity as each becomes more aware of the nature of the illusion and the place within it for each entity.

Thus, the artifacts of third density are now being used to enhance this process in many ways as those entities of inspiration bring their light to bear upon the drama now being experienced in every area of human endeavor. The exploration of the mind is under way by many who have never before considered such as a portion of their experience. The continued expansion of the interest in mind, in consciousness, in purpose for each is that motivating and central force within this entire process.

May we speak in any more specific fashion, my sister?

P: Could you comment on the difference between the hundreds of years which you just spoke of and the decades that many writers speak of as the time during which radical changes will take place?

(Side one of tape ends.)

I am Q'uo, and am again with this instrument. We would comment thusly. In the essence of this experience—that is, from the metaphysical point of view—whether the time period be that of decades or longer is but an instant of difference and we may suggest that there are no entities, ourselves included, able to accurately predict or indicate the exact timing of this process of change, for there is much that is in flux. Even the growth of those of a positive nature in numbers greater than anticipated earlier by ourselves is a phenomenon that can slow this process, in that the catastrophic nature that has been anticipated by many would then be alleviated in a degree in a direct proportion to the intensity of the positive polarity and the effect of its lightening upon this process.

There are many who are changing in ways which are fundamental to consciousness in the groupings of entities within various cultures, subcultures and movements of thoughts which explore regions of experience that are breakthrough areas, shall we say. Thus, there is no reliable way of determining the progression of this change. Only the movement of love within each heart has any hope of indicating to entities the nature of this change.

Is there a further query, my sister?

P: No. I really like your comments.

I am Q'uo, and we thank you, my sister. Is there another query at this time?

Carla: I have a personal question. I have experienced a continual exhaustion that I have not previously experienced that coincides with the accident in which I broke my ankle. My explanation is that I am not exercising as I normally do and a lack of exercise can make one tired. But this does feel like a more profound tiredness having to do with the body. I don't know what other kind of tiredness there is, but it feels different. Could you comment?

I am Q'uo. We feel that we grasp your query, my sister, and shall speak as we are able.

There is a weariness of the will which occurs as an accumulation of the exercise of the will is experienced by an entity such as yourself, one who is strong in will and uses it to motivate a physical vehicle that is somewhat weaker in the native physical energies than most of your peoples. When the will has been the primary motivating force for a physical vehicle over a long period of your time there is a weariness which is an irreversible kind of process, the price, shall we say, for being able to energize the physical vehicle time after time when it is itself without sufficient reserves. This is valuable and efficient as a means of polarization, for it is done in your case in service to others. It is detrimental in the short run of the physical incarnation for it tends to wear the physical vehicle and its connections to the spirit and mind complexes as well. Thus, there is a price for each action within your illusion, a price for each entity and each action. The cost, shall we say, for your efforts is the weariness.

Is there a further query, my sister?

Carla: Is there a way that I can be kinder and wiser to myself?

I am Q'uo, and we find that in this instance we must refrain from comment for reasons that are all too well known to you, my sister. We encourage your nature as that of one who wishes to serve.

Is there any further query, my sister?

Carla: No, thank you.

Is there a final query at this time?

(Pause)

I am Q'uo, and as we observe a lull in the questioning, we shall take this opportunity at expressing our great gratitude at having been invited to join your group this day. We thank each for the dedication and the desire to seek and to serve that has brought all of us together. At such meetings we take a great joy quite literally away with us, hopefully leaving as much as well as some words of information and inspiration that might be enjoyed by you. At this time we shall take our leave of this instrument and this group. We are those of Q'uo, and we leave each in the love and in the ineffable light of the one infinite Creator. Adonai. Adonai. ❧

Sunday Meditation
March 12, 1995

Group question: If there is a different quality that a minority group has it will be ostracized by the majority group. The differences can be sex, race, color, length of hair, creed, dressing, ideas one has in one's head, and we would like to know if this is an innate quality of humans, mammals, animals in general or whatever. Is there a way that we can look at this that would help us in dealing with the world around us?

(Carla channeling)

We are those of Q'uo. Greetings in the love and in the light of the one infinite Creator. How precious do we find the opportunity that you have given us to come and dwell within the nexus of your combined vibrations. We are most honored and we gratefully thank you. As always, we ask that those things that we offer as our thoughts be considered by you with a discriminating mind and heart, for our opinions are simply that and we would not wish to presume to know that truth which is each person's, for truth wears many clothes, yet all tends toward that truth that lies in mystery which is beyond all paths to it. If aught we say is of help to you then we are most satisfied and we thank you for this opportunity.

As we sense through this instrument's physical senses the warmth of the afternoon sun, the feeling that the sun brings is very nostalgic for us. We remember, with pleasure, our own third-density experience and our feelings of joy when the season which you would call summer approached, that wonderful feeling of life stirring and moving out from the winter's sleep into the fulfilling of the destiny that lies within each seed. Each of you, also, is a seed which has lain within the dark ground and the winter cold of times contracted and forlorn, times when there was darkness and within that darkness the chill of solitude. Each of you is a seed of infinite love and infinite light, yet your blossoming shall be a long one in coming, and you shall have many bodies and move through many densities before that blossom is finally perfect and in that perfection is lost into the All.

It is quite a journey, with many revolutions. As your planet revolves, so shall you revolve through cycles of warmth and cycles of seed time and cold. As we approach the question which you have asked us, we ask you to remember that these concerns about which we speak are those of a seed just sprouting. That seed that lies within you is expressing in this density which you enjoy at this time as self-awareness or self-consciousness. You are young in experience with self-consciousness, and so much of your attention in an inward sense is placed from that early age of childhood within the evolving attempts of the seedling to grasp its nature.

Now, the second-density animals from which you sprang in terms of your physical vehicle does indeed have ways in which it responds to threats from other selves. These responses are part of a genetic imprinting, and, shall we say, a cultural imprinting on top of the genetic base, for the mothers of the great apes and the fathers do indeed teach the young which they have born between them that this species is a threat but this one is not. And so there is for the animal, for that physical vehicle, a fairly clear-cut response: those who are not to be feared yet who are not a portion of the clan are simply ignored; those who are to be feared are avoided. Yet this response is not one in which there is the concept of the self and the other self. Rather, responses are made instinctively and appropriately. Thusly, you may see that the physical vehicle which carries your consciousness about has gone quite beyond that sensing of those which are dangerous and sensing those which are not.

As the self-aware and individualized person experiences those young years of life it begins accreting to its mental/emotional complex a growing list of entities and types of entities which impress the self as natural enemies. Your people has no natural enemies except each other. There is no animal or group of animals which threatens by its existence any human life. Yet one upon another the young soul accretes those to fear, those to avoid, those to distrust, and so forth, generalizing from one or two particulars theories which allow some entities into the charmed circle of trust and which shut the door against others.

As the person grows and has more and more experience the person acquires more and more baggage in the shape of what this instrument would call prejudices, what we would call biases. Manifestly, this is not an instinctive process, for there is no instinct towards cannibalism within your physical vehicles. There is no natural enemy in that sense amongst your peoples. The impulse to determine the degree of safety with which one may greet another has in most entities, by the time they reach their teenage years, as this instrument would say, the basic prejudices, biases and wayward opinions that form the basic floor of the prejudicial system within an entity are formed, not, shall we say, set in concrete but nailed together fairly well and ready to be used as a base upon which to build an ever more articulated system of biases and judgment.

So, there is no bodily instinct for separating from other selves. However, there is a characteristic tendency which may be seen to be close to an instinct in third density entities to develop shortcuts that aid in making quick judgments about the safety and security of any present moment. There is that instinct gone wild. The instinct, itself, is to determine for each self, "Who am I?" Yet in the process of determining the key nature of the self, the tendency is to identify the self over against others who are different.

The first prejudice is that prejudice of the very young entity who, for the first time, realizes that it is not a part of the mother or the father. Entities at this young age discover the word "no," and that impulse to negation is the crux of a process which has given your world one destructive and annihilating conflict after another. The initial impulse has no vice within it. That impulse to know the self, to define the boundaries of the self, and to become more self-aware is allowed to lower itself again and again by making judgments about others which make the self feel safer, more secure, or more comfortable. The basic point of conflict lies within the self as each self goes through repeated generations of "I am not this but that, not that but this," again and again.

There is that anxiety, that tension of the unanswered question, for each entity remains a mystery-clad being, as this instrument would say. Even, perhaps especially, to itself. This creates a primal discomfort which in some becomes anger, in some becomes pride, in some becomes an illness, or a perceived limitation, and in almost all entities defenses begin to mount. Walls to hide behind begin to seem comfortable and entire sections of the family of humankind are judged not as useful, not as important, not as good, not as smart, not as wise as the self or some group which the self identifies with.

This primal anxiety, this hunger to know the self, has within it the seeds of many densities of progressive learning and harmonizing and coming to an ever more full blooming, yet along the way humankind and all its peoples have, shall we say, legislated the necessity of projecting upon others that anxiety, that inner anger of not knowing, which is truly the business of the self with the self. Therefore, perhaps it can be seen that it is well to do whatever the individual might find useful to bring that anger, that judgment, that not-this-but-that, not-that-but-this back to the interior of the self. Those who seek peace amongst peoples first must go into the cave of the self and take the fight to the place where the arena is prepared, for the heart within is wise. And when an entity ceases judging others and accepts the responsibility of living with the dynamic of not knowing then much may be learned, much may be healed.

The job of taking the glance, taking the attention away from others which are perceived as causing judgment and, rather, putting that energy and that judgment, if you will, within the self is a powerful technique and one we encourage each to rely upon on a regular, perhaps daily, basis, for that which is outside of the self, no matter how separating or how close it may feel, is as a mirror which shows the self a dim reflection of the self to the self. Any trait or nature which is perceived as being characteristic of others or other groups is a reflection of disagreements within yourself. This is a truth which does not thrive when taken literally, for often the logic of the heart makes use of symbols, but in general it may be said that the business of humankind is the self and the numberless attempts of the self to know the self by comparing the self to other entities or groups is less useful than the practice of moving within to see the self against the backdrop, not of others, but of the one infinite Creator.

Those who seek the answer of the riddle of human nature by moving amongst humans may make any number of conclusions and offer any number of fascinating and learned narratives, yet these shall not tell the self of the self with the same depth and relevance as the self turning within and opening the heart, for there is within the heart the awareness of that seed which is the one infinite Creator. You see, you bloom not for mankind but for the one infinite Creator. As the sun shines upon you know that your greatest relationship, your central dynamic is that between the self which is individualized in you and that great Self which is the one original Thought, Love.

When the self has become content to study itself within itself, when there is no longer that running wild of the desire to protect the self from danger from without the self, then shall there be the dawning of the next density of experience for those entities who wish to move forward in their spiritual evolution at this time, for the great genius of humankind, the great gift of self-awareness is the talent, the gift, the endowment of the one infinite Creator for connection. The desire to connect, the desire to communicate, the desire to enter into communion with others, other selves, and other groups, this is the instinct, this is the true instinct of humankind, and this instinct has been trampled upon and tossed in the corner in order that entities may play those games in which masks are worn, sides are taken, and the conflicts within are given overt expression with other selves standing in for those dynamics within the self which the self has not yet accepted.

The desire for purity, for excellence is so easy to corrupt, and in that desire it is most easy, mistakenly and innocently, to project those dynamics upon the world at large instead of taking the responsibility within the self. My friends, your destiny, that which you have the deep instinct for, is unity, one with the other. Yet stumbling blocks abound, for within most of your cultures upon your planet it is accepted that there shall be groups against groups, person against person, and it is counted as folly when entities reach out too often to connect without regard for safety, security and appropriateness. The eyes of world opinion shall always see the mask, the clothing, those illusions which it wishes to see.

As each entity awakens at last from winter's sleep and knows itself once more to be a seed that shall grow, as each decides finally to disagree with the self rather than with others and to work that out in the interior safety of the self, then person by person by person consciousness shall be raised and the group that is waiting to form shall more and more begin connecting in a golden net of commonality, connection, and communion. Once the desire to disagree within the self has been accepted, grasped and loved then shall that self be ready to turn outward without fear and, little by little, shall your people take down those bricks which have built such high walls. Peace within your world must start within each heart.

There is great freedom, my friends, that awaits you. Freedom to know and to harmonize and to share the gift of life and consciousness with those other sparks of that same love which, like all seeds, are unique, each one adding a slightly different flavor to an ever-growing self. This is your destiny. We encourage each to use those resources and tools which help each in its own path towards inner unity and inner peace, for this instinct for mischief is indeed a portion of free will, and you may indulge it for as long as you wish, for as many lifetimes and as many cycles as it seems fair to do so. There is all the time in the world, yet when the self does wake up, oh, much joy awaits, and fullness of heart.

You are lovely blossoms, even as seeds. Your nature is written clearly within and you have but to free yourself to grow.

We would at this time transfer this contact to the one known as Jim. We thank this instrument and leave this instrument in love and in light. We are those of Q'uo.

(Jim channeling)

I am Q'uo, and greet each again in love and in light through this instrument. We would be honored to ask at this time if there might be further queries which any in this circle would have to offer to us. Is there another query at this time?

D: How do you contend with other entities which will not accept you?

I am Q'uo, and we believe that we grasp your query, my brother, and our response must be somewhat confusing in that the manner in which one contends with those that do not accept one is the pattern or destiny which each individual has chosen for the incarnation. The destiny, the goal, for each is to find an harmonious resolution or at least to attempt such within the being. How this is accomplished is a function of the unique nature and set of priorities in learning that each soul makes upon entering the incarnation. Thus, the means to achieve the goal are many. Again we would recommend to each that with that goal in mind that the, shall we say, intuitive capabilities be looked to for the inspiration as to how this shall be accomplished.

Is there a further query, my brother?

D: It would appear that we are all connected. It is an illusion that we are separate. Our separation is basically due to belief systems and so forth, but we are all interconnected, but there is a wall to get over to get to other individuals. And certain groups you cannot get to. What do you do to communicate with them? There is fear to get over. How do you convince other people that you are not their enemy and that you are just different than they are?

(Side one of tape ends.)

I am Q'uo, and am again with this instrument. We would suggest that the process of seating oneself within one's identity is the manner in which one can determine direction. If you retire within your own mind to the clear perception of who you feel you are and allow the inspiration of the moment that comes from this knowledge to make your direction clearer, then you will be able to move in a pattern that is in harmony with your own internal energies, which is to say that as you are true to your own self the path will be made clear to you. It may not be made easy but it shall be made clear, and the result of your efforts may not have value in the larger sense of the group that you deal with but has a greater chance of fulfilling your own pattern so that you make the effort that is appropriate and which expresses the energies that you wish to express in the manner in which you wish to express them.

Is there a further query, my brother?

D: No, Q'uo.

I am Q'uo, and we are grateful for your queries, my brother, for they touch at the heart of the experience which each of you share at this time.

Is there another query?

Carla: I was thinking about how Jesus always was quoted as saying to turn the other cheek and I was wondering how the incredible energy that he released by turning the other cheek to the point of dying has as its source the fact that he did not prejudice himself against any other person at any time. He kept the dialogue within himself for the most part.

I am Q'uo, and we believe that we grasp your query, my sister. The one known as Jesus the Christ is an example of one who has been true to the greater Self from which each springs to the degree that the words which this entity spoke were the ideal which was realized in this entity's life pattern. This entity set the goal, shall we say, in such clear statements as many others like this entity have done as well. For those who value such entities and their words and lives these goals become as the beacon which guides the journey. However, there may be many missteps upon the journey before the goal is achieved. This is the stuff of your illusion and the grist for your mill, shall we say.

Is there another query, my sister?

Carla: No, thank you, Q'uo.

I am Q'uo, and we thank you once again, my sister. Is there another query at this time?

R: I just want to say thank you for being with me when I meditate sometimes.

I am Q'uo, and we are filled with joy to be able to join you and all who ask our presence in their meditations, for in this manner we are able to share with you the essence of your experience within this illusion, and are able, thereby, to taste the many flavors of experience which are available to each portion of the one Creator.

At this time we would, again, thank each for inviting our presence this day and would take our leave of this group and this instrument, leaving each, as always, in the love and in the light of the one infinite Creator. We are know to you as those of Q'uo. Adonai, my friends. Adonai.

Sunday Meditation
March 19, 1995

Group question: Our question this evening has to do with absolute reality and relative or personal reality. We are wondering if it is possible for a person to transmit his/her reality to another person or if it is even wise to try to do so? Is it possible for us to transcend our personality, to take part in the ever-changing nature of the way we perceive the universe about us? Is there a value in this? Is there any way that we can know with some degree of certainty that what we are dealing with is true or real? And what is Q'uo's preferred perspective on reality and truth?

(Carla channeling)

We are known to you as those of Q'uo. Greetings in the love and in the light of the one infinite Creator. It is our privilege and our blessing to be able to blend our vibrations with your own at this circle of seeking. We are grateful that you desired to call us to you, for by doing so you enable us in our chosen path of service to the one infinite Creator. Thus, you give us precious treasure and we humbly thank you. If those opinions which we share at this sitting do not sit well with you we request that you leave them behind, for we are not authorities. We are neighbors walking the same path, perhaps a few steps ahead. That is all.

Thusly, we ask each to use his own discrimination and to accept truth for the self when it comes with that characteristic feeling that this is something that you knew all along and have just now remembered.

May we say that the topic which you have chosen for this sitting is a difficult subject about which to speak plainly. The structure of your language, the words which make up its arsenal of weaponry for reaching the truth, are weapons or tools created for conquering decision-making within your physical world. They become quite blunt instruments when one is attempting to speak concerning metaphysical reality or any consideration of apparent reality and real reality. With apologies for those limitations we cannot help and your continued discrimination we shall attempt to share some thoughts concerning this interesting subject.

The first level, that of apparent reality, is the level which those within this room would call consensus reality or life as it is. This manifestation, as intricate and rich as it is in texture, is but the onion skin skimming the surface of an infinite well of being. As each opens the eyes upon that common or consensus environment one finds the match of senses and objects; the creation into which humankind is born is that one which has been made relevant to humans. The creation of the Father, that second-density creation of love, in third density becomes a co-creation between Creator and yourselves. And as humankind has worn the round trail in walking many cycles of experience those many, many footsteps of manifestation again and again have worn certain biases smooth with age that they seem more real, more deeply relevant than other common experiences of humankind.

And as each sits within this domicile listening to these words each is a repository of perhaps [one] half simple sense impressions and the other half constructions upon those sense impressions created by what this instrument would call "world opinion." In other words, the onion skin of the visible and seen existence, though very tough and resistant to puncture, is quite thin, and the entity with a sharp needle of selfhood simply pierces that onion skin to move into the depths of that ocean that is being or consciousness.

Now, there are clues and hints in plenteous supply even within your everyday reality, if you would call it that. There is enough information that lies like litter about every doorpost in the ordinary of things. To create catalyst which produces the most excellent manifestation, the most complete transformation, the most satisfying epiphany for those seekers who are called to such a ministry, the everyday and ordinary surface holds every tool and resource necessary for utter realization and clarification of being.

However, most seekers prefer not to work with the ordinary and everyday but, rather, to seek that which underlies or overshadows or surrounds the everyday and the ordinary. The depth and reality of the being below the surface fascinates and attracts the seeker who is not content to be lost in bliss, gazing at the dust, at the leaves, at the air, but wishes to know more about himself or herself, which is to know how deep that self may go. Is she truly other than the everyday? What is his truth? What is his mission? The voyagers attempting to sail into that ocean which is the deep mind are seeking a truth that moves beyond limits into the ineffable. Within each seeker's mind and heart these voyages are chosen in a darkness, a blackness of shadow, and as sails are set they are set through faith or hope. And the voyager must trust the wind, must simply raise that sail which is desire and then wait patiently for the wind of spirit to fill that sail and to determine the course and the weather of the journey.

The seeker within metaphysical or time/space reality is as the miner who wishes hidden treasure. In fact, that treasure is cunningly and cleverly hidden within the self, within deep memory, yet that which is true of the metaphysical universe is true in a systematic or processional way so that the seeker who travels in this dark and shadowy sea becomes more aware only after much experience of simply sailing about metaphysical waters. The truth comes into consciousness more like a scent. An aroma is detected and the nose follows that scent and takes you to the bubbling pot of delicious food. Seeking within the metaphysical realm is of that nature. You simply must follow your intuition which is the olfactory organ of the metaphysical universe.

And we may say to the one known as N, we certainly hope that we have a pleasant smell.

Now, the one who seeks upon the onion skin of perceived reality and the one who seeks delving deeply into infinity and eternity have in common that they are dealing with illusion. We also deal with illusion. It is our limited and perhaps faulty understanding that all is illusion except the one great original Thought which is Love. If there is a "you" which is seeking, that collection of energies which is "you" is an illusion. If there is no illusion and only reality, that reality does not know Itself, for It is One. Ironically enough, then, free will dictates that anyone who seeks, by virtue of being an entity seeking is seeking an illusion. Each sees illusion, but, further, each is illusion. The manifestation that is each is an illusion. The personality that seems so deep and strong is an illusion. The photon itself that builds out of light all of the physical universe is illusion. We are illusion. All that can speak is illusion and distortion.

What we believe occurs is that through the densities more and more of the whole or entirety of all that is becomes known and the seeking soul familiarizes itself with progressively denser illusions; that is, illusions more filled with light and more articulate of truth. Yet at the point where the entity has balanced love and wisdom and integrated those blessings to become one, then it is finally that such entities turn away from manifestation and release all personality in order that they may become again the Truth, not that a seeker may know it, but that it may be it.

To move back into the density in which you now find yourselves, each in this room is aware that it has come seeking the center of things, seeking truth, yes, seeking balance also; and seeking companionship, for truly companions along the way are the greatest blessing of the spiritual path. The object of third density is, we feel, the making of a certain choice, a choice of paths. This choice is not simply a verbal one or a mental one.

In order for this choice to be made so that the entity within has truly chosen, that choice is made within the fire of unknowing, within that chasm where there is no footing but only air. The process that seekers go through in order to attain a firmly made choice is not an intellectual process nor even an intellectual/emotional process, but, rather, it is, as this instrument would say, a journey from head to heart. So that it matters not so much whether one sees clearly as it matters more that one may desire more clearly. To hone the edge of the thirst for truth is to improve that search in its efficacy.

Again, it is not what the seeker knows but what the seeker desires that creates the character of the distortions that the seeker is likely to settle upon as that which is the least distorted version of truth. Once it has been accepted that all truths are to some extent distortions of a truth that is ineffable and unknowable then there is perhaps an easier and more relaxed attitude towards this process of knowing the truth. If all things are shadows, if all things are to some extent not what they seem, then the heart is free to open in pure desire to whatever truth it may pick up with its various antennae which it does not know it has but which the being which lies within knows well how to use.

Thusly, the great tool of intuition and hunch and feeling is to be praised within the spiritual seeker, for these whimsies often are the result of the mind's making connections intuitively that make no intellectual or logical sense. Consequently, we encourage each to follow the hunches and to refrain from being concerned particularly as to whether or not that hunch is a whim or a true intuition.

It is our bias to feel that for each entity this searching for a more real reality is an entirely private matter. Each entity's journey is unique, for each entity is unique. Thusly, entities such as yourselves may sit about the circle and find many points of overlapping concept but find also that in each entity there are concepts and constructs or processes of concepts that are not repeated from person to person to person. Yet, those differences are not only acceptable but desirable, for the work of each entity and the truth of each entity is unique.

The entity that you now are has processed millions and billions, untold amounts of sense impression and through many cycles of experience, many incarnations, and not one or two densities, but three, each tiny building block of self, each input that changed the contents has sifted and compacted and built up through the many, many incarnations of a long life to the point where you are you, sitting now listening to this instrument's voice. Your path has its own characteristics and you will find truth in a way shaped by the choices you have made.

We cannot advise any as to whether to choose the deep, deep delving for self and then truth being found or that process of seeking which this instrument often experiences which is the seeing of the sacramental in the ordinary and everyday. What is important in each seeking is the validity and the purity of the choice made whenever there is an issue involving service to others versus service to self. So we do not feel that one view of reality will intrinsically place one in a better position to know truth than another. It is the usual way for entities in third density to do the seeking and the delving into the depths of self and it is at the same time quite valuable and a valid path to follow the ordinary and to find within it all that there is: the Love that is the one great original Thought.

Let your personality and your preferences [guide] you, for it is, as we said, not important that you go this way or that but only that the choices made are made with a full heart and a love in the doing. And always, when dealing with these relative matters, we encourage the glance away. The more serious and caught up that one gets in pursuit of the perfect ideal or the absolute truth the more knots that one is likely to tie in one's own mind and thinking. Therefore, let your intensity be balanced by what this instrument calls the light touch. And always we encourage each to respect the paths of others.

This is not the same thing—that is, respecting the constructs of others—as attempting to transmit one's own vision to another. In fact, the respect for another's viewpoint may well cause one to listen to what that entity has to say rather than attempting to improve the other entity's thinking, for that entity may have much to offer to you. Needless to say, the service-to-others entity is looking for a way to serve others, and often it is a real temptation to share with others some crystal vision or beautiful picture of things that may help another as it has helped you.

And it is not a mistake, precisely, to go ahead and offer advice. However, there is an innate respect which we would encourage for the free will of others and the rightness of the prohibition against infringing upon free will. When attempting to share the truth with others who are seeking, let the attempt be to remain fully open and vulnerable to the other entity's thoughts.

This frame of mind creates a place of safety for the other person in which that entity may communicate her feelings to you, and in allowing her the space and the ear to hear this verbalized inner dialogue or monologue you have aided that entity in understanding herself. Such is the value of the truly listening ear. It is far better to restrain one's self to that practice than to jump in and attempt to proselytize. However, when questions are asked it is perfectly acceptable to give all of your energies in giving your best answers, for there is great blessing for both when two are vulnerable to each other and thus able to aid each other and to become closer.

We realize from the sound of your machine that we are being wordy again and this instrument is asking us to wind things up. However, we wish to make one last point and then we shall certainly do so.

And that point is this one. The creation or world into which you came, this very one, with its apparent differences, is the environment within which you shall find the truth. This world and no other. This illusory dream world, this twilight is the absolute best environment possible for creating the opportunities for entities within third density to learn what it is to be aware and to learn what it is to love and be loved. Graduation from this density occurs when the entities have chosen how to love, how to relate to loving and being loved, and that is something which may be arrived at, as we have said, through the mystical appreciation of the ordinary and/or through the deep delving into those regions of the mind which are more profound than the conscious state of mind.

So, as always, the Creator offers a palate of many, many different colors and ways to arrive at the point of love and, breathless with it, to find that the self is loved, has always been loved, always shall be loved by Love Itself, and in that perceived love each pilgrim soul may more and more dare to love wholeheartedly, indiscriminately, and gloriously. The deepest truth that we know is love. The Creator is love. You are love that has become visible and you are able to express within the medium of your world that love which you have found within. Love each other. Care for each other. And in that giving and taking each shall know the truth.

We would at this time leave this instrument and transfer to the one known as Jim. We thank this instrument and would leave in love and light through this instrument at this time. We are those of Q'uo.

(Jim channeling)

I am Q'uo, and greet each again in love and in light through this instrument. It is our privilege at this time to ask if there might be any further queries for us from those gathered here. Is there another query?

P: How can we distinguish temptations that come before us?

I am Q'uo, and am aware of your query, my sister. We recommend that when the seeker feels any kind of confusion as to whether there is temptation or opportunity upon its path that it look as clearly as it can with the conscious mind at that which stands before it. Then, within the meditative state, look again with the deeper, intuitive, feeling mind and ask again if this is what is appropriate as the next step upon the journey.

Is there a further query, my sister?

P: Since we are talking about reality it seems that sometimes in third density we may interpret an experience one way at first and then later seems quite opposite. We have change through time, it seems. Could you comment on that? How can we distinguish what the third-density personality desires and what actually comes upon the seeker's path?

I am Q'uo, and we believe that we grasp your query, my sister. Please query further if we do not.

We would suggest that all which any entity perceives, as we said previously, is illusion, for if there is the perceiver and the perceived there is illusion, for all, in truth, is one. As each seeker moves through its own personal illusion seeking that which it can of truth it will perceive as best it can. We always recommend retiring to the meditative state for the clearest possible perception and indication of direction even though we realize that here, as well, lies illusion.

The nature of this journey seems to be moving from the greater to lesser illusion in what you might call the long run or way of viewing experience. In this process, when it is functioning efficiently there is the clarification of experience, of perception, and of desire to seek further. Thus, it would be expected that one could look, as you would say, back upon experience and see more clearly the nature of the experience as being more or less or partaking of that which is real.

Thus, we say to each seeker, value that which you have experienced, build upon it as best as you can, and seek always the heart of love within each entity and experience, knowing that you shall, even with the best and greatest of efforts, misperceive greatly and frequently. This is why we say that the qualities of faith that there is a greater reality, and will to persevere in sifting through the lesser experiences of reality, are those qualities which shall be of most aid along the path of the seeker of truth.

Is there another query, my sister?

P: Not at this time. Thank you.

I am Q'uo, and we thank you, my sister. Is there another query, my friends?

K: Is it true that there is a material soul? Is this what we are in our innermost beings, souls?

I am Q'uo, and we believe that we grasp your query, my brother. We can say to you, my brother, that each entity that moves with free will has moved along patterns of incarnation for eons of time, as you would measure it, and in this movement has had what you would call soul or [individual] spirit's experience which has gleaned the harvest of each incarnation and has grown by each harvest, and, in addition, sends forth itself into countless further illusions in order that it might accrete to it more of the one Creator's attributes which it feels are necessary and helpful in returning to the unity of all that is.

Is there a further query, my brother?

K: In referring to the returning to the unity of all that is, are you referring to the returning to the seventh-density merging of the unified body with the one Creator?

I am Q'uo, and am aware of your query, my brother. We have been referring—as you are mostly correct in assuming—to the journey that entities take through the densities of light and experience that are the path of the Creator to the Creator. These densities of light offer larger and larger arenas, shall we say, in which each seeker might seek, know and express the truth of its own beingness. When this experience has been carried out to the extent that the density of foreverness has been achieved, that in your numbering is seven, then the entity begins to turn in full to the rejoining of the one Creator, leaving the personality gained as a seed for further growth by the one Creator. The movement into total unity is that movement into what we see you have called the eighth density or that which is likened to the black hole which draws all into it in a manner which is completely unified and begins again that great cycle of creation upon another level of vibration.

Is there another query, my brother?

K: Yes, are you saying that the universe will coalesce and form a black hole, or are you giving this as an analogy to the spiritual realm of that physical process?

I am Q'uo, and if we are correct in grasping your query, my brother, we would say that both assumptions are correct, for the phenomenon which you know of as the black hole is but the completion of experience in one octave of densities that is the seed for a further octave of densities on, shall we say, the other side of the black hole, so called.

Is there another query?

K: In what sense are we all one?

I am Q'uo, and am aware of your query, my brother. We would suggest that the nature of this unity is complete. You are likened to actors upon the stage who, though remembering their lines, forget their true personality and at some point in the drama shall aid others in their remembering by their very essence and the nature of their being.

Is there another query, my brother?

(Inaudible)

I am Q'uo, and we would ask if there is another query at this time?

N: Knowing that everything is illusion, including these queries, and knowing of free will, yet knowing that there is no freedom, how you prefer to look at this situation?

I am Q'uo, and am aware of your query, my brother. Our preference as a point from which to view our experience and our universe is what you might call playful curiosity. We are infinitely amazed at the intricacy, yet the simplicity, of all creation.

Is there a further query, my brother?

N: No, thank you, and it smells very nice.

I am Q'uo, and we are grateful to you, my brother, and would also say that the scent of this group is most intoxicating to us as well.

Is there a final query at this time?

(Pause)

I am Q'uo, and we shall add our gratitude to that which has been so generously offered to us. At this time we shall take our leave of this instrument and this group in the love and in the light which has been brought forth by each. We are known to you as those of Q'uo. Adonai, my friends. Adonai. ✸

Sunday Meditation
March 26, 1995

Group question: How to communicate honestly and be true to the self when people you talk to are restricted in their point of view? How does Q'uo do this with us, for example? What about white lies? The absolute truth may hurt feelings.

(Carla channeling)

We are those of Q'uo. Greetings in the love and in the light of the one infinite Creator. We greatly appreciate your calling us to your group this day. At the time of your springtime explosion of blossoms and leaves we are ravished by the beauty which comes through your senses. Truly, those of your Earth have a fair and lovely world.

Your topic this day offers us much rich ground for comment and we would share our thoughts with you with the understanding that each of you is to choose those thoughts which seem good to you and leave the rest behind. We greatly appreciate your using your discrimination whenever you read our opinions or hear them, for we, as you, are those who seek and yet have not found all the answers.

When one attempts to communicate the truth one can be sure that if the matter has substance the full truth shall not be revealed. The arbitrary and contrary nature of this intangible called truth is such that while one may asymptotically approach truth from many angles, one cannot arrive at it in time and space. Consequently, all efforts that we are aware of to define, capture or communicate pure truth are attempts which this instrument would call quixotic, errands of the soul doomed to a noble and worthwhile attempt and failure. It is against this backdrop that the seeker comes to grapple with the issue of communicating truth to others.

The one known as Jesus the Christ, whose life this instrument is fairly familiar with from her practice of the Christian religion, tended to work with truth not by speaking plainly, but, rather, by offering little stories which had some of the characteristics of a riddle or puzzle, and which certainly were those parables which contain self-contradictory notions. One might infer, then, that this compassionate entity wished to speak a more accurate truth than could be achieved by the use of plain words. This entity, one might infer, considered the feeling behind a parable or story as the carrier of truer communication than the specific words themselves.

This was, may we say with confidence, a successful effort at communication of spiritual principles to large numbers of seekers. Was it successful at communicating due to the power of the speaker, or due to the cleverness of the parables? The effort was successful because of both of these ingredients and because of the relationship between the one known as Jesus and the material which it was presenting. The one known as Jesus felt proprietary and generous with the principles themselves. This was an entity which did indeed know itself and was able within its own mind and heart to speak accurately concerning itself, who it considered itself to be, what it considered its mission and so forth.

When an entity is comfortable with the basic questions of who she is, what she basically believes in, and where she considers her mission to be leading her, then such a person comes to the task of communication with a feeling of self-confidence. This underlying feeling is that which is to be prized and that for which it is well to work, for pure truth lies always in the area between any two entities rather than in the one or in the other. Even if they agree, yet, still, the truth itself cannot be captured.

So what entities are doing when they attempt to speak the truth to each other is relating themselves to the other through the area of concern or question. The actual truth these entities communicate is in part the truth of themselves and only in part the truth about which the words are speaking. This is how central a part personality and relationship play in the business of seeking to speak truth. Before the mouth opens on the first effort to speak, a significant portion of that which is to come has been either ratified or nullified by the being of the person communicating. Thus, that member of your group which suggested the wisdom of communication by listening is to be commended. This is, indeed, a powerful resource for communication and one, indeed, whose practice has never been enough praised and cherished by your peoples.

The words which your peoples use produce seeming clarity of meaning many times. However, each entity is aware of the slippery and often false nature which words seem to take on as they are asked to bear the weight of substantial thoughts. The great majority of entities upon your sphere have not the patience nor the personality nor the inherent gift of precise or accurate language and this is in part due to the nature of spoken language. The great efforts of your scholars, humanists and authors of every type have produced works within your cultures which continue to communicate what seems to be a deeply insightful or truth-filled body of work. The written language is as that which can be pinned down, placed upon a shelf, and referred to again and again. Spoken words have not that luxury. There is no referring back within the usual conversation.

Since the language was created by those who needed to deal with each other as a society, language is most free of confusion when dealing with those day-to-day transactions of people to people. The choice of what to eat given to the waitress is clear. Conversations concerning a specific topic which must be dealt with are usually quite clear. As long as the sensitive, emotional and spiritual nature of entities communicating is not stirred and awakened language is strong enough to bear the truth at that level. Plans can be made. Journeys can be conducted. Errands can be run. A schedule can be kept. This is what the language was developed to accomplish, and this it accomplishes.

However, as entities awaken and begin to hunger for that home which is felt to be somewhere that is not here, as these entities awaken, stirring and rousing and stretching themselves, they begin to hunger for something that is not the bread and butter of life, something that is not practical, but something that seems all the sweeter for being impractical, and that is the deeper truth, the wider perspective, the ground of being.

As this concern or galaxy of concerns matures and ripens within the seeker's mind and heart the inner landscape becomes ever more lucid and full of clarity, and as the seeker makes one mistake upon another and continues undiscouraged, layers of confusion seem to fall away within the seeker and that which is true is dimly sensed. Yet, in that dimmest sensing lies a great faith and a heightened awareness of the reality of the concept of truth. And so each as he matures spiritually and emotionally becomes more and more that which contains truth, that which holds precious gems within the earthen vessel which is the physical life. There is something about this process which makes those who would be strangers intimates upon meeting for the first time, as those who have begun to inhabit the truth, shall we say, find themselves recognizing fellow travelers whatever their background, whatever their diversity of story.

And so it is that the truest communication within the illusion which you now enjoy tends to be that shared between two seekers who recognize each other as comrades along the path, and who then are able to listen and respond with a light and free heart, not asking words to bear much but allowing words to wash over and touch upon that which is the felt and present truth. The greatest confusion lies not between two who are awakened and not between two who sleep and enjoy the illusion together in happy ignorance of its illusory quality, but rather the communication that takes place betwixt one who has awakened and one who still sleeps, and in that sleeping dreams the life.

We consider that we speak with those who are awakened. We feel that our communication with you is privileged and we assume that those listening to us take our words more as the flavor of that which we are attempting to express rather than the literal, absolute truth. We feel comfortable in fumbling for words in offering images to the channel that the channel must interpret for itself. We do not concern ourselves beyond a certain point with trying to find the right word or the right way of expressing a point. We leave that to the channel. We leave that—we should say more accurately—to the process by which the channel communicates that which has been communicated to it. We consider these communications privileged. We do not go into the marketplace, the business, the school, the church. We do not seek people to talk to. We await those who wish to communicate with us. This is our solution to the question of how to offer our truth in service to your peoples. We do not wish to change people. We wish to be there as a resource for those who are undergoing change already, and who, therefore, are seeking tools, resources and friends that may help them in their hunger and thirst after truth.

Now, when one attempts to communicate to one who is not yet awake to the spiritual journey or who feels that it already knows all that it needs to know, there are bound to be frictions and miscommunications by the score, for in this instance, no matter how pleasant the tone or how gentle the way in which points are made there is the situation where one entity seeks to improve or aid in another entity's awakening. Now, this is the prerogative of all with free will, that they have perfect right and reason to speak persuasively in the attempt to seek truth and to share it. Yet, in terms of the truth itself there is a null contract situation when the two entities do not actually have a mutual desire.

In the situation where one entity is aware of a larger viewpoint than the other, if the other has not requested communication on that point, then there will be the inevitable friction which comes from the attempt to persuade. No matter how sugar-coated this attempt is it will still be interpreted in a frictive way by the one to whom the gift of understanding is being so hopefully offered. The way to clear and pure communication, then, is the way of expressing that which one is asked concerning.

Now, if an entity sees that there shall be the inevitable friction and still desires to get the point across perhaps the best ally is the light touch. If such communication can be made in a humorous or light-hearted way which charms and disarms the hearer then the inroads might be made with the listener all unaware of the gift of larger truth it has received. So when there is the opportunity to share a truth with one who is perhaps unwilling it is well to be playful and perhaps a little silly within creativity so that ways may be found that charm and delight and then leave the taste behind of that thought which may be revisited and thought upon.

The greatest single communication which an entity ever makes is the look, the stature, the beingness, the way the seeker is. The way that expresses through the body, through the eyes, through the hands, through the expressions. Your bodies, your beings, these that you dress and wash and feed and tend, these are your wisdoms. Your inherent vibratory expression communicates more deeply, more searchingly than you shall ever know, than you shall ever be aware of, for the truth, as it becomes purer, is that which we are. And that is far beyond words.

This is a fascinating subject but we feel that we [have] gone far enough for one sitting, so at this time we would transfer to the one known as Jim that we may gather other queries at this time. We leave this instrument with thanks, in love and in light. We are those of Q'uo.

(Jim channeling)

I am Q'uo, and greet each again in love and in light through this instrument. At this time may we offer ourselves to those present for any further queries which might be on the minds.

R: I have an observation which I would like you to comment on. When I listen to the words of the channeling I find that I often drift away. I feel that I am getting the communication on a level other than the words.

I am Q'uo, and am aware of your query, my brother. As you are in the circle of seeking adding your desire and curiosity to the circle's calling for information you partake in a basic sense serving much as does the grounding device that anchors the signal. As a portion of the anchor for this signal you are, indeed, open to receiving the general sense or essence of our message upon a level which you might call the subconscious where the absorption of information takes the form more of the gestalt, shall we say. The entire picture of what we offer in our words and tones is available to your subconscious mind in a way which is not easily expressed yet which includes the foundation qualities of the message which we bring.

If you are concerned that you are not enough aware on a conscious level of the message which is being provided we can recommend that for a portion of the working you may open your eyes and listen in the normal waking sense. This shall bring you more easily remembered information for the conscious mind that then can be worked with on both the conscious and subconscious levels.

Is there another query, my brother?

R: No, Q'uo. I thank you for the suggestion and want to express my personal gratitude for your willingness to communicate.

I am Q'uo, and we are most grateful for your willingness to communicate as well, my brother.

Is there another query at this time?

(Pause)

I am Q'uo, and it appears that we are getting off easy today. We, however, are most grateful for the queries that have been offered to us and we hope that each will take the …

(Side one of tape ends.)

(Jim channeling)

I am Q'uo, and am again with this instrument. We offer opinion and do not wish any entity to take our words too seriously, but to take those which feel familiar and which feel appropriate and use them as you will, my friends.

At this time we shall take our leave, leaving each as always in the love and in the light of the infinite Creator. We are known to you as those of Q'uo. Adonai, my friends. Adonai.

L/L Research

Sunday Meditation
April 2, 1995

Group question: Today we will take general questions from our group, which has come from all corners of the planet.

(Carla channeling)

We are those of Q'uo. Greetings in the love and in the light of the one infinite Creator. It is our privilege and our blessing to join this circle, and we thank each for seeking to discover that truth that lies within and for coming together to further this divine curiosity. For truly, there is wisdom in each, yet when those of seeking mind together ponder and together discuss that truth that lies within each often becomes more accessible from each to each as those who are seemingly not at all you pluck the truth out of the thicket within those things which you have said and thought. Truly, it is a help to have friends along the way and we are honored to be among those friends.

We believe that you wish this session to be question and answer and so we shall not give you a sermonette, as this instrument would call it, but simply remind each, as always, that we are not infallible. We have our limitations, and our opinions are just that. We greatly appreciate each seeker subjecting our thoughts and all others to the personal powers of discrimination that each has. We thank you for this great courtesy. We may begin with the first query.

K: Concerning what Christianity and other groups call the mind of God, I would like to know what is the mind of God? Does it exist?

We are those of Q'uo. There are various levels of sense to possible answers to your query. Firstly, upon the level of literal word for word reality, the mind of God, as many have termed the Godhead, shall we say, is not a thing but rather a construction of the human mind which is determined to inject space and time into considerations of that which is infinite and eternal.

Perhaps a more substantive response would be to suggest that all lies within the mind of God, shall we say. That is, all that you could name and all that you might forget to name and all things whatsoever remain one thing and that one is all that there is.

Thusly, you who ask the query are the mind of God. This instrument who channels the impressions which we offer her is the mind of God, and each and every bit of stuff there is is the mind of the Creator, for it is our impression that the creation is the Creator.

And this Creator is not confined or retained within an image or form but, rather, is an infinite intelligence, what many among your peoples have called the Logos and what we have often called Love. This great original Thought or Logos which is Love is then perhaps our closest suggestion to a concept which approaches that which you have suggested as the mind of God in that it contains within its concept all unmanifest and manifest creation. However, it is well to note that within the illusions which you call the densities each of you is the mind of God in potentiation and the work done within the densities is in great part clearing away the various levels of confusion for each seeker, and in third density this clearing away is the clearing away of each seeker's self-definitions so that each may find within itself more and more the willingness and the instinct to take upon the self the role of that Love, that Logos, which is the original Thought, realizing that within the illusions the only manifestation of this Logos shall come from your words and your hands.

May we answer you more fully, my brother?

K: Is the mind of God what you would call intelligent infinity?

We are those of Q'uo. This is so, although the reverse would not be so. May we answer you in another way, my brother?

K: I can't think of a way to pursue this at this time. I do have some questions of a historical nature that relates to Christianity. Can you answer these for me?

We are those of Q'uo. It is our specialty, shall we say, to address questions concerning tools and resources that may be helpful for seekers in a metaphysical sense, those who wish to accelerate the rate of change within their own spiritual evolution. When we receive questions that ask for specific information sometimes we cannot answer because we do not know; sometimes we cannot answer because there is infringement upon free will; and sometimes we chose not to answer or to answer in a limited way because to pursue a certain point would be to allow the tuning of the circle and the instrument to suffer. With these limitations understood we are glad to have at whatever you have to discuss, my brother.

K: I appreciate what you say, and with that in mind I will ask these questions and leave the answers up to you at your discretion.

Could you describe the nature of the resurrection body that Jesus appeared in after leaving the tomb?

We are those of Q'uo, and believe that we grasp your query. We look within this instrument's vocabulary for technical words which we might make use of but we find that terms such as electrical body, astral body, and Buddha body have been so often and so variously used that we cannot call the resurrection body, as you have called it, by one of these terms without expecting confusion. However, let us say that the body which rose and walked from a cave was that body which this entity and all entities inhabit when they have not become incarnate and they are yet within the inner planes. The closest we might come to a general description would then be the electrical body or the metaphysical body. It is a body which is far more densely filled with light and therefore is able to co-exist with the third-density illusion.

Most bodies of this type are never visible to those within third-density incarnation, mostly because the entities do not know how to so clothe themselves with third-density material that they may become visible. The body of the one known as Jesus during this time was that body from which his earthly body had been made, the pattern-making body, that is. And this pattern-making or electrical body was simply picked up and put on, shall we say, but with a degree of faith that created manifestation.

You may relate this kind of body to—we search this instrument's knowledge for the closest manifestation and find that this entity has seen the so-called psychic surgery and has seen such manifestations of electrical or form-making occurrences. They are indistinguishable from normal, physical, illusory bodies. However, their actual arena of living and working is within what we would call the metaphysical universe.

May we answer further, my brother?

K: Did you say that Jesus of Galilee never incarnated but merely took on a third-density body for his work? And, also, how would that relate to what happened on the Mountain of Transfiguration?

We are those of Q'uo. No, my brother, we did not suggest that the one known as Jesus had a birth in other than the usual way. We were saying, rather, that this entity picked up and put on the form-making or electrical body in a far quicker and more decisive frame of reference than is usual for those who have left third-density incarnation by death. This was done because the one known as Jesus was aware that it was going through the processes of death and it grasped ahead of time, shall we say, what its part was, and, therefore, the faith and surety that this entity had earned allowed it to move through this process as history [has] written it for your peoples.

Do you still wish to ask the remainder of your query?

K: I do, please.

The so-called transfiguration was an event that was important to those who saw it rather than the one known as Jesus. To the one known as Jesus there was simply that basking in the light. To those who gazed upon him at this time there was the fairly articulated manifestation of earlier prophets and teachers, each of which had a ceremonial structure created about it. This was created by the great desire of those disciples who saw this to understand more clearly where the one known as Jesus fit, shall we say, into the long-standing and respected teachings of their peoples.

May we answer further, my brother?

K: Was there a UFO in the luminous cloud, or was there another meaning?

We are those of Q'uo, and we find that this instrument is aware of several luminous clouds. Do you speak of one specific instance, my brother?

K: Yes, the Bible speaks of a luminous cloud above Jesus on the Mountain of Transfiguration and a voice came out of the cloud, and I was wondering if this was a UFO or if this was a psychically projected voice, or did it not occur at all?

We are those of Q'uo. My brother, this was indeed a psychically projected manifestation and voice, yet it did occur, at the same time that it did not occur in terms of its being a flesh and blood creation rather than it being a thought form. In that particular instance there was no UFO.

Is there another query?

K: Were there two Yahwehs in the Old Testament? Or was there just one?

We are those of Q'uo. That which you have called Yahweh was, within the framework of the culture to which it came, as was understood then, God Itself. However, that personality which often was termed Jehovah or Yahweh was perhaps what you might call an angelic entity. This entity was responsible along with others for looking after the development of self-consciousness upon your planet and to aid in that development this entity chose to concern itself in the affairs of those within third density.

As the centuries passed and this very wise entity learned more about how to serve it chose to re-invent itself and did so along lines which created the possibility of the coming of the so-called Messiah. The Yahweh which many worshipped was the Creator rather than this personality. However, throughout most of the beginning, shall we say, or the Torah of the Old Testament the Jehovah character is a personality.

May we answer further, my brother?

K: Then you are saying that there was just one entity that chose to reinvent himself and that there were not two entities, one a negative and one a positive?

We are those of Q'uo. This is correct, my brother.

K: Thank you. Could you speak again on the subject of how we are all one? Could you speak without analogies and speak to the heart of the matter—how are we all one?

We are those of Q'uo, and we are most happy to attempt to speak upon this subject so very dear to our hearts.

Let us begin with things known by this instrument from her school days. The illusion is that which is real to those upon your sphere and this illusion is created of that which you call atoms. These atoms are treated as though there were little particles that, put together, become things. However, no scientist has been able to see any mass or substance when gazing at atoms or particles thereof. All that science has discovered are various fields of energy, so that the one known as Carla is a field of a certain kind of energy. The one known as K, just such another, and so forth.

These various fields seem very real, yet scientists can explain that there is no mass involved, just an arrangement of energies. Each self-conscious person is an energy field, then, which vibrates at a certain complex of levels in a characteristic way. The metaphysical identity of each person is this complex of vibrations which is the signature of each evolving self-conscious entity. So, within your density it is impossible to see that there is no separation between the clothes and the body, the body and the seat, the seat and the chair, the chair and the floor, and so forth. All these things appear separate. However, in any sense beyond energy fields there is no separation.

Now, within the mind, within the thinking and the feeling, as the mind gazes upon the creation it thinks it sees many different things, yet there are certain entities who are able, because of great similarities between them and you, to transcend the apparent separation between them and you. And such entities have been those who have supported and strengthened you. The energies, then, that seemingly separate persons from persons are those dictated by the senses which your physical vehicles have. However, as we have pointed out, these senses sense illusion, an illusion which your scientists have penetrated.

May we answer you further, my brother?

K: At your own discretion, Q'uo.

We would at this time transfer this contact to the one known as Jim, thanking this instrument and this group and leaving it briefly. We are those of Q'uo.

(Jim channeling)

I am Q'uo, and greet each again in love and in light through this instrument. We would ask at this time if there might be any further queries from any within this circle of seeking.

Questioner: What can I do to help boost my mental, emotional and spiritual energies?

I am Q'uo, and am aware of your query, my brother. We would recommend, to begin, that you review those experiences in your past that have been helpful in the revitalizing of these energies. For many entities it is helpful to find those written words of inspiration which might remind one and in the reminding may aid one to adopt a larger perspective that brings the unity and harmony of all creation more into focus for the present moment experience. The songs of inspiration are also of aid in the same regard. {As] the moving within the season of the springtime begins to make itself felt within your illusion, there is much of inspiration and revitalization that is available from your second density. There are many entities of an inspirational nature that are hidden, shall we say, within each entity's daily round of activities. To keep the inner eye open in anticipation of such entities moving within one's own path is always helpful, for the guiding hands, shall we say, that are with each entity in an unseen manner will often take the opportunity to reawaken the passion for existence and the living of the life by moving one to cross the path of such entities in what seems to be a coincidental manner.

Is there a further query, my brother?

Questioner: No, thank you very much.

I am Q'uo, and we thank you, my brother.

Is there another query?

P: Could you comment on the relation between space/time and time/space?

I am Q'uo, and am aware of your query, my sister. We hope that you realize that this is the topic which can fill volumes, my sister, for it is that which encompasses all that is. The illusion which you inhabit at this time is a reality which is constructed of the energy of love with many forms or personalities moving through the interaction and interplay of the Creator. Within this experience or classroom, shall we say, the emphasis of the Creator is upon the experience that is possible to be gained from those who momentarily create a situation in which they forget the basic truths of being and set for themselves the task with space/time of rediscovering these truths within the veil of forgetting, thus adding great weight of meaningfulness of such discoveries.

Thus, within space/time the plans created before incarnation, within the realms of time/space, are set into motion so that there is much self-awareness and awareness of all that can be gained by exploring the great darkness or seemingly so with the tiny candle of consciousness. The weight of the experience within space/time is more upon the shoulders of space so that there is movement there more possible than in the more inflexible time as it moves, or shall we say more correctly, as it is perceived in its linear fashion.

Within the realm of time/space the weight is more on the shoulders of time where more flexibility is there appreciated, movement in time being as easily accomplished as movement in space within the physical space/time illusion. Thus, the freedom and wider perspective of time/space offers the more fully experienced presence of the one infinite Creator but with less, shall we say, ability to progress along a path which is more obviously unified than is possible upon a path which is seemingly less unified as it is within the space/time illusion.

Is there any further query, my sister?

P: Am I correct in thinking that our conscious mind is in space/time and the subconscious is in time/space? Is the veil of forgetting what separates the two?

I am Q'uo, and am aware of your query, my sister. The veil of forgetting is a phenomenon which is occurring and is utilized only within the third density so that a choice of paths might be made at this point in the evolutionary path. Thus, the existence of a divided mind, that which is conscious and that which is below or subconscious, is possible only with the veil of forgetting in place which occurs, as we have mentioned, only within the third density.

Is there a further query, my sister?

P: You still didn't answer if the conscious memory is in space/time and the subconscious resides in time/space.

I am Q'uo, and believe that we grasp your query, my sister. Though it is somewhat difficult to answer in a concrete fashion, we would suggest that your assumption is in large part correct. Although it is also possible for those who are trained to travel in time/space to do so in a conscious fashion.

Is there a further query, my sister?

P: Two more questions. To do conscious work in the subconscious is what we call the sorcerer's tradition. Is it necessary for third-density people to be able to do that work?

I am Q'uo, and believe that we grasp your query, my sister. It is not necessary for third-density entities to be able to move consciously within the subconscious realms of their own minds or the time/space realms of their local creation in order to be able to be graduated from this third-density illusion to the fourth. What is necessary for such a graduation is that the entity be desirous of serving others in a loving and compassionate manner, more in a percentage, shall we say, than it desires to serve itself.

Is there a further query, my sister?

P: As we move from the third density to the fourth do we move from the present space/time into a time/space continuum?

I am Q'uo, and am aware of your query, my sister. We would suggest the pondering of the densities containing space/time and time/space from the third density through the latter portions of the sixth density so that there are experiences which can be seen as incarnational and experiences which may be seen as pre- and post-incarnational as well within each of these densities.

Is there a further query, my sister?

P: No, thank you.

I am Q'uo, and we thank you once again. Is there another query at this time?

R: Sometimes I share an inspirational image with you and I wonder if you are actually able to share it or is this just some kind of mind construct that I put together?

I am Q'uo, and am aware of your query, my brother. When a gift is offered to us it is as a calling to us and we are there and appreciate the sharing which you so generously offer and [which] gives us a taste, shall we say, of your experience that we would not have without your dedication of it to us.

Is there a further query?

R: No, thank you.

I am Q'uo. We thank you for your gift, my brother. Is there another query at this time?

P: Sometimes we receive voices, inspirations, etc. and sometimes they are of the ego and not true. How can we determine the true voices of the Creator?

I am Q'uo, and am aware of your query, my sister. We would recommend that you find that place of peace within you, whether you utilize meditation, prayer or contemplation, that you move within to that sacred room and await there the answer until it comes.

Is there a further query, my sister?

P: No, thank you.

I am Q'uo, and again we thank you. Is there a final query at this time?

Carla: I seem to have been blessed with the desire to do a whole lot more than I can do. Do you have any comments on this situation?

I am Q'uo, and am aware of your query, my sister. As we observe the well-known and well-stated preincarnative predisposition to activity and observe the choices made for the incarnation which were for the purpose of dealing with this very issue, we see now that the choices have been made conscious and you have before you much of that which you had before you before this incarnation. Thus, you are in a place of total free will where all that you desire to do lies before you as flowers in a garden, to be picked or sniffed for scent and left as they are.

Again, that meditative state is that place wherein the greatest clarity for each seeker is possible to be achieved and we would recommend that you make a time for this consideration that would coincide with a rebirthing ritual that [is] much like unto the springtime season that moves within your local environment at this time. And during this time of contemplation, prayerful thought, and the gaining of a sense of the self reborn, we would suggest that this is a means by which the subconscious mind might be alerted to the desire to know more of what is appropriate for this time for your experience within the illusion.

Is there a further query, my sister?

Carla: No, thank you.

I am Q'uo, and thank you once again, my sister.

We would take this opportunity to express our great joy and gratitude to each within this circle of seeking for inviting us this day and for giving us the gift of your queries, your concerns, and your desire to know that which is helpful on your journeys of seeking. We move with you on this journey and appreciate the desire that fuels each present and salute it as that force of motivation that is most important within each seeker's journey, not so much each experience or thought but the process of the seeking seen as a pattern, as a purpose, as a direction.

We are those of Q'uo, and would at this time take our leave of this instrument and this group, leaving each, as always, in the love and in the light of the one infinite Creator. Adonai, my friends. Adonai.

L/L Research

Sunday Meditation
April 9, 1995

Group question: The question this afternoon has to do with sexuality. We would like to know a number of things about sexuality, Q'uo. We would like to know what the natural expression of both the male and the female sexuality is—what are the archetypical images or forces that aid or cause this expression to be as it is? And we would like to know how it is most appropriate for us to work with or handle, to perceive these sexual energies in ourselves and in each other. And we would like to know if there is a way in which sexual energy exchanges can be used to experience the unity of the creation and the Creator. Is there a pathway there for evolution? And is the intelligent energy that is the creative force in the universe the same in us as sexual energy, or does it set this sexual energy in motion within us?

(Carla channeling)

Greetings in the love and in the light of the one infinite Creator. We are those of Q'uo. As always, it is a distinct pleasure and privilege to join this circle of seeking. We bless each that lends its complex of vibrations to this circle. The combined energy is most beautiful. We ask that each use its discrimination in listening to what we say. We ask that you not accept any of our opinions unless it seems to strike a chord of response within you, for truth is a deeply personal thing, and we ask you to guard your own truth carefully.

As we speak to you concerning sexual energy, we need to speak in a context so that we do not isolate this energy in thinking of it in an artificial manner, but, rather, a way that enables each to see and to feel the perfection of the sexual gift. Indeed, gifts that are large and contain great power are also those responsibilities which are equally great, for each guards and appreciates and shares this energy among others.

The wellspring of your physical vehicles is the sexual activity. The fructifier of inspiration is often the sexual activity. The healer of pain, even deep pain, is often sexual activity. And all those energies of friendship and the reaching of people unto people as societies—these need to be seated within strong and healthy sexuality in order for there to be depth to the processes by which energy moves toward that perfect light of infinite energy.

Archetypically speaking, then, sexuality for third-density entities such as yourselves begins with that dynamic between the male who reaches that outstretched hand and the female which awaits the reaching. Now, this is an archetypical structure, an archetypical logic. In truth, male and female both reach and await the reaching. But in terms of finding a way to grasp and understand the ways in which this energy arises, it is central to see this dynamic of the male which reaches and the female which awaits the reaching.

The difficulties that those who are seeking truth find in that seeking often seem to have nothing to do with sexuality, but rather with things holding one back: the spouse or something about the home situation begins to be seen as being so limiting that the seeker must leave to be free to seek unfettered by what seems to be a sea of negativity. Quite often, however, what is occurring is that the seeker has begun working upon the higher energy centers—the heart, the throat, the brow—those energies that we would call those of compassion, communication and work in consciousness. Certainly, these indeed are those energies which beckon. And oh, how hungry the student is for more wisdom, more knowledge, more insight, and more understanding! Yet, any plant begins its life within the soil, and although you no longer are attached to the earth by roots that are visible, yet the physical body which carries you about has its origin, its life, and its energy because of its oneness with the Earth plane.

The amount of sheer energy vibrating betwixt earth and physical vehicle is astounding, yet it cannot be acknowledged and used nearly so well by one who is working upon upper chakras unless that entity has the patience, the humility and the determination to come into contact with that earth, that soil of self, for the sexual identity is as powerful and as completely unique a part of the individual spirit or soul as any other incarnationally expressed energy. This is the energy which creates a healthy plant, a healthy body—the energy that gives a primal "yes" to being. This is, moreover—as are all energies—a sacred, a holy energy, and the sexual intercourse is as the Eucharist of red ray, the holy communion of the body. This union capitulates—we correct this instrument—recapitulates the oneness of earth and sky, the oneness of male and female, the oneness of reaching and waiting.

Now, when we speak of sexuality, we do not simply speak of sexual acts, for this energy is constant, and though its appearance in the conscious mind is cyclical, its place in the scheme of things, shall we say, is constant.

Now, how does one work upon the red ray? First, one simply has to become able to express to the self precisely what the attitude is, for we find among your peoples a great ability to gloss over uncomfortable subjects with generalities and half thought out concepts. There is inevitable damage done, if one would call it that. There is, shall we say, inevitable distortion that has taken place for each and every entity within incarnation, for, like the rest of the incarnational tools and resources, sex is intended to cause great catalyst, to cause entities to feel all kinds of befuddlement, anger, grief and so forth. That is one of the great virtues of sexual intercourse and the relationship between two entities concerning their sexuality and their expression, one with the other. One is intended to find this a difficult thing, at least from time to time, for the journey from head to heart must be taught at every level of energy.

So, one may work on the issue of becoming more balanced in red-ray energy whether or not one is in relationship, whether or not one is sexually active. In terms of doing one's homework, shall we say, it does not matter what the situation is, for each entity's sexuality lies at the very heart of its individuality and each entity must needs work upon its own issues, its own sexuality. It is well to attempt, then, to gently part the strands that are tangled in the process of perceiving one's relationship to another sexually, so that the other entity's issues stay with that entity, so the self works completely upon the self, and perhaps its reactions may offer that catalyst for thinking which does create lessons learned and the strength of vital energy improved.

As the Creator intended, third density is always concerned with the dualities of dynamic opposites, and the male reaching is the strongest dynamic, the female waiting is the strongest dynamic of red ray. So, let us look briefly at the reaching and the waiting.

It is not just the mind and the spirit that are involved in the processes of reaching, for the physical vehicle has instincts that are very clear. The perpetuation of the species, as this instrument would call it, is completely dependent upon that male necessity for reaching. Thus, it is that the body itself has the instinct to reach, and of course those females who have an abundance of male energy shall also find themselves involuntarily reaching out to the sexuality of a male that has caught the eye. This energy can be perceived as being very negative because it can be confrontive and because the deepest instinct of one who awaits reaching is protection.

Now, what is it for which the male reaches, beyond, that is, the obvious? What is it that is at the heart, spiritually speaking, of this energy? As always, it is that unity. The prize is great for those who wish to purify and strengthen this energy until it finds balance within the self. Thusly, males have the necessity of dealing with the catalyst of attraction to any attractive and available female. Indeed, that male energy is capable of reaching in fantasy, in thought. There does not even need to be the stimulus of the female which is present. This ensures that the species will survive as long as the planet is viable.

Meanwhile, for the female energy, there is the opposite side of this dynamic—unity there is, but an articulated unity. Males who have much female energy also find themselves involuntarily drawn into the contractions of one who protects oneself. This energy is so powerful that it—this instrument is having trouble finding a word for what we wish to say—the power of this energy is so great, that there is the necessity for the female or negative energy to be watchful, cautious and protective. Not for the female energy the indiscriminate reaching, but rather the careful protection, for the unity that is articulated betwixt male and female is that mystery which is the one great original Thought.

Female energy potentiating male energy equals subconscious energy run through conscious channels. So, each becomes a channel for the one great original Thought which is love. And in the sexual mating betwixt two who grasp the profundity and centrality of the energies of lovemaking, there is the possibility of touching intelligent energy, and in this fusion, the two truly are one. And from this rise male and female, blessed, balanced and healed.

We ask each to consider the archetype known as "The Lovers." In this figure, a male stands with a female on each side; to one side, the virginal; upon the other side, the worldly and prostituted female energy. It is the first choice, the most obvious choice, for the male who comes into possession of that sexuality which shall be its catalyst for a lifetime, to reach for that sexuality in the female which is obvious; and, indeed, there is that portion of any male energy which shall always be attracted to the prostituted and the shallow. This is natural. Yet, to the man who seeks until he finds that female which he feels he can work with in all humility, to this entity is given a great deal of aid. For, if male and female wish equally to work together at this energy level, then there is for both a constant supply of transferred energy—to the male, the inspiration, to the female, that vital energy—each giving what each has in abundance and receiving what each has not enough of.

We mention this archetype because there is a continuing need for entities to reconfigure and rebalance themselves, for there is little probability that a seeker may become perfect in this or any practice of disciplining the self again and again. That male energy which is such a blessing in its abundance and its strength may well fall into a season wherein images come and come and come into the mind and it seems that there is nothing but lasciviousness within. And for the female there is that tendency to allow the protectiveness that is appropriate to degenerate into bitterness and fear, and the separation that occurs because of these things is substantial.

Therefore, in working with each other in relationship, that energy we would call forgiveness is most important. This energy, as all energies within this illusion, has been set up to cause confusion and befuddlement, again and again. And while it is natural to experience negative emotions in response to the frustrations of failing, as one perceives one's self to fail, it may seem that the subject of sex is not worth all the work. Women have an archetypical tendency to be what this instrument would call "bitches." Males have the archetypical tendency to be what this instrument calls "pigs." These are pejorative terms. This instrument uses them because to speak them aloud takes some of the sting from that inevitable truth, for that element which seems bitchy is only the outcropping of that healthy tendency of protection. The female fights with words. That to which it is reacting is that male nature which reaches indiscriminately, and no matter how far a male has come spiritually, the physical vehicle of that male will continue to reach indiscriminately.

The student of metaphysics will, for the most part, attempt to ignore the promptings that are random and to continually re-place the attention upon the mated relationship. The male shall always fail to do this perfectly. The female may attempt to be forgiving, understanding and so forth, but again, failure is inevitable. My friends, in this way as in all others you have each other to help each other, and it is most encouraged by us that each attempt to see that dynamic that sexuality offers with a merciful and ruthful gaze, to be quick to forgive and to be willing again and again to attempt to trust.

When there is discord at this level, much energy is blocked, and it is usual for students of metaphysics that they will be blocked to some extent at this level. We have spoken to you before concerning the dangers of working in consciousness without first clearing those lower energies, and we remind each again: the first work is that work which is the lowest, the basest, and the most fundamental. The first holiness is here, where feet meet earth, where spirit meets flesh. Here, at the level where entities are born. Here, where entities express their deepest physical nature. Here is the beginning of a good work.

Working with this energy center shall last the lifetime, but we encourage each to work intensively in this level of energy until a balance is perceived by the self. Then, the process is to work upon the self's mental relationships with itself and then relationships with others, and then relationships with groups. And only when this work of balancing has been touched upon should a student move into working on opening the heart, into communicating, into work in consciousness, for the energy has a natural vector from the lower to the higher and the student needs a strong foundation.

So, we ask each to see working on sexuality as a holy occupation and part of a holy life. Let it be wonderful and fun. Free the self to rejoice in the beauty of this energy. This is a long process sometimes; however, there is much pleasure in the work.

At this time, we shall transfer this contact to the one known as Jim. We thank this instrument, and leave it in love and light. We are those of Q'uo.

(Jim channeling)

I am Q'uo, and greet each again in love and in light through this instrument. At this time it is our privilege to offer ourselves in the speaking to any further queries which may be upon the minds of those present. May we ask if there is another query at this time?

Questioner: OK, I'll ask a question … *(inaudible)*. I was thinking about the lovemaking of whales. It seems that the whales are intelligent beings and I just thought it's such an enormous thing for these huge beings. And could you please comment on the energy exchange between these beings? Is it … do they experience a total energy exchange besides just the physical … do they feel the love … for them is it an act of also reaching out besides just the progression of the physical evolution?

(Pause)

I am Q'uo, and am again with this instrument and am aware of your query, my sister. The pause in our response was due to the need for this instrument to again offer the challenge and for the process to be completed. We beg your forgiveness.

In response to your query, may we say that the entities which you know as the whale, in many of its species—though not in each species—resides a kind of consciousness which is much like your own, but in some ways is more, shall we say, advanced in that the entities are able to sense, each with the other, the nature of what you would call the emotions, the motivations, and the natural expression of them.

When this expression of energies is in the area of the red ray sexual energy exchange, there are many of these entities who have more than the red and orange and yellow centers of energy available for the moving of energy and the sharing of this energy, so that such sharings are oftentimes expressions of the unity which these entities feel with each other and with the creation about them. In such expressions, there is little of the confusions and distortions that so oftentimes plague their two-footed brothers and sisters who live upon the land surfaces. The expressions of energies are much more, shall we say, pure and clear to the point; and with clarity to the point, then there is the movement of the consciousness beyond the immediate point of the reproduction of the species and the satisfaction of the red-ray sexual urges.

Is there a further query, my sister?

Questioner: Yes, could I extrapolate from your comments that the whales are the third-density, the self-aware species? Are they also like wanderers—beings of high density who incarnate in third-density physical bodies?

I am Q'uo, and am aware of your query, my sister. This is incorrect. The achievement of the species, in some cases, of this species of whales as you call them, is a result of their own evolution upon this planetary surface.

Is there a further query, my sister?

Questioner: I would just clarify then—they are self-conscious entities who originated from Earth. Right?

I am Q'uo, and this is correct. Is there another query?

Questioner: Not at this time, thank you.

Questioner: Q'uo, I have a question. It's on another subject. I'm thinking of the nature of the soul that I asked about in a previous session. I'd like to know what is the nature of the soul and how it originates.

I am Q'uo, and am aware of your query, my brother. This query is one which spans the entire breadth of the evolutionary process as we understand it, and we would attempt to respond to your query by suggesting that the soul is that constant awareness or constant consciousness within an individualized being that is the library or repository of all experiences which this entity has accumulated in all of its incarnative expressions throughout all of its densities of progression. Thus, there is much information and much of character, shall we say, that is gathered into that concept complex which you have called "the soul."

It is as the actor upon the stage, if we may borrow again from this analogy, that has played many parts and has been moved by portions of each of them to the degree that there are characteristics or perceptions within the soul essence that are a direct result of such marks upon experience. Thus, the soul is the pilgrim upon the journey that begins with the very simple awareness of its own beingness, and begins to define its personality or identity according to those experiences that it passes through; and as the accumulation of experience, incarnation after incarnation, builds, then the soul is richer and has more to call upon for future efforts in this evolutionary endeavor.

Is there a further query, my brother?

Questioner: Is the soul created out of intelligent infinity to which it returns, or … how is the soul created? Or did I misunderstand you?

I am Q'uo, and we believe that we understand your query, my brother, and would respond by suggesting that the soul is created from that intelligent infinity from which all of creation is made, and as it is able to gather experience within one illusion after another, then there is the identifying of this soul essence as a personality of a metaphysical nature.

Is there a further query, my brother?

Questioner: Yes. Ra used the term, "the buddha body," and also "the higher self," for one of the aspects of individuals. Is the buddha body a sheath-covering for the soul? Or, what is the relationship of the buddha body and the higher self and the soul?

I am Q'uo, and am aware of your query, my brother. In the attempt to speak to this query, there is the difficulty of your language and your linear perception of time that we must deal with, for the higher self, as it is often called, is the soul at another portion of its experience in a succeeding higher density. Thus, that which is your soul—that essence of self around which all experience orbits—becomes aware of its fullness. It becomes the higher self.

This is also in close relationship to that which you have called the "buddha body," that body which is associated with the violet-ray or crown chakra energy center. This expression of the self is that portion that stands within the light at the graduation to determine the ability of the soul to accept a greater and greater light and thus be, shall we say, graduated to the fourth density. Thus, you may see a loose identity between buddha body, soul and higher self that begins to become a closer and closer equality as the soul progresses from density to density.

Is there another query, my brother?

Questioner: Q'uo, I was thinking of the soul as a kind of tablet of white paper, a mnemonic substance that was cast out of the central sun or intelligent infinity and gradually took upon identity through incarnations. Is this concept wrong … of the origin of the soul and its nature?

I am Q'uo, and we find that this concept is basically correct and thus is usable.

Is there a further query, my brother?

Questioner: Yes, thank you for that, Q'uo. I just have one more. And during this religious season I am thinking of the … what we call "the gospels" in the Holy Book: Matthew, Mark, Luke, John. I am wondering if you would speak to the people who … about the people who wrote these books and the years in which they were written. Could you do that?

I am Q'uo, and we are aware of your query, my brother, and may respond by suggesting that the entities which are responsible for the authorship of those books of your Bible called "the gospels," are entities who were working in the recording of their experiences with the one known as Jesus the Christ some two millennia previous to this present date, and who were able to glean a small portion of that entity's teachings in a manner which had meaning to them, and which they were desirous of sharing with others for that reason.

Is there a further query, my brother?

Questioner: Could you give identities of these authors?

I am Q'uo, and we are aware of your desire to know the precise nature and identity of the authors of these books of inspiration, and we are in the desire to remain without infringing upon ones' free will, and thus must withhold the specific identification, for there is some discrepancy with the accepted authors and their identity, which we find is necessary to maintain.

Is there a further query, my brother?

Questioner: I don't think so. Thank you for that. That'll be all for me. Thank you, Q'uo.

I am Q'uo, and again we thank you, my brother. Is there another query at this time?

Questioner: I have one. I had a thought, a stray thought, about sexuality … was that it kind of had a theme to it of sacrifice … a woman sacrificing, obviously, her virginity. Males used to sacrifice their virginity, too, but with the big practice of circumcision, males no longer have anything to sacrifice. But to the female it is more of a sacrifice, because of the fact that she then becomes able to have babies. And yet, to the male the sacrifice is of the whole life. Because of the sacrifice of the woman willing to give to the man, the man gives to the woman children which then he sacrifices the life to protect and support. And I wondered if there was a significance or if I was on the wrong track. It just seems to me like, almost like a woman is a priest in that ritual of sexuality.

I am Q'uo, and we are aware of a wide range of possible responses to this query, for again, the field is a large one and we cannot begin to do it justice with a short response. Thus, we are relegated to offering what must be a somewhat unsatisfactory answer.

The female of your species, indeed, does make a sacrifice which is great, for there is much of responsibility that rests with the female in that it will be the one to bear the fruit of such a joining, and must nurture and suckle this young entity for a significant portion of your time. The male makes a sacrifice in that it is desirous, in its higher motivations, of aiding in this process and building with the female the family unit that will be the teachers to the young entities born from it. The male then sacrifices what may be seen as its freedom to roam among the other female entities. This is somewhat difficult for the males of the current populations of your sphere, for there is much of confusion that follows any discussion of sexuality in all cultures upon your planet.

There are various areas of intense experience which have provided and will continue to provide catalyst of an intense nature, and the area of sexuality is, indeed, a basic area of power—and power misunderstood—within many of your cultures. Thus, there is the diluting of the sexual energy exchanges which plagues many of your peoples.

Is there a further query, my sister?

Questioner: No. Thank you, Q'uo.

I am Q'uo, and again we thank you, my sister. Is there a final query at this time?

Questioner: If no one else has a question, I'd like to ask about energy exchanges that go on in this channeling. I'd like to ask … well, the service that you provide for us is obvious *(inaudible)*. What kind of service is this to you in your spiritual growth? What kind of energy do you take from these channelings? How does it help you in your spiritual growth?

I am Q'uo, and am aware of your query, my sister. And in this query we are happy to say that the answer is quite simple, for we are served by you as you allow us to be of service to you. It is as though one hand of the Creator gives to another a touch of life, and in so touching receives that which it gives.

Is there a further query, my sister?

Questioner: That's it, thank you.

I am Q'uo, and again we thank you, my sister. And at this time we would take our leave of this group, for we are aware of the length of your time that this working has assumed and we do not wish to overtire those present. We are known to you as those of Q'uo, and we leave each, as always, in the love and in the ineffable light of the one infinite Creator. Adonai, my friends. Adonai.

Sunday Meditation
April 16, 1995

Group question: This is Easter Sunday and it is also the time of spring where the new flowers and new grass and plants start poking their heads out of the ground. We are all feeling rather inspired and inspirited, we [would] like to have some information upon this general concept of resurrection or rebirth, the coming into being of a new self, the inspiration bringing a new being, a risen being, more inspired and full of light. And we would like to have whatever information you could give us on how this process happens in our own lives, how it happens in the world around us, the interrelationship between the two and anything that you could say on rebirth or resurrection.

(Carla channeling)

We are those of Q'uo, and we greet you in the love and in the light of the one infinite Creator. It is both a privilege and a blessing for us to be sharing in your vibrations. We would thank each which has come to this circle this day for the quality and depth of the preparation of desire, for considering new thoughts and looking for new truths. Truly, when desire has been so purified that it becomes a fine instrument, then it is that the call sent out becomes clearer and stronger. And this aids us, for as the preparation is, so the energy is; and as the energy of the circle is, so the communication is. So those hours spent in thought, in prayer, in review, in contemplation, in meditation and as this instrument would say, in the sacred practice of chilling out and taking it easy, each of you has done good work, and work that enables us to do our work better. And we thank you for this most profoundly.

As we view the thrust of your opening question this day, we reflect upon how to lay the groundwork for that which we have to offer in the way of opinion. As always, we ask that each discriminate carefully and choose those things which we have to say that are useful, leaving the rest behind. Perhaps we shall begin in the dark. For the preparation for light is all important to the appreciation and resonance with that light that comes at the end of a period of watching and waiting. How necessary it is that the concepts of spirit first be nurtured and fed within the earth and ground of being.

That spiritual self that within the mythological system you call Christianity has its beginning at the birth of the Christ. The small child is deep within that darkness of winter. The beginning of spiritual seeking, or perhaps we should say spiritual learning, is always in darkness. This is quite necessary, for much ground must be laid within that darkness. Much development of the spirit takes place only within the shadows of that inner darkness which so fructifies and feeds the spirit that it gains the energy, which it then can use to seek the light.

So, as always, the beginning of discussion of equality includes its dynamic opposite. Those opposites, that seem so different one from the other, and yet are each other as two sides of the coin, in truth one object. All opposites may fruitfully be seen as unified. This practice is instructive. Now when the light lengthens upon your planet, when the sun rises earlier and sets later, the effect upon your Earth world is astounding. It is a food to green and growing things, that light which seems intangible and yet is literally food and drink to your companions of second density, that reach their leaves to the light of the sun as it rains down in a golden shower. And in that plane of the Earth world, indeed your entire planet is moving at this time within a new and previously unexperienced portion of space/time. As the inevitable cycles move, some cycles are very brief, others ponderously long. But at this particular time in your Earth history, this present moment is witness to unprecedented amounts of spiritual light and this shall continue to expand, as the cycles of time and space move relentlessly and benevolently to create ever new opportunities for seeking, for learning, for the giving and receiving of unity by unity, love by love, any quality whatsoever by its reflection in all that is seen and felt.

In a universe in which the creator moves with such order and precision it is not surprising that the rhythms of human beings move in sympathy with the rhythms of the planet and its seasons. Many of your planet's peoples celebrate a resurrection of that which was dead and is now alive. This choice, of that religion that you call Christian, of the spring as the time in which to celebrate death and resurrection of the Christ is peculiarly apt and very accurately placed, is that date that so coincides not with the rhythms of created mankind but with those fey and restless rhythms of moon and tide, of earth and the dark heart of the womb. Now is the time when that which has been in the womb, whether it be seed or embryo or spirit, has the opportunity to respond to the enlarging of the light. This is a precious time, a time to celebrate the self that is not yet unfurled, to celebrate that which is in bud, young, vulnerable and infinitely tender.

The exercise of celebration is deeply helpful to the spirit as well as being most helpful to the body and to the life of that body. For it is possible to experience the catalyst of the increasing light in such a way that there is no heightened awareness which results within the being. The preparation in the darkness is the key to the use of light. Why is that? We feel that it has to do with the nature of evolution. In the seeking for truth that which is new cannot come, cannot be realized until that which is in its place has been released. Through the cycles that are within, each seeker has moved through periods deep in the mire of personal misery and pain. And whether this has been accounted as suffering or as nothing, yet still, the work has been done. That which is dead has been released, making room for evolution. The pain of change feels like a death. The releasing of old opinion feels mortal. And the wound of leaving behind old ways of thought is fell and fatal. There is literal truth in death and resurrection in terms of the spirit. There must be the willingness to die to the old in order for that which is written already upon your heart to become visible, to become illuminated, to be in the light. Even when that which is old is a rending and separating truth, even when the new is gentler and sweeter, the death of the old is very hard to bear. And we do not wish to quibble with how hard it is to progress in relation to the letting go of that which is dead.

It is into this atmosphere that the one known as Jesus the Christ deliberately sets out to move into utter darkness, as this entity willingly and knowingly walks to its Jerusalem, to its Golgotha, to its own resurrection, which comes only after a death—a crucifixion of the entire mortal man—a going down into the darkness of the grave then, which no darkness could be blacker [than] in human consciousness. This is the fear that is beyond all fears, human: that terror of the dark which does not end. It is into this infinite darkness that the one known as Jesus moves. And when this entity again rejoins the creation of light, this entity simply expresses the normalcy, the everyday quality of the conquering of death. *(Inaudible)* life—the battle—one of darkness by light.

It is not only that there is no longer within this mythological system any death to fear, paradoxically it is also that this entity moves completely into the human condition of mortality, so completely that it accepts and undergoes the death. Now for all this entity could prove, for all that any entity can prove, this entity gave itself up to a death that had no end. Yet, words of life were given by the one known as Jesus, and it is well to heed them. The key to moving from darkness to light was given by this entity when it said of those who crucified it: "Father forgive them, for they know not what they do."

The key to using the light is forgiveness, mercy, charity, love. One may walk into the light and yet not see light. If one has confusion and puzzlement upon the mind, one can move through an entire beautiful day and see no light. And just so within. One can walk into one's own season of blossom and yet blossom not, nor see the sun, nor take food and drink from it. If one has closed one's heart, the light cannot survive and will simply be reflected and used elsewhere. Think of the darkness of winter and feel the contraction that occurs as the roots of being curl down into the earth, seeking water and nutriment. So are the roots of the self contracted and turned and curled inward, seeking and not finding nutriment. And then light comes, and the decision is made to let go of all things, save the reaching toward that light. There is expansion of self, there is the opening of the heart with these magic words: "I forgive."

Each seeker has its own seasons within, its own time of darkness and its own time of light. It is well to be most respectful towards and sensitive of these inner movements of the spirit, these trustworthy and helpful times within. As you move through your days and nights, try to remain sensitive to those rhythms, those ripples in the pond of self, those changes of weather. For all seasons, from the coldest to the hottest, from the most contracted to the most expansive are equally useful, not equally comfortable, but equally useful. However, as this instrument has said, it is possible to experience a lengthening of that inner season of light, and this instrument, however, did not find the second key to enjoying more and more light. This instrument had noted that the more one gives praise and thanksgiving for the good times the longer they are likely to stay around. But there is another truth also here.

This instrument is creating a blockage for it was concerned it would not be able to channel the other idea which it did not personally know and this has made this instrument come out of its tuning, and so we would appreciate the circle re-tuning, by perhaps singing the "Row, row, row your boat." We are those of Q'uo.

(All sing "Row, row, row your boat … ")

(Carla channeling)

We are again with this instrument and we feel that perhaps we may say what we have to say another way, and so allow this instrument the luxury of not having to know what the other part was. For the enjoyment of the good times has its basis laid in the enjoyment and positive possession of those times when all is dry and dark and without merit, seemingly. How precious it is when entities can gaze upon their pain and suffering and enter into the darkness without fear, knowing that all is illusion, knowing that both dark and light are useful, knowing that there is no place that the light is not, knowing that there is no light in which there is not the darkness of some degree of illusion.

For we ourselves are illusions. We are developed and articulated and our experience is vast, for we have been since the beginning and we shall always be, and yet we are illusion. For all that can be spoken, all that can be self-realized is by definition illusion, fields of energy, that come and go, while the Creator is in the one momentary now, that eternity in actuality is. Yet, the journey made each time the Creator flings out of Its vast and infinite potentiality those sparks of being that have become each of you, It receives in the end of that journey such a gift of whole and integrated consciousness that to the infinite riches of creation are added infinite richness more. The gift of that journey to the one infinite Creator is a perfect gift, a gift of love, that which has been reflected from love reflects at last to love and becomes One again in that sweetness of unity in which all sense is lost.

We would at this time transfer this contact to the one known as Jim, leaving this instrument with thanks and in love and light. We are those of that principle known to you as Q'uo.

(Jim channeling)

I am Q'uo, and we greet each again in love and in light through this instrument. At this time we are honored to ask if we might speak to any further queries which those present might have for us. Is there a query at this time?

Questioner: I would like to ask, there was an issue that several of us spoke of before the channeling today and a *(inaudible)* nervousness in preparation for *(inaudible)* task, that it's almost an agitation with yourself before launching on a project or before starting something. Would you comment how the self can use this particular energy in doing this work, how to best use this agitation, this nervousness?

I am Q'uo, and we believe that we grasp your query, my sister. The quality of feeling which you have mutually described as that of nervousness, is a means by which there is a contact with those portions of the conscious mind and perhaps for many of the subconscious as well, which wish to direct energy towards an expenditure of this energy that will be of such and such a nature, that nature described and defined by the conscious self. Thus, an entity which is preparing to give of itself in a manner which it hopes will be helpful and perhaps even of an inspirational nature, will begin to alert those portions of the deeper mind which may aid in this process by providing what you may call the creative motivation, the spark of energy which sets the being aflame with that which is in alignment with its nature, its passion, that which …

(Side one of tape ends.)

(Jim channeling)

I am Q'uo, and I am again with this instrument. Thus, the avenue to these deeper portions of the mind and of the self is one which has the general characteristics of the personality of the seeker, so that there is energy and inspiration available in whatever manner has been inbuilt into the patterns of the personality. This instrument has had information that describes this avenue as being somewhat indirect. This is so for each entity, because each entity has those blockages to energy flow which are in the form of lessons to be learned, tangles to be untangled. Thus, the knotted or stopped flow of energy that reaches to the deeper portions of the self is like unto a fingerprint, if you will, for the entity itself. The process of balancing which each seeker undergoes can be seen as a process that makes this way straight rather than crooked, narrowed, blocked or weakened. However, each has this access available and can utilize the inspirational and intelligent energy from the deeper portions of the self in whatever manner of self-expression is chosen.

Is there a further query, my sister?

Questioner: I just wanted to ask one short question. By balancing, then, you mean by unblocking of blockages, is that right?

I am Q'uo, and this is so. Is there another query, my sister?

Questioner: No, not at this moment. I leave it to others.

I am Q'uo, and we thank you, my sister. Is there another query?

Questioner: I just want to … and I have no question … I am just happy to be here and I don't have one.

I am Q'uo, and we are happy as well, my brother, to rest in your vibrations. For this is a gathering of energies that are at once quite potent and yet quite placid. Is there a query before us at this time?

Carla: Yes, a couple. First of all, I was wondering why it is that I was getting word by word communication for quite some time. Yet in the last couple of sessions, it's been given, ah, just by concept and not words at all but just concepts, that I have to do the words for. Is it possible for me to know why this is or what is happening in my learning of how to channel that this is been different, or any comment that you might have?

I am Q'uo, and we are aware of your query, my sister. In the channeling process there is a need to be able to move in whichever modality is most appropriate for the more advanced transmission of more complex concepts. Thus, in areas where your personal experience is somewhat lacking, we would choose to use the word by word transmission, so that the movement into the more abstract area would be accomplished with less concern than if the conceptual means of the transmission were utilized and would cause an instrument to, shall we say, panic in some degree when the concepts were unfamiliar. However, given these generalities which have been utilized in your case from time to time, there is also the desire on our parts to balance the means of transmission, so that your instrument remains able to, shall we say, play either piece.

Is there another query, my sister?

Carla: Yes, I wondered what exercise or discipline I might work at, what I ought to do I guess you would say, to work on not repeating my error of becoming concerned and then frightened, because I didn't have an idea of what was coming.

I am Q'uo, and I am aware of your query, my sister. The image which we give this instrument is to simply keep hanging your rear out on the line.

Carla: Oh, very well *(laughing)*.

Is there a further query, my sister?

Carla: Was the content that you were trying to say said to your satisfaction when I returned or is there a matter that it might be useful for us to go back and question about in a future session?

I am Q'uo, and am aware of your query, my sister. Now the student would like the grade. Well, *(Carla laughs)* perhaps there shall be some time after school. No, we are just having a bit of fun with both this instrument and yourself, my sister. We are pleased with your efforts and would not seek to alter them.

Is there a further query, my sister?

Carla: One more. Was the information that was missing having to do with one person being able to be a light to another person in darkness?

I am Q'uo, and this is well said, my sister. *(Carla laughs.)* Do you have a further query?

Carla: No, no, I am happy now. It's nice to hear the old humor, that part of you which is Latwii. I really, really enjoy that when this shines through.

I am Q'uo, and we are happy as well to be able to share in the mirth of the moment, for truly all about there is a great rejoicing and a laughter that echoes through all creation. May we ask if there is a final query?

Questioner: I would like to ask a question on how you perceive time. *(Carla laughs again.)*

I am Q'uo, and am aware of your query far more than aware of an ability to respond in a manner which would make sense. For we are aware of that which you call time when we are in the, shall we say, frame of reference that calls for the use of time. In many of our experiences there is the flow of the river of time and we may cast ourselves upon this river in whatever experiential raft that we care to construct. So that we may experience time much as do you. For we may experience a movement of time in more than one direction, at a time, if you will. Our experience is one which partakes more of the, what you may call, gestalt of the moment, where all of the factors, which are in our experiential continuum, offer themselves in the fullness of their being, which is to say, in the completeness of the experience of time; so that we are able to utilize the resources of the one Creator about us in a way which is more limitless in its nature. We may explore an avenue of time as you explore the streets of your city. We may remain in any particular street for as long as we wish or as long as is necessary. Upon the cessation of that experience we may move to other experiences and, indeed, in many instances may explore multiple experiences at once, viewing time more as a, shall we say, array of energy directions rather than a single direction. We hope that we have been able to give some indication of this experience, [as] we are aware that it is very difficult to express in the limited ambiance of any language.

Is there any further query, my sister?

Questioner: No, thanks. But I do appreciate your explanation.

I am Q'uo, and again we thank you, my sister. At this time we shall express our great gratitude, as always, for this offering of your desires, your queries and your very essence to this exploration of consciousness with us. We are thrilled at each such opportunity, for the lands through which we travel in the mind of each present are rich and fertile with a varied topography, always offering the surprise of the moment and of the experience.

We are those of Q'uo, and we would leave this instrument and this group at this time, as always, in the love and in love and in the light of the one infinite Creator. Adonai, my friends. Adonai. ☥

L/L Research

Sunday Meditation
April 21, 1995

Group question: Travelers at the crossroads. A question from P, R1, R2 and K, from various locations on the planet, and we would like to know how to be a journeyer and how to make decisions on the road, both exterior and interior-wise. How to be open to the inspiration of the moment in order to reach the destination.

(Carla channeling)

Greetings in the love and in the light of the one infinite Creator. We are those of the principle of Q'uo, and we are called to your group to speak with you, to share our thoughts, our opinions, and our presence and to blend our vibrations with yours. We greatly thank and honor each of you for this privilege. May we say that the crystalline beauty of your blended vibrations is substantial, and we thank you again and again for the opportunity of sharing this time together.

Our thoughts are not new, nor are they original. And it is important, we feel, that we express to you that we may make mistakes and we may speak in a way that does not come anywhere near your own personal truth, so as you listen and as you ask questions we ask that you continue to discriminate and use your own judgment rather than taking our word or the word of any so-called authority, for deep within you lie all your answers and, more importantly, deep within you lie all your true questions, those concerns, desires, hopes and unknown ambitions that shall create, step by step, the continuing tapestry of your experience.

This day you ask concerning ends and beginnings, times of cusp, times when there must be decisions made and vectors chosen on many levels, and indeed you are in harmony with the energies of your surroundings, for in the physical plane the energies and essences that strengthen and nurture your growing plants are in the midst of transforming that which was dead into a riot of leaf and blossom and bloom. And echoing this natural rhythm of your planet your great religions find this a beginning, a resurrection or a Passover, both being in the most literal sense great crossroads for one entity or for a people.

When one has come to the end of a pattern and one feels that itch to move, it is salutary, shall we say, both to honor that impulse and to use that impulse as a point from which to reflect. It is useful when the seeker perceives that there is a true ending to sit with that awareness, not attempting to figure anything out, not attempting to intellectually break down a situation into its logical parts, but rather allowing that situation into the full eyeshot of mind and heart and simply being with that situation, for oftentimes the things that one needs to know in order to be graceful and skillful with transformations is that peace which comes when one listens to the silence that holds the Creator's voice. Perhaps when one sits one feels nothing occurring and then comes a dream or a vision, or perhaps simply one wakes up knowing what thing it is that will balance the past and allow one to walk strong and straight and towards the light of a new horizon, with all in order as one leaves a dear and blessed situation, no matter how challenging, for that which is to come.

And as one says goodbye to times in one's life, to things which one has loved, to relationships that have changed beyond recognition, we encourage each to find strength and courage to praise and give thanks for each and every experience that has created within perhaps much pain and suffering. In the process of transformation there is almost always a great deal of sorrow and feelings of loss, for when change is going to occur naturally it simply takes one as destiny will and almost never is it a completely smooth road from that one way which was to that other way which has yet to be worked out. And yet we encourage you to have the faith to praise that which is past and to open the heart to that which is, was and shall be.

The keeping of silence, the keeping of the listening ear as part of the daily round of activity is always, we feel, an excellent practice, for in the silence, in the listening lies the key that unlocks the door of your own wisdom, that which is within the deep mind, that whose voice is silence and which can only be heard by the open and listening heart. If you can trust destiny enough to release the attempts to control it the natural waves of energy moving out from the center of that kindly destiny which is each seeker's will gradually take that seeker upon the path and in the direction which is deeply desired.

We do not need to tell you how difficult a practice it is to maintain the silent and listening receptivity to destiny in a world in which intangibles and invisible things are often given no worth or value at all. Yet, this practice is most productive of peace of mind and is very efficient in its own way at keeping the seeker upon the path chosen before the incarnative experience. It is not that your life was predestined, but, rather, that certain things were chosen by you. Certain patterns were chosen by you in order to focus on certain lessons concerning love. The energy that has moved you through various stages of life has been an energy which feels natural impulses towards some lessons and complete indifference towards others. No one else has your path. No one else has your lessons. You need no one else's lessons, so each pilgrim that is walking upon this highway is walking alone in a very deep sense.

Yet we say to you that after meditation the most important resource upon the spiritual path is the company of those who are also seeking, for one person cannot give to itself the truth. Yet the truth is in all, and entities may be instruments through which truth may travel to others. Thusly, even though you cannot offer yourself enlightenment, you can become a channel which is transparent and through which love itself may shine for others to see and to be inspired by. Your own poor opinion for yourself—for you are so into self-judgment among your peoples—has no bearing upon how other seekers may perceive the light that comes through you.

So as you feel those transforming energies moving within we suggest that you keep an awareness of the one infinite Creator, of the center of that awareness which is your conscious mind, for this clarity which is a kind of humility will allow you to be transparent so that others may see the Creator through you, and you do not get in the way but are simply the bowl in which this precious gift is offered.

There is a time for each energy within your breast—for the dark side as well as the light side. There is a time in which it is good to experience even the darkest of emotions, even the most sad failures, self-perceived, of virtue. And, likewise, there are times so lit with the golden essence of love that it seems that time and space stop, stunned by the wonder of the present moment. Such a time can occur upon a very large scale, and, indeed, your entire planet is now transforming little by little by little into a fourth-density positive environment. This shall be several centuries in the making, but the process has begun, and little by little, both positive and negative that are ready to move on are moving on. And those children being born at this time upon your planet include both Wanderers who have come to aid in this crossroads in this new beginning and those who have come from other third-density harvests to begin their fourth-density experience early on. Many of your children have both third and fourth-density vehicles of the physical kind activated.

As people feel that their children are more and more remarkable we remind each that there are many beautiful souls who seek life upon your planet at this crucial time, for all wish to aid in the birthing of the fourth density of your planet, and many have come to help, and you among them. So we ask that you continue to meditate and listen to the silence. We ask that you encourage your own faith and your own spirit of strength and joy and that you remain transparent to a destiny which is full of the grace of perfect rhythm. And if you feel, now and again, that you are moving too fast or that you are moving in the wrong direction, stop, take a deep, deep breath and say to yourself, "There are no mistakes. My lessons will come no matter what I do. My service will come no matter what I do." Say it and know it, and then let your hearts be merry and full of praise and thanksgiving, and let your arms reach out to the pilgrims that come your way upon this highway of love.

We would transfer this contact at this time to the one known as Jim. We leave this instrument, with thanks, in love and light. We are those of Q'uo.

(Jim channeling)

I am Q'uo, and I greet you in the love and in the light through this instrument. At this time it is our privilege to ask if those present may have further queries for us that we would be happy to give our attention to. Is there a query at this time?

R1: Why is one so affected by the changes in weather as I am? Is there a spiritual reason for it?

I am Q'uo, and we are aware of your query, my brother. [You are] all one in truth. The seasons of your planet at this time are changing over the entire surface as is the case at all times, yet there are cycles which begin and flourish and wane and end. And as you find yourself one portion of this great planetary consciousness you are moved much as the seasons move your flowers and trees and birds and seeds, moving into yet another expression, not only of the Creator or planet or area in which you reside but you are moved also as a portion of the one Creator which seeks knowledge of Itself in a manner which is likened to the rhythm of your music. The movement of energies occurs most naturally in pulses or rhythms, harmonic blending of vibrations which in a upward-spiraling fashion match light and love emanations of the Logos of this portion of the creation. Thus, you respond to light, to its intensity, its duration, its permutations as it is formed into one field of energy after another. So you also within your own being are moved by these pulses of energy which seek their source.

Is there another query, my brother?

R1: Is that why when I feel the wind moving past that I want to jump up and fly with it?

I am Q'uo, and am aware of your query, my brother. In short, this is so, for the movement of your air masses is a localized phenomenon that is the result of various gradients of temperatures which themselves are moving in rhythm with the changes of your sun's energy as it strikes your Earth's surface, releasing this intelligent energy in various and infinite ways. The movement of your air, for most entities, is an invigorating experience, for it seems to stir the collection of expressions of energy in a fashion which is exciting to the soul itself.

Is there another query, my brother?

R1: No, thank you.

I am Q'uo, and we again thank you, my brother. Is there another query?

K: Sometimes I talk out loud to try to communicate with my father but I don't know if he is there. Is he aware and does he understand?

I am Q'uo, and am aware of your query, my sister. We find that you are, in the central portion of your being, aware that this is so at this time, for you and the entity which served as your father upon this planet are portions of a family or, shall we say, a clan which has chosen to work in consciousness upon this plane in service to others, and this work is that which is accomplished in a manner which is difficult to describe but which is shared by many such groupings or families of entities. There is a support at the most basic level of love, shall we say, that continues between the times of incarnation as well as during the incarnation that ties each together in a manner which is most harmonious and which allows the offering of services which are not usual in that they are often intangible, of the emotions, of the intuition, of the subconscious mind. These pathways of energy which tie each are always intact so that when the heart speaks a feeling or the mind speaks a thought there is an instantaneous communication as though one portion of a body was speaking to another portion of the same body.

Is there a further query, my sister?

K: Yes. Then when I have dreams that he is in and he is talking to me, is he in fact in my subconscious mind speaking to me?

I am Q'uo, and am aware of your query, my sister. This is a reasonably accurate way of approaching or looking at this relationship, for the deeper levels of the mind offer access to those who are not of this third-density illusion at this time, much as the channels of a television will offer entry into consciousness of various images from elsewhere.

Is there another query, my sister?

K: No, thank you, Q'uo.

I am Q'uo, and we thank you, my sister. Is there another query?

Carla: I would like to follow up and ask if Don and Ron and others of our family who have died, are they together waiting for us?

I am Q'uo, and am aware of your query, my sister. Though this is so, it does not mitigate these entities also experiencing other existences and other energy expressions upon other levels of being. With this disclaimer we would answer in the affirmative to your query.

Carla: Thank you.

I am Q'uo, and we thank you, my sister. Is there another query at this time?

R2: Yes, I feel your presence. I would like to ask if being in the light is sufficient to protect against what is commonly called psychic forces?

I am Q'uo, and am aware of your query, my sister. And we would respond by suggesting that this is the greatest protection and is sufficient for those experiences which are usually described as the psychic attack or greeting. It is important for the entity upon the path of service to others to attempt to see the Creator within all beings at all times, to give praise and thanksgiving for the light of the Creator that exists in all, to seek and know that Creator in each, to offer within the meditative state the heartfelt love for all who send greetings or attacks, and to surround the self, then, in that love and light of the infinite Creator.

Is there a further query, my sister?

R2: Yes, please. You mention a couple of centuries would be needed for this consciousness shift into the fourth dimension. I know that time is man-made in a way. Is there a way that we can speed up this process even though I know it is going the way that it needs to be going? If more people tune into the light would that promote a quicker shift?

I am Q'uo, and am aware of your query, my sister. And indeed this is the experience of this planetary sphere at this time, for there is even amidst the obvious agony and suffering of many of your peoples at this time over the surface of your planet a great deal of light that is being generated by those who seek and bask within its energy at this time. To attempt to speed a process which is already moving with great rapidity is a noble desire, yet perhaps as you yourself have suggested, one fraught with a degree of impatience.

We would suggest to each that as you continue your own seeking within in order to untangle those knots of confusion and to balance the distortions from light that you aid this process greatly, and as you witness to this process to those about you in your daily round of activities there is much beneficial effect also given with this simple interchange and interplay of energies between entities.

Is there a further query, my sister?

R2: I have concern about a person who mentally knows about this process but seems to dwell in hardship for himself. Are these lessons still needed by people who are so close to lightness?

I am Q'uo, and am aware of your query, my sister. The suffering that so many of your peoples experience is likened to the tempering of the metal that gives to it its integrity, that burnishes it with a brightness and a sheen that is able to reflect great amounts of light to others as a result of the tempering. The lessons that are available within this illusion are many and are quite varied, most existing within the clouds of mystery for those who witness and for those who experience them.

The mysterious nature of all the various kinds of lessons that aid in the overall increasing of the ability to give and receive love have mystery as their salient feature in order that there be an effort necessary to penetrate to the essence the main foundation of each lesson. Thus, the effort that is necessary to deal with mystery involves many other kinds or qualities of being such as patience, perseverance, humor, joy, acceptance and so forth.

Thus, the stuff of your illusion seems to have much of grime, grit and gravity about it but is in fact the forge in which the true spirit is fired by the inspiration that is at the heart of each seeking portion of the one Creator to find again the source of its own being, the destiny of the soul.

Is there a further query, my sister?

R2: How important is a balanced, wholesome diet in elevating consciousness?

I am Q'uo, and am aware of your query, my sister. The value of such dietary procedures and selections is one which reflects, as do all such rituals and experiences that are regularized within your illusion, the ability of the experience to [express] the level of concern and respect for the nature of the experience [which] aids in the overall spiritual evolution. For as the body is shown the respect that providing certain foodstuffs offers so does this respect become available in other areas of the incarnation.

Is there a further query, my sister?

R2: No, thank you very much.

I am Q'uo, and we thank you, my sister. Is there a final query at this time?

K: I am concerned about my path. Will I find the best way to serve and will I recognize it when I do find it and stay with it?

I am Q'uo, and am aware of your query, my sister. We must be somewhat careful in giving response to this query so that we do not step over the boundary of infringement of free will but can suggest that each entity will, indeed, find the path of service that is most important to it. Whether the entity is able to recognize this path is not as certain.

Is there any further way in which we may speak, my sister?

K: No, thank you.

I am Q'uo, and again we thank you, my sister.

At this time we would thank those present for inviting us to join this circle of seeking. It has been a privilege and joy which we treasure greatly, for we walk with you on this journey and to be able to share more fully that which is your experience and to offer that which is our opinion gives us the most complete sense of joy that we have yet found as we attempt to be of service as we are called.

At this time we shall take our leave of this instrument and this group, leaving each, as always, in the love and in the ineffable light of the one infinite Creator. Adonai, my friends. Adonai. ✢

L/L Research

L/L Research is a subsidiary of Rock Creek Research & Development Laboratories, Inc.

P.O. Box 5195
Louisville, KY 40255-0195

www.llresearch.org

Rock Creek is a non-profit corporation dedicated to discovering and sharing information which may aid in the spiritual evolution of humankind.

ABOUT THE CONTENTS OF THIS TRANSCRIPT: This telepathic channeling has been taken from transcriptions of the weekly study and meditation meetings of the Rock Creek Research & Development Laboratories and L/L Research. It is offered in the hope that it may be useful to you. As the Confederation entities always make a point of saying, please use your discrimination and judgment in assessing this material. If something rings true to you, fine. If something does not resonate, please leave it behind, for neither we nor those of the Confederation would wish to be a stumbling block for any.

CAVEAT: This transcript is being published by L/L Research in a not yet final form. It has, however, been edited and any obvious errors have been corrected. When it is in a final form, this caveat will be removed.

© 2009 L/L Research

Sunday Meditation
May 14, 1995

Group question: The question today has to do with our darker sides, the part that is unknown *(inaudible)* is mysterious, sometimes it's perceived to be fearful or destructive or angry or in doubt or full of jealousy or rage or whatever. We are wondering whatever you can tell us about the darker side, how it functions, how we can shed light on it, if there is a way of becoming friends with and understanding what we see as the darker side. Is there another way of perceiving it, does it have a purpose that it plays in our spiritual evolution and how can we go about accepting ourselves and the darker side as a part of our overall growth?

(Carla channeling)

We are those of Q'uo. Greetings to each, blessings, and welcome and thanks for calling us to you. We greet you in the love and in the light of the one infinite Creator. To share in this time of meditation and thought is a most precious thing to us. And we are most appreciative of the call of that desire which each has to seek that which is the highest and the best in truth. That desire to refine and purify that which is the truth known within, that yearning, that hunger is a treasure more rich than we can express. It is riches to you, the seeker. It is riches to us and to all those who interact with you and blend their vibrations with yours. And it is a great treasure as well to offer the infinite One. We are happy to speak with you concerning the so-called dark side of personality. And we would ask, as always, that each recognize that these are our opinions. They do not carry the weight of authority; they are offered freely as flowers for the taking. Make your bouquet as you will and leave the rest behind.

We thank you for availing us the chance to learn by serving. This is our service at this time and you make it very easy for us, and for that we most heartily thank you. We are going to offer you a metaphor. This is not something to take literally but we feel that perhaps this metaphor may offer a structure that may be helpful. In this metaphor the Creator goes to sleep and in that sleep dreams. And in this world-view those dreams are peopled by all of those centers of light that we call beings or souls. It is not that the Creator sleeps in order for each of you to be awake. But in terms of the level of illusion which you now enjoy, this metaphor does a fair job of placing the experience of incarnational life in a context which makes it easier for each of you to see. That much of what is taken as real within a life is instead that which appears as on a stage and does its skit, its sketch, its scene for you, so that you are moved and shaped and given a variety of things to feel and to look at.

Now, in a dream this instrument feels that all characters are actually herself. And with that we would basically agree. In the dream which you call incarnational life, all the characters are indeed the same, they are the Creator. For it is the Creator's dream you see, and each of you is a distorted fancy that is teaching the Creator about Itself. It is in this wise that each of you is indeed precisely the same. Each comes into incarnational life from a fullness of being that includes the loss of personality and the reabsorption into the Creator. When the veil lifts, each is aware although not able to penetrate that instantaneous present moment, that instant of Creator time, shall we say, when all the billions of your years, and all the thousands of your beings occur together. The likeness of entity to entity is a congruency. You have heard so often from Confederation sources that each is the Creator, that each is a universal being. That each contains all that there is. Yet, it is difficult to make these words resonate. It is difficult to make any set of words resonate, for they are but symbols of symbols. For each of you is like a symbol, a train, a character upon the stage. Much of that which is most truly you lies safely tucked within you, accessible to you only for the most part through creative effort, not necessarily complex or occult effort. For the self reveals itself to the self that has begun a process of purifying the emotions of facing of the self as it is. It is to this basic task that each of you came here to address.

Now, if each of you were obviously congruent with each other, there would be no way for information to pass. However, since the very essence of manifestation is duality and therefore illusion, this is not a problem. The illusion is intended to be a thick soup of confusion. And we encourage each to drink as heartily as he can, with good appetite. But also, we indeed do confirm that that which you have called the dark side is the hero, or perhaps we should say the anti-hero, of the play. For all the characters which you have within, it is the villain that places the soul in the situation into which faith may come and be the deliverer, and hope the handmaiden of that deliverance. You are steeped in duality. And all that is in manifestation is steeped in that duality. As this instrument was saying earlier, it is you that label the sweet and sunny side of personality as the good side or the light side, and the bad-tempered and ugly and mean and hateful the dark side or the negative side. This is an illusion. That which is truly negative is not those angers, those frustrations or those sorrows. But rather how the entity chooses consciously to express those bitter feelings, those strong passions that are indeed dark.

Now, all of those feeling states, if we may call them that, are equally beautiful to the Creator. They are pure expressions of a self that is universal, and that universal self contains every duality, in every level, in every way that anyone has ever dreamt. How full you are, how complete and whole. And so you are plunged by choice into a school full of illusion, in which there is no text book save the self. In which there is no teacher to give homework, only teaching assistants who give vague instructions and faulty [booklists]. You are adrift upon an ocean of thought and feeling and experience with only an intermittent star to guide the way.

Now, why would the Creator choose this illusion as a way to express the love that is the Creator? When one is within the illusion it does not seem remarkable that entities are born, that they gather experiences, develop and change and then die. It seems perfectly natural, if undesirable in the end, for who wishes to die? Yet, there is hidden treasure in this being born and this dying. It is the nature of manifestation that it can only be seen in illusion. Yet in this dim illusion rivers of beauty flow. To the Creator they shine like gold. Each sorrow in each heart is felt. Each joy is shared. Each bitterness and woe is riveting to the one infinite Creator. What the Creator sees, we cannot know. But we believe, that included in that eyeshot is enormous and unending compassion for the hopelessness of manifestation ever to become correct, full or perfect.

Yet, the senses, the emotions of those who have indeed purified their personalities express truth in ways that seems beautiful to the Creator. And therefore the Creator loves most greatly each pilgrim's spirit, regardless of its circumstances, whether they be physical, mental, emotional or spiritual, for each entity is authentic in itself. Each entity expressing a unique distortion of unmanifest truth in the imperfection of manifestation. This paradox is one which can fascinate those which love riddles, for there is a deep riddle here: the riddle of manifestation itself. Yet love, that great original Thought, must use its free will, must create and so must love.

Now, within incarnation the seeker experiences itself as a good person under certain circumstances, which usually includes traits or actions or thoughts which are considered to be positive. One becomes happy at oneself if one feels that one's nature has become sweeter. When the dark side reveals itself, when there is behavior coming from mind or lips or actions that do not seem kind, that seem bitter and unlovely, the seeker naturally tends to condemn the self. And yet, each is expressing in the light and in the dark the nature of the one infinite Creator, the universal being.

Now, you do not have to like your dark side. We do not encourage that. What we do encourage is a continuing desire to know the truth and a constant willingness to separate, when thinking of the self or another self, the beingness of that dark impulse from the choices made in the expression of that darker emotion. The Creator loves to the point of no return. Entities within incarnation find that sort of love impossible to sustain. Yet, you are your first and hardest target. Loving yourself is a central and entirely difficult goal to reach, for you know those thoughts that crowd your heart, those impulses which somehow you do not act upon.

And while the world may smile upon you, yet you frown and glower at yourself for being a universal creature. Ask yourself instead: "How shall I choose to express these emotions?" For each entity has them all, no matter how pervasive may be the effort to repress and deny one or another of the traits of human nature, shall we say. And so we encourage each to refine and refine again that which you do, that which you make manifest and real within the illusion which you now share. Inwardly, we encourage each to forgive and forget, taking only the learning and leaving behind that husk of self that was shed in the learning. And as the self becomes smaller, the inner power of the self shall grow, for with each name which you cease to call yourself, more love may move through that lighter being. Beyond all punishment and debt lies a forgiveness in which all debts are paid.

This entity moves within a mythical system which is called Christianity and central to this system of thought is the concept that sacrifice is a sign of great love. And we say to you, you have made that sacrifice: you will die. You are dust and as dust you are indeed unworthy, you are indeed imperfect. You are indeed the good and the bad and the light and the dark. And you will surely die. And between the birth and the death you shall plumb the depth of every sorrow of which you fear. And you will experience those few things left beyond the touch of fear as the mountain tops of life.

The dark side, when it comes up, when it shows its head to you, is saying how would you like to change, how would you like to try to learn this lesson. That dark side is meant to get the attention of the consciousness which lies within quite beyond all duality. For you do have enough of that infinite self at your disposal at all times in order to be able to process these feelings, these thoughts and these impulses which come to you, as you receive sensory input and process it and by your choices of priority distort that incoming stream of love in this way and in that, in a beautiful dance which is spontaneous and instinctive, so that when the seeker allows itself the time to learn the rhythms of the present dance, incarnational life begins to wake up within that illusion. And the life within pokes its little head out, like a tiny chick emerging from the shell and says, "Remember me, I am you and I have lived forever and I will forever live and I am everything, every emotion, every state of mind and all of these things are love."

So we encourage each in forgiveness of self and at the same time in asking great things of the self, in asking that the self turn to the Creator and say, "Here am I, show me my destiny and I will say yes." For you planned this with the Creator before you came and it is a matter of trust and faith to take each thing as it comes and attempt to find within yourself that response which expresses love. My friends, we have a very simple message. It is always the same. Each of you is love. Each of you has a core vibration of absolute pure love. That which is consciousness is love. That which is love expresses itself in consciousness. Each of you also has heavy overlays of distortion, chosen by each over a long period. Each is rich in distortion. And these distortions are also beautiful to the Creator, each one perfect in itself. And as you mix and mingle with yourself and your various roles and with each other in the delicious and bewildering array of humankind, the love that you can share with those you meet, beginning with yourself, is the fruit and the blossom that is truth.

So, love any way that you can and praise the love that you see, and know that in loving one is never foolish, one is never wrong, one is never too naïve, for all things are beautiful and lovely in the core which is the truth. And each time that you claim that truth, you claim, yes, you claim an illusion. Yet, the illusion that you claim is indescribably more accurate in its representation of the actual truth than that expression which does not include love.

Love is often seen by your people to be a pallid emotion that contrasts to earthly love, which is not romantic, and not possessive, and so forth. Yet, we say to you that love is a beautiful and terrible thing. Out of love the Creator manifested this illusion. And out of love this illusion must end. Out of love one of your young is conceived, and in great pain oftentimes is given the chance to breath and die. But within that theater of incarnational life lies the opportunity in every breath to know the truth and to be free to turn to the one infinite Creator and to become one with that love and that light which is divine.

Love is not a nice or a pretty thing. Love is an anguished dream, a yearning, an expression that shall surely fade and fail as the rose dies, as each being has its season only to vanish. Yet in that temporal, evanescent environment comes an opportunity to believe that which is not seen and to follow the leadings of the heart, which are never logical and often resist interpretation or analysis. What wondrous love lies within each. How infinite is the richness of each and every connection that can be made between those who seek to serve. Let yourself be imperfect and focus upon the loving and the seeking of how to love better. This is our opinion, and we share it with you. For all else will die, but love is infinite, for it is all that there is. When you are engaged in seeking, you are engaged in asking how to love. It is not an easy thing. But you can help each other. You can reflect to each other honestly. You can simply be with another as that entity faces its dark side. And where that entity might not find forgiveness, you can, for you see clearly when the self is another. And the other may see clearly when you cannot see.

(Side one of tape ends.)

(Carla channeling)

So, know the treasure that you have within you when you love, and more know the treasure that you have when you do not love. For it is then that your dark side has emerged to teach you once again. Honor and praise all of yourself and know that it is your choice of how to play the instrument of self which matters. For each has the same instrument. And each has all of the abilities necessary to tune that instrument. With our hearts full of love for each, and our desire to encourage you to be easy on yourselves and forgiving of yourselves very keen, we leave this instrument in thanks.

We know that we have raised more questions then we have answered. Yet, that is inevitable for the very character of spiritual seeking is two impossible things at once, that somehow are possible. Paradoxes abound. Riddles are the very stuff of spirituality, for each is the enigma that love is. And we do praise that divine mystery that lies in the consciousness that we all share in the selfhood that we together make up.

We would at this time transfer this contact to the instrument known as Jim. And we leave this instrument in love and light. We are those of Q'uo.

(Jim channeling)

I am Q'uo, and greet each again in love and in light. At this time it is our privilege to offer ourselves in the attempt to speak to any further queries which those present may have for us. Is there another query at this time?

Questioner: I would like to ask you a question about the polarity of the entity known as Bhagwan Shree Rajneesh. Would it be possible for you to comment on the polarity of this entity and possibly those around him, those associated with him?

I am Q'uo, and we are aware of your query, my sister. So we fear we must disappoint, for we are not desirous of sharing information which may affect the decision-making of any who values our words, and we find that there is the desire upon the part of one that feels kinship with us to know that which we feel is best left for the unknown at the present time.

There are many entities who revere the words and the life of those spiritual leaders who have for them provided a pathway to truth and to knowledge and to the opening of the heart in true compassion. That each entity has those attributes which are enlightening, and also contains those attributes which are upon the topic of this evening's address concerning the darker side of the illumined self, is also without doubt a truth. We must remind each that all seeking is holy, and each entity is a teacher to another as well as being a student to yet others. If any entity can find the place to place the faith and can be inspirited and inspired by another to move forward in the evolutionary journey then who can say whether there is negativity or a positivity within the self which inspired such a step, no matter what other elements in that entity be considered. Thus, we would choose to leave this particular query unanswered, for we find there is more of service in so doing than in speaking in a specific sense.

Is there any other query, my sister?

Questioner: Not at this moment. I leave it to others. Thank you.

I am Q'uo, and we thank you my sister. Is there another query at this time?

Questioner: I would like to know, given that it seems as polarity increases, harmony increases, does it work the same in both directions, that is, if one polarizes more negatively, does that increase harmony as it does when one polarizes more positively?

I am Q'uo, and I am aware of your query, my brother. And to the best of our knowledge, which is limited we admit, as the entity who has chosen the service-to-self path becomes more efficient in this service, there is more of that which you would call a disharmony produced. For the, what we could call, the natural order of things, that is, unity of all, is broken or fragmented into manyness in order that a small portion of that manyness may govern and manipulate a larger portion of that manyness, then the natural harmony which binds all things together is seemingly shattered upon one level of existence, that is, the illusion of the creation where the many must without question obey the few who feel it is their duty to set the universe in order. Thus, we find that the quality which you would call harmony is one of the first casualties upon this path.

Is there a further query, my brother?

Questioner: Ah, on negatively polarized planets do they have more problems than we do with environmental destruction?

I am Q'uo, and I am aware of your query, my brother. It is the general run of this particular path of service that the quality of disharmony and difficulty within the illusion is experienced upon all levels of the existence, though there is more expression of the disharmonious elements within the interpersonal relationships, for it is here that those who seek power over others find the avenue to its attainment.

Is there a further query, my brother?

Questioner: No, thank you.

I am Q'uo, and we thank you again, my brother. Is there another query?

Questioner: If I may ask, OK. It's not on the topic we are talking of tonight. My question is actually about fourth density. A notion came up recently about the disappearance of nationhood befalling—of the walls between nations. I wonder if that's a necessary stage towards forming a fourth-density social memory complex of this planet. Would it be possible for you to comment?

I am Q'uo, and I am aware of your query, and we believe that we may respond by suggesting that to many entities who are experiencing the pull towards a cooperative or collective consciousness that the dissolving of such boundaries is indeed of significance along this line. There are many, however, who in their own personal journeys of seeking see such occurrences as a continuing strain or strand of confusion and disorder, which is a reflection of their own personal lack of unity in choosing a path of service. Thus, those who see with clearer eyes, those who look beyond their own personal boundaries and seek that which binds all beings into one, are those who are more able to see events about them as being significant in the achieving of this unity.

Is there a further query, my sister?

Questioner: Could we be applying what you answered to other realms of this physical *(inaudible)* reality in terms of this social/economic situation of people?

I am Q'uo, and we believe that we grasp your query, my sister. And we would suggest that this analogy may be applied in any realm or segment of third-density existence, for all of this illusion is as a mirror to the one who seeks within.

Is there a further query, my sister?

Questioner: No, unless *(inaudible)* do and so can't think of any *(inaudible)*.

Questioner: OK, I was wondering about the state of consciousness seen in literature known as nirvana, enlightenment, oneness and so forth. From what I understand in all discourses is that we as third density are here to polarize either towards service to self or service to others and that is still on the journey of duality, and yet there are people on this planet of third density, people who are beyond duality in the experience of enlightenment, the oneness. Would it be possible for you to comment on the seeming apparent conflict that I see in these two different notions, either for us as third density to polarize, say to a service to others or to surpass that, to just go beyond being part of that duality and just be one. Could you comment on that?

I am Q'uo, and we feel that we may speak most appropriately by suggesting that there is the glimpse, the taste, shall we say, that is available to any seeker of the truth that will give the inspiration of the fully experienced presence of the one infinite Creator at those times when it is most important for the mind/body/spirit complex to understand to the core of its being that the journey of seeking and polarization, as you have called it, that it is upon, is a journey which is undertaken in the full protection of the one Creator; that all in truth is one, that there is in truth no right or wrong, positive or negative, that can match the complete unity of the one Creator. Thus, the seeker is from time to time upon its journey given these moments of inspiration and unity to bolster its being and remind it that it is a participant in a great and joyous dance that has as many faces as there are units of consciousness within the one creation.

Is there a further query, my sister?

Questioner: One more. Do entities that polarize towards service to self also experience such moments of enlightenment, of oneness?

I am Q'uo, and am aware of your query, my sister. These contacts with intelligent infinity do indeed occur for those upon the negatively or service-to-self oriented path. However, the experience is one which moves past the green-ray energy center from yellow to blue, then to indigo, in order that the negatively oriented entity, who sees compassion and love for all as folly, may experience a contact with the one Creator that is in accord with its chosen path, that which sees the power, the control, and the setting in order of those about it as its duty and as that which is most desired.

Is there a further query, my sister?

Questioner: Not at this moment, thank you.

I am Q'uo, we thank you once again, my sister. Is there another query at this time?

Questioner: Is the duality of positive and negative another illusion?

I am Q'uo, and am aware of your query, my brother. And we would suggest that all is illusion, except the unity of the one Creator. All creation, all things, all other seeming entities are an illusion or distortion or portion of the one Creator which must be distorted until there is the complete realization and reunification with the one Creator.

Is there a further query, my brother?

Questioner: No, thank you.

I am Q'uo, and we thank you once again. Is there another query?

Carla: I have one. I have been assuming for years and years that the people that come to me were, let's put it this way, many people come to me and feel that they recognize me or they know me and with some people, I just … I am able to key into them very easily and it has that feeling of destiny about. Is it true that we come in what somebody has called "soul herds"?

I am Q'uo, and we are aware of your query, my sister, and can affirm that there are indeed families, groupings, clans, tribes or whatever description is considered appropriate to describe the groupings of entities that move as souls together upon the journey, having spent a great deal of time previous to the present incarnation determining the future experiences, as you would call them in your experience of time, so that the efforts that are planted in one incarnation may produce the fruits in a future effort. Thus, one builds upon another and together those who are of like mind are far more certain to discover that which they seek.

Is there a further query, my sister?

Carla: No, I just, I felt that that was the truth and that I could trust destiny to bring me the people that I want to care for. That's a very comforting thought, thank you.

I am Q'uo, and we thank you, my sister. Is there another query?

Questioner: My turn, I have a question, Q'uo, about *(inaudible)*. For some reason why did you say, that it is like a joyous dance to be in the circle of seeking … I hope that *(inaudible)* see as much light as I see in love to being together like this. Thanks for commenting.

I am Q'uo, and we also are much and truly pleased by the invitation which is offered to us at each enjoining of this group. We dance with you and listen in awe at the music of the spheres, that is always with us and this group.

Is there a final query at this time?

Questioner: Can I have the final question? I'd like to ask you if you could comment when … maybe I should ask this as a personal question. You know, when I feel something in the third chakra, you know, like a blockage or a shortness of breath of sorts, what is the best way to look at it and how to know the best way to learn from this catalyst and what?

I am Q'uo, and we are aware of your query, my sister. We can always recommend the meditative state for the place in which to accomplish this work. There is great benefit in the regular setting aside of time so that one may review the daily round of activities and explore the centers or chakras, so that there is then the possibility of discovering where openings or blockages may exist. And when these are discovered in any form such as you have mentioned, that there be a surge of those recent experiences where efforts in any particular center were offered, what the results were, how the emotions were affected and so forth, so that you look at your own experience as your guide to what centers have received the inspiration or the blockage. Looking then to see if there are deeper or connected issues that may explain or shine a greater light upon the feeling that is associated with the center, thus one can begin to set up certain avenues of exploration within the self that can be called upon to continue to offer insight, connections and a larger point of view to that which is usually experienced in the daily round of activities.

Is there a further query, my sister?

Questioner: No, thank you very much, I will meditate on that.

I am Q'uo and we again thank you and commend the regularized meditation to each entity for it is in these times of communing with the deeper self and the greater self that the vicissitudes of the daily life may be explored and experienced in their essence, that the detail of the day falls away reviewing that which is of the most import.

At this time we would express once again our great gratitude to each present for inviting us to join you in your circle of seeking. We realize that the hour is late and that there is much tiredness in need to move the muscles at this time. We shall take our leave of this instrument and this group, leaving each, as always, in the love and in the light of the one infinite Creator. We are those of Q'uo. Adonai, my friends, Adonai. ✣

L/L Research

L/L Research is a subsidiary of Rock Creek Research & Development Laboratories, Inc.

P.O. Box 5195
Louisville, KY 40255-0195

www.llresearch.org

Rock Creek is a non-profit corporation dedicated to discovering and sharing information which may aid in the spiritual evolution of humankind.

ABOUT THE CONTENTS OF THIS TRANSCRIPT: This telepathic channeling has been taken from transcriptions of the weekly study and meditation meetings of the Rock Creek Research & Development Laboratories and L/L Research. It is offered in the hope that it may be useful to you. As the Confederation entities always make a point of saying, please use your discrimination and judgment in assessing this material. If something rings true to you, fine. If something does not resonate, please leave it behind, for neither we nor those of the Confederation would wish to be a stumbling block for any.

CAVEAT: This transcript is being published by L/L Research in a not yet final form. It has, however, been edited and any obvious errors have been corrected. When it is in a final form, this caveat will be removed.

© 2009 L/L Research

Sunday Meditation
May 21, 1995

Group question: The question this week has to do with the difference between what we hold as our ideal and what we experience as our actual experience. We would like to know the most efficient way of looking at that difference that would help us most in our growth, and what Q'uo's opinion about that difference would be.

(Carla channeling)

We are those of Q'uo. Greetings in the love and in the light of the one infinite Creator. We apologize for the delay in speaking. Our instrument was confused because the one known as Oxal and ourselves both answered the question of who was to channel from the Confederation to this group. The instrument then had to challenge each entity separately. The one known as Oxal has agreed to speak last.

We thank each person in this circle of seeking for turning to the solace of the search for wisdom and truth and meaning. The faith and tenacity of this group is commendable. And you make it very easy for us to perform our service by your unflagging concern and dedication for and to the devotional life.

The question which plagues all entities who wish to excel is the question of the human failings to which the spirit does not have to be heir. The physical vehicle is an oddity, that way station betwixt nothing and infinity, that shadow world of limits and quantity. This shadow world is delicately and elegantly aligned with the needs of your density, the need to be confused, the need to strive, the need to associate with other human beings while the far reaches of intuition and dreaming discover great new galaxies every day of thought and structure and imagination.

The physical vehicle that carries this consciousness moves through one decision after another. In that gray area in which most human functions seem to take place the polarity of much of the daily round is not obvious to the physical eye. The seeking soul then moves through each day without sensing the quality which is its most fundamental, that quality which perhaps you would call ideal but we would rather term metaphysical, for it is the same quality that within the mind furnishes the touchstone, that imaginary perfection. And yet what does this perfection have to do with the everyday?

The mind is a curious tool, a great resource. Its powers of discrimination are usually well developed in humankind, and this is as it should be, for of all the incoming sense data, the trained mind selects according to priorities and judgments that have been hard won. It is only natural that there would be judgment turned towards the self, that there would be distance seen between ideal and actual. Yet the truth is neither with the judge nor with the one who refrains from judging, but rather the truth lies ineffably in the present moment.

It is difficult in words to express this concept but if you can conceive of that present moment as full of light of all that there is, full to bursting with all that ever has or that ever will be. This moment of orgasm, this moment of delight, this is the closest we have come to a knowledge of reality—no time, no space, no judgment, but pure white light, a naked manifestation of love. This is a truth available to each seeking entity, and yet the door into this present moment is locked fast against those who would judge the self or others in such a way as to injure or harm, for a judgment is in many cases an injury, whether it be inflicted upon the self or upon another. It is not to say that judging and expressing that judgment are not perfectly normal activities, and within the worldly purview judgments are expected and necessary. But if you wish to work upon yourself at the highest degree of purity then it is that the eyes turn away from the self that dangles betwixt eternity and eternity, a parentheses of manifestation within illusion. Your situation while incarnate is that of a soul who has to leave the room for just a moment. You have such a tiny instant of time in your incarnation. This is the higher truth.

Now, we would not take the power of discrimination from any, for the ability to have insight is a valuable one and it is hard-learned. However, we do encourage each first to examine judgment for kindness and compassion and then to apply that judgment sparingly and accurately, for each within incarnation is a bruised reed, a wounded and fragile living being, and to place the burden of unflinching judgment upon such a precariously alive creature is a cruelty.

We ask each to learn the value of mercy, of pity, of softness of heart and humbleness of spirit, for the judge is a proud entity, yet wisdom lies in accepting a humble, even humiliating estimate of self and self-importance. It is most healthful to abandon that effort to judge accurately the self. Or, if not abandon, moderate, de-emphasize, for you are seeking to become lighter and emptier. You are moving through a thick etheric medium, breathing the life-giving air. Metaphysically speaking, that breath is labored and thick compared to metaphysical experience. It is not at all easy to turn from the judging to look away from that comparison betwixt that which is hoped for and that which has occurred. Yet wisdom, we believe, lies not in examining that distance but rather in turning to the light and abandoning judgment for praise of the one infinite Creator, for you are equally praiseworthy when you have achieved the ideal and when you have utterly failed to achieve the ideal.

For what is more basic, more over-arching, than the sense data and all that spins therefrom is that consciousness which has half an eye upon the incarnation and the other half upon the Creator. Great peace of spirit comes to the one who is able to locate the other half of the self, the half that does indeed dwell in eternity, the half that is beyond judgment and exists rather with the eyes turned to see what may be done to serve and not that mind which looks back upon the self to find what the score was, what percentile of achievement has been achieved.

We are aware that much value has been given throughout your experience in third density to achievement, to the achievements of far-seeing men and women who have seemed to achieve their ideals, to experience and express excellence. Nor do we deny that there is value in seeing with the eyes of the world, but we ask you to consider whether or not that value is as fundamental as the turning to the present moment, to the one infinite Creator, to love, for love is the overarching truth. And if the emotional self can turn to that love and bask in it for one moment, that moment of truth shall cry, "Peace, peace," to the self-judgments of the one who wishes to run the straight race.

This instrument knows a poem that goes: "Run the straight race with God's good grace. Lift up thine eyes and seek His face. Lay hold on life and it shall be thy joy and crown eternally." My friends, we feel there is wisdom in those lines. Lift up your eyes and seek His face. That face is love. It is personified within this instrument's religious system as the one known as Jesus. This entity knew that its life was symbolic and conformed himself to that symbology. There are many other faces of that love. We encourage each to seek the face of that which most centrally symbolizes to the self that present love, that overarching compassion, that resounding cosmic "yes."

The physical vehicle, the physical brain and much of the surface of all of the bodies which you possess within incarnation are tuned to give you a certain kind of data in such a way that you shall inevitably become unable to do that which you see as perfect. The entire structure of your physical environment has as one of its characteristics the inevitable tendency to demonstrate the uselessness of the attempt to remain logical, sensible, rational and malleable. Although it is natural for humankind to try to control the environment, the personal behavior, and so forth, energies inherent within third density inevitably steer the seeking spirit into a trackless, directionless and utterly confusing frame of reference, for that which is prideful must be cast down, and that which is humble and lowly within must be lifted up.

The spiritual journey is a simple thing, yet it confounds intellectual examination, for it is, among many other things, the yielding up of that pride of self which manifests as the excellent worker, the hard-striving soul. There is an inevitability about the fall of each and every hoped for ideal, and all of this mental and emotional suffering has as its condign purpose the pulling of the energies towards the heart in order that the heart may open. Open to the present moment and to the love that is all that there is.

Honor your ideals. Honor yourself as you continue to seek to come as close as possible to those values set for the self. Yet know and allow yourself to truly to know that the actual virtue lies in doing what the Creator has called you to do, that which is in front of your face, with gladness, with a single mind and with a light heart. That lightness of heart is a gem of immense value. When you feel the sunshine pour into the heart, when you feel the heart straightening up, no longer bent under a heavy load, then you feel and know truth. The deepest truth of your human nature is love.

My friends, move in the great race. Do your best, and be glad as you fail, for there is joy in accomplishing one more step of the journey from the head to the heart. Open the hand of your compassion. Release that fluttering bird that seeks the light and the love of the one infinite Creator, that bird within the heart that your poet, Emily Dickinson, saw as hope. To hope, to trust, to abide in faith and in peace; these are the characteristics of one who has seen through judgment and pride and has released the self into that present moment. May you open that door into the present again and again.

We would at this time transfer this contact to the one known as Jim. We are those of Q'uo, and leave this instrument in love and in light.

(Jim channeling)

I am Q'uo, and greet each again in the love and in the light of the one infinite Creator. At this time we would ask if there may be further queries to which we may speak.

Carla: I would like to ask if I received accurate information about Oxal and Q'uo?

I am Q'uo, and am aware of your query, my sister. And the response is in the affirmative. We are happy to perform our regular task of speaking to the subject of the query offered us and sort of, as you may say, cleaning up with final queries. Then we will give way to the ones of Oxal that they may speak the closing for this circle through the one known as S, if this is acceptable to the one known as S.

Is there a further query, my sister?

Carla: No. I was just concerned that I had received accurate information.

I am Q'uo, and we thank you, my sister. Is there any further query at this time?

(Pause)

If there are no further queries we shall take our leave of this instrument and allow those of Oxal to speak a brief closing through the one known as S. We leave each in the love and in the light of the one infinite Creator. We are known to you as those of Q'uo.

(S channeling)

I am Oxal, and we are pleased to be given the opportunity to take up within this group a relationship which we have had for some time with those of Ra and our brothers and sisters of Latwii. We have been for some time asking of Ra a question, or series of questions, similar to the one asked by this group today, for we are those who have traveled long in the ways of wisdom and have used the judgment as a tool with which to register for ourselves those distinctions and discriminations which permit action to take place in an informed way.

And we are those who have learned the art of refinement over a long course of what you would call time and have come at last to discover that the pathways that we have followed have come back round full circle, leaving us with a sense, not of accomplishment, but of paradox. It was compassion that won us access to the world which we have since come to explore and articulate through the many wisdoms that we have made second nature. It was only when we as a social memory complex have come to see that these wisdoms are so much dust and straw that we turned in need to those who, like Ra, have found a way and a means beyond wisdom to a compassion which is a healing. We ourselves seek this healing at this time and we appreciate the dilemma in a most acute way faced by those who feel a need to act, who feel the need to refine and habituate action so as to give a stable reflection of the self to itself.

And we feel most deeply the sense of confusion when this reflection comes back shattered and incomplete, such that even the seeking out of the reflection itself must be called into question. We are beginning to learn the art of release, release of judgment of other which we have found to be rooted in judgment of self. We have begun to learn to strive without striving. We would say to those who similarly look to a higher compassion, the one truth which we feel we can add to those words of Ra which have been inspirational to us too and that … asking that is at the same time a receiving and yet again at the same time the giving of a gift. This is the grace that permits one to look at the self which in all of the ways and measures one has learned fails again and again to measure up, and to find in this self the kernel of a holy and spiritual being which could never, under any circumstances, fail to measure up for it always simply is what it is: whole and perfect.

At this time we would ask that the meditation be brought to closure by returning to the one called Carla and those of Q'uo who may bring this magical event about. We are those of Oxal.

(Carla channeling)

We greet you once again in the love and in the light of the infinite One. As the sands of the sea, as the stars in your sky, just so infinite are the shining spirits which are embodied within this creation who turn their glowing faces toward the Creator in praise and thanksgiving. At this time many, many of those not incarnate in physical vehicles flock within the inner planes of your globe. To those who ask for help they flock by the millions to offer their candle power to heighten the inner light of those in need.

Yours is third density. Ask for help and help will be given you. Reach out the hand and it will be full of invisible but real love. You are loved, not because you have achieved but because you exist, a child of the infinite Creator. You are enfolded, snuggled, by invisible nurturing arms. Every cell of your body is perfect. Your truth is that all is perfect. There is no striving necessary, for all is well.

We are motes that dance in the sunlight, but we love you with our whole heart. Ask for help. Serve each other. And the light generated shall be beautiful indeed. As you suffer, as you experience loss and limitation, all is well. Turn often to the perfection, to the integrity, and to the healing health of praise and thanksgiving within the present moment, for all that you see and know and do is done upon holy ground. That is the floor beneath the scenery.

We leave you in that ground of being, in the love and in the light of the one infinite Creator. We are those of the principle known to you as Q'uo. Adonai. Adonai. ☙

L/L Research

L/L Research is a subsidiary of Rock Creek Research & Development Laboratories, Inc.

P.O. Box 5195
Louisville, KY 40255-0195

www.llresearch.org

Rock Creek is a non-profit corporation dedicated to discovering and sharing information which may aid in the spiritual evolution of humankind.

ABOUT THE CONTENTS OF THIS TRANSCRIPT: This telepathic channeling has been taken from transcriptions of the weekly study and meditation meetings of the Rock Creek Research & Development Laboratories and L/L Research. It is offered in the hope that it may be useful to you. As the Confederation entities always make a point of saying, please use your discrimination and judgment in assessing this material. If something rings true to you, fine. If something does not resonate, please leave it behind, for neither we nor those of the Confederation would wish to be a stumbling block for any.

CAVEAT: This transcript is being published by L/L Research in a not yet final form. It has, however, been edited and any obvious errors have been corrected. When it is in a final form, this caveat will be removed.

© 2009 L/L Research

Sunday Meditation
May 28, 1995

Group question: We would like to know how learning actually takes place for humans, especially how it can happen in a positive manner for a seeker of truth. Can it be aided by paying attention to it?

(Carla channeling)

We are those of the principle known to you as those of Q'uo. We greet you in the love and in the light of the one infinite Creator. As always, it is a great blessing to us to be called to your group, and we thank you for this kindness and for your desire to seek the truth, for in answering this call you give us a way to be of service and a way to learn, and we thank you for both of these as well as for the simple joy of blending our vibrations with your own and for enjoying through your senses that physical illusion that is so beautiful and dear.

Your question this day is a broad one and in order to speak words of sense we find we need to establish a concept first. That concept is the nature of your being, for the being who learns, by its very nature will require certain kinds of learning. Now, this being that you are is like a two-story building with many basements, shall we say. The top story is something we would call consciousness. The first floor is something we call mind or brain. The basements, and there are several of them, belong some to the brain and some to consciousness and all to the blending of consciousness with the living brain so that into the incarnational experience of that consciousness which is using the brain there may come material that is useful not only to the brain or mind but also to the consciousness that overarches and undergirds and permeates your Earthly mind.

Consciousness learns in a different way than the human mind. Let us look first at the way the mind learns. We ask you to remember that these are our opinions and to choose those thoughts that seem good to you and leave the rest behind. When a spirit or consciousness fragment chooses to come into incarnation, among the things that it chooses is the acuity and ability of the physical mind. For those who are within this circle that choice has been to use a very intelligent mind and to allow that mind its prerogative of enjoying its environment. So we shall look at those whose minds are normally capable or are more intelligent than normal and more capable than normal.

These choices are made always for good reasons. However, it cannot be known by each entity what these reasons are. For some the lesson lies in the use of the mind as a skillful and precise instrument. For others the lesson is quite the opposite, and that is experienced as the entity whose mind is excellent and whose decisions are logical but whose life is constantly being overset by those things which are illogical. For the one, the strong use of mind brings more balance to an entity who has great intuition. For others the lesson is in having an excellent mind but yielding that mind to the growing awareness that that which is to be learned in life is not to be learned through the brain. Therefore, each entity must decide for itself as to the lessons of an incarnation.

Now, the way this mind works is by accretion of detail. When the entity first touches the hot stove it learns before the recoil has finished not to touch a stove when it is hot. The mind learns by repetition. The same fact told over and over and over eventually becomes a part of muscle memory, shall we say. The mind learns by sequence. First one, then two, then three and so forth. These are logical, structural ways that the mind accretes and prioritizes that which it has learned.

As these logical processes go on, another type of learning takes place within the mind which is not particularly logical but which has to do with the emotional and emotionally related portions of the mind. The emotions experienced in the course of learning about any subject affect the way that this learning is seated in the mind. Further, the bias which is gained thusly predisposes the mind to giving that subject the same priority as has been assigned to it previously. Therefore, if one has a prejudice, one is predisposed to increasing the strength of that bias. Thusly are the priorities set up by the mind.

It avoids pain and seeks comfort. It attempts to create sense or order out of randomness or disorder and it attempts to assign importance or value to each thing that it learns. This process begins immediately as the incarnation begins and the infant comes mewling from its mother's womb with prejudices in place, prejudices gained from the time within the womb. Thusly, that innocent child that breathed the air for the first time in the incarnation has already been removed from its paradise, even before that first breath.

The whole process of learning within incarnation is heavily biased, then, and is heavily subjective. Now, we speak not so much of the learning that is by memory and by rote as we are speaking of the mind's ability to configure and assign meaning to experience as it occurs. The mind was made and has been honed to make choices. And thusly the mind tends to attempt to structure things in such a way that a choice can be made and movement can be felt.

When there is no good choice, when there is no way of knowing enough to assign sense or assign priority to incoming data, the mind simply rebels much as a computer will stop all action when that which does not compute at all has been fed into it. And much of that which goes on under the threshold of consciousness as far as the physical brain is concerned has to do with the emotional reactions to being frustrated in the desire to be certain concerning choices and so forth.

This creates a kind of chatter betwixt subconscious and conscious mind, and a good deal of that which is not useful in the dreaming is the conversation which the physical vehicle's mind is carrying on with itself concerning things that do not make sense, things which do not resolve into a clear choice, things that defy logic. Now, while all this activity is going on there is at the same time and using the same physical vehicle a consciousness which was not assigned the job of making choices but rather the job of being. This consciousness is an absolute. It is eternal. It is infinite. It is all that there is. And it resides and rests in all that is. Your consciousness is a microcosm of the creation. And a macrocosm in relation to love, that still point that defies all emotion and into which all that moves yearns to go.

This consciousness learns within incarnation through harvesting the net results of the processes that the mind moves through. Within consciousness there reside what can be called archetypes of meaning. Each is familiar with the concept of the archetypical mind. This archetypical mind has two levels for the benefit of this particular consideration, the two levels being that portion of the physical mind into which memories go and that portion of the unconscious to which the larger memories of universal value go, so that there is that deep resource of the mind which holds racial memory and that deep resource of consciousness which may be approximated dimly by consideration of archetypes.

This portion of consciousness learns through the harvest of emotion and insight which has become purified or refined by the fire of experience. Usually it takes a great deal of experience to affect consciousness. There are considerations which can be taken up, which can improve the mind's use of the resources of consciousness. These techniques involve becoming aware that consciousness has a structure; that is, as the consciousness has interacted within the racial memory it has created archetypical programs, shall we say, considering the physical mind as a computer. It has created programs which when applied to conscious experience create new connections and promote the balancing and healing of distortion. These programs are archetypical. Shadows of these archetypical systems may be found within some religions, some mythologies, some philosophies.

Each entity's experiences and previous choices create an unique situation. There is no one way for minds to work. However, consciousness itself remains a constant value. However, each entity will access the great programs, or should we say, metaprograms of consciousness according to that way in which that entity alone has become used to doing. So the learning of how to make it more possible to invite these metaprograms and their wisdom is somewhat different for each person who seeks, even though the truth, the mystery of consciousness is single. One might consider consciousness itself the elephant which many people touch but cannot see. To one who touches the trunk it is a long and snaky thing. To one who touches the ear it is a big flapping thing. To one who touches the foot it is a tree trunk, and so forth. There is only one elephant, but there are many places to touch the elephant. So it is with these metaprograms.

Now, we always recommend meditation. Among the reasons that we recommend this practice is the fact that when the desire to remain silent has been potentiated by action and the effort is physically made to become silent within, a metaprogram immediately and automatically starts. A connection is made with a source outside the capabilities of the mind. There is a connection made with those archetypical metaprograms. This instrument has recently experienced the computer's e-mail and internet and we would say that it is something like being able to access the internet from one's own computer and thus be in instant touch with global resources. This is the kind of power and potential that consciousness has for that spark of consciousness that is within incarnation. The mind is local. Consciousness is universal.

Thusly, each time one goes into meditation or prayer or simply sits letting the silence be, one has automatically accessed universal mind, racial memory, archetypical structures. Suddenly there is no end to the resources available. We suggest daily meditation and we think that each entity shall, though always feeling that their meditations are no good, yet still experience that balancing and lengthening of the point of view which occurs when one has the universal perspective as opposed to the local perspective.

This entity was earlier pondering what the one known as N asked concerning passive learning. Meditation is passive learning. Tabernacling with the one infinite Creator is passive learning. It is the learning from listening to the voice one cannot hear which answers questions which one cannot ask. The process cannot be known and cannot come into consciousness in local sense, yet the learning is there. And the strength of spirit and will which comes from this learning is helpful.

We feel that we have given enough information for one lecture, shall we say, and would at this time open the meeting to further questions. We would, however, like to transfer this contact from this instrument to the one known as Jim that we may also exercise this instrument. Thusly, we transfer now to the one known as Jim, in love and light.

(Jim channeling)

I am Q'uo, and greet each again in the love and in the light of the one infinite Creator. We would at this time ask if we may speak to any further queries which may be offered to us?

Carla: I was a little puzzled by the picture I was getting of how the racial memory was partially of the mind and partially of the consciousness. Could you talk a little bit about that?

I am Q'uo, and am aware of your query, my sister. The mind is that portion of the complex of an entity which affects its evolution and adds to it through the process of learning and remembering; that is, to reconstruct from the memory experiences previously had. The consciousness of a race of beings has also within it the given, shall we say, that is from the Logos that makes a race of beings what it is to begin this third-density experience. For the case of most third-density plants, there is the graduation from second density of a group of entities that has learned to give and to receive love in sufficient degree to become enough individualized that the mind complex is able to take upon itself much of the weight of the responsibility for directing the continued evolution of this group of entities which shall become a race or a kind of being that inhabits the third-density experience. Thus, each racial mind has within it that which is given as its own kind of consciousness from the Logos and continues to develop as individualized portions of a grouping that which affects the evolution in a conscious and intelligent manner.

Is there a further query, my sister?

Carla: Yes, I'm grappling with this whole concept. When we pray, not asking for anything, just praying, are we learning? Are we accessing something about consciousness? Are we moving into an archetypical structure?

I am Q'uo, and am aware of your query, my sister. When entities engage in that process of petitioning which is called prayer there is the giving over of the self and its desire to that which is greater than the self and which has the ability to add to the knowledge of the self according to the repetition of the behavior which has associated with it certain components—the beginnings, the results.

We beg your pardon for the moment. This instrument has some difficulty. We would ask that we have a moment to work with this instrument.

We are those of Q'uo. We thank you for your efforts. This instrument was having difficulty concentrating.

I am Q'uo, and am again with this instrument. Is there a further query, my sister?

Carla: Yes, when a metaprogram kicks in is it that it makes you smarter, intensifies your intelligence, or is it that it offers alternate priorities, or is it that it offers different logical structures, or is it all three?

I am Q'uo, and am aware of your query, my sister, and suggest that each was a potential for the situation, and more as well.

Is there a further query, my sister?

Carla: Then is this a field in which we could learn more about how to use this resource skillfully?

I am Q'uo, and am aware of your query, my sister. Each of you as you seek in a conscious fashion do just this. There are layers of what you call metaprograms available according to the intensity of seeking and [that] shall be released as a kind of, shall we say, time release capsule, but more in the desired release nature.

Is there a further query, my sister?

Carla: Not at this time, thank you.

I am Q'uo, and we thank you, my sister. Is there another query?

R: No question, but I got this image of a blank piece of paper which I would begin to sketch upon and this would represent learning during the life.

I am Q'uo, and we would suggest that as you continue in your own seeking that the picture you have of your own journey, your own self, and the environment in which you move will continue to become more defined with color, with breadth of emotion, of potential, of inspiration, of joining with other pictures, so that the entire experience does become a richer experience, more filled with information and inspiration but [also] with the emotion and the passion that one feels in one's heart for the process of seeking and of becoming, realizing the unity of self with all of creation. The colors become more life-filled rather than life-like and have within them a kind of glow and depth that continues to grow with the seeker.

Is there a final query at this time?

(Pause)

I am Q'uo, and we are most thankful as well to each in this circle of seeking. At this time we shall take our leave of this instrument and this group. We are known to you as those of Q'uo and we leave you in the love and in the light of the one infinite Creator. Adonai. Adonai, my friends. ✣

Sunday Meditation
July 6, 1995

(Carla channeling)

I am Q'uo, and I greet you in the love and in the light of our infinite Creator. May we thank and bless each of you for inviting us to share in your combined life streams at this time. To be so invited to share our thoughts is a very great privilege, for it is by attempting to be of service to you that we gain in polarity and advance along our own path. We ask that you remember as always when hearing any opinion whatever that the truth is already seated in your own spirit, and if you do not recognize it in our words, it is well for you to release it from your consciousness, for we would not be a stumbling block before you to retard you in your spiritual growth. Indeed, that is far from our purpose.

We find the consciousness of those present this evening to be much aware of the day you celebrate in what you call your nation as the birth date of your nation's independence and each his own personal freedom. We find the phrase, "All men are created equal," to be written large upon your hearts and your pride at this time. Thus we would speak to you about how love, and wisdom, to a lesser extent, function through illusion to facilitate and offer tools for the facilitation of individual spiritual growth.

Each knows that the phrase, "All men are created equal"—men, of course, meaning humankind, men and women alike—to be not only an ideal but truth, for all have the same birthright, own the same Godhead in potentiation and possess all that there is within themselves. We would in no way argue with this truism, and, indeed, wish to underscore its accuracy in the sense that each of you is the Creator. And thus do you each function as each other's catalyst, for each of you is a mirror in likeness, not similar, but same, so that your other selves may gaze within your glass and see what they need to see about themselves. Indeed, it is often among your peoples that you see things in other people, not realizing that you are seeing the reflection of yourself.

However, this evening we would stress that in the illusion, which is your so-called third-density reality, all men are manifestly created unequal. In the illusion of personality, each entity is unique. This illusion is a deep illusion which will continue to hold sway through several densities of existence and many millions of your years and far, far into your spiritual development and your journey back to the one original Thought. It is an important illusion. Why, indeed, does it seem so clear that in this illusion of personality, each is unique and obviously different and therefore unequal to and from each other?

Let us consider one individual spirit. There are two basic influences which shall govern what occurs within the life experience of this individual, the first, shall we say, the "law of finished beginnings." This is not a law, but an influence. We use the term "law" advisedly and ask that you understand it as a pervasive influence rather than an unshakable law. Your vocabulary does not have such a nice word, so we must use the closest in meaning. This pervasive influence is that which indicates that that which has been previously unfinished in an entity's experience in other lifetimes shall be once again brought before the attention of the entity in order that the entity may work, consider, meditate and do whatever seems to be advisable with these pervasive influences which are familiar.

Many difficult relationships are the results of previous unfinished beginnings, and the difficulty of the relationship is much like the difficulty of a person that receives that which seems to be fresh from the grocery but which when taken home, though sweet and fresh to every physical sense, yet seems still somehow aging and putrefying. There is something ancient, something one cannot put one's finger upon, something which smacks sometimes of *déja vu*. This is that with which you deal as lovingly, compassionately, and may we say, dispassionately with in this life experience in order to finish that which has been begun, that all may be balanced with that particular relationship, or in regard to that particular point, that the entity has been attempting to learn and has yet not completely gotten, shall we say, under the belt.

As each is familiar with the so-called karmic influence, we need not dwell upon this influence, but would note only that it is well to take such influences seriously in that each entity give such challenges careful and persistent consideration, but also that the entity employ the light touch, the laughter, the seeking of joy, the discovery of love within each difficulty and each challenge.

And the other influence, although equally pervasive, is not an influence that is much noticed, however it is equally important to your development and to your understanding of the process of development. You understand already that that which you seek will come to you. This follows the basic law of finishing the beginning.

However, there is a balancing influence and [that] is the influence of finding that which has least been sought. Each of you will repeatedly during your incarnation have a new experience, [an] experience to which you come as a virgin comes to her first love. You will have no previous experience to guide you within the incarnation or within your memory, for what is occurring is a balancing process. If you have sought and sought and sought again that which is good and perfect, it is a just balance, and one with which the Creator is generous, that that which is painful shall occur to you, not because you deserve it, but because the way to transformation is the way of balancing. And for every familiar line of thought which you work upon in order to progress spiritually, there will be a brand new circumstance which has been not called for which shall occur to you also and for which you have no previously molded personal tools. This offers you the chance of assimilating new catalyst without incurring what you would call karmic responsibility or debt.

If there are very difficult lessons in your life and one thing after another has been a half-remembered nightmare through which you wearily but determinedly move in order to stop forever the wheel, as you would say, of karma, or as we would put it, to finish that which has been begun, then it is that something utterly, unexpectedly marvelous and wonderful shall occur. Not because you deserve it, but because a balance needs to be brought. And so the Creator has gifts for you to aid in transformation, to surprise you and to offer you the opportunity to teach yourself that which you have begun to learn but have not yet finished and that incalculable something which the balancing law offers as a teaching but which has been rarely spoken of and even less rarely grasped, and that is that there is such a thing as grace. There is that which rains when there is drought, and which shines to brighten an interior dim landscape. There is an inborn keel which shall manifest itself within your life experience—not when you expect it, but always as a gift. And whether these occurrences are happy or unhappy, you may find within yourself the blessing of lessons which are more simply learned because you have been learning their opposite.

When you do not recognize in a situation or relationship any half memory of any past association, when you have no personal feeling of attachment to a challenge, then it is perhaps well to consider whether or not this may or could be a gift from the Creator, that which you already have the tools to understand, if we may use a term that is incorrect in your density. Each of you has this balancing influence on hand at this time and we encourage each of you to look to such lessons with gratitude for grace which offers the easy lessons once in a while and with determination, for even though these lessons are easy, because they come as gifts, it is easy to waste them.

Therefore, be meticulous in acknowledging each gift, in seeing the balance which is internal to your own development and no one else's. Thus shall you use the illusion which makes you seem unequal, one to another. We encourage you to rejoice in this seeming inequality, for the Creator so rejoices. You are the glory which the Creator could only realize by reflection, you are the manifest of that which is and always shall be unmanifest. And while you are manifest, you are not only Creator and co-Creator, but also creation, and the Creator finds you lovely.

We ask you, my friends, to allow all those concepts which you may be learning to become seated in your consciousness by the process and discipline of regular meditation. We encourage the daily meditation, for seeking within without words is analogous to returning once again to the truth that all men are created equal, for you move into that portion of your being which is co-equal not only with your brothers and sisters, but with the Creator. And it is in this portion of your being that learning shall be seated or it shall be lost. That which skips along the top of the water does not influence the deep. Let that which you are learning sink, as the stone shall do when it ceases its headlong flight along the top of the waves.

I am Q'uo. We would like to experiment with moving this channel in order that we may answer some questions, if there be any this evening. Therefore, we shall transfer this contact at this time, thanking each of you again for requesting this particular vibration and thanking this instrument for its service. We shall transfer. I am Q'uo.

(Jim channeling)

I am Q'uo, and greet you once again in love and in light. We are pleased to have been able to make contact with this instrument and would at this time ask if we may be of further service to this group this evening by attempting to answer queries which those present may find value in the asking. May we begin with a query?

Carla: Q'uo, you feel like a fifth density contact. Are you?

I am Q'uo, and this correct, my sister. May we answer further?

Carla: Not unless you have anything that you wish to say about yourself—or yourselves.

I am Q'uo, and we have little to offer as biographical information, as you would term it, for we are as you are, that which is and that which seeks the one Creator.

May we answer another query?

L: What can you tell me about an event in our history known as the French Revolution?

I am Q'uo, and we would need to move with this instrument to deeper levels of its consciousness in order to speak in any detailed fashion concerning the event that you have called the French Revolution, for we are not historians and do not study this facet of your planet's history, as you call it, and in order to move beyond our abilities and desires to be of service in those ways which are ours to offer, we would need to be able to transmit information which was totally unfamiliar to this instrument.

That which is of the philosophical distortion, shall we say, is that which we are most able to offer, for the philosophy of one's existence and the attitude concerning the meaning in one's life pattern and life in general is that common factor which binds all who seek what you have called the truth. Therefore, we may speak upon this topic with far less difficulty than we would encounter should we move beyond these limits.

Is there some particular aspect of this event which you have called the French Revolution that we may speak upon, for as you are aware, it is an event with many, many facets and to speak in even the most general terms would be a great distortion of any one facet.

L: I think at this time I would prefer to withdraw the question. Thank you very much.

I am Q'uo, and we thank you, my brother, for your understanding and acceptance of our obvious limitations.

May we attempt any other query?

Carla: I would like to take up L's question and work with it a little bit because I think that there may be something of substance that you could answer. So what I'll do is guess at the direction that he was going, supply you with some background and then ask a question that is philosophical, if that is acceptable to you?

I am Q'uo. We are quite pleased to attempt our service in this manner.

Carla: About the middle of the eighteenth century, Europe rather exploded with revolutions having to do with freedom. Middle European nations and—I suppose England actually started it all in 1660 to 1680 with a civil revolution that didn't work out, but it started things off. In the later 1700's America declared its independence and its freedom and the idea of liberty and freedom really took hold in people's hearts. And when this came to France, it was in the 1790's and it was a rather bloody rendition of revolt, as I suppose revolutions tend to be, but there was a particularly nasty cast to this one—people got beheaded instead of merely having to go back to the old country. Nevertheless, the goals were liberty, equality, fraternity, and it has often been surmised and has been stated by some Confederation members that some within the American revolutionary movement were very, very wise souls who had no home contact with Earth. This was not their home planet, they came here as wanderers.

Jefferson, for instance, was one who was a wanderer, and who came here in order to aid the entities of this particular part of the planet in affecting a transformation of thought. The same could be said—the same could be surmised—of some entities within the French revolutionary movement, and certainly the goals were laudable. The philosophical question is: there seems to be an interweaving of souls not of this planet who come to share an increased radiance of spirit with those who may still be sleeping and who will waken to a brighter beacon. I feel that wanderers have a far more organic tie with their adopted planets than is usually thought, in other words, that wanderers to this planet take from it as well as give to it. And I wondered if you would like to comment upon the intertwining of energies of wanderers and those who are native or at least have spent many, many incarnations on this particular planet which we call Earth.

I am Q'uo, and we thank you for the opportunity to speak upon this topic, for it is one which is central to the lessons and purposes which each entity upon your planet's surface has incarnated to learn and to offer. The population of this planetary influence, being a third-density population, is one which attempts to learn the lessons of what may in general be called love. There is no better word in your language, yet it falls short. This lesson, as it makes itself apparent to those attempting to learn it, manifests in differing degrees and through various stages that one may liken to the growth of the tree which produces a fruit, and may also be likened within each human entity to the movement of light to higher and higher centers of energy within the mind/body/spirit complex.

Thus, there is a season when the gardener, shall we say, may do its work and a season when the natural evolution of the tree may take its course. Those you have called wanderers, then, have incarnated in various periods of your planet's historical past in order to aid the overall growth of the tree of mind, or of your planet's population, as it has proceeded through those stages of growth which precede that aspect of love which may be seen as manifesting in the form of the ideals of liberty and freedom and equality.

We must pause.

We shall continue. This instrument was concerned that its contact with the one known as Carla was incomplete. To continue. As the entities which comprise your population have moved through the understanding of a racial …

(Side one of tape ends.)

(Jim channeling)

I am Q'uo, and we shall continue.

As then, your planetary population has moved through the identification with groups and the giving and taking of energies between groups, and has evolved in the individual sense, as well to the appreciation of the ability to express one's own thoughts and actions without restriction, then this becomes the signal to those that you have called wanderers that there is the need and the call for assistance in aiding those who have begun to appreciate the individual expression and who now are in need of finding within their being the ability to allow that expression within others as well.

As the energies of the light move through the lower three energy centers and begin to approach the heart energy center or chakra, and that which is known as love or compassion begins to be activated within the individual and group consciousness, the ideals of liberty and equality then become paramount in a form which begins in a distorted fashion, for those who have long labored under the bonds of some form of slavery or have found themselves in a service to others [which] was not chosen but which was, shall we say, dictated to them, the desire for freedom and equality bursts forth in a fashion which first is quite gross and unrefined in its nature, thus the various tendencies towards retribution in the form of revolution begin to develop, and within this framework of transformational change that is somewhat of a chaotic nature, then those gardeners, or shepherds, shall we say, that you have called the wanderers move in order to lend their assistance in a fashion which does not infringe upon the free will of those whom they have come to serve.

Thus, the incarnational entrance into your illusion is chosen in order that only the bias to serve be remembered, and thus the service is offered as an equal to those who call for it. Thus, the concepts of liberty and equality are born in a season that is the result of a great span of experience of both the individual and collected consciousnesses of the peoples of your planet.

May we answer in any further way, my sister?

Carla: No, thank you.

I am Q'uo, and we thank you, my sister. Is there another query?

Carla: I'll ask one more and then shut up. What is the nature of infatuation compared especially with love? And what is its function?

I am Q'uo. We find that this concept which you have called infatuation is the mental and emotional analog to the natural attraction of oppositely polarized biological sexes. This may be likened unto the magnet and the iron filing. There is no thinking required to bring the two together, thus when an entity notices an attraction to one of the opposite biological sexual nature, the entity may seek further contact in order that the attraction may be explored. When further contact reinforces the initial attraction, then the mind and the emotions begin the processing of this catalyst and the beginning of what may later develop into that which you recognize as love is at hand.

The so-called infatuation period, then, serves the purpose of drawing entities of similar vibratory complexes together in order that they may proceed upon the evolutionary path in a manner which is efficient and appropriate to each, that is, in the utilizing of the daily round of activities as catalyst, that when pondered to a sufficient degree allows experience to be born and recorded within the significant portions of the self. Thus does the infatuation propel or, more correctly, provide the potential for the entities to propel themselves further along the path which each has chosen before the incarnation.

May we answer further, my sister?

Carla: The portion of the question left unanswered, perhaps deliberately, was, "What is its relationship emotionally to the human emotion that we call love?" although I understand that the creative principle, love, is not what we mean by the kind of love that people have in their eyes on their fiftieth anniversary—that's the emotion that I'm talking about.

I am Q'uo, and we see here a paradox, my sister, for in one way of looking upon infatuation, it is a pure form of love, for it accepts totally another without condition. The other, at this point in the relationship, is so desirable that the one feeling the infatuation will, shall we way, go to any length to please the one with whom the infatuation is felt. All of the self and the attention of the self is given without reservation in order that the feeling of infatuation may continue. Thus, in this sense, the period of infatuation is a pure form of love, pure, however, in the sense that it has not been tested. It, as yet, lacks the depth of experience.

When the two who have become infatuated continue the relationship and begin the processing of the catalyst which is inevitable within any life pattern, the opportunities then arise for the love to gain in strength and depth and richness and purity, for there will be many, many times in the processing of catalyst that one or the other or both entities will feel less than acceptance for the other and will need to find within the self the ability to accept that which was previously not acceptable; to forgive that within self and other self that which was unforgivable; to have compassion for that which held little interest or perhaps even dislike.

Thus, the lessons of love and acceptance make themselves known within the relationship born of infatuation and with the faith that the relationship will endure and that meaning may be found for both within it and the will to persevere in finding that meaning and growth. Thus does each entity grow in acceptance and in love, and thus does the relationship do likewise, and thus is love strengthened by testing through catalyst that each brings to the relationship. Thus, the love which results is a love which has greater strength and depth and variety of experience, shall we say.

May we answer further, my sister?

Carla: No, thank you very much.

I am Q'uo, and we thank you, my sister. Is there another query?

Questioner: Yes. You've basically covered this, so please answer briefly, but you seemingly place more importance upon the broader definition of love which is compassion, as I understand that as acceptance of people and situations and self as they are, allowing them room to grow in their own way. So for an entity who is attempting to develop love as we know it, probably the most expeditious way for them to do this would be for them to work on acceptance of others and themselves, and this is—I know this is something that I believe I know, but a simple yes or no would suffice.

I am Q'uo. This is basically correct, my brother, for within your illusion of seeming separateness and limitation there is much which offers the challenge to be accepted, much which seems traumatic, tragic and filled with sorrow, distaste horror, anger, jealousy and so forth. Yet, each entity and event is the Creator, knowing Itself in a way mysterious to most. Yet, each in any portion of the experience may increase its evolutionary progress by finding the joy, the love and the light of the Creator within that person, that moment, that event, that thought. When this can be done in a relationship, then the relationship has served as the means by which the continuing ability to expand the point of view and the acceptance, the love and the compassion for that which falls within the point of view then is also increased and the entity has moved itself further along its chosen path of evolution.

May we answer further, my brother?

Questioner: No, thank you. That was quite sufficient. Thank you.

I am Q'uo, and we thank you, my brother. Is there another query?

(Pause)

I am Q'uo, and we find that we have exhausted those queries which have been offered to us this evening, and for each query we are most grateful, for in our attempt to answer your heartfelt questions, we find further ways to know and to serve the Creator in all. We are humbly grateful for this opportunity, and we would remind each present that we are those who seek as you seek, fallible in many ways. Take those words and thoughts which have meaning to you and leave those which do not. Thus would we offer that which we have found helpful in our seeking to you in your seeking. We shall take our leave of this group at this time, thanking each again for allowing our presence. We leave you in the love and in the light of the one Creator. We are known to you as Q'uo. Adonai. Adonai.

(Carla channeling)

I am Nona. We thank you for requesting healing, and we greet you in the love and the light of the infinite Creator.

(Lovely vocal healing melody channeled by Carla from Nona.) ❧

www.ingramcontent.com/pod-product-compliance
Lightning Source LLC
Chambersburg PA
CBHW080420230426

43662CB00015B/2157